Lesson Commentary

International Uniform Sunday School Series

EDITOR
  Wesley C. Reagan

CONTRIBUTING WRITERS
  Ron Durham, Ph.D.
  Doug deGraffenried
  David Dietzel
  Phil Woodland, D.D.
  John Wright

ILLUSTRATORS
  Billy Ledet (text)
  David Chrane (cover)

The Higley Lesson Commentary, in this 69th year of its life, renews its commitment to careful and reverent scholarship, clear and understandable language, practical and insightful application, and interesting and readable writing. We send it to you with a prayer that it will be a powerful resource to you.

Higley Publishing Corporation
P. O. Box 5398
Jacksonville, FL 32247-5398
Tel. (904) 396-1918

FOREWORD

Polaris is commonly called the North Star because it **defines** due North. Everything else proceeds from there. All other directions and calculations begin there and proceed from there. Apart from its relationship to Polaris, no latitude has any significance.

In a like manner, the nature of God **defines** truth. Every teaching and command points toward God. Everything else proceeds from there. All calculations and decisions must be made on the basis of who He is. Apart from its relation to God, no command has any meaning or significance.

That is why Bible study is so vitally important. It fixes the direction of our lives on God. Without that center, one's life would be like a cork bobbling on the sea of life at the whim of wind and wave. Life would not be a progressive movement toward God, but would be rather a series of accidents and coincidences. A person would be like the man of whom it was said, "He jumped on his horse and rode off in all directions."

If we are adrift in the world with no centering on God, we will be constantly anxious and confused. If, however, all roads lead to God and we love Him with all our hearts, we will have flawless guidance in making critical decisions. They still will not be easy, but we will not be without a compass on life's sea.

The intent of **The Higley Commentary** is to help you know God better by knowing His Word better. God bless your studies!

Wesley C. Reagan, Editor

Copyright © 2001, Higley Publishing Corporation
P. O. Box 5398, Jacksonville FL 32247-5398

Soft Cover ISBN: 1-886763-19-4
Hard Cover ISBN: 1-886763-20-8
Large Print Student Book ISBN: 1-886763-21-6

Lessons and/or readings are based on International Sunday School Lessons. The International Bible Lessons for Christian Training, copyright © 1991 by the Committee on the Uniform Series.

PREFACE

My early life was one of many trials and hardships. In the midst of all of it, I always found comfort in knowing my mother was a special friend of Jesus. She had to be in order for our family to get through the storms of poverty and the environmental horrors we sometimes faced. During one of the private times we spent together before her death, she shared with me why she felt this deep friendship with Jesus.

She said that if I learn to love the Word of God and believe that God actually speaks to me and my needs through His Word, then loving Jesus is easy. Therefore, she said, my conversations with Jesus are friendly and sincere. Those words created within me a burning desire to read and study the Bible in a new way. I now study the Word of God seeking implications for my personal life. I no longer study to recite the Word. I read to listen to the Word with a receptive heart.

My personal challenge as a Christian is to build a firm foundation for my faith. I welcome opportunities to read, hear, share, and participate in activities that speak to my faith and affirm my commitment to the one true God through Jesus Christ.

I pray that your Bible study this year will renew for you the hope that God intended. Read the lessons and use the Commentary to help you apply God's Word to your life. Listen to how the editor and writers acknowledge the brokenness of human lives and the ways God uses the living word to heal and comfort us through life's storms. You will know, through these lessons, that the Lord, and He alone, is indeed your God.

Gerald V. Williams, Sr.

(Gerald V. Williams spent his early life in one of the New Orleans projects where there are few incentives to rise to spiritual stature. With the inspiration of his mother and a determination to live a good and productive life, he matured into an effective Bible teacher and Christian leader. He is a Health and Human Services Planning Consultant, President of the Louisiana Sickle Cell Anemia Association, and Executive Director of the New Orleans Sickle Cell Anemia Foundation. He regularly teaches Disciples Bible Classes at his church. He and his wife, Brenda, have a son, Jay, who is a Certified Public Accountant in Houston, and a daughter, Jakeen, who recently completed her M.D. at Louisiana State University Medical School.)

FALL QUARTER
Jesus' Ministry
Performing Miracles (Lessons 1-5)
Purpose of Parables (Lessons 6-9)
The Sermon on the Mount (Lessons 10-13)

WINTER QUARTER
Light for All People

God's Servant Will Bring Light (Lessons 1-5)
God's People Will Walk in Light (Lessons 6-9)
God's Grace is for All People (Lessons 10-13)

SPRING QUARTER
The Power of the Gospel
Justified by Faith (Lessons 1-5)
Living by Faith (Lessons 6-9)
No Other Gospel (Lessons 10-13)

SUMMER QUARTER
Worship and Wisdom for Living
Songs for Faithful Living (Lessons 1-5)
Praise the Creator and Redeemer (Lessons 6-9)
Words for the Wise (Lessons 10-13)

Sept. 2

Lesson 1

The First Miracle

John 2:1-11

And the third day there was a marriage in Cana of Galilee; and the mother of Jesus was there.

2 And both Jesus was called, and his disciples, to the marriage.

3 And when they wanted wine, the mother of Jesus saith unto him, They have no wine.

4 Jesus saith unto her, Woman, what have I to do with thee? mine hour is not yet come.

5 His mother saith unto the servants, Whatsoever he saith unto you, do it.

6 And there were set there six waterpots of stone, after the manner of the purifying of the Jews, containing two or three firkins apiece.

7 Jesus saith unto them, Fill the waterpots with water. And they filled them up to the brim.

8 And he saith unto them, Draw out now, and bear unto the governor of the feast. And they bare it.

9 When the ruler of the feast had tasted the water that was made wine, and knew not whence it was: (but the servants which drew the water knew;) the governor of the feast called the bridegroom,

10 And saith unto him, Every man at the beginning doth set forth good wine; and when men have well drunk, then that which is worse: but thou hast kept the good wine until now.

11 This beginning of miracles did Jesus in Cana of Galilee, and manifested forth his glory; and his disciples believed on him.

Memory Selection
John 2:11

Devotional Reading
Psalm 77:11-15

Background Scripture
John 2:1-11

1

There is perhaps no better way to begin a new year of Bible study than with the work and teachings of Jesus. After all, this is "the greatest story ever told." No one in any field has made such an impact on world history. He astounds us with His mighty works, and nurtures us with His teaching.

Are members of your study group too mature for a childlike "object lesson" that draws their attention to Jesus' miracle at Cana? Just bring a clear glass pitcher that is partly filled with water, and a package of cherry or grape Kool-Aid. As you pour the Kool-Aid into the water, tell the group that you are performing a miracle by making the water turn wine-colored.

Unit I, "Performing Miracles," begins at the beginning, with the miracle at Cana of Galilee. Ironically, your aim here is to point in two directions at once. Turning the water into wine is awesome evidence of Jesus' superhuman power. Providing the wine for a wedding points to Jesus' very human interest in matters of interest to humans. This "beginning of miracles" (John 2:11) is an example of the classic definition of the nature of Jesus: He was "very man, and very God."

Of course the predictable response is that your mixture is a "natural" result of combining water and food coloring. As C. S. Lewis pointed out, however, it is no more "supernatural" for Jesus to turn water to wine, as He does in this lesson, than for God to do so in the "natural" way. There are yet mysteries of how "nature" provides the chemicals in food coloring, and produces a vine that produces grapes which turn their juice into wine. When Jesus takes this power into His own hands at Cana, "the mask is off," Lewis said. Now we know who is behind the "natural" way wine is made!

Teaching Outline	Daily Bible Readings
I. Marriage Feast—vss. 1-2	**Mon.** The Word in the Beginning John 1:1-5
II. Mary's Request—3-5	**Tue.** The Word Became Flesh John 1:9-14
A. Strange reply, 3-4	**Wed.** John's Testimony John 1:15-23
B. Trusting response, 5	**Thu.** "This Is the Son of God!" John 1:29-34
III. Miracle of Nature—6-11	**Fri.** "Come and See!" John 1:35-42
A. Master of water, 6-8	**Sat.** Greater Things to Come John 1:43-51
B. Miraculous wine, 9-10	**Sun.** Water into Wine John 2:1-11
C. The power and the glory, 11	

Verse by Verse

I. Marriage Feast—vss. 1-2

1 And the third day there was a marriage in Cana of Galilee; and the mother of Jesus was there:

2 And both Jesus was called, and his disciples, to the marriage.

This event is significant enough for John to mention exactly when it occurred: "the third day" after John the Baptist's public confession of Jesus as the Messiah (when Jesus was baptized—1:29; Matt. 3:13-17). As we will be told in verse 11, the miracle (which John calls a "sign") Christ performs here marked the beginning of many others that would distinguish Him as much more than another Jewish rabbi. An important characteristic of John's Gospel is that it portrays many earthly events as "signs" of heavenly counterparts, affirming that reality consists of two "levels" or worlds. We are therefore justified in seeking "secondary" meanings to many of the events here. The first is that Jesus inaugurates his ministry of miracles at a wedding feast, an event of special joy. The Gospel writer no doubt intends for us to note that joy is one of the main themes of the Christian lifestyle.

Perhaps he is also contrasting this joyful mood with what he perceived to be the cold, joyless ritual the Jewish faith as it had come to be practiced in his day. Likewise, it can be noted that Christians often forfeit joy when they become pre-occupied with arguments about doctrinal fine points, the challenge of following the high standards Jesus set, or persecution.

II. Mary's Request—3-5

A. Strange reply, 3-4

3 And when they wanted wine, the mother of Jesus saith unto him, They have no wine.

4 Jesus saith unto her, Woman, what have I to do with thee? mine hour is not yet come.

Since Jesus' mother Mary had been invited to the wedding and the feast to follow, the host had also invited her Son, along with the disciples He was already beginning to attract. Perhaps the wine ran short because such expanded invitations had resulted in a larger-than-usual crowd. At any rate, Mary, sensing that Jesus was somehow more than just a human son, appealed to Him to see if this "something more" might include the ability to provide more wine. Jesus answer sounds abrupt in the KJV; it is more appropriately translated "Dear woman" in the NIV. Yet His reply does call Mary's timing into question. As in "the Messianic secret" when He will tell people not to announce to others how He had helped them, Jesus' had His own sense of timing about when the Messianic dimension of His ministry should be revealed. Although He will respond part-way to His mother's request, the time had "not yet come" for Him to allow the miracle fully to reveal His identity.

B. Trusting response, 5

5 His mother saith unto the servants, Whatsoever he saith unto you, do it.

Mary is not put off by Jesus' response, but proceeds confidently to enlist the servants in helping Jesus in whatever He was willing to do. Her statement here makes an appropriate motto for every believer: "Do whatever he tells you" (NIV).

III. Miracle of Nature—6-11

A. Master of water, 6-8

6 And there were set there six waterpots of stone, after the manner of the purifying of the Jews, containing two or three firkins apiece.

7 Jesus saith unto them, Fill the waterpots with water. And they filled them up to the brim.

8 And he saith unto them, Draw out now, and bear unto the governor of the feast. And they

bare it.

Many of Jesus' miracles are often categorized as "nature miracles," such as the one here, calming the storm and multiplying loaves and fishes (see Lesson 2), and walking on water. Others may be viewed as "spiritual miracles," consisting of casting out demons, and forgiving sins.

The huge stone jars, each capable of holding 20 to 30 gallons of water, were necessary for the many hand- and body-washings involved in ritual Judaism. Again, John may be peering into the heavenly realm for a special meaning behind these symbols of Judaism, asking us to contrast the blandness of the waters of cold ritual with the warmth and joy associated not only with wine (Ps. 104:15), but with the new religion Jesus is bringing.

B. Miraculous wine, 9-10

9 When the ruler of the feast had tasted the water that was made wine, and knew not whence it was: (but the servants which drew the water knew;) the governor of the feast called the bridegroom,

10 And saith unto him, Every man at the beginning doth set forth good wine; and when men have well drunk, then that which is worse: but thou hast kept the good wine until now.

The "ruler of the feast" was a kind of "emcee" or chairman of the festivities. As a modern waiter may bring a bottle of wine to a table for approval before pouring, the servants at the feast want the emcee's endorsement of the new wine—knowing, as he does not, its source. It would be a very human act to sate guests with good wine first, then, when their taste buds are somewhat dulled, to extend the supply by bringing out second-rate or watered-down wine. Instead, perceiving the second round of wine to be better than the first, the feast-chairman commends the groom, who would have been in charge of such procedures. John wants us to "overhear" a double meaning in the this enthusiastic approval of the wine's quality. He is saying subtly that the life that Jesus offers is of superior quality to the "first wine" of Judaism.

C. The power and the glory, 11

11 This beginning of miracles did Jesus in Cana of Galilee, and manifested forth his glory; and his disciples believed on him.

John mentions again that Jesus initiated His ministry of miracles in his home region of Galilee. Perhaps he emphasizes this to lay the groundwork for holding Jesus' neighbors without excuse for not believing in Him (see Matt. 13:53-58).The location of Cana has not been definitely established; two sites near Nazareth are thought by various archeologists to be its re-

mains. The story of Jesus' miracle spread far and wide, however. By the fourth century a myth had attached itself to a Christian meeting place at Jerash, far to the southeast in the Transjordan, where it was held that a fountain flowed with wine each year on the anniversary of the miracle at Cana.

John's special term for a "miracle" is *semeion*, which actually means a "sign" (see NIV "miraculous signs" at 2:11). The other gospel writers prefer the term *dynamis* or "power." John's term fits nicely into his "two-level" world-view: a miracle is not just a wonder, but a sign pointing from a temporal act to an eternal reality behind it.

That the "sign" had the desired effect is seen in the way it convinced Jesus' new disciples that the power He manifested was indeed divine, and that it glorified not the deed but the Creator behind it. No longer can believers see wine as merely "fruit of the vine," much less a drink to make one intoxicated. Instead, wine recalls the seven huge jars with more than enough provision for a life of genuine joy in contrast to dead ritual; and, later, from the "blessed tragedy" of Christ's death, the blood that cleanses in a way ritual water could never accomplish.

Evangelistic Emphasis

Jesus' response to his mother's request for more wine at the wedding feast has promoted uneasy discussion through the years. He said to her, "Woman, what have I to do with thee? mine hour is not yet come." Though that remark has been translated variously through the years, it always comes out sounding rather harsh.

Eugene Peterson's paraphrase in *The Message* certainly sounds very contemporary. He has Jesus saying, "Is that any of our business, Mother — yours or mine? This isn't my time. Don't push me." Yet, I find it difficult to hear such immature-sounding words coming from Jesus. Was he *really* becoming irritated with her nagging ways?

The New International Version provides a kinder, gentler sound: "'Dear woman, why do you involve me?' Jesus replied. 'My time has not yet come.'" Even so, there remains in the tone evidence that Mary was "pushing" Jesus to involve himself in the need. Furthermore, that should not surprise us. Has that not been one of the significant roles that mothers have filled since time began? As a mother bird will push its young from the nest, forcing it to fly, so also mothers have historically provided appropriate prompting when it is time for her young one to move on to the next stage of faith or accomplishment. It is clear from the verses that follow that Jesus complied with his mother's wishes.

Memory Selection

This beginning of miracles did Jesus in Cana of Galilee, and manifested forth his glory; and his disciples believed on him.—*John 2:11*

At precisely what point did this miracle occur? Have you ever wondered? With Naaman the miracle happened when he washed himself in the Jordan seven times (2 Kings 5:14). With the ten lepers whom Jesus healed, the miracle happened "as they went" on their way to show themselves to the priest (John 17:17). At what point, however, did the miracle occur here? Did the water become wine when the six jars had completely filled? Was it when the servants drew out the wine to take to the governor of the feast? Or, did the water change to wine "on the way" to the one who was to taste it?

I'm not sure that the answer to that question is all that important. Unfortunately, those are often the very kind of questions that preoccupy our minds when we ought, instead, to be rejoicing in the miracle that was done and thanking God for its presence.

Weekday Problems

Bill Jones and Henry Johnson are both Deacons at Blue Ridge Community Church. Until last Sunday, Henry and Bill have perceived their approach to Scripture to be as nearly identical as humanly possible. The discussion in Sunday School class last week, however, left both of the men feeling amazed at the other man's stubborn heart.

The discussion began because of Brother Johnson's off-the-cuff comment encouraging everyone to study in preparation for this week's class. What started as a light-hearted poke at "social drinking" moved quickly into a argument about drunkenness and the part that *social* drinking contributes to our society's present epidemic of alcoholism.

Bill rose to the defense of those who drink moderately, pointing out that Jesus turned water into wine at a wedding feast. Henry replied that the wine Jesus made was not alcoholic, citing Proverbs, "Look not thou upon the wine when it is red." Bill countered by noting the fact that Jesus himself acknowledged that old wine is the best wine, but Bill was not to be dissuaded. He insisted that it was sweet wine.

* Is there any way to provide sufficient evidence to bring these two men to agreement in this matter?

* If Henry is correct about this being "sweet wine," how does one account for the fact that old wine was considered better than new wine?

* If Bill is correct about this being alcoholic wine, how does one deal with the harsh realities of drunkenness in our society?

Speaking of Signs

Sign on a church marquee: THIS CHURCH IS PRAYER-CONDITIONED.

* * *

Sign in a Bible bookstore: DAVID AND BATHSHEBA . . . YOU'VE SEEN THE MOVIE, NOW READ THE BOOK.

* * *

Sign advertising a sermon topic: ARMAGEDDON: EARTH'S LAST WAR AND WHERE IT WILL BE FOUGHT AT THE FIRST BAPTIST CHURCH

* * *

Sign at a church that had been closed from lack of attendance: R.I.P. — WE SAID "NO ONE'S EVER DONE IT THAT WAY BEFORE."

* * *

Sign at a church's nursery: THEY SHALL NOT ALL SLEEP, BUT THEY SHALL BE CHANGED.

This Lesson in Your Life

Jesus was always being asked to help someone in crisis. One was seriously ill. Another had a loved one who died. Four men had a friend who was lame. Yet, other than a few invitations for dinner, people rarely included Jesus at a time of a celebration or when throwing a party.

It is strange how little that has changed over the past two thousand years. Jesus is still often invited to be involved in our lives when a crisis appears. Yes, many pray "token prayers" at mealtime or at bedtime. Unfortunately, even for those who do maintain that discipline, far too few get beyond that to more substantial conversation or relationship in prayer. As a result, prayer can easily come to be humdrum and boring. Some wouldn't dare *not* do it, but neither do they really invest themselves in it. It is difficult to cultivate a vital relationship with anyone within a humdrum context.

The time when prayer is most forgotten is in the middle of celebration! Fortunately, many marriages still retain some connection with God and faith. Unfortunately, for the most part that involvement tends to be within the context of solemnity, rather than within the context of celebration. The presence of the Lord is very much coveted at the chapel when the vows are exchanged. But as soon as the solemn vows are concluded, God is dismissed before we move on to the reception and party! We would just as soon that He politely excuse Himself before we get to the cake and punch and the wine glasses and the removal of the garter. And most certainly He is to keep his distance from the Bridal Suite after the door is closed.

Yet, when is there a more dynamic and alive time in one's life to share thankfully and consciously with Him the celebration of our hearts? John's Gospel make it clear that Jesus had been invited to this wedding and not only to witness the exchange of the solemn vows. He was asked to stay for the party and the celebration, as well! And when the party began to sag a bit, He was the one asked to take the needed action to bring it back to life!

I wonder how it would impact our marriages and homes today if we were to be brave enough to invite Jesus to stay for the parties. I wonder how it would change our prayer life (*and our relationship with Him*) if we included Him in our times of celebration as well as our times of need. Instead of reserving our prayers for "crisis petitions," what if we maintained a steady upward flow of praise and excitement for the good things going on?

STRAIGHT

1. What was the location of the wedding that Jesus attended?
It was in Cana of Galilee.

2. What did Jesus' mother tell him, and why?
Mary told Jesus that there was no more wine. Apparently she wanted him to do something about it.

3. What was Jesus' response to Mary's message?
Jesus asked Mary why she was telling him this. He told her that his time had not yet arrived.

4. What did Jesus' mother tell the servant's to do?
Mary told the servants to do whatever Jesus instructed.

5. How many jars were filled with water by the servants? How large was each jar?
Six jars were filled with water. Each jar held 20 to 30 gallons.

6. After the jars had been filled with water, what instruction did Jesus then give?
He told the servants to take some of the wine to the master of the feast.

7. Was the master of the feast aware of the source of the wine that he was being given to taste?
No. Only the servants knew its source.

8. What did the master of the feast then do?
He went to the bridegroom to inquire why he waited so late in the feast to bring out his best wine.

9. What was the usual manner of providing refreshments for such a celebration gathering?
Usually the host brought out the finest wine first. Then after everyone had his fill, the lesser quality wine was offered.

10. What does John say was the result of this miracle that Jesus performed in Galilee?
His glory was manifested and His disciples put their faith in Him.

The wedding had been marvelous! Everybody said so. There were ten attendants on each side of the bride and groom. All the men were dressed in a fully equipped tuxedo. The ladies were gorgeously attired. The bride's family had agreed to pay for all of the dresses and tuxedos, since the bride had insisted on the most expensive selections available. Even the minister had been flown in from across the country, because he was the one who had baptized the bride when she was a young girl.

Now as the wedding party and about 200 guests sat at a full-dinner reception, enjoying the finest of tenderloin and bottomless glasses of champagne, the moment came for the toasts to be offered. As usual, there was a mixture of syrupy-sentimental ones, eloquent utterances of choice wisdom, and half-inebriated attempts to say something funny. Each was accepted with gracious appreciation by the lovely bride and her properly reserved groom.

As the toasts began to wind down, the bride's father stepped up to the microphone and toasted the groom's father and thanked him for an exceptionally fine rehearsal dinner they had enjoyed the previous evening. The guests noticed that the bride beamed with pride as her father spoke. She was so proud of his sensitivity and eloquence.

Then the bride's father offered a toast to the bride and groom, who were "entering a new chapter in their lives." The mist of gentle tears gathered in her eyes. She was so pleased that God had given her such a genteel and generous dad. How had she been so fortunate?

Concluding his remarks, the bride's dad spoke directly to the reception crowd. *"After tomorrow, we, too, will be entering a new chapter in our lives,"* he informed them. *"Chapter 11."*

First Century Galileans do not have a monopoly on extravagant wedding productions. It is true that our culture doesn't usually continue the festivities for a full week, but that probably has more to do with our rush of schedule than our having a tight rein on extravagance. Our rapid pace just allows us to spend the fortune a whole lot more rapidly. Instead of its taking a full week to become bankrupt, it can now usually be accomplished in just a few hours.

If we are ever able to get couples to spend as much time and effort attempting to prepare for the *marriage* as they do preparing for the *wedding*, we might begin to make some progress toward homes that predictably last a lifetime. If we can ever get their families to invest as much emphasis and money into equipping the couple for the lifetime ahead as they do on the day they are awaiting, we will finally have priorities close to where they ought to be.

The wedding day is incredibly special and immeasurably important! Yet, unless the life that follows is constructed on wise choices and acts of mutual respect and love, the wedding will come to haunt like a New England ghost.

B/lly 00

Matthew 8:23-27; 14:14-21

A nd when he was entered into a ship, his disciples followed him.

24 And, behold, there arose a great tempest in the sea, insomuch that the ship was covered with the waves: but he was asleep.

25 And his disciples came to him, and awoke him, saying, Lord, save us: we perish.

26 And he saith unto them, Why are ye fearful, O ye of little faith? Then he arose, and rebuked the winds and the sea; and there was a great calm.

27 But the men marvelled, saying, What manner of man is this, that even the winds and the sea obey him!

14:14 And Jesus went forth, and saw a great multitude, and was moved with compassion toward them, and he healed their sick.

15 And when it was evening, his disciples came to him, saying, This is a desert place, and the time is now past; send the multitude away, that they may go into the villages, and buy themselves victuals.

16 But Jesus said unto them, They need not depart; give ye them to eat.

17 And they say unto him, We have here but five loaves, and two fishes.

18 He said, Bring them hither to me.

19 And he commanded the multitude to sit down on the grass, and took the five loaves, and the two fishes, and looking up to heaven, he blessed, and brake, and gave the loaves to his disciples, and the disciples to the multitude.

20 And they did all eat, and were filled: and they took up of the fragments that remained twelve baskets full.

21 And they that had eaten were about five thousand men, beside women and children.

Memory Selection
John 8:27

Devotional Reading
John 6:28-40

Background Scripture
Matthew 8:23-27; 14:14-21

Three more of Jesus' astounding "nature miracles—calming the storm, healing the sick, and feeding the 5,000—are the focus of this lesson.

It is wise not to take for granted that everyone in your group accepts the biblical miracles at face value. After all, in one sense they are foreign to most people's everyday lives in a scientific-minded age. Yet it may be helpful to point out that science cannot rightly claim to have explained the cause and workings of all "natural" events either. Biblical miracles may be considered more "supra-natural," showing that God is sovereign *over* nature, than "supernatural," as though they cancel the laws of nature. That is, it is just as wondrous that God can calm a storm by causing a rise in air pressure as by a word from His Son.

৯০৫

One way to introduce a lesson on miracles is to ask group members to share their sense of wonder. What events in life sometimes cause them to marvel, or to praise God? The birth of a child? The power of acceptance and love to change a life? The wonders of space travel and other scientific feats?

In one sense, "nature miracles" such as those in this lesson are no more wondrous than these more common sources of awe. Don't let the discussion get stalled on unanswerable questions about what God can or can't do. God can always stay ahead of "all that we ask or think" (Eph. 3:20). Whether we properly appreciate life's wonders, including the miracles in this lesson, depends more on the quality of our perceptive powers than on God's ability to stun us.

Teaching Outline	Daily Bible Readings	
I. Calming a Storm—8:23-27	**Mon.**	Jesus Calms a Storm Mark 4:35-41
A. A sleeping Lord, 23-24	**Tue.**	Jesus Walks on Water Matthew 14:22-27
B. Lord of wind and waves, 25-27	**Wed.**	Peter's Doubt Matthew 14:28-33
II. Healing the Sick—14:14	**Thu.**	Feeding Four Thousand Mark 8:1-13
III. Feeding a Crowd—14:15-21	**Fri.**	'Do You Not Yet Understand?' Mark 8:14-21
A. The dilemma, 15	**Sat.**	'Follow Me, Now!' Matthew 8:18-27
B. The unlikely plan, 16-17	**Sun.**	Feeding Five Thousand Matthew 14:14-21
C. Multiplied resources, 18-21		

Verse by Verse

I. Calming a Storm—8:23-27

A. A sleeping Lord, 23-24

23 And when he was entered into a ship, his disciples followed him.

24 And, behold, there arose a great tempest in the sea, insomuch that the ship was covered with the waves: but he was asleep.

The "nature miracle" emphasis now moves from turning water into wine (Lesson 1) to a portrayal of Jesus' power over the sea. Ancient peoples harbored deep fear of the unknown depths of the sea, which even in Scripture can become the symbolic source of the "dragon" of evil, Satan (Rev. 13:1). God is reassuring us here not only that His Son has power over the depths of evil, but that through Him we too can conquer our deepest fears.

Since this incident is during Jesus' Galilean ministry, we may assume that it occurs on the Sea of Galilee. Because Jesus enters the boat first, it is likely that He is on His way to another spot along the seashore (see 9:10), rather than accompanying His disciples on one of their fishing expeditions.

The word translated "tempest" here is *seismos*; and some translators ascribe the rough waters to an earthquake. This would not be surprising, since Galilee is in a geological area prone to earthquakes, and in fact is fed in part by hot springs boiling up from lava-heated depths. Whatever the disturbance, it includes strong winds (vs. 26), which is why the KJV and others describe it as a tempest or storm. Even modern visitors to the area report that the usual calm of Galilee can be violently interrupted by sudden storms with gale-force winds.

The surprising part of the story is that the superhuman Master of earthquakes and storms actually goes to sleep in the small boat. Just as Jesus showed both His humanity and his divinity in going to the wedding feast at Cana side-by-side with His divinity in turning the water into wine, both the human and the divine sides of His nature are apparent in this incident. Placed alongside the disciples' terror, the calmness that allows Him to sleep heightens the contrast. Because of this human quality, Christ's disciples can draw courage from the fact that even in storms Jesus "is in the same boat" with us.

B. Lord of wind and waves, 25-27

25 And his disciples came to him, and awoke him, saying, Lord, save us: we perish.

26 And he saith unto them, Why are ye fearful, O ye of little faith? Then he arose, and rebuked the winds and the sea; and there was a great calm.

27 But the men marvelled, saying, What manner of man is this, that even the winds and the sea obey him!

"Disciples" means learners; and these closest followers of Jesus have just emerged from an intense learning session about putting Him first (vss. 19-22). It is significant, however, that they do not cry out here, "Teacher, instruct us!" but "Lord save us!" The peril of life's storms is too great for us to think we can save ourselves merely by learning more; at times we can only cry out for salvation from a source more powerful than our minds.

As stunning as this miracle is, believers should not have difficulty believing that the word of the Son could act on creation, when it was His Word that spoke creation into existence (John 1:1-3). Although Jesus' "rebuke" is aimed first at the wind and waves, His words also seem to rebuke the disciples by calling them, literally "little-faiths." The tone here is in contrast to the frequent passive sense in which faith is spoken of in modern times, as though it either "happens" to us or doesn't. Actually, having faith requires a certain amount of courage and aggressive willingness to believe. Jesus scolds His followers here for having so little confidence in Him. Yet the real point of the story is that even in our "little-faith" Jesus responds to His followers' appeals.

II. Healing the Sick—Matt. 14

14 And Jesus went forth, and saw a great multitude, and was moved with compassion toward them, and he healed their sick.

In order to focus on two more "nature miracles," our lesson now moves to the time when King Herod had put John the Baptist to death (Matt. 14:1-12). Apparently Jesus is so moved by this incident that He needs to draw away from the crowds who followed Him, for reflection and prayer (vs. 13). Although He does so by ship, a multitude trail Him from the shore, and when His boat puts in they throng about Him again. They have heard that He is a healer; and they have physical needs.

The word translated "moved with compassion" describes heart-felt sentiment so deep that it gives rise to the King James expression "bowels of compassion" (as in 1 John 3:17), which sounds strange to modern ears. Although the term reflects the ancient belief that the liver or physical heart was the seat of the emotions, it accurately describes the inner depths of Jesus' feelings toward the needy. One of the reasons He sometimes needed to get away from the crowds was that their plight was literally "gut-wrenching" to Him. Instead of holding Himself aloof from the suffering of others, He allowed Himself to hurt with them. Hence, in this scene, He foregoes His need for rest, and heals (from Grk. *therapeuo*) those who approach Him.

III. Feeding a Crowd—14:15-21
A. The dilemma, 15

15 And when it was evening, his

14

disciples came to him, saying, This is a desert place, and the time is now past; send the multitude away, that they may go into the villages, and buy themselves victuals.

The urgent need of some in the crowd for healing had caused them to follow Jesus around Galilee with no thought of packing picnic lunches. Suddenly it was "past time" for them to eat, prompting Jesus' disciples to urge the Lord to send the crowds into nearby villages. They may have had enough food with them for Jesus and the Twelve, but hardly for the multitudes who had followed them.

B. The unlikely plan, 16-17

16 But Jesus said unto them, They need not depart; give ye them to eat.

17 And they say unto him, We have here but five loaves, and two fishes.

Jesus does not meet hunger by preaching another sermon, but by feeding the people—an example that is so important to the Holy Spirit that this miracle is the only one recorded in all four Gospels. It stands as a model for believers today, who sometimes had rather meet "spiritual" needs than become involved in the often more difficult task of meeting physical needs.

Jesus plan, however, is designed to meet another need as well. His disciples need to know that because they follow Him they have the power to "give ye them to eat"—to help others in ways that transcend the natural. Because they are challenged to

use only five loaves and two fishes to feed a multitude, their task is more than "social work"; it takes on a glory of its own because it is a task that is not only miraculous but commissioned by Jesus—another important lesson for modern believers.

C. Multiplied resources, 18-21

18 He said, Bring them hither to me.

19 And he commanded the multitude to sit down on the grass, and took the five loaves, and the two fishes, and looking up to heaven, he blessed, and brake, and gave the loaves to his disciples, and the disciples to the multitude.

20 And they did all eat, and were filled: and they took up of the fragments that remained twelve baskets full.

21 And they that had eaten were about five thousand men, beside women and children.

The few loaves and fishes become adequate not because of a feat of magic but because they are blessed by the Lord of the material world. Although we may not always be able to feed all who are hungry, the principle we are to learn from this story is that the limited resources of Jesus' followers become more than enough (note the leftovers) when we use what we have in His name.

Jesus' blessing of the loaves and fishes is similar to the blessing He used in instituting the Lord's Supper (Matt. 26:26), reminding Christians eating at the Table of their duty also to feed the hungry, as Jesus does here.

Evangelistic Emphasis

The words "marveled" and "astonished" are found often in the Gospels. Different people were impressed by different kinds of things. Some marveled at Jesus' teaching, because he taught with such a voice of authority. Some were astonished at His level of understanding. Not a few marveled at His healing of the sick. Peter was particularly impressed at His directing them to a location where they made a fabulous catch of fish. Here the disciples marveled at Jesus' command of the storm, that even the wind and waves obeyed Him!

Perhaps, we would be well served by remembering this amazing variety of things that impressed people as we go about the task of attempting to introduce people to Jesus. We have no reason to believe that everybody today will be impressed by the same facet of the message of Jesus that impresses us. If we limit our proclamation of Christ only to those truths that stir our own soul, then we will reach only those few who are stirred the same way we are stirred. In essence, we are insisting that people marvel as we marvel, or not receive the message, at all.

Instead, the proclamation of the Gospel ought to wear at least as many faces as it wore when Jesus walked the dusty roads of Palestine. Only then can the great variety of masses hear Him and come to Him as they are moved.

☜☞

But the men marveled, saying, What manner of man is this, that even the winds and the sea obey him! —*Matthew 8:27*

Little children are sometimes easily impressed. I remember well the first time I watched a man lift the front end of a car. I was impressed! "Marveled" would probably be a more accurate word. My jaw dropped and my mouth gaped open in disbelief.

Brute strength doesn't impress us so much, once we become adults. What impresses us as adults is *command*—not simply the voicing of a command, but rather command successfully executed. The Kindergarten teacher who quietly commands the rapt attention of 20 five-year-old children for hours at a time causes our jaw to drop and our mouth to gape open in disbelief. We marvel that these are the same children who reveled in chaos at our child's birthday party, in spite of all we could do.

The disciples marveled that Jesus spoke quietly to the wind and waves, and they were silenced.

Weekday Problems

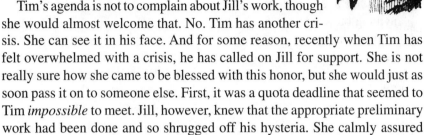

As Jill glances up from her keyboard, she spots Tim headed toward her desk. "Oh, no! Not again!" she feels the light-headed panic beginning to build within her. This is the third time this week!

Tim's agenda is not to complain about Jill's work, though she would almost welcome that. No. Tim has another crisis. She can see it in his face. And for some reason, recently when Tim has felt overwhelmed with a crisis, he has called on Jill for support. She is not really sure how she came to be blessed with this honor, but she would just as soon pass it on to someone else. First, it was a quota deadline that seemed to Tim *impossible* to meet. Jill, however, knew that the appropriate preliminary work had been done and so shrugged off his hysteria. She calmly assured him that the quota would be met.

Next, Tim was livid because "somebody" had failed to write on his calendar that he was to deliver a speech. Jill calmly handed him a folder of notes he would need and a computer disk with PowerPoint graphics. She assured him that he would do "just fine."

As Tim nears Jill's desk, she wonders what the crisis is this time. "He really does need to do something about his blood pressure," she whispers under her breath.

* What causes some people to operate at the level of "panic" most of the time, while others move calmly from problem to problem with relative ease?

* To what degree does *faith* or the lack of faith influence one's "panic threshold?"

* How can Jill help Tim to have more confidence within himself that it will all be OK?

Speaking of Miracles . . .

The thoroughly modern man told his minister he was having trouble believing in the miracles in the Bible. "What, really, is a miracle, anyway?" he asked.

"Turn around," the minister ordered; and then gave the man a swift kick in the pants. "Did you feel that?" he asked.

"I sure did!" the man replied.

"Well, it would have been a miracle if you didn't," the minister explained.

* * *

Did you hear about the guy who miraculously crossed a parrot with a tiger? He can't understand what the animal is saying, but when it talks, *everybody* listens!

This Lesson in Your Life

As Jeff read over his Sunday School lesson last night, he wished ever-so-hard that life could be so simple for him. To be on the Sea of Galilee amidst a vicious storm with life hanging in the balance sounded to him like a real treat—because the storm going on all around him is anything but simple.

For the past 20 years, life for Jeff had run with unusual smoothness. Though he has watched the lives of many of his friends come crumbling down around them, his own life has continued to sail the high seas without so much as a rough gale. More than once, he has congratulated himself for his careful "life engineering" that has proven his unusual level of wisdom. "Discipline" and "control" have been his slogans of emphasis.

Saturday night, August 11, Jeff's carefully engineered life began to crumble. First, he got a call at 11:30 p.m. that his son, Jim, had been picked up by the local police, charged with drug possession, and suspected of being part of a burglary ring. After nearly seven hours and two cell phone batteries later, Jeff was finally able to pick up his son from the county jail. Never in his wildest nightmare, had he ever dreamed that he would be faced with something like that! Though the storm began that night, it did not end there. It only began to rage.

Two days later, a detective knocked on his door with a warrant for his son's arrest for a convenience store holdup that had been under investigation for about two months. The fingerprints that had been taken two nights earlier when he was arrested matched up with prints lifted following the holdup. This time a bail bond would not come so easily. His savings account was running low, and he still needed to hire a good attorney.

Since that Monday night, life for Jeff has been a hurricane of Texas proportions. Raised voices and accusations and blaming have blown through his house unlike anything within memory. He has attempted to fasten down the shutters to keep out further unpleasantries but without much success.

Jeff and his wife have argued just about every evening until bedtime. At work, the boss is on his back to "not bring his family troubles to the office." Yet, those family troubles seem all-consuming right now. They are the "storm" in his life. And the Lord seems to be sleeping through it all. Oh, how he wishes that Jesus would wake up from His nap in the rear of the boat, and silence his storm.

1. Who initiated the boat trip that gave rise to this story's events?

Jesus. He got into the boat and his disciples followed him.

2. What prompted the disciples to awaken Jesus?

A storm suddenly arose that frightened them.

3. Upon being awakened, what was Jesus' response to His disciples?

"Why are ye fearful? O ye of little faith!"

4. After Jesus chastised His disciples, what did He do?

Jesus then got up and rebuked the wind and the waves, and it became completely calm.

5. How did Jesus' disciples respond to what they had observed?

They were completely amazed and wondered what kind of man this was whom they were following.

6. What news prompted Jesus to seek a solitary place?

Jesus had been brought the message that John the Baptist, his relative, had been executed.

7. What means of transportation did Jesus use to arrive at this "solitary place?"

He traveled by boat.

8. When Jesus arrived at his "solitary place," what did He find awaiting him there?

He found a large crowd of people who were waiting for him to arrive.

9. What one word most nearly describes Jesus' reception to the people who awaited him?

Compassionate.

10. How did Jesus show compassion to the crowd: (a) initially? (b) ultimately?

Jesus showed compassion initially by healing their sick. Ultimately, His compassion was exhibited by feeding them.

I heard a story a few months ago about a Mother who noticed that it was about time for school to dismiss. Since it looked like it was going to rain, she drove toward the school to pick up her eight year old daughter. As she turned down the street, she saw her daughter running toward her down the sidewalk.

As a lightning bolt flashed, the little girl looked up towards the sky, smiled, and then began running towards her mother's car again. Another lightning bolt flashed and again the little girl looked towards the sky, smiled, and resumed running. This happened several times until the little girl finally arrived at where her mother was parked. The young mother promptly inquired as to the strange behavior.

"Why did you keep stopping and smiling at the sky?" the mother asked.

"Because," the young girl proudly replied, *"God was taking my picture!"*

There is something delightfully innocent and true-to-life about that story. At the age of eight, we automatically assume the best of God. There is no shame within us that we wish to hide. As the lightning fills the sky we presume them to be "God's fireworks of celebration" or "His searchlight for seeking the lost" or as with that little girl, He must be "taking our picture."

It isn't long, however, before we do have shame to hide. We've eaten of the tree and shudder in the bushes, scared that God will find out what we've done. Suddenly, lightning bolts are warped by our fears into "God's missiles, aimed for our carcass." We just know that "we're toast!" The many other kinds of storms that come upon us in life also cause us to want to hide. When filtered through our fears and our shame, they seem to us to be God's way of punishing us or even destroying us.

What a blessing it would be if, as Christians, we could reflect on such storms with the same innocent welcome as that little girl in the story. Instead of interpreting the lightning bolts that come our way as missiles intended to kill us, perhaps we ought to receive them as flashes from God's camera.

After all, isn't that the message behind the story of Job? Job's friends interpreted Job's problems as the punishment of God due to some terrible sin in Job's life. And though even Job is never fully informed about what is going on, the readers (you and I) are allowed to peek behind the curtain to see that, *actually*, God is taking Job's picture. At least He is expressing great confidence in Job to prove his loyalty *even in the face of severe trial*. Or to put it another way, God is displaying his "champion" Job for all the host of heaven to see and applaud. So perhaps that little girl's interpretation of lightning was not that far off, after all!

Healing Miracles

Sept. 16

Mark 3:1-6; John 9:1-12

And he entered again into the synagogue; and there was a man there which had a withered hand.

2 And they watched him, whether he would heal him on the sabbath day; that they might accuse him.

3 And he saith unto the man which had the withered hand, Stand forth.

4 And he saith unto them, Is it lawful to do good on the sabbath days, or to do evil? to save life, or to kill? But they held their peace.

5 And when he had looked round about on them with anger, being grieved for the hardness of their hearts, he saith unto the man, Stretch forth thine hand. And he stretched it out: and his hand was restored whole as the other.

6 And the Pharisees went forth, and straightway took counsel with the Herodians against him, how they might destroy him.

John 9:1-12

1 And as Jesus passed by, he saw a man which was blind from his birth.

2 And his disciples asked him, saying, Master, who did sin, this man, or his parents, that he was born blind?

3 Jesus answered, Neither hath this man sinned, nor his parents: but that the works of God should be made manifest in him.

4 I must work the works of him that sent me, while it is day: the night cometh, when no man can work.

5 As long as I am in the world, I am the light of the world.

6 When he had thus spoken, he spat on the ground, and made clay of the spittle, and he anointed the eyes of the blind man with the clay,

7 And said unto him, Go, wash in the pool of Siloam, (which is by interpretation, Sent.) He went his way therefore, and washed, and came seeing.

8 The neighbours therefore, and they which before had seen him that he was blind, said, Is not this he that sat and begged?

9 Some said, This is he: others said, He is like him: but he said, I am he.

10 Therefore said they unto him, How were thine eyes opened?

11 He answered and said, A man that is called Jesus made clay, and anointed mine eyes, and said unto me, Go to the pool of Siloam, and wash: and I went and washed, and I received sight.

12 Then said they unto him, Where is he? He said, I know not.

Memory Selection
Mark 3:5
Devotional Reading
John 4:46-54
Background Scripture
Mark 3:1-6; John 9:1-12

Although a brief reference to a "healing miracle" was included in the previous lesson, healing miracles are often distinguished from Christ's "nature miracles" because they involve the human element. Just as a nature miracle shows Jesus' power over creation, so the focus on this lesson is to exalt His power over all human "dis-ease."

Two important religious principles accompany the healings here. In the first incident, focus on the priority of meeting human needs over religious ritual (in this case, not working on the Sabbath). In the second miracle, correct the universal tendency to think that all human plights can be traced to particular sins. Although sin in general can be traced to the Fall, Jesus warns against making judgments that relate particular cases of suffering to particular sins.

ଽୠଔୠ

You can draw attention to this lesson by asking a question that invites a false either-or answer: Does God or science heal people today? As most Christians will testify, the healing sciences grow out of the fact that a loving God stands behind creation. As even many scientists are admitting these days, there is also scientific evidence that prayer can be a valid component of the healing process. The obvious answer to the misleading question is simply Yes!

These dual truths should not detract from the superhuman power of Jesus exhibited in the two miracles in this lesson. However, the incidents invite us to learn other lessons in addition to the fact that Jesus is divine. Challenge group members to listen to other conclusions awaiting them in these texts.

Teaching Outline	Daily Bible Readings
I. Suffering and Ceremony—Mark 3:1-6	**Mon.** Healed Through Friends' Faith Mark 2:1-12
A. Set-up in the synagogue, 1-2	**Tue.** Wanting to Be Healed John 5:2-9a
B. Penetrating questions, 3-4	**Wed.** Healing a Demoniac Mark 5:1-15
C. Hard hearts, 5-6	**Thu.** Healing Jairus' Daughter Mark 5:21-24, 35-43
II. Suffering and Sin—John 9:1-12	**Fri.** Faith that Makes Us Whole Mark 5:25-34
A. Universal question, 1-2	**Sat.** Healing Through Prayer Mark 9:17-29
B. Jesus' answer, 3-5	**Sun.** Healing on the Sabbath Mark 3:1-6
C. From blindness to sight, 6-7	
D. Quest for certainty, 8-10	
E. A man called Jesus, 11-12	

Verse by Verse

I. Suffering and Ceremony—Mark 3:1-6

A. Set-up in the synagogue, 1-2

1 And he entered again into the synagogue; and there was a man there which had a withered hand.

2 And they watched him, whether he would heal him on the sabbath day; that they might accuse him.

The fact that Jesus entered "again" into the synagogue implies a habit: he modeled obedience to God for His followers by keeping the Law of Moses, even while preparing to mediate the "new covenant" of love (see Heb. 9:15).

Apparently the setting of this scene is Capernaum, the city on the northwest shore of the Sea of Galilee, where Jesus' ministry was headquartered (2:1). Archeologists have uncovered the remains of a first-century synagogue in the ruins of Capernaum—a building that could be the very place where this incident occurred.

Jesus' repute as a miracle-worker attracted a man with a "withered" (NIV "shriveled") hand. Where better to find this Healer than at the place where faithful Jews regularly gathered? Verse 6 will tell us that it was the Pharisees who watched Jesus to see whether he would heal the man

on the Sabbath. Not working on the Sabbath had become a kind of litmus test of Jewish faithfulness. Rabbis debated the definition of "work," and had developed a vastly detailed list of forbidden activities. For Jesus even to reach out His hand to heal the man could be interpreted as violating the Sabbath laws; so His critics watch Him closely here.

B. Penetrating questions, 3-4

3 And he saith unto the man which had the withered hand, Stand forth.

4 And he saith unto them, Is it lawful to do good on the sabbath days, or to do evil? to save life, or to kill? But they held their peace.

Jesus' favorite way of answering His critics was to pose questions that placed them "between a rock and a hard place," involving them in error however they answered. Failing to heal the man's hand would have been to do evil; so Jesus asks if it would be better to "break" the Sabbath with an evil deed or one that was good. With such skillful questions Jesus was not only challenging their practice of adding tradition to the Law; He was also preparing them to accept a "law of love," or of doing good, as of higher priority than the law of religious ritual. He taught the same lesson in the parable of the good Samaritan and when He defended His disciples for eating grain on the Sabbath: meeting people's needs is a law of higher priority than ritual correctness.

The Pharisees see the point, but decline to answer Jesus' question. If they admit that it would be better to "work" good on the Sabbath than not to work at all, it would compromise their tradition.

C. Hard hearts, 5-6

5 And when he had looked round about on them with anger, being grieved for the hardness of their hearts, he saith unto the man, Stretch forth thine hand. And he stretched it out: and his hand was restored whole as the other.

6 And the Pharisees went forth, and straightway took counsel with the Herodians against him, how they might destroy him.

If the Pharisees had admitted that it is better to do good than evil on the Sabbath, they would have betrayed a "soft heart"; and since Jesus is more concerned about the state of the heart than about over-scrupulously tending to religious detail, He is understandably angry and grieved. Without further attention to their hard-hearted position, He heals the man—and because this is working on the Sabbath, He incurs the wrath of His politically powerful opponents.

Nothing else is known about "Herodians" outside of Scripture. Presumably the Pharisees counsel with them because they are close to

King Herod, who has the power to use force in restraining anyone convicted of civil disobedience. The collaboration between these parties will grow more crucial over the question about paying taxes to Caesar (Mark 12:13ff.).

II. Suffering and Sin—John 9:1-12

A. Universal question, 1-2

1 And as Jesus passed by, he saw a man which was blind from his birth.

2 And his disciples asked him, saying, Master, who did sin, this man, or his parents, that he was born blind?

The second miracle in our lesson deals with the age-old tendency to explain suffering by saying that the sufferer has incurred the wrath of God (or "the gods," since pagans and worshipers of God both have a long tradition of this kind of thinking).

This time it is not an opposition party like the Pharisees who question Jesus, but His own disciples. Their question is understandable. They knew the story of the Fall, and the consequences of a "fallen" earth resulting from the sin of Adam and Eve. They also knew that children sometimes suffer at least the consequences of the sins of their parents (Exod. 34:7)—as when a pregnant mother who uses drugs may deliver a baby that is already addicted.

B. Jesus' answer, 3-5

3 Jesus answered, Neither hath this man sinned, nor his parents: but that the works of God should be made manifest in him.

4 I must work the works of him that sent me, while it is day: the night cometh, when no man can work.

5 As long as I am in the world, I am the light of the world.

Despite the fact that sin in general descends on us all because of the Fall, Jesus denies that in this particular case the man's blindness stems from specific sin. He is blind in order to display the work of God—to be the subject of Jesus' miraculous healing. Verses 4 and 5, in which Jesus connects His work as the light of the world with God's work of salvation, should caution us against developing a full-blown "theology of evil" from this incident. The man is a vehicle to authenticate Christ's work, not a lesson on the general theory of suffering. Still, can we not allow our own ills to point also to Jesus' power by responding to them positively?

C. From blindness to sight, 6-7

6 When he had thus spoken, he spat on the ground, and made clay of the spittle, and he anointed the eyes of the blind man with the clay,

7 And said unto him, Go, wash in the pool of Siloam, (which is by interpretation, Sent.) He went his way therefore, and washed, and came seeing.

There is no more significance in the clay with which Jesus anoints the man's eye than there was in the gesture with which He healed the withered hand of the man at the synagogue in Capernaum. The healings could have been accomplished with a thought; the visual elements are for our benefit, allowing us to be sure the miracle was done by Jesus Himself.

D. Quest for certainty, 8-10

8 The neighbours therefore, and they which before had seen him that he was blind, said, Is not this he that sat and begged?

9 Some said, This is he: others said, He is like him: but he said, I am he.

10 Therefore said they unto him, How were thine eyes opened?

Amid the excitement of the healing are the attempts to verify that the man who now can see is the same man Jesus anointed. No doubt his demeanor and actions were different. After identifying him, the "neighbors"—and no doubt Jesus' enemies as well—want to know how the healing was accomplished. Of course we do not really know *how*, but only *who*. The method is Jesus Himself.

E. A man called Jesus, 11-12

11 He answered and said, A man that is called Jesus made clay, and anointed mine eyes, and said unto me, Go to the pool of Siloam, and wash: and I went and washed, and I received sight.

12 Then said they unto him, Where is he? He said, I know not.

Although the man whose sight is recovered does not know where Jesus is, the incident has contributed to the build-up of Messianic excitement that will both reveal Jesus' identity as Savior and, because of His enemies, lead Him to the Cross.

25

Evangelistic Emphasis

I first became aware of Bruce, passing him on the streets of Searcy, Arkansas, as he jogged early in the morning. Not being quite so health-conscious as Bruce, I was always in a car. One of the things that caught my attention was his "short arm." His right arm was smaller than his left arm in every way. His hand was not fully developed.

As my college years passed, Bruce and I became friends. Times of quiet "heart-talk" revealed his own personal struggle with his "deformity." Though he had learned to accept his physical limitations, he confided that one of the most difficult struggles that he encountered was the ignorance of people who interpreted his "defect" as a punishment from God.

Even though Jesus Himself addressed that superstition as having no validity, it still is often found among religious and superstitious people. My friend's own confrontation with that issue has opened many doors to him to minister to others who struggle with the same kinds of deformity stereotypes. He has found that for some, these illusions of God's punishment have been barriers to their understanding the Gospel and their coming to faith.

ഇൻറ

And when he had looked round about on them with anger, being grieved for the hardness of their hearts, he saith unto the man, Stretch forth thine hand. And he stretched it out: and his hand was restored whole as the other.—*Mark 3:5*

Faith inevitably demonstrates itself in the form of obedience. For Noah, it produced an ark. Abraham carried his son to a top of a mountain. Moses responded by providing leadership to the people of Israel. Rahab was moved by her faith to hide the spies of Israel from those who would have captured them. Nehemiah rebuilt the city walls. John the Baptist began immersing people in water, waiting for the appearance of a dove. He had been told that the one on whom the dove descended would be the one who was promised.

Every one of those Biblical heroes were heroes *because* they were individuals of faith. It was not an idle faith, however, but in each case the faith present prompted the believer to actions pleasing to God. So too, the man with the withered hand had a faith that prompted him *automatically* to stretch out his hand at the word of Jesus. The end result was that his faith brought wholeness to his life. If our faith is to be pleasing to God, it too must prompt us to action that pleases Him.

Weekday Problems

Jim and Susan McCoy tried to become parents for seven years. During that time, their lives were a roller coaster of emotions. More than ten times their hearts leaped with joy at the thought that they were finally going to become parents. Each time, however, their hopes were dashed on the hard rocks of reality. Their excitement had been premature.

Finally, after four miscarriages last year Susan carried a baby full-term. Unfortunately, when little Jeffery was born, the doctor informed Susan and Jim that their baby had Down's syndrome. Following the thrill of nine months of anticipation, it was almost more heartbreak than they could endure. Earlier, both Jim and Susan had wondered if their childlessness was the result of God punishing them for some sin. Now they are asking why He is punishing their baby.

* Do you believe that Jim and Susan's childlessness was the result of God's punishment? What evidence would you find conclusive—one way or the other?

* Do you believe God is punishing Jeffery for something that Jim and Susan has done? Why? Why not?

* What kinds of physical or mental illnesses have you heard people cite as evidence of God's punishment? How do you typically respond to such allegations?

Over-Eaters Synonymous

Overeating: the destiny that shapes our ends.

* * *

I am not overweight. I'm just six inches too short.

* * *

He was so overweight that the only job he could get was piloting the Goodyear blimp.

* * *

I don't want to say that she's fat, but she is definitely over-emphasized.

* * *

He's a do-it-yourself man. He made a bay window with a knife and fork.

***

She's on a garlic diet. She hasn't lost any weight, but she's lost quite a few friends.

This Lesson in Your Life

It has been years since Gertrude has felt the touch of human kindness against her weather-worn skin. There was a time when men paid handsomely for her companionship. She was one of the highest paid "call girls" in San Francisco—too expensive for most men even to consider. Her attention was reserved for only the most successful business men and politicians. That was a very long time ago, however. That was when she used the professional name, "Rochelle," rather than "Gertrude," the name that her Arkansas parents had given her.

Today, though Gertrude lives just on the other side of the bay in Oakland, she is a thousand miles away from that life in San Francisco. Somehow, life got away from "Rochelle." She never thought about her bad choices catching up with her. Neither did she think about getting old and losing her natural allurement that provided her livelihood. But it all finally caught up with her—wrinkles, venereal diseases, liquor, drugs, severe beatings by unsatisfied or insane customers, and jail time. In a matter of months she went from "Rochelle, the top-dollar San Francisco call girl" to "Gertrude, the Oakland street addict/hooker."

More than seven years have passed since Gertrude moved to Oakland. She's spent time in every shelter in town at least once. Several of those shelters require daily Bible study and attendance at the evening preaching service. Gertrude has been "saved" more times than she can count, because she quickly learned that "getting saved" was an easy ticket to receive some better meals in the homes of real families. After awhile, though, her "salvation routine" stopped working. Her crassly, unrepentant heart eventually became common knowledge and shelters were found to be always mysteriously full when she tried to get a room.

The only times that Gertrude has had a bath during the past two years came when she found herself in jail (twice) and when she was hosed down by some neighborhood children because of her bad smell. Oh, how she would love to feel the embrace of love again—even if it could be only the artificial kind that the prostitute knows. How painfully Gertrude remembers her mother rocking her on the cool mornings and kissing her goodnight. Gertrude remembers stories from some of those preachers about lepers that no one would touch, and she thinks she knows pretty much how they felt. She wonders whether this Jesus would be willing to touch her, or if the smell would drive him away. Though she suspects that all that "Jesus talk" was just stories that those preachers made up, a part of her desperately wants to believe that theywere true. She needs so much to believe that some Jesus-kind-of-person will one day find her. And if he does, perhaps, he will touch her with a tenderness for which she so much longs.

STRAIGHT

1. Where was Jesus when He encountered the man with the withered hand?
He was in the synagogue.

2. Why were some of in the synagogue closely watching Jesus?
They were seeking to find some accusation to bring against Him.

3. What did Jesus instruct the man with the withered hand to do?
Jesus instructed him to stand in front of everyone.

4. What question did Jesus then ask those who were seeking to accuse him?
He asked whether it was right to good or evil on the Sabbath day—to save life or to kill?

5. What emotion does the Bible say Jesus had on that occasion?
Anger. The Bible says that He was deeply distressed by their hardness of hearts.

6. Once Jesus had healed the man's hand, how did the Pharisees respond?
They immediately went out to begin to plot to kill him.

7. What question did Jesus' disciples ask Him when they encountered the blind man on the road?
They asked, "Who sinned" (causing his blindness)? Himself or his parents?

8. Which did Jesus point to as "guilty?"
Neither. He said that neither had sinned (causing his blindness).

9. What did Jesus put on the eyes of the blind man?
He made some mud out of saliva and put it on the man's eyes.

10. Where did Jesus tell the man to go to wash his eyes?
He told him to wash his eyes in the Pool of Siloam.

I once read that "What sunshine is to flowers, hugs are to humanity." Perhaps most parents have run across Shel Silverstein's poem, "Hug O' War:"

I will not play Tug O' War,
I'd rather play Hug O' War;
Where everyone hugs, instead of tugs,
And everyone giggles and rolls on the rug.
Where everyone kisses,
and everyone grins;
everyone cuddles,
and everyone wins.

One "prescription" praising the value of the "human touch" or ordinary "hugs" comes from Mark Katz, M.D., Member of L.A. Shanti's Advisory Board. He has written:

How important are hugging and physical and emotional contact for people affected by life -threatening illnesses? In my work, I have found that people who receive nurturing maintain a better outlook on their situation—and historically, positive attitude is an important factor in long-term survival. Hugging and physical contact make a difference in a person's frame of mind, and may help his medical condition. Best of all, hugging has no side effects and does not require a trip to the doctor.

The most impressive testimonial that I have seen recently was an article that appeared in a variety of places, including *Life*, *Ensign*, *Readers' Digest*, and in a host of e-mail forwards that were sent my way. It was entitled, "The Rescuing Hug." The article details the first week of life of a set of twins that were patients at Massachusetts Memorial Hospital in Worcester, Massachusetts. Apparently, each was in her respective incubator, and one was not expected to live. A hospital nurse fought against the hospital rules and placed the babies in one incubator. When they were placed together, the healthier of the two threw an arm over her sister in an endearing embrace. The smaller baby's heart rate stabilized and her temperature rose to normal.

Both of the infants survived, and went on to thrive! A follow-up report testified that after the two girls were taken home, they continued to sleep together and snuggle. The hospital changed its policy after they saw the effect of putting the two girls together. Now they bed multiples together.

As one reads the Gospel record of Jesus' ministry, it is obvious that 2,000 years ago Jesus understood fully the importance of human touch that modern medical science is just now beginning to discover. I wonder if it is possible that His insights could have anything to do with the fact that He participated in our original design and formation.

...GREAT IS YOUR FAITH!
Billy 00

Mother's Faith

Matthew 15:21-31

Then Jesus went thence, and departed into the coasts of Tyre and Sidon.

22 And, behold, a woman of Canaan came out of the same coasts, and cried unto him, saying, Have mercy on me, O Lord, thou Son of David; my daughter is grievously vexed with a devil.

23 But he answered her not a word. And his disciples came and besought him, saying, Send her away; for she crieth after us.

24 But he answered and said, I am not sent but unto the lost sheep of the house of Israel.

25 Then came she and worshipped him, saying, Lord, help me.

26 But he answered and said, It is not meet to take the children's bread, and to cast it to dogs.

27 And she said, Truth, Lord: yet the dogs eat of the crumbs which fall from their master's table.

28 Then Jesus answered and said unto her, O woman, great is thy faith: be it unto thee even as thou wilt. And her daughter was made whole from that very hour.

29 And Jesus departed from thence, and came nigh unto the sea of Galilee; and went up into a mountain, and sat down there.

30 And great multitudes came unto him, having with them those that were lame, blind, dumb, maimed, and many others, and cast them down at Jesus' feet; and he healed them:

31 Insomuch that the multitude wondered, when they saw the dumb to speak, the maimed to be whole, the lame to walk, and the blind to see: and they glorified the God of Israel.

Memory Selection
Matthew 15:28

Devotional Reading
Luke 4:16-21

Background Scripture
Matthew 15:21-31

The twin focus of this story from the life of Jesus is (a) His power over the demonic world, and (b) the value of persistent faith. Jesus at first denies the request of a Gentile woman who begs Him to cast a demon out of her daughter. Yet the woman stubbornly maintains her case, and Jesus relents, exorcising the daughter by "long distance."

Although this much is clear, the effective teacher will also focus on questions that arise from the story. What was "demon-possession," and does it occur today? Why does the Master Healer seemingly have to be begged to respond to the request of a genuine seeker? And does He finally give in just because she "out-argues" the very Son of God? In addition to affirming the awesome power of Jesus over demons, the answers to such questions also deserve emphasizing as you present this lesson.

ഇⓒ

Try a quick TV trivia quiz to introduce this lesson. Ask what anyone in the group can remember about the comedian Flip Wilson. He had audiences roaring with laughter by his use of the excuse "The devil made me do it." The gimmick was an effective satire on the way many people try to avoid personal responsibility by attributing evil impulses to Satan.

Point out that Satan's influence is no laughing matter in today's lesson. He had taken over the daughter of one of the story's main characters. You may also want to bring up the question of whether demon possession occurs today, although it will add to the build-up of interest as the lesson progresses if you leave the question unanswered until the plight of the woman's daughter arises in the verse-by-verse discussion.

Teaching Outline	Daily Bible Readings
I. Possessed by a Demon—15:21-22 II. Parrying the Appeal—23-24 　A. Silence, 23a 　B. 'Send her away,' 23b 　C. Exclusive mission, 24 III. Persistent Plea—25-28 　A. Jesus' position, 25-26 　B. Winning retort, 27-28 IV. Physical miracles, 29-31	**Mon.** 'Come to Me, Ye Weary' 　　Matthew 11:25-30 **Tue.** A Son Restored 　　Luke 7:11-17 **Wed.** Cured, but 'Don't Tell' 　　Matthew 12:15-21 **Thu.** Healing by What Authority? 　　Matthew 12:22-28 **Fri.** Breaking with Tradition 　　Matthew 15:1-9 **Sat.** Things that Defile 　　Matthew 15:10-20 **Sun.** A Woman of Great Faith 　　Matthew 15:21-31

Verse by Verse

I. Possessed by a Demon—15:21-22

21 Then Jesus went thence, and departed into the coasts of Tyre and Sidon.

22 And, behold, a woman of Canaan came out of the same coasts, and cried unto him, saying, Have mercy on me, O Lord, thou Son of David; my daughter is grievously vexed with a devil.

Jesus' behavior in this account will be less perplexing if we note that the incident follows a discussion of the Jewish practice of ritual washings (Matt. 15:1-2). This rite was often performed not only before meals but as a sign of cleansing oneself of spiritual impurity supposedly caused by associating with Gentiles. Before this Canaanite woman came to Jesus, He had taught His disciples that sin consists of impurity that arises from within the heart, not from externals such as eating or associating with the "wrong" kind of people (vs. 11). This background will be crucial for understanding why Jesus deals with the woman's request as He does.

The coastal areas of Tyre and Sidon had never been fully occupied by the Jews who conquered most of the "Promised Land." As a Canaanite whose ancestors had lived in Palestine before the Jews arrived, the woman was despised by proper Jews.

She typified the reason a good Jew would wash his or her hands after being in a Gentile's presence. The plight of her daughter, along with Jesus' reputation as a healer, must have driven from her mind any concern about her "inferior" social status offending these Jews whom she approaches.

Stated literally, the daughter is "badly demonized" (KJV "vexed with a devil;" NIV "suffering terribly from demon-possession"). Although this condition was sometimes accompanied by physical illness, it is incorrect to assume that all biblical references to being "demonized" reflect a primitive view that all sickness was to be attributed to demon-possession.

The presence of the Messiah apparently brought a rash of Satanic activity. The devil's ability to inhabit a person was severely curtailed by Christ's death and resurrection (Col. 2:15); yet the condition continued to some degree, for it was after His resurrection that Jesus specifically promised that His disciples would have the power to cast out demons (Mark 16:17). Responsible persons sometimes report this condition even today, especially from missionaries in areas that are in the grip of paganism.

33

II. Parrying the Appeal—23-24
A. Silence, 23a

3 But he answered her not a word.

At first Jesus seems to ignore the woman. It is more likely that He is silent in order to give time for His disciples to react. They will be more susceptible to the truth of the lesson He will teach them if they are allowed first to express their erroneous view.

B. 'Send her away,' 23b

And his disciples came and besought him, saying, Send her away; for she crieth after us.

More than once, Jesus' disciples try to protect Him from those who would accost Him (see Matt. 14:15). Here they advise Him to send the woman away, not because their Master is tired, but because she is a Gentile, and thus "unclean." She is also a loud woman whose incessant crying out is irritating.

C. Exclusive mission, 24

24 But he answered and said, I am not sent but unto the lost sheep of the house of Israel.

At first it seems that Jesus will agree to send the woman away since, as a Gentile, she is not included in His mission to be a Jewish Messiah. He had expressed this same limited scope of His work in the "limited commission" (Matt. 10:5-6). Some commentators think that His larger, worldwide purpose dawned on Jesus only gradually. It seems more in tune with His usual self-awareness that He views His mission as proceeding in stages, like that of Paul, "to the Jew first, [but then] and also to the Greek (Rom. 1:16, etc.) If this is correct, Jesus is agreeing that His disciples have a point, and seemingly adding a good theological reason for sending this Gentile woman away. As we shall see, however, He is likely only setting them up for a larger view of His role as Messiah.

III. Persistent Plea—25-28
A. Jesus' position, 25-26

25 Then came she and worshipped him, saying, Lord, help me.

26 But he answered and said, It is not meet to take the children's bread, and to cast it to dogs.

Now the woman proves not only to be a loud Gentile woman, but "pushy" as well! Her need is so urgent that she pushes past both Jesus' and the disciples' apparent rejection. She also proves to be a well-informed and pious Gentile. She knew that Jesus was the "Son of David" (vs. 22), and now she acknowledges His divinity by worshiping Him.

Jesus' reply seems surprisingly blunt. Jews often referred to Gentiles as dogs, and while He uses a diminutive form of the word here (perhaps something like "house-dog" as opposed to a stray cur), it still seems designed to put the woman in her place. However, knowing what we do about Jesus' overall kindness toward all, we should see what comes of His reply before concluding that He is prejudiced or rude.

B. Winning retort, 27-28

27 And she said, Truth, Lord: yet

the dogs eat of the crumbs which fall from their master's table.

28 Then Jesus answered and said unto her, O woman, great is thy faith: be it unto thee even as thou wilt. And her daughter was made whole from that very hour.

Now the woman proves not only to be a loud, pushy Gentile female, but a smart-alec as well. She actually dares to try to out-argue the Son of God, accepting His having called her a dog but turning it into a reason He should help her. And it works! Against His disciples' advice and His own recitation of His Jewish mission, He relents. In contrast to the "little faith" of His own disciples at times (see Matt. 8:26 and Lesson 2), He commends the "great faith" of this Gentile woman. Without even having to go to the girl in person, He uses His divine power to exorcise the woman's demonized daughter.

What has happened here? Did Jesus allow Himself to be outsmarted or ground down by this persistent Gentile woman? It is more likely that He deliberately went into Gentile territory (vs. 21) to set up the entire scene. He wanted to illustrate for His disciples what He had taught earlier about uncleanness coming from within, not from externals such as food or Gentiles. He seemed to go along with their view of His (at first) limited commission, then corrected it with a miraculous healing that forecast a mission to Gentiles as well as Jews.

Jesus' act is in line with the broader mission seen from the beginning by old Simeon, who foresaw that the Christ-child would be a "light to lighten the Gentiles," in direct fulfillment of prophecy (Luke 2:32; Isa. 9:2). Faced with the task of teaching prejudiced Jews this truth, Jesus had allowed Himself to side with them even to the point of appearing rude to the woman—but only in order to more dramatically portray His acceptance of her and other non-Jews.

IV. Physical miracles, 29-31

29 And Jesus departed from thence, and came nigh unto the sea of Galilee; and went up into a mountain, and sat down there.

30 And great multitudes came unto him, having with them those that were lame, blind, dumb, maimed, and many others, and cast them down at Jesus' feet; and he healed them:

31 Insomuch that the multitude wondered, when they saw the dumb to speak, the maimed to be whole, the lame to walk, and the blind to see: and they glorified the God of Israel.

After the dramatic encounter with the Canaanite woman, Jesus returns to a more familiar Jewish area to resume His healing ministry. In a more general sense, the ailments listed here are also of Satan, who instigated the Fall that brought physical as well as spiritual infirmities. From showing His power over demon-possession, Jesus turns to more physical manifestations of the evils from which He was sent to free the world.

Evangelistic Emphasis

One ingredient of speech that is often a forgotten element when we read Scripture is tone. Yet, tone is as important to appropriate understanding of the intended message as are the words that are spoken. A sentence of only a few words can communicate any of a wide array of messages.

Consider for a moment the words, "I love you." Those three words may convey the gentle affection of friendship, or the heated passion of lust. They may hold rich tenderness of a grandmother speaking to her grandson, or the mocking humiliation of a spurned suitor. Most of the time, these words bless those on the receiving end. Occasionally, the sarcasm they carry can inflict wounds that scar for a lifetime.

How did Jesus' words sound as he spoke to this woman whose daughter was ill? In print, they can sound so callous--so uncharacteristic of Jesus. Yet, with what tone did he speak those words? Was it a tone that hardened the callous nature of the words? Or, was it a tone that softened the words into a welcoming caress?

As I try to listen to the text with ears conditioned by hearing Jesus in a host of other conversations with people, I hear words with the expected rejection that the culture dictated. Yet, I hear a tone that tenderly contradicted the expectation, inviting her to be persistent in her request.

ഇരുൽ

Memory Selection

Then Jesus answered and said unto her, O woman, great is thy faith: be it unto thee even as thou wilt. And her daughter was made whole from that very hour.—Matthew 15:28

Jennifer Long is presently struggling with her faith. It's *not* the usual kind of struggle she has known before. This struggle is linked with a coworker, whom she perceives to have a much stronger faith than her own. She has observed her friend endure heavy stress amidst in an unusually threatening situation, yet without wavering even slightly in her trust in God. Jennifer is not at all sure her own faith would be so enduring.

The reason this is troubling to Jennifer is that according to her own doctrine, her coworker is not really a Christian. The religious group of which she is a member does not meet the rules of orthodoxy as she understands them. How can this friend who is not a "real Christian" have a faith that is deeper and richer than her own?

Weekday Problems

As Linda reads this week's lesson from Matthew 15, she can understand very well the disciples' recommendation that Jesus send away the woman of Canaan. Two weeks ago, Linda made a very similar recommendation to Pastor Andrews. Since she works as church secretary, it is her responsibility to screen calls and "protect his time." One woman who came to the office on that Tuesday, however, would not take "no" for an answer. She insisted on talking with the Pastor.

Linda had a bad feeling about the woman, however. Perhaps it was the way she was dressed, or the way she carried herself. She wasn't really sure. She just knew that her sense was that *the woman was trouble.* Linda told Pastor Andrews that, too, before she admitted the woman to his office. Unfortunately, he did not listen to her advice. He was beguiled by the woman's' crocodile tears and baby-doll eyelashes. What will come of all of this is yet to be seen, but it will come. Linda is convinced of it!

* Are there times when someone "in need" should be sent away? If so, what are some examples of such times? If not, how does one deal with situations where questions arise about one's claimed need?

* Is it possible that Linda was attempting to be overly protective of Pastor Andrews? How can one in her role determine what is appropriate and what is inappropriate?

* How could "the way one is dressed" or "the way she carries herself" legitimately raise questions about whether she should be helped? Give examples.

Slips of the Lips

Q: What did the German clock-maker say to the broken cuckoo clock?
A: Ve haff vays of making you tock.

* * *

Q: What did the man do after his cat was run over by a steam roller?
A: He just sat there with a long puss.

* * *

Q: How do you make a glowworm happy?
A: Cut off its tail. It'll be delighted.

* * *

A tiger was walking through the jungle and saw two men relaxing under a tree. One was reading a newspaper; the other was typing on a portable typewriter. The tiger leaped on the man with the newspaper and ate him up, but he didnÆt bother the other man at all. Why? Because any predator knows that readers digest, but writers cramp.

This Lesson in Your Life

Cheryl's high school basketball coach was unusually loud and verbally abusive. He yelled and screamed at everyone, but Cheryl was the only one who yelled back. Her parents had strongly mixed feelings about the matter. They were proud of her for standing up for herself, yet they were not sure that they were comfortable about her being involved in such verbal jousting. Observing the situation regularly, however, they consoled themselves that it wouldn't last long. They knew that she was an above-average player, but they also knew that the relationship between her and the coach was more than a little strained. Either their daughter would quit or she would get cut from the team. Much to her parents surprise, Cheryl actually made the team.

When the regular playing season began, not much changed in the face-off between Cheryl and her coach. He continued to bark loudly and often at all of the players. Some of them would cry. Some of the parents complained at his verbal outbursts. Cheryl continued to reply to his attacks with counter-attacks equal in volume and determination.

The contention between the two in no way diminished Cheryl's playing time, however. In fact, the tougher the competition became, the more the coach leaned on Cheryl. At the same time, the more he looked to her for performance, the more he tended to be in her face, yelling.

When the basketball season was finally over and it was time for the awards dinner, Cheryl left with the "Most Valuable Player Award" for the season. And when the word came back from the school district that spring that the coach's contract was not being renewed, Cheryl led the petition to have his contract renewed.

Relationships are each unique. In an odd way, I suspect that the contention that was so strong between that coach and Cheryl brought out the best in both of them. Even though he sometimes became furious with Cheryl's "back talk," it was obvious, also, that he respected her feisty tenacity. And although Cheryl was often furious at the coach for yelling at her on the basketball court in front of her whole school, she respected the strong way that he pushed her to do her absolute best. He wasn't trying to break her, but to push her "to the max."

As one reads the account of Jesus and the Canaanite woman all the way to its conclusion, it becomes obvious that Jesus never intended to "break" that woman, either. His verbal bantering was well gauged, instead, to bring to light the unequaled measure of her strength. Rather than humiliating her, Jesus highly praised her in the presence of all.

1. To what region of the country did Jesus withdraw?
To the region of Tyre and Sidon.

2. A woman of what ethnic group approached Jesus for help?
A Canaanite woman.

3. What was the need that prompted the woman to cry out?
Her daughter was suffering from what she judged to be demon-possession.

4. How did Jesus initially respond to the woman's pleas?
He remained silent in response to her cries.

5. How did Jesus' disciples want Him to respond to her pleas?
The disciples wanted Jesus to "send her away."

6. To whom did Jesus say He had been sent to minister?
He said that he had been sent only to the lost sheep of Israel?

7. What did the woman then do?
She knelt before him and begged.

8. What reason did Jesus give to the woman for not helping her?
He told her that it was not right to take the children's (the Jews') bread and to give it to the dogs (Gentiles).

9. What was the woman's ready reply?
The woman told Jesus that even the dogs eat the crumbs that fall from their master's table.

10. Did Jesus heal the woman's daughter?
Yes.

Stan and Jessica Johnson paced their son's hospital room floor, unsure what God had awaiting them. They did know that the previous two months had been the most difficult of their lives. Stan held in his arms Gregory, his motionless son, who was less than a year old.

At eight months of age little Gregory had become mysteriously ill. Fifty-five days and hundreds of tests later, it was finally determined that he had a bad case of "infant botulism." Unfortunately, by then the disease had taken a heavy toll on Gregory's little body.

Stan Johnson had stayed with his son since his son had been admitted. One great comfort was that the people at church where Stan preached had been faithfully praying for Gregory since he became ill. As Stan paced the floor with Gregory in his arms, it was the seventieth day since he was admitted to the hospital and more than two weeks since the diagnosis was made. The future did not look promising for the deathly still infant. His condition had taken a sharp turn for the worse a few days earlier, and the doctors began to suspect that he might be brain-dead. Once that possibility was mentioned, representatives from several departments had promptly approached the Johnsons in petition of the child's organs. Church members divided into teams and t ook turns standing watch beneath Gregory's window, praying around the clock in unbroken prayer.

Because of the extensive nature of the testing, the results were considered to be conclusive. Since the Johnsons were resistant to the idea, they were given 48 hours to come to terms with reality. Their response to this wrenching news was more prayer. Now, 48 hours later, it was with heavy hearts that Stan and Jessica prayed and paced. No signs of life had appeared. Instead, as they prayed the hospital room door opened. Twelve doctors and hospital personnel entered the room to take the child forcibly if necessary. The team had assembled to reap the child's organs.

It was with one last petition of desperation that the Johnson's cried out to God that He not allow this to be so. As the hospital staff reached to take the child, Stan called out, *"Wait! I saw him open his eyes!"*

Of course, that could not be. The doctors had established officially that he was brain-dead 48 hours earlier. The situation became confrontational. Fortunately, the evidence was on Stan's side that day. Gregory *had* opened his eyes! Furthermore, 18 days later he was dismissed from that hospital. Today, he is age 14 and doing quite well, showing no signs of having ever been sick. Like the woman who approached Jesus, the Johnsons had a faith that refused to give up in behalf of their child.

Raising Lazarus

John 11:1-6, 11-15, 38-44

Now a certain man was sick, named Lazarus, of Bethany, the town of Mary and her sister Martha.

2 (It was that Mary which anointed the Lord with ointment, and wiped his feet with her hair, whose brother Lazarus was sick.)

3 Therefore his sisters sent unto him, saying, Lord, behold, he whom thou lovest is sick.

4 When Jesus heard that, he said, This sickness is not unto death, but for the glory of God, that the Son of God might be glorified thereby.

5 Now Jesus loved Martha, and her sister, and Lazarus.

6 When he had heard therefore that he was sick, he abode two days still in the same place where he was.

11 These things said he: and after that he saith unto them, Our friend Lazarus sleepeth; but I go, that I may awake him out of sleep.

12 Then said his disciples, Lord, if he sleep, he shall do well.

13 Howbeit Jesus spake of his death: but they thought that he had spoken of taking of rest in sleep.

14 Then said Jesus unto them plainly, Lazarus is dead.

15 And I am glad for your sakes that I was not there, to the intent ye may believe; nevertheless let us go unto him.

38 Jesus therefore again groaning in himself cometh to the grave. It was a cave, and a stone lay upon it.

39 Jesus said, Take ye away the stone. Martha, the sister of him that was dead, saith unto him, Lord, by this time he stinketh: for he hath been dead four days.

40 Jesus saith unto her, Said I not unto thee, that, if thou wouldest believe, thou shouldest see the glory of God?

41 Then they took away the stone from the place where the dead was laid. And Jesus lifted up his eyes, and said, Father, I thank thee that thou hast heard me.

42 And I knew that thou hearest me always: but because of the people which stand by I said it, that they may believe that thou hast sent me.

43 And when he thus had spoken, he cried with a loud voice, Lazarus, come forth.

44 And he that was dead came forth, bound hand and foot with graveclothes: and his face was bound about with a napkin. Jesus saith unto them, Loose him, and let him go.

Sept. 30

Memory Selection
John 11:25-26

Devotional Reading
John 11:17-27

Background Scripture
John 11:1-44

All of Jesus' miracles astound and amaze us. Preceding lessons have advanced in a crescendo of wonder, from calming a storm to feeding the hungry, healing the sick, and casting out demons. Each of these "signs," as John calls them, grip our attention because they show Jesus conquering enemies of the good life and connecting with the universal human experience of fear, hunger, illness, and encounters with evil.

Now, in a miracle that crowns them all, Jesus addresses the ultimate human predicament: death. People everywhere ask hopefully, "If a man dies, will he live again?" (Job 14:14). In response to this universal question Jesus not only rises from the dead Himself; He raises His friend Lazarus from the dead. Focus in this lesson on the Gospels' answer to Job's question: Jesus' followers will experience a glorious resurrection.

ഇന്ദ്ര

Start this session by announcing that "We are all invited to a funeral today." Ask what we expect of such a service. We assemble family and friends to commemorate the life of the deceased. Words and music offer comfort to the bereaved. Flower arrangements are designed to remind us that beauty and hope exist amid grief and despair. Finally, a burial service hopefully adds "closure" to the experience as an encouragement to get on with our lives.

Note, however, that the order of today's "service" has a slight interruption. The deceased is raised from the dead! Like the hymns, sermon, and flowers, however, this too is designed not just for the dead, but for us. In John's hands the event becomes a "sign"—a "portent" of the Christian hope. In this sense, all who attend this "funeral" are brothers and sisters of the deceased.

Teaching Outline	Daily Bible Readings

I. Death of Lazarus—John 11:1-6
   A. Lazarus and his sisters, 1-2
   B. Jesus is summoned, 3-6
II. Dead or Asleep?—11-15
   A. Resting vs. Dying, 11-14
   B. That you may believe, 15
III. Defeat of Death—38-44
   A. Sadness at the tomb, 38
   B. Directions for life, 39-40
   C. Jesus' prayer, 41-42
   D. Lazarus is raised, 43-44
	Mon. Jesus: Sinner or Prophet?
	   John 9:13-17
	Tue. Once Blind, Now I See
	   John 9:18-25
	Wed. Who Sees? Who Is Blind?
	   John 9:26-41
	Thu. Death of Lazarus
	   John 11:1-16
	Fri. 'I Am the Resurrection'
	   John 11:17-27
	Sat. 'If You Had Been Here'
	   John 11:28-37
	Sun. The Dead Arises
	   John 11:38-44

I. Death of Lazarus—John 11:1-6

A. Lazarus and his sisters, 1-2

1 Now a certain man was sick, named Lazarus, of Bethany, the town of Mary and her sister Martha.

2 (It was that Mary which anointed the Lord with ointment, and wiped his feet with her hair, whose brother Lazarus was sick.)

Bethany, was a town just a mile and a half out of Jerusalem (15 "furlongs," literally, *stadia*, vs. 18, KJV). Today it is called El Azariyeh after the main character of this story; and visitors are still shown a site that is supposedly Lazarus' tomb. Bethany was Jesus' "home away from home." It was there that, as verse 2 tells us, Mary anointed Jesus' feet; and since this event doesn't occur until 12:3, the author either assumes the reader knows of it, or verse 2 was added by a later editor.

B. Jesus is summoned, 3-6

3 Therefore his sisters sent unto him, saying, Lord, behold, he whom thou lovest is sick.

4 When Jesus heard that, he said, This sickness is not unto death, but for the glory of God, that the Son of God might be glorified thereby.

5 Now Jesus loved Martha, and her sister, and Lazarus.

6 When he had heard therefore that he was sick, he abode two days still in the same place where he was.

Lazarus' sisters send for Jesus because Jesus is a good friend of the family, as verse 5 indicates. Jesus, however, perceives that God has singled Lazarus out for another of John's "signs"—this time a resurrection from the dead. He may be reflecting on this and speaking within himself when He notes that Lazarus' case "will not end in death" (v. 4, NIV), but has been pre-arranged to witness to the power and glory of God. By faith that death is not "for death," but only a phase of the "eternal life" Christ gives us when we come to Him, all believers' death can be a testimony to God's glory.

Why does Jesus stay two days where He is instead of rushing immediately to Lazarus' bedside? Some think the delay is to give Lazarus time to die, so Jesus can raise him to life. However, in discussing the case with His disciples in verse 14 (below), Jesus says plainly that His friend had died before He heard he was ill.

Some ancient rabbis taught that the spirit of a dead person lingered three days over the body before finally accepting the separation called "death" and departing to "Abraham's bosom" (Luke 16:22). Burial rites therefore did not conclude until the fourth day after death, to be sure the person did not revive, but was actually dead. Knowing His disciples might believe this, perhaps Jesus postpones his arrival until everyone perceives that Lazarus' spirit did not return to his body. Counting a day to get the message to him, the two days' delay, and a day to return, Jesus will not arrive at Bethany until the fourth day (vs. 39). In this way critics could not say that Lazarus merely revived from a coma.

II. Dead or Asleep?—11-15
A. Resting vs. Dying, 11-14

11 These things said he: and after that he saith unto them, Our friend Lazarus sleepeth; but I go, that I may awake him out of sleep.

12 Then said his disciples, Lord, if he sleep, he shall do well.

13 Howbeit Jesus spake of his death: but they thought that he had spoken of taking of rest in sleep.

14 Then said Jesus unto them plainly, Lazarus is dead.

By saying that Lazarus "sleepeth," Jesus is not deliberately trying to mislead His disciples but using a term that was a common way to speak of death (see also 1 Thess. 4:13-15). However, the disciples take Him literally, saying that if Lazarus is only sleeping "he shall do well"—literally, he will be "saved (from death) or restored to health. In order for the miracle of raising Lazarus really to give glory to God, Jesus quickly corrects the disciples' misunderstanding, saying plainly that the situation has already become more serious than a faint or a coma.

B. That you may believe, 15

15 And I am glad for your sakes that I was not there, to the intent ye may believe; nevertheless let us go unto him.

It must have shocked the disciples to hear that Jesus was "glad" that He was not there to heal Lazarus when he was merely ill. Yet he could not be raised if had not died; so Jesus explains that his death was for their sake, so their faith in Him as God's Son (vs. 4) could be strengthed by witnessing Lazarus' rising from the dead. With this in mind, Jesus and His disciples finally set out for Bethany.

III. Demise of Death—38-44
A. Sadness at the tomb, 38

38 Jesus therefore again groaning in himself cometh to the grave. It was a cave, and a stone lay upon it.

Verse 35 has noted that Jesus wept, and here he moans inwardly—not in sorrow for the loss of Lazarus, who was about to be raised from the dead, but for the pain of his loved ones.

B. Directions for life, 39-40

39 Jesus said, Take ye away the stone. Martha, the sister of him that was dead, saith unto him,

44

Lord, by this time he stinketh: for he hath been dead four days.

40 Jesus saith unto her, Said I not unto thee, that, if thou wouldest believe, thou shouldest see the glory of God?

The Jews buried their dead with spices to delay the stench from a rotting corpse (in contrast to the Egyptians, who embalmed the dead to resist decay). But by the fourth day the spices would have lost their pungency, bringing Martha's protest that the body would smell from decay if the stone were removed from the cave-tomb's entrance.

Jesus' reply to Martha's protest echoes His conversation with her in the intervening verses, when He earnestly solicited her strong faith that "whosoever liveth and believeth in me shall never die" (vs. 26). The glory of God is visible to those with the courage to believe.

C. Jesus' prayer, 41-42

41 Then they took away the stone from the place where the dead was laid. And Jesus lifted up his eyes, and said, Father, I thank thee that thou hast heard me.

42 And I knew that thou hearest me always: but because of the people which stand by I said it, that they may believe that thou hast sent me.

Setting an example for us at funerals, Jesus has wept at others' grief, and now He prays. He has already asked in spirit for the life of His friend; knowing that His prayer will be answered, He now expresses gratitude. This indicates that Jesus' very life was such a constant prayer that "answers" were an accomplished fact even before verbalized. Praying aloud was merely for the benefit of those who listened.

D. Lazarus is raised, 43-44

43 And when he thus had spoken, he cried with a loud voice, Lazarus, come forth.

44 And he that was dead came forth, bound hand and foot with graveclothes: and his face was bound about with a napkin. Jesus saith unto them, Loose him, and let him go.

The famous Shroud of Turin gives us a glimpse of ancient burial wrappings even if it is not, as many believe, the one in which Jesus was wrapped. A long, narrow strip was laid with one end under the feet of the dead, then stretched under the body to the head and folded down toward the feet again. Then smaller strips were wound crossways around the body to secure the arms to the body.

None of these bindings were equal to the power of Christ's call to "Come forth!" The scene echoes again in 1 Thessalonians 4:16-17: "For the Lord himself will come down from heaven, with a loud command, with the voice of the archangel and with the trumpet call of God, and the dead in Christ will rise first."

Evangelistic Emphasis

Bill Brotherton tells everybody he meets that he is a 21st Century Lazarus. No, Bill was not in the grave four days like the Lazarus in John 11. Yet, Bill will tell you emphatically that he was as dead as people can get. His deadness was from drugs.

For more than seven years, Bill's life was one of numb existence. His whole world revolved around getting his next fix. As the addiction set in, the preoccupation began to take over his life, intruding into his work setting. For the past nine years, Bill has not had a "work setting," except for picking up cans and bottles for re- demption. For the past eight and a half years, he has lived in shelters and on the street. Bill is not sure exactly when, but somewhere along the way, Bill stopped having a life.

Then one day, by way of a chance encounter, Bill came into contact with an old street crony who was now clean. He bragged that he had been clean for more than two years. Nar- row Gate was the drug treatment pro- gram that had helped him and in the process had introduced him to Jesus Christ.

It wasn't easy for Bill to believe that life could be different than it seemed it had always been. Eventu- ally, though, he accepted his friend's invitation to put him into contact with Narrow Gate. In a matter of just a few months, Bill Brotherton was *raised from the dead.*

୫୬୯୧

Memory Selection

Jesus said unto her, I am the resurrection, and the life: he that believeth in me, though he were dead, yet shall he live: And whosoever liveth and believeth in me shall never die. Believest thou this?—*John 11:25-26*

The concept of resurrection is in a strange position in our time. Though there are many Christian-educated people in our circle of friends and church, the concept does not interface well with our scientific world view. Though people tend to dig out their resurrection language when their grandmother dies, many of them don't live with an ongoing consciousness of the eternal.

"Resurrection talk" is for church! As long as it is kept within the walls of Sunday's religious scene, people don't find themselves compelled to blend logically their faith with their secular outlook. Though they sing with vigor the words of "When We All Get To Heaven" and would love really to believe what they sing, they live with strong suspicion that it's all a pipedream. Consequently, they are driven to live as though the grave is the end of it all.

Weekday Problems

For years Helen has been intrigued by stories that she has heard of "near-death experiences." She has wondered whether there is really any truth in them. She finds it uncanny that nearly every testimonial she has ever heard or read tells much the same thing. Predictably, there is something about a "bright light at the end of a dark tunnel," and the closer one gets to the light, the more at peace one is found to be. Unfortunately, Helen has never really known any one *personally* who had such an experience. At least, that was true until last week.

The new accountant in Helen's office was introduced as one who had "come back from the dead." She testifies that five years ago she was in a head-on collision and was pronounced dead on the scene by a medical doctor who just "happened" to stop to help. When the paramedics arrived, however, they dutifully administered CPR anyway. Much to everyone's amazement, she revived, even though she had been clinically dead for more than 10 minutes.

* How do you explain the fact that nearly all of the much publicized "back-from-the-dead" experiences share the same story line? Does this confirm the facts, or is a "copy cat" process being played out in all of this?

* Do you know anyone *personally*—whose word you trust totally—who testifies to an after-death experience?

* How does one account for the fact that one's faith, religion, or lack of it does not seem to alter the story told much, at all?

Lazarus, the Next Day . . .

Where was the doc? I had to die myself, without his help.

* * *

Nothing's ever improved my appearance as much as the photograph the newspapers used with my obituary.

* * *

Hey, everybody! Drive carefully. Motorists can be recalled by their Maker.

* * *

I could have done this earlier if I hadnÆt stopped smoking and eaten so much oat bran.

* * *

He has a supernatural voice. His hollering would raise the dead.

* * *

Sorry folks. You thought I'd put a period after the sentence, and it was only a comma.

This Lesson in Your Life

"If only" are some of the saddest words to be spoken. In a setting where there has been a death, they will almost always be heard in some of the conversations pertaining to the loved one's passing.

"If only I had been there," someone says, *"perhaps I could have done something." "If only the doctor had arrived in time,"* someone else will add. The specific words that follow are really not all that important. The refrain, *"If only"* provides the doorway for us either to claim responsibility or to direct blame.

"I might have prevented her from dying, had I been here! I sure wish I had been here." During a time of grief, one is apt to accept responsibility for something far beyond his control. On the other hand, grieving can prompt the laying of blame that is neither reasonable nor acceptable. *"You could have prevented her from dying had you been here! Why weren't you here?"* the charge is laid.

These were the words spoken separately by both Mary and Martha. If only Jesus had been there, they said, their brother would not have died. Jesus held the power to keep their brother alive. He had the power to heal him. In a sense, then, Jesus was to blame for their brother's death. Or at least that's the way one twist of logic would interpret the circumstances.

Jesus, of course, understood the emotions behind the two women's complaint. At some point in the process of grieving, most of us—even if only momentarily—will be tempted either to claim responsibility or to point a finger of blame. It is during that phase of the grieving process when malpractice lawsuits are filed. It is during that time when families are often scarred for life by allegations and counter-allegations as blame is passed back and forth from one relative to another.

There is no indication that Jesus was offended by the remarks of Mary and Martha, nor do we hear bitterness or rancor in the women's words. Instead, there is a note of disappointment that Jesus had not come before Lazarus' death. While they waited and prayed and wrung their hands in anxious anticipation, Lazarus died. All their hoping, they thought had been in vain—until Jesus raised Lazarus from the dead.

When we find ourselves desperately praying in behalf of a grimly ill loved one, we need to remember this story. We need to remember that Jesus does not have to come to keep our loved one from dying. He has the power to come later as He did with Lazarus and to raise him from the dead. In fact, it seems as though that is often his plan.

1. What was the situation in Bethany when Jesus arrived in town?

Jesus' friend, Lazarus, had died four days earlier. His sisters and their neighbors were mourning his death.

2. When Mary and Martha heard that Jesus was coming to town, what did they do?

Martha went to meet Jesus. Mary stayed at home.

3. What did Martha say to Jesus when she met him?

Martha said that if He had been there earlier, her brother would not have died.

4. What did Martha add to modify this initial comment?

She said that she knew that even now God would give to Jesus whatever He asked.

5. What did Jesus then tell Martha?

Jesus told Martha that her brother would rise again.

6. After telling Martha that He was the resurrection and the life, what did Jesus then ask her?

He asked her if she believed this.

7. What was Martha's response?

She said, "Yea, Lord: I believe that thou art the Christ, the Son of God, which should come into the world."

8. What did Martha tell her sister, Mary?

Martha told Mary that Jesus was asking for her.

9. What did Mary say to Jesus when she first saw him?

As her sister, she said that had He been there her brother would not have died.

10. What emotion did Jesus display when He saw Mary also weeping?

He wept.

Most people try to avoid cemeteries. For Henry Johnson, the Marion County Cemetery is his least favorite place on earth. For as long as he can remember, he has heard tales of the Marion County Cemetery and the various ghosts that reside there. He was only 5 when his uncle Winston told him about Shotgun Sam, who had murdered his whole family. After being executed, his body was buried in a county plot. Ever since, stories have circulated that Shotgun Sam's ghost stalks the cemetery seeking his next victim.

Then there was Grandma Garland who went crazy following her child's death. Now buried at County, she stalks the cemetery to find a child to accompany her in the next life. These and many more stories like them provided Henry with plenty of reason to stay as far away as possible from Marion County Cemetery. And he was quite successful until one fateful night when he was 10.

That night Henry was spending the night with his cousin, Teddy Hamilton. Shortly before midnight, Teddy and Henry climbed out of Teddy's bedroom window to seek some adventure. A new girl had moved into town a couple of weeks earlier. She was without a doubt the prettiest girl they had ever seen. A year or so older, she epitomized "mature beauty," they thought.

As the boys climbed out of the window that night, they "crossed their hearts and hoped to die" that would not return until they had *met* this new beauty and claimed a token of their meeting. Before the night was over, Henry began to think that the "to die" part was going to come true.

Unfortunately, the new girl lived a distance from Teddy's house *on the other side of Marion County Cemetery.* It was Teddy Hamilton's idea to cut through the Cemetery to save time. Against his better judgment, Henry agreed to go. All went well until they were just about half-way across.

Suddenly, Teddy heard a yell and a thud; then all was quiet. He called for Henry, but Henry did not respond. Without a second moment's hesitation, Teddy broke into a run back to the safety of his house. It seemed to Teddy as though the stories about Marion County Cemetery were true.

Meanwhile, Henry had fallen into an open grave and had the wind knocked out of him. The grave was ready for a burial that was to take place the next morning. Regaining consciousness, Henry yelled with all the volume he could generate but to no avail. Being 10 years old, he was too short to climb out of the hole. It wasn't until the funeral party arrived the next morning that he was able to get free. During the night, Henry wondered about Lazarus, trapped in that tomb for four days. He was sure glad that for Henry Johnson, resurrection came with the morning.

Lesson 6

Purpose of Parables

Matthew 13:1-13, 34-35

The same day went Jesus out of the house, and sat by the sea side.

2 And great multitudes were gathered together unto him, so that he went into a ship, and sat; and the whole multitude stood on the shore.

3 And he spake many things unto them in parables, saying, Behold, a sower went forth to sow;

4 And when he sowed, some seeds fell by the way side, and the fowls came and devoured them up:

5 Some fell upon stony places, where they had not much earth: and forthwith they sprung up, because they had no deepness of earth:

6 And when the sun was up, they were scorched; and because they had no root, they withered away.

7 And some fell among thorns; and the thorns sprung up, and choked them:

8 But other fell into good ground, and brought forth fruit, some an hundredfold, some sixtyfold, some thirtyfold.

9 Who hath ears to hear, let him hear.

10 And the disciples came, and said unto him, Why speakest thou unto them in parables?

11 He answered and said unto them, Because it is given unto you to know the mysteries of the kingdom of heaven, but to them it is not given.

12 For whosoever hath, to him shall be given, and he shall have more abundance: but whosoever hath not, from him shall be taken away even that he hath.

13 Therefore speak I to them in parables: because they seeing see not; and hearing they hear not, neither do they understand.

34 All these things spake Jesus unto the multitude in parables; and without a parable spake he not unto them:

35 That it might be fulfilled which was spoken by the prophet, saying, I will open my mouth in parables; I will utter things which have been kept secret from the foundation of the world.

Oct. 7

Memory Selection
Matthew 13:13

Devotional Reading
Matthew 13:18-23

Background Scripture
Matthew 13:1-35

This lesson introduces a unit on the parables of Jesus, and focuses on the famous "Parable of the Soils."

As the Verse by Verse section indicates, parables are stories that in one sense are designed to clarify and illustrate a point. In another sense, however, they can mystify and puzzle. Because parables do not state the point itself literally, they require something more than mere hearing to understand. As Jesus used them, that "something more" is a *willingness to understand*—a spirit that says "I want to understand this story so I can embrace its truth."

Jesus' parables also invite the hearer into the story, offering the opportunity to identify with one of its characters. Because these extra dimensions are often neglected, you may want to focus on the importance of attitude and identification as you discuss these lessons.

Consider introducing this lesson by telling the story of "The Emperor's New Clothes," by Hans Christian Andersen. An emperor hires two tailors to make him a suit that will be invisible to the incompetent and the stupid. The unscrupulous tailors actually make nothing, and only pretend to dress the king in his new clothes. Afraid he will be considered stupid if he admits he cannot see the suit, he parades through town undraped. Afraid of his wrath, the people acclaim his new clothes—all but a child who finally cries, "The king has on no clothes!"

Point out that such tales have a moral that is tied to our ability to identify with a character. By identifying with the lad, we learn the importance of courage and truth-telling. By identifying with the king, we learn the folly of vanity.

Jesus was the master of this kind of parable. Invite group members to identify the elements in the Parable of the Soils whose "moral" best fits them.

Teaching Outline	Daily Bible Readings
I. Parable of the Soils—Matt. 13-1-9	**Mon.** Weeds Among Wheat Matthew 13:24-30
A. The setting, 1-2	**Tue.** Parable of the Weeds Explained Matthew 13:36-43
B. Of parables and seeds, 3-4	**Wed.** What the Kingdom Is Like Matthew 13:31-33, 44-46
C. In stony places, 5-6	**Thu.** More Kingdom Parables Matthew 13:47-53
D. Among thorns, 7	**Fri.** Having Ears that Hear Mark 4:21-29
E. The good ground, 8-9	**Sat.** Parable of the Soils Explained Matthew 13:18-23
II. Power of Parables—10-13	**Sun.** So He Told a Parable Luke 15:1-10
A. Chosen to understand, 10-12a	
B. Consigned to confusion, 12b-13	
III. Prophetic Fulfillment—34-35	

Verse by Verse

I. Parable of the Soils—Matt. 13-1-9

A. The setting, 1-2

1 The same day went Jesus out of the house, and sat by the sea side.

2 And great multitudes were gathered together unto him, so that he went into a ship, and sat; and the whole multitude stood on the shore.

By this time, Jesus' miracles and His simple but profound teaching were attracting so many people that He borrowed a fishing boat moored nearby and pushed out a little way from the shore (probably at Galilee). This gap of a few feet between Him and His audience, plus His sitting down to teach, established an appropriate combination of intimacy and distance—for it was the rabbis' style to sit down when they taught authoritatively. Also, the water would help carry Jesus' voice so all could hear.

B. Of parables and seeds, 3-4

3 And he spake many things unto them in parables, saying, Behold, a sower went forth to sow;

4 And when he sowed, some seeds fell by the way side, and the fowls came and devoured them up:

A parable is a short story with a point that may be either plain or obscure, depending on the attitude of the hearer. The make-up of the Greek word *parabole* is instructive. *Para* means "beside" and a *bole* is a toss

or throw. In Jesus' parables, a story is "thrown alongside" a certain truth for our comparison, much like a potter "throws a pot"—tossing a lump of clay onto a potter's wheel and shaping it. The "verbal vase" the Master Potter throws only approximates the ideal He has in mind. As hearers, we are invited to "finish" the work, or shape it to match the ideal. This requires us to catch something of the vision the Master Artist has in mind for us, implying a certain degree of willingness or commitment rather than passivity or resistance. The hearer's role as "co-creator" is why parables were Jesus' favorite way to teach—and why they put special responsibility on the hearer (see vss. 10-13).

Although the parable here is classically named "The Parable of the Sower," it is more aptly called "The Parable of the Soils." The emphasis is not on Jesus as the Sower but on the different kinds of "soil" represented by the hearts of those who receive the "seed," the Word of God (Luke 8:11).

Jesus uses four kinds of soil as illustrations, explaining each one in verses 19-23. The first kind of heart is "hardened," like soil along a pathway (vs. 19)—areas that are beaten down by the trampling of many feet.

As any gardener knows, seed sown in spots like that simply lie on top of the ground instead of nestling into the earth. Exposed, they are vulnerable to being snatched up by the birds that typically follower a sower. Although in verse 19 Jesus will compare these scavengers with Satan ("the wicked one"), the hearer is held responsible for not having a heart soft or receptive enough to take the seed of the Word into itself and nourish it until it is understood. The millions who know about Jesus but lack the interest to investigate, understand, and accept His teaching are typical of this pathway soil.

C. In stony places, 5-6

5 Some fell upon stony places, where they had not much earth: and forthwith they sprung up, because they had no deepness of earth:

6 And when the sun was up, they were scorched; and because they had no root, they withered away.

"Stony places" have soil that is soft enough to receive the seed, but not deep enough to allow it to take root. In Jesus' later explanation (vss. 20-21), this soil represents people who may initially receive the Word joyfully, but abandon it at the first sign of "rocky" experiences such as persecution. Many who have worked with converts at exciting evangelistic campaigns know that something besides excitement is required if they are to remain faithful when the applause of the crowds gives way to criticism by co-workers at the office.

D. Among thorns, 7

7 And some fell among thorns; and the thorns sprung up, and choked them:

Moving on, the Sower's "broadcast" method of planting means that some seed—some echoes of the Word—falls on thorn-choked soil. In verse 22, these thorns are identified with "the care of this world, and the deceitfulness of riches." Jesus realistically acknowledges that people hear a vast number of other messages and weigh many other claims in addition to the Good News. What will others think if I commit my life to Jesus? How can I keep up with my competitors if I close the shop on Sunday morning for worship? How can I maintain Christian values such as honesty and integrity and still advance in a career in which bribery and cheating are commonplace? As Jesus warns, placing such worldly concerns above the claims of the faith is to choke it out of our lives and to be "unfruitful" (vs. 22).

E. The good ground, 8-9

8 But other fell into good ground, and brought forth fruit, some an hundredfold, some sixtyfold, some thirtyfold.

9 Who hath ears to hear, let him hear.

Finally, the fourth type of "soil" or heart is the kind that is productive. People with such hearts receive the Word, nurture it so it germinates, and accommodate its roots deep within their souls (vs. 23). The result is what any gardener or farmer longs to see—not to mention Christ, the

Sower—an abundant crop. Note that not all "good soil" is required to produce in the same proportion. Some will yield more than others. The important thing is to use our ears not just to receive the sound waves from the call of the Sower, but to transmit the sound to the heart, responding to and obeying the message.

II. Power of Parables—10-13
A. Chosen to understand, 10-12a

10 And the disciples came, and said unto him, Why speakest thou unto them in parables?

11 He answered and said unto them, Because it is given unto you to know the mysteries of the kingdom of heaven, but to them it is not given.

12 For whosoever hath, to him shall be given, and he shall have more abundance:

Sometimes we hear that Jesus taught in parables to make His message easy to understand. This is true only for those who care enough about Jesus to follow Him and put His teaching into practice. It is these who are "given" the ability to understand. The "mysteries" of the Kingdom are not riddles requiring cleverness or complex doctrines only sages can understand; but they do require a heart that is willing to practice them before they can be fully understood. For example, it may seem nonsense to "turn the other cheek" when unfairly criticized. Yet one has only to practice and experience the sense of victory at having been strong enough to stand above base arguments to "learn" the power of Jesus' teaching.

Those who have such willingness will be given more understanding; but there is also the other group.

B. Consigned to confusion, 12b-13

12b but whosoever hath not, from him shall be taken away even that he hath.

13 Therefore speak I to them in parables: because they seeing see not; and hearing they hear not, neither do they understand.

Jesus is not refusing to accept any honest seeker, but requiring honesty and willingness as conditions of understanding His Word and His ways. Far from using parables only to make His way "simple," He uses them to separate the wheat of willingness from the chaff of hard hearts.

III. Prophetic Fulfillment—34-35

34 All these things spake Jesus unto the multitude in parables; and without a parable spake he not unto them:

35 That it might be fulfilled which was spoken by the prophet, saying, I will open my mouth in parables; I will utter things which have been kept secret from the foundation of the world.

The "prophet" cited here is, perhaps surprisingly, Asaph the psalmist, who describes himself as a teacher of parables (Ps. 78:2). Matthew probably identifies Jesus with this quotation from the Psalms because the whole collection is identified with King David. He thus reminds us that Jesus, the parable-teacher par excellence, is the authoritative Son of David, the Messiah.

Evangelistic Emphasis

When Pastor David Dalton arrived at Needles Community Church, he was overflowing with excitement. Fresh out of seminary and bubbling with optimism, he envisioned quickly building that store-front church into a booming center of activity. His seminary studies focused specifically on this type of ministry. His dream was to change people's lives through face-to-face evangelism.

It has now been nearly three years since Dalton arrived in Needles. The dynamic church he had dreamed of building seems now like a reckless fantasy. Though the numbers at church are a few more than when he came, the numerical growth has not been overwhelming. Though he has knocked on nearly every door in Needles, the reception he has received has remained cool. Even the few who have shown excitement initially when he shared with them the gospel, have rarely moved beyond that point to a life-changing commitment.

Pastor Dalton is beginning to wonder whether his call to the ministry was "all in his imagination." His wife attempts to reassure him that the seed he has been sowing will eventually bear fruit. She reminds him that one cannot manufacture Christians on an assembly line. Rather, one plants the Word of God in the community as *seed*. Some of that seed will find its way into good hearts, and when the time is right, it will grow.

ဆာၛ

Memory Selection

Therefore speak I to them in parables: because they seeing see not; and hearing they hear not, neither do they understand.— *Matthew 13:13*

According to Martin Thielen, "Effective preaching is not ultimately about points, outlines, and information as much as about helping people make contact with God." He calls mind-focused preaching, "Infosermons." Such preaching operates under the illusion that if one's minds *understands* thoroughly, one's heart will automatically respond spiritually. Such reasoning is no less foolish than that of an aspiring comedian supposing that if he sufficiently *explains* the joke, people will be sure to laugh.

When Jesus told a parable, the things of God were made more plain and easy to those willing to be taught. At the same time they became more difficult and obscure to those who were willingly ignorant. Those willing to learn had their hearts moved and their lives changed. For those determined to remain unchanged, his parables were *"just stories."*

Weekday Problems

Thelma Washington has always been puzzled by the concept of "seed and soil." Her frustration especially is with the idea of sowing seed recklessly in various kinds soils. "Why not sow *only on good ground?*" she demands. "If rocky soil is not going to produce, why would one want to waste good seed there? Farmers would soon go broke if they failed to choose carefully where to plant. Should not Christians choose just as carefully?"

When thinking of her own neighbors, Thelma tries to assess the potential of each for receiving the gospel. The Wilson family across the street is quickly excluded, because they are much too heavily involved in the weekend party crowd ever to be interested in going to church on Sunday. The Franklins next door are consumed with making money. Thelma knows they wouldn't be good soil.

Even good old Mr. Hubbard who lives on the corner *would never* be interested in religion! Though nice enough, he is a crusty old fellow who *"just wouldn't fit in at church."*

The only person Thelma can think of who *might* be "good soil" is Mrs. Johnson down the street. Widowed a few years ago, Mrs. Johnson is very lonely and grasps desperately for any form of human interaction.

* Is Thelma Washington correct in her thinking about the need to choose carefully the soil for sowing the Gospel? Why?

* Is Thelma likely correct in her assessment of the Wilson family? The Franklins? Mr. Hubbard? Mrs. Johnson? Why?

* Can you think of anyone within your neighborhood with whom you should find a way to share the gospel? Who?

The Wise and the Otherwise

Joe: You mean ol' Red never completed his education?
Moe: Nope. He lived and died a bachelor.

* * *

Did you hear about the young woman who spent two years learning how to behave in polite society, and the rest of her life trying to locate it?

* * *

Teaching children to count isn't as important as teaching them what counts.

* * *

A college education never hurt anyone who was willing to learn after he got it.

* * *

We need enough education not to have to look up to anyone, and enough wisdom not to look down on anyone.

This Lesson in Your Life

Carolyn Winters was flabbergasted last week when the new minister made a visit to see her. It wasn't his visit that surprised and angered her, but his *insolence*. After some initial chit chat, he told her he was calling on all the *"wayward members."* He said that he "had studied her attendance record" and found himself wondering whether she was *really* a Christian. Perhaps, he suggested, she is merely "a fair-weather Christian" who is easily distracted by the cares of the world. He then read to her from Matthew 13 and told her that if she was allowing the gospel to be choked out by thorns, she should not consider herself to be part of the Christian fold.

Carolyn cannot remember a time when she was more angry. Why, she has been a Christian as long as she can remember! As a little girl, her mother took her to Sunday School. No. They did not go every Sunday, but they did go several times each year. They were always there for Easter, and sometimes even the Sunday or two after Easter! Usually they would go a few times during the Christmas season, too! Carolyn even went once as a teenager during the annual revival. She even answered the altar call and gave her heart to the Lord. Yes. She definitely considers herself to be a Christian!

Since becoming an adult, Carolyn Winters has continued to attend church with some regularity. It is important to her that her own three children receive a Christian upbringing, although she cannot go to worship as often as she would prefer because her husband is not interested. But she goes more often than a lot of people, and she definitely considers herself to be a Christian.

Every time Carolyn thinks of that minister's visit, she becomes angry all over again. As much as she has tried to dismiss the matter from her mind, his infuriating suggestion that she is *"not really"* a Christian keeps haunting her. Returning to read Matthew 13 more than a half dozen times during the past 10 days, the question that really haunts her is the one asking if she might have a heart that is filled with thorns. She knows that, periodically, she becomes very excited about serving the Lord, only to have other distractions choke out her good intentions. *Surely the Lord understands that she means well!* Is it possible that she has never really given her heart to the Lord? Though the minister's question angers her, Carolyn cannot let go of it. *Could it be true?*

1. Why did Jesus get into the boat to teach?
Because of the press of the crowd.

2. What method of teaching did Jesus use mostly?
He taught using parables. Parables are stories containing imbedded messages.

3. On what four different kinds of soil or surface did the seed fall?
Soil by the wayside (path), rocky soil, thorny soil, and good soil.

4. What was the end result of each seed group?
Birds ate the seed on the path. Seed on the rocky soil was sun-scorched. The thorns choked their seed. The good soil produced 100 fold.

5. What reason did Jesus say that He spoke in parables?
He said, "Because it is given unto you to know the mysteries of the kingdom of heaven, but to them it is not given."

6. Which prophet had prophesied that Jesus would speak in parables?
Isaiah.

7. Why did some people not understand the parables that Jesus told?
Their hearts were calloused, their hearing dull, and their eyes dim.

8. Why did Jesus say that the disciples were blessed?
Because their eyes could still see and their ears could still hear.

9. What kind of believer compares to the "thorny soil?"
One who allows the cares of this world and the deceitfulness of riches to choke the Word, making him unfruitful.

10. What kind of things was Jesus revealing through his parables?
"Things which have been kept secret from the foundation of the world."

Frank Harrison and Jack Morgan have been neighbors in Dawson, Georgia, for more than 30 years. They've shared back-fence discussions about every topic imaginable. Together, they speculated whether or not Governor Carter would actually become President. Later, they each contended that he always knew that Carter would be elected. They talked about the economy, the strike at the local factory, and the school bond drive.

During all those years, however, Mr. Harrison and Mr. Morgan talked about gardening more than anything else. Each of them prided himself in being unusually good at the art. Frank Harrison probably bragged the most. He was always trying something new, sending off for some new seed that was supposed to be rare and exotic. Jack Morgan listen patiently as Frank daily boasted how beautifully the plant was developing. Last summer Jack got his turn.

Early in the planting season, Frank began bragging about some new vegetables that he had imported from Spain. Supposedly, they would look a lot like beans when they were ready to harvest but had the flavor of fine asparagus. Actually, the seed that Frank showed Jack looked more like peas than either beans or asparagus.

Since Frank was reliable to give Jack a daily update, Jack knew exactly when and where Frank had planted his prized crop. Late that night, Jack crawled over the back fence and went to work. It was a more time-consuming job than he had planned, but he was able to finish before the break of dawn. Very carefully he dug up as many of Frank's new seeds as he could find and planted beans in their place. The next day, he replanted Frank's seeds in his own garden.

As the days passed, Frank kept Jack informed about every shoot to peak through the ground and every bud to appear. Each time Jack would take the extra trouble to go over to Frank's garden to see for himself. Each time he said to Frank, *"Frank, those just look like beans to me."* And each time, Frank chided him for his country ignorance.

When finally the day arrived for harvest, Jack made sure that his wife invited the Harrisons for dinner. He knew Frank well enough to know that he would bring his prized dish for all to enjoy.

After the dinner prayer, Frank passed his exotic dish around for everyone to sample. He had asked his wife to steam it according to directions. The verdict of everyone at the table was the same, *"Frank, those are nothing but ordinary green beans!"* And so they were.

Not all tares (or beans) that are sown in our garden are quite so benign. We are blessed if they are only sown by friends as a harmless joke.

The Good Samaritan

Luke 10:25-37

A nd, behold, a certain lawyer stood up, and tempted him, saying, Master, what shall I do to inherit eternal life?

26 He said unto him, What is written in the law? how readest thou?

27 And he answering said, Thou shalt love the Lord thy God with all thy heart, and with all thy soul, and with all thy strength, and with all thy mind; and thy neighbour as thyself.

28 And he said unto him, Thou hast answered right: this do, and thou shalt live.

29 But he, willing to justify himself, said unto Jesus, And who is my neighbour?

30 And Jesus answering said, A certain man went down from Jerusalem to Jericho, and fell among thieves, which stripped him of his raiment, and wounded him, and departed, leaving him half dead.

31 And by chance there came down a certain priest that way: and when he saw him, he passed by on the other side.

32 And likewise a Levite, when he was at the place, came and looked on him, and passed by on the other side.

33 But a certain Samaritan, as he journeyed, came where he was: and when he saw him, he had compassion on him,

34 And went to him, and bound up his wounds, pouring in oil and wine, and set him on his own beast, and brought him to an inn, and took care of him.

35 And on the morrow when he departed, he took out two pence, and gave them to the host, and said unto him, Take care of him; and whatsoever thou spendest more, when I come again, I will repay thee.

36 Which now of these three, thinkest thou, was neighbour unto him that fell among the thieves?

37 And he said, He that shewed mercy on him. Then said Jesus unto him, Go, and do thou likewise.

Oct. 14

Memory Selection
Luke 10:36-37

Devotional Reading
Deuteronomy 15:7-11

Background Scripture
Luke 10:25-37

The parable of The Good Samaritan may well be the most familiar of all Jesus' teachings. Even those who make no claim to being Christian know it and like it, perhaps because of its implied criticism of religious people for not living up to their message.

This familiarity calls for the teacher's creativity in not only focusing on the story's point ("Who is my neighbor?") but on the way a changing world challenges us to keep redefining "neighbor." As new ways of communication and travel place the entire world at our doorstep, we must focus not only on helping the needy but on prioritizing needs.

It will also be important to focus on who the "Samaritan" is in our day and culture. Jesus deliberately selected a Samaritan as the hero of this story because his audience looked down on them. Who would He select if He were to tell the story today?

🙖🙘

To introduce this session, ask group members to name people from whom they would find it most difficult to accept counsel. A dyed-in-the-wool Democrat might name a leading Republican such as George Bush, while a dedicated GOP member might think of Bill Clinton or Al Gore. A basketball fan who longs for the game to be played decently and in order might name self-confessed "bad boy" Dennis Rodman.

Be sure to nudge the discussion beyond national boundaries. How readily would we accept moral council from Iraq's Saddam Hussein, Libyan dictator Qadafi, or Yasser Arafat? Point out that we can ready ourselves to hear Jesus best if we imagine hearing this lesson from some such anti-hero. For in choosing "The Good Samaritan" as the hero of this story, Jesus chose someone whom the Jews loved to hate.

Teaching Outline	Daily Bible Readings
I. Discussion with a Lawyer—Luke 10:25-29 A. Eternal Question, 25-26 B. The Law's answer, 27-28 C. 'Is that all there is?', 29 II. Definition of a Neighbor, 30-37 A. Crisis and response, 30-35 1. The priest, 30-31 2. The Levite, 32 3. The Samaritan, 33-35 B. Pointed conclusion, 36-37	**Mon.** Neighbor in Need Deuteronomy 15:7-11 **Tue.** Sadness of a Rich Man Luke 18:18-25 **Wed.** Follow; Don't Look Back Luke 9:57-62 **Thu.** Hidden from the Wise Luke 10:17-24 **Fri.** Love God Deuteronomy 6:4-9 **Sat.** Love Your Neighbor Leviticus 19:13-18 **Sun.** Who is My Neighbor? Luke 10:25-37

Verse by Verse

I. Discussion with a Lawyer—Luke 10:25-29

A. Eternal Question, 25-26

25 And, behold, a certain lawyer stood up, and tempted him, saying, Master, what shall I do to inherit eternal life?

26 He said unto him, What is written in the law? how readest thou?

A "lawyer" in Jewish society of the day was not an attorney so much as an expert on the Law—the Pentateuch, or first five books of the Jewish Scriptures. Such professionals researched both law and tradition to help officials and ruling bodies such as the Sanhedrin settle disputes in conformity with the Law of Moses. That he "stood up" implies that he was among a group of people seated to listen to Jesus teach, although his question and attitude indicate that he was not a disciple.

The lawyer's question has been on the lips of everyone in any religion who is concerned to share the "eternal life" of the God they worship. As used in the Gospels, this term refers to life that is like the Eternal One, not just life unending. It is clear, however, that the questioner is not interested in defining terms, but in testing Jesus to see if His answer conforms with Jewish orthodoxy.

As He often did, Jesus answers the question by turning the issue back to the questioner. As any good teacher knows, students remember answers longer and apply them more effectively when allowed to participate in discovering the answer themselves.

B. The Law's answer, 27-28

27 And he answering said, Thou shalt love the Lord thy God with all thy heart, and with all thy soul, and with all thy strength, and with all thy mind; and thy neighbour as thyself.

28 And he said unto him, Thou hast answered right: this do, and thou shalt live.

Whether he is testing Jesus or not, the lawyer is not a superficial student of the Law. Out of its bewildering number of commandments (some rabbis would count 630), he was aware of a central core consisting of two grand statutes—love God and neighbor. Jesus Himself quoted these same passages from Deuteronomy and Leviticus in His own summary of the Law (Mark 12:30-31), and is therefore able to commend His questioner's answer. Note that Jesus does not even add being justified by grace, instead of works, simply because the man's answer was correct given the fact that he lived in the Mosaic dispensation. The underlying principle of love the man referred to would lead to the development of justification by grace after Christ's death fulfilled the Law.

C. 'Is that all there is?', 29

29 But he, willing to justify himself, said unto Jesus, And who is my neighbour?

Most translations have the lawyer wanting either to commend ("justify") himself in Jesus' eyes for having kept the right commandments, or to justify his question, lest it be thought too simple. It is also possible, however, that, like many scrupulous Christians who do all the good works they can but lack assurance of salvation, the lawyer felt spiritually empty and uneasy even after keeping all the commandments he could. Perhaps he is asking whether he has missed something that would bring peace to his soul. If so, he presses Jesus to define the term "neighbor" in hopes of discovering some missing piece—or peace—to justification.

II. Definition of a Neighbor, 30-37
A. Crisis and response, 30-35
1. The priest, 30-31

30 And Jesus answering said, A certain man went down from Jerusalem to Jericho, and fell among thieves, which stripped him of his raiment, and wounded him, and departed, leaving him half dead.

31 And by chance there came down a certain priest that way: and when he saw him, he passed by on the other side.

Master Teacher that He is, Jesus knows the man can learn the definition of a "neighbor" better from a story than a dictionary. Jericho was about 17 miles from Jerusalem, down a road that drops 3,000 feet and passes through badlands that hid bandits lying in wait. We assume the thieves robbed the traveler of his money as well as leaving him stripped, beaten, and half dead.

For the priest, this last term is crucial. The Law forbade a priest from touching a dead body unless the deceased was a member of his immediate family (Lev. 21:1-4). The beaten man was no doubt unconscious, so the priest could not be sure he was dead; but he avoided touching him because of the mere possibility. Obviously, ritual cleanness was more important to the priest than human life—a priority that Jesus opposed more than once (see Mark 2:27).

2. The Levite, 32

32 And likewise a Levite, when he was at the place, came and looked on him, and passed by on the other side.

By Jesus' day, a distinction between priests and Levites had become ingrained enough in Jewish practice to be useful in this story; but the history of the distinction has been lost. All priests were Levites in the sense that they were descendants of the tribe of Levi. In practice, however, not all Levites were priests. Some were specially chosen for a higher office that included animal sacrifice—a function from which "lesser" Levites came to be prohibited (see Num. 4:5-15).

Whatever the distinction, Jesus' main point is that both were "clergy" —and his use of them as characters in His story shows the expectation that professional religious leaders would be faithful representatives of the faith. Jesus is drawing sharply the question of whether ritual cleanness in not touching the possibly dead man is in fact as "religious" as stopping to see if can be helped.

3. The Samaritan, 33-35

33 But a certain Samaritan, as he journeyed, came where he was: and when he saw him, he had compassion on him,

34 And went to him, and bound up his wounds, pouring in oil and wine, and set him on his own beast, and brought him to an inn, and took care of him.

35 And on the morrow when he departed, he took out two pence, and gave them to the host, and said unto him, Take care of him; and whatsoever thou spendest more, when I come again, I will repay thee.

We can imagine that ordinary Israelites among Jesus' hearers are by now anticipating with delight that one of their class will be the hero of the story, putting the "clergy" in their place. Instead, the man who keeps the law of love to one's neighbor is a despised Samaritan! These were the descendants of Jews who had been captured by the Assyrians some 800 years earlier, then resettled north of Judea to intermarry with non-Jews. "Proper" Jews therefore had contempt for them, considering them "half-breeds." Jesus Himself had contrasted Jewish faithfulness with Samaritan heresy (John 3:23).

The wine administered to the man's wounds would act as an antiseptic, while the oil would have helped seal them from further contaminants. Putting the victim on his own beast meant the Samaritan was willing to walk to Jericho and find an inn. After caring for the wounded man himself until his business trip required him to leave, the Samaritan pays the inn-keeper to be sure the convalescence is complete. Some estimate that the two "pence" (literally denaria) may have been enough to care for the man for three or four weeks if necessary.

B. Pointed conclusion, 36-37

36 Which now of these three, thinkest thou, was neighbour unto him that fell among the thieves?

37 And he said, He that shewed mercy on him. Then said Jesus unto him, Go, and do thou likewise.

Although the lawyer began this episode wanting to "test" Jesus, he is forced to admit the obvious: it is the Samaritan, not the "proper" Jews, who proved to be a true neighbor. Jesus' definition, then, is that a neighbor is anyone whose needs we can meet—as in the modern saying, "Opportunity plus ability equals responsibility."

Jesus may also be implying that putting human needs above mere rule-keeping is not only being a true neighbor; it provides that "something more" the lawyer may have sought—the feeling of fulfillment, though not smugness, we experience when we go beyond the minimum requirements of law.

Evangelistic Emphasis

It's not necessarily the one who boasts loudest about his credentials who proves to reflect the best influence. Jill has become embarrassingly aware of this at the office where she works. Every since she began work there three years ago, Jill has attempted to win her immediate supervisor to Christ. Unfortunately, it seems that every time she begins to feel as though she is making progress, one of the other "Christians" in the office exhibits very *un*christian behavior. Jill knows what response she will hear from her supervisor even before her supervisor has spoken a word. *"Even I would never do that!"* she inevitably says. How can Jill argue with her. She, herself, is mortified at how her fellow -Christians sometimes behave.

Though the word "hypocrites" echoes hauntingly in Jill's ears, she is reminded that the situation about which Jesus spoke was probably not all that different. Samaritans were "unorthodox" and "unacceptable" by the upstanding religious folks of Jerusalem. Yet, when the story was finished, it was the Samaritan who proved to be more obedient to God's law for showing mercy than those who grew up in the temple. The priest and Levite passed by the man in need much as a Gentile pagan would have done. The Samaritan, however, lived the Law of which the Priest and the Levite boasted.

৪৩৫

Memory Selection

Which now of these three, thinkest thou, was neighbor unto him that fell among the thieves? And he said, He that showed mercy on him. Then said Jesus unto him, Go, and do thou likewise. —*Luke 10:36-37*

The most difficult part of this verse is the final phrase, *"Go, and do thou likewise."* Virtually every principle of religion is easier to theorize than it is to do. It is easier to talk about serving than it is to serve. It is easier to plan evangelism than it is to evangelize. It is easier to affirm the idea of ministering to the homeless than it is actually to minister to the homeless.

If we could exchange, hour-for-hour, the time that we Christians have spent talking religion for time spent acting out the principles of our faith, Christianity would be thriving in every church and in every town across America. Rather than churches dying in the intercity and in the small rural communities, they would abound. Our problem has never been a lack of talk. Our problem is too little "do."

Weekday Problems

Franklin Hoover remembers fondly the many times his parents stopped along the road to help strangers. Sometimes they were people whose car had broken down. At other times, it was to pick up a hitchhiker or to offer food and water to someone who was walking. Though they usually offered to take those walking to their destination, sometimes there was an obvious hesitation in the walkers to climb into a car with strangers. This hesitation neither surprised nor offended Franklin's parents. Their quick reply was always an offer of nourishment.

Unfortunately, those memories were from many years ago. Today, Franklin finds himself almost ashamed that he does not stop to help, as he saw his parents do. He tells himself that "It's a different world now!" Yet, even that reassurance does not sufficiently soothe his conscience. Franklin wonders if his faith is just weak. Perhaps, the only difference between then and now is the seriousness with which his parents trusted God to protect them as they responded to those in need, whereas he does not sufficiently trust.

* Is there really a significant difference in the level of personal risk involved in helping a stranger now as opposed to then?

* What factors ought one to consider as he weighs the decision of whether or not to follow the Samaritan's example?

* If one decides that it is simply not wise for him/her to stop along the road to help a stranger, how then can he/she respond appropriately to Jesus' teaching in this text? What other options are open?

The Samaritan Spirit

The roots of happiness grow deepest in the soil of service.

* * *

True religion is love in work clothes.

* * *

Service is the rent we pay for the space we occupy in this world.

* * *

The only way some people are willing to serve God is in an advisory capacity.

* * *

"Pure and lasting religion in the sight of God our Father means that we must care for orphans and widows in their troubles, and refuse to let the world corrupt us."—James 1:27, *New Living Translation.*

This Lesson in Your Life

Princes and princesses merged with paupers and prostitutes to listen to Catherine Booth, the "mother" of the Salvation Army. The story is told that one night when she was speaking a great crowd of "publicans and sinners" was there. Her message prompted many responses so that there was an outpouring of repentance and prayer.

After the meeting, Mrs. Booth went to be entertained at a fine home. The lady of the manor said, "My dear Mrs. Booth, that meeting was dreadful."

"What do you mean, dearie?" asked Mrs. Booth.

"Oh, when you were speaking, I was looking at those people opposite to me. Their faces were so terrible, many of them. I don't think I shall sleep tonight!"

"Why, dearie, don't you know them?" Mrs. Booth asked.

"Certainly not!" the hostess replied. She was offended that Mrs. Booth would even ask such a question.

"Well, that is interesting," Mrs. Booth said. "I did not bring them with me from London; they are your neighbors!"

The wish to be selective as to who is to be accepted as one's neighbor is not new. It was attempted in the hearing of Jesus when he called attention to the Law of God to love neighbor as self. The defensive question that emerged was, "And who is my neighbor?" Luke informs us that the man was attempting to justify himself. There was an "attitude" present, reflecting the notion that "neighbor" is a role for which one must qualify. In other words, *"If you expect me to treat you as a neighbor, then you must meet the qualification for being accepted as a neighbor."* To put it another way, *"If you don't measure up to the qualifications, then I don't owe you anything."*

Jesus' not-so-subtle response to this attitude in this parable was essentially, *"You've misunderstood your role."* Your and my responsibility is not to screen applicants, deciding whether or not they are worthy to be accepted as our neighbors. Our responsibility is to be neighbor to any whom God brings into our path, not to pick and choose from among them. Too often our selection would be based on something as incidental as one's economic status, race, social circle, how one dresses, or even one's taste in music or amusement. We must not tell ourselves that, if all the credentials are in order, then we will accept the responsibility of being a neighbor to the worthy. The parable of the Samaritan informs us that this kind of selection is not our prerogative. It belongs to God.

GETTING THE FACTS STRAIGHT

1. What was the initial question that led to this parable?
"Master, what shall I do to inherit eternal life?"

2. How did Jesus respond to that question?
"He said unto him, What is written in the law? how readest thou?"

3. What was the lawyer's answer to Jesus' question?
He quoted to him "the two great commandments."

4. How did Jesus commend the lawyer at this point?
"And he said unto him, Thou hast answered right: this do, and thou shalt live."

5. What was the lawyer's next question? Why did he ask it?
"And, who is my neighbor?" He was attempting to justify himself.

6. Why did the priest and the Levite pass by on the other side of the road, not helping the injured man?
The Bible does not say why. We can only speculate on possible reasons.

7. Why did the Samaritan stop to help the man?
He was moved with compassion.

8. What did the Samaritan do to the injured man?
He bound up his wounds, pouring on oil and wine, and set him on his own beast, and brought him to an inn, and took care of him.

9. What promise did the Samaritan make to the inn keeper?
"Take care of him; and whatsoever thou spendest more, when I come again, I will repay thee."

10. After telling the parable, what question did Jesus ask the lawyer?
"Which now of these three, thinkest thou, was neighbor unto him that fell among the thieves?"

When I got ready to go to Harding College, my parents moved to Searcy, Arkansas, so I could live at home, and save "room and board" costs. Actually, I moved them to Arkansas in a large U-Haul trailer, pulled behind my '58 Mercury. That U-Haul was loaded far beyond its recommended load limit. On the way from West Virginia to Arkansas, we detoured through Ohio to visit a host of family relatives.

Having made the rounds of family, we finally departed late one evening for Arkansas. We left at night to have cooler driving and less traffic, but we hadn't gotten 10 miles before the car suddenly died. I used to have this obsession with trying to use all 20 gallons of a 20-gallon tank. Much to my embarrassment, I had failed to account for the fact that I was pulling an extra 3,000 pounds behind my car. I had run out of gas!

It was dark, and according to the road sign it was 11 miles to the nearest town. Unfortunately, there weren't many options open. I was much too embarrassed to return to my uncles's house which we had just left. So, I left my parents in the car, got a gas can out of the trunk, and started walking.

I hadn't gotten a quarter of a mile when two friendly young men stopped to see if I wanted a lift. Their '56 Pontiac was even more a pile of bolts than my nine-year-old Mercury, but it beat walking! So, I thankfully got in.

This was a secondary road with rolling hills, the kind that give your stomach a thrill if you go fast enough. The speed limit was 60 miles per hour during the day and 50 miles per hour at night—and it was night. Much to my dismay, it was obvious before we had gone a mile that the driver of that car thought that the speed limit sign was referring to 50 miles per hour per person. He seemed to have a terrible obsession for keeping the speedometer above the 100 mark. My knuckles turned blue from holding onto the seat. I fully expected to die that night!

Much to my surprise, we actually arrived in town and at a service station with all of our parts still in place. And, graciously, those two fellows offered to wait for me to get the gas and then take me back to my car. I didn't know what to say. I was very impressed with their unusual generosity. With sincerely expressed gratitude, however I turned them down. There was no way that I was going to get back into that car. I had placed my life in their hands once and survived it. I would never be so foolish to do that again! I preferred to walk that 11 miles back to the car.

We worry about stopping along the road to help someone in need. We tell ourselves that *"It's not like it used to be. It's not safe any longer."* What we fail to consider is the fact that it is as much a risk for the one being aided by a stranger as it is for the one aiding the stranger.

Parables on Prayer

Luke 18:1-14

And he spake a parable unto them to this end, that men ought always to pray, and not to faint;

2 Saying, There was in a city a judge, which feared not God, neither regarded man:

3 And there was a widow in that city; and she came unto him, saying, Avenge me of mine adversary.

4 And he would not for a while: but afterward he said within himself, Though I fear not God, nor regard man;

5 Yet because this widow troubleth me, I will avenge her, lest by her continual coming she weary me.

6 And the Lord said, Hear what the unjust judge saith.

7 And shall not God avenge his own elect, which cry day and night unto him, though he bear long with them?

8 I tell you that he will avenge them speedily. Nevertheless when the Son of man cometh, shall he find faith on the earth?

9 And he spake this parable unto certain which trusted in themselves that they were righteous, and despised others:

10 Two men went up into the temple to pray; the one a Pharisee, and the other a publican.

11 The Pharisee stood and prayed thus with himself, God, I thank thee, that I am not as other men are, extortioners, unjust, adulterers, or even as this publican.

12 I fast twice in the week, I give tithes of all that I possess.

13 And the publican, standing afar off, would not lift up so much as his eyes unto heaven, but smote upon his breast, saying, God be merciful to me a sinner.

14 I tell you, this man went down to his house justified rather than the other: for every one that exalteth himself shall be abased; and he that humbleth himself shall be exalted.

Oct. 21

Memory Selection
Luke 18:1

Devotional Reading
Genesis 32:22-30

Background Scripture
Luke 18:1-14

Prayer has become so commonly associated with the Christian faith that it's easy to treat it like a pet kitten instead of the tiger it can be. We cannot assume that no one in a Christian study group has trouble believing that a universal God can hear individual prayer. We cannot take for granted that seemingly unanswered prayer is not a problem for some, or that everyone even prays regularly.

That is why it is important to focus honestly on these two parables Jesus taught about prayer. Although your main task is to dwell on His emphasis on persistent prayer and praying with humility, do this in an atmosphere that invites the participation of group members who struggle with prayer. The second prayer especially models for us this essential attitude of honesty and integrity on a subject that is often taken for granted.

ഇൻൽ

Lead into this lesson on the *inner* attitudes of prayer by a discussion of group member's preference for *external* positions. Ask what postures are considered appropriate for prayer. Do some prefer to kneel in prayer? To fold their hands, or lift them heavenward? For some, perhaps their usual posture is actually lying in bed as they go to sleep!

Then note that while a variety of postures might be conducive to prayer, the two parables of Jesus in this lesson are more concerned with the inner attitudes of persistence and humility. Point out that we can be discouraged about unanswered prayer even with folded hands, and arrogant even while on our knees; and that these two parables are designed to help us pray with faith and integrity.

Teaching Outline	Daily Bible Readings	
I. Pray Without Ceasing—Luke 18:1-8	**Mon.**	Ask in Faith James 1:2-8
A. Hard-hearted judge, 1-2	**Tue.**	David's Prayer 1 Chronicles 29:10-14
B. Reluctant response, 3-5	**Wed.**	Pray in Secret Matthew 6:1-8
C. Speedy answer, 6-8	**Thu.**	Pray in This Way Matthew 6:9-14
II. Pray Without Pride—9-14	**Fri.**	Ask and It Will Be Given Luke 11:9-13
A. Self-righteous prayer, 9		
B. Proud Pharisee, 10-12	**Sat.**	Persistence in Prayer Luke 18:1-8
C. A sinner's prayer, 13	**Sun.**	Humility in Prayer Luke 18:9-14
D. The law of opposites, 14		

Verse by Verse

I. Pray Without Ceasing–Luke 18:1-8

A. Hard-hearted judge, 1-2

1 And he spake a parable unto them to this end, that men ought always to pray, and not to faint;

2 Saying, There was in a city a judge, which feared not God, neither regarded man:

The occasion for Jesus' teaching on prayer here may well have been the healing of the 10 lepers in Luke 17:12-14. No doubt many of the disciples who witnessed this miracle could recall situations when they had prayed for healing or made any number of other requests, without apparent answers. Jesus assures them—and us—that while God may not answer prayer in the way we wish, He does hear us when we pray persistently.

The parable invites us to compare a judge in Israel's court system with God, the Supreme Judge. However, this comparison can be confusing if we forget a fundamental rule for interpreting parables: They are designed to teach a single point, rather than asking us to find a spiritual parallel to every detail. In this case, the single point is that, like the judge in the parable, God will answer persistent prayer. Obviously we are not to press further and assume that the judge's hard-hearted and unfeeling attitudes are like God.

B. Reluctant response, 3-5

3 And there was a widow in that city; and she came unto him, saying, Avenge me of mine adversary.

4 And he would not for a while: but afterward he said within himself, Though I fear not God, nor regard man;

5 Yet because this widow troubleth me, I will avenge her, lest by her continual coming she weary me.

Jesus chooses a widow because she is an easy target for unjust judicial decisions—so easy, in fact, that the Law expressly forbade taking advantage of widows (along with orphans, Exod. 22:22; see also 1 Tim. 5:3ff.; James 1:27).In a patriarchal society, when business women such as the woman in Proverbs 31 were rare, a woman whose husband and bread-winner died was especially vulnerable. Typically, this widow's "adversary" would be someone who tried to obtain her property because it was in her deceased husband's name.

Yet it was easy for the judge in our parable to ignore her claim. No doubt she had little or no political clout that might influence his continuing appointment to the bench, and no money with which to bribe him. If he had no fear of judgment from God, and no love for people made in God's image, what motivation could he have for responding to the woman's plea?

The answer is only that the woman's "continual coming" exasperated and exhausted this hard-hearted judge. Again, the single point we are to keep in mind as we apply this very human story to God and our prayers is that, like the judge, God answers persistent prayer—not that we have to wear Him down before He does so.

C. Speedy answer, 6-8

6 And the Lord said, Hear what the unjust judge saith.

7 And shall not God avenge his own elect, which cry day and night unto him, though he bear long with them?

8 I tell you that he will avenge them speedily. Nevertheless when the Son of man cometh, shall he find faith on the earth?

Applying the judge's action to His heavenly Father, Jesus specifically contrasts the judge's disinterest with the Father's love. While the judge responded only after being worn down, God hears "speedily," or immediately. Jesus does not say that God will give what we ask immediately, but that we do not have to "wear Him out" to get His attention. He does ask for persistence in prayer, not because He does not know how earnestly we desire relief, but so we may assess our own level of earnestness. Jesus

is promising that God, more like a Father than a judge, immediately gather us up and consoles us, even though what we request may not be how He plans to answer our prayer.

The use of the term "elect" and their anguished crying "day and night," may indicate that the immediate application of this parable was to the Messianic hopes of God's chosen people in Jesus' day. Warning about the severity of God's judgment against unfaithful Israel (which included the destruction of Jerusalem, with its treasured Temple), Jesus says that those dreadful days would be shortened "for the elect's sake" (Matt. 24:22). He also says that only those who endured to the end, or persisted as in this parable, would be saved (vss. 9-13). This application makes Jesus' question in the latter part of verse 8 all the more relevant. Because the destruction of Jerusalem was such a catastrophe it qualified as a "coming of the Son of Man," the faith and love of those who did not persist in prayer would "wax cold" (Matt. 24:12) if they did not persist in prayer, as this parable teaches.

II. Pray Without Pride—9-14
A. Self-righteous prayer, 9

9 And he spake this parable unto certain which trusted in themselves that they were righteous, and despised others:

Turning immediately to another topic having to do with prayer, Jesus shows that He is as concerned about prideful prayers as about prayers that are discontinued because of discouragement. Here is the height of irony and hypocrisy—pretending to bow our knees and express dependence on God while inwardly considering ourselves already to have the righteousness we so desperately need from Him.

B. Proud Pharisee, 10-12

10 Two men went up into the temple to pray; the one a Pharisee, and the other a publican.

11 The Pharisee stood and prayed thus with himself, God, I thank thee, that I am not as other men are, extortioners, unjust, adulterers, or even as this publican.

12 I fast twice in the week, I give tithes of all that I possess.

Some scholars think the very name "Pharisee" means "separatist," denoting those who felt their superior piety required them not to associate with sinners. Such pride is naturally fed by looking not within one's heart, but around at others—so this Pharisee's eyes of proud comparison fall on a publican (see below); and this only fuels his arrogance. He not only refrains from sins of which he is sure the publican is guilty; he participates in the rituals of fasting and tithing that were external "proofs" (to himself at least!) of his piety.

The Pharisee's prayer echoes in the hearts of people today who are proud that their religion is better than that of others. The insidious thing about this is that it may be true!—until boasting about it suddenly voids the good points of our faith and makes it worse than those with whom we compare ourselves.

C. A sinner's prayer, 13

13 And the publican, standing afar off, would not lift up so much as his eyes unto heaven, but smote upon his breast, saying, God be merciful to me a sinner.

In contrast to the righteous "separatist" or Pharisee, another person stands praying in the Temple. He is a "publican" or tax collector (NIV), a class of people who were virtually excommunicated by all Jews. These tax agents were authorized to collect taxes for Rome, but were allowed to extort any amount over that which was due the government and keep it for themselves. The reference to this despised publican prepares us for the next chapter's account of Zaccheus, who was a "chief publican"—and therefore considered a chief sinner. Contrast this publican's confession of sin with the "righteous list" of the Pharisee, above.

D. The law of opposites, 14

14 I tell you, this man went down to his house justified rather than the other: for every one that exalteth himself shall be abased; and he that humbleth himself shall be exalted.

Driving home the point of the parable, Jesus gives a simple requirement for God to hear our prayers. He states it in the form of an ironic "law of opposites." Those who "exalt" (the Greek word also gives us our word "hype"!) themselves cannot be justified, while only those who confess that they are sinners can be justified.

Evangelistic Emphasis

The sinner's prayer" is actually an elaboration of Revelation 3:20. There Jesus said, "I stand at the door, and knock: if any man hear my voice, and open the door, I will come in to him, and will sup with him, and he with me." The sinner's prayer, then, is understood as opening the door for Him to come in.

Luke 18:13, however, may provide even a better foundation for a sinner's prayer. Here the tax collector with bowed head cried out to God words that all of us need to learn to voice. "God be merciful to me a sinner,"he begged. Jesus even makes it clear that this man went away justified because of his humble appeal.

We make a mistake, though, if we think this is a prayer *only* for those who have not yet publically confessed their faith in Jesus. This is the prayer that needs to be learned, also, by the deacon who struts before the congregation in obvious pride in his position. This prayer needs to find its place on the lips of the soprano who sang so beautifully last Sunday, and then basked in the sunshine of her own glory. And yes, these words need to be prayed by Aunt Matilda who proudly holds the record for perfect attendance at church, while she secretly fantasizes herself to be the finest Christian who ever lived.

Two others need to learn and speak this prayer regularly. *I* need to pray this prayer. It must be sincerely prayed, not simply as a sham. *You* need to pray it, too.

෨෩

Memory Selection

And he spake a parable unto them to this end, that men ought always to pray, and not to faint;—*Luke 18:1*

Her name is Gloria and she is an alcoholic. That is the first thing she says each week when she identifies herself at her regular AA meeting. The fact that she has been "dry" for five years does not mean that Gloria has life "totally together." Some of her problems, she can admit, are her own fault. She has not always made good choices.

Still, Gloria struggles with the haunting idea that she "was dealt a bad hand in life, and praying to God really doesn't do a whole lot of good." She suspects that either He doesn't really listen or doesn't really care. She has tried praying, but was never able to document any tangible results.

As Gloria sits once again in The Women's Shelter, she tells her tales of woe about how her boyfriend kicked her out of the house, leaving her nowhere to go.

Weekday Problems

Julie has heard of people being in a "catch 22" situation. She is certainly in one now! The awkwardness of it all causes her to feel bewildered. To make things worse, it's her mother's fault!

Several months ago, one of Julie's friends in the Youth Group pointed out to her how self-righteous Julie's mother and her friends act when they talk about other religious groups. Though Julie had found herself uncomfortable in the past when overhearing such conversations, she had never thought of it in terms of "self-righteousness." The more she listened with that word in mind, however, the more mortified she became. And of all her mother's age group and circle of friends, her own mother was *the absolute worst!* When she speaks of members of other denominations, there is an obvious sneer included. Julie is embarrassed, but doesn't really know how to "correct" her mother. Julie is certainly glad that she and her own friends are not self-righteous like that.

* What could possibly be said to Julie's mother to alert her to the way she is being heard by her child's peer group?

* Since self-righteousness almost always tends to be invisible to the person who wears it, how can another help her/him see it?

* Who else in this picture needs to become aware of their own self-righteousness? How can we better guard ourselves from this "spiritual fungus"?

Hypocrisy and Humility

Hypocrisy:
    Actors are the only honest hypocrites.
    A hypocrite preaches by the yard, but practices by the inch.
    A measure of hypocrisy is the ability to appear shy while indicating how wonderful you are.
    It's hypocritical to look up to God and down on people.

       * * *

Humility:
    The person who does things that count never stops to count them.
    To grow tall spiritually, a person must first learn how to kneel.
    Humility is like underwear. We should have it, but not let it show.
    Humility is like a fragile plant. The slightest reference to it causes it to wilt and die.

This Lesson in Your Life

Charles Hodge, a minister friend, once made a sage observation as he spoke to an audience of "cutting-edge truth-seekers." Hodge said, "I have never met a humble conservative. Every conservative that I have met has been very proud of his conservatism. His chest swells with the knowledge that he has remained sound, without compromise to the changes brought by time." As he paused to take a breath, the room literally echoed with silent amens. Heads nodded approvingly. Glances and smiles were exchanged.

Then with little more than a moment's enjoyment of our self-satisfaction, Hodge thundered the rest of his observation. "And I have not yet met a humble liberal. Every liberal I know is quite proud of the fact that he is not nearly as narrow-minded as his poor, less-informed brethren."

And so it is. Some of us kneel before our beds at night in gratitude, praying, "Thank you, Lord, that I am not like most men—atheists, agnostics, secular humanists and especially those deceptive liberals. Keep me as I am, Lord, a simple, Bible-believing Christian."

Meanwhile, others of us counter, "Thank you, Lord, that I am not like other men—legalists, tradition-bound conservatives, and especially those self-righteous witch-hunters. Always let me remain as I am, Lord, a simple, Truth-seeking Christian."

Perhaps, the most maligned character in all of the Bible (other than Pilate) is this Pharisee who "went up to the temple to pray." We read this text and promptly think of the most self-righteous person that we know. The ugliness of his egotism is strangely magnified by this verbal rebuke of Jesus. Shuddering with disgust deep within our soul, we breath a silent prayer of thanks that we are not like that!

Each of us, rank with our own form of self-righteousness, imagines himself to be a truer, more honest and godlier disciple than his brothers. We fancy ourselves to be just a little closer to the throne room of the Lord. We imagine the Father on Judgment Day calling our group to the front of the assembly. Then, standing proudly before the entire watching universe, we listen as He informs the grand body of Christendom, "This group got it right!" In reality, each of us, just like that Pharisee, is due to be humbled by God.

1. Who are the two main characters in the first parable of Luke 18?
A city judge and a widow with a petition.

2. Other than living in the city, how is the judge described?
He is said to be a judge who "feared not God, neither regarded man."

3. What was the judge's initial response to the widow's petition?
Initially he refused to grant her wishes and give her justice in her case against her adversary.

4. What finally motivated the judge to grant the widow's petition, in spite of his unconcern for the woman?
The judge finally granted the woman's petition because he did not want to be worn out with her continual petitioning.

5. What was the moral of the parable?
Jesus' point was that God will certainly avenge His own elect, who cry day and night unto Him.

6. Who are the two main characters in the second parable in Luke 18?
A Pharisee and a publican (tax collector).

7. To whom did Jesus address this parable?
He spoke this parable to certain individuals who "trusted in themselves that they were righteous, and despised others."

8. What was the essence of the Pharisee's prayer?
"I thank you that I'm so much better than most men."

9. What was the essence of the publican's prayer?
"Lord, have mercy on me, for I am a sinner."

10. Which man of prayer did Jesus commend? Why?
The publican, because "every one who exalts himself shall be abased; and he that humbles himself will be exalted."

You may remember when it was published in the local newspaper. For years it hung over the desk of my secretary. I'm speaking of a Kudzu comic that has to be one of the most poignant every published.

In the first frame Reverend Will B. Dunn is shown on his knees praying. His prayer is for the Lord to zap his enemy—*"My own worst enemy,"* he says. The next frame shows a lightning bolt coming from on high.

What follows is a view of one charred and mangled Reverend Will B. Dunn. In the last frame, Will B. Dunn is saying, *"Let me rephrase that."*

Have you ever asked God to *zap* somebody? Be truthful, now! I suspect that at least a large minority of us have. Jonah certainly wanted God to zap his enemy, Nineveh. James and John once asked Jesus if He wanted them to call down fire from heaven onto a Samaritan village (Luke 9:54). Apparently, they had ideas of asking God to "zap" them.

But of course, we more commonly misuse prayer in a host of other ways. Like the Pharisee, for some of us prayer becomes the stage for our pompousness. Perhaps, it is a public display of our eloquence. Or it may be that in private we secretly echo our feelings of superiority and perception of preference in God's sight.

How often does our prayer life deteriorate into a "gimme list" where we lay our needs and our whims before His throne for satisfaction. Some of our requests are material in nature. We ask for clothes and cars and jewelry and the latest electronic gadgetry. Somehow, we think ourselves justified in our exercise of self-indulgence.

On other occasions, our prayers petition for privileges or prominence or the favorable attention of someone of the opposite gender who has caught our eye. Such prayers always sound crass when we hear them verbalized by others. The Pharisee's prayer causes us to snicker at his audacity. Yet, somehow, we never seem to notice how inappropriate similar words are coming from our own lips. When we pray them, they always seem to be justified.

Fortunately, God is not quick to strike us down for our inappropriate prayers. His rebuke is firm but gentle. Jesus rebuked James and John for their inappropriate wish to misuse prayer, but He did not reject them as His disciples. The Father rebuked Jonah for his pouting wish for God to destroy Nineveh, but He never disowned Jonah as his prophet. Jesus spoke a word of rebuke about the Pharisee for his self-acclaim, but it was a gentle word that allowed room for a wiser tomorrow. Isn't it grand that our Lord is so gracious with us!

...YOU DID IT TO ME...

Billy 00

The Sheep and the Goats

Matthew 25:31-46

When the Son of man shall come in his glory, and all the holy angels with him, then shall he sit upon the throne of his glory:

32 And before him shall be gathered all nations: and he shall separate them one from another, as a shepherd divideth his sheep from the goats:

33 And he shall set the sheep on his right hand, but the goats on the left.

34 Then shall the King say unto them on his right hand, Come, ye blessed of my Father, inherit the kingdom prepared for you from the foundation of the world:

35 For I was an hungred, and ye gave me meat: I was thirsty, and ye gave me drink: I was a stranger, and ye took me in:

36 Naked, and ye clothed me: I was sick, and ye visited me: I was in prison, and ye came unto me.

37 Then shall the righteous answer him, saying, Lord, when saw we thee an hungred, and fed thee? or thirsty, and gave thee drink?

38 When saw we thee a stranger, and took thee in? or naked, and clothed thee?

39 Or when saw we thee sick, or in prison, and came unto thee?

40 And the King shall answer and say unto them, Verily I say unto you, Inasmuch as ye have done it unto one of the least of these my brethren, ye have done it unto me.

41 Then shall he say also unto them on the left hand, Depart from me, ye cursed, into everlasting fire, prepared for the devil and his angels:

42 For I was an hungred, and ye gave me no meat: I was thirsty, and ye gave me no drink:

43 I was a stranger, and ye took me not in: naked, and ye clothed me not: sick, and in prison, and ye visited me not.

44 Then shall they also answer him, saying, Lord, when saw we thee an hungred, or athirst, or a stranger, or naked, or sick, or in prison, and did not minister unto thee?

45 Then shall he answer them, saying, Verily I say unto you, Inasmuch as ye did it not to one of the least of these, ye did it not to me.

46 And these shall go away into everlasting punishment: but the righteous into life eternal.

Oct. 28

Memory Selection
Matthew 25:40

Devotional Reading
1 John 4:7-21

Background Scripture
Matthew 25:31-46

We read or hear daily about wrong-doers who seemingly go scot-free. The popular magazine, *The Reader's Digest*, even has a regular feature called "That's Outrageous!" which includes accounts that defy any sense of justice. The helpless and the poor too often have no recourse against the crimes of the powerful, the wealthy, and the privileged.

This lesson, however, is part of a long section of Matthew (chapters 22–25) that focus on a Day when justice will at last be realized. Although the pleas of the abused may be ignored in this life, God is keeping a Book of Judgments against their abusers. While scoffers ask, "Where is the promise of his coming?" (2 Pet. 3:4), Jesus teaches here the certainty of a Day of Reckoning.

Focus especially on the human element of the Last Judgment. In this scene, judgment is not rendered on the basis of what we believe, think, or feel, but on whether we have tended to human needs.

༄༅

Sketch for your group the storyline of a recent TV movie in which a rapist assaulted and killed a seven-year-old girl. After the police had charged a man with the horrible crime, her mother took judgment—as well as a gun—into her own hands and killed the accused as he was being arrested.

Discuss what passions raged in the heart of this mother. Note that in such situations the feelings go deeper than anger, hatred, and loss. In the hearts of most people is also the sense that such criminals must be brought to judgment. Of course this did not justify the distraught mother's taking the law into her own hands. Christians know that "'Vengeance is mine; I will repay,' says the Lord" (Rom. 12:9).

Some people protest that a truly good God would not administer eternal punishment. In this lesson, however, Jesus insists on a "Yes" answer to the question raised in the preceding lesson: "Shall not God avenge his own elect?" (Luke 18:7).

Teaching Outline

I. Promise of Judgment–Matt. 25:31-33
  A. The Son on the throne, 31
  B. The gathering of the nations, 32-33
II. Reward of the Faithful—34-40
  A. For service to Christ, 34-36
  B. In the form of others, 37-40
III. Punishment of the Neglectful—41-45
  A. For neglecting Christ, 41-43
  B. In the form of others, 44-45
IV. The Two Destinies—46

Daily Bible Readings

Mon.	Signs of the End	Matthew 24:1-8
Tue.	Enduring to the End	Matthew 24:9-14
Wed.	No One Knows the Hour	Matthew 24:36-44
Thu.	The Faithful and the Wicked	Matthew 24:45-51
Fri.	Parable of the Bridesmaids	Matthew 25:1-13
Sat.	Parable of the Talents	Matthew 25:14-29
Sun.	'When Did We See You?'	Matthew 25:31-46

I. Promise of Judgment—Matt. 25:31-33

A. The Son on the throne, 31

31 When the Son of man shall come in his glory, and all the holy angels with him, then shall he sit upon the throne of his glory:

"Son of man" was Jesus' favorite way of referring to Himself, perhaps because the phrase blended both the divine and human elements of His nature. In the Old Testament, "son of man" is most often used to describe a mere human being in contrast to God (see Ps. 8:4). In the book of Ezekiel the term begins to take on a more noble cast, as God honors the prophet Ezekiel with the title, designating him as the recipient of divine messages. Finally, the book of Daniel envisions the "Son of man" as a powerful, divine figure who seems to be God Himself (see Dan. 7:13-14).

It is in this glorious aspect that Jesus uses the term for Himself in the great Judgment scenes of Matthew 24-25. Accompanied by angels and seated on the throne of judgment, we can at last see that the humble "son of man" is none other than the divine Son of God. The title "Son of man" includes this entire transformation.

B. The gathering of the nations, 32-33

32 And before him shall be gath-ered all nations: and he shall sepa-rate them one from another, as a shepherd divideth his sheep from the goats:

33 And he shall set the sheep on his right hand, but the goats on the left.

During Jesus' ministry, He has gradually expanded His followers' initial perception of Him as a local Messiah who will save only the Jews. Now, in powerful imagery depicting the end of the Age, Jesus states plainly that His Messianic role is extended to all the world. He will not only honor them by being their Savior; they are also subject to the Son of man's standard of judgment.

The mysterious signs of the Second Coming of Jesus now give way to a clear statement of the basis by which all shall be judged: how they acted on Jesus consistent teaching that love is the "greatest command-ment." Since this Last Judgment scene is the final story in Jesus' teach-ing ministry, perhaps He is saying that how we respond to human need is more important than deciphering codes that may tip us off as to the *time* of His coming.

Although this scene is starkly real, the language pushes beyond the con-straints of this-wordly categories such as time and space. We can hardly imagine a literal gathering of people in which all can see the Judge of all peoples; but in His divine power, the Judge will make it so. Similarly, the gathering of the good "sheep" and the evil "goats" asks us to use our imagination. As in many cultures, sheep were valued more highly than goats. Even in our society, the butt of a joke is the "goat"; and it is a lamb, not a kid, that the Good Shepherd rescues (Luke 15:4ff.).

II. Reward of the Faithful—34-40
A. For service to Christ, 34-36

34 Then shall the King say unto them on his right hand, Come, ye blessed of my Father, inherit the kingdom prepared for you from the foundation of the world:

35 For I was an hungred, and ye gave me meat: I was thirsty, and ye gave me drink: I was a stranger, and ye took me in:

36 Naked, and ye clothed me: I was sick, and ye visited me: I was in prison, and ye came unto me.

The reference to the divine King and His kingdom at Judgment Day does not mean that His kingdom is only then to appear. The Kingdom of God has long been present in seed form. The concept grew out of God's having chosen the descendants of King David to sit on an eternal throne (2 Sam. 7:12-13). When Jesus came of "the seed of David" and fulfilled His ministry, He was elevated to David's throne, by God's right hand (Acts 2:30-36). Ever since, people who are saved are "translated" into this Kingdom (Col. 1:13-14). The judgment scene before us now is the final phase of this Kingdom.

On what basis are "the sheep" granted entrance into this heavenly phase of the Kingdom? On the basis that they have cared for Jesus! As He will explain, He identifies Himself here with "the least, the lost, and the last"—those who are hungry, thirsty, lonely, naked, ill, and imprisoned. No doubt these specific descriptions of the needy stand for all human needs that are so commonly overlooked by the contented, the wealthy, the powerful, and the wellfed.

B. In the form of others, 37-40

37 Then shall the righteous answer him, saying, Lord, when saw we thee an hungred, and fed thee? or thirsty, and gave thee drink?

38 When saw we thee a stranger, and took thee in? or naked, and clothed thee?

39 Or when saw we thee sick, or in prison, and came unto thee?

40 And the King shall answer and say unto them, Verily I say unto you, Inasmuch as ye have done it unto one of the least of these my brethren, ye have done it unto me.

Now Jesus makes explicit His identification with the needy of the world, and reinforces the teaching that His followers are to see their Lord in the face of every needy person. They have often been ignored because they went unrecognized; now, at Judgment Day, the abusers and neglectful of the world see that in mistreating the needy they have been mistreating the Son of man.

This basis of judgment does not exclude the fact that we are saved by faith through grace, not works. Jesus' assumption seems to be that the "sheep" are those who not only tend to the needy but who follow the Shepherd. The sheep know that it is only by the Shepherd's grace, and, changing the figure, by the grace of the cleansing blood of the Lamb, that they are privileged to share grace with the needy. Years later, the epistle of James will reinforce the picture here, insisting that those saved by grace respond with works: "faith without works is dead" (2:20), and "pure religion [is] . . . to visit the fatherless, and widows in their affliction . . ." (1:27).

III. Punishment of the Neglectful—41-45

A. For neglecting Christ, 41-43

41 Then shall he say also unto them on the left hand, Depart from me, ye cursed, into everlasting fire, prepared for the devil and his angels:

42 For I was an hungred, and ye gave me no meat: I was thirsty, and ye gave me no drink:

43 I was a stranger, and ye took me not in: naked, and ye clothed me not: sick, and in prison, and ye visited me not.

In perfect balance, the story of Judgment is reversed as the Judge reviews the goats on His left hand. Just as the sheep have tended to Jesus Himself, the goats have neglected Him in precisely the same ways. Note that we do not have to be actively "evil" to be placed among the goats; this is a sin of *omission*. Again a figurative element is introduced into the scene: ordinary, literal "fire" creates light, not darkness; and the language leaves room for various interpretation on whether "everlasting fire" means eternal banishment from God's presence or eternal conscious torment.

B. In the form of others, 44-45

44 Then shall they also answer him, saying, Lord, when saw we thee an hungred, or athirst, or a stranger, or naked, or sick, or in prison, and did not minister unto thee?

45 Then shall he answer them, saying, Verily I say unto you, Inasmuch as ye did it not to one of the least of these, ye did it not to me.

Earlier teachings on Judgment have contained the message, "Watch!" Here we see that watching involves seeing the face of Jesus in the faces of the needy. Now the opportunity for such discernment is over; it is time for sentencing.

IV. The Two Destinies—46

46 And these shall go away into everlasting punishment: but the righteous into life eternal.

The eternal destiny of the goats is punishment, while that of the sheep is eternal life. This quality of life has already been as real as the promise of Jesus (John 3:16); now the Judge pronounces it as their final destination, not just a quality of life.

Evangelistic Emphasis

Jim Hunt has not been in church since he was a boy, until today. This morning, he attended as a favor to Bill Franklin, a good friend. Church has been a real turn-off for Jim through the years, because it has seemed to him as if it were a thoroughly self-serving racket. He found it a real surprise that he actually attended. Even more so, it surprised Jim that he came away from the experience with a different perception of church.

During the course of the morning's class and worship time, Jim was made aware of a great variety of outreach ministries of Bill's church. There were ministries to children, to the homeless, to victims of domestic violence, and to alcoholics and addicts who are trying to get their lives together again. Jim decided that the community could not help but be made a better place by Bill's church. Almost all the work was being done by volunteers, who invested huge amounts of time, as well as funding the program financially.

Thought Jim is not ready to endorse church *in* general, he must admit that he is a lot more open-minded than he has ever been before. Should Bill Franklin invite him to return for another visit, it will be a welcome invitation.

୫୦ଔ

Memory Selection

And the King shall answer and say unto them, Verily I say unto you, Inasmuch as ye have done it unto one of the least of these my brethren, ye have done it unto me.— *Matthew 25:40*

Isn't it amazing! Our Lord places completely within the reach of every one of us the ability to serve Him with royal acclaim. That privilege is not restricted to a pious few. One need not first work one's way up a "pecking order" to a position of Cardinal, Bishop, or even Deacon. The young Christian that sits on the back pew can be the cup-bearer for the King. The middle-aged widow who sits on the fourth row is able extend to Him the hospitality of her table. The 50-year-old alcoholic who is desperately seeking to remain dry can visit Him in the hospital or bind up His wounded side.

It is easy for us to envy Mary, Martha, Peter, or Joseph of Arimathaea. Yet, Jesus places within the reach of each of us the ability to minister to Him as they did. We minister to Jesus by ministering to His brethren.

Weekday Problems

Clark Oberlin is as close to being homeless as anyone at Riverside Christian Church. He lives alone in a wretched apartment. At 47, Clark lives on SSI and a state-funded subsidy. He is mentally incapable of holding a job due to drug abuse during his adolescence. Clark is aware of fact that his disabilities are due to his own bad choices and will tell you so without hesitation.

Though Clark became a Christian several years ago during one of Riverside's evangelistic campaigns, not everyone at the church is thrilled that he is a member there. His clothes are always shabby. Due to the brain damage caused by the drugs, his behavior is often socially inappropriate. Clark's hygiene is not always up to Riverside's standards. Several of the members at Riverside wish that Clark would go to the storefront church that is much nearer the part of town where he lives.

* Is Clark's choice to attend Riverside inappropriate since he does not really "fit" culturally?

* What is a good way for those at Riverside who are uncomfortable with Clark to deal with the problem in a way that is best for Riverside?

* If the pastor at Riverside learns of this "problem," how can he best help both Clark and those uncomfortable members?

Judgment Calls

A sailor's ship sank and he was set adrift on a raft in the ocean. Facing death and the Last Judgment, he lifted his eyes to heaven. "O Lord," he said, "I've been unkind to my wife, I've neglected my children, and I haven't contributed to Your work as I should. But if you'll save me, I promise . . . ." Suddenly, from the corner of his eye, the sailor spotted something on the horizon. "Never mind, Lord," he said, "I think I see land."

* * *

Judgment will come to the wicked in many forms:

Electricians will be delighted.
Cashiers will be distilled.
Piano tuners will be unstrung.
Orchestra leaders will be disbanded.
Artists' models will be deposed.
Office clerks will be defiled.
Mediums will become dispirited.
Dressmakers will be unbiased.

This Lesson in Your Life

The day had gone well for Adam Alexander. His first call that morning had been at the office of a potential client his boss had been trying to sign for more than five years. His boss had asked him to make this call even though he didn't expect anything to come of it. But somehow he had the signed contract in hand before 9 o'clock.

Following that initial call, his life seemed to be charmed. Before lunch, he had signed two additional contracts. They were small ones, but they too were token "duty calls." When 2:00 rolled around, life was purring so sweetly, Adam decided he owed himself a treat. Starbucks coffee shop caught his eye as he drove down Pacific Avenue. What sounded good to him was an iced latte.

As Adam pulled into Starbucks parking lot, however, Adam cringed as he noticed a man with only one leg headed towrd him. He tried not to make eye contact as he hurried toward Starbucks door. Unfortunately, he was not fast enough. "Hey Mister!" the one-legged man called. "Hey Mister! Can you spare a dollar or two? I'm mighty hungry."

Adam wanted so much to get back into his car and forget the iced latte. "Why me?" he thought to himself. "Why does my perfect day have to be spoiled by some nobody, a bum? It's not fair!"

Between that thought and a moment later when the one-legged man touched his shoulder from behind, a thousand thoughts rushed through his mind. "Why can't people like him get a job and earn a living like the rest of us?" "Probably, he just wants the money for cheap wine, anyway!" "Why should I be responsible for funding the dregs of society who are leeches on the community?" "Why does Starbucks allow such panhandlers to operate on their premises and bother their customers? There ought to be a law!"

As the one-legged man pulled on his shoulder, Adam reached into his pocket, pulled out a dollar bill and handed it to the man. Without speaking a word, he then hurried into the coffee shop door. Rather than getting his latte to go, as he had planned, he decided to sit at one of the tables inside. His thought was that, perhaps, the bum might be gone by the time he finished. Certainly, he wanted to avoid feeling compelled to fork over another dollar as he attempted to get to his car.

While enjoying his iced latte, Adam decided it wise to use the time to get part of his Sunday School lesson read. As he finished Matthew 25, his disposition suddenly changed. Perhaps, the day had not *made,* not ruined, by the crippled man!

1. Before whom did Jesus say all nations would be gathered?
The Son of Man.

2. When did Jesus say this "gathering" would take place?
When the Son of Man comes in his glory and sits on his throne of glory.

3. What will be the initial action taken by the Son of Man when the nations gather before him?
He will separate them as one separates sheep from goats–one group at his right hand, the other at his left.

4. According to this passage, on what basis will that separation be made?
The separation will be made according to how one has responded to his needy fellow human.

5. Why will those at his right hand be commended?
They responded to His need by tending to the hungry, thirsty, stranger, naked, sick, and imprisoned.

6. Why will those at his left hand receive rebuke?
They did not respond "Him" by meeting the needs of the hungry, thirsty, stranger, naked, sick or imprisoned.

7. What question was asked by those who were commended for their good response?
When did we see You in times of such need, and respond?

8. What question did those who were rebuked ask?
When did we see You in such times of need and not help?

9. What was Jesus' reply to the inquiries of the two groups?
Inasmuch as ye have done it [or "did it not"] unto one of the least of these my brethren, ye have done it unto me.

10. What did Jesus say would be the destiny of each of the two groups?
The wicked will go away into everlasting punishment: but the righteous into life eternal.

Martin of Tours was a Roman soldier and a Christian. The story is told that one cold winter day as Martin was entering a city, a beggar stopped him and asked for alms. Martin had no money, but his heart ached for the beggar, who was blue and shivering with cold. Having nothing in the way of silver, Martin gave the beggar what he had. He took off his worn and frayed soldier's coat and cut it in two, giving half of it to the beggar.

That night Martin had a dream. In his dream he saw the heavenly places and all the angels and Jesus in the midst of them. Jesus was wearing half of a Roman soldier's cloak. One of the angels asked Jesus, *"Master, why are you wearing that battered old cloak? Who gave it to you?"*

Jesus replied to the angel, *"My servant Martin gave it to me."*

A great many of us dream of doing something heroic for King Jesus, yet we fail to take seriously the instruction He provided for *how* we might do it. We serve Him by serving our fellow human beings. Ironically, it is in the process of selflessly giving ourselves away that we most successfully capture life's fulness for ourselves.

A fascinating study on the principle of the Golden Rule was conducted by Bernard Rimland, director of the Institute for Child Behavior Research. Rimland found that "The happiest people are those who help others." Each person involved in the study was asked to list 10 people he knew best and to label them as happy or unhappy. Then they were to go through the list again and label each one as selfish or unselfish, using the following definition of selfishness:

> A *stable tendency to devote one's time and resources to one's own interests and welfare—an unwillingness to inconvenience one's self for others."* (Rimland, "The Altruism Paradox," *Psychological Reports* 51 [1982]: 521.)

In categorizing the results, Rimland found that all of the people labeled happy were also labeled unselfish. He wrote that those "whose activities are devoted to bringing themselves happiness are far less likely to be happy than those whose efforts are devoted to making others happy." Rimland's conclusion sounds quite familiar to the Bible student. He said that the bottom line as a prescription for happiness is, "Do unto others as you would have them do unto you."

What Bernard Rimland discovered through scientific research, Martin of Tours discovered through responding out of compassion for a man in need. What they both discovered, Jesus had taught many years earlier for the benefit of those who were willing to listen. Are we willing to listen?

LET YOUR LIGHT SHINE BEFORE OTHERS...

Lesson 10

Rewards and Responsibilities

Matthew 5:1-16

And seeing the multitudes, he went up into a mountain: and when he was set, his disciples came unto him:

2 And he opened his mouth, and taught them, saying,

3 Blessed are the poor in spirit: for theirs is the kingdom of heaven.

4 Blessed are they that mourn: for they shall be comforted.

5 Blessed are the meek: for they shall inherit the earth.

6 Blessed are they which do hunger and thirst after righteousness: for they shall be filled.

7 Blessed are the merciful: for they shall obtain mercy.

8 Blessed are the pure in heart: for they shall see God.

9 Blessed are the peacemakers: for they shall be called the children of God.

10 Blessed are they which are persecuted for righteousness' sake: for theirs is the kingdom of heaven.

11 Blessed are ye, when men shall revile you, and persecute you, and shall say all manner of evil against you falsely, for my sake.

12 Rejoice, and be exceeding glad: for great is your reward in heaven: for so persecuted they the prophets which were before you.

13 Ye are the salt of the earth: but if the salt have lost his savour, wherewith shall it be salted? it is thenceforth good for nothing, but to be cast out, and to be trodden under foot of men.

14 Ye are the light of the world. A city that is set on an hill cannot be hid.

15 Neither do men light a candle, and put it under a bushel, but on a candlestick; and it giveth light unto all that are in the house.

16 Let your light so shine before men, that they may see your good works, and glorify your Father which is in heaven.

Nov. 4

Memory Selection
Matthew 5:16

Devotional Reading
Psalm 24

Background Scripture
Matthew 5:1-16

The next four lessons focus on what may well be the most influential single piece of writing in the world—Jesus' "Sermon on the Mount." What Matthew records in three chapters (Matt. 5-7) has prompted countless commentaries and books, life-changing decisions, and peaceful revolutions.

This first lesson in the series examines "The Beatitudes." This is a lesson on how to experience *blessedness*, or what Jesus may have called "shalom"—peace, joy, and wholeness. These character traits challenge conventional views of happiness. Unfortunately they have become so familiar to many Christians that we forget how radical they are—how they stand the world's values upside down. In one sense they serve as the "Ten Commandments" of the New Covenant, since they capsule so much of the rest of the teaching of Christ and His apostles.

෨෬

A good way to begin this session is to illustrate the role of "digests." If available, show the group one of the large paperback manuals of instruction about how to operate some of today's complicated computer equipment. Ask if group members have ever struggled with the size and complexity of such manuals. Then show a "How to Get Started," abbreviated version, which is often only a few pages; and note that it boils down and simplifies the larger manual.

Alternatively, bring a copy of *The Reader's Digest*, and show how its popularity stems in part from the way it "digests" good articles from a massive number of other sources. Do a word-association exercise, calling for synonyms for "digest" (core, gist, abridgment, brief, precis, synopsis).

Now note how grateful we can be for Matthew 5-7, which is also a digest—of the Bible's most important teaching.

Teaching Outline	Daily Bible Readings	
I. Beginning the Sermon—Matt. 5:1-2	**Mon.**	Called to Holy Living 1 Peter 1:10-16
A. Mount vs. 'plain,' 1a	**Tue.**	What Truly Endures 1 Peter 1:18-25
B. The new Moses?, 1a-2	**Wed.**	A Spiritual House 1 Peter 2:1-8
II. Blessed Believers—3-12	**Thu.**	To Inherit a Blessing 1 Peter 3:8-15a
A. Inward attitudes, 3-6	**Fri.**	Suffer for God, Not Evil 1 Peter 3:17-22
B. Outgoing dynamics, 7-12	**Sat.**	Support Faith with Goodness 2 Peter 1:3-11
III. Believers' Situation—13-16	**Sun.**	'Blessed Are You When . . .' Matthew 5:1-11
A. Salt, 13		
B. Light, 14-16		

Verse by Verse

I. Beginning the Sermon—Matt. 5:1-2

A. Mount vs. "plain," 1a

1 And seeing the multitudes, he went up into a mountain:

Some interpreters hold that this event is the same as Jesus "Sermon on the Plain" in Luke 6:17-23, and assume that the "plain" was a level place on the mountainside. The present approach, however, treats these as two different events because of the difference in content. For example, in Luke's account the Beatitudes apply more to literal situations ("blessed be ye poor,") vs. the "poor in spirit" here.

B. The new Moses?, 1a-2

1a and when he was set, his disciples came unto him:

2 And he opened his mouth, and taught them, saying,

Many commentators find special significance in Jesus' delivering His sermon from a mountain. They compare this with Moses delivering the Ten Commandments from Mount Sinai, and suggest that Jesus is presenting Himself as the "new Moses," or Law-giver. Some support this view by finding five divisions in the Gospel of Matthew, and comparing these with the "Pentateuch," or first five

books of the Old Testament, traditionally held to have been written by Moses. Whether such speculations are true or not, the three chapters devoted here to Jesus' sermon are powerful enough in themselves to claim a level of attention and obedience as loyal as that of any Jew who placed himself under the law Moses brought down from Sinai.

II. Blessed Believers—3-12

A. Inward attitudes, 3-6

3 Blessed are the poor in spirit: for theirs is the kingdom of heaven.

4 Blessed are they that mourn: for they shall be comforted.

The Greek word for "blessed" is *makarios*, which can mean simply "happy" (as in the Phillips translation, "Happy are ye . . ."). However, the word is from a root that goes more deeply into the human psyche with the meaning of "supremely blessed." This definition recalls the Hebrew word *shalom*, "peace" or "fullness of well-being," and some have suggested that Jesus may have used this word as He spoke.

The point is that all these traits of "blessedness" characterize, or should characterize, those who proclaim their allegiance to Jesus by becoming citizens of the Kingdom of heaven—living under God's rule on earth in a way that leads to living with Him in heaven. Each trait, it should be noticed, calls into question many popular, secular understandings of what characterizes happiness in the sense of "the good life."

In referring to the "poor in spirit" and "they that mourn," Jesus must have had in mind those hearers who were deeply saddened by their own sins, or by the degraded moral and civic state of the Judaism of the day. Leading with these traits, Jesus emphasizes that only those who realize their failure can throw themselves onto the mercy of Jesus.

This does not mean that Christians cannot have an "upbeat" or buoyant spirit. As Frederick Dale Bruner writes, "Jesus beatifies mourning, not moping" (*The Christbook*, p. 139). Jesus is warning against the arrogance that blinds us to sin and injustice, insisting that only those who are sensitive enough to mourn the wrong can truly rejoice in the right.

5 Blessed are the meek: for they shall inherit the earth.

The word "meek" does not describe a pushover, but a person who is not arrogant but willing to subject his will to that of Jesus. Moses, the classic Bible example of a meek person (Num. 12:3), was one of Israel's most powerful and dynamic leaders. "The earth" corresponds to "the kingdom of heaven" in other Beatitudes, indicating that their inheritance will be the future "new heaven and a new earth" (Rev. 21:1).

6 Blessed are they which do hunger and thirst after righteousness: for they shall be filled.

Here Jesus promises fulfillment for all those who have the sense that they could be more like Jesus, and whose appetite is for the spiritual over the material. When they hear the title of the old song, "Is that All There Is?", they answer No!—affirming that this life's rewards pale in the light of the joys in the world to come. They therefore gladly set their highest hopes on the future that will dawn when Christ returns.

B. Outgoing dynamics, 7-12

7 Blessed are the merciful: for they shall obtain mercy.

Moving from more passive attitudes of "blessedness," Jesus now pronounces blessedness on those whose Kingdom commitment dares to press beyond the standard of "an eye for an eye and a tooth for a tooth." Here He anticipates His teaching on loving our enemies, in verses 43-47; and His insistence in 6:14-15 that we must forgive if we expect to be forgiven.

Questions immediately arise: Should we forgive the impenitent? Does this teaching forbid going to war? Without providing answers to our endless questions, Jesus simply puts forth the principle and leaves His followers to apply it to their own life situation.

8 Blessed are the pure in heart: for they shall see God.

The pure in heart also depart from

94

standard world standards by seeking the good in others, not turning every thought into something debasing, not engaging in the relational murder of gossiping, not harboring grudges.

9 Blessed are the peacemakers: for they shall be called the children of God.

Since Jesus was the Prince of Peace, His followers are to follow His example in trying to pour the oil of calm on the stormy waters of disputes. Of course this describes the overall intent and policy of a child of God, who must sometimes stand for the right instead of making peace with evil. We recall that Jesus Himself was sometimes driven to stormy action, as when He took a whip and drove the moneychangers from the Temple.

10 Blessed are they which are persecuted for righteousness' sake: for theirs is the kingdom of heaven.

11 Blessed are ye, when men shall revile you, and persecute you, and shall say all manner of evil against you falsely, for my sake.

12 Rejoice, and be exceeding glad: for great is your reward in heaven: for so persecuted they the prophets which were before you.

These three verses describe the single "blessed" trait of being persecuted or reviled for being faithful to Christ. Indeed, embracing the preceding traits will entail opposition, since they challenge the majority view and standard values of the world. Yet we are to face such opposition with the strength of love, forgiveness, and re-

joicing, since that was Christ's own reaction to persecution.

III. Believers' Situation—13-16
A. Salt, 13

13 Ye are the salt of the earth: but if the salt have lost his savour, wherewith shall it be salted? it is thenceforth good for nothing, but to be cast out, and to be trodden under foot of men.

Of what influence on the world will we be if we live in the spirit of the Beatitudes? They are values that have the power to "save" the world as salt preserves meat from decay.

B. Light, 14-16

14 Ye are the light of the world. A city that is set on an hill cannot be hid.

15 Neither do men light a candle, and put it under a bushel, but on a candlestick; and it giveth light unto all that are in the house.

16 Let your light so shine before men, that they may see your good works, and glorify your Father which is in heaven.

Changing the metaphor of Christian influence from salt to light, Jesus continues to describe the impact enlightened "Beatitude" people can have in a world of darkness. Note that while His followers are to live out their "blessed" lifestyles boldly, their purpose is not to attract attention to themselves but to glorify the Father.

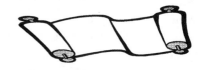

Evangelistic Emphasis

"Blessed *are* the pure in heart: for they shall see God." Those are the words that Miriam Abdy remembered most from the preacher's sermon. She had never before been to a Christian worship service, and she would not have come this time if it had not been for her yearning to understand Bill Thompson better.

Miriam was reared in Iran's world of Islam. Bill claims to believe in Jesus. Even though Miriam now lives in America, which is highly influenced by Christianity, she is not sure she could ever accept it. Yet, something deep inside her wants to find out more.

Miriam wonders if she is "pure in heart." Her interest in Christianity, after all, is prompted more by her interest in Bill than in Jesus. Still, this remark of Jesus haunts her. What exactly does it mean? She tries to remember something from the Koran that echoes the same sentiment, but she cannot think of anything.

Miriam feels awkward about asking Bill to explain the statement. *"He would probably think me stupid,"* she thinks. She wonders how she might find out more about this Jesus. Fortunately, Miriam lives in a time and place when her options are many. It is possible for her search to take her to the public library for some books. She can invest in some reputable journals. The story of Jesus is even readily available on tape. She is determined, however, that she will somehow learn more.

৩০০৪

Memory Selection

Let your light so shine before men, that they may see your good works, and glorify your Father which is in heaven.—*Matthew 5:16*

This is one of two principles from Jesus' teaching that really troubles Janet. Neither concept would trouble her if it stood alone. That one should *"let his light shine to be seen by men"* sounds reasonable. And the other principle that teaches one not to give alms, pray, or fast *"to be seen by men"* also seems reasonable. But how can we follow faithfully the one principle without breaking the other?

If Janet does her acts of righteousness out in the open so that the light of her life will be observable to others, is she then living *to be seen by men?* On the other hand, if she does all of her good deeds anonymously, is she then *hiding her light under a bushel?* Surely, there must be something that she has failed to understand. Janet cannot accept the idea that Jesus was as inconsistent in his teaching as this seems to her.

Weekday Problems

Henrietta knows that Jesus said that those who are persecuted for righteousness sake are "blessed," but she does not feel very blessed. These past two years working at Web-Soft have been a real trial. Every time she incidentally mentions church or something about faith, an echo of snickers can be heard resonating throughout the workforce. Initially, Henrietta found it hard to believe that she was the only believer at Web-Soft. Yet, during the past two years she had concluded that she obviously is.

It has been Henrietta's attempt not to make her faith "an issue" in the work setting. Though she would love to have other believers working in the same setting with her, she has never been preachy. In fact, Henrietta has gone out of her way to avoid mentioning faith, at all. Yet, her faith is so much a part of whom she is, it naturally is reflected in the words she speaks and how she does her work.

* Is there a difference between living one's faith *naturally* and "wearing one's religion on her sleeve?" How does one make that distinction?

* Should we try to avoid talking about our faith on the job? Or, ought one to use the workplace as one place to sow the seed of the Kingdom?

* What is the best way for one to respond to co-workers when belittling of one's faith is obviously taking place in subtle ways?

Tru(thful) Love

He: If you'd give me your phone number, I'll call you.
She: It's in the book.
He: Good. What's your name?
She: It's in the book, too.

* * *

She: Would you like to take a walk?
He: I'd love to!
She: Don't let me detain you.

* * *

She: You know, you remind me of the ocean.
He: You mean, wild, restless, and romantic?
She: No, I mean you make me sick.

* * *

"If you won't marry me, I'll die," said the earnest young lover. And sure enough, 50 years later, he died.

This Lesson in Your Life

How can one tell whether or not the church is being effective in its ministry? Is it obvious by whether its membership is going up or down? Can one tell by counting those who were saved during the past year? Ought one to focus on the attendance figures for Sunday School? Each of these benchmarks have been used through the years.

Is it possible, however, that while some of the above criteria (or perhaps even all) might indicate positive results, a closer investigation could reveal that the church has been predominately ineffective? Sometimes the church is swelling rapidly in size, but coming apart internally. It is easy to be so positively impressed with a church's "growth" that we fail to see beyond what impresses us. Only later does it come to be painfully clear that what we thought was growth was, instead, *bloating*.

For example, large numbers can profess "salvation" without there being any noticeable life change. The church becomes a revolving door for sinners to soothe their consciences, while they go on with their life of sin as before.

Several years ago Ray Stedman said: "It bothers me greatly to come into a city and find it filled with church buildings on every side, but to find also that the city is locked into patterns of violence and hatred, riot and bloodshed. It tells me that there is something seriously wrong with the churches of that city, for God always aims at the world."

What Stedman was highlighting was the fact that Christians are to be "salt in the world." As churches, we do not abide in our communities simply as decorations on the landscape. We have a work to do. Part of that work is to *retard the decay* that threatens our communities. The salt of the Gospel is so rubbed into the meat of the neighborhood that it does not spoil, even though neighborhoods all around it are rank with stench. Those who are not even Christians are impacted by the lives of Christians. Consequently, *love* and *caring* and *trust* and *kindness* and *stewardship* are perceived—even though outsiders may call it something such as "community pride."

This kind of effectiveness will sometimes appear long before the numbers of those in church increase or the Sunday School rosters swell. Stedman went on to say, "It is wonderful to have things happening within the congregation, but that is not the mark of success. The church is successful only when things start happening in the world . . . . Until something starts happening in the community, the church is a failure."

GETTING THE FACTS STRAIGHT

1. What posture did Jesus assume before beginning this "sermon?"
He sat down.

2. Upon whom did Jesus pronounce the first "blessing?" What was that blessing?
Upon "the poor in spirit." Jesus declared that theirs is the kingdom of heaven.

3. What blessing was pronounced upon "the meek?"
Jesus said that they shall inherit the earth.

4. Whom did Jesus say would be called the children of God?
The peacemakers.

5. Why were "the merciful" said to be blessed?
Because they will receive mercy.

6. Whom did Jesus tell to rejoice and to be exceedingly glad?
His followers, when they are reviled, persecuted, and falsely charged with evil for their commitment to Jesus.

7. Why did he tell those who were reviled and persecuted to rejoice?
Because they will receive a great reward in heaven.

8. Whom did Jesus say was the "salt of the earth" and the "light of the world?"
"Ye"—His followers, those to whom He was speaking.

9. According to Jesus, what is the value of salt that has lost its saltiness?
It is "good for nothing."

10. According to Jesus, what ought *not* be done with a candle?
It ought not be hidden (i.e., put under a bushel basket).

One of the "blessings" of e-mail in recent years has been the proliferation of readily available humor. The first lesson one learns after getting online is that "junk mail" has taken on a whole new meaning. Having said that, however, it needs also to be said that mixed in with all of the trivia are also gems of worth.

Recently I received a story by e-mail that said that Jesus took His disciples up the mountain and, gathering them around him, taught them saying:

- Blessed are the poor in spirit: for theirs is the kingdom of heaven.
- Blessed are they that mourn: for they shall be comforted.
- Blessed are the meek: for they shall inherit the earth.
- Blessed are they which do hunger and thirst after righteousness: for they shall be filled.
- Blessed are the merciful: for they shall obtain mercy.
- Blessed are the pure in heart: for they shall see God.
- Blessed are the peacemakers: for they shall be called the children of God.
- Blessed are they which are persecuted for righteousness' sake: for theirs is the kingdom of heaven.
- Blessed are ye, when men shall revile you, and persecute you, and shall say all manner of evil against you falsely, for my sake.

When Jesus had finished speaking, the crowd was thoroughly impressed with his sage words, but his students began to ask those questions that students ask:

- Simon Peter said, "Do we have to write this down?"
- And Andrew said, "Are we supposed to know this?"
- And James said, "Will we have a test on it?"
- And Philip said, "What if we don't know it?"
- And Bartholomew said, "Do we have to turn this in?"
- And John said, "The other disciples didn't have to learn this."
- And Matthew said, "When do we get out of here?"
- And Judas said, "What does this have to do with real life?"
- Then one of the Pharisees present asked to see Jesus' lesson plan and inquired of Jesus his terminal objectives in the cognitive domain.
- And Jesus wept . . . .

It would be wonderful if we could dismiss such humor as having no relevance to our world. Unfortunately, it gets so close to where we live that our laughter is inevitably a nervous laughter. Pointing to the obvious offenses of others, we hold our breath, hoping no one will notice our own.

...BUT TO FULFILL

Billy

'But I Say to You'

Matthew 5:17-20, 38-48

Think not that I am come to destroy the law, or the prophets: I am not come to destroy, but to fulfil.

18 For verily I say unto you, Till heaven and earth pass, one jot or one tittle shall in no wise pass from the law, till all be fulfilled.

19 Whosoever therefore shall break one of these least commandments, and shall teach men so, he shall be called the least in the kingdom of heaven: but whosoever shall do and teach them, the same shall be called great in the kingdom of heaven.

20 For I say unto you, That except your righteousness shall exceed the righteousness of the scribes and Pharisees, ye shall in no case enter into the kingdom of heaven.

38 Ye have heard that it hath been said, An eye for an eye, and a tooth for a tooth:

39 But I say unto you, That ye resist not evil: but whosoever shall smite thee on thy right cheek, turn to him the other also.

40 And if any man will sue thee at the law, and take away thy coat, let him have thy cloke also.

41 And whosoever shall compel thee to go a mile, go with him twain.

42 Give to him that asketh thee, and from him that would borrow of thee turn not thou away.

43 Ye have heard that it hath been said, Thou shalt love thy neighbour, and hate thine enemy.

44 But I say unto you, Love your enemies, bless them that curse you, do good to them that hate you, and pray for them which despitefully use you, and persecute you;

45 That ye may be the children of your Father which is in heaven: for he maketh his sun to rise on the evil and on the good, and sendeth rain on the just and on the unjust.

46 For if ye love them which love you, what reward have ye? do not even the publicans the same?

47 And if ye salute your brethren only, what do ye more than others? do not even the publicans so?

48 Be ye therefore perfect, even as your Father which is in heaven is perfect.

Nov. 11

Memory Selection
Matthew 5:17

Devotional Reading
Amos 5:4-15

Background Scripture
Matthew 5:17-48

Everyone lives by rules. Even the anarchist lives by the rule, "There shall be no rules." Although Jesus was far from being an anarchist, He did claim to have the authority to reinterpret the rules—that is, the Old Covenant. This lesson focuses on what He meant when He affirmed that His mission was "to fulfill the law"—the Law of Moses.

This affirmation has prompted a vast amount of study and writing on the role of the Old Covenant in the life of the Christian. Even the apostle Paul, who taught firmly that salvation is by grace, not by Law, insisted that the Old Covenant writings are to instruct Christians (Rom. 15:4). The teacher's challenge here is to show that the best way to show respect for the Law is to follow Jesus as the One who fulfilled its purpose.

ഇരു

Discuss with your group the role that rules played in their maturing from children to adults. Ask, "What rules that your parents made have you reinterpreted or redefined?" For example, were some group members forbidden to go to the movies, only to find that the advent of television caused them to redefine that rule? Have some who were raised by parents who used tobacco made rules against

it as they saw increased evidence of its danger to health? Point out that while many such rules may change, they grow out of an unchanging allegiance to good spiritual and physical health.

Likewise, Jesus calls us in this lesson to discover the underlying spirit of the Law. He found that the intent of some rules was being ignored, while others were being kept superficially. Just as our own understanding of life-related rules has grown since we were children, so Christ beckons us to follow Him in rediscovering the essence of the Law.

Teaching Outline	Daily Bible Readings	
	Mon.	The Law in Perspective Galatians 3:19-29
I. Fulfilling the Law—Matt. 5:17-20	**Tue.**	Burdensome Barriers Luke 11:37-52
A. Fulfilled, not destroyed 17-18		
B. Deepened, not broken, 19-20	**Wed.**	Hypocrisy Doesn't Work Luke 12:1-7
II. Reinterpreting the Law—38-48		
A. How to react to wrong, 38-42	**Thu.**	Murder, Anger, Reconciliation Matthew 5:21-26
B. How to treat enemies, 43-47		
1. Love them! 43-44	**Fri.**	Lust: Adultery in the Heart Matthew 5:27-32
2. Like Father, like child, 45-48	**Sat.**	'Do Not Swear at All' Matthew 5:33-37
	Sun.	To Fulfill, not Abolish Matthew 5:13-20

Verse by Verse

I. Fulfilling the Law–Matt. 5:17-20

A. Fulfilled, not destroyed, 17-18

17 Think not that I am come to destroy the law, or the prophets: I am not come to destroy, but to fulfil.

18 For verily I say unto you, Till heaven and earth pass, one jot or one tittle shall in no wise pass from the law, till all be fulfilled.

"Law and prophets" was a common way of referring to the Jewish Scriptures. Because Jesus did not emphasize the correct sacrifice, rituals, and formal prayers associated with these holy writings, as did other rabbis, some thought He was antino-mian," or against keeping the Law that was the very foundation of both Judaism and the universal moral order. Thus it was essential for Jesus to explain His position relative to their Scriptures.

Jesus says that the Scriptures must be kept down to the smallest "jot" (Grk. *iota*) and brush-stroke. Yet He will proceed to show in the rest of this chapter that "keeping the Law" must mean something different than salvation by works—as the apostle Paul will emphasize. Also, Jesus says that the Law is to be in effect only until "heaven and earth

pass away" and "all be fulfilled"; while, in contrast, His own words are forever valid (Matt. 24:35).

Before His death, Jesus Himself was under the Law, including its system of sacrifice, circumcision, and other rituals. As the only person ever to keep the Law perfectly, Jesus "fulfilled" or "filled full" these requirements, preparing the way for the abolishment of these "legal" or "ceremonial" aspects of the Law by His death on the Cross (Col. 2:15; Gal. 3:5). The "moral" aspects of the Law, such as embodied in the Ten Commandments, are reaffirmed in New Covenant teaching—not as works salvation but as the believer's heart-felt response to salvation. It is in these ways that the Law is "established" forever (Rom. 3:31).

B. Deepened, not broken, 19-20

19 Whosoever therefore shall break one of these least commandments, and shall teach men so, he shall be called the least in the kingdom of heaven: but whosoever shall do and teach them, the same shall be called great in the kingdom of heaven.

20 For I say unto you, That ex-

cept your righteousness shall exceed the righteousness of the scribes and Pharisees, ye shall in no case enter into the kingdom of heaven.

To fairly grasp the importance of not teaching that the Law can be ignored, we must again allow Jesus to redefine what that means, as in the rest of the Sermon on the Mount. Instead of merely giving outward or formal obedience, ("the righteousness of the scribes and Pharisees") He will define obedience as a matter of the heart. Instead of trusting in the blood of animals to remove sin, "keeping the Law" will be defined as trusting in the blood of Christ (Heb. 9:13,14; 10:4).

II. Reinterpreting the Law—38-48
A. How to react to wrong, 38-42

38 Ye have heard that it hath been said, An eye for an eye, and a tooth for a tooth:

39 But I say unto you, That ye resist not evil: but whosoever shall smite thee on thy right cheek, turn to him the other also.

40 And if any man will sue thee at the law, and take away thy coat, let him have thy cloke also.

41 And whosoever shall compel thee to go a mile, go with him twain.

42 Give to him that asketh thee, and from him that would borrow of thee turn not thou away.

From verse 21, Jesus has been teaching one aspect of what it means for Him to "fulfill" or "fill full" the Law. He does this by stating what the Old Covenant Law said (or in some cases how it had been interpreted), then giving its true interpretation. At times, as here in the law of "an eye for an eye," Jesus' reformulation is so different that this section is often called "the antitheses."

The examples here partly reflect the presence of Roman soldiers in Palestine. They could coerce citizens into running errands, and confiscate personal property such as a cloak. Jesus' teaching, however, extends beyond such military contacts into all personal relations. It is an extension of "the Golden Rule," a call to go beyond the minimum retaliation authorized by most civil laws with the spirit of the forgiving Christ. The main reason for a "turn the other cheek" ethic is that this was the way Jesus responded to His own persecutors (1 Pet. 2:23). Here is another way in which Jesus "filled full" the Law.

Some authorities point out that Jesus' teaching here is best understood as the individual Christian's ideal response to wrongs done against him personally, rather than as a universal "social ethic." This interpretation allows a society, for example, to exact the death penalty against a wrong-doer, while personally having a spirit of forgiveness.

B. How to treat enemies, 43-47
1. Love them! 43-44

43 Ye have heard that it hath been said, Thou shalt love thy neighbour, and hate thine enemy. 44 But I say unto you, Love your enemies, bless them that curse you, do good to them that hate you, and pray for them which despitefully use you, and persecute you;

Although the Old Covenant Scriptures never say "Hate thine enemy," some of the Psalms and other passages call for God to treat one's enemies hatefully (see esp. Pss. 58 and 109). Some rabbis may have made the short step from hating evil to hating evil's perpetrators; and it is this that Jesus corrects.

This teaching has led some devout Christians to oppose going to war. All must admit that when put into practice this teaching has the otherwise unheard-of power to change not only the heart of the offended believer, but of the offender. Others, again, would apply it to an individual believer's attitude—which would require the Christian not to hate even those whom nations classify as the enemy.

2. Like Father, like child, 45-48

45 That ye may be the children of your Father which is in heaven: for he maketh his sun to rise on the evil and on the good, and sendeth rain on the just and on the unjust.

46 For if ye love them which love you, what reward have ye? do not even the publicans the same? 47 And if ye salute your brethren only, what do ye more than others? do not even the publicans so? 48 Be ye therefore perfect, even as your Father which is in heaven is perfect.

Now the radical nature of Christian behavior is seen in its starkest contrast with that of the world. Jesus says that refusing to retaliate against wrong treatment, and loving one's enemies, are the way to identify God's true children. He tells us to leave "natural" tendencies to strike back and to hate enemies to the "publicans," the collectors of public taxes, who were universally viewed as having the lowest possible standards of morality.

Verse 48 has often been mistaken as a "counsel of perfection," leaving many Christians laboring under an unnecessary burden of guilt. The expression translated "perfect" can also mean "complete," "mature," or "fulfilled." This reminds us of the context here. Christ is the only "perfect" person who ever lived, both by nature and by fulfilling the letter and the spirit of the Law. Here He calls His followers to fulfill their own role, not as perfectionists but as those who strive for perfection by daring to follow the one Person who perfectly fulfilled the Law.

Evangelistic Emphasis

Jesus' words, "Whosoever looketh on a woman to lust after her hath committed adultery with her already in his heart" cause many Christian men to despair. Making things seem even more desperate, Jesus follows those words with the admonition, "If thy right eye offend thee, pluck it out, and cast it from thee: for it is profitable for thee that one of thy members should perish, and not that thy whole body should be cast into hell."

Perhaps the only thing that keeps the church from being filled with one-eyed men is the fact that most of us realize that we are also quite capable of lusting with just one eye. Yet, it is a painfully fearful thought that, even when one is determined to guard one's mind from any illicit venturing, illicit venturing will probably happen. In fact, it sometimes seems as though the more one determines not to lust, the more he is prone to lust. It's a little like trying not to think of polka-dotted elephants. The harder one tries *not* to think of them, the more such thoughts are generated.

Perhaps what we need most to gain from Jesus' statement here is not despair, but humility. Rather than encouraging us to "just do it," He is calling for us to understand that all of us sin—even those who are exceptionally disciplined in their conduct. Consequentially, all of us are in desperate need of a Savior.

෪ඍ

Memory Selection

Think not that I am come to destroy the law, or the prophets: I am not come to destroy, but to fulfil.—*Matthew 5:17*

As long as Linda Skipp can remember being aware of this Scripture, she has struggled with it. It does not fit very well into her method of subdividing history into dispensations. Neither does she understand how the statement of Jesus here harmonizes with what Paul wrote. When he spoke of "the handwriting of ordinances that was against us" being "nailed to the cross," wasn't he speaking of the Law? Yet, in the memory passage for today, Jesus seems to be strongly "pro-law."

As Linda ponders the implications of Jesus' remarks, she wonders how that ought to effect her devotion. Should she "keep the Sabbath holy? and observe the various dietary restrictions of the Law? These questions worry her as she attempts to come to peace with her faith. Is it possible that she and most of the Christian world have been wrong about these issues? Or, is it possible that there is something involved that Linda does not understand?

Weekday Problems

Harry and Jeanette Weber have a good marriage and, for the most part, have pretty much seen eye-to-eye in matters related to rearing their children. There is one topic, however, that has prompted frequent disagreements. It involves training their eight-year-old son, Tommy, how best to deal with confrontational situations. Harry argues that a boy must learn to "stand up for himself." Jeanette maintains that "there is never an excuse for fighting."

Harry is not a "Bible scholar," but he knows that there is a whole lot in the Bible that has to do with military defense. "David didn't back down from Goliath!" he reminds Jeanette. "If Tommy doesn't stand up for himself, he will get pushed around all his life," he says.

Jeanette replies, "That's nonsense. Jesus was very clear in what he instructed. "If someone hits Tommy on the right cheek, Jesus tells him to offer his other cheek to be hit also," she insists.

* Since both Harry and Jeanette seem to be making arguments based on their understanding of specific Scriptures, how can they resolve the matter?

* How does Jesus' admonition to "turn the other cheek" apply to Timmy, who is being beat up every day by the class bully?

* How does David's killing Goliath speak to Jeanette's desire to instill peace in her son, rather than violence?

Getting Around the Law (?)

The following excerpts were taken from actual comments on insurance claim forms:

- I collided with a stationary streetcar coming the opposite direction.
- A pedestrian hit me and went under my car.
- The guy was all over the road. I had to swerve a number of times before I hit him.
- My car was legally parked as it backed into the other vehicle.
- An invisible car came out of nowhere, struck my vehicle, and vanished.
- The pedestrian had no idea which way to go, so I ran over him.
- The telephone pole was approaching fast. I was attempting to swerve out of its path when it struck my front end.
- Coming home, I drove into the wrong house.

This Lesson in Your Life

Virginia Henderson is a young attorney. She worked hard getting through Law School, and is proud of her profession, in spite of all the "lawyer jokes" told in her presence by her friends. She gets teased a lot by those with whom she grew up in Albany. And for the most part, Virginia accepts the teasing in a good spirit. She just teases them back, assuring them that the day will come when it will be she who is called to come to the rescue. The only one to seriously challenge her self-confidence and sense of success is her own father.

In every way except her career choice, Virginia's father was always her greatest encourager and fan. He never missed a piano recital or a volleyball game. A bumper sticker was permanently attached to the rear of his pickup bumper, announcing to the world that his daughter was an honor student in school. When she medaled in The Academic Decathlon he proudly announced it at church.

Since Virginia decided to pursue a Law degree, however, her father has echoed only disapproval. According to him, Jesus disapproved lawsuits. "If Jesus disapproves of lawsuits, then a Christian ought not have anything to do with them," he reasoned.

Virginia has attempted to reason with her dad many times. The argument skills that she learned in Law School, however, have not helped much in her discussions with him. He keeps reciting the same Scriptures to her over and over again. In addition to this passage, 1 Corinthians 5 and 6 provide his primary argument.

Virginia is bewildered as to how to respond. When she began Law School, she convinced herself that he would eventually "come around." It does not seem to her, though, that he has budged an inch. Virginia so much wants her dad's approval, but she has invested far too much into this career just to throw it away.

Though Virginia may not realize it, the result of her dad's persistent disapproval of her career has not been all negative. It has really challenged her to search her own soul in the matter. In the process, choices have been made that have nudged her career in a different direction than it would have otherwise gone. Her strong sense of ethics has been refined and purified, rather than merely compromised by the sleaze that is so prevalent in the undercurrents of her profession. For this she is very thankful.

Virginia may never win her dad over in this matter. She only prays that the day will come when her polished skill will show that she is not only successful at her profession, but also a blessing to her family.

1. Who did Jesus say would be called great in the kingdom of heaven?

He who keeps the commandments of the Law and teaches them.

2. Jesus said that not one jot or tittle would pass from the Law until what happen?

Until heaven and earth pass away.

3. What level of righteous did Jesus say must be exceeded in order to enter into the kingdom?

The righteousness of the scribes and Pharisees.

4. Who did Jesus say was in danger of hell fire?

He who calls his brother a fool.

5. According to Jesus, of what is one guilty who looks on a woman to lust after her?

Committing adultery with her in his heart.

6. What response did Jesus give to the contemporary guideline pertaining to swearing?

He said, "Swear not at all," but simply let Yes mean Yes (in other words, to become known as one who speaks the truth).

7. What rule does Jesus offer in place of "an eye for an eye" retaliation?

He said that if someone hits you, to turn the other cheek, or not retaliate.

8. How did Jesus say we ought to respond to someone who wishes to borrow from us?

He said that we should not turn that person away.

9. What did Jesus say would result from loving our enemies and blessing those who curse us?

We would be behaving like children of our Father in heaven.

10. To whom did Jesus compare those who love only those who love them in return?

Publicans. Even they love like that, he said.

109

My good friend Charles Turner is a preacher turned attorney. For several years he was a member of a church that I served in the Houston area. As time passed, Charles was found to be a real asset to the church. Several of the members needed to have wills processed, and Charles was someone they trusted with that very important task. My wife and I engaged him to do our will, as well.

Just because Charles left full-time ministry to enter the law profession does not mean that he "flunked preaching." Actually, he did a pretty good job. I frequently called on him to speak in my place when I had to be out of town.

On one such occasion, my trip was canceled at the last minute, so I warmed a pew that morning. After the service was over, however, I made my way to the lobby to greet visitors and members as they left. One of the first to exit was a middle-aged woman who was almost ecstatic. "Wasn't he wonderful!" she said.

I concurred that Charles had done a fine job. She did not leave it there, though. "I just wish he preached for us every week!" she blurted. But as soon as she said it, it dawned on her to whom she was speaking. "Or maybe, every other week," she added timidly.

Perhaps, amid all our cynicism and humor about attorneys, we have forgotten how much we depend on them. Beyond "fill-in preaching," lawyers bring to Christians the expertise needed to process legal papers needed for the purchase of a home or the starting of a business. They write our wills and deeds of trust. They scrutinize labor contracts to make sure that we didn't miss something of which we should be aware. They defend the church against frivolous lawsuits and the preacher against malpractice lawsuits.

In addition to all this, whole new fields of law have opened in recent years that focus on bringing opposing parties together to find a mutually satisfying solution to their problem, rather than capitalizing on the adversarial relationship that already exists. It's called "dispute resolution" or "mediation," and it is the practice of *peacemaking*.

Should there remain a reluctance to give up the idea that Jesus is bashing lawyers in this sermon, it might be helpful for us to consider the word "advocate." In 1 John 2:1 Jesus himself is described by this term. He is at the Father's throne interceding for us—a function that also describes the task of the lawyer. Jesus is our lawyer, representing us in Heaven's court. He approaches the bench not as a novice who is lacking valuable experience. Rather, He stands to defend us as one who has been at the front lines of battle and understands our plight. That's not a bad description of a good lawyer, too.

STRIVE FIRST FOR THE KINGDOM OF GOD...

Concerning Treasures

Matthew 6:19-21, 25-34

Lay not up for yourselves treasures upon earth, where moth and rust doth corrupt, and where thieves break through and steal:

20 But lay up for yourselves treasures in heaven, where neither moth nor rust doth corrupt, and where thieves do not break through nor steal:

21 For where your treasure is, there will your heart be also.

25 Therefore I say unto you, Take no thought for your life, what ye shall eat, or what ye shall drink; nor yet for your body, what ye shall put on. Is not the life more than meat, and the body than raiment?

26 Behold the fowls of the air: for they sow not, neither do they reap, nor gather into barns; yet your heavenly Father feedeth them. Are ye not much better than they?

27 Which of you by taking thought can add one cubit unto his stature?

28 And why take ye thought for raiment? Consider the lilies of the field, how they grow; they toil not, neither do they spin:

29 And yet I say unto you, That even Solomon in all his glory was not arrayed like one of these.

30 Wherefore, if God so clothe the grass of the field, which to day is, and to morrow is cast into the oven, shall he not much more clothe you, O ye of little faith?

31 Therefore take no thought, saying, What shall we eat? or, What shall we drink? or, Wherewithal shall we be clothed?

32 (For after all these things do the Gentiles seek:) for your heavenly Father knoweth that ye have need of all these things.

33 But seek ye first the kingdom of God, and his righteousness; and all these things shall be added unto you.

34 Take therefore no thought for the morrow: for the morrow shall take thought for the things of itself. Sufficient unto the day is the evil thereof.

Nov. 18

Memory Selection
Matthew 6:33-34

Devotional Reading
Philippians 4:4-9

Background Scripture
Matthew 6

Many people in our society seem to embody the old tongue-in-cheek saying, "Money isn't everything, but it's 'way above whatever's in second place." The focus of this lesson is to put wealth and what it will buy into proper "place" or perspective, giving priority to the spiritual over the material.

The importance of this topic is obvious when we remember that Jesus taught more on it than on any other. Obviously, putting these teachings into practice depends partly on our cultural context. For example, a lower-income American would be considered rich in parts of India and Africa. Yet Jesus' teaching is relevant to all cultures, since He focuses more on the quality of our attitudes toward the material than on the quantity of our possessions. Challenge group members to identify what Jesus is teaching them in their own situation.

ഏറെ

Get this session off to a lively start by wearing an old, worn-out and even ragged jacket. Standing before the group in such a castaway garment, start the lesson as though nothing is different. Then recognize whispered comments, stares, or giggles, and invite group members to share their first impressions. Some may have suspected a joke, others may have wondered if your regular attire didn't make it back from the cleaners, or if you were trying to win sympathy.

Make two points as you respond to comments. (1) We often make unfair judgments about people's worth by their appearance; yet (2) our appearance can help or hinder how we represent our Christian calling. In this lesson Jesus warns against elevating the material above the spiritual. Yet He does not say that the material is wrong. Although we are not to dress "for show," neither are not to allow shoddy appearances to detract from the gospel. We are to use the material in service to the spiritual.

Teaching Outline

I. True Treasures—6:19-21
  A. Risky investments, 19
  B. Lasting treasure, 20-21
II. True Trust—25-34
  A. For true life, 25-26
  B. For true glory, 27-30
  C. For the future, 31-34

Daily Bible Readings

Verse by Verse

I. True Treasures—6:19-21

A. Risky investments, 19

19 Lay not up for yourselves treasures upon earth, where moth and rust doth corrupt, and where thieves break through and steal:

In Jesus' day, a common way to store wealth was simply to hide gold and silverware, coins, and costly garments under the floor of one's house, or in a cave on one's property. Banking as we know it was not a highly-developed industry, although archeological evidence has been discovered from ancient Babylonia indicating that some Jews were bankers there. That some limited kinds of banking were in use in Jesus' day is indicated in the "Parable of the Talents," where He actually commends the practice of investing (see Matt. 25:27; the KJV "usury" simply means "interest"). Such references, plus the positive references to people of substance such as Joseph of Arimathea and Lydia, are evidence that Jesus is not teaching that wealth is wrong in itself. Instead, He is warning that the material is unsafe to build a life on, or to make it our first priority.

Whether material wealth is stored in a bank or a cave, the problem is that it is impossible to guarantee its safety. Precious metals rust, costly silks become moth-eaten, and anything stored is subject to theft. Even in the modern U.S., with the government insuring many accounts, bank failures are not unknown and stock market losses are notorious. In using the phrase "on earth" Jesus encourages us to ask, "If my treasure is not safe here, then where?"

B. Lasting treasure, 20-21

20 But lay up for yourselves treasures in heaven, where neither moth nor rust doth corrupt, and where thieves do not break through nor steal:

21 For where your treasure is, there will your heart be also.

The only truly safe place to store our "treasure," Jesus says, is "in heaven." Of course since heaven is a spiritual realm, we know that Jesus is speaking of spiritual riches—the opposite of "mammon" or material wealth (see vs. 24). What does it mean to store up spiritual wealth? According to verse 33, it means putting "kingdom treasures" above material wealth. We make "kingdom investments" when we put service to others ahead of serving ourselves, when we explain to them how to access the supreme treasure of salvation, and when we develop in ourselves Christian character traits. Although none of these "treasures" would be accepted by any bank as collateral for a loan, neither are they subject to decay or theft; and Jesus assures us that heaven is a safe depository for them.

Verse 21 underscores the obvious truth that our hearts are invested in that which is highest priority in our value system. A proper attitude toward the material is ensured by investing our interest in the non-material. When we treat people as things, or hoard our wealth instead of "investing" a portion in the needs of others, it is obvious that our heart is set on earthly, not spiritual, things.

II. True Trust—25-34

A. For true life, 25-26

25 Therefore I say unto you, Take no thought for your life, what ye shall eat, or what ye shall drink; nor yet for your body, what ye shall put on. Is not the life more than meat, and the body than raiment?

26 Behold the fowls of the air: for they sow not, neither do they reap, nor gather into barns; yet your heavenly Father feedeth them. Are ye not much better than they?

"Take no thought" is better translated "Do not worry," as in the NIV. Jesus' counsel is directed not at being thoughtless, but at being unduly anxious—which is inevitably the result of placing all our concern on the material. Note that Jesus does not fall into the trap of the "dualist" or gnostic who holds that the spirit is good and the flesh is evil. In fact, He

insists that not worrying about the material but giving first place to the spiritual is good for "the body" as well as for the totality of "life" (Grk. *psyche*).

The value of not being totally focused on externals is illustrated by the way God cares for the birds of the air. If He "giveth to the beast his food, and to the young ravens which cry" (Ps. 147:9), then will God not care for the needs (not the luxuries!) of believers?

B. For true glory, 27-30

27 Which of you by taking thought can add one cubit unto his stature?

28 And why take ye thought for raiment? Consider the lilies of the field, how they grow; they toil not, neither do they spin:

29 And yet I say unto you, That even Solomon in all his glory was not arrayed like one of these.

30 Wherefore, if God so clothe the grass of the field, which to day is, and to morrow is cast into the oven, shall he not much more clothe you, O ye of little faith?

Whether we think of clothing in particular or our outward looks, in general, there is an obvious limit to how much we can improve the looks with which we were born. (This revelation comes as a shock to the cosmetic industry, which insists that there is no limit to the number and kind of potions and ointments that can improve our appearance, and that, above all, "We're worth it!")

Jesus does not say that our appearance is unimportant, but that there are limits to how much we can really change it by giving it obsessive concern. His use of King Solomon as an example also shows that the lesson for us here is not that wealth is wrong, but that it is not achieved by making it our first priority. "Whoever loves money never has money enough; whoever loves wealth is never satisfied with his income" (Eccl. 5:10, NIV). Yet Solomon, who put his desire for wisdom above material abundance, was given both.

This line of reasoning is too often seized on and exploited by "name it and claim it" teachers, who advise us to expect to grow wealthy by positive thinking or giving to their favorite charity (often themselves). Jesus, however, is not giving us a formula for growing rich but insisting that God has whole-life concern for those who put Him first.

C. For the future, 31-34

31 Therefore take no thought, saying, What shall we eat? or, What shall we drink? or, Wherewithal shall we be clothed?

32 (For after all these things do the Gentiles seek:) for your heavenly Father knoweth that ye have need of all these things.

33 But seek ye first the kingdom of God, and his righteousness; and all these things shall be added unto you.

34 Take therefore no thought for the morrow: for the morrow shall take thought for the things of itself.

Sufficient unto the day is the evil thereof.

By referring to "Gentiles" Jesus is not being racist but speaking of those who, unlike those Jews who faithfully served their God, seek material gain over the spiritual. He is criticizing the priorities of those who beseech multiple gods to tend to their welfare instead of trusting the One God to care for them, body, mind, and soul. Yet believers in this One God must be sure that they get the point: becoming obsessed by what we eat, drink, or wear (or by luxury cars, TV, movies, cosmetics, houses, ad infinitum) is to live like pagans! That is, worrying about material goods is an indication that we are substituting material "gods" for the true God.

In verses 33-34, *time* is added to materialism as part of what competes with our putting God's Kingdom first in our lives. We think that treasuring up material gain is a way of controlling the future, staving off "the wolf at the door" or other evils. Just as Jesus' teaching that we should "hate" our parents (Luke 14:26) is to be taken as over-statement for emphasis, so verse 34 does not forbid us from saving a reasonable amount of funds for tomorrow. It is a warning against trying to find security in the material goods treasured by those whose allegiance is to earthly life instead of the Kingdom of heaven.

Evangelistic Emphasis

Jesse has not always been blind. Until he was 23, Jesse could see better than most of the members of his family. Most of his family members wore glasses or contacts. Jesse was the exception. He seemed to be the lucky one who did not inherit the "near-sighted gene." During duck-and dear-hunting season, Jesse always came back with the prize.

All that ended, however when Jesse was 23. He doused some stubborn charcoal too liberally with lighter fluid, then failed to allow enough time for the fluid to soak in. When Jesse struck the match, the fumes from the fresh fluid flash-burned, leaving Jesse's face and eyes badly burned. His face healed without any ugly scars, but Jesse has been blind since that day.

It seems such an irony to Jesse. Only his eyes were permanently injured, yet his whole world is now dark. The insight that reality has given him, however, has been a real "eye-opening" experience. He now understands better why he has found it impossible to reach his good friend, Joe, with the gospel. Joe is a good man. He has a good heart. Yet, his eyes have been blinded to the gospel due to an unfortunate experience he had with a pedophile at church when he was just a young boy. Jesse now understands that he must find a way to repair the perception that Joe has of the church.

ഇൗരു

Memory Selection

But seek ye first the kingdom of God, and his righteousness; and all these things shall be added unto you. Take therefore no thought for the morrow: for the morrow shall take thought for the things of itself. Sufficient unto the day is the evil thereof. — *Matthew 6:33-34*

Pastor Henry Washington made it his goal at the age of 15 to allow this passage to be his guiding light of life. At 15, it never dawned on him that he might have difficulty doing that. Now as the age of 32, however, Henry is not at all sure that he will succeed at his goal. His life as a minister has not been an easy one. Last week, he was fired from his third church since leaving seminary. With a wife and two preschool children to support, he does not know what he should do. Though his heart tells him that the Lord will provide, his head is not so sure.

Loretta, Henry's wife, no longer trusts church people to supply their livelihood. Pastor Washington feels heavily the pressure of his present joblessness. Though he wants to seek first the Kingdom, he's not sure that he can do that and hold his family together, too.

Weekday Problems

Often, when we think of "materialism," our minds immediately target those of the tycoon set. We think of individuals who spent their lives amassing wealth. Perhaps, it was gained at the expense of their family life or even their own health and sanity. We might even think of those who prostituted their virtue or ethics in order to close a prized deal or to get a choice job.

Is it possible, though, that materialism is really much closer to us than any of those categories? Is it possible that it nips at our own heels regularly, much as does our neighbor's pet Chihuahua?

There are times when I convince myself that I won't truly be happy until I acquire a certain gadget. Is that materialism? It may be a new tool for the garage or a new appliance for the kitchen. For a lot of folks these days, the target of desire is something computer-related. What ever the item of interest, it often seems to as though it will bring quality to our lives—until we actually obtain it! Too often it brings disillusionment instead of fulfillment.

* What material "want" has a particular hold on your interest these days?

* What specific yearning can you think of that once consumed you, but which subsequently proved to be a major disappointment?

* What can you think of that might help to curb your battle with "the wants"?

Money Talks

Most money is tainted. 'Taint yours and 'taint mine.
* * *
There's something bigger than money—bills.
* * *
Money talks. Mine says, "Bye."
* * *
It takes twice as much money to live beyond your means as it used to.
* * *
There are some things sweeter than money, but they won't go out with you if you're broke.
* * *
Promises, promises. In January the politicians promised that things would improve by the last quarter. Well, I'm down to my last quarter and things haven't improved.
* * *
I hope the standard of living isn't raised. I can't afford it now.

This Lesson in Your Life

It is most difficult to see accurately into one's heart by looking at his possessions. We like to think that we can. With envy we watch the vice-president of the company climb into his Porsche and easily chalk him up as "a materialist." It probably has never dawned on us that the Viet Nam veteran, sitting on the corner, begging for quarters, made exactly the same judgment about us when we drove past him on the way to church in our minivan. Yet from his economic position as a homeless veteran, that seemed like a justifiable conclusion.

Our critical judgment of the company vice-president failed to consider the possibility that buying the Porsche was not an exorbitant expenditure for him. Or was the car a gift from his grown son who wanted to give to his dad something he knew his dad would never buy for himself? Or was it an award that he received from the company for outstanding production in last year's quota challenge?

Gary Freeman once wrote, "A materialist is not someone who makes a lot of money, or even someone who has a lot of it. He is someone who thinks more of it than it is worth." It is difficult for one to know how highly someone else thinks of money by looking at him from across the cul-de-sac.

At no point in Jesus' sermon on the mountain did He call for all of his disciples to take a vow of poverty. He did not ban the rich from following Him. Rather, his call is for the allegiance of our hearts.

Jerry Watkins and Jim Holt live directly across the street from one another. They paid almost exactly the same price for their houses. Both Jerry and Jim drive late model Buicks. Both men are members at Arch Road Community Church and attend with similar regularity. They even work out of similar offices selling insurance.

If you were to meet Jerry and Jim at church or at a neighborhood cookout, you would not necessarily be more highly impressed with one over the other. Both are "nice guys." It is not blatantly obvious that Jerry holds as his number-one priority the goal of pleasing God. Yet, that priority is the driving force of every thing he does. It is the guiding light for every insurance sale that he makes.

At the same time, it would not be obvious that Jim is totally sold-out to the "almighty dollar." Always, that ranks first in his life. Every friendship he makes at church is prompted by the materialist agenda hiding in the shadows. One man serves God. The other Mammon. Yet, to the casual eye, they seem to be very much alike.

STRAIGHT

1. What reason did Jesus give for calling His disciples to lay up their treasures in heaven?
Because, He said, where your treasure is, there will your heart be also.

2. What did Jesus describe as "the light of the body"?
The eye.

3. What did Jesus say would be the consequence if one's eye is evil?
His body will be full of darkness.

4. What did Jesus say that no man could do?
Serve two masters

5. How did Jesus define His the warning, "Take no thought for your life"?
Not to be unduly focused on what we will have to eat, drink, or wear.

6. To which items of creation did Jesus refer as evidence that God can be trusted to provide?
The fowls of the air and the lilies of the field.

7. The glory of what king is exceeded by the glory of the lilies of the field?
Solomon.

8. What happens to the grass of the field tomorrow?
It is cast into the oven.

9. Who did Jesus say focused on what they would have to eat, drink, and wear?
The Gentiles.

10. Complete this sentence: "Sufficient unto the day is . . . ."
". . . the evil thereof."

The story is told of a fisherman who was lying on a beautiful beach with his fishing pole propped up in the sand. He reclined peacefully, enjoying the warmth of the afternoon sun and the possibility of catching a fish. Soon a businessman came jogging down the beach, trying to relieve some of the stress of his workday. He decided to take a break to get his breath and to find out why this man was fishing instead of working.

"You aren't going to catch many fish that way," said the businessman to the fisherman. "You should be working rather than lying on the beach!"

The fisherman looked up at the businessman, smiled and replied, "And what is that going to get me?"

"Well, you can get bigger nets and catch more fish!" was the businessman's answer.

"And what is that going to get me?" asked the fisherman, still smiling.

The businessman replied, "You will make money and you'll be able to buy a boat, which will then result in larger catches of fish!"

"And then what is that going to get me?" asked the fisherman again.

The businessman was beginning to get just a tad irritated with the fisherman's questions. "You can buy a bigger boat, and hire some people to work for you!" he said.

"And then what is that going to get me?" repeated the fisherman.

The businessman was getting angry. "Don't you understand? You can build up a fleet of fishing boats, sail all over the world, and let all your employees catch fish for you!"

Once again the fisherman asked, "And then what is that going to get me?"

Now in frustration the businessman was shouting at the fisherman, "Don't you understand that you can become so rich that you will never have to work for your living again! You can spend all the rest of your days sitting on this beach, looking at the sunset. You won't have a care in the world!"

The fisherman, still smiling, looked up and said, "And what do you think I'm doing right now?"

Dr. Tammie Fowles has noted that we have a tendency to live on "the deferred payment plan." That is, we are waiting for the day when we've accumulated enough money to do what we really want to do. Sadly, this often causes us to project so much of ourselves (and our spirit) into the future that we fail fully to appreciate (and perhaps, even to live in) the present. All too often, at the end of a lifetime of fretfully "making a living," we discover that our lives ended without our ever having lived at all.

Big Mouth Billy Bass's song may not be all that different from the advice Jesus: "Don't worry. Be happy."

Do Unto Others

Matthew 7:1-5; 12-20

Judge not, that ye be not judged. **2** For with what judgment ye judge, ye shall be judged: and with what measure ye mete, it shall be measured to you again.

3 And why beholdest thou the mote that is in thy brother's eye, but considerest not the beam that is in thine own eye?

4 Or how wilt thou say to thy brother, Let me pull out the mote out of thine eye; and, behold, a beam is in thine own eye?

5 Thou hypocrite, first cast out the beam out of thine own eye; and then shalt thou see clearly to cast out the mote out of thy brother's eye.

12 Therefore all things whatsoever ye would that men should do to you, do ye even so to them: for this is the law and the prophets.

13 Enter ye in at the strait gate: for wide is the gate, and broad is the way, that leadeth to destruction, and many there be which go in thereat:

14 Because strait is the gate, and narrow is the way, which leadeth unto life, and few there be that find it.

15 Beware of false prophets, which come to you in sheep's clothing, but inwardly they are ravening wolves.

16 Ye shall know them by their fruits. Do men gather grapes of thorns, or figs of thistles?

17 Even so every good tree bringeth forth good fruit; but a corrupt tree bringeth forth evil fruit.

18 A good tree cannot bring forth evil fruit, neither can a corrupt tree bring forth good fruit.

19 Every tree that bringeth not forth good fruit is hewn down, and cast into the fire.

20 Wherefore by their fruits ye shall know them.

Memory Selection
Matthew 7:12

Devotional Reading
Romans 13:8-14

Background Scripture
Matthew 7

Nov. 25

121

Christianity is a faith designed for human relationships. Some other faiths encourage the serious believer to draw apart from others in order to seek God in the solitude of private meditation and contemplation. Although such disciplines are not foreign to Christianity, the focus of this lesson is on how faith changes the way the believer relates to others.

Think of how each of the relational aspects in this lesson would change the home, the workplace, and the world if it were seriously practiced. How life would change for the better if all were less judgmental, more willing to practice "the Golden Rule," more eager to seek the right way than the easy way, more willing to hold ourselves accountable for the results of our faith instead of merely pleading that we have good intentions! These are a few of the relational aspects of Jesus' teaching.

⅏

Consider introducing this session by citing the "The Golden Rule in Many Creeds" on page 127, showing how the essence of the Golden Rule, one of the parts of this lesson, appears in several other world faiths, as well as in the philosophy of Socrates.

You may want to note that the fact that other religions have teachings similar to

the Bible does not mean that Christianity merely "borrowed" from previous teachings. More often than not, it's the other way around: later faiths such as Islam borrowed from the Hebrew and Christian Scriptures. It should also be kept in mind that many gems of wisdom are discoverable through experience, by means of God's "general revelation." The message that Jesus of Nazareth is the only begotten Son whom God sent to save the world is a matter of "special revelation," and is unique to the Bible. Otherwise God often reveals Himself both through His world and His Word.

Teaching Outline	Daily Bible Readings

I. Decide Fairly About Others—1-5
  A. Reciprocal standards, 1-2
  B. Judging yourself, 3-5
II. Do as You Want to Be Done to—12
III. Dare to Be Different—13-14
  A. The wide way, 13
  B. The narrow way, 14
IV. Discern False Prophets—15-20
  A. Faithful fruit, 15-18
  B. Future judgment, 19-20
	Mon. Love Your Enemies
	      Luke 6:27-36
	Tue. Don't Be Judgmental
	      Luke 6:37-42
	Wed. Enter by the Narrow Door
	      Luke 13:22-30
	Thu. Love Fulfills the Law
	      Romans 13:8-14
	Fri. Welcome the Weak
	      Romans 14:1-6
	Sat. Ask, Search, Knock
	      Matthew 7:6-11
	Sun. Who Will Enter?
	      Matthew 7:21-28

Verse by Verse

I. Decide Fairly About Others—1-5
A. Reciprocal standards, 1-2

1 Judge not, that ye be not judged.

2 For with what judgment ye judge, ye shall be judged: and with what measure ye mete, it shall be measured to you again.

Scripture consistently elevates God alone as the one Judge of all hearts, and warns against the persistent human tendency to presume to take on the task ourselves (see Acts 10:42; Rom. 2:1; Jas. 4:12). Too often, however, well-meaning people take this to mean that we should not even be discerning or discriminating. In this very lesson Jesus challenges us to "judge" or discern by the fruits of a prophet's teaching whether he or she is a false or true prophet (vss. 15-20). Furthermore, He said that we should "judge (with) righteous judgment" (John 7:24); and Paul will later counsel Christians to judge good and bad actions among themselves (1 Cor. 5:12).

Therefore Jesus' blunt statement here is a warning not to judge in the sense of being "judgmental." That is, we are not to be harshly critical in spirit, nor to judge the thoughts and intents of the heart.

Verse 2 also prompts questions when it is made to apply to salvation. If we are to be eternally judged by God on the basis of whether we are harsh and judgmental toward others, how can salvation be by grace through faith? It is possible that Jesus is not referring here to the standard of eternal judgment, but simply warning us that being judgmental toward others will prompt them (not God) to be judgmental of us. Still, there is a moral edge to His teaching that should stand as a warning, again, to leave judgment in general to God instead of presuming to be able to look into another's heart and pronounce judgment ourselves. Even if we decide (judge) that a false prophet's teaching is to be rejected, it is not ours to pronounce final judgment upon him as a person. As Jesus said in the Beatitudes, "Blessed are the merciful" (5:7).

B. Judging yourself, 3-5

3 And why beholdest thou the mote that is in thy brother's eye, but considerest not the beam that is in thine own eye?

4 Or how wilt thou say to thy brother, Let me pull out the mote out of thine eye; and, behold, a beam is in thine own eye?

5 Thou hypocrite, first cast out

the beam out of thine own eye; and then shalt thou see clearly to cast out the mote out of thy brother's eye.

In a second warning against being judgmental, Jesus uses a very pointed illustration to remind us that even discrimination should begin with ourselves. Taking Jesus' question seriously, "Why *are* we judgmental?" Sometimes we are quicker to judge others than ourselves because it is more painful to face sin in our own lives than in the lives of others. Also, it is simply easier to see sin in others than in ourselves because we are so subjective, and introspection does not come as easily as inspecting others.

Another good question is why people who will not tend to their own problems so often want to solve the problems of others. Whatever the reason, Jesus says that it is like trying to get a tiny splinter out of the eye of another while trying to peer around a stick in our own eye. The attempted "operation" is not only foolish; again a moral edge is injected as Jesus calls it *hypocritical*. Among Greek-speaking people of Jesus' day, this word referred first to an actor in a drama, then to a person who "played a role" by pretending to be something he is not. In this case, the pretense is in judging others by showing a concern for their righteousness while not being righteous ourselves. Jesus adds that the first step to qualifying ourselves to help another sinner is to first take care of our own sin problem.

II. Do as You Want to Be Done to–12

12 Therefore all things whatsoever ye would that men should do to you, do ye even so to them: for this is the law and the prophets.

This "Golden Rule" is rightly famous as the "gold standard" of Christian ethics, the essence of Christian behavior toward others. By adding that "This is the law and the prophets," Jesus shows that it is really the essence of a Jewish ethic of relationships as well. While it is also, with slight variations, a part of other world religions (see p. 127), Jesus states it in a uniquely positive way.

In our day we have seen the spread of the popular acronym "WWJD"—What Would Jesus Do?—on everything from T-shirts to bracelets. The Golden Rule would have us add the acronym "HDOWTBT?"—How Do Others Want to Be Treated? By affirming this standard, Jesus affirms a standard for deciding what to do in ethical situations that is available to every believer, not just to highly-trained specialists in theology or ethics.

III. Dare to Be Different—13-14
A. The wide way, 13

13 Enter ye in at the strait gate: for wide is the gate, and broad is the way, that leadeth to destruction, and many there be which go in thereat:

Unfortunately the power of the King James translation has enthroned this famous saying in the minds of many as "straight" in the sense of not crooked. The word actually means "narrow" (NIV "small"), and is in con-

124

trast to the "broad way" that leads to destruction. It should come as no surprise that more people walk along the "broad way," since it is the way of permissiveness, undisciplined behavior, and "doing what comes naturally." Yet many who have fallen into this "easier" way of dissipation learn that it can lead to destruction even in this life—as in the case of those who become addicted to substance abuse.

B. The narrow way, 14

14 Because strait is the gate, and narrow is the way, which leadeth unto life, and few there be that find it.

The higher standards of Jesus constitute a "road less traveled." Yet, in contrast to the broad way, the narrow path of self-discipline and service to others leads to life, rather than to destruction. Jesus affirms one of life's ironies: the path of discipline leads to freedom, while the path of unbridled behavior often enslaves us to our appetites.

IV. Discern False Prophets—15-20

A. Faithful fruit, 15-18

15 Beware of false prophets, which come to you in sheep's clothing, but inwardly they are ravening wolves.

16 Ye shall know them by their fruits. Do men gather grapes of thorns, or figs of thistles?

17 Even so every good tree bringeth forth good fruit; but a corrupt tree bringeth forth evil fruit.

18 A good tree cannot bring forth evil fruit, neither can a corrupt tree bring forth good fruit.

The closing verses of the Sermon on the Mount are warnings about dangers along the "broad way" that leads to destruction. The first concerns the guides that are all too ready to give us advice about what way to take. How are we to discern the true guide from the false? Jesus' answer here does not constitute the full range of answers to this question, but does underscore one of the most fundamental. He calls us to observe the fruits of a prophet's teaching. For example, does his teaching produce followers who observe the Golden Rule, above? And does the prophet or guide follow in his own life what he prescribes for others? The Pharisees of Jesus' day were an example of false guides, for "they say and do not"; and Jesus therefore urged their audiences to beware of them (see Matt. 23:1-4).

B. Future judgment, 19-20

19 Every tree that bringeth not forth good fruit is hewn down, and cast into the fire.

20 Wherefore by their fruits ye shall know them.

Jesus bluntly warns that those who deliberately misguide others will be destroyed, referring no doubt to the fiery end reserved for "blind guides," or teachers who do not bear the "fruit" of living by their own counsel (see also Matt. 23:16, 33). While eternal destruction is prepared for all who deliberately reject Christ's way, teachers are especially vulnerable because of the influence their "bad fruit" has on others (see Jas. 3:1).

Evangelistic Emphasis

Nothing has played a bigger role in keeping Loretta from taking Christianity seriously than judgmentalism. When she was about 10 years old, Loretta's mother divorced her father. It was then that she began to see the ugly side of many of the people at church. Tongues began to wag, speculating about the "worldliness" of her mother. Divorce was not nearly so common in those days. Certainly, it was not acceptable for a Christian woman to divorce "her fine Christian husband."

What very few people knew, however, was that Loretta's mother filed for divorce only after trying for several years to make her marriage work. Loretta's father beat her mother regularly when he got angry or was just in a bad mood. More than once her mother had to be hospitalized because of the severity of the beating. It was finally in fear for her life that Loretta's mother accepted defeat and ended her marriage. None of those things were commonly known, however. Loretta's mother was much too ashamed to allow it to be known by anyone outside the family.

Harsh criticism from the ladies at church often brought Loretta's mother to tears. Eventually she stopped going to church, and ever since, Loretta has not been willing even to consider attending church.

&)CR

Therefore all things whatsoever ye would that men should do to you, do ye even so to them: for this is the law and the prophets.—*Matthew 7:12*

Ginger Green is the mother of three children. Ten-year-old Ben is her middle child and only son. As a single mother, Ginger has really appreciated the fact that Ben's very best friend in all the world is 13-year-old John Appleby. John has been a "big brother type" of mentor for Ben. Recently, however, she's become concerned about the kinds of things John might be teaching her son. Mostly her concerns have involved adolescent-type attitudes that she suspects Ben is mimicking from John.

Though all of this has been nebulously eating at her for some time, it suddenly bulldozed urgently into her consciousness last week when she accidently saw John shoplift a music CD from the mall. Suddenly, she knows that she must find a way to end her son's relationship with John, at least for now. The question that troubles her is should she tell Betty, John's mother, what she saw? Ginger does not want to get John into trouble. Yet, as a mother, she knows that *she* would want to know if her son needed correction.

Weekday Problems

Melba Hughes has struggled with her understanding of Matthew 7:1-2. On the surface, at least, it seems fairly straightforward in its message—we will be condemned if we condemn others. Nevertheless, Melba has been taught that each of us is saved by the grace of God based on faith in Jesus Christ, and that salvation is **not** *performance-based* in any sense of the term. Yet, reading what Jesus preached about judging prompts her to wonder. It sounds to her as though Matthew 7:1-2 is saying that there is at least *something* about judgment that will be performance-based—namely, whether we refrain from judging others..

"If I judge my brother harshly, then God will judge me harshly," Melba contends . *"How then can I continue to insist that I am saved by grace, not on the basis of how well I have performed in my Christian walk?"* she asks.

Melba's frustration has recently reached the point that she doubts her salvation. She sincerely wants to refrain from judging others, but down deep she is aware that certain judgmental attitudes have been ingrained in her heart since childhood.

* Is Jesus teaching that *if* we've proven harsh in our judgements of our brother, *then* God will judge us with the same level of harshness?

* Is it possible that our own tendency to judge others harshly *will tend to* prompt others to be harsh in their judgment of us?

* If Melba's understanding of grace is correct, how then does our own judgmentalism impact the judgment we receive?

The Golden Rule in Many Creeds

Judaism: "Thou shalt love thy neighbor as thyself" (Levit. 19:18); "What is hateful to you, do not to your fellow man. This is the law: all the rest is commentary" (The Talmud).

Buddhism: "Hurt not others in ways that you yourself would find hurtful."

Hinduism: "This is the sum of duty: do naught unto others which would cause you pain if done to you."

Shintoism: "The heart of the person before you is a mirror. See there your own form."

B'hai: "Ascribe not to any soul that which thou wouldst not have ascribed to thee."

Confucianism: "Do not do to others what you do not want them to do to you."

Socrates: "Do not do to others that which would anger you if others did it to you."

This Lesson in Your Life

Last Sunday morning Jeremiah Watson had the television on in his bedroom, listening to some gospel music and preaching as he dressed for church. This has been his routine for more than five years. Last Sunday the message caused him to stop what he was doing and to listen even more attentively. Talking about the "best known of all Scriptures," the minister asserted that John 3:16 may no longer be the most treasured verse among Christian people. Especially among the younger generation, the best-known, most often quoted of all scripture verses is Matthew 7:1--*"Judge not, that ye be not judged."*

Though Jeremiah's initial reaction was a mild, *"That's interesting,"* the more he thought about it, the more it bothered him. Certainly, Matthew 7:1 is just as much *Scripture* as John 3:16. Yet, as long as Jeremiah can remember, John 3:16 has been the verse that was learned earliest by children and the treasured most by adults. It is, after all, a very concise statement of the gospel: *"For God so loved the world, that he gave his only begotten Son, that whosoever believeth in him should not perish, but have everlasting life."*

At first it seemed almost as though the gospel itself had been demoted. During the following week, however, Jeremiah had to admit that the minister had a point. It explained a "live and let live" attitude among many people that had troubled Jeremiah. He realizes that it makes him seem like some kind of bigot or prude to make such a complaint, so he really hasn't said much. Yet, it bothers him when he sees some Christian making a very bad choice and nobody steps forward to alert him to the foolishness of his choice.

Everyone was thrilled when Deacon Franklin, who had been widowed for three years, began dating a woman from a neighboring congregation. Jeremiah, too, was happy for him. When he learned, however that the deacon and the widow were living together, he was suddenly less thrilled. Yet, the primary attitude that others at church echoed was, "Ah, mind your own business!"

Much the same attitude was reflected when he expressed concern about a high school girl showing up at church in a maternity dress. And no one seemed concerned enough about the last dozen or so divorces in the congregation to ask, *"Is there something that we need to be doing better to strengthen our families?"* It seems to Jeremiah that even raising such a question is not acceptable. He wonders, *"In the attempt to be 'open minded,' have we allowed our brains to fall out?"*

STRAIGHT

1. What did Jesus say would be the measure of judgment by which we would be judged?
The measure of judgment by which we judge others.

2. What should we remove from our own eye before we attempt to remove the mote from our brother's eye?
The beam.

3. What is a good "rule of thumb" for how we ought to treat others?
As we would like for them to treat us.

4. What word best describes the way that leads to destruction?
Broad.

5. To what does the strait gate and narrow way lead?
To life.

6. What kind of clothing do false prophets wear?
Sheep's clothing.

7. What are false prophets *inwardly*?
Ravening wolves.

8. How did Jesus say one could recognize false prophets?
By their fruit.

9. What can a good tree *not* bring forth?
Evil fruit.

10. What will happen to every tree that does not bear good fruit?
It will be hewn down and cast into the fire.

For some reason, it is easier to jump to negative conclusions about people than it is to assume the best about them. My suspicions can cause my mind to run away from all reason. I begin to imagine sinister intentions and evil purposes that have no foundation of truth. Before much time has passed, an innocent remark or action can be enlarged in my analysis of it so as to cause panic. When I allow my imagination to run wild like this, I am also revealing something significant about myself. Often, the faults I see in others are actually a reflection of my own.

In his little book, *Illustrations of Bible Truth,* H. A. Ironside pointed out the folly of judging others. He related an incident in the life of a man called Bishop Potter. As Ironside told the story, Bishop Potter was sailing for Europe on one of the great transatlantic ocean liners. When he went on board, he found that another passenger was to share the cabin with him. After going to see the accommodations, he came up to the purser's desk and inquired if he could leave his gold watch and other valuables in the ship's safe. He explained that ordinarily he never took advantage of that privilege, but he had been to his cabin and had met the man who was to occupy the other berth. Judging from his appearance, he was afraid that he might not be a very trustworthy person.

The purser accepted the responsibility for the valuables and then remarked, *"It's all right, bishop, I'll be very glad to take care of them for you. The other man has already been up here and left his valuables with me for the same reason!"*

That story reminds me of a real-life couple I once knew who were engaged to be married. Both Karen Harnack and Ted Thompson had been widowed several years earlier, but had been reluctant to pursue any new relationship due to their large accumulation of wealth. Fearful of someone marrying them just for their money, they each had buried themselves in their projects of interest. Yet, in spite of their fears, these two had fallen in love with each other.

As the wedding approached, however, both Karen and Ted independently struggled with how they might tactfully request of the other a prenuptial agreement. Neither felt good about making such a request, but both felt that far too much was at stake for them to neglect insisting on it.

Finally, one evening at dinner, after several awkward false starts, they both in chorus blurted out their insistence on a prenuptial. Ironically, once the request was made, they both were so offended at the other's request, the wedding plans were canceled.

Dec. 2

Lesson 1

The Servant's Mission

Isaiah 49:1-12

Listen, O isles, unto me; and hearken, ye people, from far; The LORD hath called me from the womb; from the bowels of my mother hath he made mention of my name.

2 And he hath made my mouth like a sharp sword; in the shadow of his hand hath he hid me, and made me a polished shaft; in his quiver hath he hid me;

3 And said unto me, Thou art my servant, O Israel, in whom I will be glorified.

4 Then I said, I have laboured in vain, I have spent my strength for nought, and in vain: yet surely my judgment is with the LORD and my work with my God.

5 And now, saith the LORD that formed me from the womb to be his servant, to bring Jacob again to him, Though Israel be not gathered, yet shall I be glorious in the eyes of the LORD, and my God shall be my strength.

6 And he said, It is a light thing that thou shouldest be my servant to raise up the tribes of Jacob, and to restore the preserved of Israel: I will also give thee for a light to the Gentiles, that thou mayest be my salvation unto the end of the earth.

7 Thus saith the LORD, the Redeemer of Israel, and his Holy One, to him whom man despiseth, to him whom the nation abhorreth, to a servant of rulers, Kings shall see and arise, princes also shall worship, because of the LORD that is faithful, and the Holy One of Israel, and he shall choose thee.

8 Thus saith the LORD, In an acceptable time have I heard thee, and in a day of salvation have I helped thee: and I will preserve thee, and give thee for a covenant of the people, to establish the earth, to cause to inherit the desolate heritages;

9 That thou mayest say to the prisoners, Go forth; to them that are in darkness, Shew yourselves. They shall feed in the ways, and their pastures shall be in all high places.

10 They shall not hunger nor thirst; neither shall the heat nor sun smite them: for he that hath mercy on them shall lead them, even by the springs of water shall he guide them.

11 And I will make all my mountains a way, and my highways shall be exalted.

12 Behold, these shall come from far: and, lo, these from the north and from the west; and these from the land of Sinim.

Memory Selection
Isaiah 49:6

Devotional Reading
Isaiah 49:8-13

Background Scripture
Isaiah 49:1-12

One of the distinctive features of biblical faith is that it fuels enthusiasm for better times to come. The next 13 lessons focus on this hope, as expressed in passages from Isaiah, Luke, Jonah, and Nahum.

Christians affirm that the power and love of God through Jesus of Nazareth is the basis for this hope. Yet this faith is rooted deeply in Old Testament prophecy, and the role of God's chosen people, Israel, as the "Servant" through whom the Messiah was to come. This first lesson therefore focuses on God's Old Covenant people, who were destined to extend His Covenant to all people. This emphasis inescapably leads also to the challenge for Christians, God's Covenant people today, to extend the promise of God's glorious future to the world.

ଔ

For an object lesson to start off this session, take a flashlight and a world globe to class. With the lights dimmed, shine the light on the Middle East. Note that this is the part of the earth where the Star of Bethlehem first signaled that Jesus of Nazareth would be "the light of the world."

Now slowly turn the globe toward the left, causing the light to spread to the Mediterranean Sea as far as Spain. Note that the apostle Paul may have gone that far west, spreading the gospel. Reverse the motion of the globe from left to right until the light illuminates India, noting that tradition says that the apostle Thomas planted churches in India, and that the light eventually spread to all the world. Tell the group that this quarter's lessons will discuss various aspects of Jesus as the light of the world; and that this first lesson is about the nation of Israel's role in that great adventure.

Teaching Outline

I. Israel's Call—1-3
   A. Origin of the plan, 1
   B. Commissioned as a servant, 2-3

II. Exiles' Plight—4-5
   A. Trust amid woe, 4
   B. From darkness to light, 5

III. Reversal of Fortune—6-7
   A. From a nation to the world, 6
   B. The glory of election, 7

IV. Mission to the World—8-12
   A. Covenant to the people, 8-9
   B. Promise to the nations, 10-12

Daily Bible Readings

Mon.	God's Purpose Will Stand Isaiah 46:8-13
Tue.	Hear New Things Isaiah 48:1-11
Wed.	Draw Near and Hear Isaiah 48:12-16
Thu.	Your God Teaches You Isaiah 48:17-22
Fri.	You Are Chosen Isaiah 49:7-12
Sat.	God Will Comfort Isaiah 49:13-22
Sun.	God's Servant Will Suffer Isaiah 50:4-9

Verse by Verse

I. Israel's Call—1-3

A. Origin of the plan, 1

1 Listen, O isles, unto me; and hearken, ye people, from far; The LORD hath called me from the womb; from the bowels of my mother hath he made mention of my name.

The "me" here is the nation of Israel, according to verse 3. Isaiah chapters 40–55 are widely known for their "servant songs"—poetic prophecies of an anointed servant of God who will save His people. These prophecies refer ultimately to Christ, as in chapters 40, 42, and 53. Once, Cyrus, king of Persia is identified as God's "anointed" servant (44:28–45:1), because of his role in restoring to their homeland Jews who had been carried away into Babylonian captivity. The present passage says the nation of Israel itself is God's anointed servant (see also 41:8-9; 44:1-2, 21). Isaiah envisions the day when the Chosen People were scattered among the "isles" of the Mediterranean Sea, as well as in other parts of the ancient world. Yet, from their dispersion and captivity they are given the role of reminding the nations that God has called them "from the womb"—probably from their birth as a nation in the Exodus from Egypt—to be His special agents for the salvation of the world. Christians know this role to have been fulfilled in the coming of Jesus through God's chosen race.

B. Commissioned as a servant, 2-3

2 And he hath made my mouth like a sharp sword; in the shadow of his hand hath he hid me, and made me a polished shaft; in his quiver hath he hid me;

3 And said unto me, Thou art my servant, O Israel, in whom I will be glorified.

Even though they are in captivity, Israel's true destiny is to be a sword and an arrow in God's hands. As a nation, Israel is being disciplined in exile to be God's obedient servant through whom God will be glorified. Little did those who first heard this prophecy realize that this glory would eventually appear in the form of Jesus of Nazareth, from whose mouth the Word will issue as a sharp sword (Rev. 1:16).

II. Exiles' Plight—4-5

A. Trust amid woe, 4

4 Then I said, I have laboured in vain, I have spent my strength for nought, and in vain: yet surely my judgment is with the LORD, and my work with my God.

Again, this is Israel speaking. We can well imagine how dejected the Israelites were in "the Diaspora"—the scattering among the nations that God allowed because of their idolatry and disobedience. The prophet Isaiah peers into their mind in captivity and quotes them as feeling that it has been in vain for them to have been chosen by God to accomplish His purposes. Yet the faithful among them commit the judgment that befell them to God, and trust that He will yet reveal a role for them in His plan.

B. From darkness to light, 5

5 And now, saith the Lord that formed me from the womb to be his servant, to bring Jacob again to him, Though Israel be not gathered, yet shall I be glorious in the eyes of the Lord, and my God shall be my strength.

Now God speaks to the remnant of faithful Israel to reassure them that even though they are now scattered, they will be gathered again to be used gloriously. As Bible history recounts (in the books of Ezra and Nehemiah), a remnant of the Israelites were indeed allowed to return to the Promised Land. There they rebuilt the Temple, and through them came Jesus, the Messiah, whose resurrection proclaimed God's power to fulfill His promise to Israel.

III. Reversal of Fortune—6-7

A. From a nation to the world, 6

6 And he said, It is a light thing that thou shouldest be my servant to raise up the tribes of Jacob, and to restore the preserved of Israel: I will also give thee for a light to the Gentiles, that thou mayest be my salvation unto the end of the earth.

As further reassurance that God has not abandoned His servant-people, a two-level mission is outlined for them. First (the "light thing"), a remnant will marshal the nation in a restoration to the Promised Land. Second, this light or limited mission will become infinitely more "weighty" as they become a beacon to the whole world. This prophecy finds explicit fulfillment in Acts 13:47. Paul and Barnabas preach Christ to the Jews in the city of Antioch, in Pisidia, but are rejected. They then turn to the Gentiles, citing this very verse as justification.

Although only a "remnant of the remnant" of the Jews who were allowed to return from captivity accepted the Christian message, this glimpse of early Christian missions shows that God fulfilled His promise that although His chosen people were in captivity in Isaiah's vision here, their election would be vindicated in the proclamation of the Messiah who came from their ranks. It is in this way that Christ can often be referred to, along with Israel, as God's Servant in Isaiah's prophecies.

B. The glory of election, 7

7 Thus saith the Lord, the Redeemer of Israel, and his Holy One, to him whom man despiseth, to him whom the nation abhorreth, to a servant of rulers, Kings shall see and arise, princes also shall worship, because of the Lord that is faithful, and the Holy One of Israel, and he shall choose thee.

The identification of God's Servant ("his Holy One") seems to shift now from Israel to the Servant Messiah. It is He who will be despised and abhorred by the majority of the nation of Israel, even to the point that He will be slain. Yet He will arise from the dead, and His Kingdom will become so powerful that princes will bow down to Him. All this should encourage the faithful in Israel, even though they do not personally live to see the prophecy fulfilled.

IV. Mission to the World—8-12
A. Covenant to the people, 8-9

8 Thus saith the Lord, In an acceptable time have I heard thee, and in a day of salvation have I helped thee: and I will preserve thee, and give thee for a covenant of the people, to establish the earth, to cause to inherit the desolate heritages;

9 That thou mayest say to the prisoners, Go forth; to them that are in darkness, Shew yourselves. They shall feed in the ways, and their pastures shall be in all high places.

God's encouraging words continue as He indicates that He has heard the cries of captive Israel. The "acceptable time" may refer both to God's having heard Israel's prayer at a time appropriate for a remnant to be restored to Israel, and, looking ahead, to the "fullness of time" (Gal. 4:4) when the world would be ready for the Messiah to be revealed from heaven.

The important point here is that from having made His Covenant with Israel (through the patriarchs Abraham, Isaac, and Jacob), *God will now use Israel to extend the Covenant to "the people" in general—the Gentiles* (referred to here as among those who were "prisoners" to sin).

This element of "universalism" was not easy for the Jews to accept. The Jewish apostle Peter was used in specific fulfillment of the prophecy here by extending the good news of the Messiah to the Gentile Cornelius (Acts 10:34-35). Yet Peter was slow to put this acceptance into practice (Gal. 2:11-14).

B. Promise to the nations, 10-12

10 They shall not hunger nor thirst; neither shall the heat nor sun smite them: for he that hath mercy on them shall lead them, even by the springs of water shall he guide them.

11 And I will make all my mountains a way, and my highways shall be exalted.

12 Behold, these shall come from far: and, lo, these from the north and from the west; and these from the land of Sinim.

These verses seem to be figurative descriptions of the salvation to be extended to all people. We recall that the wise men came to worship the Christ-child from "the east", where lay the "land of Sinim" (perhaps China). Sadly, although God wanted to use Israel as a missionary tool, the single reference to such activity in the New Testament portrays their work in a negative light (Matt. 23:15); and at any rate, a majority rejected the message that Jesus was the Messiah.

Evangelistic Emphasis

Bookstores abound with materials on reaching goals and achieving results. We live in a "bottom line" world that judges us in terms of numbers. The number game is won by those having the most, whether money or people. The church lives and works in the midst of this number mania. We are guilty of judging ourselves by the same standards by which society makes judgments.

Isaiah's servant felt the frustration of feeling that his ministry was having no effect on his audience. I wonder if he looked out at the sparse Sunday crowds and wondered if all the work was worth the results. Many of today's ministers and lay workers resonate with the frustration of sparse results. Encouragement would be unnecessary if we saw the results of our efforts more clearly.

The truth of our Evangelistic Emphasis is that we are planting the seeds of faith in Christ. We feel affirmed when we plant the seed and can immediately plan and execute a harvest. In the kingdom of God, things don't work that quickly. Converted souls cannot be instantly produced through our efforts. God has called us to be faithful seed planters and faithful harvesters of His crop. God has not said He would hold us responsible for making the seed grow.

Frustration grows out of our inability to control the working of God's Spirit. It is one of the job hazards of sharing Jesus Christ with others.

ॐ

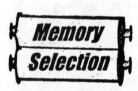

Memory Selection

I will also give thee for a light to the Gentiles, that thou mayest be my salvation unto the end of the earth.— *Isa. 49:6*

Light has probative and redemptive power. Have you ever kicked over a rock and watched all the varmints scatter? That is the probative power of light. Those varmints like the darkness and will flee from the light. Some things in our souls like to be hidden in darkness. The deeds of which we are least proud are those most fond of the darkness. Jesus warned that deeds done in the darkness will be exposed to the light. God uses light to probe the dark places of our souls.

Light has redemptive power. Most toddlers require a night-light. Children feel safe and secure with the light on. When God bathes our souls in the light of His love and grace we feel better because the "light is on." Jesus came as the light of the world, not only to probe the dark places in our souls, but also to lead us to redemption.

Jesus is the light leading us away from danger and toward the safe harbor of His kingdom.

Weekday Problems

Pastor Buster Weatherly was not looking forward to the evening's finance committee meeting. He had already seen the agenda for the meeting.

Dave Freeman was making the motion that the church close the Adult Day Care Center that was housed in their building. The Center was a ministry that provided care for senior adults who could not be left alone during the day. The Center allowed for caregivers and others to work during the day. It was a ministry that was nearly 20 years old. The church had experienced both good times and bad times with this particular ministry.

Dave's own mother had been at the Center for nearly two years before her death. Now Dave was heading the effort to remove the Center from the church. His argument was based on the financial drain of supplying electricity, maintenance of the building, the church's continuing underwriting of the financial short-fall of the ministry, and the lack of numbers attending. Dave had spreadsheets loaded with facts and figures to back up his position. He felt passionately that the church would be better served by standing empty five days a week than having the Day Care Center housed at the church.

Buster Weatherly knew that the finance committee would be impressed with the financial arguments against the continuing relationship with the Adult Day Care Center. He also knew that his arguments about "doing the work of Christ" would fall on deaf ears.

* Has your community of faith made decisions based on numbers only?
* How would you describe a "successful" program at your church?

Good Advice

Remember that "overnight success" is the result of at least 10 years' hard work.

* * *

Be positive when faced with a tough challenge. If you're going after Mob Dick, take along the tartar sauce.

* * *

Be willing to lose a battle in order to win a war.

* * *

Resist giving advice regarding matrimony, finances, and hair styles.

* * *

If you're on a budget, don't go grocery shopping when you're hungry.

* * *

Take a blind date to lunch, not an evening out. If things turn out badly you won't waste so much time.

This Lesson in Your Life

The only thing remaining the same is change. Some changes cause the church to make choices we have never before considered. We long to find safety in an ever-changing world. Our safest bet is often to take the riskiest choice. Our frustration in ministry comes when we try to manage and control changes and choices.

The Franciscan Jean Buridan had a famous parable, "Buridan's Donkey," that demonstrated how one has to risk choosing one thing over another if he wants to proceed forward. The story goes like this: A donkey had two heaps of hay in front of him, both of the same size and both located at equal distances. He could not make a decision as to which heap of hay should be eaten first. He continued asking himself which was the better choice until finally he died of hunger, being unable to find a logical reason for choosing one heap over the other, unable to risk making a choice of one over the other. The story demonstrates both that mere logical deduction is insufficient for making any decision whatsoever and that risk is sometimes safer than security.

There is no safety in safety; there is only safety in the risk and dare of a life of faith. Faith is but another word for "risk."

In this changing world we look for leadership that is fearless in being faithful. Isaiah's image of a suffering servant is an image for that kind of leadership. This is the kind of leader who had faith that God was working. This leader could make a decision to follow the will of God.

Today it is hard to discern where the movement of God may be found. Multitudes lay claim to being the people of God. They are as numerous as persons who claim that God is no longer active in the world. A servant leader has the gift of discernment. He understands where God is moving and where He is leading His people. He can discern the difference between sheep and wolves.

Servant leaders have the gift of brokenness. They understand the frustrations of the people he is leading. Frustration has always been a part of ministry. The servant in Isaiah lamented, "I have labored to no purpose; I have spent my strength in vain and for nothing." (Isaiah 49: 4) Can you almost hear the Junior High Sunday school teachers joining this lament? A leader understands the frustration of working in the church today.

A leader must understand his calling. Isaiah's servant was certain that he was known before he was born. "Before I was born the Lord called me; from my birth he has made mention of my name" (Isa. 49:1). A sense of calling and purpose are powerful antidotes to the frustration present in ministry.

1. Who was commanded to listen to the message of the Servant?

The coastlands and people who live far off were the audience to whom the servant's message was addressed.

2. At what point was this Servant called into his ministry by the Lord?

From the time the Servant was in the womb of his mother.

3. What else was unique about the Servant's name?

The name of the Servant was given to His mother, prior to his birth.

4. Naming a child prior to its birth was common in Scripture. Whose name was revealed to Mary, in the New Testament?

Jesus' name was revealed to His mother Mary before His birth. This text foreshadows that event.

5. In reading verses 2 and 3, how are you reminded of the ministry of Jesus Christ?

Jesus came speaking words of truth. His ministry showed the splendor of God. God protected His ministry.

6. What was the feeling of the Servant toward His ministry?

Verse 4 indicates the frustration the servant felt with His ministry, but His ultimate vindication came by the hand of God.

7. What limitations were placed on the ministry of the Servant?

His ministry was primarily to "raise up the tribes of Jacob and to restore the preserved of Israel."

8. How was the ministry of the Servant expanded?

Beyond his original mission (question 7), He was called to bring the salvation of the Lord to the ends of the earth.

9. How does this two-phase ministry remind you of the ministry of Jesus and the Church?

Although Jesus ministered to some Gentiles, His ministry was primarily to His own people . The church expanded on that ministry, taking the gospel to the ends of the earth.

10. How will the salvation of the Lord reach to the ends of the earth?

It will come as God's people shine as lights. Those in darkness will see this light, and be drawn to it.

139

Light is powerful. Today phone companies send both voice and digital information over fiber optic circuits. This wizardry of technology allows for information to be sent over streams of light. It is amazing. Doctors are now operating on people using lasers. They do everything from eye surgery to heart surgery using this powerful form of light. Light has the ability to make us feel more energetic.

Light is also protective. Many homes have installed motion sensors on their outdoor lighting. These sensors cause the light to come on when there is movement around the light. It is very convenient for those of us who can't fumble for our keys in the dark. It is inconvenient for those persons who are hanging around our home for nefarious purposes. Light protects us from stubbing our toes as we go on our nocturnal pilgrimages to the refrigerator. The "nightlight" comforts children and adults alike.

Light is personal. Light can be seen and experienced by an individual. When you turn on a light in a darkened room you have a personal experience with the light. What had been theory or something you "knew" about suddenly becomes part of your personal objective experiences of living. If you don't believe in this powerful objective reality, I challenge you to change the color theme of the lights on your Christmas tree and find out if there is a reaction. Add lights to the outside of your home and see if you get noticed. Light causes us to have a personal experience.

Look at the stars on a clear night. No matter what mundane frustrations have caused you to look up, seeing the stars momentarily transforms you. It is amazing to think that the light we see from stars is hundreds, in some cases, thousands of years old. Isn't it true that stargazing is another of life's personal pleasurable experiences?

Since we believe that Jesus is the light of the world, we affirm that He also is personal, powerful, and protective. Christ came into this world to have a personal relationship with us. That is what the Christmas season is about—God coming as a baby. Has anyone been threatened by a baby? Do people fear approaching a baby? Most of us like getting very close to a baby. There is something about that innocence and pure love that is attractive.

Christ came so we might know Him personally. He came in power. It was a muted power not fully seen until His resurrection. He came with the ability to forgive sin, heal hurts, and offer new life. His power is offered to His disciples through the presence of the Holy Spirit.

Christ's power means that He is protective of His people. In scary times, we live fearlessly because we know that Jesus hold's our future. We know that nothing can separate God from His people in Jesus Christ. He is watching over us as a shepherd watches over his flock. There is nothing in our world or in our lives that will surprise our Lord. He is prepared to help us with any eventuality.

The Light has come into the world.

The Peaceful Kingdom

Dec. 9

Isaiah 11:1-11

And there shall come forth a rod out of the stem of Jesse, and a Branch shall grow out of his roots:

2 And the spirit of the LORD shall rest upon him, the spirit of wisdom and understanding, the spirit of counsel and might, the spirit of knowledge and of the fear of the LORD;

3 And shall make him of quick understanding in the fear of the LORD: and he shall not judge after the sight of his eyes, neither reprove after the hearing of his ears:

4 But with righteousness shall he judge the poor, and reprove with equity for the meek of the earth: and he shall smite the earth with the rod of his mouth, and with the breath of his lips shall he slay the wicked.

5 And righteousness shall be the girdle of his loins, and faithfulness the girdle of his reins.

6 The wolf also shall dwell with the lamb, and the leopard shall lie down with the kid; and the calf and the young lion and the fatling together; and a little child shall lead them.

7 And the cow and the bear shall feed; their young ones shall lie down together: and the lion shall eat straw like the ox.

8 And the sucking child shall play on the hole of the asp, and the weaned child shall put his hand on the cockatrice' den.

9 They shall not hurt nor destroy in all my holy mountain: for the earth shall be full of the knowledge of the LORD, as the waters cover the sea.

10 And in that day there shall be a root of Jesse, which shall stand for an ensign of the people; to it shall the Gentiles seek: and his rest shall be glorious.

11 And it shall come to pass in that day, that the Lord shall set his hand again the second time to recover the remnant of his people, which shall be left, from Assyria, and from Egypt, and from Pathros, and from Cush, and from Elam, and from Shinar, and from Hamath, and from the islands of the sea.

Memory Selection
Isaiah 11:6

Devotional Reading
Isaiah 12

Background Scripture
Isaiah 11:1-11

The text for this lesson is one of the many passages in Scripture that promise hope in hard times. It is set in the eighth century B.C., when the prophet Isaiah foresaw both the oppression of Israel by the nation of Assyria, and God's deliverance from their oppressive rule.

Yet the focus of the passage strains beyond the facts of the day. Again and again, God's people and their rulers return to their back-sliding ways despite being delivered temporarily from their oppressors. The faithful ask whether a truly righteous ruler will ever appear. Isaiah's answer here is Yes: one day, a descendant of David, the Messiah, will establish a righteous and peaceful kingdom. That reign began with the coming of Christ, born of the royal family of David. Although the world does not yet enjoy the final state of peace Isaiah envisioned, believers now, as they did then, trust that the time will one day come.

ജരു

Ask members of your group to think of living things that are the most opposite. Which pairs of living things seem instinctively pitted against each other? Wolves against sheep, or lions vs. lambs? Cats vs. mice, or cats vs. dogs? Wiley E. Coyote vs. the cartoon road runner? Or, moving into the human realm, man against woman? Mothers-in-law against sons-in-laws? Cowboys vs. Indians?

Note that against such deeply-ingrained hostilities, the Bible points toward a time when creation will be at peace with itself. Today's lesson contains the classic prediction of the wolf and the lamb lying down with each other. What could such a word picture mean? Is it to be taken literally? While some answers may elude us, we can rely on the New Testament to help us interpret this intriguing language from 800 years before Christ.

Teaching Outline	*Daily Bible Readings*

I. The Coming King—11:1-5
A. A Davidic branch, 1
B. Personal qualities, 2
C. Kingly traits, 3-5
  1. Insight, 3
  2. Righteousness, 4-5
 	
II. A Kingdom of Peace—6-11
A. Among all creation, 6-8
B. In fullness of knowledge, 9
C. From a remnant to the Gentiles, 10-11
	Mon. Rebellious Children
	Isaiah 1:1-9
	Tue. Justice over Rituals
	Isaiah 1:10-20
	Wed. An Age of Peace
	Isaiah 2:1-5
	Thu. Give Thanks to the Lord
	Isaiah 12:1-6
	Fri. Compassion for the People
	Isaiah 14:1-7
	Sat. Hope for the Remnant
	Isaiah 11:1-9
	Sun. A Second Chance
	Isaiah 11:10-16

Verse by Verse

I. The Coming King—11:1-5
A. A Davidic branch, 1

1 And there shall come forth a rod out of the stem of Jesse, and a Branch shall grow out of his roots:

From preceding sections of Isaiah, we know that the great eighth-century B.C. prophet foretold that God would allow the Assyrians to conquer the rebellious northern kingdom of Israel (10:5). This occurred in 722-21 B.C. Yet the Assyrians were no model of righteousness either, and God said through Isaiah that they would be punished for their arrogance (10:12-13). Although most of the Israelites in the northern kingdom will be carried into captivity, a remnant would return— signifying that God has not abandoned His people (10:20-21). Now, Isaiah 11 describes a blossoming and extension of this reassuring note.

The immediate fulfillment of this prophecy apparently occurred under the reign of King Hezekiah in Judah. He cleansed the land of idol worship, which had been one of the primary reasons for Israel's fall, and rebelled against the Assyrians (2 Kings 18:1-7). Note also that Hezekiah was a descendant of King David (18:3). It is for this reason that Isaiah 11:1 can call the new king who will bring peace a "stem" or "branch" of Jesse; for Jesse was the father of David and thus the "stump" or ancestor of Hezekiah.

Yet Christians cannot leave the prophecy at this point because the New Testament applies the language of the righteous "branch" not to Hezekiah but to Jesus, the Messiah. In a "secondary fulfillment" it is Christ who ultimately is the true "root of David" or of his father Jesse (Rev. 5:5; 22:16). Both the genealogies of Jesus (as in Matthew 1) and early gospel sermons emphasize that Jesus was born of the tribe of Judah and was a direct descendant of David, in direct fulfillment of prophecies such as this one in Isaiah 11. We can therefore assume that the "peaceable kingdom" described in the following verses was not realized in Hezekiah's day, nor will it be a reality until the Second Coming of Christ envisioned in the passages in Revelation.

B. Personal qualities, 2

2 And the spirit of the LORD shall rest upon him, the spirit of wisdom and understanding, the spirit of counsel and might, the spirit of knowledge and of the

fear of the LORD;

The personal traits of this "branch" from David's roots also seem too illustrious to apply only to King Hezekiah. They are, however, a perfect description of Christ. We recall that His wisdom began to be manifest early, as in His questioning of the Jewish leaders in the Temple (Luke 2:46-47); and the rest of His life and teaching testify to the might of His counsel and to His fear of God.

C. Kingly traits, 3-5

1. Insight, 3

3 And shall make him of quick understanding in the fear of the LORD: and he shall not judge after the sight of his eyes, neither reprove after the hearing of his ears:

While lesser rulers make decisions on outward appearance or hearsay, this coming Branch (first Hezekiah, then Jesus) will make judgments out of deep spiritual insight. We have only to recall how Jesus looked into the soul of the penitent woman taken in adultery (John 8:3-11). Her other "judges" would have stoned her, based on the outward facts of the case—what they saw and heard. Jesus, however, with insight based on reverence for God and respect for people created in God's image, looked into the woman's heart and extended grace and forgiveness.

2. Righteousness, 4-5

4 But with righteousness shall

he judge the poor, and reprove with equity for the meek of the earth: and he shall smite the earth with the rod of his mouth, and with the breath of his lips shall he slay the wicked.

5 And righteousness shall be the girdle of his loins, and faithfulness the girdle of his reins.

In many ancient courts, merely accusing the poor of a crime meant sure conviction, for they lacked the means to hire competent counsel or bribe the judge. The "Branch" of David, however, will be closed with righteousness and truth as He takes His place on the judgment seat (see Rev. 19:11). The language here may be echoed in Ephesians 6:14, where Paul lists "the full armor of God."

II. A Kingdom of Peace—6-11

A. Among all creation, 6-8

6 The wolf also shall dwell with the lamb, and the leopard shall lie down with the kid; and the calf and the young lion and the fatling together; and a little child shall lead them.

7 And the cow and the bear shall feed; their young ones shall lie down together: and the lion shall eat straw like the ox.

8 And the sucking child shall play on the hole of the asp, and the weaned child shall put his hand on the cockatrice' den.

This word picture of the universal peace that will be the result of the coming righteous "Branch" of David has been taken both literally and figuratively. The literal view takes seriously the fact that elements of creation set at odds with each other by the Fall will be put back into harmony under the rule of the Messiah. Self-taught Quaker painter Edward Hicks painted an estimated 100 versions of this scene, believing in a literal interpretation. Figurative interpretations hold that the scene describes normally hostile people and nations living in peace under the rule of Christ either in heaven or on an earth that has been renovated by the Prince of Peace.

B. In fullness of knowledge, 9

9 They shall not hurt nor destroy in all my holy mountain: for the earth shall be full of the knowledge of the LORD, as the waters cover the sea.

The prophet Jeremiah joined Isaiah in foreseeing a day when the knowledge of God will result in "peace on earth, good will to men." Jeremiah said that this state of affairs will be a result of the New Covenant God would make with His people, when "they shall teach no more every man his neighbor . . . for they shall all know me" (Jer. 31:31). Here is another indication that what Isaiah foresees in 11:1ff. was too large a picture to be confined to King Hezekiah's reign.

C. From a remnant to the Gentiles, 10-11

10 And in that day there shall be a root of Jesse, which shall stand for an ensign of the people; to it shall the Gentiles seek: and his rest shall be glorious.

11 And it shall come to pass in that day, that the Lord shall set his hand again the second time to recover the remnant of his people, which shall be left, from Assyria, and from Egypt, and from Pathros, and from Cush, and from Elam, and from Shinar, and from Hamath, and from the islands of the sea.

A final indication that this prophecy presses beyond immediate fulfillment through an Israelite king is that the "peaceable kingdom" will be extended to the Gentiles. Recall that even Christ's closest followers had difficulty in conceiving that He was a Messiah for the world, not just for the Jews. It was left for the apostle Paul to become the champion of taking the gospel to non-Jews; yet here is a clear indication that this was the intent of the "righteous Branch" of David.

This universal aspect is to be accompanied by a second gathering of God's people. Just as God retrieved the faithful from Egypt, He would gather them from the nations where they had been dispersed by later captors. This seems to refer to the Day of Pentecost in Acts 2, where Jews "from every nation under heaven" assembled to hear to first gospel sermon after Christ's resurrection—the "shot heard 'round the world" that would eventually result in the full incoming of Gentiles into the peaceable kingdom envisioned here by the prophet Isaiah.

Evangelistic Emphasis

What standards do you use when making value judgments about people? The Bible condemns having a judgmental spirit toward people, not making judgments about issues. The difference is between being safe and self-righteous. Good judgment keeps us out of certain areas of the city at certain times of the night. Being judgmental says that we are better than those people living in that certain area. There is a difference.

We have a very limited ability to make correct value judgments about people. While we can see their actions, we cannot discern their motivations. That is why Jesus warned about "judging" people at all. The tendency is that we will become judgmental.

Isaiah brings us good news. We will not be judged by what is seen with the eye. We will not be judged by our external appearance. We will not be judged by what is heard with the ear. We will not be evaluated on the basis of rumor, gossip, or reputation. We will be judged on the basis of righteousness.

Our judgment comes, as we are held accountable for our relationship with God and our relationship with each other. We are responsible for our own actions. We will be held accountable for the things that we have done.

In a world that hides behind victimization and blame, this is good news. We are accountable for what we have done. We will be judged rightly, with mercy and grace. A loving God will judge us, which is good news.

୫୦୦୫

The wolf shall live with the lamb, the leopard shall lie down with the kid, the calf and the lion and the fatling together; and a little child shall lead them.—*Isaiah 11:6*

Christmas time seems to focus attention on the possibility of the miraculous. Real miracles happen every day, but at this time of year we seem to be more in tune with them. We note with amazement that notorious misers become generous benefactors. Stories abound of groups and organizations bringing hopes and dreams to families who had no hopes and dreams. The power behind these miracles is the birth of Jesus Christ.

Isaiah sees a day when the forces of nature will be harnessed, when natural enemies will lie down as friends. These miracles will happen through the power of God's presence in the little child. Technology and science lay claim to the power of making "new" miracles happen, but their "miracles" are of human origin. The miracle of harmony is of divine origin. The next time you see two people getting along, hear of deeds of kindness, or see a smile on a child's face, understand through these signs that God is at work in His world.

Weekday Problems

With military precision Theo Carpenter awoke her grand-children. They were her responsibility this particular week-end as her daughter and son-in-law were enjoying a week-end getaway. Theo loved her grandchildren, but expected them to "get with the program" on Sunday morning.

She got them up and fed them well. Their next assignment was to dress for Sunday school and church. That task, while difficult, was handled with the skill of a drill sergeant leading the troops. At the appointed hour, the kids and car were ready for departure. Theo went about collecting children. She had to get Lindsey off of the computer. Lindsey had been surfing the net while waiting for church time. She was also "chatting" with some of her on-line friends. In the car, Lindsey pulled out her Game boy and was deeply engaged in some game that was "saving the world from sure doom." As they pulled in the parking lot of the church, Theo confiscated the appliance. As they walked toward the Sunday school building, Lindsey's phone paged her to make a call to her best friend. Theo confiscated the phone as well.

Lindsey, in the sixth grade, entered Miss Hope's class. In the class the children made felt cut outs of the lion and the lamb lying down together. Miss Hope showed off pictures from an old book illustrating the story from Isaiah.

Lindsey refused to ever come to Sunday school again.

*How can the lion (technology) and the lamb (your church) learn to lie down together?

Church Chuckles

"Who was the first man?" the Sunday School teacher asked.
"Hoss," said little Willie.
"Wrong," said the teacher. "It was Adam."
"Shucks," said Willie. "I knew it was one of those Cartwrights.

* * *

An usher was showing a visitor the church. "This plaque," he said proudly, "is for those who have died in the service."
"Which one?" the visitor said, alarmed. "Morning or evening?

* * *

Member to Minister: "How'd you get that cut on your face?"
Minister: "I was thinking about my sermon this morning and cut myself while I was shaving."
Member: "Next time you'd better think about your shaving and cut your sermon."

This Lesson in Your Life

As the chaos that is Christmas continues around us, we wonder when Isaiah's vision of a coming peaceful kingdom will arrive. Many are dealing with this annual rite designed to separate us from our money under the guise of "giving meaningful gifts." The Hallmark card image of people enjoying the season wrapped in the glow of a near by fire singing Christmas carols rings hollow. The precious commodity of peace on earth is as rare as an empty front row parking spot at the mall.

We are living in a time in which information is the main product of our economy. New information delivered faster than ever is the rule of the day. We used to live in isolation in our own towns and communities. Now, with technology, a problem half way around the world is on our local news in the evening. We find ourselves worrying about "other people's problems."

Our problem lies partially in our definition of peace. As a little boy I remember my grandmother telling us that she desired "peace and quiet." She usually needed that late in the day, after chasing grandchildren all morning. In that setting, "peace" was the absence of noise. As a teenager, I watched news stories about Henry Kissenger going to Paris to make "peace" with the Vietnamese. In that context, "peace" was the absence of military conflict.

We struggle with the notion of peace because we try to make it the "absence of any kind of pain" in our lives. The Bible knows no such definition of peace. In the biblical languages, the words for peace do not mean the absence of conflict, but the assurance of God's care in any situation. We, as Christians, have the promise that God is with us in any circumstance that we face. It is the knowledge of His presence that allows us to face any difficulty that comes to us.

The lion and the lamb can lie down together, not only because their natural instincts are absent, but also because the presence of God allows them to experience a new relationship with each other. This relationship is based on a divine peace, which will be created between them.

In your life, the lion and the lamb at peace might symbolize God creating a loving relationship where you are experiencing conflict. The symbol may mean that God can bring order in places where you are experiencing chaos. This biblical image might mean that a struggle in your life could come to an end if you would hand that struggle over to God.

The symbol could mean that there is hope in a place where you had given up. These promises are possible because God though Jesus Christ has brought His kingdom, with its new rules, into our midst.

1. What was the significance of the mention of Jesse?
Jesse was the father of David, the greatest king of Israel. The Messiah came from the lineage of David.

2. What image described the family of Jesse from which this leader came?
The leader did not come from a full plant, but from a tree that appeared to have been cut down.

3. What was the significance of Messiah coming from the "stump" and the "root?"
Although springing up from the tree of Jesse, He would come in a way that would not appear as obvious to those looking, but as a surprise.

4. What were the results of the "Spirit resting" on the Messiah?
The Spirit would give the Messiah wisdom and understanding, counsel and might, the spirit of knowledge and the fear of the Lord.

5. What character traits would the Spirit of the Lord give the Messiah?
The gift of understanding within the context of the fear of the Lord. He would judge His people with mercy.

6. How will the Lord judge His people?
He will not use His eyes nor His ears. His judgment will not be based on external actions, but on internal righteousness.

7. What would result from the word that the Messiah would speak?
"He will strike the earth with the rod of His mouth. With the breath of His lips he will slay the wicked."

8. As a result of the leadership of this child, what would the lion do that was out of character?
The meat-eating lion would eat grass.

9. What is the meaning of Isaiah 11: 6?
Enemies would relate to each other in new ways, indicating the Messiah's righteousness and pattern for creation.

10. What two items of clothing are mentioned in this passage?
The girdle of righteousness and the girdle of faithfulness. In modern vernacular, one might be a T-shirt and the other running shorts.

What is the meaning of the lion and the lamb lying down together? When you read on in the 11th chapter of Isaiah, it appears as though a bunch of crazy stuff happens in the animal kingdom. The natural animosity within the animal kingdom disappears. A divine peace settles in on the created order.

Earlier I suggested that the "lion and the lamb" lying down together could be our use of "technology" for the advancement of the kingdom of God. Technology appears to be the modern "boogie man" of which church-going people are afraid. We live, work, and minister in a world that is filled with gadgetry. I wonder how much of this scientific gadgetry we are using for the kingdom of God?

When I wrote my first set of lessons for this commentary, I sat at a typewriter. In a matter of less than six years, I have gone from typewriter to computer. I have learned phrases like "web page" and "dot com." I have been amazed and amused as retirees have bought computers and found themselves "on line." I have watched as church libraries have become "media centers" which house all kinds of information distribution systems. We contact members with voice mail and automated phone systems. We produce "streaming" video of our worship services and have "web sites." We don't send messages by "snail mail" but by "e-mail."

The new economy is said to be an "e-economy." We are living through a revolution of information not seen since the advent of the printing press. Do we face these days with chagrin or with faith? Could the Lord be providing the Church the means by which we can reach lives in a way never before imagined? Could it be that the Lord is the author of this revolution and is calling His people to use all means possible to share the good news of His love and grace?

Could the image of the "lion and the lamb" together encourage us to put aside our animosities and worries and get busy with the work of the Messiah? We answer, "yes" to all of those rhetorical questions only to the extent that we are working for the purposes of God.

Rather than lament the situation in which we live, we are called to be faithful servants of the times. We are called to proclaim the Day of the Lord in the ways that are available. We are to claim not only our time but also the technology of our time for the Lord's service.

This means that we can be creative with our use of technology in the Church. Indeed, we have an obligation to use the most current methods possible to lead our world to faith in Jesus Christ. This next generation has been playing with computers since they could walk. They understand the technology and don't fear its use. The Church needs to talk to the next generation about our Lord in a way that generation can understand.

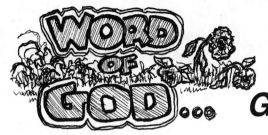

Comfort for God's People

Isaiah 40:1-11

Comfort ye, comfort ye my people, saith your God.

2 Speak ye comfortably to Jerusalem, and cry unto her, that her warfare is accomplished, that her iniquity is pardoned: for she hath received of the LORD's hand double for all her sins.

3 The voice of him that crieth in the wilderness, Prepare ye the way of the LORD, make straight in the desert a highway for our God.

4 Every valley shall be exalted, and every mountain and hill shall be made low: and the crooked shall be made straight, and the rough places plain:

5 And the glory of the LORD shall be revealed, and all flesh shall see it together: for the mouth of the LORD hath spoken it.

6 The voice said, Cry. And he said, What shall I cry? All flesh is grass, and all the goodliness thereof is as the flower of the field:

7 The grass withereth, the flower fadeth: because the spirit of the LORD bloweth upon it: surely the people is grass.

8 The grass withereth, the flower fadeth: but the word of our God shall stand for ever.

9 O Zion, that bringest good tidings, get thee up into the high mountain; O Jerusalem, that bringest good tidings, lift up thy voice with strength; lift it up, be not afraid; say unto the cities of Judah, Behold your God!

10 Behold, the Lord GOD will come with strong hand, and his arm shall rule for him: behold, his reward is with him, and his work before him.

11 He shall feed his flock like a shepherd: he shall gather the lambs with his arm, and carry them in his bosom, and shall gently lead those that are with young.

Memory Selection
Isaiah 40:8

Devotional Reading
Isaiah 40:25-31

Background Scripture
Isaiah 40:1-11

from their enemies.

The preceding chapter has identified the enemy here as Babylon. The traditional dating of Isaiah in the eighth century B.C. results in the view that the prophet looks forward more than a century, and foresees the Babylonian captivity described in 2 Kings 25:1ff.; then predicts the return to the Promised land described in Ezra and Nehemiah. It is the promise of this period of "restoration" that is the comfort of which the prophet sings here.

This beautiful and timeless passage grows out of the pattern of Israel's behavior throughout the Old Testament. The people and their leaders rebel against God, then repent, and God restores their fortunes. Isaiah 40 begins an entire section focusing on this third phase of the cycle, when God will deliver His people

శిం(ఇ

The theme of this lesson might be called "Homecoming," and introduced by drawing members of your study group into a discussion of memorable homecomings in which they have participated. Be prepared to accept negative comments as well as positive, since some group members may have memories of

homecomings at which Mom was judgmental, Dad was gone, and the kids misbehaved badly!

Generally, however, point out that home is recalled by many people as a place where their roots were nourished, and where they return to be refreshed by warm memories and renewed relationships. Point out that when the southern kingdom of Judah was carried into Babylonian captivity in 587-86 B.C. they were cut off from their roots in the Promised Land. How they must have rejoiced to hear God's promise in this lesson that a grand Homecoming was just ahead!

Teaching Outline	Daily Bible Readings
	Mon. Turn and Be Saved Isaiah 45:18-25
	Tue. Better Days Promised Isaiah 44:1-8
I. Punishment Is Ended—1-2	
II. Prepare the Lord's Way—3-5	
A. A straight and level path, 3-4	**Wed.** The Folly of Idols Isaiah 44:9-20
B. Our eyes shall see the glory!, 5	
III. Priority of the Word—6-8	**Thu.** God Who Redeems Isaiah 44:21-28
A. All flesh is grass, 6-8a	
B. God's Word is eternal, 8b	**Fri.** The Incomparable God Isaiah 40:12-17
IV. Preach the Glad Tidings!—9-11	**Sat.** Idols vs. God Isaiah 40:18-24
A. Joy to Jerusalem, 9	
B. Feed for the flock, 10-11	**Sun.** The Everlasting Creator Isaiah 40:25-31

Verse by Verse

I. Punishment Is Ended—1-2

1 Comfort ye, comfort ye my people, saith your God.

2 Speak ye comfortably to Jerusalem, and cry unto her, that her warfare is accomplished, that her iniquity is pardoned: for she hath received of the LORD's hand double for all her sins.

Along with verses from Isaiah 9, this beautiful and comforting passage becomes a tender strain in Handel's famous "Messiah." Yet an already comfortable audience at a Christmas program can hardly reap as much comfort from this promise as did the Israelites languishing in Babylonian captivity. Their idolatry and injustice has caused God to allow them to be taken into a land so foreign that many cannot even sing the old songs of Zion (Ps. 137:4). For 70 years they endured this bondage and oppression, just as the prophet Jeremiah predicted (Jer. 25:11-12; 29:10). Now Isaiah foresees the day that Israel will have served her sentence, which must have seemed twice as severe as their sin. Their "warfare" against God, or their "hard service" (NIV) in the "prison" of Babylonia is about to come to an end.

II. Prepare the Lord's Way—3-5
A. A straight and level path, 3-4

3 The voice of him that crieth in the wilderness, Prepare ye the way of the LORD, make straight in the desert a highway for our God.

4 Every valley shall be exalted, and every mountain and hill shall be made low: and the crooked shall be made straight, and the rough places plain:

Isaiah describes Israel's approaching return to the Promised Land in terms of a great king entering a city his forces have just conquered. Some of the roads in the ancient world began as just such "highways," as laborers would literally level small hills and straighten sharp curves to make a more passable road for a king and his entourage.

This verse is seen by the Gospel writers as an analogy for the work of John the Baptist, who "built" such a highway for King Jesus, crying "Prepare ye the way of the Lord, make his paths straight" (Mark 1:3). **B. Our eyes shall see the glory!, 5**

5 And the glory of the LORD shall be revealed, and all flesh shall see it together: for the mouth of the LORD hath spoken it.

The life of Jews who had been carried into Babylonian captivity had been anything but glorious. Yet they are called on to have the faith to accept God's promise that He will overrule rulers, as He in fact did in the case of the Persian King Cyrus, who conquered Babylon, then was persuaded to allow the Jews to return. This decision ranks as one of the great miracles in Scripture, for it flew in the face of "the flesh," or what we might ordinarily have expected. The event can be compared with the modern collapse of the Soviet Union, which virtually ended the Cold War. Convincing captive Jews that God would soon rescue them must have been comparable to assuring a victim of Soviet oppression living behind the Iron Curtain in 1985 that in only four short years the wall would fall and democracy would come.

III. Priority of the Word—6-8
A. All flesh is grass, 6-8a

6 The voice said, Cry. And he said, What shall I cry? All flesh is grass, and all the goodliness thereof is as the flower of the field:

7 The grass withereth, the flower fadeth: because the spirit of the LORD bloweth upon it:

surely the people is grass.

8a The grass withereth, the flower fadeth:

These verses are probably to be read as a dialog that Isaiah has with himself. God tells him to "Cry," and when the prophet asks what he should cry, the answer comes, "All flesh is grass." The "conversation" seems to answer the question of God's people in Babylon, "Why has this happened to us?" The answer is that they are weak and fleshly people; but that, in contrast (vs. 8b), God's Word is Spirit; and that in His power and grace He can rescue the people from their fleshliness and captivity. We can also suppose that those who hear Isaiah's prophecy respond with fleshly doubt. Their low expectations were natural enough, but the way of the natural is the way of "the flesh"; and Isaiah is told to remind the people of how undependable life is when limited by the fleshly dimension.

Centuries later, the apostle Peter will use this passage to emphasize again that "All flesh is as grass . . . but the word of the Lord endureth for ever" (1 Peter. 1:24-25).

B. God's Word is eternal, 8b

8b but the word of our God shall stand for ever.

In contrast, despite predictions based on the power of "the flesh," the word from God through Isaiah that Israel will be restored to the Promised Land is a word of Spirit, hence a word that will stand.

IV. Preach the Glad Tidings!—9-11
A. Joy to Jerusalem, 9

9 O Zion, that bringest good tidings, get thee up into the high mountain; O Jerusalem, that bringest good tidings, lift up thy voice with strength; lift it up, be not afraid; say unto the cities of Judah, Behold your God!

It is not uncommon for the prophetic and poetic writings to personify a city, especially one so famous as Jerusalem. Zion, the name at least since the time of David, refers to one of the two main hills or ridges on which the Holy City was built. Here Zion and Jerusalem are called to join their own voices to those who sing a new song of victory as the Babylonian captives return.

Some scholars believe that the word "Zion" means "citadel," while others say it is derived from a term meaning "sunny mountain." The name takes on poetic power in the Psalms, and becomes a symbol of the place where the victorious "144,000" will stand at the Second Coming of Christ (Rev. 14:1).

It would have been another challenge to the captive Israelites to believe that their beloved city would again be restored to its position of leadership among the cities of Judah. The long Babylonian siege had reduced the city to rubble, and its people to starvation (see 2 Kings 25:1-4, 9-10). Again they are challenged to believe God's promise over what perishable "flesh" would tell them.

B. Feed for the flock, 10-11

10 Behold, the Lord GOD will come with strong hand, and his arm shall rule for him: behold, his reward is with him, and his work before him.

11 He shall feed his flock like a shepherd: he shall gather the lambs with his arm, and carry them in his bosom, and shall gently lead those that are with young.

God's Word of encouragement through Isaiah becomes more personal in stages. Verse 9 had promised that Jerusalem as a city would rejoice. Now verse 10 affirms that God as a powerful general will rule in favor of these deportees who had so long been out of favor. Then verse 11 promises that at the return from Babylon the individual citizen, long starved for spiritual nourishment, will be fed by God as a shepherd pastures his sheep, with those too weak to walk gently carried to the sheepfold.

All these events, which the oppressed Israelites must have had difficulty believing, actually occurred only a few years after Isaiah's prophecy, as King Cyrus allowed Ezra and Nehemiah to lead hundreds of Jews back to Israel to rebuild both their capital city and its Temple.

Evangelistic Emphasis

The words of Isaiah offer the promise that God will comfort His people. Written to the Hebrew exiles, who were separated by distance from the familiar landscape of home, Isaiah's words offered hope in a hopeless situation. The exiles were in a place where the worship of God was foreign. They were in a hostile environment. Families had been broken apart. Futures had been taken captive and there was little hope for the restoration of the Hebrews to their homeland.

In the middle of this pain, the prophet spoke the words from God of comfort.

The same promise of comfort is available to us. This comfort comes not in the changing of our circumstance but in the understanding that God sees our pain and will one day "make it all right." This promise of God's love and comfort sees its final fulfillment in words found in the last chapters of our Bible.

"He will wipe every tear from their eyes. Death will be no more; mourning and crying and pain will be no more, for the first things have passed away" (Rev. 21:4). The ultimate comfort of God comes at the end of time, when He wipes away all the tears we have shed.

The good news is that God knows our pain and one day will wrap us in His arms and dry our tears.

ℰ◌ℛ

Memory Selection

The grass withereth, the flower fadeth: but the word of our God shall stand for ever.—*Isaiah 40:8*

Back in 1995 I bought a big screen television. My wife told me that I could buy one in 1995, so I found a store opened on New Year's Day and made my purchase. By 2005 my big screen television set will be obsolete, or so the experts say.

The computer I use to write these lessons is a year old. I spent large sums of money purchasing this machine and at the time, it was the best. Computer people tell me that computers are obsolete as soon as you take them from the store. My computer is now considered a dinosaur.

I have a map of the world. It was printed in the 1970s. I'm told that my map is not longer valid.

So much of what we buy and what we have is no longer "valid." We need to constantly update our "stuff."

The promise from Isaiah is that God's Word is as powerful and as penetrating as the day it was spoken. There is something we can count on as always being there—God's word.

Weekday Problems

John Masters stared at his bank statement in disbelief. There on the bottom was the message that the bank would now be charging two dollars for every transaction that involved a teller. The flyer in the statement was touting the bank's new "electronic" banking services. John's life kept changing as a result of technology. His job was becoming computerized. John was having a hard time imagining a car mechanic working primarily to fix a computer in a broken down car. That was his new reality. Now he couldn't talk to his favorite bank teller without paying for that privilege.

John Masters was pondering his predicament in church on Sunday morning. John had decided to attend the new "contemporary" service that Pastor Buster Weatherly had started at First Church. John wasn't given a bulletin when he entered the room. He looked around and saw only drums and guitars. The microphone stands on the stage looked like a forest. Then as the service began, the words to the songs magically appeared on a screen

Knowing the words to the songs comforted John. While the tunes were different, "Amazing Grace" was still John's favorite song. He found himself singing it to a new tune. Pastor Weatherly had his sermon outline on the screen, and John found himself comforted by hearing and now seeing God's word.

*In a changing world, how can the church proclaim the unchanging nature of God's word?

~~Marching~~ Limping to Zion

A member of the congregation had dozed off during the sermon, and didn't hear the preacher say, "Will all who want to go to heaven please stand?" All stood but the man who was asleep.

"Now be seated," said the minister, "and will all who believe they are going to hell please stand?"

No one stood, but someone dropped a song book and awoke the man, causing him to jump to his feet facing the pastor. Looking about him he said sheepishly, "I don't know what we're voting for, but looks like we're the only ones for it."

* * *

"Lot was told to take his family and flee from the cities of Sodom and Gomorrah," explained the Sunday School teacher. "But his wife looked back and was turned into a pillar of salt."

"But teacher," said one little boy, "what happened to the flea?"

This Lesson in Your Life

This lesson has several places that touch our daily walk. It's about sin. The Hebrews found themselves in the predicament of captivity because of their sin. God saw the evil of His people and raised up prophets. The prophets preached in clear ways the message of God's displeasure. They proclaimed the need for the people to repent of their sins. The people with stubborn determination refused to acknowledge their sins and turn from them. God, being faithful to His word, punished the Hebrews by allowing them to be carried off into captivity. This came as no surprise to the people who had been listening to the preaching of the prophets.

Today sin still has natural and normal consequences. It is not a subject widely discussed because it is painful and embarrassing to admit that sin still lurks in our souls. God's word condemns sin while boldly proclaiming that God loves the sinner. That is a dichotomy that we, as His people, have yet fully to grasp.

Perhaps some of the things that have happened to you are the result of sin. You must live with the natural consequences of your actions. The eternal consequences of sin are forgiven when we seek God's grace.

A secondary point related to the first is the issue of suffering. Isaiah would affirm that some suffering is the direct result of sin. Other kinds of suffering are indirectly related to sin. The caveat to those statements is that not all suffering is related to sin. Paul would write, "for as all die in Adam, so all will be made alive in Christ" (1 Cor. 15:22). There is something about being related to Adam that brings pain and suffering into our lives. The relationship we have with Adam is that we are all sinners.

If sin and suffering are parts of this lesson in your life, so too is comfort and consolation. God told Isaiah that the Hebrews had suffered enough in captivity and that the prophet should proclaim God's restoration. There is a limit to the pain and suffering in our lives.

The cross of Calvary shows that God has intervened in our sinfulness in a way that brings us relief. The grace of God restores our relationship to the Father through Jesus Christ. When God speaks to our souls the word of comfort and consolation, He brings to an end the spiritual suffering in our lives. There are times when we must endure the physical sufferings that result from our sinfulness, but we are no longer estranged from God. We can make the pilgrimage through pain, even when it is the consequence of sin, because we know that at the end of our journey God is there to bring us comfort.

1. What message of comfort was to be proclaimed to Jerusalem?

That "her term has been served" and "her penalty is paid" (Isa. 40:2).

2. How, in terms of severity, was the sentence carried out against Jerusalem described?

Jerusalem had received a "double" portion for her sin and folly (Isa. 40:2).

3. Although the source of suffering often remains a mystery, according to Isaiah 40:2 who was the source of the woe falling upon Jerusalem?

Jerusalem's sentence and penalty came from "the Lord's hand."

4. According to Luke 3:-6, John the Baptist uttered words from the prophet Isaiah. Which verses did John quote?

John the Baptist was quoting from Isaiah 40:3-4. His ministry was to prepare the people for the coming Christ.

5. "Preparing the way of the Lord" involved what actions?

The way of the Lord was prepared by making straight the highway, lifting up the valley, bringing down the mountain and leveling the uneven and rough ground (Isa. 40:3-4).

6. How was the faith of the people of God described?

Their faith (constancy) was like the grass and flowers of the field. Both of these things wither and die (Isa. 40: 6-8).

7. What is the only enduring truth in our world?

"But the word of our God will stand forever" (Isa. 40:8).

8. What was the essence of the message to be preached by Zion and Jerusalem?

They were both to proclaim to the world and to the people of Israel, "Here is your God!" (Isai. 40:9).

9. How was the Lord described as coming to Judah?

He was described as a mighty ruler. His reward was with Him. His recompense was before Him. (Isa. 40:9.)

10. What contrast does Isaiah 40:11 offer to verse 10?

In verse 10, God was described as a mighty conqueror. In verse 11, God was pictured as a shepherd tending His sheep.

Tucked in this text from Isaiah is a beautiful pattern for the ministry of the Church: "He will feed His flock like a shepherd; He will gather the lambs in His arms, and carry them in His bosom, and gently lead the mother sheep" (Isa. 40:11).

Isaiah was describing the ministry of the Suffering Servant. In His ministry on earth, Jesus adopted this picture and described himself as the Good Shepherd. In His discussion with Simon Peter, Jesus continued to lift up the shepherd image as a pattern for ministry. "When they had finished breakfast, Jesus said to Simon Peter, 'Simon son of John, do you love me more than these?' He said to Him, 'Yes, Lord; you know that I love you.' Jesus said to him, 'Feed my lambs.' A second time He said to him, 'Simon son of John, do you love me?' He said to Him, 'Yes, Lord; you know that I love you.' Jesus said to him, 'Tend my sheep.' He said to him the third time, 'Simon son of John, do you love me?' Peter felt hurt because He said to him the third time, 'Do you love me?' And he said to Him, 'Lord, you know everything; you know that I love you.' Jesus said to him, 'Feed my sheep'" (John 20:15-17).

Most pastors see their ministry as shepherding the sheep. By extension, the ministry of the Church is to shepherd the sheep and seek and save the lost lambs. Some other functions of ministry follow this primary pattern, but they can actually cause a drain on the real purpose of ministry.

There is the *"veterinarian"* function of our ministry together. There are some sick sheep that we are called to heal. This is not a glamorous part of our ministry and often the sick sheep take years of care before they achieve wholeness. The veterinary function is one that takes too much time and keeps our shepherding ministry from being visionary. We try to cure sheep of diseases from which they have already been set free by the grace of God. We find ourselves treating their symptoms rather than letting the Good Shepherd heal their souls. In this mode of ministry we find ourselves running to those sheep that make the most noise, rather than seeking out those who are silently lost.

Another image is that of *"rancher."* We find ourselves spending much time taking care of the "sheep pens." Ranchers are involved in tending to the fence posts and the wire protecting the sheep. They spend much time building barns in which the sheep are housed. They are busy with bringing food and water to the flock. They take care of the day-to-day needs of the sheep pen.

Our calling as Christians is to shepherd the flock of God. Jesus told us to tend the little lambs. How much time is actually spent with the flock and how much time is given to making sure the flock is "comfortable"? Is a great deal of what we do and call "ministry" actually foreign to what we should be doing as "shepherds"?

The Prince of Peace

Isaiah 9:2-12

The people that walked in darkness have seen a great light: they that dwell in the land of the shadow of death, upon them hath the light shined.

3 Thou hast multiplied the nation, and not increased the joy: they joy before thee according to the joy in harvest, and as men rejoice when they divide the spoil.

4 For thou hast broken the yoke of his burden, and the staff of his shoulder, the rod of his oppressor, as in the day of Midian.

5 For every battle of the warrior is with confused noise, and garments rolled in blood; but this shall be with burning and fuel of fire.

6 For unto us a child is born, unto us a son is given: and the government shall be upon his shoulder: and his name shall be called Wonderful, Counseller, The mighty God, The everlasting Father, The Prince of Peace.

7 Of the increase of his government and peace there shall be no end, upon the throne of David, and upon his kingdom, to order it, and to establish it with judgment and with justice from henceforth even for ever. The zeal of the LORD of hosts will perform this.

8 The Lord sent a word into Jacob, and it hath lighted upon Israel.

9 And all the people shall know, even Ephraim and the inhabitant of Samaria, that say in the pride and stoutness of heart,

10 The bricks are fallen down, but we will build with hewn stones: the sycomores are cut down, but we will change them into cedars.

11 Therefore the LORD shall set up the adversaries of Rezin against him, and join his enemies together;

12 The Syrians before, and the Philistines behind; and they shall devour Israel with open mouth. For all this his anger is not turned away, but his hand is stretched out still.

Memory Selection
Isaiah 9:6

Devotional Reading
Luke 2:8-20

Background Scripture
Isaiah 9:1-12; Luke 2:1-20

Like Isaiah 7:14, this lesson focuses on a coming Deliverer who will save God's people from hard times. "The Prince of Peace" is among the titles of this Savior (9:6), tying in with this season when we celebrate the birth of Jesus.

The setting is the eighth century B.C. At times, both Judah and Israel were assaulted by Assyria. Isaiah warns that de-liverance will not come through alliance with other governments (see 31:1). Instead, God Himself will provide a child who will become Israel's Deliverer (as in 7:14).

Although many scholars believe this passage predicts the godly reign of King Hezekiah, who succeeded the faithless King Ahaz, the language presses beyond a merely human deliverer. Thus, the New Testament will cite our passage as a prophecy of the Messiah. Far beyond any earthly ruler, de-liverance for God's people comes through Jesus.

❧❧

The courageous teacher can focus attention on today's lesson by leading a brief discussion of the hot topic of religion and politics. Ask such questions as, *Should our government endorse Christianity? What about prayer at government-sponsored events such as the* public schools? Is America a "Christian" nation?

Before the group disintegrates in disagreement, point out that the prophet Isaiah had a great deal to say about the difference between politics and religion. Judah was supposed to be a "*theo*cracy," a nation ruled by God, rather than a *demo*cracy. However, in this lesson Isaiah will affirm that in hard times God's people should not count on political schemes for deliverance, but look to Him who is called the Prince of Peace.

Teaching Outline	Daily Bible Readings	
I. A Light in the Darkness—9:2-3	**Mon.**	Moving Worship Time Isaiah 6:1-5
II. Deliverance from Oppression—4-5	**Tue.**	Answering God's Call Isaiah 6:6-13
III. The Child to Come—6	**Wed.**	God's Special Sign Isaiah 7:10-17
IV. The Eternal Kingdom—7	**Thu.**	Wounded for Our Sins Isaiah 53:1-9
V. Judgment on Israel—8-12	**Fri.**	'The Lord Is with You' Luke 1:26-38
A. False confidence, 8-10	**Sat.**	'My Soul Magnifies the Lord' Luke 1:41-55
B. False allies, 11-12	**Sun.**	The Birth of Jesus Luke 2:1-7

Verse by Verse

I. A Light in the Darkness—9:2-3

2 The people that walked in darkness have seen a great light: they that dwell in the land of the shadow of death, upon them hath the light shined.

3 Thou hast multiplied the nation, and not increased the joy: they joy before thee according to the joy in harvest, and as men rejoice when they divide the spoil.

"The people that walked in darkness" are the faithful Jews Isaiah addressed in the southern kingdom of Judah, in the eighth century B.C. They are in darkness because of threatened invasion from the north. Looking into the future with prophetic vision, Isaiah can speak of coming events as present facts. One of the "dark" truths is that the king of Assyria has captured (or will capture) the northern 10 tribes, often known now as Israel or Ephraim. Verse 1 also refers to them as "Galilee of the nations" or Gentiles, because non-Jews have been brought in to intermarry with the Israelites.

Assyria has made an alliance with these mixed-blood Jew/Gentile people, and together they plan to invade Judah. The darkness and gloom over the land is increased by the fact that Ahaz, king of Judah, shamelessly tried to appease the king of Assyria, even going so far as to import idolatrous Assyrian worship into Judah (see 2 Kings 16:7-10).

Verse 3 describes a change in the mood of the people from sadness to joy (see the NIV: "You have enlarged the nation and increased their joy," instead of the KJV's reference to no increase in joy). This is because, in the midst of this darkness, Isaiah sees a light which many scholars believe is to be applied first to Hezekiah, King Ahaz' son, who would bring a dramatic reform to Judah. When Hezekiah succeeded his father on the throne, he cleansed the land of idolatrous worship, reinstated the worship of the true God, and trusted in Him, instead of alliances with other nations, to deliver Judah from its enemies (see 2 Kings 18:1-8).

While Hezekiah's reform was certainly significant, the New Testament shows that the "light" which Isaiah foresaw was not exhausted in the person of the king. Rather, the beam extends down the long years into the Christian era. Matthew 4:12-16 affirms that the light that began with Hezekiah culminated in the ministry of Jesus, the Messiah. The Jews un-

163

der Ahaz therefore become a "type" of those who lived in the darkness of Roman oppression in first-century Palestine; and Hezekiah becomes a type of the even greater deliverance that came in the form of Jesus, the Messiah.

II. Deliverance from Oppression –4-5

4 For thou hast broken the yoke of his burden, and the staff of his shoulder, the rod of his oppressor, as in the day of Midian.

5 For every battle of the warrior is with confused noise, and garments rolled in blood; but this shall be with burning and fuel of fire.

Again claiming the prophetic future as the present, Isaiah asserts that the rule of the coming king would break the yoke of oppression under which his people labored. This victory is compared with the "day of Midian," when the judge Gideon won the great battle with Israel's arch-enemies, the Midianites (Judg. 7:19-22).

Again, however, the language can hardly be limited to Isaiah's day. Verse 5 refers to the destruction of the weapons and battle-garments of warriors by fire—a vision of universal peace that would come only under the spiritual victory of the Messiah. Although this victory began to be apparent in the resurrection, it will not be culminated until God's foes are cast into the "lake of fire" (Rev. 20:8-10).

III. The Child to Come—6

6 For unto us a child is born, unto us a son is given: and the gov-ernment shall be upon his shoulder: and his name shall be called Wonderful, Counseller, The mighty God, The everlasting Father, The Prince of Peace.

Again, while the language here may have been understood first as applying to the birth of a righteous king such as Hezekiah, the terms describing him are far too full of divinity to be contained in a person of mere humanity.

Although Hezekiah took the government of Judah upon his shoulders, he did not claim, as Jesus would later do, that "all power has been given unto me in heaven and in earth" (Matt. 28:18). In cleansing the land of idolatry, Hezekiah worked wonders, but not to the extent that he was called "Wonderful." While the king was a wise counselor (partly because he consulted God's counsel, through Isaiah), he was not *the* Counselor, as Jesus would one day serve in His role as Mediator between God and man.

Also, while an earthly Jewish king was referred to as "lord," "father," and a "prince," it would only be the Messiah who would elevate these terms into titles of divinity. Hence Handel's famous "Messiah" appropriately makes verse 6 the centerpiece of what has become a beautiful and moving Christmas event attributing these terms to Jesus of Nazareth.

IV. The Eternal Kingdom—7

7 Of the increase of his government and peace there shall be no end, upon the throne of David, and upon his kingdom, to order it, and to establish it with judgment and

with justice from henceforth even for ever. **The zeal of the LORD of hosts will perform this.**

Once more, the comparison and contrast between King Hezekiah and the coming Messiah are sharply drawn. God had promised David that he would never lack a ruling descendant (2 Sam. 7:12-13). Although the throne of David did come to an end under the human kings of Israel, the ascension of Jesus to His heavenly throne is taken to be the final fulfillment of the David lineage (Acts 2:29-36). It is only in the transference of the "kingdom promise" to spiritual Israel, both Jews and Gentiles who are "grafted" into the kingdom under the rule of Jesus Christ, that God's promise of an eternal kingdom is fulfilled.

V. Judgment on Israel—8-12

A. False confidence, 8-10

8 The Lord sent a word into Jacob, and it hath lighted upon Israel.

9 And all the people shall know, even Ephraim and the inhabitant of Samaria, that say in the pride and stoutness of heart,

10 The bricks are fallen down, but we will build with hewn stones: the sycomores are cut down, but we will change them into cedars.

Now Isaiah turns from encouraging Judah to pronouncing God's wrath on Israel, the 10 northern tribes. They had already suffered numerous invasions, and the cities of Samaria had been plundered. Yet idolatrous rulers refused to return to God, but boasted of their ability to rebuild the cities. The materials they planned to use included the famous "cedars of Lebanon"—perhaps a sly claim to equal buildings as magnificent as the Temple in Jerusalem, which had also been constructed of those storied timbers.

B. False allies, 11-12

11 Therefore the LORD shall set up the adversaries of Rezin against him, and join his enemies together;

12 The Syrians before, and the Philistines behind; and they shall devour Israel with open mouth. For all this his anger is not turned away, but his hand is stretched out still.

Although Israel had allied itself with Rezin, king of Damascus in Syria, he will prove to be a weak friend. Rezin and Prince Pekah of Israel had joined in an attack against Judah (2 Kings 16:5). Shortly afterward, he met God's judgment by being slain at the hands of the Assyrians, who conquered Syria (16:9). Despite the woes God sent against Israel, the people and their leaders were unrepentant. Hence God's anger was not "turned away," and eventually allowed the Assyrians to devour Israel and take the people into captivity (17:5-6).

Evangelistic Emphasis

Isaiah 9:2 tells us that people who walked in darkness saw a great light. Darkness keeps us from understanding the joy and grace of God's light. Actually, darkness is not the problem, but the lesser lights that blind us to the true light. On the darkest of nights, my neighbors "security light" glows in my window. In my own home, there are a number lights that stay on at night. On the darkest of nights we live with the glow of all of our artificial lights.

On a spiritual level we can understand how people living in darkness can see a light. We see signs around us that God is still taking people from their sinfulness and moving them into eternal life. He does this through His grace and love. We might not understand their conversion because we have never known spiritual darkness. Those who have had this conversion experience talk about a time when "the light went on and I saw myself as I was."

A good spiritual exercise would be to sit in the darkness for a while and understand the power of a light that penetrates the darkness. We take light for granted. There are people today walking in darkness while we hoard the light.

To a world that is lost in the darkness of sin, that light is good news. We are called to let our light shine!

ଛୁଙ୍କ

Memory Selection

For unto us a child is born, unto us a son is given: and the government shall be upon his shoulder: and his name shall be called Wonderful, Counselor, The mighty God, The everlasting Father, The Prince of Peace.—*Isaiah 9:6*

When I was a young boy I didn't know what my middle name was all about. Eventually I learned that I was named for my father, and it was a family name. That was significant because I have discovered relatives I never knew before who share that same family name.

Names are important. If you don't believe me, try making introductions and watch as a name departs your memory as that person enters the room. To the government and to our creditors we might be a number; but to the people who matter we have a name.

God has many names. We use His different names as we call upon Him for different things. In moments of praise we call Him "Wonderful." In moment of pain and confusion we call Him "Counselor." When we are feeling alone and helpless we call Him, "Mighty God."

Our God, who has many names, knows us by name. Since we are on a first name basis, shouldn't we be spending more time with Him?

Weekday Problems

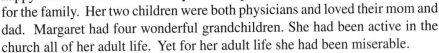

Buster Weatherly found his mind wandering as Margaret Johnson poured out her soul. He knew that a loving pastor should be listening to a member of his flock as she shared from her soul, but he had heard this sad story before.

Margaret had everything a person could want to be happy. Her husband was wealthy and had provided well for the family. Her two children were both physicians and loved their mom and dad. Margaret had four wonderful grandchildren. She had been active in the church all of her adult life. Yet for her adult life she had been miserable.

Margaret Johnson's problem was that she didn't know how to enjoy the blessings that God had placed in her life. She had actually decided to be miserable. Buster found himself again listening to a litany of things that would have made anyone else rejoice, but seemed to make Margaret miserable. He had tried to be a patient pastor, but had read someplace that being a "veterinarian" to sheep was contrary to a good model for ministry.

He asked Margaret, "why can't you see the joy that God has placed in your life?" He realized by the look on her face that his question had shocked her.

*Do we rejoice at the goodness that God has placed in our lives?

*Do we more easily see joy or pain in our lives?

Significant People and Events During Isaiah's Ministry

Judah (Southern Kingdom)

Uzziah (Azariah; reigned 52 yrs.; Isaiah's call to the prophetic ministry came the year Uzziah died.

Jotham (16 yrs.)

Ahaz (16 yrs.)

Hezekiah (29 yrs.)

Northern kingdom falls, 722-21 B.C.

Manasseh (55 yrs.)
Isaiah's death. (Tradition holds that Manasseh had Isaiah sawed in two with a wooden saw.)

Israel (Northern Kingdom)

Pekah (reigned 20 yrs.)
Unsuccessfully attacked Judah.

Hoshea (9 yrs.)
The 10 northern tribes carried into Assyrian captivity, 722-21 B.C.

This Lesson in Your Life

Poor Buster Weatherly had to listen to Margaret Johnson complain when she should have been counting her blessings. Unfortunately, there are many people like that in the Church. They count up every pain but fail to give God the credit for every joy that comes their way. They live with blinders on. When joy does come in their lives, rather than receiving it they live as though they are waiting for the "other shoe to drop."

As a minister I have sat in meetings listening with great joy as missions committee shared what work has been done in the church. They will tell about successful efforts in reaching out in service and concern to our world. They will talk about certain ministries have changed the lives of both the recipients of ministry and those performing the tasks. After several moments of celebration, "Chicken Little" will show up. You remember Chicken Little, don't you? He was the chick that was wrongly convinced that "The sky is falling, the sky is falling!" There is always a Chicken Little on a missions committee. No matter how great the rejoicing, Chicken Little will remind the committee that there are people starving in some third world country and that we are not doing enough.

One Sunday I was bragging on the church in my sermon. I was talking about how well things were going and how many souls were being touched for Jesus Christ. I had the actual numbers in front of me. As I was leaving the church that morning, I overheard our "Chicken Little" talking about how terrible things were in the church. I began to wonder if we were talking about the same congregation. Then I focused in on Chicken Little and found out she was simply a negative person.

Negativity in the kingdom of God is a dangerous thing. I would never diminish the problems the church faces, but I think that negative people do something far more dangerous. Negativity in the church means that we don't believe that God is able to provide for us. We see problems rather than opportunities for service. When we see these "problems" we immediately assume they are bigger than God.

The lack of joy in the Church comes when we give in and declare something "bigger than God can handle" . . . when we give in to the negativity of Chicken Little . . . when we fail to praise God for what He is doing in our midst. There is enough pain and suffering in the world already; we don't need to be resuing the joy God places in our path.

Are you living joyfully? Or do you see your "mission" as keeping people "honest"? If you are "keeping people in the Church honest" is it bringing you and others joy?

168

STRAIGHT

1. What was the only hope for Israel's desperate situation?
The coming of a divine child was the only hope Israel had.

2. Into what two realms had the "light of God" entered?
The light had been seen by those who "walk in darkness" and by those "in the land of the shadow of death."

3. What "earthly" activities brought some joy, according to the prophet?
People rejoiced when they gathered the harvest, and when they divided the spoils of war.

4. What might the modern parallels to "gathering the harvest" and "dividing the spoils"?
This would make a good discussion question for your class.

5. What threefold image was used to describe the freedom that God brought when He delivered His people?
God broke the "yoke" the "staff" and the "rod."

6. What burden would the child carry?
The government "will be upon His shoulder."

7. What names would be used for this child?
"His name shall be called Wonderful, Counselor, The Almighty God, the Everlasting Father, The Prince of Peace."

8. Which one of these names means the most to you in your personal faith pilgrimage?
You might have the class discuss this.

9. From whence would this child rule?
The child would rule from the throne of David, because His Kingdom would be an extension of the prophesied kingdom of David.

10. How long would this child reign as king?
His reign would be forever, over an everlasting Kingdom.

It's time to find our Christmas heroes and heroines. Only a few days are left. Don't you admire all those people who have their shopping done? Some have had it done for months! What about those brave souls who fight the mobs in the malls? Don't you admire the warriors of the pre-Christmas shopping who maintain their joy? They are heroes and heroines of this season. Maybe you're waiting until Christmas morning to open some gifts, to find out who your heroes are.

Christmas shopping does tend to separate the men and women from the boys and girls. Now think with me about some other images of Christmas. Ponder the persons who might need heroes and heroines. Visualize the child running around the mall on Christmas Eve looking for the perfect gift for mommy and daddy. Or should he spend the money on himself? Who would know? the child reasons. Mom and Dad will love the trinket. If they really wanted something valuable, they could buy it. So the child stands at the arcade using gift money for his or her own pleasure. Does this child need a hero?

Picture a child standing in the front door of a home. This disheveled child is gazing into space. He is wondering whether Santa will visit his home this Christmas, or if it will be just another day of poverty and misery? How about those adults sitting in a line of traffic trying to get into a mall? They wonder what to give that special person in their life. Do they need a hero?

Again, look over the shoulder of a mother in the kitchen. Her shoulders are shaking as she sobs at the sink. She knows that her children won't have a Christmas. How can she tell them? How can she face those excited looks of anticipation? They can't read a check registry, but they certainly have learned to read a calendar.

Or transport yourself to a busy airport. Watch that college kid. He is loaded with luggage and book sacks. He is hoping for a standby seat. This was the tough kid who wasn't coming home for the holidays. But now is praying for that last stand-by seat. The lure of mom's cooking and dad's generosity is more powerful than his professed independence. Christmas trees and family are stronger than the urge to be a tough Joe College guy.

Do any of these images resonate in your soul? If so, you can be someone's hero this Christmas. It will only take a moment. After all, the heroic event of the birth of Jesus happened in a **moment**. In a most remarkable moment, God changed human history. The birth was announced to the shepherds, the simpliest of people.

That is why my Christmas heroes are the shepherds. They remind me that God came for people like them, like me . . . people who need not just heroes, but a savior.

HERE IS MY
SERVANT,
WHOM I UPHOLD...

Justice for the Nations

Isaiah 42:1-9

Dec. 30

Behold my servant, whom I uphold; mine elect, in whom my soul delighteth; I have put my spirit upon him: he shall bring forth judgment to the Gentiles.

2 He shall not cry, nor lift up, nor cause his voice to be heard in the street.

3 A bruised reed shall he not break, and the smoking flax shall he not quench: he shall bring forth judgment unto truth.

4 He shall not fail nor be discouraged, till he have set judgment in the earth: and the isles shall wait for his law.

5 Thus saith God the LORD, he that created the heavens, and stretched them out; he that spread forth the earth, and that which cometh out of it; he that giveth breath unto the people upon it, and spirit to them that walk therein:

6 I the LORD have called thee in righteousness, and will hold thine hand, and will keep thee, and give thee for a covenant of the people, for a light of the Gentiles;

7 To open the blind eyes, to bring out the prisoners from the prison, and them that sit in darkness out of the prison house.

8 I am the LORD: that is my name: and my glory will I not give to another, neither my praise to graven images.

9 Behold, the former things are come to pass, and new things do I declare: before they spring forth I tell you of them.

Memory Selection
Isaiah 42:1

Devotional Reading
Isaiah 43:1-7

Background Scripture
Isaiah 42:1-9

This lesson deals with the crowning theme of the prophet Isaiah's message: *one day, God's Servant will come and set things right.*

Several passages in Isaiah 40-55 speak of this Servant. At times, He is identified as Israel; and at other times as a Person who will restore Israel's fortunes and provide a system of justice for Gentiles as well. As we shall see, the New Covenant Scriptures point to Jesus, the Messiah, as the final fulfillment of these Servant prophecies.

The present text reminds us that the Servant calls us to be concerned not just with personal salvation but with justice for those who have been wronged by imperfect human systems, and with healing for those who have been wounded by Satan in a fallen world. Standing for such rightness in a world of wrong, we not only identify the Servant, but identify ourselves *with* Him as well.

ഇരു

Citing examples of gross injustice is a good way to begin this lesson on God's Coming Servant who would bring justice to the world. The leader and class members might mention the paupers in 18th-century England who were shipped to Australia for life imprisonment for stealing a loaf of bread . . . cases of racial discrimination . . . the American Indians' loss of land in the Westward Expansion . . . recent DNA evidence proving the innocence of some who had received the death penalty . . . older workers illegally fired because of age.

Alternately, use the quips in the "No Justice" section on page 177 to introduce the lesson. The point is that Isaiah predicts that one day God's Servant will bring healing and justice. Christians seen the fulfillment of such prophecies in Jesus Christ. It remains for His followers to stand with Him in upholding justice in their own time.

Teaching Outline	Daily Bible Readings	
I. Traits of the Servant—1-4	**Mon.**	Good News of Great Joy Luke 2:8-14
A. Personal traits and mission, 1	**Tue.**	Amazing Announcement Luke 2:15-20
B. Gentle demeanor, 2-3		
C. Firm determination, 4	**Wed.**	A Light of Revelation Luke 2:25-35
II. Commission of the Servant, 5-7	**Thu.**	Sing a New Song! Isaiah 42:10-17
A. Commissioner's credentials, 5		
B. Call and Covenant, 6-7	**Fri.**	Israel's Blindness Isaiah 42:18-25
III. Authority Behind the Servant, 8-9	**Sat.**	Called by Name Isaiah 43:1-7
A. The One God, 8		
B. The only Creator, 9	**Sun.**	The One and Only Savior Isaiah 43:8-15

Verse by Verse

I. Traits of the Servant—1-4
A. Personal traits and mission, 1

1 Behold my servant, whom I uphold; mine elect, in whom my soul delighteth; I have put my spirit upon him: he shall bring forth judgment to the Gentiles.

Although the prophet Isaiah lived in the sixth century B.C., the scene here jumps ahead some 150 years to Babylon, where the southern kingdom of Judah has been taken into captivity. Some scholars believe the scene is described by a later author who wrote in Isaiah's name, while others believe the original Isaiah was empowered to see these events in the future.

Ironically, God allowed His people to be conquered because of their widespread immorality, idolatry, and injustice. Now they are slaves, experiencing injustice themselves; but God shows that He has not totally abandoned them and that through a special Servant He will bring judgment upon their Gentile captors, as well as justice from which all nations will benefit.

This "Servant" is often identified as the nation of Israel itself (as in 41:8). If we had no other guide for identifying Him, we would interpret this verse to mean that God had chosen Israel to model justice for the Gentiles. However, the New Testament applies several of the Servant passages to Jesus as the Messiah. Matthew confirms Jesus' "justice" in healing a man despite His critics objecting that it should not be done on the Sabbath by citing this very verse (Matt. 12:18-21).

We can therefore conclude that while the nation of Israel was God's "Servant" in bringing the Messiah into the world, its role became personified in Jesus, God's Servant *par excellence*. (The supreme example showing that Jesus is the Servant of Isaiah is in His role on the Cross, suffering for our sins—Isaiah 53:4-12 and Mark 15:28.)

B. Gentle demeanor, 2-3

2 He shall not cry, nor lift up, nor cause his voice to be heard in the street.

3 A bruised reed shall he not break, and the smoking flax shall he not quench: he shall bring forth judgment unto truth.

In contrast to attempts to bring peace and justice through violence, God's Coming Servant would bring His just "revolution" about with gentleness and in peace. This was why many in Jesus' day would not accept Him as Messiah—He refused to take up arms against the Romans. Worst of all, He challenged His followers to love their enemies, and "turn the other cheek." He made His way through life as gently as a man walking through rushes so carefully that he does not break tender reeds that were already bent. He would pass by a smoking torchlight so carefully that the brush of His garments would not snuff it out.

C. Firm determination, 4

4 He shall not fail nor be discouraged, till he have set judgment in the earth: and the isles shall wait for his law.

The gentle nature of the Servant described above is not to be mistaken as weakness. His peaceful methods are shored up by inner strength and strong determination. Although He will be put to death on a Cross without resisting, His resurrection will prove the power of His gentleness. Although societies throughout the world that are built on the Servant's teachings have surely proved to be more just than those who ignore them, the full extent of His influence will not be revealed until the end of time. Meanwhile, the Servant's followers are called to take His just system to the far-flung "isles" and nations.

II. Commission of the Servant, 5-7
A. Commissioner's credentials, 5

5 Thus saith God the LORD, he that created the heavens, and stretched them out; he that spread forth the earth, and that which cometh out of it; he that giveth breath unto the people upon it, and spirit to them that walk therein:

In verses 1-4 God is the speaker; here, the speaker is the prophet. He is concerned first to quote God on the important question, *Under whose authority will the Coming Servant judge the nations?* God replies: *On the authority of Him who created them, and the land they occupy.* This verse contains the important philosophical principle that faith in God is the most solid basis for civil justice and political morality. He who "giveth breath unto the people" knows better than anyone else what principles should guide them.

B. Call and Covenant, 6-7

6 I the LORD have called thee in righteousness, and will hold thine hand, and will keep thee, and give thee for a covenant of the people, for a light of the Gentiles;

7 To open the blind eyes, to bring out the prisoners from the prison, and them that sit in darkness out of the prison house.

Remembering the significance of the word "LORD" written in capitals and small capitals leads to a second confirmation of the Servant's authority. "LORD" is the "Tetragrammaton," or four-letter name YHWH, or Yahweh, the name held to be so holy by the Jews who copied the Scriptures that they would not pronounce it. When they came to the term in Scripture they would say *"Adonai,"* Hebrew for "Lord"; hence the way it is written here. We can count on the Servant's righteousness because

He is sent by Yahweh, who personifies righteousness.

Again, the fact that Jesus is ultimately the Servant referred to here is confirmed by the New Testament. When old Simeon, the devout Jew awaiting the Messiah, was told that the infant Jesus was indeed the One, he quoted this very verse, recognizing that he had finally seen the "light to lighten the Gentiles" (Luke 2:32).

Note that the Servant's commission is in the form of a *covenant*, reminding us of the prophet Jeremiah's prediction that Messiah would bring with Him a new covenant (Jer. 31:31-33). Specifically, this "promise-law" from God is that mankind can discover, in the Servant-Messiah, the healing of body and soul and the justice we long for if we will but follow Him. Obviously this too has elements that will be finally fulfilled only at the end of time.

Until then, the Servant's followers are to work for the health and justice of society as a sign that they live under this covenant. This fact is emphasized by the apostle Paul, who takes a stunning step in applying this Servant-prophecy to his and Barnabas' missionary efforts. When Jews hardened their hearts against the message that Jesus was the Messiah, Paul quoted Isaiah 42:6 to justify turning to the Gentiles and sharing the message with them (see Acts 13:46-47). This identification of the Church's outreach with the Servant passages in Isaiah reveals to Christians their own kinship with the Servant Himself, and comprises a mission and reason for existing that cannot be over-emphasized.

III. Authority Behind the Servant, 8-9
A. The One God, 8

8 I am the LORD: that is my name: and my glory will I not give to another, neither my praise to graven images.

Our passage closes with another affirmation that Yahweh Himself is sending the Servant to establish justice. Refusing to share divine glory with "another" is a not-too-subtle swipe at the historical tendency of Israel to give glory to idols. It also reminds us of the principle of "ethical monotheism." Grounding our behavior on the belief that God is One, not many, gives it a consistency of motive and action that is impossible when life is directed by many gods. Thus, holding that there is only One God is not just a sign of doctrinal orthodoxy; it affects in concrete and personal ways the justice a society renders to its people.

B. The only Creator, 9

9 Behold, the former things are come to pass, and new things do I declare: before they spring forth I tell you of them.

How can the prophet's hearers know that the Servant will perform the commission God is giving Him? Because He is being sent by the God who predicted events in the past which came true. This is the God who promised to deliver His people from Egypt, who created the path through the Sea for their escape. We can therefore believe He will also do the "new things" He has in mind for all people through His Servant-Messiah.

Evangelistic Emphasis

Tim Allen's character on the show *Home Improvement* is a comic reminder of how some people want to do evangelism. The Tim Allen character was always looking for something with "more power." The more powerful the tool the more effective the tool, was his underlying life assumption.

I wonder if we don't approach the idea of evangelism with that same kind of mentality. We have a mass marketing approach to leading people to Jesus Christ. If we can find something big, well attended, and loud, we may think that this is the quickest way to make a "conversion."

The Suffering Servant was pictured as being a gentle person. While this servant had all the power of God available to him, he approached others in gentle kindness. The servant was not loud nor forceful in his ministry.

The good news is the God comes to us not in loud forceful ways. God comes to us as the "still small voice." In our ministry to the world, we should follow that pattern of quiet gentleness as we seek to show others God's love in Jesus Christ.

A gentle ministry will be a personal ministry. It is hard to be gentle when you are trying to herd a big audience to the altar. It is easy to be gentle when you are talking to a friend over a cup of coffee about the love of God in Jesus Christ.

৪)এ

Behold my servant, whom I uphold; mine elect, in whom my soul delighteth; I have put my spirit upon him: he shall bring forth judgment to the Gentiles.—*Isaiah 42:1*

While this verse speaks of the Suffering Servant and formed the tone for Jesus' ministry, the words also apply to you as you serve God.

We serve God in a fast-paced, quickly changing world. The source of our strength for ministry comes from God. He has placed His Spirit upon us so that we might live for Him and serve Him.

The church is constantly discovering new ways of sharing the "old, old story of Jesus and His love." It is the Spirit of God resting on the church that is responsible for those discoveries. God is still active with His people.

As long as there is ministry and service needed, God will be providing His Spirit to answer those needs. This means that we don't serve God alone; God is working with us as we are ministering for Him. Our source of strength for service is an eternally available resource.

Weekday Problems

Wendy Williams and Gay McKnight were a study in contrast. They both were from similar backgrounds and families. They did similar work in the same office; but their work was held in very different regard by management.

Wendy was always working late, making sure that every job was done right. It didn't matter that something was given to her beyond a deadline, she would make every effort to make sure the task was accomplished. Wendy was a stickler for details. She expected nothing less than perfection from herself and from others. Even with this kind of drive, people in the office loved her. It seemed that Wendy was always smiling and ready to give a hand.

On the other hand, Gay was sullen. Her work, while done, never showed concern for detail. She could always be counted on to miss a deadline. Gay had a habit of getting a migraine as a deadline approached. Around the office, people stayed away from Gay because she tended to stir up trouble. She was quick to find fault and slow to help. She never understood why Wendy received all the attention while she seemed to be left out of the fun.

One day she confided, "people don't understand what I have to deal with."

*Contrast people who make excuses with those who take responsibility in the area of Christian service and ministry.

No Justice

Joe: I was so poor when I was a boy that I had to wear hand-me-down clothes.
Chloe: So what? Most kids have to do that.
Joe: Yeah, but all I had were older sisters.

* * *

Jill: I *really* came from a poor family.
Bill: How'd you know you were poor?
Jill: Every time I'd pass a neighbor they'd say, "There goes Jill. Pity her poor family."

* * *

Nick: I caught a fish that weighed 250 pounds!
Rick: That's nothing. I hooked a lamp while I was fishing. It turned out to be 100 years old, and the light was still burning!
Nick: We gotta quit lying. I'll take 200 pounds off the fish if you'll blow out the light.

* * *

Shoe salesman, after dragging out 24 boxes for his customer to try on: Mind if I take a break? Your feet are killing me!

This Lesson in Your Life

This lesson lends itself to a discussion of "servant leadership." This phrase is being used to describe a new generation of Christian leaders. A servant leader is one who has experienced suffering. When he talks about the power of God to heal and deliver, it is not theoretical. It is personal. His suffering may take many forms, but the result is that multiplies his compassion for God's people. Suffering is the school in which this kind of leader learns to trust God and to look to Him for power and comfort.

A servant leader is one who has a sense of God's calling in his life. We are attracted to people who have vision for ministry. The great leaders are those people who seem to be able to see beyond the trends of their day and look to the possibilities of the future. They also have the gift of being able to articulate clearly that vision to others. A servant leader who can't communicate his vision is only a dreamer. Dreamers rarely are able to motivate people to deepen their discipleship.

A servant leader has a clear understanding of the power of the Holy Spirit in his life. The Spirit produces the fruits that make leadership winsome. A Spirit-filled servant leader will draw people to his leadership. His spirituality points beyond himself to the Christ living within him.

This servant leader may be dynamic but is also gentle. The leadership of the suffering servant does not harm the weak. It is the kind of leadership that brings everyone on the journey of discovery. It is the kind of leadership that goes about its business in a quiet way.

The task for the Church is twofold. When it becomes obvious that God has sent servant-leadership to a congregation we have a choice. We can follow or get out of the way. One of the great renewal movements in the church today is the purposeful extinction of committees. Having their visions refined in committee has thwarted many potential church leaders. When we understand that servant leadership is in our midst our response should involve prayer for that leader. Too often we still don't understand that people are looking for community and that the church seems capable of offering only committees.

The second task before the Church is to call out servant leaders. Ask the question of your class. "How long has it been since someone from this congregation has been ordained in the ministry?" If leadership for the next generation is not being called out from your congregation, you must ask some tough questions as to why this is so.

Each of us could become a servant leader at any time. God is the One who issues the call. Is He calling you?

STRAIGHT

1. Why did the Lord rejoice in His servant?
The servant was God's elect, and His Spirit dwelt within the servant.

2. What do you think it means that the servant "shall not cry, not lift up, nor cause his voice to be heard in the street?"
The words of the servant will be gentle words that are softly spoken, calling attention only to God.

3. What two images of brokenness indicate the gentleness of the preaching and the work of the servant?
The preaching would not harm the bruised reed or the dimly burning wick.

4. How long would the ministry of the servant last?
Until he establishes justice in the earth and the coastlands wait for His law.

5. How is the image found in verse 4 true of the ministry of Jesus Christ?
Discuss ways that Christ can continue to minister through His people.

6. Verse 5 pictures God as One who did what?
God was a creator God. He formed the earth and all life upon the earth.

7. How does verse 6 picture God?
As nurturing and protecting His people because of His righteousness.

8. How are these two images (creator and righteous protector) related?
God would not allow His creation to be destroyed. The ultimate act of nurture and protection was sending His Son to us.

9. What familiar theme is sounded again in verse 7?
The Lord would bring light to the nations, open the eyes of the blind, and set the prisoners free.

10. According to verse 9, when did God make declarations to His people?
God declared things to His people before they happened. If the future is good, we are promised it will happen. If bad, we are warned.

The servant of Isaiah 42 was a person of kind words. He spoke in such a manner as to be almost inaudible. His words did not thunder across the creation. They did not bring damage to the fragile souls who heard them.

We learn in this passage that God's words are gentle yet powerful. We need to be reminded of the same truth about our words. Verse 5 of the text indicates God's creative power. He brought all of the cosmos into being as well as all who inhabit that cosmos. From Genesis, we learn that He created His universe with a word. He literally spoke creation into being. Verse 9 indicates that God had both warned and promised His people certain things. Both the warnings and the promises came into being because God spoke them. While gentle, when His word goes forth, it does so with the power to bring about all that was spoken.

While all of that might sound rather distant and theoretical, we have the same power in our words. They too have the ability both to create and to destroy. Remember the story of Jesus and the Roman Centurion? The Centurion's daughter was ill and he went to Jesus seeking help. He told the Lord, "Just speak the word and she will be healed." And sure enough, just by speaking the word Jesus healed the girl.

On the other side of the coin, words are destructive. An insidious type of real abuse is verbal. We all have painful memories of times we were "dressed-down" or "chewed-out." Even the words to describe those events bring about their own set of images. Think about times when words hurt you. Now the lesson we learn is that our words can hurt as much as they can heal. In many cultures words are seen as living things. I'm not sure they are not. Once a word is out, it is out forever. The damage a word can do can last for a lifetime.

You can illustrate from stories you know in which people were hung with words, words that became negative realities in their lives. Words such as "drunk," "loose," "lazy," or "incompetent" have been hung on persons. While they might not have been true, those labels have the ability to become true. The apostle James talked about the tongue as a fire that could destroy the whole body.

God used His words carefully. Maybe you have noticed that God is often silent. Our Lord might have wanted us to learn the lesson of your face. If you will look in a mirror, you will discover you have two ears and one mouth. You should use your ears and mouth in that proportion— listening twice as much as you speak! Be like God, and remember that silence is always better than a word misspoken.

Lesson 6

Good News for All Nations

Isaiah 60:1-3; 61:1-6

Arise, shine; for thy light is come, and the glory of the LORD is risen upon thee.

2 For, behold, the darkness shall cover the earth, and gross darkness the people: but the LORD shall arise upon thee, and his glory shall be seen upon thee.

3 And the Gentiles shall come to thy light, and kings to the brightness of thy rising.

61:1 The Spirit of the Lord GOD is upon me; because the LORD hath anointed me to preach good tidings unto the meek; he hath sent me to bind up the brokenhearted, to proclaim liberty to the captives, and the opening of the prison to them that are bound;

2 To proclaim the acceptable year of the LORD, and the day of vengeance of our God; to comfort all that mourn;

3 To appoint unto them that mourn in Zion, to give unto them beauty for ashes, the oil of joy for mourning, the garment of praise for the spirit of heaviness; that they might be called trees of righteousness, the planting of the LORD, that he might be glorified.

4 And they shall build the old wastes, they shall raise up the former desolations, and they shall repair the waste cities, the desolations of many generations.

5 And strangers shall stand and feed your flocks, and the sons of the alien shall be your plowmen and your vinedressers.

6 But ye shall be named the Priests of the LORD: men shall call you the Ministers of our God: ye shall eat the riches of the Gentiles, and in their glory shall ye boast yourselves.

Jan. 6

Memory Selection
Isaiah 60:1

Devotional Reading
Isaiah 60:17-22

Background Scripture
Isaiah 60–61

A Golden Age is coming for the People of God. When will this Age come? Do the prophecies in this lesson refer to the Messianic Age brought in by Jesus, or to the "new heavens and new earth" that are to accompany His Second Coming? What do the terms "dark-ness" and "light" refer to?

The present approach assumes that such questions may have three sets of answers. (1) The prophecies originally applied to the Restoration of the Jews from Babylonian captivity. (2) The New Testament applies the prophecies to the Messianic Age that began with the coming of Jesus. (3) The ultimate fulfillment of these glad predictions await Christ's Second Coming.

୫୦ଓଽ

The following object lesson can introduce the principle of "multiple fulfillment" of prophecy employed in this lesson.

On a chalkboard or whiteboard, draw three mountains of similar shape, the second and third partially obscured by the one in front—like this:

Now ask group members to describe the mountains. ("A level place is on the left side; the lower left side of the mountain is steeper than the right.") Since the descriptions are similar, note that a person in front of the first mountain might describe it, while those observing from afar might think the description fits the second or the third.

The Isaiah prophecies in this lesson may be viewed like these mountains. The first represents the glad return of the Jews to the Promised Land after Babylonian captivity. The second stands for the Golden Age introduced by Christ; and the third for heaven, the most golden age of all.

Teaching Outline	Daily Bible Readings

I. Arise and Shine!—60:1-3
  A. From darkness to light, 1-2
  B. From Jews to Gentiles, 3
II. Anointed to Preach and Serve—61:1-4
  A. Messianic ministry, 1-2
  B. Beauty for ashes, 3
  C. Building anew, 4
III. Acknowledging Debt to Jewry—5-6
	Mon. Messianic Mission
	      Luke 4:14-21
	Tue. God's People Will Prosper
	      Isaiah 60:4-9
	Wed. Open Gates
	      Isaiah 60:10-15
	Thu. God Will Be Your Light
	      Isaiah 60:17-22
	Fri. Anointed for Good News
	      Isaiah 61:1-7
	Sat. Righteousness in the Nations
	      Isaiah 61:8-11
	Sun. Worshipers from Afar
	      Matthew 2:1-12

Verse by Verse

I. Arise and Shine!—60:1-3
A. From darkness to light, 1-2

1 Arise, shine; for thy light is come, and the glory of the LORD is risen upon thee.

2 For, behold, the darkness shall cover the earth, and gross darkness the people: but the LORD shall arise upon thee, and his glory shall be seen upon thee.

Once again, our studies in Isaiah find the people of God in Babylonian captivity, which occurred in 521 B.C. Since Isaiah himself died more than a century earlier, some scholars think a later prophet, writing in the spirit of Isaiah but during the Captivity, described this prediction that the "darkness" of captivity will be overwhelmed by the "light" of the Restoration to Israel led by Ezra and Nehemiah. Others say that God inspired the original Isaiah, who wrote the first part of the book, to peer into the future and see both the burden of slavery in Babylon and the fact that the Restoration would occur.

The books of Ezra and Nehemiah provide an account of the Restoration, which occurred some 70 years after captivity. Yet this account does not seem as monumentally glorious as the present text implies. Also, it is remark-able that the Jews who returned did not engage in extensive missionary activity to spread "the light" throughout the earth. Many scholars therefore see a secondary fulfillment of this passage in the coming of the Messiah, and the spread of the light of the Gospel. Thus, as in the case of the prophecy in 61:1-4, this text forecasts the Golden Age ushered in by the Messiah.

B. From Jews to Gentiles, 3

3 And the Gentiles shall come to thy light, and kings to the brightness of thy rising.

The application of the passage to the Messianic Age is strengthened by this reference to the Gentiles being included among the People of God. The story of the Restoration in Ezra and Nehemiah actually portrays Gentiles as opposing the work of rebuilding Jerusalem and a Jewish nation in Palestine (see Ezra 4:1-6). As noted in Lesson 5, the New Testament actually applies the concept of the Jews as a "light to the Gentiles" to the coming of Jesus, the Jewish Messiah, and the spread of His message by the apostles (Luke 2:32; Acts 13:46-47).

II. Anointed to Preach and Serve— 61:1-4

A. Messianic ministry, 1-2

1 The Spirit of the Lord GOD is upon me; because the LORD hath anointed me to preach good tidings unto the meek; he hath sent me to bind up the brokenhearted, to proclaim liberty to the captives, and the opening of the prison to them that are bound;

2 To proclaim the acceptable year of the LORD, and the day of vengeance of our God; to comfort all that mourn;

It is easy to imagine an Old Testament prophet using this language to proclaim hope to God's people by envisioning their liberation from the Babylonian captivity. While this is probably the primary application of the passage, Christians must not ignore how it is later applied to Jesus.

This occurs, significantly, at the very beginning of Christ's ministry. At a Sabbath-day service in the synagogue in Nazareth, Jesus is asked to read from the Scriptures. He deliberately selects the present verse, reads it, and says, "This day is this scripture fulfilled in your ears" (Luke 4:18). Now the "broken-hearted" (vs. 1) and those "that mourn" (vs. 2) become those who mourn the sad state of Jewry and long for the purity of the Kingdom of God (Matt. 5:4). The "captives" are not just Jews under the rule of Babylon but those who are imprisoned to sin. The "acceptable year of the Lord" is not just the Restoration to Palestine but the inauguration of the Messianic Age; and "the day of vengeance" becomes the prophecy, and the eventual fulfillment at the Second Coming, that those who deliberately spurn Messiah's message will be punished.

B. Beauty for ashes, 3

3 To appoint unto them that mourn in Zion, to give unto them beauty for ashes, the oil of joy for mourning, the garment of praise for the spirit of heaviness; that they might be called trees of righteousness, the planting of the LORD, that he might be glorified.

Again the prophet turns to those who mourn because of the sad state of affairs among God's people. Again employing the principle of "multiple fulfillment," these are (1) the remnant in Jerusalem, or among "Zion" in captivity, who lament the fact that the people's faithlessness has resulted in bondage; (2) those who mourned their sins in Jesus' day (Matt. 5:4); and (3) those at the end of time who mourn the sin that brings on the destructive wrath of God.

A strong case can especially be made for the second application in the phrase "beauty for ashes." What more apt description could be found for the grace of God revealed through Jesus Christ? As sinners we can bring Him only the burned-out remains of wasted lives; but as we offer our lives to Him, we receive in exchange the beauty of a new creation in Christ (see Rom. 6:3-6; 2 Cor. 5:17).

C. Building anew, 4

4 And they shall build the old wastes, they shall raise up the former desolations, and they shall repair the waste cities, the desolations of many generations.

Now the focus seems to be on the Jews' Restoration to the Promised Land, as the prophecy's emphasis goes back and forth among the three possible applications cited in the present approach. The prophet knows the devastation that befell Judah as their enemies laid waste the capital, Jerusalem, and surrounding cites. Empowered by the Spirit, however, he sees these citadels rebuilt; and in the spirit or rebuilding perhaps envisions also the reconstruction of a spirit of obedience in the hearts of the people.

III. Acknowledging Debt to Jewry–5-6

5 And strangers shall stand and feed your flocks, and the sons of the alien shall be your plowmen and your vinedressers.

6 But ye shall be named the Priests of the LORD: men shall call you the Ministers of our God: ye shall eat the riches of the Gentiles, and in their glory shall ye boast yourselves.

This part of the prophecy likely belongs only to the second and third "phases" of the three fulfillments envisioned here. A long tradition of Christian interpretation sees these verses as a description of Gentile indebtedness to the Jews for the benefits of the Messiah's rule. In this view, "aliens" (vs. 5) or Gentiles (vs. 6) bring food and other blessings to Jews as God's priests or ministers, just as the Levites were served under the Old Covenant. The commentator Matthew Williams, a standard source of several generations ago, said of this passage:

The wealth and honour of the Gentile converts shall redound to the benefit and credit of the church, v. 6. The Gentiles shall be brought into the church. Those that were strangers shall become fellow-citizens with the saints; and with themselves they shall bring all they have, to be devoted to the glory of God and used in his service; and the priests, the Lord's ministers, shall have the advantage of it. It will be a great strengthening and quickening, as well as a comfort and encouragement, to all good Christians, to see the Gentiles serving the interests of God's kingdom. (*PC Study Bible, no page ref.*)

Those who support this interpretation point to Ephesians 2:12, which also refers to Gentiles as "aliens." Further, in Christ's Kingdom, all Christians have been "named the priests of the Lord" or "holy priesthood" (1 Pet. 2:5). Yet Gentile members of this Kingdom are to honor the Jews as God's original root, of which Gentiles are branches (Rom. 11:16-20).

Evangelistic Emphasis

This is the first lesson of 2002. Could it be that this is the "year of the Lord's favor?" The coming Messiah was to proclaim the "year of the Lord's favor." As you face this year to come, how are you looking at it?

This is a complete year with possibilities and opportunities. In this year you will experience both birth and death. It happens all around us. You will experience both joy and tears. You will experience both blessing and suffering. You will have all of these experiences because they are common to the human experience.

For some people this year will represent the year of their rebirth. They will look back on 2002 as a time when they met Jesus as Savior and Lord. They will look back on this as the culmination of the work of the Spirit in leading them to faith in Christ. They will see this year as the beginning of their discipleship pilgrimage.

What has all of this to do with you?

Will you be remembered as a person through whom God decided to do His bidding? You might be remembered as the Sunday school teacher who prayed with others and stood by them. You might be remembered as that person whose act of kindness modeled the love of Christ.

God will do something great though you this year if you let Him. Will you help God proclaim the "year of the Lord's favor?"

%%

Memory Selection

Arise, shine; for thy light is come, and the glory of the LORD is risen upon thee.—*Isaiah 60:1*

The Hebrews had been in captivity for years. The daily grind of that experience had dulled their hope of ever returning to their homeland. Jerusalem lay in ruins and existed only in their memory. It appeared to the Hebrews as though God had forgotten them.

This verse is a powerful affirmation to claim God's promises. He promised to return the people to their land. He promised that redemption was coming to the Hebrews in captivity. This verse is a clarion call for the people of that day to get up and claim the victory that had been provided to them by God.

Today we would tell someone that his or her time to "shine" has come. In our walk with the Lord, there are times when we are to grasp the moment and give our all for the kingdom.

When God has called you, are you willing to stand up and say, "Here I am Lord, send me?

Weekday Problems

There is an old story told of a man who was caught in the a flood. He was very devoted to God, and was certain that God would deliver him from any harm during this flood. The floodwaters continued to rise and eventually forced the man to stand on the roof of his house. Even standing that far above the ground the waters continued to rise.

As the waters reached his knees a man came by in a rowboat and offered the fellow on the roof a ride to safety. The endangered man graciously replied, "No thank you, God will take care of me." The fellow in the rowboat left this staunch believer on the roof.

As the waters rose to the man's waist, a motorboat happened by. Again the man was offered rescue, but again he refused, saying "God will take care of me." A helicopter showed up about the time the water got to the man's neck, but he sent the helicopter away, saying again, "God will take care of me."

Eventually the man drowned. When he arrived at the Pearly Gates he was furious. He told Saint Peter, "How could you let me drown like that?"

Saint Peter replied, "I don't see why you are angry. We sent a rowboat, a powerboat, and a helicopter. What more did you want us to do?"

*How do we participate in our "working out our own salvation"?

*What is an appropriate response to God's call to "Arise and shine?"

Pop Quiz

Q: What would you get if you crossed a porcupine with a cow?
A: A steak with a built-in toothpick.
* * *

Q: What animal can jump higher than a house?
A: Any animal. A house can't jump.
* * *

Q: What did one casket say to the other casket?
A: Is that you coffin?
* * *

Q: On which side does a chicken have more feathers?
A: On the outside.
* * *

Q: What would you get if your crossed a flea with a rabbit?
A: A Bug's Bunny.
* * *

Q: Why do cows wear bells?
A. Because their horns don't work.

This Lesson in Your Life

There is an adage about everyone getting the chance to be famous for 15 minutes. With modern media, many people who should not be famous at all seem to get their 15 minutes in the sun. I would never begrudge someone fame and fortune, but I have a problem when what brings them fame is not something of which they should be proud.

For a minute, allow me a "rant" about the afternoon television shows hosted by "one-named" people. At writing we had "Oprah," "Jerry," "Sally," and others. Their talk shows consist of people who have no business being in public without men in white coats standing close by, whining about being "misunderstood." These same shows pander to humanity's basest desires. They advertise for people who have certain kinds of problems to call their show and sign up. People, it seems, will do almost anything to have their time in the sun, or at least to have a moment in the television spotlight. Things normal people would hide in a closet, these persons go on television and reveal to all. You would think they are fulfilling the words of Jesus" "Arise and shine for your light has come."

Children of God are not called to a moment of fame but to a moment of faithfulness. My hope is that if I ever get my 15 minutes it will be a time when I can be faithful to the Lord. I am not worried about my fame.

How about you?

"Arise and shine for your light has come." In one sense this is a call to get busy. Our time to "shine" has come. The Church in the 21st century must be a Church firmly grounded in the traditions of the past while boldly taking risks to insure our future. The Bible uses the word "crisis" time to describe these days in which we live. Every generation of Christians has lived in its own "crisis" time. Each generation has faced tough decisions and uncertain futures, but it also seems that God provides each generation with the resources to remain faithful in the times in which it lives.

Our time to "arise and shine" is now. God has placed His light in our world for those living in darkness to see. He has placed His light on us for the world to see. This is our time not to seek fame, but to be found faithful in His service.

In your faith community, what are the issues that must be faced head-on to insure that your witness remains vital? What obstacles must be overcome? What new skills must be acquired or talents learned in order that your church can stay on the cutting edge of ministry?

On the personal level, how will you respond to "your time" in God's spotlight? As the year 2002 unfolds, do you believe that this will be the "year of the Lord's favor?"

STRAIGHT

1. According to Isaiah, what was the source of the light that was shining in the believer?
The source of the light was the glory of the Lord.

2. What effect would the light have in the darkened world?
The nations of the world as well as their kings would be drawn to the light.

3. After the nations and the kings were drawn to the light, what other group would be attracted to this light?
The children of the Hebrews in captivity would be drawn to the light.

4. Why would the Messiah preach glad tidings to the poor and release to the captives?
The Spirit of the Lord had come upon the Messiah, leading Him into this ministry with these groups.

5. What do Isaiah 61:1 and Luke 4:18-19 have in common?
In Luke 4 Jesus quotes Isaiah 61:1.

6. Why do you think Jesus chose the words from Isaiah to describe himself and His ministry?
Jesus' concept of His ministry was that of a servant ministry as opposed to being a kingly kind of ministry.

7. Describe the state of the people prior to the ministry of the Messiah.
They were in sitting in ashes and mourning. Their spirits were faint.

8. Once the Messiah came, how would the attitude of the people change?
They would have garlands rather than ashes, oil of gladness instead of mourning, and a mantle of praise rather than a faint spirit.

9. What would these renewed persons do?
They would build up the ancient ruins and repair the ruined cities.

10. When would these blessings occur?
Isaiah didn't give any definite time-frame. However, we know these words were fulfilled in the life of Christ.

A friend of mine was telling about a golf experience recently. He said he was playing with two other men he didn't know on an exclusive golf course. One of the fellows was a good player. The other fellow was not much of a golfer, but he could use profanity well. He would curse when he hit a bad shot. When he would miss a short putt, he would curse. It was both amusing and embarrassing for the other two golfers.

On the seventh hole, the trio began to talk about their work. My friend explained that he was a computer software salesman. The other fellow said he was an electrical engineer. Then the foul-mouthed man blushed, hung his head, and said, "I hate to admit it, but I am a preacher."

Beyond the amusement of this story is the message we all must hear and bear. We are accidental witnesses for or against Jesus Christ. Accidental, because most of our witnessing is done when we think people are not watching.

As we think about our time to "shine" we must understand that sometimes we are "shining" when we are unaware of it. People see Jesus in us or fail to see Him during moments when we are unaware they are watching. The world is not interested in our many words about God's love in Jesus. The world needs to see our faithful and loving actions as we reflect the love of Jesus.

The Hebrews showed God's glory in the way they lived in captivity and returned from it. They either affirmed their belief in an all-powerful God, or confirmed what the pagans said about Him. People all around us are looking for excuses not to believe in or follow Christ. Don't you give them the excuse they need! Live as though people were watching you every moment of your life, because they are. I have a friend who tells me that I should dance like "no one is looking" and live my faith as though "everyone were looking."

Our witness must be an incarnation of the Spirit of God. As Christ brought "good tidings to the afflicted, bound up the brokenhearted and proclaimed liberty to the captives" (Isa. 61:1), our witness should consist of the same actions. We are being watched to see if our bold words about loving Jesus give rise to bold actions of love on behalf of those who are outcasts. The test of our faith is never our words but our actions.

In this coming year, make your resolutions not just in terms of your life, but in terms of others. Plan to be involved with people. You will discover the joys of service that cannot be explained, only experienced. Reach out to the lost, to the sinner, to the outcast with the love of God in Christ Jesus. As you do so, you will notice that your witness is being watched. The glory of God is will shine through you as you seek to bring light into a darkened life.

In 2002, pray that the Lord will show you the people around whom your light needs to shine.

Seek the Lord

Isaiah 55:1-13

Ho, every one that thirsteth, come ye to the waters, and he that hath no money; come ye, buy, and eat; yea, come, buy wine and milk without money and without price.

2 Wherefore do ye spend money for that which is not bread? and your labour for that which satisfieth not? hearken diligently unto me, and eat ye that which is good, and let your soul delight itself in fatness.

3 Incline your ear, and come unto me: hear, and your soul shall live; and I will make an everlasting covenant with you, even the sure mercies of David.

4 Behold, I have given him for a witness to the people, a leader and commander to the people.

5 Behold, thou shalt call a nation that thou knowest not, and nations that knew not thee shall run unto thee because of the Lord thy God, and for the Holy One of Israel; for he hath glorified thee.

6 Seek ye the Lord while he may be found, call ye upon him while he is near:

7 Let the wicked forsake his way, and the unrighteous man his thoughts: and let him return unto the Lord, and he will have mercy upon him; and to our God, for he will abundantly pardon.

8 For my thoughts are not your thoughts, neither are your ways my ways, saith the Lord.

9 For as the heavens are higher than the earth, so are my ways higher than your ways, and my thoughts than your thoughts.

10 For as the rain cometh down, and the snow from heaven, and returneth not thither, but watereth the earth, and maketh it bring forth and bud, that it may give seed to the sower, and bread to the eater:

11 So shall my word be that goeth forth out of my mouth: it shall not return unto me void, but it shall accomplish that which I please, and it shall prosper in the thing whereto I sent it.

12 For ye shall go out with joy, and be led forth with peace: the mountains and the hills shall break forth before you into singing, and all the trees of the field shall clap their hands.

13 Instead of the thorn shall come up the fir tree, and instead of the brier shall come up the myrtle tree: and it shall be to the Lord for a name, for an everlasting sign that shall not be cut off.

Jan. 13

Memory Selection
Isaiah 55:6

Devotional Reading
Psalm 85:4-9

Background Scripture
Isaiah 55

Previous lessons in Isaiah have painted a rosy picture of a "Golden Age" awaiting the faithful. At times, the prophecies seem to describe the Restoration of the Jews to Israel. At other times the scenes depict the Messianic Age begun when Christ would come into the world. Still other portraits seem to be of heaven itself.

The focus in today's lesson includes this view of good times to come, but also qualifies it significantly. Here God recognizes that what we *want* is not always what we *need*. He insists that the Golden Age He has in mind can be appreciated only by those who seek Him on His terms. He warns against dissipating our search for happiness on the temporal values when He can provide eternal joy. Ask members of your study group if they are ready to depend totally upon God—which is the price of entering into His glory.

ഇരു

Sometimes we marvel at how God's teachings make such "common" sense. At other times, however, we are drawn to confess that His thoughts, as this lesson states, "are not [our] thoughts."

The aspect of God's "otherness" in this lesson can be introduced effectively by asking group members to discuss events in life, or teachings in God's Word, that prompt them to wonder, to worship, to express awe, to ask hard questions. Perhaps it's the birth of a child, the beauty of creation, or the awesome power of "natural" events such as tornadoes, earthquakes and volcanoes. Perhaps we marvel at God's providence when He transforms evil into good, or want to ask Him why good people suffer evil.

Lead into the lesson by noting that it points to a Golden Age ahead for believers, but that since God's ways are above our ways, He insists on defining what that involves.

Teaching Outline	Daily Bible Readings	
I. Eternal Values—1-2	**Mon.**	I Sought; God Answered Psalm 34:1-10
A. Priceless principles, 1	**Tue.**	Thirsting for God Psalm 63:1-8
B. Sound investments, 2		
II. Everlasting Covenant-3-5	**Wed.**	Seek God's Strength Psalm 105:1-7
A. The mercies of David, 3-4		
B. Inclusion of the Gentiles, 5	**Thu.**	The Holy One Redeems Isaiah 54:4-8
III. Different Direction—6-11	**Fri.**	Heritage for God's Servants Isaiah 54:9-17
A. Timely repentance, 6-7		
B. God's otherness, 8-9	**Sat.**	Accept God's Grace Isaiah 55:1-5
C. God's guarantee, 10-11		
IV. Peaceable Kingdom, 12-13	**Sun.**	Return to the Lord Isaiah 55:6-13

Verse by Verse

I. Eternal Values—1-2

A. Priceless principles, 1

1 Ho, every one that thirsteth, come ye to the waters, and he that hath no money; come ye, buy, and eat; yea, come, buy wine and milk without money and without price.

The Jews who had been carried into Babylonian captivity have suffered long enough. The prophet has predicted that God would restore their fortunes; but now it is time to recall why He had allowed them to be captured, and to ask whether they are enough attuned to His ways to accept the free gifts He offers. If they will but commit themselves to Him, He will give living waters and spiritual nourishment so beyond price we cannot buy them. They can be dispensed only by amazing grace.

B. Sound investments, 2

2 Wherefore do ye spend money for that which is not bread? and your labour for that which satisfieth not? hearken diligently unto me, and eat ye that which is good, and let your soul delight itself in fatness.

Had God's people fallen into materialism even in their captivity? Archeologists have discovered evidence of a bank that had been established by Jews in Babylon, perhaps in this period (sixth-to-fifth-century B.C.). Here God asks through the prophet why anyone would devote himself to material goods that do not sustain the spirit. It is all too easy to fall under the scope of the prophet Haggai's judgment: "You have planted much, but have harvested little. You eat, but never have enough. You drink, but never have your fill. You put on clothes, but are not warm. You earn wages, only to put them in a purse with holes in it"(Hag 1:6, NIV).

II. Everlasting Covenant-3-5

A. The mercies of David, 3-4

3 Incline your ear, and come unto me: hear, and your soul shall live; and I will make an everlasting covenant with you, even the sure mercies of David.

4 Behold, I have given him for a witness to the people, a leader and commander to the people.

Abandoning all metaphors, God now uses plain language in a direct appeal for the people to indicate by "listening" (hearing with the intent of obeying) to Him that they want to enter the Golden Age He has awaiting them. He offers to renew the "everlasting covenant" He made with King David, who brought their ancestors into an earlier Golden Age. This pact was God's solemn promise that David's lineage as a king would never die—a promise that the apostle Peter would later say was fulfilled when Jesus ascended to the throne of the Father (Acts 2:29-36).

The prophet speaks in the "prophetic past" of things to come as though they have already occurred. Giving "him" as a witness seems to refer first to David, then by typology to the Messiah, who came of the tribe of Judah and a descendant of David. Both David, whom Scripture says was a man after God's own heart (1 Sam. 13:14), and Jesus bore witness to the world of the love and might of God. David was a commander of literal armies, while Christ led spiritual forces.

B. Inclusion of the Gentiles, 5

5 Behold, thou shalt call a nation that thou knowest not, and nations that knew not thee shall run unto thee because of the Lord thy God, and for the Holy One of Israel; for he hath glorified thee.

From speaking of David and Jesus as "him" the prophetic voice now seems to speak directly to the Servant Messiah, whom the New Testament affirms is spoken of in these sections of Isaiah. In the absence of any significant Jewish mission after the return to Palestine, this prophecy seems to apply to the Kingdom reestablished by Christ and the Gentiles—nations who formerly did not know God but who came to be grafted as branches onto the root of Judaism, through Christ.

III. Different Direction—6-11

A. Timely repentance, 6-7

6 Seek ye the Lord while he may be found, call ye upon him while he is near:

7 Let the wicked forsake his way, and the unrighteous man his thoughts: and let him return unto the Lord, and he will have mercy upon him; and to our God, for he will abundantly pardon.

The prophet turns now to the people themselves with an urgent call to repentance. Although His offer to restore them is a gift of pure grace, the people must accept it with heartfelt willingness to follow where God leads. This simple invitation becomes a confrontation: are the people, who have previously all too easily followed idols, ready now to be true to the true God?

B. God's otherness, 8-9

8 For my thoughts are not your thoughts, neither are your ways my ways, saith the Lord

9 For as the heavens are higher than the earth, so are my ways higher than your ways, and my thoughts than your thoughts.

Now it is time to confront the otherworldly awesomeness of God, as suggested in the section "For a Lively

Start." The books of Ezra and Nehemiah describe the slow and often dangerous progress the people made in rebuilding the walls of Jerusalem. Looking forward to such difficulties, God knows it will be all too human for the people to become discouraged and quit. The task of Restoration would take a people who could confess that it was too great a task for mere humans, but one that could be accomplished if they would but commit their untrustworthy human ways to the divine ways of God.

C. God's guarantee—10-11

10 For as the rain cometh down, and the snow from heaven, and returneth not thither, but watereth the earth, and maketh it bring forth and bud, that it may give seed to the sower, and bread to the eater:

11 So shall my word be that goeth forth out of my mouth: it shall not return unto me void, but it shall accomplish that which I please, and it shall prosper in the thing whereto I sent it.

It is easy to imagine "nay-sayers" among the captives in Babylon—people who would question the truth of the prophet's predictions that God would lavishly bless them if they commit their ways to Him. How can God conquer their doubts? By reminding the people of His faithfulness in the "natural" realm—in sending moisture for a parched earth, and enabling seeds to be nurtured into bread. Surely a God of such grace and power can keep His promise to restore the people if they would commit themselves to His "higher" ways.

IV. Peaceable Kingdom, 12-13

12 For ye shall go out with joy, and be led forth with peace: the mountains and the hills shall break forth before you into singing, and all the trees of the field shall clap their hands.

13 Instead of the thorn shall come up the fir tree, and instead of the brier shall come up the myrtle tree: and it shall be to the LORD for a name, for an everlasting sign that shall not be cut off.

The prophet closes the section with a joyful psalm depicting the earth resounding with the victory of those who entrust themselves to God's faithful promises. Just as the wilderness blossomed in welcome to the Jews on the way to the Promised Land under Moses, so the prophet envisions all nature responding joyfully to the good things God has in store for the faithful. In Isaiah 11 the picture of restoration was of wild animals existing peaceably with each other, so gentle that "a little child shall lead them." Here the imagery is extended, with the very earth coming alive for the very joy of being touched by its Creator—a picture that surely points beyond the Restoration to Palestine, even beyond the peace established by the first coming of the Prince of Peace, and on to the eventual eternal peace of heaven.

Evangelistic Emphasis

Several years ago a member of my congregation was in the final stages of a terminal disease. This person was still in her right mind, as her major organs began to shut down. One of the things most painful for the family was that their mother was thirsty all of the time. Because the condition had adversely affected her kidneys, the doctors had limited her intake of fluids. They were afraid that too much fluid would hasten her death, which was certain.

The family was in anguish when their mother asked them for a drink of water and they couldn't give it to her. After a couple of days, the valiant struggle with the terminal disease came to an end. The family was both very sad and very much relieved. Their mother was a woman of great faith in Jesus Christ.

At the funeral, the text I chose was from Isaiah. "Come all you who are thirsty, come to the waters." With water such a ready resource we have a tough time imagining people being thirsty. The words were written to people who lived in an arid climate. To the first audience, these words were describing an oasis in the middle of the desert. God came to us in our greatest need and supplies us with abundance. To people who are thirsty He gives water. To people who are walking in darkness God brings light.

The good news is that God knows what we need and willingly provides for us.

ഇൗരു

Memory Selection

Seek ye the LORD while he may be found, call ye upon him while he is near.—*Isaiah 55:6*

On a recent cruise, I witnessed something that reminded me of this passage of Scripture. We were cruising from the Caribbean back to our port in New Orleans. For two days we had been in the Gulf with no land in sight. About sunset we arrived at the mouth of the Mississippi River for our trip back to New Orleans.

We were about 10 miles up the river when people on the boat started breaking out their cell phones. The news traveled quickly around the boat that we were "within range" of a repeater tower. People who had been separated from loved ones for a week were calling and checking in. Dozens of phone calls were being made from all parts of that cruise ship.

I am glad that the Lord is near, as we need to call upon Him. He is never "out of range." We are never "out of the calling area." Remember the nearness of the Lord the next time you are in a bind and need divine deliverance.

Weekday Problems

Buster Weatherly was shocked when Tom Richards walked into his office. Tom was one of the wealthiest people in the community. While he was a member of the church, Pastor Weatherly could count on his fingers the number of times he has actually attended church. Tom was too busy with the affairs of his business. He was cordial to the minister but wanted to talk only of financial matters. He was known for giving financial advice to preachers, while keeping his money safely in his wallet.

Tom was approaching retirement and looking forward to getting out of the rat race. Still, Buster was surprised to see Tom in his office. "Preacher, I've got a couple of problems with which I need help."

As Tom talked several things became evident. First, this was a lonely man. He told his preacher that he really didn't make any good friends during his lifetime. He was estranged from his family. They had all gone about living their lives and had done so without Tom. He told the preacher that they were simply "treating him as he had treated them" earlier in their lives.

In short, Tom Richards was a man who had achieved every material success that could be imagined; yet he found himself spiritually and emotionally bankrupt. Now facing an uncertain future, he had turned to the church and to the Lord for help.

*What advice would you give Tom?

*Do you know of people who have labored for things that cannot satisfy?

Heaven Help Us

(From *Heavenly Humor* by Bob Phillips, used by permission)

The distance from earth to heaven isn't so much a matter of altitude as it is attitude.

* * *

Almost everybody is in favor of going to heaven, but too many people are hoping they'll live long enough to see an easing of the entrance requirements.

* * *

An exasperated mother whose son was always getting into mischief finally asked him, "How do you expect to get into heaven?"

The boy thought it over and said, "Well, I'll just run in and out and in and out and keep slamming the door until St. Peter says, 'For heaven's sake, Jimmy, come in or stay out.'"

This Lesson in Your Life

The text for this lesson begins with a beautiful promise. "Ho, everyone who thirsts, come to the waters; and you that have no money, come, buy and eat! Come, buy wine and milk without money and without price" (Isa. 55:1). The promise begins with a word to those seeking life's basic needs. Nothing is more basic to life than water. You might be able to live up to 40 days without eating, but you can't last much more than five or six days without water. In an arid world, not only was water basic. It was precious. Those traveling in this kind of geography could only find water in an oasis. Those who had control over the oasis had control over the water and hence could make a fortune, while depriving persons of this life giving necessity. The promise of God begins with the very basics of life. God will provide water. In a desert land God will provide water without cost. We can't imagine that. Most of us in some way pay for our water today. Persons who have wells had to pay to have those wells drilled. Water, while plentiful in most places, is not free.

Poor people, who "have no money," are invited to come and eat. This is the second thing one must do in order to live. We must eat. In a country famous for fast foods, this image does not quickly resonate with us. Yet the point is the same that God provides the necessities of life for His people. Remember that the people who first heard these words lived in a desert where life is very hard.

The text continues with wine and milk provided again at no cost to the people. Not only does God provide the basics for His people, God brings abundance to His people. Wine and milk were luxuries of that day. They were symbols of abundance. Yet, God provided these elements of abundance for His people.

God will provide abundantly everything we need to be healthy and happy, if we but trust in Him. That kind of trust in God's willingness to bless stands in stark contrast to the second verse of this chapter: "Why do you spend your money for that which is not bread, and your labor for that which does not satisfy? Listen carefully to me, and eat what is good, and delight yourselves in rich food" (Isa. 55:2).

The contrast is simple. You trust God for the things of life, or you make your own provision for the things of life. Tragically, persons who feel they must provide the basic of life for themselves are rarely satisfied with the things they have. If you trust God to give you part of His abundance you will be satisfied. If you trust yourself to provide abundance you will never be satisfied. The message from this text is that God is generous in providing for His people.

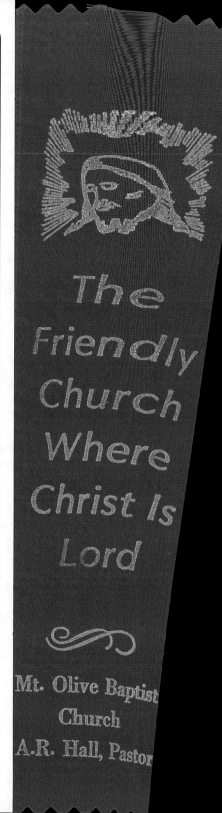

The
Friendly
Church
Where
Christ Is
Lord

Mt. Olive Baptist
Church
A.R. Hall, Pastor

GETTING THE FACTS STRAIGHT

1. An invitation was issued in Isaiah 55:1. Was there a limitation on the invitation?
No. The invitation was issued to all who are thirsty and to all who have no money.

2. What three specific invitations were given here?
The thirsty were invited to drink. The hungry were invited to eat. All were invited to have wine and milk.

3. What price was to be paid for all of this eating and drinking?
The people were invited to eat and drink without cost.

4. In light of verse 1, what was the strong warning issued at the beginning of verse two?
Since verse 1 made it clear that God provided the basics, people were warned about seeking satisfaction through material gain.

5. What is the implication of the phrase "your soul will delight in the richest of fare?"
The implication was that not only will God provide for our basic needs, He will provide abundant blessings for His people.

6. What did God offer as evidence that He would be faithful to His promise?
God evoked images of the covenant made with King David. The rule of David was considered a high point in Israel's relationship with God.

7. The children of Israel were encouraged to call upon the Lord and to seek Him, under what circumstances?
While He may be found and while He is near.

8. In contrast to the people of God, what were the wicked encouraged to do?
The wicked were encouraged to forsake their ways and the evil encouraged to give up their wicked thoughts.

9. What was the promise of the prophet to the wicked who wanted to make a change?
The promise was that the Lord would have mercy on the wicked and would freely pardon him.

10. The Lord gave a reason for His gracious actions that are articulated in this chapter. What was that reason?
The Lord's way are not our ways. The Lord's thoughts are not our thoughts. God has a divine way of doing things.

A way of talking about the first part of this passage is to address the concept of stewardship. God said: "Ho, everyone who thirsts, come to the waters; and you that have no money, come, buy and eat! Come, buy wine and milk without money and without price. Why do you spend your money for that which is not bread, and your labor for that which does not satisfy? Listen carefully to me, and eat what is good, and delight yourselves in rich food" (Isa. 55: 1-2).

The first two verses of this chapter speak to the abundance of God and His provision in our life. However, the passage has a warning for those who are looking to material possessions for their happiness and fulfillment. There is a strong stewardship message in this passage for those willing to hear it.

The Bible has over 2,300 references to money and possessions. The same Bible has only 500 references to prayer. While prayer is the very breath of the soul, stewardship and our attitude toward possession are signs of the vitality of our faith. It may be time for Christians to have their vital signs checked. The average member of most churches gives between 2 and 4 percent of his income to the Lord through the church. That is not very good stewardship, considering that God had set the tithe, 10 percent, as the basic unit of giving.

You know all the reasons often offered for not giving generously to the Lord. Another reason is our attitude toward the abundance of God. If we believe that God not only provides for our basic need but also provides the "extras" that bring joy, our giving will reflect that belief. If we believe that "God helps those who help themselves," our giving will likewise reflect those beliefs. In looking at the giving of the average church member, it seems that most people believe the latter while hoping for the former.

Our generosity, or lack of it, is a reflection of what we believe about God.

The passage from Isaiah affirms that God will supply our basic needs. If we take the passage literally, God will supply our needs without our having money. God will provide the extras to us at "no cost." There is no fine print in this promise from God. There are no loopholes for God to wiggle out of His promise. His promise is made; it is up to you to respond in faith to this great promise. Yet most of us are living "below the poverty line" when it comes to the abundance and blessings that God could provide. It is only as we turn our money over "in faith" that we will see His promise of abundance come to pass.

In the words of Jesus, "give and it shall be given you . . .for the measure you give will be the measure you get back." This is the Lord who also told His people not to worry about what they would eat, or wear. He promised that God would provide everything for those making the Kingdom of God their priority.

Where are your priorities?

True Worship

Isaiah 58:3-9a, 12-14

Therefore have we fasted, say they, and thou seest not? wherefore have we afflicted our soul, and thou takest no knowledge? Behold, in the day of your fast ye find pleasure, and exact all your labours.

4 Behold, ye fast for strife and debate, and to smite with the fist of wickedness: ye shall not fast as ye do this day, to make your voice to be heard on high.

5 Is it such a fast that I have chosen? a day for a man to afflict his soul? is it to bow down his head as a bulrush, and to spread sackcloth and ashes under him? wilt thou call this a fast, and an acceptable day to the LORD?

6 Is not this the fast that I have chosen? to loose the bands of wickedness, to undo the heavy burdens, and to let the oppressed go free, and that ye break every yoke?

7 Is it not to deal thy bread to the hungry, and that thou bring the poor that are cast out to thy house? when thou seest the naked, that thou cover him; and that thou hide not thyself from thine own flesh?

8 Then shall thy light break forth as the morning, and thine health shall spring forth speedily: and thy righteousness shall go before thee; the glory of the LORD shall be thy rereward.

9 Then shalt thou call, and the LORD shall answer; thou shalt cry, and he shall say, Here I am.

12 And they that shall be of thee shall build the old waste places: thou shalt raise up the foundations of many generations; and thou shalt be called, The repairer of the breach, The restorer of paths to dwell in.

13 If thou turn away thy foot from the sabbath, from doing thy pleasure on my holy day; and call the sabbath a delight, the holy of the LORD, honourable; and shalt honour him, not doing thine own ways, nor finding thine own pleasure, nor speaking thine own words:

14 Then shalt thou delight thyself in the LORD; and I will cause thee to ride upon the high places of the earth, and feed thee with the heritage of Jacob thy father: for the mouth of the LORD hath spoken it.

Jan. 20

Memory Selection
Isaiah 58:6

Devotional Reading
Isaiah 58:10-14

Background Scripture
Isaiah 58

201

The argument is ever with us: Is religion mainly about worship or service? Instead of allowing the question to be framed in this either/or way, this lesson focuses on the answer, Yes!

In the prophet Isaiah's day, many people had lapsed into mere formalism in worship. They went through the motions of sabbath observances, sacrifice, prayer, and fasting, but for self-centered reasons. This meant that they failed to consider the plight of the poor and oppressed. As a result God did not accept their worship.

Of course God's remedy was not to stop praying and fasting, but for the people to express their devotion and worship to God by serving those who have been created in His image. Then, and only then, "shalt thou delight thyself in the Lord" (Isa. 58:14).

ഇൽ

Introduce this lesson by putting the false "either/or" question in the Focus section to your group: *Is religion mainly about worship or service?* Guide the response and discussion to the truth taught in today's lesson: It's "both/and," not "either/or."

Support the discussion with the following specifically Christian points. God's covenant is with His people, the Body of Christ. The religion of these people is *personal*, but not *private*. God has therefore ordained that we assemble together, observing certain ordinances in worship (Acts 2:41-42; 20:7). However, the sacrifice of Christ in our behalf is a pattern that should move us to sacrifice ourselves for others, serving the poor and the oppressed. This life-pattern, along with purity of life, constitutes "pure religion" (see James 1:27).

Teaching Outline	Daily Bible Readings	

I. Superficial Rituals—3-5
  A. 'Why do You not hear?' 3a
  B. 'Your worship is self-centered,'
   3b-5
II. Satisfactory Rites—6-7
  A. Result in justice, 6
  B. Result in ministry, 7
III. Subsequent Blessings-8-9a, 12
  A. God's glory and presence, 8-9a
  B. Restoration in Zion, 12
IV. Satisfying Worship—13-14
  A. God first, not convenience, 13
  B. Being delighted with God, 14
	Mon.
	
	Tue.
	
	Wed.
	
	Thu.
	
	Fri.
	
	Sat.
	
	Sun.
		Worship in Spirit and Truth
		John 4:19-26
		Worship with Honor
		Malachi 1:6-14
		Worship in Righteousness
		Amos 5:18-24
		A Heritage for All
		Isaiah 56:1-5
		A Place for Outcasts
		Isaiah 56:3-8
		Not too Late to Repent
		Isaiah 57:14-21
		Honoring the Sabbath
		Isaiah 58:9b-14

Verse by Verse

I. Superficial Rituals—3-5

A. 'Why do You not hear?' 3a

3 Therefore have we fasted, say they, and thou seest not? wherefore have we afflicted our soul, and thou takest no knowledge?

The worship of the Jews asking this quesion, apparently those in Babylonian captivity, was not fulfilling. Perhaps most Christians have also had the experience of prayers seeming to rise no higher than the sanctuary ceiling, and the whole worship service leaving them as empty as they came. Even the active worship of the Jews, which involved offering animal sacrifice and fasting, which represented the affliction of the soul, seemed to prompt no response from God. Why was their worship neither delightful to them nor delighting to God?

B. 'Your worship is self-centered,' 3b-5

3b Behold, in the day of your fast ye find pleasure, and exact all your labours.

4 Behold, ye fast for strife and debate, and to smite with the fist of wickedness: ye shall not fast as ye do this day, to make your voice to be heard on high.

5 Is it such a fast that I have chosen? a day for a man to afflict his soul? is it to bow down his head as a bulrush, and to spread sackcloth and ashes under him? wilt thou call this a fast, and an acceptable day to the LORD?

God's answer is that the people have been going through the motions of worship for their own purposes, not to glorify God. When they fasted, they found some other way to satisfy their appetites. Even when they "afflicted their souls" it was in order to *get* something from God instead of to demonstrate their love and devotion. According to verse 4, their fasts even disintegrated into "quarreling and strife" (NIV). We can imagine arguments over who is best at fasting, with one worshiper claiming to be "hungrier than thou."

Just as Jesus would often do many years later, God answers the people's question in the form of questions. Do we really think that He delights in self-sacrifice with the self at the center? Do we really expect Him to find our worship acceptable when it consists of competing with each other to see who can appear the most abased, or even the most pious? Jesus also taught this very lesson in the Sermon on the Mount (Matt. 6:1-7, 16-18).

II. Satisfactory Rites—6-7

A. Result in justice, 6

6 Is not this the fast that I have chosen? to loose the bands of wickedness, to undo the heavy burdens, and to let the oppressed go free, and that ye break every yoke?

God specifies that the kind of religious rituals that please Him result in doing justice and working in behalf of the oppressed and unfairly imprisoned. This is no doubt because *worship is not designed to change God, but the worshiper.* Praising God for lifting our own burden of sin should result in our lifting someone else's burden. Thanking Him for liberating us from the prison of our sins should prompt us to go about setting free those who have been unjustly imprisoned. It is no accident that some New Testament words for "worship" are also translated "service."

B. Result in ministry, 7

7 Is it not to deal thy bread to the hungry, and that thou bring the poor that are cast out to thy house? when thou seest the naked, that thou cover him; and that thou hide not thyself from thine own flesh?

God also calls the true worshiper to be so grateful that God has met his needs that he help meet the needs of those who lack the basic sustenance required to sustain life. Fasting, for example, should set us free from thinking about our own need for food so we can focus on feeding the hungry. The message here is essentially the same as that of Amos, through whom God even said that He "hates" worship that is self-centered instead of resulting in concern for others (see Amos 5:21-24).

III. Subsequent Blessings-8-9a, 12

A. God's glory and presence, 8-9a

8 Then shall thy light break forth as the morning, and thine health shall spring forth speedily: and thy righteousness shall go before thee; the glory of the Lord shall be thy rereward.

9a Then shalt thou call, and the Lord shall answer; thou shalt cry, and he shall say, Here I am.

Just as many Christians know the experience of empty worship, so those who allow their gratitude to God to overflow in service to others know how fulfilling this can be. Few joys can equal feeding a hungry man, then finding him beside you in joint worship of a God who has fed you. The answer to "empty worship" is thus often to be found not in changing the service but in changing what the worshiper habitually does for others.

Only in such service do we experience God as our "rereward"—a KJV word that meant "rearward," referring to the rear guard of an army. The figure of speech is of an army feeling that it has made a successful march only when the last of its soldiers have closed ranks with those who went before. Worship that results in service "closes up" those empty spaces of the soul that result from realizing that our worship has not changed us.

B. Restoration in Zion, 12

12 And they that shall be of thee shall build the old waste places: thou shalt raise up the foundations of many generations; and thou shalt be called, The repairer of the breach, The restorer of paths to dwell in.

Another result of worship that results in service is promised to the remnant of the Jews in Babylonian captivity. It would be such dedicated worshipers whom God would marshal to return to Palestine to rebuild the holy city that had been laid waste by the invaders. For two full generations, counting 35 years each, the faithful had longed to return. Now God assures them that true worship that prompts them to serve others will result in their repairing the breaches and restoring the walls of Jerusalem (a promise that was fulfilled under the leadership of Ezra and Nehemiah).

IV. Satisfying Worship—13-14

A. God first, not convenience, 13

13 If thou turn away thy foot from the sabbath, from doing thy pleasure on my holy day; and call the sabbath a delight, the holy of the LORD, honourable; and shalt honour him, not doing thine own ways, nor finding thine own pleasure, nor speaking thine own words:

To "turn away thy foot from the sabbath" means to stop "kicking" or breaking the sabbath (see the NIV). The intent of keeping the Sabbath under the Law of Moses was that the people stop focusing on their own needs and continuing to tend to their own business in order to focus on worship—which was also to result in tending to the needs of others. This verse simply restates the

Fourth Commandment, "Remember the sabbath day, to keep it holy" (Exod. 20:8).

Under the New Covenant, Christians are still called to focus on worship, now on the first day of the week instead of the seventh. (Paul waited nearly a week to meet with the saints on "the first day of the week," Acts 20:7.) Unfortunately, many Christians can recall homes that had so many burdensome restrictions on what they could do on what was mistakenly called the "Christian Sabbath" that they could not enjoy God on it—which was the Sabbath's main purpose. At the other extreme, our own times offer so many diversions on Sunday that a special day for glad times with God seems equally elusive.

B. Being delighted with God, 14

14 Then shalt thou delight thyself in the LORD; and I will cause thee to ride upon the high places of the earth, and feed thee with the heritage of Jacob thy father: for the mouth of the LORD hath spoken it.

"High places" in the Old Testament usually refers to mountain tops devoted to the worship of idols. Here, however, God reasserts His authority over "mountaintop experiences," promising them to those worshipers who answer His "call to worship"— to observe His ordinances and to engage in praise and thanksgiving in ways that prompt them to serve others. Only then can we expect our assemblies to "feed" us as God promises they can.

Evangelistic Emphasis

What is the purpose of worship? There are many answers to that question, and most will have points of validity and truth. To some extent, your answer will be unique to you. We worship to glorify God. We worship to be in harmony with His will for our lives. We worship as an expression of our response to God's love for us. We worship to show others God is a priority for us.

Have you ever thought about worship as being evangelistic?

We worship to center our hearts on and in the purpose of God for His people. We are blessed by God to become a blessing for others. We have been saved by God to become instruments of God's salvation message.

The essence of the message in these verses from Isaiah is that worship that does not express itself in some form of evangelism, is not what God intends.

Worship must find expression in evangelism, in mission, in outreach, and in social justice or we are simply participating in an empty ritual act.

This is good news for those who need a savior. God wants His people to be His witnesses. It is bad news for people who want to worship and be comfortable with the status quo.

෨෬

Is not this the fast that I have chosen? To loose the bands of wickedness, to undo the heavy burdens, and to let the oppressed go free, and that ye break every yoke?—*Isaiah 58:6*

Have you ever fasted?

I don't fast while writing these lessons. I eat. My excuse is that I think better. Fasting is foreign to the American Christian experience. We view it as a curiosity of a bygone era. Now before you get excited and reach for that second donut, read on.

God chose a fast not related to our normal understanding of fasting. God's fast consists of actions that involve helping the less fortunate. God's fast is found in four actions. God's fast is found in actions that loose, undo, let go and break every yoke. God is interested in our worship leading us into acts of compassion and service. These acts of compassion and service are not necessary for our salvation. They are a reflection of our desire to be like Jesus.

He defined God's love in His loving action of going to the cross. He defined our faithfulness to God in terms of our actions on behalf of hurting people.

Something to think about when you are having that second donut!

Weekday Problems

A discussion raged in the worship committee. It seemed that Lamar Robertson wanted to move the piano to the left side of the pulpit area. The piano, given in memory of one of the favorite sons of the church, had stood for 40 years on the right side of the pulpit. Lamar wanted to move the piano so that the Hand Bell Choir would have more room for the patriotic program they were planning for the Sunday before the fourth of July.

Peggy Hunt would hear nothing of moving the piano. She was the foundation of the worship committee. She had been a member of the church for as long as anyone could remember. Her family had given the piano in memory of her brother who was killed in action during World War II. To suggest moving the piano was an affront to everything that Peggy Hunt held dear.

Pastor Buster Weatherly walked into the discussion about the time Peggy was about to unload on Lamar for such an un-American, un-Christian suggestion as moving the piano to the left side of the church.

After listening to a few minutes of Peggy's articulation of American and Church liturgical history, Buster interjected. "I'm sorry I was late for the meeting. I was helping a homeless family secure housing for this evening. You know they are predicting record cold tonight."

The minister made his point with the committee.

*Do you understand what point Buster Weatherly was trying to make?

*Is worship that doesn't lead to changed lives, valid worship?

'On the First Day of the Week . . .'

Sweet young thing trying to flirt with the minister: I'm afraid I've sinned—I couldn't focus on the sermon for thinking about how pretty I am.
Minister: That's no sin, that just a mistake.

* * *

Minister to deacon: I hear you went to the ball game this morning instead of coming to church.
Deacon: That's a lie, and here's the fish to prove it.

* * *

"I have a question," said Johnny after his first day at Sunday School. "Sure, son, what is it?"

"Well, the teacher told us all about the children of Israel crossing the Red Sea, the children of Israel offering sacrifices, the children of Israel building the Temple. What I want to know is, didn't the grown-ups do anything?

This Lesson in Your Life

Jesus said, "Not everyone who says to me, 'Lord, Lord,' will enter the kingdom of heaven, but only the one who does the will of my Father in heaven. On that day many will say to me, 'Lord, Lord, did we not prophesy in your name, and cast out demons in your name, and do many deeds of power in your name? Then I will declare to them, 'I never knew you; go away from me, you evildoers'" (Matt. 7: 21-23).

How many times do you suppose the word "Lord" is used in your church services? I wonder if the people who use the word feel like these verses from Matthew would ever apply to them. Isaiah pictures worship that arises out of praise for God but expresses itself in acts of compassion for others. These are tangible acts of compassion that make a difference in the lives of those touched by them. Worship without this kind of work would have been foreign to Isaiah's understanding of worship.

This same pattern of worship giving rise to righteous work is present in the teaching of Jesus. He did not automatically accept those affirming Him as Lord, or those who preached without righteous actions. A long and uncomfortable list in Matthew 7 describes people who should have been high on Heaven's list but and didn't make the cut. All the things done in Matthew 7:21-23 were works of power and might. There is nothing mentioned in this section about works of compassion for those less fortunate, nothing about people seeking to right injustice, nothing about dealing with poverty. Instead, we find a very chilling warning for people who try to worship while locking the hurting world out of church. According to the Rabbi Jesus, those people are in danger of locking themselves out of the Kingdom of God.

This is not a call to give up worship for social justice ministries. I don't believe such a choice exists in Scripture. This is a call to make our worship give rise to acts of compassion. What good is it to sit in our comfortable pews and sing "Amazing Grace" if we are not willing to work to share that grace with others? Worship that does not move us or change us is not worship. It is "doing time" in the pew. The aim of worship is to put us in touch with the transforming power of God's Holy Spirit. Unless that transformation is expressed outside the doors of the church, it is doubtful it has taken place.

The kind of worship that is energizing is the kind that changes people. When we have experienced God's transforming power in worship, we long to share that good news with everyone. Worship then gives rise to righteous work for the kingdom of God.

STRAIGHT

1. What question did the people have for God according to Isaiah 58:3? why did the people question whether God had accepted their worship?

The people of Israel had humbled themselves and fasted before the Lord, and the Lord had not honored their worship.

2. What were those who fasted also doing on the day they were fasting?

They were exploiting their workers even though they were fasting.

3. According to Isaiah 58:4, what problem arose among those who were fasting?

The problem that arose among the fasters was a fistfight.

4. Why were the people who were fasting also fighting?

The fight arose out of the quarreling and strife that occurred after the fast.

5. What are the implications of the words, "You cannot fast as you do to-day and expect your voice to be heard on high"?

Because of the duplicity of the people God would not honor their worship.

6. What acts of worship are listed in verse 5?

The acts related to worship are fasting, bowing the head, and lying on sack-cloth and ashes.

7. Were these acts of worship acceptable to the Lord?

Verse 6 implies that these acts of worship were not acceptable to the Lord.

8. In verse 6, what is the meaning of the words, "Is not this the kind of fast I have chosen?"

The words indicate that the Lord desired a different kind of fast.

9. What were the elements of the fast that the Lord had chosen?

Bringing freedom and help to those suffering from injustice and bondage.

10. What were the actions that were pleasing to God?

God wanted His people to share food, shelter, and clothing to the needy.

The author of Isaiah 58 could resonate with the discussions going on in the Church regarding worship. Many members of worship committees come out of meetings feeling like the situations described in verse 4: "Look, you fast only to quarrel and to fight and to strike with a wicked fist. Such fasting as you do today will not make your voice heard on high" (Isa. 58:4).

The debate that almost causes fights today is over contemporary versus traditional forms of worship. This debate has created many strange alliances. It has also caused the Church to rethink and debate the very meaning and purpose of Sunday morning worship. As with all of our debates, while we decide what to do on the inside of the Church, the world is dying outside. Our debate over worship sounds petty when compared with the suffering we should be addressing.

Debate is loud in many denominations today as to the nature of worship. Congregations are asking questions about worship never before addressed or contemplated. As a new generation looks for a clear word from Jesus, the Church finds herself unwilling or unable to speak the language of a new generation. This is especially true as congregations attempt to reach the demographic age group of 18-36. This is a generation largely raised outside the Church. They grew up watching television. They have little knowledge of the worship traditions that many readers of this commentary hold sacred. The question before the Church is: How shall we worship in a way that touches this age group?

Many congregations are finding that two types of worship, contemporary and traditional, seem to address this issue. The debate in committee is tradition versus new styles of worship. Both sides of this debate seem to have their heels dug in and their territory well marked off.

From Isaiah, we learn that a debate over the style of worship begs the point. Worship could be in Latin with incense or using guitars and drums, but if it doesn't change lives can it be called worship?

The word "worship" comes from an Old English word roughly translated "worth-ship." As we worship, we are showing the world God's worth by celebrating what He has done in our lives. Failing to continue to worship God outside the doors of the church negates that worth. If our worship is not translated into actions then we have devalued the worth of God, and failed in our charge to bear witness to His grace.

We are good about debating, but we could do better about just letting worship happen, then allowing that experience to overflow into the world that surrounds the Church.

Sometimes it seems that we would rather argue than serve, rather debate than minister. We are all in need of some transformational worship.

God's New Creation

Isaiah 65:17-25

For, behold, I create new heavens and a new earth: and the former shall not be remembered, nor come into mind.

18 But be ye glad and rejoice for ever in that which I create: for, behold, I create Jerusalem a rejoicing, and her people a joy.

19 And I will rejoice in Jerusalem, and joy in my people: and the voice of weeping shall be no more heard in her, nor the voice of crying.

20 There shall be no more thence an infant of days, nor an old man that hath not filled his days: for the child shall die an hundred years old; but the sinner being an hundred years old shall be accursed.

21 And they shall build houses, and inhabit them; and they shall plant vineyards, and eat the fruit of them.

22 They shall not build, and another inhabit; they shall not plant, and another eat: for as the days of a tree are the days of my people, and mine elect shall long enjoy the work of their hands.

23 They shall not labour in vain, nor bring forth for trouble; for they are the seed of the blessed of the LORD, and their offspring with them.

24 And it shall come to pass, that before they call, I will answer; and while they are yet speaking, I will hear.

25 The wolf and the lamb shall feed together, and the lion shall eat straw like the bullock: and dust shall be the serpent's meat. They shall not hurt nor destroy in all my holy mountain, saith the LORD.

Jan 27

Memory Selection
Isaiah 65:17

Devotional Reading
Revelation 21:1-7

Background Scripture
Isaiah 65:17-25

ised Land. Half a millennium later, the apostle John finds this text also speaking of heaven as the "new creation."

Today's text is another of the prophecies in the latter chapters of Isaiah that affirm that God's people can look to the future in hope. The text brings us again to the principle of "multiple fulfillment" of Bible prophecy. It finds its first fulfillment in the return of a remnant of the Jews in Babylonian captivity to the Prom-

Some interpreters also believe the text applies to the new spiritual creation, the Church, inaugurated at the ascension of Christ. Still others see in it the glorious reign of Jesus in His pre-millennial Second Coming. The common thread in all these views is that dark days in any age need not cause the faithful to despair. They serve the God who makes all things new, the God of hope.

ഇരുൽ

Today's study can be introduced by leading a free-for-all discussion of specific hopes that group members have of eternal life in heaven with God. You may be surprised at how few mention standard pictures of people with wings strumming a harp and sitting on a cloud. More likely, their hope of heaven will be re-

lated to their most severe trials in this life. The person with chronic back pain looks forward to having no illness in heaven. The aged sometimes dream of heaven preserving them as they were in their prime. And what about work? Will we idle away the days, or joyfully engage in the work that most fulfilled us here on earth?

The point is that life hereafter can be envisioned in many ways. In today's study, the prophet Isaiah uses one of the most stunning images of all. He looks forward to "new heavens and a new earth."

Teaching Outline	Daily Bible Readings

I. New Day of Joy—17-19
   A. New heavens and earth, 17
   B. New Jerusalem, 18-19
 	
II. Life as It Was Meant to Be—20-23
   A. Fullness of years, 20
   B. Fruits of one's labors, 21-23
 	
III. Harmony and Peace—24-25
   A. Between God and man, 24
   B. Among all creation, 25
	Mon. 'While You Wait...'
	2 Peter 3:11-18
	Tue. All Things New
	Revelation 21:1-8
	Wed. A New Spirit Within
	Ezekiel 11:14-20
	Thu. Cleansed People, New Hearts
	Ezekiel 36:22-28
	Fri. Redemption of Jerusalem
	Isaiah 52:7-12
	Sat. Nations See God's Glory
	Isaiah 66:18-23
	Sun. New Heavens and Earth
	Isaiah 65:17-25

Verse by Verse

I. New Day of Joy—17-19

A. New heavens and earth, 17

17 For, behold, I create new heavens and a new earth: and the former shall not be remembered, nor come into mind.

Although it makes common sense to seek an application of any prophecy first in the experience of those who heard it, some expressions press beyond immediate application. We have seen this to be true when the prophet sees a coming "child" who will bring a golden age (Isa. 9:6). While Hezekiah may have been the first application of this hope, his names ("Wonderful, Counselor, the Mighty God," etc.) strain the language so much that they point ahead to another fulfillment in the Messiah, the Son of God.

In a similar way, the hope of "new heavens and a new earth" may first have been used to inspire a remnant of the Jews in Babylon to return to the Promised Land, rebuild the city and its capital, Jerusalem, and restore to its former fertility farmland which had been sown with salt by enemies. A new heaven and earth was an apt way to describe the sharp contrast between the Jews' dismal state in captivity and the total newness of the day dawning in the Restoration.

Again, however, the language seems "oversized," too grand to be contained in that event. Hence, the apostles Peter and John will find in the phrase a picture of heaven (2 Pet. 3:13; Rev. 21:1-54).

How totally "new" will the heavens and earth of that Great Day be? Some interpreters take "earth" literally, and believe the fiery end of the present earth that is to precede the new earth will be only a renovation; and that the ultimate "heaven" will be on this restored planet. Others take 2 Peter 3:10 more literally, and predict that the earth will be burned up, or consumed, and that heaven will be life with God "in the air." They cite 1 Thessalonians 4:17 to support this view, while others say the passage applies to the "rapture." The common ground between the welter of views about the end time and the hereafter is that the ultimate life to come for the faithful will be so glorious that it will blot out all memory of our struggles in the various "Babylonian captivities" of life.

B. New Jerusalem, 18-19

18 But be ye glad and rejoice for ever in that which I create: for, be-

hold, I create Jerusalem a rejoicing, and her people a joy.

19 And I will rejoice in Jerusalem, and joy in my people: and the voice of weeping shall be no more heard in her, nor the voice of crying.

Here a God of continuing creation is depicted. When God "rested" on the seventh day of creation, He merely stopped that session of "work." He wasn't so tired that He determined to stop creating new things. He later showed His continuing creative power by creating a "path through the sea" at the exodus from Egypt; and by enabling believers to be "created anew" in Christ (2 Cor. 5:17). Now the promise is that He will create anew the Holy City of Jerusalem and its people, changing them from sad exiles to joyful citizens.

Once more, the actual Restoration was not quite as glorious as the language here. As joyful as was the rebuilding of the Temple under Ezra and Nehemiah, the new work lacked the glory of the old, and those who remembered the former Temple wept (Ezra 3:12). The passage must therefore point beyond the Israel's return to Palestine and to the ultimate "Restoration" of the people of God in heaven, where there will be no crying (Rev. 21:4).

II. Life as It Was Meant to Be— 20-23

A. Fullness of years, 20

20 There shall be no more thence an infant of days, nor an old man that hath not filled his days: for the child shall die an hundred years old; but the sinner being an hundred years old shall be accursed.

In a figurative way, this verse may describe the scene of "fulfillment" both the young and the old will find when the Jews return to Babylon. It seems, however, more appropriate to view it as the total *shalom*—peace, wholeness, fulfillment—awaiting the faithful in heaven.

One of the tragedies of this life is when children live "but a few days" (NIV), dying before they can reach their potential. Such tragedies will not occur in heaven. The prophet here offers the hope of complete age and moral appropriateness. The faithful will reach their full potential, while there will be no room for the willfully sinful, no matter their age.

B. Fruits of one's labors, 21-23

21 And they shall build houses, and inhabit them; and they shall plant vineyards, and eat the fruit of them.

22 They shall not build, and another inhabit; they shall not plant, and another eat: for as the days of a tree are the days of my people, and mine elect shall long enjoy the work of their hands.

23 They shall not labour in vain, nor bring forth for trouble; for they are the seed of the blessed of the LORD, and their offspring with them.

One of the most anguished memories in Babylon must have been of "the family farm" that was laid waste by the invaders. After working long, hard years to build up the soil and to grow vineyards and olive groves, all was lost when the enemy sowed the land with salt and ignored deeds of ownership. In the cities, after years of labor building their homes, wave after wave of invaders tore them down.

In the Restoration, and ultimately in heaven, such losses will be nonexistent. The prophet makes a word play on the term "seed." While the seed of crops was wasted in the invasion, God's people are an eternal seed, guaranteed to "sprout" under His loving nurture.

III. Harmony and Peace—24-25
A. Between God and man, 24

24 And it shall come to pass, that before they call, I will answer; and while they are yet speaking, I will hear.

Throughout their long history, God accused Israel of being hard-hearted and deaf to His pleas that they live faithfully. Even through the prophet Isaiah God said that while the people's ears were open, they failed really *to hear* in the sense of obeying (Isa. 42:20). When God punished them for such deliberate deafness, they cried out; but He "stopped His ears" or refused to listen to their cries. Now the prophet says the hearts of the people will be so attuned to His will that He will respond to their needs even before they can ask for them to be met.

The ultimate fulfillment of such a prophecy must have come with Jesus, the Messiah, who taught His followers that God was a step ahead of them when they prayed. If they asked in faith, and in accordance with His will, the answer will have already been anticipated and provided. Because of the tense of the verbs in the famous saying in Matthew 18:19, the verse can be understood to mean, "Whatever you ask for on earth will be that which is already provided in heaven."

B. Among all creation, 25

25 The wolf and the lamb shall feed together, and the lion shall eat straw like the bullock: and dust shall be the serpent's meat. They shall not hurt nor destroy in all my holy mountain, saith the LORD.

Now the picture of "the peaceable kingdom" drawn in Isaiah 11:6-9 is repeated. For the remnant preparing to return and reclaim the Promised Land, the scene must have been taken as beautiful but figurative language portraying that God's *shalom* would come not only upon the people but on the whole land. That the earth can respond to the way people live is seen even in our day, when proper conservation practices result in a balance of nature. Ultimately, however, the scene must describe the peace among all living things in heaven, when hurtful treatment of earth, mankind, or beast will dissolve in the all-consuming love of new heavens and the new earth.

Evangelistic Emphasis

When I was ordained, I received a chalice as a reminder of that night. The chalice was made out of pottery. Since I was ordained with a large group of people, we all had chalices. At the reception for our new group of ministers, the newly ordained minister next to me knocked over my chalice, and it broke into two pieces. I remember being very disappointed about my chalice being broken and hoped it was not a harbinger of my coming ministry.

By the time I had arrived back home, news of my broken chalice had spread to the person who made the original chalice. This person called and asked about my broken chalice. When I described the damage, she told me that it was terminal, but that I shouldn't worry.

Not a full week passed before I received a new chalice in the mail. Now I have two chalices. I glued the original one back together. Because of how it was broken I can't use it for communion. But the broken chalice sits right beside the replacement chalice. I keep them together because they remind me of the powerful work of God's grace.

God is in the business of fixing what we have broken. He is in the business of making all things new. He offers you a fresh start. He offers to take the brokenness in your life and heal it.

Have you responded to the good news that God makes all things new?

ℰℭ

Memory Selection

For, behold, I create new heavens and a new earth: and the former shall not be remembered, nor come into mind.—*Isaiah 65:17*

Memory is an interesting thing. I can remember growing up and spending time at my favorite fishing hole. While I can remember what I did 25 years ago, I can't remember where I left my car keys. Do you have the same trouble?

I can remember things I have done wrong. Late at night in the silence of my soul, sins of the past sometimes pop to mind. I take the opportunity to pray about them and to ask God's forgiveness. I have spent some nights making lists of people from whom I needed to seek forgiveness. There are things I have done that I wish I could forget.

The promise of Isaiah that brings me the most excitement is that part about "the former things shall not be remembered."

When I confess my sins, God forgives them. Not only does He forgive my sins, He forgets them as well. In the new creation, some of our memories will be gone. Praise the Lord!

Weekday Problems

When she heard the name of her new boss, Sharon Todd was flabbergasted. She had worked for Bob Whybray, manager of operations, for 15 years. She knew he was efficient with the customers, honest with the employees, and good to his family. But he had recently had a number of health-related problems and his doctor had demanded that Bob take early retirement. It meant that Sharon Todd would soon have a new boss.

Marilyn Toups was given the job. Sharon knew Marilyn to be the type who would do anything to get what she wanted. She had wanted Bob's job. Sharon couldn't say anything about Marilyn to people who asked, because it would have seemed "catty." When they began working together, Sharon was relieved to find out that Marilyn only viewed this position as a stepping-stone to a higher position. With disdain, Sharon listened as Marilyn "worked" once loyal customers. She listened with patience as employees regaled her with tales of Marilyn's duplicity toward them. She wondered how someone could rise so high and be so grossly mismatched for the job.

*Do you know a case of a person who has achieved something without working for it?

*Isaiah addressed the issue of people who build houses in which they never live. What would Isaiah say about this Weekday Problem?

More About Heaven

Atheist: How do you know hell is real?
Believer: When I get to heaven I'll ask Jesus.
Atheist: And what if heaven isn't like that?
Atheist: Then you ask about it yourself.

* * *

A golfer who died and went to heaven marveled at its glory. It had everything a golfer could want—green fairways, calm winds, clear skies. He carried on and on about how glad he was go be there.

"Well," said St. Peter. "You could've played here a lot sooner if you hadn't eaten all that oat bran."

* * *

People wonder what they will do in heaven, assuming that it will be complete, finished to the last bit of gilding. Of course it won't.—*J. B. Priestley,* adapted.

* * *

Heaven—the Coney Island of Christian imagination—*Elbert Hubbard.*

This Lesson in Your Life

At one level the passage for this lesson address the unfairness that is a part of life. "They shall not build and another inhabit; they shall not plant and another eat" (Isa. 65:22). We all know people who got jobs, promotions, homes, and the lives that we dreamed we might have, although they did not earn them. Some people get ahead at the expense of others. Especially in the economic realm, life often seems unfair.

Isaiah was addressing a greater issue. Beyond actions that are unfair, some events are painful. Earlier in the text, the prophet referred to children who die before maturity. No pain is greater than for a parent to experience the loss of a child. The grief remains for a lifetime. The prophet wrote about adults who die "before their time." These are real events today. We hear of premature deaths and the unspoken thought is of unfairness. People, we believe, should have the opportunity to live out long and productive lives. It is tragic when life is cut short.

Some persons choose not to believe in God because of all the pain and suffering in the world. Their "logical" position is reached by claiming a loving God could not allow His people to experience all the pain they do. They must reason that a loving God would only allow His people to live a utopian existence and know no pain. I have never bothered to ask people with this belief what God should allow His people to experience.

The Bible is honest as it acknowledges pain as a part of human existence. We don't live long before experiencing the pain that is associated with being a resident of this planet. Throughout our lives, pain and heartache will color the tapestry of our lives. Isaiah's writings were honest as the prophet admitted to the reality of pain.

If there were only pain and suffering then we might have cause to doubt our God. The passage from Isaiah is a balanced and true picture of a spiritual reality. There is pain in this life, but this life is not all there is to life in the Kingdom. In response to the hurt of this world, God will bring a new heaven and a new earth. Life on this orb will not be remembered in that new day. We live with the hope that God has seen the suffering of His people. He has witnessed our faithfulness in the days filled with turmoil. We have turned to Him for our help and for our comfort. Because of God's love for us, He has prepared a place for His people where we will be freed from the possibility of pain. We will be delivered from the twists of fate. We will dwell with God in a place prepared of us.

GETTING THE FACTS STRAIGHT

1. In the beginning God created. According to Isaiah 65:17, what would God be doing again?
God will create a new heaven and a new earth.

2. How would people in the new heavens and the new earth relate to their life in this world?
The tragedies experienced in this life would not be remembered in the life to come.

3. What is the comfort found in the phrase "the former things will not be remembered?"
The pain and suffering experienced in life will not be remembered in the world to come.

4. What was the purpose of the re-creation of Jerusalem?
Jerusalem would be re-created to be a delight and its people to be a joy.

5. What would be the response of the people to the new heaven and earth, and the New Jerusalem?
God's people would "be glad and rejoice forever in what I will create."

6. How would God respond to this New Jerusalem?
"I will rejoice over Jerusalem and take delight in my people.

7. What would be absent in this new creation of God?
"The sound of weeping and of crying will be heard in it no more."

8. In terms of lifespan, what two promises were made about life in New Jerusalem?
In New Jerusalem no longer would "infants live only a few days or an old man . . . not live out his years."

9. A long life on earth was "three score and ten," How will a long life be defined in the new creation?
Someone dying at a hundred years of age would be said to have died in his or her youth.

10. What would the people do in the new creation?
They would plant crops and harvest them, and they would build houses and live in them.

A woman who had been diagnosed with cancer and had been given three months to live. Her doctor told her to start making preparations to die, so she contacted her pastor and had him come to her house to discuss certain aspects of her final wishes.

She told him which songs she wanted sung at the service, what Scriptures she would like read, and what she wanted to be wearing. The woman also told her pastor that she wanted to be buried with her favorite Bible. Everything was in order, and the pastor was preparing to leave when the woman suddenly remembered something very important to her. "There's one more thing," she said excitedly.

"What's that?" came the pastor's reply.

"I want to be buried with a fork in my right hand," the woman said.

The pastor stood looking at the woman, not knowing quite what to say.

"That shocks you, doesn't it?" she asked.

"Well, to be honest, I'm puzzled by the request," said the pastor.

The woman explained. "In all my years of attending church socials and functions where food was involved, my favorite part was when whoever was clearing away the dishes of the main course would lean over and say, 'You can keep your fork.' It was my favorite part because I knew that something better was coming. When they told me to keep my fork, I knew that something great was about to be given to me. It wasn't Jell-O or pudding. It was cake or pie. Something with substance.

"So," she continued, "at my funeral I want people to see me there in that casket with a fork in my hand, and I want them to wonder, 'What's with the fork?' Then I want you to tell them: *Something better is coming, so you keep your fork, too.*"

The preacher then hugged the woman goodbye. He knew this would be one of the last times he would see her alive. But he also knew that she had a better grasp of heaven than he did. She knew that something better was coming.

At the funeral, people were walking by the woman's casket, and they saw the pretty dress she was wearing and her favorite Bible and the fork placed in her right hand. Over and over, the pastor heard the question, "What's with the fork?" Over and over, he smiled. During his message, the pastor told the people of the conversation he had with the woman shortly before she died. He also told them about the fork and about what it symbolized to her. The pastor told the people how he could not stop thinking about the fork, and told them that they probably would not be able to stop thinking about it, either. He was right.

So the next time you reach down for your fork, let it remind you that there is something better coming.

Lesson 10

Ruth Chose Naomi's God

Ruth 1:1-8, 16-18

Now it came to pass in the days when the judges ruled, that there was a famine in the land. And a certain man of Bethlehem-judah went to sojourn in the country of Moab, he, and his wife, and his two sons.

2 And the name of the man was Elimelech, and the name of his wife Naomi, and the name of his two sons Mahlon and Chilion, Ephrathites of Bethlehem-judah. And they came into the country of Moab, and continued there.

3 And Elimelech Naomi's husband died; and she was left, and her two sons.

4 And they took them wives of the women of Moab; the name of the one was Orpah, and the name of the other Ruth: and they dwelled there about ten years.

5 And Mahlon and Chilion died also both of them; and the woman was left of her two sons and her husband.

6 Then she arose with her daughters in law, that she might return from the country of Moab: for she had heard in the country of Moab how that the LORD had visited his people in giving them bread.

7 Wherefore she went forth out of the place where she was, and her two daughters in law with her; and they went on the way to return unto the land of Judah.

8 And Naomi said unto her two daughters in law, Go, return each to her mother's house: the LORD deal kindly with you, as ye have dealt with the dead, and with me.

16 And Ruth said, Intreat me not to leave thee, or to return from following after thee: for whither thou goest, I will go; and where thou lodgest, I will lodge: thy people shall be my people, and thy God my God:

17 Where thou diest, will I die, and there will I be buried: the LORD do so to me, and more also, if ought but death part thee and me.

18 When she saw that she was stedfastly minded to go with her, then she left speaking unto her.

Feb. 3

Memory Selection
Ruth 1:16

Devotional Reading
Psalm 8

Background Scripture
Ruth 1

The lovely story of Ruth focuses on the priority of following God over national and tribal ties. In some ways the book is an ancient missionary tract, describing the choice made by Ruth, a woman of Moab, to follow Yahweh, the God of her Jewish mother-in-law, instead of the national gods of the Moabites.

Historically, the book has been important to both Jews and Christians. It has prompted debates among Jews on the issue of intermarriage. The two sons of the Jewish Naomi marry Moabite women, apparently in defiance of the prohibition against marrying non-Jews in the books of Ezra and Nehemiah.

Christians find the book of Ruth important because it places a Gentile woman, Ruth, in the lineage of the Messiah (4:17-22)—a forecast of how Jesus is a Messiah to the world, not just to Israel.

≫◊≪

The story of Charlie "Two Shoes" makes a good introduction to this lesson. As a Chinese boy, Charlie had befriended American soldiers stationed in the Far East during a crisis between Communist China and Formosa. Unable to pronounce the boy's name, the soldiers called him "Charlie Two Shoes." They took up a collection to send Charlie to school, where he converted to Christianity.

Of course the Chinese Communist authorities took a dim view of the lad's loyalty to Americans, and to his new-found faith. However, Charlie resisted pressure to deny his new friends, and eventually came to America and made a new life for himself. For years he worked to bypass immigration laws that prevented his becoming a U.S. citizen. Finally, just last year, he succeeded. Charlie Two Shoes is now a citizen in a land that allows him to be loyal both to faith and freedom.

Loyalty, faith, and freedom are also central to the story of Ruth.

Teaching Outline	Daily Bible Readings	

I. Flight from Famine—1-2
  A. The setting, 1
  B. Moab and Israel, 2
II. Forlorn in Moab—3-5
III. Decision to Return—6-8
  A. Three on the way, 6-7
  B. 'Go, return,' 8
IV. Determination to Follow—16-17
  A. Ruth's decision, 16-7
  B. Naomi's willingness, 18
	Mon.	Strangers in Egypt
		Deut. 10:12-22

	Tue.	Caring for Others Deut. 26:1-15
	Wed.	Call to Just Living Jer. 7:1-7
	Thu.	Protect the Weak Jer. 22:1-8
	Fri.	Provide for the Needy Deut. 24:14-21
	Sat.	Three Widows in Moab Ruth 1:1-14
	Sun.	Your God, My God Ruth 1:15-22

Verse by Verse

I. Flight from Famine—1-2
A. The setting, 1

1 Now it came to pass in the days when the judges ruled, that there was a famine in the land. And a certain man of Bethlehem-judah went to sojourn in the country of Moab, he, and his wife, and his two sons.

"In the days when the judges ruled" places the setting of the book of Ruth before the time when kings ruled over the Jews in the Promised Land. In our present Old Testaments, the book therefore is placed appropriately between Judges and the books of Samuel. The unknown author may insert this historical note to hint that the story of Ruth and her family's temporary migration to the often hostile land of Moab occurred during a time when "every man did that which was right in his own eyes" (Judg. 21:25). Borders between Israel and Moab may have been more closed during later times when kings ruled the land.

Although Palestine was a land "flowing with milk and honey" when compared with the desert wastes in much of the Middle East, famine was not unknown. It is possible that one of the reasons the book of Ruth was included in the Hebrew canon of the Bible is that it shows that Yahweh is a universal God; sometimes He blesses unbelievers such as the Moabites with rain while allowing famine to remind His own people of their dependence upon Him. Since Moab was just to the southeast of Israel, across the Dead Sea, it was near enough to attract refugees from Bethlehem, in the hill country of Judah.

B. Moab and Israel, 2

2 And the name of the man was Elimelech, and the name of his wife Naomi, and the name of his two sons Mahlon and Chilion, Ephrathites of Bethlehemjudah. And they came into the country of Moab, and continued there.

Relations between Moab and Israel had not always been conducive to immigration from one to the other. A Moabite king hired the seer Balaam to curse Israel as it was poised to cross the Jordan and enter Canaan (Num. 22:1ff.). Yet some Israelites forsook true worship to take part in the sexual immoralities of Chemosh, the Moabites' god, who also demanded child sacrifice (Num. 25:1-9; 2 Kings 3:27). Still, the relationship between the two nations allows Moses to be buried on Mount Nebo, which was in Moab (Deut. 34:1); and the future king, David sojourned in Moab, the native land of his ancestor Ruth, while fleeing from King Saul (1 Sam. 22:3-4).

II. Forlorn in Moab—3-5

3 And Elimelech Naomi's husband died; and she was left, and her two sons.

4 And they took them wives of the women of Moab; the name of the one was Orpah, and the name of the other Ruth: and they dwelled there about ten years.

5 And Mahlon and Chilion died also both of them; and the woman was left of her two sons and her husband.

Because of the Moabites' hostility to Israel, they were excluded "from the congregation" (Deut. 23:3-4); that is, from becoming proselyte Jews. This exclusion was extended to intermarriage according to Ezra 9:1ff., so Mahlon and Chilion are not in strict conformance with the Law when they take Moabite wives. Yet, as subsequent Bible history shows, this does not prevent God from being able to make good come out of their situation.

The KJV expression "left of" means "left without," as in the NIV. The term carried with it an ominous hint that the women had lost their primary means of support. Even in our society a woman whose husband and wage-earner dies can be thrown on hard times. In patriarchal days, when it was even less customary for women to own property or to learn a trade, the situation of Naomi and her daughters-in-law would have been even more difficult.

III. Decision to Return—6-8
A. Three on the way, 6-7

6 Then she arose with her daughters in law, that she might return from the country of Moab: for she had heard in the country of Moab how that the LORD had visited his people in giving them bread.

7 Wherefore she went forth out of the place where she was, and her two daughters in law with her; and they went on the way to return unto the land of Judah.

With considerable courage, the three women bereft of their husbands form a family without male leadership. When Naomi hears that the famine in Judah is over, she determines to return; and apparently both Orpah and Ruth at first intend to go with her. We learn later (in 4:3) that another attraction back in Israel is that Naomi, perhaps at the death of her husband, has inherited a parcel of land.

B. 'Go, return,' 8

8 And Naomi said unto her two daughters in law, Go, return each to her mother's house: the LORD deal kindly with you, as ye have dealt with the dead, and with me.

We are not told why Naomi decides

to urge her daughters-in-law to return to their Moabite homes. Perhaps she foresees that they may not be accepted in Israel, or that they will have a harder time making it on their own there than back at their families of origin.

Naomi's blessing is an example of effective "cross-cultural communication" in evangelism. The blessing is in the name of the true God Yahweh, not just in the name of *El,* a more common name for "God" that could have included any god, including the Moabite deity Chemosh. Yet she hopes that God will show the same lovingkindness (Heb. *chesedh*) to Orpah and Ruth that they showed to Naomi's sons. In other words, Naomi acknowledges goodness and worth in these pagan women while being true to the God of Israel.

IV. Determination to Follow—16-17
A. Ruth's decision, 16-17

16 And Ruth said, Intreat me not to leave thee, or to return from following after thee: for whither thou goest, I will go; and where thou lodgest, I will lodge: thy people shall be my people, and thy God my God:
17 Where thou diest, will I die, and there will I be buried: the LORD do so to me, and more also, if ought but death part thee and me.

It sometimes comes as a surprise to learn that these tender words of commitment and dedication are not between husband and wife, as the words are commonly used at marriage ceremonies, but from a daughter-in-law to her mother-in-law.

The full power of Ruth's statement can be realized by noting that it encompasses such major rites of passage: (1) *following,* or making any moves from place to place that Naomi may decide; (2) *lodging,* or taking part in the everydayness of settled life; (3) *peoplehood,* casting her lot with Naomi's people, the Israelites, regardless of how they may look upon her as a non-Jew; and (4) chosen God ("the LORD," again using the name "Yahweh"; and (5) *death and burial,* one of the most clan-related rituals of all.

Apparently living as part of this Jewish family has been such a rewarding experiencing for this Moabite woman that she has converted to their practice of worshiping the true God. She takes an oath ("The Lord do so to me and more also") to show her determination.

B. Naomi's willingness, 18

18 When she saw that she was stedfastly minded to go with her, then she left speaking unto her.

How can Naomi resist such passionate commitment not only to her but to her faith? Her acceptance and Ruth's determination take them back to their homeland, and into a future that will include the formation of the ancestry of the Messiah.

Evangelistic Emphasis

Some members of the church vote with their wallets and their feet when they are displeased. These persons will become "crossed" with the agenda or direction of the church and rather than trying to affect change they quit. There is a whole new category of persons visiting the church on any given Sunday. I have labeled these persons as "tire kickers." The myth of buying a used car somehow involved the kicking of tires to see if the car was worthy of purchase. Tire kickers basically do the same activity in the church. They will come to your church this Sunday because they are mad about something that happened (or didn't) in their church last Sunday. These people have a lack of loyalty.

The good news is that some of the tire kickers eventually will become loyal to the church. The better news is that God has complete and unchanging loyalty to us. He does not change based on "how He is feeling" at the moment. He will not leave you when you need Him.

God is old-fashioned. He believes in loyalty. He is loyal to us to the end. "Behold, I am with you always" is the promise of our Lord. The story of Ruth and Naomi is a story of loyalty. This moving story of personal and religious loyalty might seem strange in today's world. But it reminds us of a God who never has to hunt us down. The loyalty of Christ to His Church and people is something we can take with us as we travel and move.

ℰᏨ

Memory Selection

Entreat me not to leave thee, or to return from following thee; for whither thou goest, I will go; and where thou lodgest, I will lodge: thy people shall be my people, and thy God my God.—*Ruth 1:16*

How many friends do you have?

Friendship is a valuable expression of our need for one another. We need persons who are our friends. Friendships can develop and overlap other relationships in our lives. My suspicion is that these two women were more than relatives. They had become friends.

Friendship grows in the soil of trust and loyalty. Those chords build a strong connection, which can live and grow over a lifetime.

Jesus talked about friendship in His parable of the Good Samaritan. The question posed to Jesus was about who is my friend. The answer Jesus gave was a more pointed question for us: "To whom are you a friend."

Friendship happens when we decide we want to be a friend. We have few friends or many friends based as much on our friendliness as any other factor.

Weekday Problems

Steve was a very successful high school football coach. He was a faithful member of Buster Weatherly's church. That fall, the football team had its best season ever. Everything was going well in Steve's life. He was the father of a two year old and a newborn. His name was being mentioned as a possible candidate for the head coaching position at a university located near by.

All of that came to a halt one afternoon. Steve and his wife were good friends with a family down the street. Their daughter was Steve and Lisa's babysitter and a junior at the School where Steve coached. Steve had offered to pick their daughter up from her gymnastics' class and drive her home, since the class was taught near the football stadium. On the way home the daughter asked Steve if they could stop for a minute, so they could talk. As they were having a conversation about one of the boys on Steve's team, a police car pulled up.

Because they were sitting in a corner of a deserted parking lot the officer became suspicious. Although nothing had happened, the officer decided to take Steve to the police station for further questioning. By 6 p.m., newscasts were filled with the story of the coach and the coed. "My life is ruined by innuendo," Steve told his pastor.

*Would you stand beside Steve?

*How could the church support him?

*How should Christians respond to friends who are, rightly or wrongly, accused of moral indiscretions?

Mothers-in-Law

My mother-in-law certainly isn't one for those mother-in-law jokes. She is never outspoken.

* * *

My mother-in-law sent me two sweaters for Christmas. When she came for a visit, I put on one of the sweaters. The first thing she said to me was, "What's the matter? You didn't like the other one?"

* * *

Ike: My mother-in-law died last week.
Mike: What was the complaint?
Ike: No complaint. Everybody was satisfied.

* * *

I didn't mind it when my wife and my mother-in-law both said "I do" at the wedding; but when I had to carry the two of them over the threshold, that was too much.

This Lesson in Your Life

There is a play on words at the beginning of the book of Ruth, one that is lost to us in the English language. "In the days when the judges ruled, there was a famine in the land, and a certain man of Bethlehem in Judah went to live in the country of Moab, he and his wife and two sons" (Ruth 1:1). Did you catch the play on words? I didn't think so.

"Bethlehem" means literally "house of bread." The play on words occurs when it is said that there is actually a famine in the "house of Bread"! (You might also ponder the contrast of Jesus, the "bread of life," being born hundreds of years later in Bethlehem, "the house of bread.) In Ruth's day, the famine drove the family from the familiar confines of their home to a foreign land. They traveled to Moab in search of food. There are some priorities that take precedence over our desire to stay "at home" or "in place." When our family is threatened, or when we need to make a change for their benefit, we will travel to a foreign land. The family of Elimelech found itself in such a predicament.

Spiritual famines sometimes occur, too. Would you feel it accurate to describe America as being in the midst of a moral famine? In a country which claims to be "one nation under God," we find Christians not having the right to display the Ten Commandments on a courthouse wall. There is something wrong in the land. A famine of freedom has broken out in the home of the free. Bravery can't be found in the land of the brave. Something in our nation is amiss.

That was the point the writer was trying to make in the first verse of the book of Ruth. The family of Elimelech was living in dire times. Drastic measures had to be taken for the family to survive. The only way for this family to make it was to enter enemy territory. The Moabites and the Israelites mixed like water and oil. They were bitter, long-term enemies.

When the family stayed awhile in Moab, long enough for the sons to take Moabite wives. That is the rub in the story of Ruth and Naomi. These two women should have been enemies. Because of marriage they became related. Because of love and respect they became friends. A relationship that never should have happened came to exist between people who had every excuse to dislike each other.

More than a beautiful friendship, the story of Ruth and Naomi is the story of king David's great grandmother.

The story of Ruth is about a God who went into hostile territory, lost His Son, but redeemed His people. The story of Ruth is also a story about Jesus and His saving act as our kinsman-redeemer.

1. Why does the book of Ruth follow the Book of Judges?

The story took place during the time when the judges ruled the land of Israel (Ruth 1:1).

2. Give the names of the persons living in Bethlehem who fled to Moab during the national famine?

Elimelech, who was married to Naomi, and their two sons, Mahlon and Chilion.

3. Given that "Mahlon" means "to be sick" and Chilion means "pining" or "failing," what does this indicate about the children?

Both of these boys were probably "sickly." This was further indicated by their early demise.

4. How long did Mahlon and Chilion live in Moab with their mother and wives?

They lived in Moab for about 10 years (Ruth 1:4).

5. What were the names of the Moabite wives who were taken by Mahlon and Chilion?

The wives were Orpah and Ruth. There is no indication as to who was married to whom.

6. Why did Naomi leave the land of Moab with her daughters-in law?

She had heard that "the Lord had visited His people" back in Bethlehem, and the famine had been relieved.

7. What indications are given about the age of Naomi when she returned to Bethlehem?

She told Ruth and Orpah that she had no more "sons in her womb" and that she was "too old to have a husband" (Ruth 1:11-12).

8. What happened to Orpah?

Orpah traveled part of the way to Bethlehem and pledged her loyalty. However, she eventually turned back to Moab.

9. What was the pledge that Ruth made to Naomi?

That she would stay with her until death.

10. What was Naomi's prayer and wish for her two daughters-in-law?

She prayed that the Lord would deal kindly with them, and that He would provide them with homes and husbands (Ruth 1: 8-9).

During his days as President, Thomas Jefferson and a group of companions were traveling across the country on horseback. They came to a river that had risen above its banks because of a recent downpour, and had had washed the bridge away. Each rider was forced to ford the river on horseback, fighting for his life against the rapid currents. The very real possibility of death threatened each rider.

After several men had plunged in and made it to the other side, a stranger asked President Jefferson if he would ferry him across the river. The President agreed without hesitation. The man climbed on Jefferson's horse, and soon the two of them made it safely to the other side. As the stranger slid off of the saddle onto dry ground, one man in the group asked, "Tell me, why did you select the President to ask this favor of?"

The man was shocked, admitting that he had no idea it was the President who had helped him. "All I know," he said, "is that on some of your faces was written the answer "No" and on some of them was the answer "Yes." In Jefferson the man had found a "yes" face.

I can imagine that Naomi had a "yes" face. Can you see her as the type of person who was always cheerful? Can you see her as the famine takes hold in Bethlehem, trying to make the best of a worsening situation? Can you see her entertaining the children as they travel to this foreign land? There must have been something about her that added stability to her family life.

There must have been something about her that attracted Ruth to her. Remember Ruth left her country and followed this widow to the land of Israel. Others could see something powerful in Naomi. We know that powerful presence was faith in her God. She returned to her home when she heard that God had visited her people and was again supplying the land.

What makes people come to faith in Jesus Christ? Certainly it is the work of the Holy Spirit, but we are instruments of the Spirit's work. People come to faith in Jesus Christ not because they have been convinced by some preacher's eloquent theological argument, but because they see Him living in His followers. People want to look at us and have our faces say, "yes." They want to know that God loves them. When a person has sinned and destroyed his life, he wants to know that God provides a second chance. When we give him a second chance and offer him forgiveness, we are saying "Yes, God loves you."

People see Jesus in us. That is both a thrilling and an awesome statement. It means that each moment is charged with possibility, because in each moment we are making a witness for our Lord.

What does YOUR face say?

God's Blessing for Ruth

Ruth 2:1, 8-12; 4:13-17

And Naomi had a kinsman of her husband's, a mighty man of wealth, of the family of Elimelech; and his name was Boaz.

8 Then said Boaz unto Ruth, Hearest thou not, my daughter? Go not to glean in another field, neither go from hence, but abide here fast by my maidens:

9 Let thine eyes be on the field that they do reap, and go thou after them: have I not charged the young men that they shall not touch thee? and when thou art athirst, go unto the vessels, and drink of that which the young men have drawn.

10 Then she fell on her face, and bowed herself to the ground, and said unto him, Why have I found grace in thine eyes, that thou shouldest take knowledge of me, seeing I am a stranger?

11 And Boaz answered and said unto her, It hath fully been shewed me, all that thou hast done unto thy mother in law since the death of thine husband: and how thou hast left thy father and thy mother, and the land of thy nativity, and art come unto a people which thou knewest not heretofore.

12 The LORD recompense thy work, and a full reward be given thee of the LORD God of Israel, under whose wings thou art come to trust.

4:13 So Boaz took Ruth, and she was his wife: and when he went in unto her, the LORD gave her conception, and she bare a son.

14 And the women said unto Naomi, Blessed be the LORD, which hath not left thee this day without a kinsman, that his name may be famous in Israel.

15 And he shall be unto thee a restorer of thy life, and a nourisher of thine old age: for thy daughter in law, which loveth thee, which is better to thee than seven sons, hath born him.

16 And Naomi took the child, and laid it in her bosom, and became nurse unto it.

17 And the women her neighbours gave it a name, saying, There is a son born to Naomi; and they called his name Obed: he is the father of Jesse, the father of David.

Feb. 10

Memory Selection
Ruth 2:12

Devotional Reading
Psalm 126

Background Scripture
Ruth 2–4

Evangelistic Emphasis

The story of Ruth, with its emphasis on *being faithful to tend to family obligations,* has special relevance for society in general as well as for Christians in particular. Boaz performs the duty of "Levirate" marriage—the responsibility of the nearest kinsman to bring up children by the widow of a near relative. Although Naomi is the widow, she is past child-bearing age; so Boaz marries her daughter-in-law Ruth, instead.

As indicated in the previous lesson, this story was no doubt included in the Hebrew canon because Ruth, a Gentile (Moabite) woman, becomes an ancestor of King David, and hence the Messiah. On a lesser scale, who knows what eternal significance might also come from men and women today who, in the midst of fragmented families, choose to fulfill their duty to hold their own family together?

ᘓᘔ

FOR A LIVELY START...

This session can be introduced by a discussion of relatives that have been important in the lives of members of your group. Some may recall that a godly mother never failed to read them a Bible story at bedtime, or worked a second job so her children could attend college. . . a father who always made it to his son's Little League baseball games . . . an uncle or aunt, brother or sister, grandfather or grandmother who in other ways showed their commitment to family.

Not all group members will have positive memories of immediate relatives. Accept any such comments that arise in the discussion, then note that believers with the worst family backgrounds have God as the Father and Jesus as their Brother (Mark 3:35). Lead into the story of Boaz and Ruth as an example of family members caring for their own.

Teaching Outline	Daily Bible Readings	
	Mon.	Gleaning in the Right Field Ruth 2:1-7
	Tue.	A Safe Place to Work Ruth 2:8-13
I. Boaz, Man of Strength—2:1	**Wed.**	Generous Kinsman Ruth 2:14-23
II. Blessing for Ruth, 8-9		
III. Boaz' Benediction, 10-12	**Thu.**	Obedient Daughter-in-Law Ruth 3:1-5
IV. Birth of a Son, 4:13	**Fri.**	A Worthy Woman Ruth 3:6-18
A. 'It takes a village,' 14-16	**Sat.**	Boaz Marries Ruth Ruth 4:1-12
B. Link with David, 17	**Sun.**	Heritage of a King Ruth 4:13-22

I. Boaz, Man of Strength—2:1

1 And Naomi had a kinsman of her husband's, a mighty man of wealth, of the family of Elimelech; and his name was Boaz.

We last left Naomi as she was returning from the land of Moab with her daughter-in-law Ruth to Naomi's home in Bethlehem (Ruth 1:19; see Lesson 10). Having lost her husband and two sons in Moab, Naomi told her friends no longer to call her Naomi, which means "pleasant," but Mara, which means "bitter"(1:20; cp. Exod. 15:23). Although Naomi feels bereft of God, the story that follows shows that He is tenderly caring for her.

The name Boaz means "Strength is in him," which he apparently exemplified since the text calls him a "mighty man of wealth" (cp. NIV "man of standing"). The story will also show that Boaz was a mighty man of morality and responsibility, too. He will fulfill the duties of a brother of Elimelech, Naomi's late husband, although the text only identifies him as a member of the same family or clan; another relative was more closely kin, as we shall see.

II. Blessing for Ruth, 8-9

8 Then said Boaz unto Ruth, Hearest thou not, my daughter? Go not to glean in another field, neither go from hence, but abide here fast by my maidens:

9 Let thine eyes be on the field that they do reap, and go thou after them: have I not charged the young men that they shall not touch thee? and when thou art athirst, go unto the vessels, and drink of that which the young men have drawn.

In verse 2 we learned that Ruth had shown herself to be an enterprising daughter-in-law by taking advantage of the Jewish law that allowed the poor to follow harvesters to "glean" or pick up leftovers (Lev. 19:9-10). This served in much the same way as public assistance programs do in our day. As it happened, God led her to a field owned by Boaz, Naomi's kinsman by marriage. Boaz inquires about the young woman, discovers her identity, and kindly urges her to remain in his field to glean instead of moving from field to field, as was the custom. As a bonus, he warns the young male reapers not to molest her, and invites her to join them when they slake their thirst.

III. Boaz' Benediction, 10-12

10 Then she fell on her face, and bowed herself to the ground, and said unto him, Why have I found grace in thine eyes, that thou shouldest take knowledge of me, seeing I am a stranger?

11 And Boaz answered and said unto her, It hath fully been shewed me, all that thou hast done unto thy mother in law since the death of thine husband: and how thou hast left thy father and thy mother, and the land of thy nativity, and art come unto a people which thou knewest not heretofore.

12 The LORD recompense thy work, and a full reward be given thee of the LORD God of Israel, under whose wings thou art come to trust.

In verse 2, Ruth had said that she would glean "after him in whose sight I shall find grace," indicating that she may have hoped for just such acceptance by a land-owner as that extended to her by Boaz. Now she melts in gratitude before the man to whom God had guided her. She thanks Boaz for the consideration extended to a mere "stranger," not yet knowing, as Boaz does, of the family connection. For his part, Boaz commends Ruth for her courage in leaving her homeland and accompanying her mother-in-law Naomi back to Israel. The warmth of his welcome indicates that Boaz did not share the common Jewish prejudice against Gentiles.

IV. Birth of a Son, 4:13

13 So Boaz took Ruth, and she was his wife: and when he went in unto her, the LORD gave her conception, and she bare a son.

So much has happened between 2:12 and this passage that we must summarize the events. Ruth returns from Boaz' field to tell Naomi of his special kindness; and Ruth reveals that he is a "kinsman" (2:20). This word, from *go'el*, is sometimes translated "redeemer" (see Job 19:25), since it implied the duty of a relative to "redeem" the lot of a widowed female relative by marrying her and raising up children in her late husband's name. This is the "Levirate" marriage described in Deuteronomy 25:5-10 (see also Mark 12:19). As her actions will show, Naomi no doubt cherished early on the hope that Boaz would serve in this role, just as he will do.

Instead of passively waiting for this to occur, Naomi has instructed Ruth to go into Boaz' tent near the threshing floor and "uncover his feet," or lie down with him as he slept (3:4). Although this is the only reference we have to such a custom, it was apparently an acceptable way for a woman eligible for Levirate marriage to show to a kinsman that she was available.

Boaz was all too ready to accept the role of "redeemer" or kinsman, and marry Ruth, although, legally, it will be in order to raise up a child for Naomi. He knew, however that he was not the nearest of kin. Perhaps he knew that Elimelech had a living brother, while Boaz was perhaps only a cousin or nephew. A fascinating portrayal of Boaz going through the required procedure to obtain a release from the nearer relative is described in 4:1-12. All this precedes the announcement here, in 4:13, that Boaz and Ruth married, and that God blessed them with a son.

A. 'It takes a village,' 14-16

14 And the women said unto Naomi, Blessed be the Lord, which hath not left thee this day without a kinsman, that his name may be famous in Israel.

15 And he shall be unto thee a restorer of thy life, and a nourisher of thine old age: for thy daughter in law, which loveth thee, which is better to thee than seven sons, hath born him.

16 And Naomi took the child, and laid it in her bosom, and became nurse unto it.

The women of Bethlehem react to the birth as though the infant belongs not to Ruth but to Naomi —reminding us that Levirate marriage was for the benefit of the widow. Suddenly Naomi's original name, "Pleasant," becomes more appropriate than Mara, "bitter." At least she has become a grandmother, a mother once-removed. In fact, the women predict that the grandson and his mother, Ruth, will prove more valuable to Naomi than "seven sons," and that he will nourish and provide for her in her old age.

The text does not draw a parallel between Naomi helping to raise the child and Moses' mother, who helped raise him even though he was known as the child of Pharaoh's daughter. Yet the resemblance is clear. Both Moses and this child are destined to figure in God's plan for redeeming His people.

B. Link with David, 17

17 And the women her neighbours gave it a name, saying, There is a son born to Naomi; and they called his name Obed: he is the father of Jesse, the father of David.

We are not told whether some Jewish custom gave the women of the village the right to name Naomi's son, or Naomi and Ruth deferred to them because of the warmth and enthusiasm of their support. At any rate, the name they gave the child, Obed, was significant. The word means "servant," and in God's providence it is given here to one whose lineage will include King David, the servant-king. Of course Christians also connect this remarkable family tree with the Messiah, as shown in the genealogies of Jesus in the Gospels (Matt. 1:5-6; Luke 3:31-32).

This connection shows again the importance of the book of Ruth, and explains why such a story was included in the Bible. Even Jews who do not accept the claims of Jesus have seen in the inclusion of a Moabite woman, Ruth, in the lineage of King David a sign that even while nourishing the Jews as His specially chosen people, God was planning for a Messianic descendant of David to reach out to Gentiles. In Ruth, we can see that such a universal mission was imprinted in the very genes of the Davidic Messiah.

Evangelistic Emphasis

A woman who traveled called home to check on things. She asked about the kids, her mom, and the dog. The husband said, "The dog is dead." The wife was sad and angry at the abrupt way her husband broke the news.

She said, "When I called from New York you should have said, 'the dog is on the roof.' When I called from Atlanta you should have told me, 'The dog fell off of the roof.' When I called from Dallas you should have told me the dog had died.' "From now on, I want you to be more gentle in your communication," she said. "By the way," she added, "how is Mom?" "She's on the roof!" her husband said.

Our Lord has shared His kindness with us in the ministry of Jesus Christ. One of the fruits of His Spirit is kindness. Share a kind word, or a thoughtful action with someone you know. They need it.

We do live in a world where kindness appears to be a scarce commodity. We don't stop and help stranded travelers because we fear for our safety. We don't tip waiters and waitresses because they don't report the tips. We have all kinds of excuses and reasons for not practicing the gift of kindness.

The story of Ruth and Boaz is a story of kindness. It is a love story of King David's great-grandparents. We shudder to think what would have happened had Boaz not been kind to Ruth.

We shudder to think what would happen to us had God not been kind in offering His son for our sins.

✺

Memory Selection

The LORD recompense thy work, and a full reward be given thee of the LORD God of Israel, under whose wings thou art come to trust."—*Ruth 2:12*

I consider myself an adult. After all I have been writing Sunday school lesson for you for more than five years now. I pastor a very wonderful church. I have a wife and a couple of children. One of my children is in college. I know I am an adult. The calendar and the candles on my birthday cake say so.

So I am amused that my mother still wants to "mother" me. When I am down she sees it as her duty to give me a lift. When I neglect to call, she gives me gentle reminders. When I am having difficulty with certain members of the church, mom will ask, "Do you want me to come and hit them with my purse?" She would too! Mom's purse is registered in several states as a lethal weapon!

Until one of us goes on to glory, Mom will be my mom. She is still sheltering me under the shadow of her wing.

What a beautiful image for God. God is like a mother who will always be there for us and will protect and care for us. As adults God is still "mothering" us.

Weekday Problems

Hope Lewis was struggling with her faith. Actually, she was mad at God. Hope had grown up in First Church. She had done all the things one is suppose to do to nurture her faith. Yet, her life was not working out the way she had planned. Now her grandmother had died rather suddenly. Hope was very close to her grandmother.

"Just one more thing on top of this mound of trouble," Hope thought as the family gathered to clean out Granny's home. They all were struggling with the fond memories they had of Mrs. Mary Grace Lewis. She was one of God's angels. She loved everyone and never had a harsh word to say about anyone.

As she emptied out an old chest in her room, Hope found one of Mrs. Mary Grace's old Bibles. The cover was missing. The pages were frayed. The Bible had her grandmother's handwriting all over it. Notes she taken during sermons, notes she'd written for her Sunday School classes, and thoughts she had during her morning and evening devotional times, all were there in the Bible.

On the back page, Hope found a birth announcement glued to the back page of the Bible. It was the announcement of her birth. Suddenly the anger was gone; Hope felt the warmth of a presence she'd never known before. Hope took the Bible and lovingly placed it in her purse. She didn't care what the others would say, that Bible was going to be hers.

*Why would Hope be so moved by that birth announcement?

*How can the faith of one person, inspire and uplift the faith of another?

All in the Family

Asked whom they admire most, 79 percent of American kids say it's Mom and Dad; and additional 19 percent name their grandparents. Athletes, musicians, and movie stars don't even come close. Also, 95 percent of children ages 6-14 say they believe in God. On the other hand, almost 1 of every 4 children are being raised by a single mom.—*Time Almanac 2000.*

* * *

The number of accidents in the home is rising. People aren't spending enough time there to know there way around.—*Anonymous*

* * *

The best way to keep children home is to make the home atmosphere pleasant—and to let the air out of the tires.—*Dorothy Parker*

* * *

The three stages of modern family life are matrimony, acrimony, and alimony.—*The Virginian-Pilot*

This Lesson In Your Life

Kindness is its own reward. Kindness is treating persons with respect and dignity. Kindness is also reciprocal. In the jargon of the streets, "What goes around comes around." That idiom is used to describe what happens to the town bully when that bully is finally brought to justice. It is axiomatic that people who live at the edges of the law will be finally convicted of breaking the law.

Kindness that goes around also comes around. The kindness that Naomi showed was sent back to her. It didn't come directly, but through the love that Ruth had for her. Holding her grandson rewarded the mother, who was deprived of the love of her two sons. The kindness that Boaz showed to Ruth led to the beginning of a relationship and eventually a marriage. Kindness was multiplied in this story and kept coming back to those who were being kind.

There were moments where Naomi could have been consumed by her bitterness and grief. In this short saga she lost much. She was displaced from her home because of a famine. Her sons married foreign women on foreign soil. Eventually her husband and both of her sons would die, leaving her as a widow in a strange land. If anyone was qualified to be the poster child for bitterness, it would be Naomi. The kindness she had shown to her daughters-in-law was about to come back to her.

It is one of those great spiritual truths that we reap what we sow. When we plant the seeds of the Spirit the crop produced is the fruit of the Spirit. If we want the good things of God coming to us, we have to send out those good things. Have you noticed that people are drawn to kindness, gentleness, meekness, and people with self-control? People with those manifestations of the fruit of the Spirit become people-magnets. We live in a harsh word, filled with jagged edges and edgy people. Finding someone who is practicing kindness in his or her life is like finding an oasis in the middle of the desert. It is purely refreshing.

In your walk with the Lord are you practicing kindness to others? It is a gift of the Spirit. It is also an activity of human will. You can learn to be kind. You can learn to treat all persons with the dignity, worth, and respect they deserve. And when you practice kindness it will return to you.

The book of Ruth begins with terrible things going on. There was a famine in the land. The book ends with the genealogy of King David. Between those events we find much kindness. We live in a world with similar contrasts. As a child of God, bring kindness to the world in which you live.

1. How was Boaz related to Naomi?
Boaz was a kinsman of Naomi's husband Elimelech.The specific relationship is not mentioned.

2. What was the first act of kindness that Boaz showed to Ruth?
Boaz allowed Ruth to glean in his fields following, close behind the harvesters he had hired.

3. What other deeds of kindness did Boaz offer to Ruth?
Boaz protected this widow from the young men who might molest her. He also allowed her to drink water from a special vessel.

4. What did Boaz say was the motivation for his kindness?
Boaz knew of all the kindness that Ruth had shown to Naomi since the death of her (Ruth's) husband.

5. What prayer did Boaz offer for Ruth?
That the Lord would repay her for all she had done for others (Ruth 2:12).

6. What eventually happened to Ruth and Boaz?
They were married, and had a son named Obed.

7. In terms of Israel's history, why was this story important?
Ruth and Boaz were grandparents to king David.

8. In terms of Israel's history, why would this story be disconcerting for the Hebrews of that day?
David's grandmother was a Moabite, who were enemies of Israel.

9. In what other place do the names of Boaz, Ruth, and Obed appear?
These names were mentioned in the genealogies of Jesus found in the first chapter of Matthew and the third chapter of Luke .

10. What was Naomi's reward for her faith?
She was allowed to raise the child Obed as her very own.

I love going to the movies! I must confess that I saw the movie *Titanic* several times. I loved it because it had a happy ending. Well, not the kind of happy ending that most people like. I know that the boat sank. There were over fifteen hundred people who lost their lives. But the story of the movie ended with the implication that love was rewarded in the end. Jack and Rose were together for eternity. I love happy endings.

I am naive enough to believe that happy endings are possible in most situations. Where there is pain and suffering, a happy ending can still happen when the grace of God is allowed into a situation. The great news of grace is that the work of God in our lives and in our world is never finished. Unfortunately, in our cynical world, even believers sometimes are doubtful about happy endings, feeling that they may happen to other people, but not to them.

The story of Ruth is the story of a happy ending. It is a story as real as your life. The pain in the book is almost unimaginable. Naomi was in a foreign land trying to eke out a life after a famine drove her from her home. Once in this strange land, with strange customs, Naomi's sons decided to marry women from that locale. The proudest moment of her life could not be shared with her extended family because she was away from them. There was no one to invite to her son's weddings. The sons got married and moved out of the house. Naomi was left alone with her husband. The sons got sick and died. Her husband died. Naomi was left alone with her two daughters-in-law and had to support them.

A Hebrew woman alone in a foreign land with the responsibility of her two daughters-in-law had no chance. She must have wondered what she had done wrong for God to have laid such burden on her life. She must have felt that she had been abandoned by her God in a foreign land. Her feelings of abandonment showed through in her words. "Call me no longer Naomi, and call me Mara, for the Almighty has dealt bitterly with me" (Ruth 1:20).

Could you think that this woman could ever have a happy ending? Her life was in shambles. Her faith was being tested. There was little hope for a bright future. There were few options she had for a happy ending.

The story of Naomi and Ruth is the story of two persons who would not quit until God had moved in their lives. They leaned on each other and were faithful to each other in their friendship. They sustained each other until they saw the blessings of God realized in their life. A woman who had no husband or children kept the faith until God could finish His work. This woman who had nothing held in her arms the grandfather of the greatest king in Israel's history.

God continues to work in "impossible" situations. God will be faithful to us if we cling to Him. Our lives are not finished until He calls us home—and that is the ultimate happy ending.

Jonah Rejects God's Call

Jonah 1:1-4, 11-17; 2:1, 10

Now the word of the LORD came unto Jonah the son of Amittai, saying,

2 Arise, go to Nineveh, that great city, and cry against it; for their wickedness is come up before me.

3 But Jonah rose up to flee unto Tarshish from the presence of the LORD, and went down to Joppa; and he found a ship going to Tarshish: so he paid the fare thereof, and went down into it, to go with them unto Tarshish from the presence of the LORD.

4 But the LORD sent out a great wind into the sea, and there was a mighty tempest in the sea, so that the ship was like to be broken.

11 Then said they unto him, What shall we do unto thee, that the sea may be calm unto us? for the sea wrought, and was tempestuous.

12 And he said unto them, Take me up, and cast me forth into the sea; so shall the sea be calm unto you: for I know that for my sake this great tempest is upon you.

13 Nevertheless the men rowed hard to bring it to the land; but they could not: for the sea wrought, and was tem-

pestuous against them.

14 Wherefore they cried unto the LORD, and said, We beseech thee, O LORD, we beseech thee, let us not perish for this man's life, and lay not upon us innocent blood: for thou, O LORD, hast done as it pleased thee.

15 So they took up Jonah, and cast him forth into the sea: and the sea ceased from her raging.

16 Then the men feared the LORD exceedingly, and offered a sacrifice unto the LORD, and made vows.

17 Now the LORD had prepared a great fish to swallow up Jonah. And Jonah was in the belly of the fish three days and three nights.

2:1 Then Jonah prayed unto the LORD his God out of the fish's belly,

10 And the LORD spake unto the fish, and it vomited out Jonah upon the dry land.

Memory Selection
Jonah 1:3
Devotional Reading
Psalm 40:1-8
Background Scripture
Jonah 1–2; Nahum 3

Feb. 17

The story of Jonah emphasizes God's sovereignty over both nations and people. He is not only Lord of His chosen people, the Jews, but over the Gentile nation of Assyria and its important city, Nineveh. He is also Lord over His messengers, although, like Jonah, they sometimes try to flee their commission. Whether we flee or obey, God will accomplish His purpose.

The part of this ancient story to be focused on in this lesson is Jonah's attempted flight from responsibility. The group leader should avoid getting bogged down in endless discussions of whether, and how, a "great fish" literally swallowed Jonah whole. Although this is no doubt the most remembered feature of the book, in the actually story it is only a tool to show both God's care of the rebellious prophet and His insistence that he get on with his task.

೮೦೧೪

The story of Jonah is so familiar that the leader can start this discussion with a free-for-all word association. Ask, *What one word comes to mind first when you think about the story of Jonah?* Predictably, some group members will answer *whale*, giving an opportunity to point out that the text itself only says "great fish,"

although some translations of the Bible, including the KJV, use "whale" in Matthew 12:40. Other useful responses include *obedience . . . Nineveh . . . missions . . . rebellion . . . storm at sea . . . God's ability to intervene miraculously..*

As in Jesus' parables, what individual people see and remember about this story says as much about their own focus and expectations as it does about the story itself. Guide the discussion to the focus of this lesson: *God's plan will be accomplished, with or without the willingness of His servants.*

Teaching Outline

I. Flight from Duty—1:1-4
  A. Jonah and Nineveh, 1-2
  B. Attempted flight, 3-4

II. Furious Storm—11-16
  A. Tempest at sea, 11-12
  B. Heroic struggle, 13-14
  C. 'Thy will be done,' 15-16

III. Further Opportunity—17–2:1, 10
  A. Whale of a time, 17–2:1
  B. Second chance, 10

Daily Bible Readings

Mon. Good News for an Ethiopian
Acts 8:26-40

Tue. 'What God Has Made Clean...'
Acts 10:1-6

Wed. Peter with a Gentile
Acts 10:19-33

Thu. God Is Not Partial
Acts 10:34-48

Fri. Fleeing from God's Call
Jonah 1:1-6

Sat. Man Overboard!
Jonah 1:7-17

Sun. Prayer in a Fish's Belly
Jonah 2:1-10

I. Flight from Duty—1:1-4

A. Jonah and Nineveh, 1-2

1 Now the word of the LORD came unto Jonah the son of Amittai, saying,

2 Arise, go to Nineveh, that great city, and cry against it; for their wickedness is come up before me.

The prophet Jonah is mentioned in 1 Kings 14:25 as having served in the northern kingdom of Israel (often called "Samaria") during the reign of King Jeroboam II. This would place the events in the book of Jonah in the late eighth-century B.C., not long before the northern kingdom was invaded and captured by the Assyrians.

Nineveh was one of the most important cities of Assyria. Although the people of Nineveh would not have appreciated being described as wicked, the story of Jonah actually portrays God as graciously extending to them an opportunity to repent, through the preaching of Jonah. The book of Jonah is therefore important in showing that even under the Old Covenant, God showed Himself to hold accountable all nations, not just the Jews, and to compassionately give them opportunity to serve His moral law even

though they were not under the Mosaic Covenant.

B. Attempted flight, 3-4

3 But Jonah rose up to flee unto Tarshish from the presence of the LORD, and went down to Joppa; and he found a ship going to Tarshish: so he paid the fare thereof, and went down into it, to go with them unto Tarshish from the presence of the LORD.

4 But the LORD sent out a great wind into the sea, and there was a mighty tempest in the sea, so that the ship was like to be broken.

Although Joppa is easy enough to identify as a port city on the Palestinian coast, Tarshish cannot now be definitely identified. Some scholars believe that it was "Tarsus," the city in what is now southeastern Turkey and the home town of the apostle Paul ("Saul of Tarsus"). Others say it was "Tartessos," a Phoenician colony on the Atlantic coast of southwestern Spain. The main point to notice is that both places are *west* and *north* of Israel, while Nineveh was *northeast*. In other words, Jonah is going in almost the opposite direction from where God told him to go.

It should come as no surprise that the prophet resists the mission God gives him. Not only would he have viewed the Assyrian Gentiles as "unclean," political tensions were mounting between the two nations. Also, Jonah's reluctance may have had a personal aspect. Several Old Testament prophets responded reluctantly to their calling; for example Moses (Exod. 3:1ff.), Isaiah (Isa. 6:5); and Jeremiah (Jer. 1:6). They seem to have forgotten that despite their personal inadequacy, where God guides, God provides.

II. Furious Storm—11-16

A. Tempest at sea, 11-12

11 Then said they unto him, What shall we do unto thee, that the sea may be calm unto us? for the sea wrought, and was tempestuous.

12 And he said unto them, Take me up, and cast me forth into the sea; so shall the sea be calm unto you: for I know that for my sake this great tempest is upon you.

Verses 5-9 have described the sailors' terror. Living in a day when God sometimes revealed His will partially through seers and various forms of occult practices, they had cast lots and determined that the storm had arisen because of God's anger at their passenger Jonah. Hence they approach him to ask how to appease his God. Jonah's answer is self-sacrificial enough. We can imagine that a tempest is also raging in his soul, torn as it was between duty and personal desire. He is not reluctant to die, both to calm his inner storm and to save the ship and the lives of the sailors.

B. Heroic struggle, 13-14

13 Nevertheless the men rowed hard to bring it to the land; but they could not: for the sea wrought, and was tempestuous against them.

14 Wherefore they cried unto the LORD, and said, We beseech thee, O LORD, we beseech thee, let us not perish for this man's life, and lay not upon us innocent blood: for thou, O LORD, hast done as it pleased thee.

Now we can note again how the story of Jonah portrays God's concern and esteem for non-Jews. The sailors are more righteous than the fleeing prophet, trying with all their might to save his life. The fact that they "rowed hard" to bring the ship to shore indicates that it was not a large vessel, but was powered by oars as well as sails—like the "bi-remes" (galleys with two banks of oars) and "tri-remes" (three banks) used by the ancient Greeks and Phoenicians.

Also, while the sailors are pagans (vs. 5), and they had at first urged Jonah to pray to his own "god" because of the fierce storm (vs. 6), after Jonah's confession they apparently recognize that his "god" is in fact *the* God, Yahweh. Having determined to sacrifice Jonah to appease God's wrath and calm the tempest, they call Him now to have mercy on them for this desperate act.

C. 'Thy will be done,' 15-16

15 So they took up Jonah, and cast him forth into the sea: and the sea ceased from her raging.

16 Then the men feared the LORD exceedingly, and offered a sacrifice unto the LORD, and made vows.

Carrying out Jonah's advice explicitly, the sea-farers consign him to the sea. Recognizing in this case the connection between a "natural disaster" and Jonah's sin of rebellion does not mean that we can always make this connection. Sometimes disaster strikes in order to show God's glory in overcoming them (see John 9:1-3)

III. Further Opportunity—17–2:1, 10

A. Whale of a time, 17–2:1

17 Now the LORD had prepared a great fish to swallow up Jonah. And Jonah was in the belly of the fish three days and three nights.

2:1 Then Jonah prayed unto the LORD his God out of the fish's belly,

Skeptics have from earliest times protested that this part of Jonah's story cannot be taken literally. Some interpreters have gone so far as to suggest that "The Great Fish" was a tavern or inn on shore near the spot where Jonah was cast overboard. Others, who take the story literally, note that several kinds of sharks and whales have stomachs large enough to accommodate a man. (A 19th-century story of a whaler surviving being swallowed by a whale was denied by his wife after his death.)

A further question is how a person could survive the action of the digestive juices at work in the beast's stomach. Note that 1:17 says that God "prepared" the great fish; obviously a miracle-working God could have included a gastric adjustment in this preparation.

Whether figurative or literal, the story depicts God's willingness to allow this sobering experience to make Jonah reassess his rebellion. For it is from the belly of this leviathan that Jonah reflects on his experience and prays to God in the form of the eloquent psalm in chapter 2. He cries for release "out of the belly of hell" (2:2)—meaning literally "the grave" (NIV), not the place of eternal torment.

B. Second chance, 10

10 And the LORD spake unto the fish, and it vomited out Jonah upon the dry land.

Distasteful though it may seem to modern sensibilities, this simple statement actually shows God's patience and grace in giving Jonah a second chance. By now Jonah has had time to reflect on his plight and repent of his rebellion. Through his experience he has learned to "look again toward thy holy temple" (2:4). Although, as the story continues, he will encounter his stubborn will again, he is on the way to being faithful to his calling.

Evangelistic Emphasis

God has called us to share His message of love and forgiveness with the world. None of us would argue that point. However, our execution of God's purpose of His people is a little less bold than our words.

The essence of Jonah's message is lost when people get bogged down trying to figure out what kind of fish would be large enough to swallow a man. If you have ever known a fisherman, and listened to his tales, the one that got away was big enough to have swallowed Jonah. The point of this story is not the fish.

This story is about a man who would not obey the call of God because he didn't like the people to whom he was being sent. Jonah thought the love of God should stay within the bounds of the land of Israel. It was this feeling of nationalistic ownership of God's message that caused the prophet to run away from his assigned duty. It was on his journey to flee from God that he ran into problems of the fishy kind.

Of all the characters in the story it is the fish that is most obedient to God. The fish became an instrument of Jonah's rehabilitation as a prophet.

Eventually Jonah did land on the shores of Nineveh and preached to the great city. His preaching was so powerful that there was city-wide repentance.

The good news is that God has called us to proclaim His love to everyone. We might not like the people to whom we minister, but we are called to love them.

୫୦ର

But Jonah rose up to flee unto Tarshish from the presence of the LORD, and went down to Joppa; and he found a ship going to Tarshish: so he paid the fare thereof, and went down into it, to go with them unto Tarshish from the presence of the LORD."—*Jonah 1:3*

Jonah was a silly prophet. He was playing a childish game. The assumption he made is still made today—that there is a place we can go to flee from the presence of the Lord. If you want to understand the foolishness of fleeing from the Lord, watch some children playing hide and seek. The kids are out there for everyone to see, but they think they are well hidden.

Adults try to hide from God, too. They try to hide in their careers and the sport of accumulating assets. Others will hide from God in seeking the pleasures of the world. They even seek to hide from God in church—right there on a pew. The feeling is that God certainly won't see them there, and if He does He won't ask them to do anything.

Have you played hide and seek from God?

Weekday Problems

Buster Weatherly was tired. It had been a long week. The sermon just wouldn't come. He had two weddings and a couple of funerals. In the middle of the week he discovered that his Higley deadline had come and gone. His Sunday school lessons would be late getting to the editor.

In the middle of all the things that happen to a minister in the middle of a week, Buster got a phone call from Jean. Jean was in charge of the "church information system." Actually, she was the head of the gossip network, and the prime cause of much trouble in the church. When Jean called it was always with bad news.

This call was no exception. Jean had heard that the Smiths were upset at the preacher. The Smiths were on the church roll, but only showed up for church on Christmas and Easter. They were upset because the preacher had not come and visited in their home.

Buster Weatherly was wondering what good a pastoral visit would do in the case of people who only showed up in church once every six months. He caught himself groaning audibly.

Jean was the type that would pass along this tidbit about the preacher if he didn't show up at the Smiths' house. She loved to tell stories.

Buster went to visit. When he left, he was glad he visited. He discovered some real needs in the Smith's life; and the next Sunday, they came to church.

*In what other ways does God surprise us when we minister to people who are "hopeless"?

Love Life

Flo: Is it true that you're engaged to two different guys?
Jo: Yes, it's true. I can hardly wait until after Christmas to get things straightened out.

* * *

I wrote my girl Suzie every day for a year, and you know what happened? She married the mailman.

* * *

I took my date home in a cab last night, and she was so beautiful I could hardly keep my eye on the meter.

* * *

Ray: I bet you wouldn't go out with me in a million years.
Mae: That's not true.
Ray: Wow! You mean you might go out with me?
Mae: Sure. Call me after a million years.

This Lesson In Your Life

I saw an interesting thing in a worship service. At the time of the offering a lady took out a $20 bill. She held it dutifully in her hand, and dropped it in the offering plate when it arrived. Then I watched her take out $18 dollars in change! It is the first time I have ever seen someone make change out of an offering plate.

Her actions were scary to me because that kind of mentality about God has crept into many churches, where people seem to want to "make change" in their commitment to God. We want to slide through life on a couple of dollars worth of God. We figure that is enough to get us to heaven and keep us out of trouble here.

We want a God who makes change, a God who doesn't demand more than we are willing to give. We desire a deity who conveniently fits into our modalities of thinking and our decisions about living. We want a God who doesn't mind that a person makes change out of the offering plate and out of His commandments for living. We want a God who is not offended by our hedonistic actions. We think we have a God who would be comfortable with compromise. How about a God who doesn't care that we spend more on our hunting and fishing than we give to our Lord and His church?

We don't have such a God! The Lord of heaven and earth is not a negotiator. A thing is either right or wrong, faithful or slothful, good or evil. There are no gray areas with the Almighty. There is no room for discussion and debate. That is a human trait.

Jonah found out about the nature of God. Jonah was not thrilled when God commanded him to go to the biggest, meanest, most Hebrew-hating city of that day, Nineveh. The message to Nineveh was simple, "Repent or be destroyed." We don't know if Jonah went to the Spanish coast to pray about it, or whether he was running away from God. But Jonah boarded a ship to flee, at least for a while, the assignment given him. In his own mind he might have felt perfectly justified in his actions. Justified or not. God was not pleased.

The story is familiar. The storm blew up. After casting lots, the sailors decided to throw Jonah overboard. God commanded a great fish to swallow Jonah. That is where most of us lose the story. We've seen some big ones, but not that big. Don't let the details trip you up. There is something important here. Every character in this story is obedient to God, *except for Jonah.* Finally, in the belly of the fish, Jonah prayed. That's all he could do. He found himself in an impossible situation, of his own making. He found out that God doesn't "make change."

1. What did God command Jonah to do?
To go to Nineveh and cry out against her wickedness.

2. What alternate plan did Jonah devise?
He tried to flee from his commission by catching a ship to Tarshish.

3. From what port did Jonah embark on his ill-fated journey?
Jonah caught a ship at the port of Joppa bound for Tarshish .

4. How did the Lord get the attention of His wayward prophet and the members of the ship's crew?
The Lord sent a great storm that threatened to destroy the ship.

5. How did the sailors save their ship?
They got rid of the object of the Lord's wrath by throwing Jonah overboard.

6. What happened to Jonah once he was cast into the sea?
The Lord appointed a great fish to swallow the prophet.

7. How long was Jonah in the belly of the fish?
Jonah was in the belly of the fish for three days and three nights.

8. What New Testament event parallels the time Jonah was in the fish's belly?
Jesus was in the tomb for three days. The Lord made reference to the "sign of Jonah."

9. List Jonah's travel itinerary.
From Joppa he caught a boat. Thrown off the boat, he was swallowed by a great fish. From the belly of the fish, he was cast out on the shore.

10. In this section of Scripture, who was the only being that was obedient to the Lord?
The fish.

With his back against the wall, Jonah prayed. There is not much else one can do in the belly of the fish. In that prayer, Jonah recognized his responsibility. In an attitude of contrition, he looked to God to deliver him from the situation.

Unfortunately, God is the last one we want to talk to when we find ourselves with our backs against the wall. Too often, when push comes to shove, we try pushing harder, trying to extricate ourselves from our predicament. But to his credit, Jonah prayed!

When you feel the cold mortar at your back, do you turn to the Lord? Or do you try logically to figure out a solution to your own problems? Jonah turned to the only One who could get him out of trouble. He turned to God, knowing that ultimately death might be the result of his disobedience, but believing that even in death God would deliver him. However, God heard the prayer of His stubborn prophet and delivered him from the belly of the fish. I am amused that the fish spit him out right at the destination God had in mind in the first place.

If you don't believe the Jonah story, how about the story of a man whose back was against a cross? He was being crucified with two other fellows that day. He looked over to the one in the middle. Jesus, the claimant to the throne of God, was on the middle cross. In an act of desperate faith this man prayed. "Lord, remember me when you come into your kingdom." Right now there is a forgiven convict walking the streets of heaven who knows more about grace than a hundred theologians. God hears and honors our honest prayers.

God's grace reaches over the walls of our lives and rescues us. That is why when one's back is against a wall, he should pray. God is listening. He has delivered and saved His servants in the past. He will deliver and save you now.

God does not "make change," as discussed in "This Lesson in Your Life." He will hold us accountable for all of life's choices and actions. Yet He does make a way for *us* to change when we find ourselves with our backs against the wall. He offers us a second chance at living life faithfully.

This is both good news and a challenge to us. God has called us to share His message of grace with all people. Too many of us are guilty of walking past the people in the neighborhoods in which we worship, without ever opening our mouths about God's mercy. We would rather relocate our church to the suburbs than to reach out to the neighborhoods in which some churches find themselves. It is much more palatable to move, than to have "those" kind of people in our churches.

Jonah found it easier to try to flee from God than to think God could love and forgive the people of Nineveh. How many misplaced value judgments have we made about the people who surround our very churches?

YOU ARE A GRACIOUS GOD...

God's Mercy to Nineveh

Jonah 3:1-5, 10; 4:1-5, 11

And the word of the LORD came unto Jonah the second time, saying,

2 Arise, go unto Nineveh, that great city, and preach unto it the preaching that I bid thee.

3 So Jonah arose, and went unto Nineveh, according to the word of the LORD. Now Nineveh was an exceeding great city of three days' journey.

4 And Jonah began to enter into the city a day's journey, and he cried, and said, Yet forty days, and Nineveh shall be overthrown.

5 So the people of Nineveh believed God, and proclaimed a fast, and put on sackcloth, from the greatest of them even to the least of them.

10 And God saw their works, that they turned from their evil way; and God repented of the evil, that he had said that he would do unto them; and he did it not.

4:1 But it displeased Jonah exceedingly, and he was very angry.

2 And he prayed unto the LORD, and said, I pray thee, O LORD, was not this my saying, when I was yet in my country? Therefore I fled before unto Tarshish: for I knew that thou art a gracious God, and merciful, slow to anger, and of great kindness, and repentest thee of the evil.

3 Therefore now, O LORD, take, I beseech thee, my life from me; for it is better for me to die than to live.

4 Then said the LORD, Doest thou well to be angry?

5 So Jonah went out of the city, and sat on the east side of the city, and there made him a booth, and sat under it in the shadow, till he might see what would become of the city.

11 And should not I spare Nineveh, that great city, wherein are more than sixscore thousand persons that cannot discern between their right hand and their left hand; and also much cattle?

Memory Selection
Jonah 4:2

Devotional Reading
Psalm 113

Background Scripture
Jonah 3–4

Feb. 24

251

This lesson provides a good opportunity to focus on a consistent trait of both people and God. It portrays the human tendency to try to justify our own prejudices even in the face of God's will; and it shows that Yahweh is a God of graciousness, love, and of second chances.

We reviewed in the previous lesson Jonah's attempt to flee God's charge to go to Nineveh to proclaim God's love and the danger of His wrath. Although the prophet repented after his stormy experience at sea, this lesson finds him protesting that he knew all along the trip would be wasted!

The lesson closes with a reminder that bringing people the message of God's love and of His high expectations is of the highest priority—far more important than justifying our own tendency to let them "stew in their own juice."

ဆာ

Ask members of your group what people, especially children, often do when they don't get their own way. Responses might include *pouting*, a practice in which Jonah freely participates in this lesson; *getting angry*; retreating into an *accusing silence*; or the healthier reaction of *trying to cooperate*.

In this lesson, the prophet Jonah sulks when God accepts the penitent spirit of the people of Nineveh. "I knew that would happen," Jonah pouts to God. "Why did I waste a trip here if You're not going to destroy them as I warned? You could have saved them without my going to all this trouble to preach to them."

God's reply at the end of the story suggests a better way to handle matters when we don't get our way: *respecting people with whom we disagree as being as capable as we are of choosing the right.*

Teaching Outline	Daily Bible Readings

I. Second Chance—3:1-2
 II. Obedient Response—3-5, 10
  A. Preaching God's Word, 3-4
  B. Penitent people, 5
  C. Gracious God, 10
 III. Pouting Prophet—4:1-5
  A. 'I knew it!' 1-2
  B. 'Take me, Lord!' 3-5
 IV. God's Priority—11
	Mon. Good News for Gentiles
	 Acts 15:1-11
	 Tue. Wonders Among Gentiles
	 Acts 15:12-21
	 Wed. No Further Burdens
	 Acts 15:22-35
	 Thu. Ninevites Repent
	 Jonah 3:1-5
	 Fri. Nineveh Is Spared
	 Jonah 3:6-10
	 Sat. Grumbling About Grace
	 Jonah 4:1-5
	 Sun. God's Love for Nineveh
	 Jonah 4:6-11

Verse by Verse

I. Second Chance—3:1-2

1 And the word of the LORD came unto Jonah the second time, saying,

2 Arise, go unto Nineveh, that great city, and preach unto it the preaching that I bid thee.

With infinite patience, God picks up at the point where Jonah had previously rebelled, telling the prophet again to preach to the Gentile city of Nineveh, in Assyria (see 1:2).

Giving Jonah a second chance to fulfill the ministry to which God had ordained him raises modern questions. When God's ministers fall into disobedience that is publicly known, are they also to be given a second chance, or summarily relieved of their ministry? The question can be finally answered only by considering the individual case; but as a general principle the way God dealt with Jonah seems to indicate that however harsh the discipline meted out to a fallen minister, God can still use him.

A second issue concerns the practice of ordination. Some Protestants have inherited something of the Roman Catholic notion of ordination as a "sacrament" that depends more on the call of God than the approval of man. This sacramental view of ordination has resulted in the idea of "once a priest always a priest." Various denominations answer differently the question of whether a minister who for one reason or another resigns his post can later be reinstated.

II. Obedient Response—3-5, 10
A. Preaching God's Word, 3-4

3 So Jonah arose, and went unto Nineveh, according to the word of the LORD. Now Nineveh was an exceeding great city of three days' journey.

4 And Jonah began to enter into the city a day's journey, and he cried, and said, Yet forty days, and Nineveh shall be overthrown.

As noted in the previous lesson, Jonah had to overcome his Jewish prejudice against Gentiles in order to take up God's commission to preach to the Ninevites. The importance of the book of Jonah's being included in the canon of Scripture is its insistence that God was as concerned about Gentiles as He was about the Chosen Race. This does not mean that the Ninevites themselves would automatically praise the Jewish God for being concerned about them; for Jonah's message is one of doom if they do not repent of their sins (1:2). The Assyrians in general were widely feared as ruthless and vicious, and their worship of idols was a given. According to Romans 1:17ff., God had a moral covenant with Gentiles as well as a moral and ritual covenant with Jews. He is as outraged over Gentile breaches of this Law as He is about the Jews' slighting of His covenant through Moses.

According to 4:11, about 120,000 people lived in Nineveh. Some scholars therefore say it could not have taken Jonah "three days" to journey through the city. Others defend this reference by noting that Jonah may have taken his time, preaching in market places along the way. Others say that the term "Nineveh" included surrounding areas that could easily require three days to encompass.

The word translated "overthrown" (NIV "overturned") basically refers to any kind of dramatic reversal; so some would say the line should read "in forty days Nineveh will change its mind" or "repent"— which in fact is exactly what happened. Yet this reading seems to rob Jonah's message of the its confrontational tone and warning.

B. Penitent people, 5

5 So the people of Nineveh believed God, and proclaimed a fast, and put on sackcloth, from the greatest of them even to the least of them.

Although Jonah claims later not to be surprised by the penitent spirit of the Ninevites that led to God's graciously lifting His sentence of doom, it must have been remarkable to other Jews that such a warlike people would heed the Jewish prophet wandering through their city. Imagine a street corner preacher in New York City walking about with "Repent" on a body-sign effecting this kind of change! Nineveh remains the classic reminder to modern believers to simply proclaim God's Word without deciding beforehand what kind of people will respond.

C. Gracious God, 10

10 And God saw their works, that they turned from their evil way; and God repented of the evil, that he had said that he would do unto them; and he did it not.

To say that God "repented" is to say that He changed His mind, not that He was remorseful for sin. This short statement stands in profound contradiction to both ancient and modern views that God is an impersonal Being "out there," a mere "Force" that is unmoved by and uninvolved with what occurs on earth. Abraham's impassioned plea in behalf of Sodom and Gomorrah implies that God could hear prayer and even change His mind, just as He postponed judgment against Nineveh here when the people repented.

III. Pouting Prophet—4:1-5
A. 'I knew it!,' 1-2

1 But it displeased Jonah exceedingly, and he was very angry.

2 And he prayed unto the LORD, and said, I pray thee, O LORD, was not this my saying, when I was yet in my country? Therefore I fled before unto Tarshish: for I knew that thou art a gracious God, and merciful, slow to anger, and of great kindness, and repentest thee of the evil.

Now it becomes clear that Jonah's reluctance to preach to Nineveh was based on a suspicion that God would unleash His love on non-Jews! Jonah's description of God as gracious, merciful, slow to anger, and kind is accurate, but it places God beyond Jonah's comfort zone. His narrow nationalism left no room for divine grace to be poured out on Gentiles.

B. 'Take me, Lord!,' 3-5

3 Therefore now, O LORD, take, I beseech thee, my life from me; for it is better for me to die than to live.

4 Then said the LORD, Doest thou well to be angry?

5 So Jonah went out of the city, and sat on the east side of the city, and there made him a booth, and sat under it in the shadow, till he might see what would become of the city.

Jonah now joins that pitiable group of people who cherish preconceived ideas about God over life itself. The prophet no longer wanted to live in a world in which God was not exclusively the God of the Jews. He is so despondent that he retreats to a spot outside the city where he can nurse his grudge and watch to see if perhaps God will change His mind again and destroy the city as Jonah had warned might happen. Jonah seems to value his prophetic denunciation more than God's sparing the Ninevites. He builds a temporary shelter to shield himself from the sun while he waits.

IV. God's Priority, 11

11 And should not I spare Nineveh, that great city, wherein are more than sixscore thousand persons that cannot discern between their right hand and their left hand; and also much cattle?

In a fascinating "story within a story" in verses 6-10, God "prepared" a small tree or bush to shade Jonah while he pouted, then caused a worm to destroy it—perhaps to test the prophet's response. Sure enough, Jonah was more disturbed at the loss of his shade than about the plight of the formerly impenitent Ninevites! Now, with painful irony, God confronts Jonah for this dismal display of mistaken priorities. Can the fate of 120,000 people be compared with the loss of Jonah's material comfort?

This is also a question hanging over modern Christians. In a world that surely needs God as much as the Ninevites, we often seem more concerned about maintaining our material prosperity than about the fate of people who also "cannot discern between their right hand and their left hand" when it comes to knowing the truth that God longs to redeem them through Christ.

Evangelistic Emphasis

One has to admire Jonah. He didn't get the call of God right the first time, so God called him again. This time, dripping with the stuff in a fish's belly, Jonah decided that he'd better obey God. Admittedly, although he preached against Nineveh, he still didn't fully appreciate what God had called him to do.

Still, he did it. When his doubts grew, all Jonah had to do was to think about those three days in that intestinal tract. That was enough encouragement for him. Jonah, we could say, "learned from his mistake." Jonah is the story of a second chance.

Before we are too hard on ourselves or someone else, let's look at how this man got to "start over." That is what the good news is all about, telling a lost world that in Christ we can start anew. If Jonah got a second chance after going in the opposite direction from the way God's calling demanded, don't you think that you are worthy of God's second chance? If you decide that you are worthy of a second chance, how about a friend? Does he deserve another chance? If you give second chances to yourself and to a neighbor, how about the stranger?

When you tell that stranger about the second chance of God you have understood the evangelistic emphasis.

ഇറ

And he prayed unto the Lord, and said, I pray thee, O Lord, was not this my saying, when I was yet in my country? Therefore I fled before unto Tarshish: for I knew that thou art a gracious God, and merciful, slow to anger, and of great kindness, and repentest thee of the evil." —*Jonah 4:2*

My grandmother would make me choose my switch! When I was being particularly rowdy, she would tell me to go out back and get a switch for her to use on my backside. In my memory, I can't recall her ever using one of the switches on me. Knowing I had gotten to the point of her telling me to get the switch changed my behavior. I don't remember ever going past the back porch, before confessing my sins and promising to be good.

My grandmother taught me about God. You see, the injured party is the only one who can offer forgiveness. The powerful party is the only one who can offer mercy. God is all-powerful and yet is the injured party. Our sin and mischief is against Him. He therefore is the only one who can offer forgiveness and mercy. Enter the door of His house, confess your sins and you will find a God who " . . .is abounding in steadfast love, and ready to relent from punishing." (Jonah 4:2)

Weekday Problems

Weekday problems are my favorites. I love writing this section because I can write about real problems of which I am aware.

My hero in the stories is Buster Weatherly, who is my real life cousin. He is not a minister, but his dad is. My favorite part of writing this section is wondering if you use them in your class discussions or if you use them to ask questions about your real life situation. Some times I like to get people in an impossible bind just to imagine how you would help them straighten them out. How have you done with some of the characters you have met in this section since December?

My hope is that you have learned to be willing to give second chances. That is the whole point of the book of Jonah. The people of Nineveh needed a second chance. Jonah was the reluctant prophet nominated by God to deliver that gracious message. In your own life, think about persons you need to give a second chance. In the life of your church, where are second chances needed?

For anything in the Higley Commentary to matter, you have to apply God's Word to your daily walk. Are you being obedient to the call He has issued? Are you being God-like and offering the people around you a second chance?

When you do, the results are going to surprise you. God will take your offering of that second chance and use it as a seed to turn a life around. Isn't it wonderful that God participates in our weekday problems?

Shades of Jonah:
Here Come da Judge!

Visitor: Pastor, how many active members do you have?
Pastor: They're *all* active. A few are active for the Lord and the rest are active for the devil.

* * *

A Sunday School teacher asked the children to draw a picture illustrating a Bible story. One lad turned in a drawing of a speeding car with a driver who had a long beard, and a man and woman sitting in the back seat.
"What's this Johnny?" the teacher asked.
"Oh," said Johnny. "That's God driving Adam and Eve from the Garden of Eden."

* * *

The prison chaplain was walking through a workroom where inmates made clothing.
"Sewing?" the chaplain asked a prisoner.
"No, chaplain," was the reply. "Reaping."

257

This Lesson in Your Life

This is the modern version of the Jonah story. God tells a Cajun Baptist preacher to go to Baghdad and preach to the Iraqis. At first he naturally refuses, because a respectable preacher wouldn't be caught dead in a place like that among people like them. Yet God keeps hounding the poor man, hardly giving this modern Jonah a moment's peace until the preacher sullenly relents, saying to God and himself, "Well, I'll go if it will make you happy, but the whole thing is a big waste of time."

In Baghdad, this Jonah preaches a short sermon with a bad attitude. He gives the benediction and plans to make a beeline back to his bass boat and head for home. To his shock and consternation, he can't get out of the auditorium. Scarcely has he given the benediction when all these people rush to him, telling him how they are going to change their ways, wanting to give their lives to Jesus, demanding to be baptized. The Bible says that everyone in town—120,000 people— repented. Even the cattle repented. Have you ever seen a cow repent? If you preach in such a way as to provoke bovine repentance, that's impressive!

"Jonah's" reaction? He's absolutely livid. How dare God change His mind and not obliterate Nineveh! How dare He forgive the unforgivable! How dare He love people Jonah hated! So now, Jonah is having a whale of a time. He pouts like a fool sitting beside a withered castor bean plant.

Who is this Jonah? He is the **patron saint** of anyone who secretly smiles when the High School prom queen shows up for the 20th year reunion with 60 extra pounds and her third husband. He is the **soul mate** of the employee who feels delicious pleasure when the boss is suddenly sacked and given 15 minutes to clean out his office. He is the **poster child** of all who appreciate reading in the newspaper about the "family values" politician who winds up being photographed in a hot tub with a "woman not his wife."

Jonah reminds us that even those of us in the community of faith may confuse what *we* hate with what *God* hates. Do we, like Jonah, find pleasure in hating, joy in our enemy's misfortune? Do we find ourselves working for our own self-interests rather than God's glory and the growth of the kingdom?

Jonah provides a new mirror for us to examine ourselves. Jonah presents a painfully clear reflection of slice-of-life malevolence. While war criminals and deranged zealots display glaring, colorful hatefulness for the entire world to scorn, Jonah reminds us that hate also takes shape in souls that appear respectful and faithful. Souls like ours.

1. How many times did God have to tell Jonah to preach to Nineveh?
Jonah had to hear the call of God twice before he preached against Nineveh.

2. How large was the city of Nineveh?
Verse 3 says that it would take three days to walk around the city.

3. How far into the city limits did Jonah travel before preaching?
Jonah traveled "a day's journey" inside the walls of the city before he began his sermon.

4. How long was the period of time between the preaching of the sermon and the destruction of the city?
The Ninevites had 40 days before the city would be overthrown.

5. What was the king's response to the preaching of Jonah?
The king "arose from this throne, removed his robe, and covered himself with sackcloth and sat in ashes" (Jonah 3:6).

6. What was Jonah's response to the results of his preaching ministry?
Jonah was "displeased exceedingly and angry" because the people of Nineveh had heard the message and repented.

7. What did Jonah give as his excuse for not obeying the first time?
He said he knew God would forgive the people of Nineveh and not bring destruction. Why preach destruction if God is a God of mercy? (Jonah 4:2).

8. What did Jonah say he wanted to do as a result of the events in his life recently?
Jonah said, "I beseech thee, for it is better for me to die than to live."

9. How did God show mercy to Jonah after his angry request to die?
God sent a plant to cover his head and give him shade.

10. When God caused the plant to die, what message was He "acting out" for Jonah's behalf?
God was showing Jonah that life and death, judgment and forgiveness, are topics for His control, not Jonah's; and that the spiritual condition of the people of Nineveh was more important than Jonah's physical comfort.

Sybil Canon recalls an experience from her teenage years reminiscent of the second son. Her Uncle Chester was an alcoholic. In fact, in their small Mississippi town he was known as the town drunk. When Sybil was 15, Uncle Chester and Aunt Mattie came to live with her. Sybil had become a Christian as a small girl and had shortly thereafter dedicated her life to Christian service. She was the president of the youth group in her church. She could hardly bear the sight of her uncle. Let alone treat him kindly.

Uncle Chester came to a revival service where Sybil was the soloist. The evangelist asked those who were Christians to stand. Sybil proudly did so. The next morning as Uncle Chester fried the breakfast bacon, he said, "Some people at church last night misunderstood the preacher's directions. He asked for all the Christians to stand. Many people who aren't Christians stood up too."

Sybil knew his quiet comment was aimed at her. It called forth all her bitter resentment. "Do you dare doubt my Christianity?" she screamed. "Your wife has to support you, and everybody in town laughs at you. You can't walk straight! You can't talk without slurring and slobbering. You smell like the gutter. I can't stand having you in my mother's house. I can't stand seeing Aunt Mattie put up with you. The truth is, I can't stand *you*! Do you know what you are, Uncle Chester? You're a drunk, a worthless drunk!"

Chester didn't look up from his frying pan. But he answered quietly, "Sybil, I know what I am. *But do you know what you are?"*

Sybil Canon remembers that as the question that changed her life. She realized that with all her claims to Christianity and her parading of her religion, she had never shown Christian love to her Uncle Chester.

The story hurts because I know of so many people who have not been shown Christian love. Some persons we don't share with because we fear them. Prejudices keep us from sharing the love of God with other people. Still other people fall through the cracks because we look at them and make an assumption that they are people of faith. That diabolical assumption is that if they look like me, talk like me, think like me, then they must believe like me.

Jonah made some serious assumptions about the people of Nineveh. Those assumptions reflected more the truth of his relationship with God than that of the people of Nineveh. In much the same way, when we fail to share God's love it says more about our faith than we are ready to admit. It says that we have determined whom God should and should not love, that if we have decided a person is unfit for the kingdom then God should at least ratify our decision. For such modern people, we certainly can possess a backward theology.

You can get swallowed whole when you try and play God.

the righteousness of God is revealed through FAITH...

Lesson 1

Mar. 3

God's Righteousness Revealed

Romans 1:1-13, 16-17

Paul, a servant of Jesus Christ, called to be an apostle, separated unto the gospel of God,

2 (Which he had promised afore by his prophets in the holy scriptures,)

3 Concerning his Son Jesus Christ our Lord, which was made of the seed of David according to the flesh;

4 And declared to be the Son of God with power, according to the spirit of holiness, by the resurrection from the dead:

5 By whom we have received grace and apostleship, for obedience to the faith among all nations, for his name:

6 Among whom are ye also the called of Jesus Christ:

7 To all that be in Rome, beloved of God, called to be saints: Grace to you and peace from God our Father, and the Lord Jesus Christ.

8 First, I thank my God through Jesus Christ for you all, that your faith is spoken of throughout the whole world.

9 For God is my witness, whom I serve with my spirit in the gospel of his Son, that without ceasing I make mention of you always in my prayers;

10 Making request, if by any means now at length I might have a prosperous journey by the will of God to come unto you.

11 For I long to see you, that I may impart unto you some spiritual gift, to the end ye may be established;

12 That is, that I may be comforted together with you by the mutual faith both of you and me.

13 Now I would not have you ignorant, brethren, that oftentimes I purposed to come unto you, (but was let hitherto,) that I might have some fruit among you also, even as among other Gentiles.

16 For I am not ashamed of the gospel of Christ: for it is the power of God unto salvation to every one that believeth; to the Jew first, and also to the Greek.

17 For therein is the righteousness of God revealed from faith to faith: as it is written, The just shall live by faith.

Memory Selection
Romans 1:16-17
Devotional Reading
Psalm 34:1-8
Background Scripture
Romans 1

daism. The rediscovery of Paul's teaching by the Reformers of the 16th century also made justification by faith a distinctive tenet of Protestantism. Few topics, therefore, are more basic than those explored here.

This lesson introduces 13 sessions on "The Power of the Gospel." It is also the first of five lessons on the classic Reformation topic of "Justification by Faith," drawn from the apostle Paul's letters to the Romans and the Galatians.

Paul's distinction between faith and works became the doctrinal basis of the difference between Christianity and Ju-

Throughout these lessons, the thoughtful teacher will raise questions about how to understand Paul's teaching. Is accepting Christ's work on the Cross itself a kind of "mental" work? Does being saved by faith mean that it doesn't matter how we live? Such questions have won Paul an important if controversial position in the annals of religious history.

ഇൗരു

Bring a pocketful of change to class to introduce Paul's emphasis on justification by faith. First, recall Jesus' question, "What shall a man give in exchange for his soul?" (Matt. 16:26). Then suggest that perhaps you would "pay" a quarter to save your own soul . . . then twice that . . . then a dollar . . . and so on until you have made

clear the point that even the wealthiest person doesn't have enough money to "buy back" or save his soul.

If we can't save our soul with money, what about good deeds? Ask the group to list the worthiest deeds—helping the poor, working for great social causes, righting wrongs, saving someone's life. Then note that Jesus' question implies that none of these deeds is sufficient for salvation, either.

Finally, note that this lesson is about the good news that in our inability to pay enough or do enough to save ourselves, "Jesus paid it all."

Teaching Outline	Daily Bible Readings

I. Paul's Mission—1-5
  A. His apostleship, 1, 5
  B. The Gospel in the Law, 2-3
  B. The witness of the resurrection, 4
II. The Romans' Faith—6-13
  A. Called to be saints, 6-7
  B. Reputation of faithfulness, 8-9
  C. Intent to visit, 10-13
III. God's Power to Save—16-17
  A. First Jews, then others, 16
  B. Justification by faith, 17
	Mon. Hold to Sound Teaching
	      2 Timothy 1:8-14
	Tue. God's Righteousness
	      2 Timothy 2:1-13
	Wed. The Lord Knows His Own
	      2 Timothy 2:14-22
	Thu. The Power of the Gospel
	      Romans 1:11-17
	Fri. Judged in Righteousness
	      Acts 17:22-31
	Sat. On Not Judging Others
	      Romans 2:1-11
	Sun. Law Written on the Heart
	      Romans 2:12-16

Verse by Verse

I. Paul's Mission—1-5

A. His apostleship, 1, 5

1 Paul, a servant of Jesus Christ, called to be an apostle, separated unto the gospel of God,

5 By whom we have received grace and apostleship, for obedience to the faith among all nations, for his name:

Unlike modern letters, in which we sign our names at the end, letters (or "epistles") in the ancient world began with the name of the author. From the outset, Paul identifies himself as an apostle. Hard experience has taught him that some will question his authority to explain such issues as justification by faith. "Judaizing teachers" have especially dogged his steps, wanting Gentiles to come to Christ through the Law. Paul therefore insists on his authority to teach otherwise.

He supports his case by saying that he has been both "called" and "separated" (NIV "set apart"). In modern terms, Paul is saying that he is not a "free-lance" or self-proclaimed minister but has been officially "ordained." In verse 5 he maintains that this appointment was by none other than Christ himself. As he explains in 1 Corinthians 9:1, he fits the qualifications of an apostle as one who has "seen the Lord," no doubt referring to his conversion experience on the Damascus Road (Acts 9:1-5).

B. The Gospel in the Law, 2-3

2 (Which he had promised afore by his prophets in the holy scriptures,)

3 Concerning his Son Jesus Christ our Lord, which was made of the seed of David according to the flesh;

Part of Paul's defense of his apostleship against Jewish opponents was to show that what he preached was rooted in the Scriptures of the Old Covenant. Perhaps he was thinking especially of the prophet Isaiah, often called "the Messianic prophet" because of the many references to the coming One who would bear the sins of the world. From His birth in Bethlehem to His dying for others, the story of Christ could be reconstructed from the Old Testament.

In verse 3, Paul connects his message about Jesus to God's promises to King David. God had promised that His Kingdom would always have an heir of David on the throne (2 Sam. 7:12-14). Both Matthew and Luke are therefore careful to show through detailed genealogies ("according to the flesh") that Jesus was a descendant of David.

B. The witness of the resurrection, 4

4 And declared to be the Son of God with power, according to the spirit of holiness, by the resurrection from the dead:

Not only did the Old Testament testify that the seed of David would come as the Messiah, the fact that Jesus was raised from the dead authenticated him as that Coming One who was promised. Although in His human nature He endured death, the fact that the grave could not hold Him testified also to His divine nature as the Son of God. In a tightly-packed verse or two, Paul has summarized the preaching in the book of Acts: Jesus Christ fulfilled Old Testament prophecy, and although He was crucified He was raised again to prove that He was no mere man.

It was important for Paul to lay this foundation at the very beginning of his letter. He will affirm that salvation rests on the work not of persons but of Jesus, on the Cross. If He were not who He claimed to be, Paul's case cannot be built on a firm foundation.

II. The Romans' Faith—6-13

A. Called to be saints, 6-7

6 Among whom are ye also the called of Jesus Christ:

7 To all that be in Rome, beloved of God, called to be saints: Grace to you and peace from God our Father, and the Lord Jesus Christ.

Here Paul refers to the Romans as being among those among all nations who respond in obedient faith (vs. 5) to this message that Jesus is Messiah and Savior. Using the same word he

used in verse 1 to say he was "called" to be an apostle," he twice says that these believers are also called to be followers of Jesus, or "saints." This word had not yet been reserved for especially venerated examples of holiness and faith. Originally, "saints" (lit. "holy ones") referred to all believers, since they had been "made holy" or set apart by the work of Christ.

"Grace and peace" was a common Christian salutation near the beginning of a letter, much like "Yours in Christ" might be used today at the end.

B. Reputation of faithfulness, 8-9

8 First, I thank my God through Jesus Christ for you all, that your faith is spoken of throughout the whole world.

9 For God is my witness, whom I serve with my spirit in the gospel of his Son, that without ceasing I make mention of you always in my prayers;

Before plunging into the sometimes heavy doctrinal content of his letter, Paul takes time to commend his readers' reputation for faithfulness. We are not told exactly when and by whom Christianity was taken to Rome. Although early tradition has it that Peter visited the city, Galatians 2:7 implies that he did not found the church there; and according to verses 10-11 Paul had not yet been there either. We do know that Christians were in Rome as early as A.D. 49 when the emperor Claudius expelled both Jews and Christians (see Acts 18:3). Apparently the believers there rebounded strongly to have already had a worldwide reputation (meaning the Mediterranean world).

C. Intent to visit, 10-13

10 Making request, if by any means now at length I might have a prosperous journey by the will of God to come unto you.

11 For I long to see you, that I may impart unto you some spiritual gift, to the end ye may be established;

12 That is, that I may be comforted together with you by the mutual faith both of you and me.

13 Now I would not have you ignorant, brethren, that oftentimes I purposed to come unto you, (but was let hitherto,) that I might have some fruit among you also, even as among other Gentiles.

It may seem surprising for Paul to go to such lengths to explain his frustrated plans to visit Rome. Apparently a visit from the apostle was highly prized among the early churches. In the case of Corinth, he was accused of faithlessness when he did not visit as planned (1 Cor. 1:15, 2:1). Clearly, he does not want such a charge to arise among Christians at Rome. His heavy church-planting and church-strengthening schedule had simply "let" him (which meant "disallowed" instead of "allowed," in King James English).

At any rate, Paul had longed to visit these highly reputed Christians in Rome, both to impart and to receive spiritual enrichment and so Paul could reap some "fruit" or results among these Gentile Christians.

III. God's Power to Save—16-17
A. First Jews, then others, 16

16 For I am not ashamed of the gospel of Christ: for it is the power of God unto salvation to every one that believeth; to the Jew first, and also to the Greek.

This famous verse lays down near the start of Paul's letter the principle he will expound throughout. Paul is proud to be a proponent of the Good News that both Jew and Greek can be saved not by keeping the Law but by trusting and obeying ("obedience to the faith" vs. 5) Jesus. This message is for "the Jew first" since Jews were first to be chosen as God's Covenant people. It was through them that Messiah had come. Thus it was Paul's practice to go first to a Jewish synagogue when entering a city for the first time. Only after being rejected there did he typically go to Gentiles (see Acts 13:14, 44-46).

B. Justification by faith, 17

17 For therein is the righteousness of God revealed from faith to faith: as it is written, The just shall live by faith.

The difficult phrase "from faith to faith" probably refers to the *origin* of faith in Christ in the Old Testament, of which Paul spoke in verses 3-4, and the *outcome* of faith in Jesus. Paul's main point is in the final phrase. Quoting Habakkuk 2:4, he again grounds his position in the Old Testament, showing that even there the faithful were justified by faith, not by works of human righteousness. This claim becomes the main thesis in Romans, as Paul moves from a simple letter to an elaborate essay on justification by faith.

Evangelistic Emphasis

Paul writes that through Jesus "and his name's sake, we received grace and apostleship to call people from among all the Gentiles to the obedience that comes through faith" (ROM. 1:5, NIV). Paul declares that he received the grace of God and was called as an apostle to encourage the Gentiles to faithful obedience.

We receive that grace as well. Paul wrote in Ephesians 2:8-9 that we are saved by grace through faith. But, he goes on to say in Ephesians 2:10 that we are created to do good works. Therefore, the work of God's grace within us produces good works.

Now, what is the most important good work a Christian can do for others? I suspect the most important work the Christian can do is to tell someone else about the good news of Jesus Christ. Jesus Himself told all who call themselves disciples, not just apostles like Paul, to go into the world and make other disciples.

Paul received grace and a call to apostleship. We also receive grace and a call to spread the gospel of Jesus Christ among those who do not know. May we always be about the business of sharing the good news of the grace of God in Christ Jesus.

ଓଓ

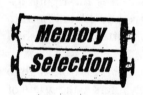

Memory Selection

For I am not ashamed of the gospel of Christ: for it is the power of God unto salvation to every one that believeth; to the Jew first, and also to the Greek. For therein is the righteousness of God revealed from faith to faith: as it is written, The just shall live by faith.—*Romans 1:16-17*

In our day and age, it seems that more and more people are becoming ashamed of the gospel of Jesus Christ. It seems that we have let the world convince us that the gospel (which means "good news") has become a negative thing. We have become timid in the sharing of the gospel, as if we are trying to talk someone into doing something that will ruin their lives.

Of course, we know that living according to the gospel of Jesus Christ is the greatest thing a person can do. Living the gospel brings meaning to an otherwise meaningless existence. The gospel brings purpose to one who is drifting in life. The gospel brings blessing upon blessing, in this life as well as the next.

The gospel is not something of which we should be ashamed. The gospel is something we should be willing to shout from the rooftops in our own hometowns. The gospel is good news.

Weekday Problems

The professor was becoming more and more agitated as he spoke. "I do not see how any thinking person can believe there is such an entity as 'God!' You can't see God. You can't touch God. You can't taste God. Ignorant people invented God centuries ago in order to explain what was at that time unexplainable. In today's world, science has altogether explained away God. Science has proved the idea of a 'God' to be false! Religion is only for fools." The professor glared around the room, as if daring any student to do anything but swallow what he was saying without question.

Robert was squirming uncomfortably in his seat. He felt his face growing redder the longer the professor talked. Robert was a Christian as well as a pastor's son. Everything the professor was saying went against what Robert believed and had experienced. Also, by association, the professor was calling Robert's father a fool.

Robert looked around. Although there were several students who seemed uncomfortable by the professor's words, nobody spoke up.

Robert felt he must not keep silent. He cleared his throat. "Professor," he said. "I think you are wrong."

*Would you have spoken up? Explain why or why not?

*Name some ways you defend the gospel in your community.

'Waiter! There's a Fly in My Soup!'

. . . Don't worry, sir, the spider in the bread will take care of it.

. . . So don't worry. Here's a flyswatter.

. . . Just a moment, madam. I'll bring some fly spray.

. . . Now *there's* a fly that knows good soup!

. . . Don't worry. He won't each much.

. . . That's OK, go ahead and eat him. It's on the house, and there's more where it came from.

. . . And that's just the first course. Just wait 'til you see what's in the main entree.

. . . Oh, dear. I told the chef not to strain the soup through the flyswatter.

. . . That's funny. There were two of them when I left the kitchen.

. . . Half a fly would be worse.

. . . Shhhh! Everyone will want one.

From *The All-New Clean Joke Book*, by Bob Phillips.
Used by permission.

This Lesson in Your Life
Getting Right with God

Paul begins this letter to the Romans by telling them who he is and by what authority he is instructing them. This was probably important, for Paul had not yet been to Rome at the writing of this letter. He needed for them to know and recognize his credentials. Certainly, we understand that. We are much more apt to believe and/or respond to instruction that comes from a credible, authoritative source.

Paul expects the Romans to accept that the letter is from him. He also expects the Romans to believe what he says. That is, to accept what he says "by faith." We must live that way as well. There is not a person alive today that was on the earth when Paul went on his missionary journeys. There is not a person alive today who witnessed Peter preach on the day of Pentecost. There is not a person alive today who personally heard Jesus teach or watched Him make the blind man see. No one alive has touched the resurrected body of Jesus.

We accept the veracity of these events by faith. We are convinced these things happened only by our faith. There are no eyewitnesses still around today. We live by faith.

Faith is the foundation of the Christian life. We must trust that God will do what He promises He will do. We count on the fact, by faith, that God will provide. Thus, we willingly give money and time to God knowing that He will see to it that we have enough of both.

We live by faith in Jesus Christ. We trust in His merits alone for our salvation. We count on His righteousness to clothe us in the presence of a Holy God that will not tolerate unrighteousness. We trust that Jesus will come to take His people to live in their heavenly home, just as He said He would in John 14.

We live by faith in the Holy Spirit. We count on Him to work within us to guide us into truth, to convict us of sin, and to give us the power to live lives in victory over the bondage of sin.

All of this comes by faith. That is how we get right with God. It happens by faith. We do not make ourselves more righteous. As we draw closer to God by faith, He works within us to make us better people. It is in the faith relationship with our Heavenly Father through Jesus Christ by the Holy Spirit that we live the Christian life.

There is no Christianity without faith. Paul reminds us, "it is by grace you have been saved, ***through faith*** . . . " (Eph. 2:8). The Christian walk begins with faith. The Christian walk is maintained by faith.

STRAIGHT

1. In verse one Paul says three things about himself. What are they?
Paul says that he is a servant of Jesus Christ; he is called to be an apostle; and he is set apart for the gospel of God.

2. How did God give the promise of the gospel before Jesus?
Through the prophets in the Holy Scriptures.

3. According to verse 4, how did God declare that Jesus was God's Son?
God declared with power that Jesus was the Son of God by His resurrection from the dead.

4. Paul received grace and apostleship for what purpose?
According to verse 5, Paul's apostolic purpose was to call people from among all the Gentiles to the obedience that comes from faith.

5. Were the Romans a faithful people? Explain your answer.
Yes, we know they were faithful because verse 8 tells us their faith was being reported all over the world.

6. Paul describes himself as a servant of Christ. According to verse 9, how is Paul serving?
By serving God with his whole heart in preaching the gospel of Jesus Christ.

7. What was Paul praying for, according to Romans 1:16?
Paul was praying that he might be able to visit Rome in person.

8. Why does Paul want to visit Rome so badly?
So that he may give to Christians there some spiritual gift, and so that he and they may be mutually encouraged by each other's faith.

9. Paul says in verse 16 that he is not ashamed of the gospel. What is the gospel of which he speaks?
The gospel is the power of God for the salvation of everyone who believes. The power of the good news of Jesus is the only way to salvation.

10. What does it take to begin a righteous life and to live a righteous life?
It takes faith. Habakkuk 2:4 (which Paul quotes) says, "The righteous will live by faith."

Isn't it exciting to receive an invitation to a party or special occasion get-together that you have been dying to attend? When we receive an invitation it often means that the person issuing the invitation is a friend. An invitation shows that the folks issuing it want you to be with them to share in their special event. We usually get a positive feeling when we receive an invitation from a friend.

How much more exciting is it to receive an invitation from the King of Kings! Jesus has issued an invitation to each of us to share in the great banquet that will one day be held in His honor. Jesus wants us to be there. It is His fervent desire for *all* of us to be there.

It could be said that Jesus signed the invitation with His own blood. We know that He died on the Cross for the sins of the whole world. Jesus died for all. In His death was the invitation for every person to become a part of the Kingdom of God . . . every person. Have you accepted His invitation?

In our passage we read Paul's testimony about "God, whom I serve with my whole heart. . . ." In that phrase we are reminded that our God is someone to whom we can give all of ourselves. We enter the abundant Christian life when we give all we have to the Master. That is a foreign concept to many. In the natural realm, we are taught we gain more by hanging on to what we have. In the spiritual realm, we gain more by releasing more. The more we give to God of ourselves, the more God gives back to us of Himself.

God is definitely the only agent worthy of our wholehearted dedication. He is worthy of our wholehearted service, as Paul discovered. And when we serve God without holding anything back, we discover that God blesses us in ways we may not even have been able to imagine before.

Paul speaks of imparting to the Romans a "spiritual gift." A gift is something one gives away. Most gifts are something we want to receive. The gift of God's love is interesting. We have more of it if we give it away. The more of God's love we share, the more we have for ourselves. What a unique gift! At Christmas time we search for just the right gift, "the gift that keeps on giving." We really do not need to look any further than God's love. It is the perfect gift. It is the ultimate gift that keeps on giving. It is a gift of which we have more when we give it away.

Jesus Christ invites us all to come into His Kingdom. He offers us the benefits of His Kingdom as we serve Him with our whole hearts.

Often, when one gets an invitation, he is expected to bring a gift. Isn't it great? Jesus sends us the invitation and He gives us the gift, too.

Gift of Grace

Romans 3:1-4, 19-31

What advantage then hath the Jew? or what profit is there of circumcision?

2 Much every way: chiefly, because that unto them were committed the oracles of God.

3 For what if some did not believe? shall their unbelief make the faith of God without effect?

4 God forbid: yea, let God be true, but every man a liar; as it is written, That thou mightest be justified in thy sayings, and mightest overcome when thou art judged.

19 Now we know that what things soever the law saith, it saith to them who are under the law: that every mouth may be stopped, and all the world may become guilty before God.

20 Therefore by the deeds of the law there shall no flesh be justified in his sight: for by the law is the knowledge of sin.

21 But now the righteousness of God without the law is manifested, being witnessed by the law and the prophets;

22 Even the righteousness of God which is by faith of Jesus Christ unto all and upon all them that believe: for there is no difference:

23 For all have sinned, and come short of the glory of God;

24 Being justified freely by his grace through the redemption that is in Christ Jesus:

25 Whom God hath set forth to be a propitiation through faith in his blood, to declare his righteousness for the remission of sins that are past, through the forbearance of God;

26 To declare, I say, at this time his righteousness: that he might be just, and the justifier of him which believeth in Jesus.

27 Where is boasting then? It is excluded. By what law? of works? Nay: but by the law of faith.

28 Therefore we conclude that a man is justified by faith without the deeds of the law.

29 Is he the God of the Jews only? is he not also of the Gentiles? Yes, of the Gentiles also:

30 Seeing it is one God, which shall justify the circumcision by faith, and uncircumcision through faith.

31 Do we then make void the law through faith? God forbid: yea, we establish the law.

Memory Selection
Romans 3:23-24

Devotional Reading
Psalm 33:13-22

Background Scripture
Romans 3

Shockingly, the apostle Paul has just redefined the term "Jew." Formerly, a person was born into the "chosen race," or became a proselyte. Now, Paul asserts, it's a matter of the heart (Rom. 2:28-29). That is, we become a part of the people of God by accepting Christ, the Jewish Messiah.

Now, in Romans 3, Paul deals with predictable questions raised by this radical redefinition. Why did God even call the Jews if anyone can now become a "Jew" by faith? What about the Law of Moses? Does it apply only to the Jews, or to everyone?

Actually, the definition of God Himself is also at stake. Is He the God only of the Jewish race, or a universal God concerned about all people? The breadth of Paul's redefinition of both God and His chosen people make this section a crucial part of his entire theology.

ଛଠର

Paul's rejection of racial superiority would have shocked and angered many Jews of his day. To enable members of your group to identify with how they must have felt, lead them in a discussion of modern feelings of racial superiority. Initial examples may deal with relations among U.S. racial groups—blacks and whites, Hispanics and native Americans.

Point out that feelings of racial superiority are worldwide. People from Japan to the Navajo tribes of America have referred to themselves as *"The* People," implying special status. Primitives of many nations have viewed their land as "the navel of the earth."

Such views would have been magnified among the Jews of Paul's day because of their having been the chosen race under the Old Covenant. Imagine their shock as Paul now asserts that "there is no difference"!

Teaching Outline

I. Priority of the Jews—1-4
  A. Safekeeping God's will, 1-2
  B. Proving God's love, 3-4
II. Provision for All—19-31
  A. Old Covenant law, 19-20
  B. Old Covenant gospel, 21-22
  C. Universal judgment and grace, 23-26
  D. Paul's conclusion, 27-31
    1. Justification is by faith, 27-28
    2. Faith fulfills the Law, 29-31

Daily Bible Readings

Mon. Grace Freely Bestowed
Ephesians 1:3-14

Tue. Called to Hope
Ephesians 1:15-22

Wed. Saved by Grace
Ephesians 2:1-10

Thu. No Longer Strangers
Ephesians 2:13-22

Fri. Under Sin's Power
Romans 3:1-9

Sat. Sin Revealed by Law
Romans 3:10-20

Sun. Justified by Grace
Romans 3:21-31

Verse by Verse

I. Priority of the Jews—1-4
A. Safekeeping God's will, 1-2

1 What advantage then hath the Jew? or what profit is there of circumcision?

2 Much every way: chiefly, because that unto them were committed the oracles of God.

God was justified in selecting the Jews, the descendants of Abraham, Isaac, and Jacob, in order to have a single people who would protect His "oracles" against rampant paganism and unbelief. This "racial preference" had nothing to do with rejecting other peoples, but everything to do with preserving a model for them also to enjoy the blessings of God.

Circumcision was an outward mark of the Jewish "advantage." However, far from being a mark of superiority or exclusion, it was a sign that anyone willing to "cut off" moral and spiritual depravity could become a part of "the Israel of God," a term which Paul applies to Gentiles as well as Jews in Galatians 6:6-16.

B. Proving God's love, 3-4

3 For what if some did not believe? shall their unbelief make the faith of God without effect?

4 God forbid: yea, let God be true, but every man a liar; as it is written, **That thou mightest be justified in thy sayings, and mightest overcome when thou art judged.**

God's Covenant with the Jews stemmed from His unconditional love for them, not their performance. "The LORD did not set his love upon you, nor choose you, because ye were more in number than any people; for ye were the fewest of all people: But because the LORD loved you, and because he would keep the oath which he had sworn unto your fathers" (Deut. 7:7-8a). Therefore the frequent unfaithfulness of even a majority of Israel's kings and people did not annul the Covenant. Yet God reserved the right to redefine, as Paul brings out, the subjects of the Covenant. Including believing Gentiles in it only expanded the Covenant and justified God against those who accused Him of canceling it.

II. Provision for All—19-31
A. Old Covenant law, 19-20

19 Now we know that what things soever the law saith, it saith to them who are under the law: that every mouth may be stopped, and all the world may become guilty before God.

20 Therefore by the deeds of the law there shall no flesh be justified

in his sight: for by the law is the knowledge of sin.

Just as God had singled out the Jews to be His Covenant people, so His Law through Moses applied specifically to them. His universal moral law also applied to Gentiles; but from Abraham to Christ it was the Jews, not the Gentiles, who were held especially accountable to the very Law through which they also enjoyed God's special favor.

Yet both the Jewish and Gentile "laws" carried judgment with them. Gentile nations had rejected God's moral law as freely as many Jews rejected the Law of Moses. Hence "all the world [became] guilty before God" (see vss. 9-18). Yet this very guilt meant that both Jew and Gentile alike needed, and could be the recipients of, not just of law but of God's saving grace, or justification.

This word is so basic to Paul's theology that it deserves a special note here. Originally it was an accounting term, coming from a root we still use today when we speak of "logging" an entry into a set of accounting books. Justification comes not when we keep the Law perfectly, but when God in His grace "logs" the righteousness of Christ, and the perfect way He kept the Law, to our account.

Why could not the Law of Moses "log" this grace? Because, verse 20 affirms, its purpose was not to save but to supply a knowledge of sin. For example, "I had not known lust," Paul will say in 7:7, "except the law had said, Thou shalt not covet." This is similar to the little old lady who said she never read the Ten Commandments "because they put such evil ideas in my head." Certainly the Law was necessary, to define sin; but to attribute salvation to it is to go beyond its intent.

B. Old Covenant gospel, 21-22

21 But now the righteousness of God without the law is manifested, being witnessed by the law and the prophets;

22 Even the righteousness of God which is by faith of Jesus Christ unto all and upon all them that believe: for there is no difference:

Paul frequently shows that his message of grace was actually foreseen by the "law and prophets" (the Old Testament) itself. For example, God predicted through the prophet Jeremiah that the old written Covenant would be replaced by a new covenant written in the heart (Jer. 31:31-33). This is the sense in which the Old Law was not "destroyed" but "fulfilled" by the New (see Matt. 5:17).

C. Universal judgment and grace, 23-26

23 For all have sinned, and come short of the glory of God;

24 Being justified freely by his grace through the redemption that is in Christ Jesus:

25 Whom God hath set forth to be a propitiation through faith in his blood, to declare his righteousness for the remission of sins that are past, through the forbearance of God;

26 To declare, I say, at this time his righteousness: that he might be just, and the justifier of him which believeth in Jesus.

Since the Jews had not kept Moses' Law, nor the Gentiles the moral law, all people are law-breakers. This concept is necessary to pave the way for Paul's next affirmation: since law has failed to save anyone, then everyone may hope in Christ's fulfillment of the law *for* them. They could not enjoy redemption without facing their previous condemnation.

The term "propitiation" means "sin-offering." Paul asserts that the sacrifices of neither Jew nor Gentile were sufficient to atone for our sins; only Christ's death on the Cross suffices. Theologians have long grappled with the question of whether this offering was made to Satan, to redeem us from his clutches, or to God, to appease His wrath. Both Scriptures and logic can be cited on both sides of the argument; but Paul's predominant view seems to be that Jesus' death redeemed us from Satan instead of rescuing us from the wrath of an angry God.

D. Paul's conclusion, 27-31

1. Justification is by faith, 27-28

27 Where is boasting then? It is excluded. By what law? of works? Nay: but by the law of faith.

28 Therefore we conclude that a man is justified by faith without the deeds of the law.

We can imagine both Jews and Gentiles of high moral character "boasting" that this is what saves them. Paul, however, rejects such claims. However righteous we are, we are not perfect; and he who breaks one point of law is a lawbreaker (Jas. 2:10). The only refuge from this dilemma is accepting the work of Christ as our justification, instead of our own deeds.

2. Faith fulfills the Law, 29-31

29 Is he the God of the Jews only? is he not also of the Gentiles? Yes, of the Gentiles also:

30 Seeing it is one God, which shall justify the circumcision by faith, and uncircumcision through faith.

31 Do we then make void the law through faith? God forbid: yea, we establish the law.

Paul's "universalism," or the belief that all people are responsible to God alone instead of to various national gods, was by no means accepted by everyone, either among Jews or Gentiles. Yet is important to establish the point that one God stands behind the one principle that both Jew and Gentile are saved by faith, not works.

Paul's last word here returns to the principle that justification by faith, not works, is supported not only by the apostle's claims but by the Law itself. Actually, the article "the" is omitted in the original. Both the Law of Moses and law in general are incapable of saving sinners. Neither the moral law that applied to the Gentiles nor the Mosaic Law of the Jews had proved adequate. A new day has dawned. Although it does not release us to live lawlessly, it frees us from the eternal burden of knowing that since we are imperfect people we cannot perfectly keep the Law. This unburdening is supplanted by the joy of knowing that we can throw ourselves on the mercy of the One who, unlike any law, can administer grace.

Evangelistic Emphasis

In the state where I live we are required to have our cars inspected annually to ensure their roadworthiness. When the car passes inspection, the mechanic places a small sticker on the front windshield to show that the car has passed.

One year I failed to get my car inspected on time and I was stopped by a state trooper. He wrote me a ticket for the expired sticker and sent me on my way. I went the next day and had my car inspected without any problems. However, I still had a fine to pay for the traffic violation.

I wished I did not have to pay the fine, but I was guilty of the offense, and the law of Louisiana had to be satisfied. Now, the law does not specify that I had to pay the fine. The law simply states that the fine be paid. It would have been nice if someone else had paid my fine, but nobody offered. I paid it myself.

In the spiritual realm every person except Jesus, has violated God's law. There is a penalty for the violations. However, nobody has enough riches of any kind to pay the fine. We need somebody to pay the fine for us.

Jesus has done that. Jesus, who never violated God's law, has paid the fine for those who have violated God's law, and that's all of us.

"Jesus paid it all. All to Him I owe. Sin had left a crimson stain. He washed it white as snow."

ଯ୦ର

Memory Selection

For all have sinned, and come short of the glory of God; Being justified freely by his grace through the redemption that is in Christ Jesus.—*Romans 3:23-24*

Paul says we are justified by God's grace. That term "justified" is a legal one. It means that the law has been satisfied.

Notice, the term does not mean that we have not committed the violation. It can mean either that the penalty has been forgiven or the penalty has been paid by one other than the party who committed the infraction.

In Christ Jesus, we see both senses of the definition of "justified." He has forgiven our sins. It is not by accident that some of the last words uttered on the cross were, "Father, forgive them for they know not what they do."

Also, Jesus paid the penalty for our sins. The Law stated that the blood of a sacrificial animal without blemish or spot must be shed for the sins of the people. Jesus was that perfect sacrifice.

Jesus is both the forgiver and the sacrifice.

Weekday Problems

John just did not understand what all the fuss was about. David was trying to explain to John the fact that all humans are in need of God's grace through Jesus Christ. David was telling John that all folks are guilty of breaking God's laws and are deserving of punishment.

"I go to church," John said. "I'm basically a good person."

"That's not the point," David insisted. "Most people are basically good people. But there is within each person the desire to do what 'I' want to do instead of what God wants done. When you do what you want to do instead of what God wants you to do, that is disobedience. Disobedience is sin."

"Well, I'm not a sinner," John snorted. "I'm better than most of the so-called Christians."

"You're not a sinner? Then, let me ask you," David countered. "Have you ever told a little white lie? Maybe you told your kids to tell your boss you weren't at home if he called."

"Sure," John replied. "Everybody does that."

"Well," David responded, "How many lies do you think it takes to make you a liar?"

*Was David being too hard on John? Explain.

*Have you ever tried to witness to someone that was "too good" for the gospel? What was the outcome?

Amazing Grace in the Law of Nature

A young boy in the woods watched in horror as his parents drowned in a boating accident. Forced to spend the night in the freezing cold, he was trying to sleep when he felt a furry body snuggle against him. Supposing it was a stray dog, he hugged the animal and slept soundly. The next morning he found three beavers who had snuggled around him . . . and saved his life.

* * *

A woman, the sole survivor of a shipwreck, faced drowning. Suddenly she spotted a giant sea-turtle approaching her. She held onto the turtle's shell while it pulled her toward land. Although turtles normally dive in search of food, this one did not eat for two days, until, nearing the shore, it was able to deliver the woman safely into the hands of the crew of a passing ship.

This Lesson in Your Life
Admitting Need

Okay, men, I'm about to pick on you. Picture this. Your family is with you on vacation. You are in an unfamiliar metropolis. Your sister-in-law gave you directions to her house, but the names on the street signs you are passing do not match up at all with the street names she listed. Your wife and kids notice your look of insecurity. About that time you pass a McDonald's.

"Hey!" your son shouts from the back seat. "Didn't we just pass that McDonald's 20 minutes ago?" Of course, your son is right.

"Dear, are we lost?" your wife asks tentatively.

"No, of course not," you reply in your most confident voice.

"Maybe we ought to stop and ask directions," she suggests.

Now, we all know that most men will not admit they are lost. Fewer still will ask for directions even if they will admit they are lost. I am not sure why. I suspect we refuse to ask for directions because that is an admission that we do not exactly have everything under control.

Refusing to ask for directions while lost can waste time when one is trying to reach his destination. Refusing to admit one is lost can be an eternal tragedy in the spiritual realm. In the spiritual realm, recognizing you are lost is quite often the biggest and most difficult step in the salvation process.

We Americans have been taught all our lives to stand on our own two feet. We have been taught to be independent. We have been taught that nobody owes us a handout, a person has to work for what he gets. Yet, there are times in our lives when we need help. There are times in our lives when we are faced with things we simply cannot accomplish on our own. Being good enough to get to heaven is one of those things we cannot accomplish on our own.

We need a Savior—". . . for all have sinned and fall short of the glory of God" (Rom. 3:23). "As it is written: 'There is no one righteous, not even one. . .'" (3:10). Not even Billy Graham, Mother Teresa, or the Pope himself have been good enough to gain heaven on their own merits. They need the Savior.

We all need Jesus. When we recognize that fact, repent, and turn our lives over to Christ, Jesus graciously forgives us of our sins and empowers us to live lives of righteousness through faith in Him.

It all starts when we admit we are lost and need His direction.

STRAIGHT

1. What did Paul say is the first advantage of being a Jew?
The Jews have been entrusted with the very words of God.

2. If people are not faithful to God, will God still be faithful?
Yes, indeed. Neither the Jews' lack of faith nor ours will nullify the faithfulness of God.

3. According to verse 19, who will be held accountable to God?
Paul says the whole world will be held accountable to God.

4. The law cannot make us righteous. What *does* it do for us? (vs.20).
The law makes us conscious of sin. Without the law we would not know when we sin.

5. What is the source of the righteousness of God apart from the law?
The righteousness from God apart from the law comes through faith in Jesus Christ to all who believe.

6. Not including Jesus, list all humans who have lived sinless lives.
There are none, and there never will be any. "All have sinned" (Rom. 3:23).

7. What term does Paul use in verse 24 to mean that believers are declared "not guilty" in God's eyes?
The term "justified" means "declared not guilty." By faith we are justified and declared righteous in God's eyes.

8. What term in verse 24 means "bought with a price"?
The term "redemption." Christ's death redeemed us from slavery to sin.

9. By whose merits are we justified, and who paid the price for our redemption?
Of course, the answer is Jesus Christ. (If nobody in the study gets this answer right, stop immediately and explain the Gospel again!)

10. Are we justified by our observance of the law or by faith?
We are justified only by faith in Jesus Christ. Paul reminds us in verse 23 that no person can keep all the law perfectly.

Once upon a time there was a young man who had been caught shoplifting at a store. The store had a zero-tolerance policy towards shoplifters, so the police were called in and the young man was arrested and taken to jail. The young man was ashamed to call anyone to tell them he had been arrested, so he spent a few nights in jail awaiting his appearance before the judge.

His day in court came up. The young man walked in to the courtroom and his eyes opened wide with surprise. The presiding judge was none other than the young man's own father.

"How do you plead, young man?" the judge asked.

"Dad, you know. . . ."

"Young man, in this courtroom you will address me only by "Judge" or "Your Honor," the judge interrupted sternly. "How do you plead?"

Now the young man was thinking fast. "Your honor, store security picked up the wrong guy. I wasn't even in the department they said the shoplifter was in. I didn't have any of the stuff they said the shoplifter had taken. I haven't done anything. They picked up the wrong guy."

"Your honor," the prosecutor spoke up. "We have videotapes of this young man stealing, then discarding the merchandise seconds before our officers caught up with him."

Sure enough, when they showed the videotape there was no doubt they had the right person for the right crime. The young man simply hung his head. "I plead guilty, your honor. I took the merchandise. I didn't even need it. I had enough money in my wallet to pay for all that stuff. I'm sorry. I'm guilty."

The judge looked across the bench at the defendant, his own son. "For an infraction of this nature I sentence you to 10 days in jail or a $500 fine." With that he rapped the gavel and the case was closed.

"Dad—I mean, your honor! I don't have that kind of money and I sure can't go to jail!" the young man gasped.

With that, the judge got up from the bench and took off his robe. "Son, I know you can't pay the fine. But I can." The judge came around to where his son was, pulled his own checkbook out, and paid the fine for his son.

In a sense, that is what God did for us through Jesus Christ. We cannot be good enough that we never, ever commit a sin. We break God's law. There is no question about it, we are guilty. We are lawbreakers. A penalty has to be paid for our transgressions. However, we do not have the resources to pay the penalty. We need someone to pay the fine for us. Jesus has done that. God then declares us "not guilty" because of the righteousness of Christ. His payment is credited to our account. Praise God!

ABRAHAM BELIEVED GOD...

Heirs of the Promise

Mar. 17

Romans 4:2-3, 13-25

For if Abraham were justified by works, he hath whereof to glory; but not before God.

3 For what saith the scripture? Abraham believed God, and it was counted unto him for righteousness.

13 For the promise, that he should be the heir of the world, was not to Abraham, or to his seed, through the law, but through the righteousness of faith.

14 For if they which are of the law be heirs, faith is made void, and the promise made of none effect:

15 Because the law worketh wrath: for where no law is, there is no transgression.

16 Therefore it is of faith, that it might be by grace; to the end the promise might be sure to all the seed; not to that only which is of the law, but to that also which is of the faith of Abraham; who is the father of us all,

17 (As it is written, I have made thee a father of many nations,) before him whom he believed, even God, who quickeneth the dead, and calleth those things which be not as though they were.

18 Who against hope believed in hope, that he might become the father of many nations; according to that which was spoken, So shall thy seed be.

19 And being not weak in faith, he considered not his own body now dead, when he was about an hundred years old, neither yet the deadness of Sara's womb:

20 He staggered not at the promise of God through unbelief; but was strong in faith, giving glory to God;

21 And being fully persuaded that, what he had promised, he was able also to perform.

22 And therefore it was imputed to him for righteousness.

23 Now it was not written for his sake alone, that it was imputed to him;

24 But for us also, to whom it shall be imputed, if we believe on him that raised up Jesus our Lord from the dead;

25 Who was delivered for our offences, and was raised again for our justification.

Memory Selection
Romans 4:3

Devotional Reading
Psalm 32:6-11

Background Scripture
Romans 4

In Paul's day, submitting to the Law of Moses had become a kind of "deal" between the Jews and God. Many considered God to be obligated to reward them with salvation if they carefully kept Moses' laws that included circumcision, Sabbath-keeping, sacrifice, and tithing.

In this passage, Paul shows that even the Jews' revered ancestor Abraham was not saved that way! God's promise to save Abraham and make of him a great nation came long before the law was given through Moses. Abraham even became a father not by following the "law" of procreation, but by believing his wife Sarah could bear a child when she was long past the normal age of child-bearing.

Paul's point is not that obeying the rules is unimportant, but that God's promises depend on His grace, not our ability to keep the rules. Those who want to be true heirs of Abraham are not those who keep the Law perfectly, but those who believe like Abraham did, even before the Law was given.

ॐ

Introduce this lesson by illustrating how Paul connected positively to His Jewish audience's desire to cling to the past, then pointed them to the future.

Ask what there is about the past that members of your group would like to keep. People look to the past for the very good reason that some old ways have been tried and found true. Yet ask also what elements of the past group members might want to leave behind. What bad elements did the "good ol' days" actually include?

In this lesson Paul wants the Jews to affirm Abraham's faith, but to leave behind later interpretations of his life that led to "legalism" and works salvation—elements in their history, that, when clung to, would actually cancel the best of Abraham's sacred heritage.

Teaching Outline	Daily Bible Readings
I. Ruling out Boasting—2-3 II. Role of the Law—13-15 　A. Faith in a promise, 13 　B. Wrath from the Law, 14-15 III. Receiving the Promise—16-18 IV. Righteousness by Faith—19-25 　A. Grace overcomes nature, 19-22 　B. Heirs of the promise, 23-25	**Mon.** Descendants Like the Stars 　Genesis 15:1-5 **Tue.** 'Unto thy Seed' 　Genesis 15:12-18 **Wed.** God Chose Our Ancestors 　Acts 13:13-25 **Thu.** Set Free by Jesus 　Acts 13:26-39 **Fri.** 'Continue Your Heritage' 　2 Timothy 3:10-17 **Sat.** Faith as Righteousness 　Romans 4:1-8 **Sun.** Heirs Through Faith 　Romans 4:13-25

Verse by Verse

I. Ruling out Boasting—2-3

2 For if Abraham were justified by works, he hath whereof to glory; but not before God.
3 For what saith the scripture? Abraham believed God, and it was counted unto him for righteousness.

As a learned Jew himself, Paul knew his Jewish audience very well. He knew that in their better moments throughout the centuries they had taken pride in being "the children of Abraham." At this period in their history, many Jewish families could trace their family tree all the way back to "the patriarchs," Abraham, Isaac, and Jacob. Paul therefore introduces the arguments in this passage by referring in verse 1 to Abraham as "our father." He is wisely connecting with the way God related to Father Abraham in order to lead Jews to a better understanding of how God wants to relate to them now.

How *did* God relate to Abraham? Did He promise to make his descendants a great nation (Gen. 12:1-2) after Abraham had kept such rules as the law of circumcision? If so, Abraham would have been able to "glory" or boast (NIV) that he had wrested such a promise from God by keeping the

rules. This was not the case, however, As Paul will argue in verses 9-12, God promised to make of Abraham a great nation some 500 years before Moses gave the Law from Mt. Sinai—the Law that included circumcision. Then how did Abraham obtain the promise? *By believing God*—an act of faith, not a work such as circumcision, or tithing, or sacrifice, or any other element in Moses' Law.

II. Role of the Law—13-15
A. Faith in a promise, 13

13 For the promise, that he should be the heir of the world, was not to Abraham, or to his seed, through the law, but through the righteousness of faith.

Although we might expect Abraham to be called "the ancestor" of the world of the faithful, Paul calls him *the heir* of the world—in the sense that he received the world through God's "seed" promise. The main point, however, is that neither Abraham nor his seed "achieved" this status through achievement at all, but only by faith.

Modern discussions have somewhat changed our view of faith from the way Paul usually used the term.

Some, for example, would distinguish between faith and belief; but both words are actually used to translate the same word (*pistis*). It is also popular to view faith as a merely mental process. However, as a Jew, Paul's view of persons did not distinguish between mind and body as much as we do. It is more accurate to define Paul's view of faith as *active trust* or *acceptance*.

B. Wrath from the Law, 14-15

14 For if they which are of the law be heirs, faith is made void, and the promise made of none effect:

15 Because the law worketh wrath: for where no law is, there is no transgression.

If God "accepts acceptance" or active trust as righteousness, what of those who try to earn righteousness by keeping the Law of Moses? Paul's answer is that they make void the promise to Abraham to save the world through him and his "seed," since the promise depends not on the Law but on faith. The reason stated here is that Law *defines sin*, making the need for salvation obvious, but lacks the power to save from the sin of which the Law makes us aware.

III. Receiving the Promise—16-18

16 Therefore it is of faith, that it might be by grace; to the end the promise might be sure to all the seed; not to that only which is of the law, but to that also which is of the faith of Abraham; who is the father of us all,

17 (As it is written, I have made thee a father of many nations,) be-fore him whom he believed, even God, who quickeneth the dead, and calleth those things which be not as though they were.

"It" refers to God's promise to Abraham, and thence to His promise to save all others the same way He saved Abraham—by grace through faith. (Grace and faith are partners in Paul's teaching, just as law and works are paired in what he opposes.)

If this means of salvation were not available to all, God would not be a universal God, saving both Jews and Gentiles—since the Law of circumcision was given only to the Jews. Now that it is clear that God saves even the Jews by faith, we can believe that God "creates" an entire world family out of those who believe instead of out of only the circumcised, raising from spiritual death Gentiles whose sin had "slain" them just as surely as He raises Jews. This gracious act is compared to creating the world out of nothing.

18 Who against hope believed in hope, that he might become the father of many nations; according to that which was spoken, So shall thy seed be.

"Who" refers to Abraham. He hoped and believed even when he could not see the God who called him out of Ur of the Chaldees; and even, as Paul will say in more detail in the next verses, when he and his wife Sarah were "too old" to give him a child through whom the "seed" promise might be fulfilled.

IV. Righteousness by Faith—19-25
A. Grace overcomes nature, 19-22

19 And being not weak in faith, he considered not his own body now dead, when he was about an hundred years old, neither yet the deadness of Sara's womb:

20 He staggered not at the promise of God through unbelief; but was strong in faith, giving glory to God;

21 And being fully persuaded that, what he had promised, he was able also to perform.

22 And therefore it was imputed to him for righteousness.

Abraham was 99 and Sarah was 90 when God appeared to them to renew His covenant that He would make of their descendants a great nation (Gen. 17:1-4, 17). Obviously they could be considered "dead" as far as their childbearing capacity was concerned. Looking back, we can conclude that God deliberately waited until their old age to give them their son Isaac, so His gift of a child could be seen to be of *grace* instead of *nature*. Thus, Abraham's faith was neither in his natural virility nor his ability to save himself by works of righteousness.

The phrase "imputed" was an accounting term, used when a sum of money was "credited" (NIV) to an account. We might think of a man in Abraham's day harvesting 10 bushels of grain, selling it, and taking the proceeds to the bank. The "work" of harvesting would then be credited to the man's account. Paul, however, teaches that God "credited" righteousness to Abraham's account in heaven's divine log-book as righteousness when he accepted God's promise, not when he "worked" to build up his account.

B. Heirs of the promise, 23-25

23 Now it was not written for his sake alone, that it was imputed to him;

24 But for us also, to whom it shall be imputed, if we believe on him that raised up Jesus our Lord from the dead;

25 Who was delivered for our offences, and was raised again for our justification.

Paul has not just been delivering a history lesson on the life of Abraham. He has explained that God related to Abraham by faith, not works, as an object lesson for our own salvation. If we show active trust that Jesus is God's Son, and that He died and was raised from the dead for our sins, we, too, have an account in heaven to which righteousness has been imputed—again, "credited" or logged.

Paul ordinarily affirms that it is the *death* of Christ that atones for our sin or justifies us. In verse 25 he adds that we are also justified by Christ's *resurrection.* If Christ had remained in the tomb, how would we have known that God accepted His atoning act on the Cross? The resurrection justifies our trust in the entire event, showing that just as God raised Jesus, so He will also give eternal life to those who trust in His sacrifice.

Evangelistic Emphasis

Have you ever stopped to think about how much of our lives depend on living by faith? Much of our lives are lived depending on both faith and law. For instance, we see our traffic light turn green. We enter the intersection having faith the person coming at right angles will see his red light and obey the traffic laws and stop.

Again, we hear that a local bank is paying 7.5% interest on certificates of deposit. We know the laws of advertising. If the bank says it will pay 7.5% it must pay 7.5%. We place our faith in that bank and deposit our money there, trusting we will receive our original deposit plus the 7.5% interest when the certificate matures.

God's law reminds us that we must live by faith in Him also. First, we become Christians only by faith in Jesus Christ. God's Word tells us that. We cannot work ourselves into Christianity. There are not enough good works a person can do to earn the title of Christian. We are reminded that it is by grace through faith that we become Christians in the first place (see Eph. 2:8-9).

After we have become Christians by faith, we walk in our Christianity by faith. We trust God for our salvation. Subsequently, we trust God to guide us, lead us, provide for us, and teach us in our daily Christian walk.

Without faith it is impossible to live a Christian life.

ഇരു

For what saith the scripture? Abraham believed God, and it was counted unto him for righteousness.—*Romans 4:3*

During most of the Old Testament times, a person's adherence to the Law, as set forth by the Ten Commandments, was the measure of that person's righteousness. If one kept the Law that one was considered righteous. If one failed to keep the Law that one was considered a sinner.

According to many scholars, Moses received from God the Ten Commandments, God's Law, on Mt. Sinai around 1445 B.C. However, Abraham died some 550 years before the Law was ever introduced. Thus, Abraham's righteousness could not have been based on his obedience to the Law.

Abraham heard from God. He believed God meant what God said. Abraham acted on that belief. Thus, he was considered righteous. Like Abraham, our righteousness is not based solely on our strict obedience to the Law. No one can keep the Law perfectly. Our righteousness is based on faithfully trusting the One who *was* able to keep the Law perfectly, Jesus Christ.

Weekday Problems

Anne had been praying for weeks that God would show her what He wanted her to do in her church. A visiting preacher told the congregation that every person who has been called by God to be a Christian has also been called to be in ministry. So Anne began to pray. She believed she was earnestly seeking God's direction.

Three weeks ago the teacher for the Searchers Class was transferred to another city. Frank, the Sunday School director, began praying about a new teacher. Every time he prayed Anne's name came into his mind. "Could it be that God is directing me to ask Anne to teach?" he asked himself.

After another week of praying and seeking God's will, Frank felt sure he had heard from God. He arranged a meeting with Anne.

"Anne," he said, "I have been praying about this for a month. I believe God has been telling me to ask you to lead and teach the Searchers Sunday School class."

Immediately Anne blurted out, "Oh, I could never do that! I don't have the ability. I don't have the time. I've never taught before! I just couldn't!" Then, a loving voice in Anne's head whispered, "Anne, remember what you asked God for."

*Could Frank's invitation be God's answer to both Frank's and Anne's prayers?

*Does Anne's "no" answer demonstrate her faith or doubt? Explain your answer.

Daffynitions

Stalemate—A spouse who is beginning to smell musty.

Claustrophobia—The fear that Santa Claus and Fidel Castro may be the same person.

Committee—A group of the unprepared, appointed by the unwilling, to do the unnecessary.

Comedian—A person who has a good memory for old jokes.

Cloverleaf—California's state flower.

Church—A place where you encounter nodding acquaintances.

Brat—A child who acts like your own, but belongs to someone else.

Bore—A person who opens his mouth and puts his feats in.

Bachelor—A person who is footloose and fiancee free.

Alarm clock—A small device designed to wake up people who have no children.

This Lesson in Your Life
Following an Example of Faith

God called Abraham, back when his name was Abram, and promised to make his offspring as numerous as the stars. Abram questioned God about this promise, since he was an old man and was childless. God repeated Himself, "A son coming from your own body will be your heir. . . . Abram believed the Lord, and He credited it to him as righteousness" (Gen. 15:4,6).

Abram's wife, Sarai, was in her mid-70s at this time. She was convinced she was past her childbearing years. At first, they decided they would have to help God build a family. Sarah gave her maid, Hagar, to Abram as a wife and asked for a child through her. Ishmael was born to Hagar a year later. This was not God's promise.

Eventually, Abraham and Sarah were convinced that God could do what God said He would do even if it went against all natural laws. As a result, Isaac, the child of promise, was born to the two old people in a miraculous way.

When Abraham and Sarah tried to do things in their own strength and intellect, what followed only resulted in more problems. When they decided to do things God's way, according to God's promise and direction, blessing upon blessing followed.

Following God's commands, promises, and guidance always is the best way. God's way, the way of faith, is always the best way even if it goes against what might seem natural. Proverbs 16:25 tells us, "There is a way that seems right to a man, but in the end it leads to death." God's ways are always right, even if they go against so-called conventional wisdom. We must be people of faith and trust God's ways.

You remember David's battle with Goliath from 1 Samuel 17. David, although still a youth, said he would fight the giant warrior, Goliath. David stated his faith that "The Lord who delivered me from the paw of the lion and the paw of the bear will deliver me from the hand of this Philistine" (vs. 37). This is why David had faith. He said to Goliath, "You come against me with sword and spear and javelin, but I come against you in the name of the Lord Almighty. . . . This day the Lord will hand you over to me . . . and the whole world will know there is a God in Israel" (vss. 45-46).

Today you may be facing trials that seem impossible to overcome. There may be circumstances that seem to overwhelming. You may be facing giants in your own life, even if they are not in the form of nine-foot tall warriors. Yet you can count on God to help you overcome. We must trust in Him and follow His leading. As we walk with Him in faith, He will gain the victory for us. God did it for Abraham. God did it for David. God will do it for you.

GETTING THE FACTS STRAIGHT

1. What was the basis upon which Abraham was counted righteous?
Abraham's belief in God, who had made promises to him, was credited to him as righteousness.

2. Through what medium did Abraham receive the promise that he would be heir of the world?
The promise of Abraham's inheritance came through the righteousness that comes by faith.

3. Who are considered heirs to Abraham's promise: those who live by law or by faith?
The heirs are those who live by faith. If those who live by law are heirs, faith has no value and the promise is worthless.

4. What does Paul mean, "where there is no law there is no transgression"?
No one can break a law that does not exist. Whenever law is introduced, transgression follows.

5. Who is included in the term "Abraham's offspring"?
Both Jewish Christians, those of the law, and Gentile Christians, those who share Abraham's faith but do not possess the law.

6. To what is Paul referring when he says "God who gives life to the dead"?
Paul could be referring to Isaac's birth to Abraham and Sarah. He is certainly referring to the resurrection of Jesus Christ.

7. How old was Abraham when his son of promise, Isaac, was born?
Abraham was 100 years old. Sarah was 90.

8. How does Paul describe Abraham's faith according to verse 21?
Abraham was fully persuaded that God could do what He had promised.

9. The words, "it was credited to him" were written of Abraham and of whom else (vs. 23)?
They were written to us, that is, all who believe in Jesus whom God raised from the dead.

10. According to vs. 25, what was the significance of Jesus' death and resurrection?
He was put to death for our sins and raised to life for our justification.

Faith might be defined as the confidence that what God has promised or said will come to pass. All through the Bible we see this concept.

God told Abraham that Abraham and Sarah would have a son of their own in their old age. At first they did not believe. Eventually they came around to believing that God would do exactly as He promised. Sure enough, God did what He said He would do.

At first, Abraham and Sarah could not believe God would perform that miracle. They tried to take things into their own hands. They did not accept God's plan. They had what they thought was a better plan. However, Abraham and Sarah eventually came around to believe God. Then, they had their son, Isaac.

For Abraham and Sarah, faith was required for them to receive what God had for them. God did what was impossible without God. God worked in that manner many times in the Holy Scripture.

God had a plan for the Israelites to come out of Egypt. It was an impossible plan. Still, God rolled back the waters of the Red Sea, guided the Israelites by cloud and fire, fed the masses with manna and quail, and even brought them water out of a rock. All of these things were impossible without God.

Remember Joshua? He was supposed to defeat the city of Jericho. Do you remember the battle plan? Of course you do! What a crazy plan! It was to march around the city in silence once a day, every day for six days. Then, on the seventh day they marched around the city seven times with the priests blowing trumpets. On the last time they shouted . . . and the walls came tumbling down. Impossible? Well, it was impossible for everyone but God.

The point is, God can do what He says He will do. We can trust that today. I know there have been times in your life where circumstances have beaten you down to the point it seems there is no escape. Don't give up. Keep walking with God in faith. When we are walking with our hands in God's hand, there is nothing that is too big, too tall, or too impossible. God can!

The Scripture reminds us that God calls things that are not as though they were. God can make a way where there is no way. He can make a straight highway out of a wilderness. He can raise a valley up and make a mountain low. He can make rough ground level and rugged places a plain. Our God can!

He is able. We can trust Him. We can place our complete faith in Him. There is no problem too big for God. There is no solution too hard for God. Our task is simply walk with Him daily in faith and watch to see what He does.

Our God *can!*

WE WERE RECONCILED THROUGH THE CRUCIFIXION...

Christ Died for Us

Romans 5:1-11, 18-21

Mar. 24

Therefore being justified by faith, we have peace with God through our Lord Jesus Christ:

2 By whom also we have access by faith into this grace wherein we stand, and rejoice in hope of the glory of God.

3 And not only so, but we glory in tribulations also: knowing that tribulation worketh patience;

4 And patience, experience; and experience, hope:

5 And hope maketh not ashamed; because the love of God is shed abroad in our hearts by the Holy Ghost which is given unto us.

6 For when we were yet without strength, in due time Christ died for the ungodly.

7 For scarcely for a righteous man will one die: yet peradventure for a good man some would even dare to die.

8 But God commendeth his love toward us, in that, while we were yet sinners, Christ died for us.

9 Much more then, being now justified by his blood, we shall be saved from wrath through him.

10 For if, when we were enemies, we were reconciled to God by the death of his Son, much more, being reconciled, we shall be saved by his life.

11 And not only so, but we also joy in God through our Lord Jesus Christ, by whom we have now received the atonement.

18 Therefore as by the offence of one judgment came upon all men to condemnation; even so by the righteousness of one the free gift came upon all men unto justification of life.

19 For as by one man's disobedience many were made sinners, so by the obedience of one shall many be made righteous.

20 Moreover the law entered, that the offence might abound. But where sin abounded, grace did much more abound:

21 That as sin hath reigned unto death, even so might grace reign through righteousness unto eternal life by Jesus Christ our Lord.

Memory Selection
Romans 5:1

Devotional Reading
Psalm 32:1-5

Background Scripture
Romans 5

In this passage, the apostle Paul continues to explain the doctrine of salvation by grace through faith, apart from the works of the Law. Here he moves from the argument, which he knows from bitter experience will be challenged by many, to practical application and illustration. As every Christian knows, it is one thing to accept grace in theory, but another to *live* in grace.

Thus, Paul shows the difference grace can make in the life of a person being persecuted for his faith (vss. 3-5). He shows how much more comforting it is to know that God extended His grace and power to us even while we were sinners, not waiting for us to "earn" it by works (6-11). Finally, he illustrates the importance of grace by comparing and contrasting God's gift of His own Son with Adam, continuing to use Old Testament history to connect with his readers.

෨෨ඏ

Draw your group into this lesson with this unverifiable story illustrating Romans 5:7. During the Vietnam War, a bomber with a four-man crew was hit in the midsection by anti-aircraft flak, and broke in two. The two crew members in the rear of the plane fell to their death, leaving only the pilot and co-pilot aloft. The pilot was a black man from the south, and the co-pilot was a white man from Vermont. Unfortunately, they hated each other.

As the two prepared to eject from the plane, they realized that the explosion had damaged the co-pilot's parachute beyond repair. Without a word, the black man forced his own chute on to the co-pilot's shoulders, and triggered the eject mechanism, giving his life for a man he could not respect.

In this text, Paul acknowledges that giving one's life for someone we love is *admirable*, but affirms that doing so for someone who is unlovable is *miraculous*.

Teaching Outline	Daily Bible Readings
I. Peace with God—1-2 II. Power amid Troubles—3-5 III. Sacrificial Love—6-8 IV. Saved by His Life—9-11 V. Comparison and Contrast—18-21 　A. Adam and Christ, 18-19 　B. Law and Grace, 20-21	**Mon.** The Blessing of Forgiveness 　Psalm 32:1-5 **Tue.** By the Grace of God 　1 Corinthians 15:1-11 **Wed.** Made Alive in Christ 　1 Corinthians 15:20-28 **Thu.** Justified by Faith 　Romans 5:1-11 **Fri.** Free Gift of Righteousness 　Romans 5:12-17 **Sat.** A King on a Donkey 　Zechariah 9:9-13 **Sun.** 'Hosanna in the Highest!' 　Matthew 21:1-11

Verse by Verse

I. Peace with God—1-2

1 Therefore being justified by faith, we have peace with God through our Lord Jesus Christ:

2 By whom also we have access by faith into this grace wherein we stand, and rejoice in hope of the glory of God.

It may be difficult for modern Christians to imagine how a Jew in Paul's day would have puzzled over the statement in verse 1. Typically a Jew would have said that peace with God is obtained by keeping the Law. As the previous lesson and in fact most of the book of Romans shows, Paul's object in writing is to say that we are "accounted just" not by law-keeping but by accepting "the Christ event"—not just His death, but also His resurrected life, as verse 10 will affirm.

Why would not we be able to "stand" (vs. 2) in a secure place of grace by keeping the Law? Because of our human weakness. Rules are important, and no one is more eager than Paul to live a righteous life. Yet those whose sense of peace and security with God depends on keeping the rules are always aware of something, however small, they should not have done, or something more they could have done.

On the other hand, accepting God's grace by faith that *Christ's* perfection, not ours, is the basis of salvation, enables us to live a life of joy and hope.

II. Power amid Troubles—3-5

3 And not only so, but we glory in tribulations also: knowing that tribulation worketh patience;

4 And patience, experience; and experience, hope:

5 And hope maketh not ashamed; because the love of God is shed abroad in our hearts by the Holy Ghost which is given unto us.

Now Paul turns to the very practical issue of how depending on grace, not works, for our salvation applies to a life beset by difficulties. In a day when Jews and Christians were in constant danger of official or unofficial persecution under Roman rule, this was an especially crucial issue. Paul is aware that the person whose security is based on law-keeping lacks the spiritual resources to stand up under this pressure.

Meeting this need, he outlines a five-step "protection plan" available to those whose security is based on the grace-faith system instead of the

293

old law-works regime. We can accept (1) *tribulation* because we know God did not bring it on us to punish us for not being perfect. This leads to (2) *patience*, which is increased by (3) *experience*. Instead of a trembling insecurity, wondering whether God is as opposed to us as our persecutors, we are led to (4) *hope*, which points us toward (5) *confidence,* the opposite of being "ashamed" before God. The end result of the process is rejoicing that we have had the privilege of suffering for the Name (see also James 1:2-4).

III. Sacrificial Love—6-8

6 For when we were yet without strength, in due time Christ died for the ungodly.

7 For scarcely for a righteous man will one die: yet peradventure for a good man some would even dare to die.

8 But God commendeth his love toward us, in that, while we were yet sinners, Christ died for us.

To reinforce the idea of salvation by grace, Paul turns to the most powerful illustration of all: the *timing* of God's gift of His Son for the sins of the world. If salvation were by works, or keeping the Law, God would have waited until the Jews lived perfect lives before sending the Messiah. As every morally and religiously sensitive Jew knew, however, they were far from perfect. Yet God sent His Son not only *despite* their imperfection, but *because* of it!

This is the reason Paul can say that this gift was "in due time." This phrase translates the Greek word *kairos,* and means literally "according to the right moment." That moment came not only for the sin-laden Jew, but for all of us now. God's gift of salvation comes not when we finally reach perfection, but when we finally confess our imperfection.

It is not unheard of for a parent or other loved one to exhibit the kind of courageous love that leads him to give his life for someone he loves or admires. For example, an older brother may see a sibling about to drown, and jump into an icy torrent to save him—only to lose his own life in the process. God's love, however, exceeds such acts of heroism in that He and His Son "jumped in" to rescue us in our wholly unlovable and sinful condition. (See also the illustration in "For a Lively Start.")

IV. Saved by His Life—9-11

9 Much more then, being now justified by his blood, we shall be saved from wrath through him.

10 For if, when we were enemies, we were reconciled to God by the death of his Son, much more, being reconciled, we shall be saved by his life.

11 And not only so, but we also joy in God through our Lord Jesus Christ, by whom we have now received the atonement.

Here Paul skillfully weaves the death of Christ and His subsequent resurrection into a single cloth. We are not only saved by the blood shed in His death; we are also buoyed up in hope by the fact that He was raised from the dead. If Christ's death accomplished our salvation theoretically, His resurrection provides experiential proof that our trust is well-placed. Now we know that instead of being left to die in well-deserved punishment for sin, we, like Jesus, shall be raised to eternal life. Carrying the illustration further, just as grace enlivened Christ's lifeless body and brought it from the tomb, so grace enlivens people who are "dead in sin" (see also Rom. 6:9-11).

The joyful life referred to in verse 11 was an ideal under the Law, but was rendered difficult by the system. The book of Psalms especially rings with the joy of salvation and fellowship with God. Yet *realizing* such joy was constantly threatened by the believer's realization that he had failed to keep some law, however minute. In contrast, the new People of God could rejoice in the fact that Christ Himself had fully kept the Law, and experience more unreservedly a life of gladness and joy. This was a constant theme of the early disciples, despite the persecutions they endured (see Acts 2:46; 5:41).

V. Comparison and Contrast—18-21
A. Adam and Christ, 18-19

18 Therefore as by the offence of one judgment came upon all men to condemnation; even so by the righteousness of one the free gift came upon all men unto justification of life.

19 For as by one man's disobedience many were made sinners, so by the obedience of one shall many be made righteous.

Thoughtful Jews in Paul's day frequently reflected on how one individual often represented and reflected the group of which he or she was a member. For example, in what has been called "corporate personality," Jacob represented the whole of his descendants, Israel (see Num. 24:5). Now Paul uses this way of thinking to compare and contrast Adam and Jesus, and their effect on their "corporate" whole. Just as Adam's sin "infected" the whole race, so Christ's sacrifice for sin takes the place of any future sacrifices for everyone. In this sense, Jesus can be considered "the second Adam," reversing the corporate inheritance of the first sin (see also 1 Cor. 15:21-22, 45).

B. Law and Grace, 20-21

20 Moreover the law entered, that the offence might abound. But where sin abounded, grace did much more abound:

21 That as sin hath reigned unto death, even so might grace reign through righteousness unto eternal life by Jesus Christ our Lord.

In a final word to questioning Jews, Paul moves from a comparison of Adam and Christ to contrasting the Law with grace. Returning to a theme introduced in 3:20, he notes that just as Adam's sin infected the race, so the Law reinforces our awareness of this spiritual sickness. Yet, although sin "abounded" among Adam's descendants, its long-term effects are now canceled by grace. This grace will "reign" not because of the righteousness of those who claim it, but because of the eternal nature of the righteous Christ.

The little child asked her father, "Do you love me, Daddy?"

Her father answered, "Yes, sweetheart. I love you this much." And he held his hands only about six inches apart.

"Daddy," the child grinned, "stop teasing. I know you love me more than that."

"Do I love you this much?" the father asked, holding his hands about two feet apart.

"No, Daddy, you love me more than that."

"Do I love you *this* much?" the father asked, stretching his hands out on both sides of his body as far as he could reach.

"Yes, Daddy," the child answered, bounding into her father's arms. "That's how much you love me."

I'm sure you have noticed. When a person stretches his hands out to the side as far as they can, the person naturally forms the shape of a cross. Jesus showed us how much He loved us not simply by stretching out his hands. He stretched His hands out . . . and died for us. We have a Savior that loves us so much that He gave His life for us on the Cross. In a sense, He stretched out his arms and said to each of us, "I love you this much."

ഓരു

Memory Selection

Therefore being justified by faith, we have peace with God through our Lord Jesus Christ—*Romans 5:1*

I once read a church sign that said, "Know Jesus, know peace. No Jesus, no peace." Friends, there is no source of peace like that of knowing Jesus Christ as our savior. That peace which comes from our faith is not merely a subjective feeling, such as our expression "peace of mind." The peace from knowing Christ truly settles our souls.

We no longer have to prove our goodness by frenzied efforts. We no longer have to accomplish one more good work to demonstrate how deserving we are of God's favor. We simply have to accept by faith the fact that Jesus did for us what we could not do for ourselves. He settled our account with God. We owe nothing more. Therefore, we can live at peace with our God and with ourselves.

Weekday Problems

It certainly sounded too good to be true. In fact, Robert refused to believe it at first. The pastor had come into the prison telling some story about how Jesus loved him so much that Jesus had paid the price for Robert's sins.

"Ain't no way that can be true," Robert told himself. Reflecting over his life, he knew it had been one long trail of criminal activity. He had committed his first crime at the age of 13. He had been in and out of detention centers for the last 10 years. He had lied, stolen, fought, and used and sold drugs.

He had been high on drugs when he beat a woman almost to death just to steal a few dollars from her purse. He had stood before a prosecutor who told him he was guilty. Twelve honest citizens on a jury believed he was guilty. A black-robed judge declared him guilty with the wooden "crack" of his gavel. Now Robert is in a medium security correctional facility in the far end of the state. It really is a living hell.

Now this pastor comes and tells Robert that God will forgive him of all he has done. The pastor says all Robert has to do is ask for forgiveness and accept in faith that he has received it. Surely the pastor had left something out. Were there no good deeds to be assigned, to make up for all the evil he had done? Although it all sounded too good to be true, there is a strange peace coupled with excitement churning in Robert's heart.

*Can a person as bad as Robert be saved by grace?

*Where does repentance come into a situation such as this?

Boy Meets Girl

One girl to another: There's never a dull moment when you're out with Wilbur. It lasts the whole evening.

* * *

The young man's car conked out on a lonely road. "That's funny," he said to his date. "I wonder what that knocking was."

Replied the girl, icily: "Well I can tell you one thing. It wasn't opportunity."

* * *

Girl, looking at menu: I wonder what "filet mignon" is.

Boy, strapped for cash: It's pickled goat's liver. Why?

* * *

Boy: Whisper those three little words that will make me walk on air.

Girl: Go get lost.

This Lesson in Your Life

Reaping the Benefits

I have been on a diet lately. I need to lose some weight. My clothes are getting too tight. I don't like the way I look. The crowning blow came when I applied for a new life insurance policy. The insurance company informed me that I was not eligible for the lowest rates because I was too heavy.

I really, truly do not like to diet. However, I really, truly enjoy the benefits of being of a normal weight for my height and age. There are times when we must endure things in order to gain something else we desire more. Paul addresses this concept here. "We rejoice in our sufferings, because we know that suffering produces perseverance; perseverance, character; and character, hope" (vs. 4). Nobody wants to suffer, but Christians seek the ability to stick with Christ to the end. Nobody wants to suffer, but we do desire to be people of pure character. Nobody wants to suffer, but we do look forward to better things in the future. In my walk with the Lord, I have discovered that God is much more concerned with my character than He is with my immediate comfort. Just as I am doing without the pleasure of stuffing myself with food in order to gain something I want more, we often endure suffering in our spiritual lives to gain more of the character of Christ.

We hope for better things in the future. Paul reminds us that this hope will not disappoint us. You see, a believer's hope is not to be equated with unfounded optimism. On the contrary, it is the blessed assurance of our future destiny and is based on God's love. God's love is revealed to us by the Holy Spirit and has been demonstrated to us by the death of Jesus Christ. Our hope is also strengthened when we remember God's track record. As we read God's Word we are reminded over and over how God has taken care of His people.

Even if there may be suffering, God will gain the victory. Listen to God's Word from Isaiah 43: 1-3a, "Fear not, for I have redeemed you; I have summoned you by name; you are mine. When you pass through the waters, I will be with you; and when you pass through the rivers, they will not sweep over you. When you walk through the fire, you will not be burned; the flames will not set you ablaze. For I am the LORD, your God, the Holy One of Israel, your Savior."

Sometimes we must go through troubles. Yet, we must never fear, God will take care of His people. We can count on Him.

STRAIGHT

1. In Romans 5:2-3, Paul says we should rejoice in two things. What are they?

We rejoice in the hope of the glory of God and in our sufferings.

2. Why would anyone rejoice in suffering?

Because suffering produces endurance which produces character which produces hope.

3. How does God continue to demonstrate His love in our hearts?

His love is "shed abroad in our hearts by the Holy Ghost which is given us."

4. What can we do to gain justification from our sins?

Actually, we are powerless to gain justification on our own merits. We are justified by faith alone.

5. Did Jesus die only for good people?

Of course not. Christ died for the ungodly. Jesus died for all.

6. According to Romans 5: 8, what is the ultimate demonstration of Christ's love to us?

While we were still sinners, Christ died for us. Long before we loved Him, He loved us enough to die for us.

7. Can one be reconciled to God by Christian service and good works?

No. One can only be reconciled to God through the death of Jesus. Our trust in the merits of that death leads to our reconciliation.

8. Does Christ's "one act of righteousness" automatically guarantee eternal life for all?

No, not necessarily. This life is *available* to all, but we must accept it by faith, trusting in the merits of Jesus Christ.

9. It was through the one man Adam's disobedience that we became sinners. How are we made righteous?

The one person Christ's obedience made it possible for us to become righteous. Through our obedience we continue to grow in righteousness.

10. Is it possible to be such a terrible sinner that God cannot forgive and save?

Indeed not. When sin is at its greatest, God's grace is even greater. No sin nor sinner is beyond the reach of God's grace.

Did you know that the God of the universe wants you to be His friend? You see, our friendship with God got all messed up back when Adam and Eve ate that forbidden fruit in the Garden of Eden. Humanity's relationship with God was broken at that point. Yet immediately after that, God began working on restoring that relationship. He has been working since that day to reconcile us to Himself. He is willing to do almost anything to gain back that close bond .

Once upon a time there were two sisters who lived next door to each other. They had not spoken civilly to each other in four years. Their relationship was broken over a rose bush that was growing right on top of the property line. Each sister believed the rose bush to be her own, although neither remembers actually planting the flower. Both watered it. Both fertilized it. Both cared for it. But when it came to picking the beautiful blooms, each wanted them all for herself.

One afternoon, one sister was looking through a photo album their mother had given her. She saw the many pictures of two sisters smiling as they enjoyed the love of the other.

"I've had enough," the sister thought. "I would rather have my sister than that old rose bush any day." So she walked out her front door, down her walk, across the sidewalk, and up the walk to her sister's house. She rang the doorbell and waited expectantly.

"What do *you* want?" was her sister's cool greeting.

"Sis, I've been thinking. I am really sorry that we have been fighting over that rose bush. I would rather have my sister back. Please forgive me. You can have the bush with my blessing."

With those words the other sister melted into tears as she reached out for a hug. "Oh, I don't want that old bush. I want *you!*" They held each other for a long moment and wept. Then they did something else they hadn't done in years. They had a cup of tea and talked for hours.

That story almost parallels our story in relation to God. We broke the relationship with God. God was not wrong. We were. Still, God made every effort to bring us back into His arms. In fact, He had to do something because we had neither the ability nor strength to restore that broken fellowship with God.

God loves you and me so much that He did and will do almost anything to restore any breach in our relationship. I don't know about you, but the realization of that fact makes me love God even more.

New Life in Christ

John 20:1, 11-17; Romans 6:3-8

The first day of the week cometh Mary Magdalene early, when it was yet dark, unto the sepulchre, and seeth the stone taken away from the sepulchre.

11 But Mary stood without at the sepulchre weeping: and as she wept, she stooped down, and looked into the sepulchre,

12 And seeth two angels in white sitting, the one at the head, and the other at the feet, where the body of Jesus had lain.

13 And they say unto her, Woman, why weepest thou? She saith unto them, Because they have taken away my Lord, and I know not where they have laid him.

14 And when she had thus said, she turned herself back, and saw Jesus standing, and knew not that it was Jesus.

15 Jesus saith unto her, Woman, why weepest thou? whom seekest thou? She, supposing him to be the gardener, saith unto him, Sir, if thou have borne him hence, tell me where thou hast laid him, and I will take him away.

16 Jesus saith unto her, Mary. She turned herself, and saith unto him, Rabboni; which is to say, Master.

17 Jesus saith unto her, Touch me not; for I am not yet ascended to my Father: but go to my brethren, and say unto them, I ascend unto my Father, and your Father; and to my God, and your God.

Romans 6:3-8

3 Know ye not, that so many of us as were baptized into Jesus Christ were baptized into his death?

4 Therefore we are buried with him by baptism into death: that like as Christ was raised up from the dead by the glory of the Father, even so we also should walk in newness of life.

5 For if we have been planted together in the likeness of his death, we shall be also in the likeness of his resurrection:

6 Knowing this, that our old man is crucified with him, that the body of sin might be destroyed, that henceforth we should not serve sin.

7 For he that is dead is freed from sin.

8 Now if we be dead with Christ, we believe that we shall also live with him:

Mar. 31

Memory Selection
Romans 6:4

Devotional Reading
Romans 6:9-13

Background Scripture
John 20:1-18; Romans 6

This timely session blends the current study of Paul's letter to the Romans with the Easter celebration of the resurrection of Jesus.

The lesson focuses first on the Gospel of John's account of Mary Magdalene's discovery that the tomb that had held the body of her Lord was now empty (John 1:1, 11-17). Help group members capture both Mary's initial dismay, then her unparalleled joy when Jesus appears in His resurrected body.

Transition to Romans 6:3-8 by noting that Paul's account of baptism parallels Mary's abrupt transformation from despair to joy. Just as Jesus' lifeless body was buried, so despairing, sinful souls can be "buried" in baptism; and just as Christ was raised from the dead, so new believers are raised to the joy of new beginnings.

෨෬

Start this session by reminding the group that one of Jesus' most arresting commandment was the simple command, *"Follow me."* Point out that many of us may have been quite happy to do this as long as we could partake of benefits such as loaves and fishes, find a comfortable seat on a grassy hillside to listen to Him teach. Ask, however, how we would have felt when we learned that we were to follow Jesus even to the Cross.

As this season emphasizes, however, there is Good News in this command. The earliest Christians found they could "crucify" and bury their sinful selves in the waters of baptism; and, in being raised, answer Jesus' call to new life as well. Just as in Jesus' transformation from death to life, when we leave behind our old ways to follow Jesus, "old things are passed away; all has become new."

Teaching Outline	Daily Bible Readings

I. Resurrection Reality—John 1:1, 11-17
  A. The empty tomb, 1, 11
  B. Angels' announcement, 12-13
  C. Tear-dimmed vision, 14-15
  D. The risen Lord, 16-17
 	
II. Re-enactment, Rebirth—Romans 6:3-8
  A. From death to life, 3-5
  B. Dead to sin, 6-7
  C. Alive to Christ, 8
	Mon. Alive to God in Christ
	Romans 6:1-11
	Tue. Eternal Life in Christ
	Romans 6:15-23
	Wed. Sin Brings Death
	Romans 7:7-13
	Thu. Thanks Be to God
	Romans 7:14-25
	Fri. The Empty Tomb
	John 20:1-10
	Sat. Seeing the Living Lord
	John 20:11-18
	Sun. Jesus Among the Living
	John 20:19-23

Verse by Verse

I. Resurrection Reality—John 1:1, 11-17

A. The empty tomb, 1, 11

1 The first day of the week cometh Mary Magdalene early, when it was yet dark, unto the sepulchre, and seeth the stone taken away from the sepulchre.

11 But Mary stood without at the sepulchre weeping: and as she wept, she stooped down, and looked into the sepulchre,

According to tradition, this "first day of the week" was the morning of the third day after the crucifixion of Jesus on Good Friday. The other Gospel writers mention other women who accompanied Mary Magdalene to the tomb, bringing "sweet spices" (Mark 16:1) to anoint Jesus' body, since this work was forbidden on the seventh day, the Sabbath. Perhaps John mentions only Mary Magdalene because it is she who will first leave the site and report to Peter and John that the tomb had been opened (vss. 2-3), then to the other apostles that she had seen the risen Lord (vs. 18).

Although Mary, along with the apostles, had no doubt heard Jesus' predictions that He would arise from the dead, they did not yet "know"

them in the sense of understanding them (vs. 9). Since they could not conceive how the Messiah expected to establish the Kingdom could be cut off after only three years' ministry, the disillusioned apostles drifted away from the tomb, leaving Mary in tears, stooping to gaze into the empty tomb and wondering what could have happened to the body.

B. Angels' announcement, 12-13

12 And seeth two angels in white sitting, the one at the head, and the other at the feet, where the body of Jesus had lain.

13 And they say unto her, Woman, why weepest thou? She saith unto them, Because they have taken away my Lord, and I know not where they have laid him.

While Matthew mentions only one angel outside the tomb (28:2), two are present inside by the time Mary Magdalene enters. While it was obvious that she is weeping both because Jesus had died, and because she thought someone had stolen the body, no doubt the angels ask about her tears to prepare her for the joyful discovery that she has no reason to despair. Only later will Mary realize that the divine beings' presence indicates that God, not robbers, is involved in the empty tomb.

C. Tear-dimmed vision, 14-15

14 And when she had thus said, she turned herself back, and saw Jesus standing, and knew not that it was Jesus.

15 Jesus saith unto her, Woman, why weepest thou? whom seekest thou? She, supposing him to be the gardener, saith unto him, Sir, if thou have borne him hence, tell me where thou hast laid him, and I will take him away.

As Mary turns to leave the tomb, she sees, but does not recognize Jesus. Because He, along with the angels, knows she has no real reason for grieving, he again confronts her with the question about her tears. It will be recalled that the two disciples on the road to Emmaus also did not at first recognize Jesus after His resurrection (see Luke 24:15-16). It is often pointed out that He may have been too emaciated to recognize since He had not eaten for nearly three days and had endured savage beatings. Mary also may have simply been blinded by her tears. She volunteers to take responsibility for the body if the "gardener" will tell her where he took it; for unlike many pagans, the Jews were especially concerned to honor the dead by tending properly to their bodies.

D. The risen Lord, 16-17

16 Jesus saith unto her, Mary. She turned herself, and saith unto him,

Rabboni; which is to say, Master.

17 Jesus saith unto her, Touch me not; for I am not yet ascended to my Father: but go to my brethren, and say unto them, I ascend unto my Father, and your Father; and to my God, and your God.

"Rabboni" was an extended form of "rabbi," which, as John explains, means "Master" in the sense of school-master or "Teacher" (NIV). No doubt Mary reached out toward Jesus, engulfed with love and gratitude at seeing that her Lord was alive after all; and perhaps intending to throw herself to the ground and seize him by the feet in a sign of devotion, as the disiples did in Matthew 28:9.

Jesus, however, restrains her, for reasons that are not absolutely clear. Some believe it was because His fleshly body had already started to decay since he had not yet ascended to receive His resurrection body. Others suppose that He did not want Mary to restrain Him or delay His ascension. This raises the possibility of two "ascensions." Did He ascend to receive a body He can invite others to touch, to prove that He is not a ghost, or the figment of their imagination (see vs. 27); then finally ascend to the right hand of God (Acts 1:9)?

II. Reenactment, Rebirth—Romans 6:3-8

A. From death to life, 3-5

3 Know ye not, that so many of us as were baptized into Jesus Christ were baptized into his death?

4 Therefore we are buried with him by baptism into death: that like as Christ was raised up from the dead by the glory of the Father, even so we also should walk in newness of life.

5 For if we have been planted together in the likeness of his death, we shall be also in the likeness of his resurrection:

It is not as much of a gap as it might seem to move from the resurrection of Christ to Romans 6. For here the apostle Paul shows how believers can personally get in touch with the event that saves them—the death, burial, and resurrection of Christ—by re-enacting that event in baptism.

The importance of being "baptized into his death" is that it was in His death that Christ's blood was shed, and it is that blood that "washes away" sin (5:9; Heb. 9:12-15). The obvious connection between the "washing of water" (Eph. 5:26; Tit. 3:5) and the forgiveness of sins purchased by Christ's death has classically related baptism to salvation, although various religious heritages differ on the precise nature of the relationship.

The re-enactment of the saving event is continued in being "raised" from baptism, just as Jesus was raised from the dead. As Paul has already said, we are not only saved by Christ's death, but by His life (4:24-25). The post-baptismal "newness of life" is parallel to Jesus' "new birth." The believer faces the future, cleansed of sin and ready to live for Christ instead of for self and sin.

B. Dead to sin, 6-7

6 Knowing this, that our old man is crucified with him, that the body of sin might be destroyed, that henceforth we should not serve sin.

7 For he that is dead is freed from sin.

Paul began this chapter defending himself against the charge that his position on salvation by grace means that it doesn't matter how we live (vss. 1-2). Here he expands on the concept of "death" in the imagery of baptism to further clarify the relationship between faith and works. He could say "God forbid" that the Christian ignore good works and continue to sin, because the old self with which he sinned has been buried. It is "dead" to the allure of the flesh. "Henceforth" shows that Paul emphasizes the importance of good works *after* salvation; they are not what *earns* salvation.

D. Alive to Christ, 8

8 Now if we be dead with Christ, we believe that we shall also live with him:

Paul's message is not primarily the negative counsel, "Don't sin," but the positive, "Be alive!" Does he refer here to living with Christ in holiness after dying with Him in baptism, or to the resurrected life after the Second Coming? Probably both. We begin in this life to allow Christ to reign in our bodies, then "lean" into the eventual incorruptible body of the resurrection (1 Cor. 15:54).

Evangelistic Emphasis

A man named Nicodemus once met with Jesus. Nicodemus was a Pharisee and a member of the Jewish ruling council. Jesus told Nicodemus, "I tell you the truth, no one can see the kingdom of God unless he is born again" (John 3:3).

This confused Nicodemus. He supposed Jesus was talking about physical birth. Jesus was actually talking about a spiritual rebirth.

We meet people every day who need new life in Christ: people with whom we work, people we meet at the store, family members, or good friends. They need to be born again, for no one will see the kingdom of God if they have not been reborn.

Folks also need to know that Jesus gives new life in this life, too. There are people whose lives have no meaning, no purpose, and no passion. There are folks who are dying to know that Jesus can give them a second chance.

One of the lessons the resurrection of Jesus proved is that there is new life for those willing to trust Christ. Jesus can also perform the miracle of "resurrecting" those whose lives are withering away on the inside.

We must be about telling others of the new life to be found in Jesus. We must be about showing others the new life we ourselves found in Jesus.

છાલ્સ

Memory Selection

Therefore we are buried with him by baptism into death: that like as Christ was raised up from the dead by the glory of the Father, even so we also should walk in newness of life.—*Romans 6:4*

I have read accounts of people who have had near-death experiences. In almost every account I read, the person was very grateful to have been given another chance at this life. Also, they were quite willing to talk about their experiences.

Paul tells us that we Christians have experienced somewhat of a near-death event. Our baptism demonstrated that we have died to self. Now we live the rest of our lives not for ourselves but for Christ.

The persons who had near-death experiences expressed gratitude and a willingness to tell their stories. We Christians have died to self and been given new life in Jesus Christ. We must live our new lives in Christ with a heart filled with gratitude and the story always on our lips.

Weekday Problems

Janet sat in the hospital room next to her mother's bed. The only sounds were the hiss of the breathing apparatus and the steady beep of the heart monitor. Janet's mom, Mrs. Jacobs, had slipped into a coma since the last stroke.

The first stroke was bad, but Mrs. Jacobs had recovered from it somewhat. She had lost the use of the left side of her body, but her mind and her speech had rebounded. She told Janet after the first stroke, "Sweetheart, if this should happen to me again and it's worse, please don't put me on life support. If I can't be here with you and the family, I want to be with Jesus in heaven."

Mrs. Jacobs had given her life to Christ many years before. She had walked with the Lord all her adult life. She and her husband had raised their children in the church. But Janet had turned away from Christianity.

Janet didn't see any need for faith in Jesus Christ. "I can take care of everything on my own, thank you," Janet had often told her mother. But now, here was something Janet could not take care of at all. Someone she loved was slipping away. Janet realized that her mother might never regain consciousness. She might never see her mother again.

*How would you witness to Janet about eternal life in Christ Jesus?

*Have you ever lost a loved one who was a Christian? How did you handle it?

Who's That Knocking at My Door?

Knock-knock.
Who's there?
Duane.
Duane who?
Duane the tub—I'm dwowning.

Knock-knock.
Who's there?
Freeze.
Freeze who?
Freeze a jolly good fellow.

Knock-knock.
Who's there?
Olive.
Olive who?
Olive you.

Knock-knock.
Who's there?
Mayonnaise.
Mayonnaise who?
Mayonnaise have seen the glory of....

Knock-knock.
Who's there?
Gorilla.
gorilla who?
Gorilla my dreams, I love you.

Knock-knock.
Who's there?
Della.
Della who?
Della Katessen.

This Lesson in Your Life
Experiencing New Life

Everybody knows the story of Jesus' death and resurrection. We have seen "Passion Plays," and the story as it is portrayed on television and in movies. But the story does not stop with the resurrection of Jesus. The message must continue to include our own resurrection life. Now, when I refer to "resurrection life" I am not limiting that phrase simply to life after death. As important as that is, Christ's resurrection also gives new lives for old, right here and now. Lives are changed by His living presence.

Have you experienced new life in Christ? Do others see in you new life, or do they see the same type of life in you that they see in everybody else? I suspect that at least one reason folks are not flocking to churches to experience new life is that they do not see evidence of the new life in Christians!

We would not listen much to a physician who smokes, hacking with every breath, telling us the evils of lung cancer, would we? We would not respond too readily to a fat, sloppy aerobics instructor with high blood pressure telling us how important exercise and weight control are to good health, would we? We would not invest all our money with a financial advisor who asks for a couple of bucks to tide him over until payday, would we?

Neither will people come to Christ if it seems that Christ makes no difference in a person's life. Furthermore, people are dying to see that difference in us. They want to see evidence of one who is born again; who has experienced resurrection life; who is living a new life.

The resurrection of Jesus Christ changed the world. Before His resurrection, the disciples could see no hope. Their leader was dead. They were convinced that all was lost—until they encountered the risen Christ. Shortly afterward they were filled with the Holy Spirit and they became unstoppable.

If we view the resurrection of Jesus as an event locked behind the doors of 2,000 years of history, then our view is incomplete. There was only one resurrection of Jesus, but because of that resurrection, we are able to experience new life. People need to see that new life in us. The message of second chances and fresh starts needs to be proclaimed and demonstrated to a lost and dying world. New life in Christ is a life anchored with the promise of heaven. It is also a life filled with meaning, direction, and purpose in this life.

Have you experienced new life?

1. According to John, who first discovered the stone had been rolled away from the tomb?

John says it was Mary Magdalene. Matthew lists Mary Magdalene and "the other Mary." Mark says it was the two Marys and Salome.

2. On what day and at what time of the day did Mary discover the empty tomb?

Mary discovered the empty tomb on Sunday, apparently very early in the morning because it was still dark. Mark says, "just after sunrise."

3. According to John, who first spoke to Mary at the tomb?

John reports two angels in white. Matthew has one angel, Mark a young man, and Luke has two men who were angels.

4. At first, what did Mary think was the explanation for the empty tomb?

She thought someone had carried away the body of Jesus . (See John 20:15.)

5. What was the message Jesus asked Mary to deliver to His brothers?

"I am returning to my Father and to your father, to my God and your God."

6. According to Romans 6:4, what happens at our baptism?

We are buried with Christ through baptism into death, in order that, just as Christ was raised from the dead, we may have new life.

7. According to Romans 6:5, if we are united in Christ in His death to sin, what do we gain?

Union also with Him in His resurrection.

8. When Paul speaks of the "old self," what does he mean?

The "old self" refers to our lives before we become born again, that is, before we became Christians.

9. When our "old self" is crucified with Christ, what also dies at the same time?

When the "old self" dies, so dies the "body of sin." When the pre-Christian self is put to death, so is the life that was dominated by sin.

10. If we "die with Christ" what do we gain?

If we die with Christ we believe we will live with Christ, both in this life and in Heaven.

The fact of the resurrection of Jesus Christ demonstrates to us that God is able to give new life. God is able to bring things that were dead back to life. He does that every spring. We see grass, trees, plants, and flowers that formerly had no life at all burst into new life and glorious bloom.

Jesus demonstrated that God is also able to give new life to those who have died. We count on the fact that every person who died in Christ will live again with Christ for all eternity. We know that Christians will live again in that perfect place we call Heaven. We will live again where God "will wipe every tear from our eyes. There will be no more death or mourning or crying or pain, for the old order of things has passed away" (Rev. 21:4). Life in Heaven is offered through faith in Christ Jesus.

New life on this earth is offered as well.

When I was a kid we used to play baseball in the vacant lot behind my house. We had no formal teams, no uniforms, no base-on-balls, no fans, no umpires. Sometimes a play at first base would be so close that we could not agree on whether the runner was out or safe. Sometimes we would almost fall out and fight over a call. But then, usually, a peacemaker would say, "Do-over! I call a do-over!" And we would agree. The batter would go back to the batter's box. The runners would go back to their bases. The pitcher would throw the ball as if the play never took place.

New life in Jesus Christ is a divine "do-over." It is a second chance. Jesus takes the past mistakes and erases them.

Just listen to Psalm 103:11-12, "For as high as the heavens are above the earth, so great is his love for those who fear him; as far as the east is from the west, so far has he removed our transgressions from us." Hear God's Word from Jeremiah 31:34, "No longer will a man teach his neighbor, or a man his brother, saying, 'Know the LORD,' because they will all know me, from the least of them to the greatest," declares the LORD. "For I will forgive their wickedness and will remember their sins no more."

God gives divine "do-overs." No matter what a person might have done, no matter how low a person might have sunk, no matter how far away from God a person might have strayed, God will give that person a second chance. God will enable a person to begin a new life today.

God gives new lives for old. He gives healing to those that others may have given up for dead. He takes broken lives and mends them. He redeems the past, reconciling memories and soothing them with His touch.

God has made new life possible. We simply must die to self (the old life) and live for Jesus. That's new life in Christ.

Lesson 6

God's Glory Revealed

Romans 8:18-27, 31-34, 38-39

For I reckon that the sufferings of this present time are not worthy to be compared with the glory which shall be revealed in us.

19 For the earnest expectation of the creature waiteth for the manifestation of the sons of God.

20 For the creature was made subject to vanity, not willingly, but by reason of him who hath subjected the same in hope,

21 Because the creature itself also shall be delivered from the bondage of corruption into the glorious liberty of the children of God.

22 For we know that the whole creation groaneth and travaileth in pain together until now.

23 And not only they, but ourselves also, which have the firstfruits of the Spirit, even we ourselves groan within ourselves, waiting for the adoption, to wit, the redemption of our body.

24 For we are saved by hope: but hope that is seen is not hope: for what a man seeth, why doth he yet hope for?

25 But if we hope for that we see not, then do we with patience wait for it.

26 Likewise the Spirit also helpeth our infirmities: for we know not what we should pray for as we ought: but the Spirit itself maketh intercession for us with groanings which cannot be uttered.

27 And he that searcheth the hearts knoweth what is the mind of the Spirit, because he maketh intercession for the saints according to the will of God.

31 What shall we then say to these things? If God be for us, who can be against us?

32 He that spared not his own Son, but delivered him up for us all, how shall he not with him also freely give us all things?

33 Who shall lay any thing to the charge of God's elect? It is God that justifieth.

34 Who is he that condemneth? It is Christ that died, yea rather, that is risen again, who is even at the right hand of God, who also maketh intercession for us.

38 For I am persuaded, that neither death, nor life, nor angels, nor principalities, nor powers, nor things present, nor things to come,

39 Nor height, nor depth, nor any other creature, shall be able to separate us from the love of God, which is in Christ Jesus our Lord.

Apr. 7

Memory Selection
Romans 8:18
Devotional Reading
Romans 8:1-11
Background Scripture
Romans 8

For seven chapters Paul argued that we are saved by grace-faith, not the works-law system his opponents wanted to preserve. He produced a monumental doctrinal essay that ever since has been a mainstay of Christian theology.

With 8:1, the apostle turned from the theology of being *saved* by grace to the practical effects of *living* by grace. He moves from the tone of a prophet confronting error to that of a pastor offering reassurance. He shows that all creation awaits the grace Jesus offers to us now. No longer should we be insecure in our relationship with God because we make mistakes. No longer do we live in fear that a divine Law-giver will strike us down because we cannot keep His rules perfectly. Now we can emphasize the Spirit over the Law. Now we can live in the joyful freedom of those who know that their security depends not on their own righteousness, but on Christ's.

ଆର

A modern parable can serve to introduce this session. A brilliant young apprentice artist contracted to do a huge mural. Halfway through, however, he knew he would be unable to finish. He could not execute what he pictured in his mind. His brush trembled as he contemplated his failures.

Then a Master Artist came to the apprentice's assistance. At times he assured the young painter that he was doing well. He supplied technique and advice when the younger man was failing. Suddenly the project seemed do-able after all! The aid the young man received did not make him quit work, but, reassured, he was inspired to paint as never before.

Having taught that our spiritual security depends not on our own ability but on the Master's, Paul now shows that grace not only comforts and reassures us; it inspires us to work more effectively than when we trusted in our works, instead of the work of Christ.

Teaching Outline	Daily Bible Readings

I. Creation Hopes—18-22
  A. From suffering to glory, 18-19
  B. From groans to deliverance, 20-22
II. The Spirit Sustains—23-27
  A. Awaiting adoption, 23
  B. Saved by hope, 24-25
  C. The Spirit intercedes, 26-27
III. If God Be for Us—31-34
  A. He gives freely, 31-32
  B. He justifies, 33-34
IV. Nothing Can Separate Us—38-39
	Mon. The Greater Glory
	2 Corinthians 3:1-11
	Tue. From Glory to Glory
	2 Corinthians 3:12-18
	Wed. The Power Is God's
	2 Corinthians 4:1-5
	Thu. Walk by the Spirit
	Romans 8:1-8
	Fri. The Spirit Is Life
	Romans 8:9-17
	Sat. Glory to Be Revealed
	Romans 8:18-30
	Sun. More than Conquerors
	Romans 8:31-39

Verse by Verse

I. Creation Hopes—18-22

A. From suffering to glory, 18-19

18 For I reckon that the sufferings of this present time are not worthy to be compared with the glory which shall be revealed in us.

19 For the earnest expectation of the creature waiteth for the manifestation of the sons of God.

Since 8:1, Paul has exalted living in the Spirit by grace over living in the flesh. Now he seems to anticipate the very practical issue that the flesh is the very arena in which many believers were suffering and being persecuted; and the realm in which we suffer temptations.

Paul deals with this issue first by saying that the future glory promised to those who stand fast in God's grace through the Spirit far outweighs any suffering we may incur. The suffering we experience is part of what Martin Luther would call "the order (or system) of creation." The NIV makes this clear, using the word "creation" instead of "creature" in these verses. Christians, however, can endure present suffering because they already live in the superior "order" of grace.

Paul is actually continuing to contrast "law" with "grace." The fallen world in which we live is governed by "natural law." Hence, Paul can say that the creation awaits in eager anticipation to see the revealing of the victory that grace promises to Christians, to see them possess in actuality what they already have in potentiality: the "new heavens and new earth."

B. From groans to deliverance, 20-22

20 For the creature was made subject to vanity, not willingly, but by reason of him who hath subjected the same in hope,

21 Because the creature itself also shall be delivered from the bondage of corruption into the glorious liberty of the children of God.

22 For we know that the whole creation groaneth and travaileth in pain together until now.

Again referring to the fallen creation (not "creature"), Paul notes that it has been subjected to the vain rule of Satan. It is vain because Satan only thinks he is in control. Creation did not ask to be punished along with Adam and Eve. Yet, although God did not *cause* the fall, He allowed it; and He tucked into Satan's temporary victory the principle of *hope,* His plan to liberate fallen creation through Christ's work on the Cross. Although

313

Paul affirms that hope will eventually win out, that bright future can be affirmed only by admitting that living by the law of nature offers no hope.

The dirty haze that hangs over every major city, the waterways that are too polluted to swim or fish in, the strip-forested and mined land that washes away in the rain—these are some of creation's cries. In the human realm, the "natural" or fleshly person who lives only by the law of selfish desires, or who is quite willing to hurt others on his way to the top—these too are evidence that creation "groans." Salvation from the abuse of nature and from sin comes not from groaning nature itself, but by grace.

II. The Spirit Sustains—23-27
A. Awaiting adoption, 23

23 And not only they, but ourselves also, which have the firstfruits of the Spirit, even we ourselves groan within ourselves, waiting for the adoption, to wit, the redemption of our body.

"They" apparently refers to those of the groaning creation, perhaps angels. With them, even the first-generation Christians who received grace by the Holy Spirit are burdened by the fallen world in which the righteous suffer. Paul himself gave an excellent example of the moral groaning that arises from wanting to live "in the Spirit" while bound by natural law. In chapter 7 he confessed the agony in his own life of being unable to do the good he wanted to do because of the law of the flesh (7:18-25). Although living "in Christ" puts us on the upward path, we will be totally free of the shackles of the flesh only when we are "adopted" by heaven itself.

B. Saved by hope, 24-25

24 For we are saved by hope: but hope that is seen is not hope: for what a man seeth, why doth he yet hope for?

25 But if we hope for that we see not, then do we with patience wait for it.

Here Paul confesses that the bright light of hope we see in the Good News of grace is not precisely the same as *possessing* that for which we hope. By definition, hope represents the longing for something that lies ahead. As Paul will emphasize below, this does not mean that we do not have the assurance of God's love and protection in this life; but that as long as we live in the flesh the total consummation of our hope is in the future. This in turn means that we must have patience as we lean toward hope's fulfillment in the next life.

C. The Spirit intercedes, 26-27

26 Likewise the Spirit also helpeth our infirmities: for we know not what we should pray for as we ought: but the Spirit itself maketh intercession for us with groanings which cannot be uttered.

27 And he that searcheth the hearts knoweth what is the mind of the Spirit, because he maketh intercession for the saints according to the will of God.

Just as Christ, the Second Person of the Godhead, stands in for us because we cannot earn salvation by keeping the Law, so the Holy Spirit, the Third

Person of the Godhead, stands in for us as we pray. Picking up on the imagery of groaning, Paul puts a more positive face on it when he says we aren't the only ones who "groan," in the sense of voicing unutterable pain. The Spirit perceives what we want and need even when we cannot articulate it, translating our prayers to the Father.

III. If God Be for Us—31-34

A. He gives freely, 31-32

31 What shall we then say to these things? If God be for us, who can be against us?

32 He that spared not his own Son, but delivered him up for us all, how shall he not with him also freely give us all things?

So what if the early Christians were persecuted for their faith? What if we today are burdened by other "laws" that operate in a fallen world? How can we possibly despair, when the God who created the world and called it "good" is still on His throne? Against the fallen nature that would pull us down, God is on our side. What better proof of this is there than God's action in Christ? If "God so loved the world that He gave His only begotten Son," how can we doubt that He will see us through the burdens of this life? Though Jesus died, God raised and enthroned Him. Likewise, even though life slays us, God will give us, with His Son, life with Him in the next world.

B. He justifies, 33-34

33 Who shall lay any thing to the charge of God's elect? It is God that justifieth.

34 Who is he that condemneth? It is Christ that died, yea rather, that is risen again, who is even at the right hand of God, who also maketh intercession for us.

Those whom Paul addressed knew about "charges." Jews charged that they worshiped multiple gods. Pagans charged them with incest (overhearing them say they loved each other as brothers and sisters); cannibalism (hearing them say, at the Lord's Supper, "This is the body of Christ"); and treason (because they worshiped a King other than Caesar). Paul urges a persecuted Church to ignore such charges on grounds that the Christ who was raised despite the judgment of the world against Him is in fact our Advocate.

IV. Nothing Can Separate Us—38-39

38 For I am persuaded, that neither death, nor life, nor angels, nor principalities, nor powers, nor things present, nor things to come,

39 Nor height, nor depth, nor any other creature, shall be able to separate us from the love of God, which is in Christ Jesus our Lord.

This classic passage deserves to be memorized, as so many millions of believers have done. Here Paul assembles all the dark powers of a fallen world, and affirms that none of them can divide us from God's love. Some of these entities, such as "height" and "depth," were "principalities and powers" that would later be worshiped by gnostics. Anticipating such deification of natural forces, Paul insists that they are no match for God's gracious love through Jesus Christ His Son.

Evangelistic Emphasis

In our society today lawyers often get a bad rap. We hear lawyers referred to by names like "ambulance chaser" and "shyster." I hope none who reads this has ever needed a lawyer except maybe to take care of the paperwork on a home purchase or to settle the estate of a loved one.

Yet, there are times when we need a good lawyer to defend us in court. Lawsuits may be brought against us even if we really have not done anything against the law. Accidents happen. Sometimes a person needs an advocate.

We need an advocate in our spiritual lives as well. There are times when we just mess up. There are times when we sin against God. We break God's laws, maybe by accident, maybe on purpose, or maybe we are just too weak at the time to do right. God understands. God has made provision for those times when we might sin. "My dear children, I write this to you so that you will not sin. But if anybody does sin, we have one who speaks to the Father in our defense--Jesus Christ, the Righteous One. He is the atoning sacrifice for our sins, and not only for ours but also for the sins of the whole world" (1 John 2:1-2).

God's plan is for us not to sin, but if we do, He has made a way for us to be forgiven.

৪৩০৫

Memory Selection

For I reckon that the sufferings of this present time are not worthy to be compared with the glory which shall be revealed in us. (Romans 8:18)

There are some things that make this world a tough place to live. We see violence all around us. People we know are stricken with AIDS or cancer or heart conditions or some other deadly malady. You have probably noticed that even Christians have some of these same problems on this earth. We suffer right along with the general population. Being one of God's children does not automatically exempt us from earthly problems.

However, being one of God's children does guarantee us a better life in Heaven. Just listen to what Paul tells us,: "However, as it is written: 'No eye has seen, no ear has heard, no mind has conceived what God has prepared for those who love him'" (1 Cor. 2:9).

We cannot even imagine how good Heaven is going to be. It will make us forget about any hardships we may have experienced on this earth.

Weekday Problems

The bell over the door jingled as Harry walked into the air conditioned coolness of the barber shop. The barber had a man in his chair, and three others were waiting. As Harry picked out a magazine and sat down to wait, one man snickered, "Did you hear? Ol' Bob Smart got religion."

"Yeah," another added, "he went down to that revival meeting and walked the aisle. I know what he's trying to do. He and his wife are having problems. He's trying to look like he's straightening up so that if she leaves him he won't have to pay so much alimony." Everybody except Harry had a good laugh.

Bob Smart had been coming to Harry's discipleship group for about a year now. Harry knew Bob's reputation when Bob joined the group. One night, long before the revival meeting, Bob sensed he needed Jesus in his life. The folks in the group prayed with Bob and he received forgiveness for his sins. Since that time, Harry had seen a remarkable change in Bob. Bob's wife even started coming to the Bible study. Harry knew those things the men were saying about Bob were no longer true. He sensed God urging him to defend Bob's commitment to Christ.

*Should Harry speak up to defend Bob? Explain.

*Have you ever needed someone to stand up for you when someone else was accusing you? Explain.

The Family Feud

Wife: You're the laziest man I ever saw. Can't you do anything quickly?
Hubby: Oh yes. I get tired fast.

* * *

Wife, sniffing: I smell B.O. Did you take a bath today?
Hubby: Why? Is one missing?

* * *

Little girl: Granddad, make like a frog.
Grandfather: What do you mean?
Little girl: Mommy says we're going to make a lot of money when you croak.

* * *

Ted: My wife and I have worked out an arrangement that cuts down on our arguments.
Fred: How does it work?
Ted: We haven't spoken for five years.

317

This Lesson in Your Life
Is There Hope?

One of the problems that is seen in the United States today is obesity. We tend be an overweight nation. I suspect that none of us plans to be overweight. It just seems to happen. We have another donut . We order fries with that hamburger. We take second helpings. We couple that with a lack of sufficient exercise and, "Voila!" we are overweight.

This year I have gone on a diet to try to lose some of my flab. I needed to lose about 30 pounds when I started. I lost 10 pounds rather quickly. It was hard. I plan to continue my diet until I reach my target weight.

Do I enjoy dieting? No! But I do enjoy how I look when I am near the normal weight for a person my height. I do enjoy how I feel when I am not so heavy. I enjoy knowing how much less stress is put on my cardiovascular system when I am not overweight and I enjoy that knowledge. I have decided I want to be thinner more than I want to eat without restraint. Thus, I suffer a little now to gain that which I desire more in the future.

Paul reminds us that we Christians may suffer some on this earth, but what we gain from our sufferings will far exceed any discomfort we may endure. When God gives something to us it is so much better and more satisfying than anything this world can come up with.

Even in our sufferings on this earth, we can trust that Christ is with us. I remember a story about a child who was in bed during a thunderstorm. The lightning would flash then the thunder would crash. The child called out for her mother. When the mother came in the room she comforted the little girl by saying, "It's okay. Remember Jesus is right here with you." The mother tucked the child in and left the room.

As soon as the next clap of thunder came the little girl cried out again, "Mom! I need you!"

When her mother came back in she said, "Now, didn't I tell you Jesus was with you?"

"Yes, ma'am," the child replied. "But right now I need to be with someone with skin on."

Even though Christ may not have skin on, we have confirmation through the Holy Spirit that Jesus is with us. The Holy Spirit witnesses to our hearts that Christ is with us through thick and thin.

And nothing can separate us from Him. One of the most powerful passages of scripture validates that fact. Paul writes, "For I am convinced that neither death nor life, neither angels nor demons, neither the present nor the future, nor any powers, neither height nor depth, nor anything else in all creation, will be able to separate us from the love of God that is in Christ Jesus our Lord" (Romans 8:38-39).

STRAIGHT

1. Which should we focus on: the sufferings of this world or the glory that will be revealed?

We should definitely keep our eyes on the glory that will be revealed. The present sufferings cannot compare with the future glory.

2. At what time or event was creation cursed?

All of creation came under the curse during the Fall of Adam and Eve through their sin in the Garden of Eden.

3. To what does Paul compare creation's desire to be liberated from the bondage of corruption?

Paul compares the "groaning creation" to the pangs of childbirth.

4. According to verse 26, when does the Spirit step in to help?

The Spirit helps us in our weakness and our infirmities.

5. What is one of the Holy Spirit's ministries according to verse 26?

The Holy Spirit intercedes for us with groans that words cannot express when we do not know what we ought to pray for.

6. Why is it important to pray in the Spirit (vs. 27)?

We should pray in the Spirit because the Spirit always intercedes for the saints according to God's will. God knows the mind of the Spirit.

7. Why should Christians be bold when we face opposition (vs. 31)?

We know that if God is for us no one can stand for long against us.

8. How do we know that God will give us all things, even His best (verse 32)?

We know that God will give us all things because He did not spare His best. He has already given up His Son, Jesus Christ, for us.

9. Who intercedes for the saints?

Jesus Christ (vs.34) and the Holy Spirit (vs.27) both intercede.

10. What can separate us from the love of God that is in Christ Jesus our Lord?

Nothing! Not anything in all creation can separate us from the love of God in Christ Jesus.

I remember an old song that told the story of a man lost in the desert. The man had been walking for days. His food and water had both run out. He was close to collapse. Up ahead he saw something sticking out of the sand. As he got closer he realized it was an old hand-operated pump. He stumbled up to the pump and discovered a bucket full of water. There were insects in the water. A film of scum was over the surface. The man's thirst was so great that he was about to drink this filthy water when he noticed a note attached to the pump. The note read, "I know you're tempted to drink this water, but don't do it. You need the water in this bucket to prime the pump. Just pour the whole bucketful into the top of the pump while you work the handle. After a minute, you'll have more water than you need. Drink all you want, then fill up the bucket. Have faith, my friend. There's water down below. You have to give before you get. Prime the pump." The note was signed, "Jezzard T."

Well, the wanderer was in a terrible fix. He had a bucketful of water right there in his hands. As nasty as that water was, it was still water. What if, after pouring the whole bucket out to prime the pump, it still wouldn't work? He could die of thirst. Should he trust a handwritten note from someone he had never heard of? Thoughts raced through his mind as he tried to make what might be a life or death decision.

He read the note again. With trembling hands he began to pour the water into the pump as he worked the handle. At first, there was just the creaking of the rusty parts. Then, he heard a gurgling sound. "There really is water down below!" he said to himself.

In just a few seconds the water came gushing forth. Pure, clear, cold water came flowing from that pump. The man drank and drank and drank. He filled his canteen. He lay there for a few minutes, then he drank some more.

"It was true," he thought as he refilled the bucket to leave for the next wanderer. "I really did have to give before I could get."

Friends, this is just a story. But it makes a spiritual point. Much like the man wandering in the desert, we sometimes find ourselves in a dry, dusty place searching for a drink of cold water. We may try to quench that thirst with things of this world. But that is only a temporary fix. To be filled to overflowing with good things, we must give ourselves up. And when we do give ourselves up to the Master, he fills us with good things. He gives us things that satisfy us. He provides purpose, direction, and meaning to our lives. He blesses us beyond measure.

But you have to give before you get. Give yourself to God and receive God's abundant blessings.

SALVATION BY FAITH IN CHRIST IS AVAILABLE
TO ALL WHO CALL ON CHRIST IN FAITH.

Proclaim the Gospel

Romans 10:1-10, 13-17

Brethren, my heart's desire and prayer to God for Israel is, that they might be saved.

2 For I bear them record that they have a zeal of God, but not according to knowledge.

3 For they being ignorant of God's righteousness, and going about to establish their own righteousness, have not submitted themselves unto the righteousness of God.

4 For Christ is the end of the law for righteousness to every one that believeth.

5 For Moses describeth the righteousness which is of the law, That the man which doeth those things shall live by them.

6 But the righteousness which is of faith speaketh on this wise, Say not in thine heart, Who shall ascend into heaven? (that is, to bring Christ down from above:)

7 Or, Who shall descend into the deep? (that is, to bring up Christ again from the dead.)

8 But what saith it? The word is nigh thee, even in thy mouth, and in thy heart: that is, the word of faith, which we preach;

9 That if thou shalt confess with thy mouth the Lord Jesus, and shalt believe in thine heart that God hath raised him from the dead, thou shalt be saved.

10 For with the heart man believeth unto righteousness; and with the mouth confession is made unto salvation.

13 For whosoever shall call upon the name of the Lord shall be saved.

14 How then shall they call on him in whom they have not believed? and how shall they believe in him of whom they have not heard? and how shall they hear without a preacher?

15 And how shall they preach, except they be sent? as it is written, How beautiful are the feet of them that preach the gospel of peace, and bring glad tidings of good things!

16 But they have not all obeyed the gospel. For Esaias saith, Lord, who hath believed our report?

17 So then faith cometh by hearing, and hearing by the word of God.

Apr. 14

Memory Selection
Romans 10:14-15

Devotional Reading
Romans 11:1-6

Background Scripture
Romans 10:1-17

The apostle Paul's teaching that righteousness comes not from keeping the Law but through faith in Christ was radical to many Jews. They considered themselves the exclusive heirs of at least 1,500 years of history, enjoying special status as God's "chosen people" ever since God called their father Abraham. If God now calls people to be members of His family through faith in Christ regardless of their racial heritage, even Gentiles can be adopted into this family. What, now, of God's relationship with the Jews? And what relationship is there between Jew and Gentile?

This lesson is an excerpt from Paul's complex answer to such questions in Romans 9–11. It focuses on the fact that since Christ fulfilled the demands of the Law, all who hear and respond to Him may be a part of God's Covenant People. What remains, therefore, is to sound out the glad message!

ഇൻയ

This session can be introduced by challenging your group to consider their reaction to someone who proclaimed, during the days of the Cold War, that the Russians were God's "chosen people." Recall the concept of "manifest destiny" affirmed by many founders of the United States. God had chosen our country as a special witness to the world. With that destiny came the authority to subdue Native American opposition and to cleanse the land of English, Spanish, and French colonies.

Compare this widely-held view with the Jewish sense that they were God's chosen people. How would such people respond to Paul's claim that anyone could become a child of God by faith in Jesus Christ? What repercussions would this have in communities in which Jews and Gentiles lived alongside each other?

Teaching Outline	Daily Bible Readings
I. Human Efforts—1-3	**Mon.** All Can Be Saved Acts 2:14-21
II. Heavenly Help—4-10	**Tue.** Jesus, Killed but Raised Acts 2:22-33
A. Christ vs. the Law, 4-5	**Wed.** The Word from the Beginning John 1:1-5
B. Nearness of the Word, 6-8	**Thu.** The Advocate to Come John 16:4-15
C. The good confession, 9-10	**Fri.** Take Up God's Armor Ephesians 6:10-23
III. Hearing the Word—13-17	**Sat.** The Message of John 1 John 1:1-10
A. A missionary message, 13-15	**Sun.** The Word Is Near You Romans 10:5-17
B. Hearing and obeying, 16-17	

Verse by Verse

I. Human Efforts—1-3

1 Brethren, my heart's desire and prayer to God for Israel is, that they might be saved.

2 For I bear them record that they have a zeal of God, but not according to knowledge.

3 For they being ignorant of God's righteousness, and going about to establish their own righteousness, have not submitted themselves unto the righteousness of God.

It should not surprise us that Paul wants Israel to be saved. After all, he was an Israelite himself, with impressive credentials (see Philip. 3:4-6). What may be surprising is that Paul's thinking has taken him so far from his Jewish heritage that he can speak of Jews as "they" instead of "we." The apostle's Damascus Road conversion experience, along with subsequent revelations, have resulted in a huge "we-they" gulf. God showed him that salvation is by grace through faith, not through keeping the Law; and he had to take a stand against those of his own race who held otherwise.

If zeal and human efforts could achieve salvation, Paul's wish for Israel to be saved could come true. Thousands of sincere Jews were careful to keep all the hundreds of details of the Law, from circumcision to Sabbath-keeping, tithing to ritual hand-washing. Unfortunately, Paul says all this was "zeal without knowledge."

To what knowledge does Paul refer? In verse 3, he implies that it is the fact that even under the Old Covenant people were saved by faith in the righteousness of God, who gave the Law, rather than in the human ability to keep the Law perfectly. As Paul argues in Galatians 2:11, the Old Covenant itself said "the just shall live by faith" (Hab. 2:4; see also Gal. 2:6). When we put our faith in correct religious practices, or in our good works, religion becomes an attempt to "establish our own righteousness" instead of trusting in God's righteousness.

II. Heavenly Help—4-10
A. Christ vs. the Law, 4-5

4 For Christ is the end of the law for righteousness to every one that believeth.

5 For Moses describeth the righteousness which is of the law, That the man which doeth those things shall live by them.

Although the principle of justification by faith can be cited from the Old Covenant, as Paul has argued, the Law can also be quoted to put an emphasis on works-salvation. Here Paul poses as opposites the principle of accepting the righteousness of Christ (vs. 4) and thinking that righteousness is achieved by doing the works of the Law (vs. 5, loosely quoted from Lev. 18:5).

The term "end" (Grk. *telos*) in verse 4 can be taken to mean either "goal" or "termination." It is therefore parallel with "fulfill" in Matthew 5:17, where Jesus said He did not come to abolish the Law but to fulfill it. Either way, Paul clearly shows that the works of the Law were fulfilled by Jesus, and that it is like trying to live in the past to "earn" one's salvation by law-keeping.

B. Nearness of the Word, 6-8

6 But the righteousness which is of faith speaketh on this wise, Say not in thine heart, Who shall ascend into heaven? (that is, to bring Christ down from above:)

7 Or, Who shall descend into the deep? (that is, to bring up Christ again from the dead.)

8 But what saith it? The word is nigh thee, even in thy mouth, and in thy heart: that is, the word of faith, which we preach;

In another contrast with Christ's way over Moses', Paul quotes again from Moses himself to argue that justification by faith was not foreign to the Old covenant Scriptures. The quotation is from Deuteronomy 30:11ff., where Moses is appealing to the people to accept the Law because God personally revealed it to them instead

of requiring them to discover it on their own.

There seems to be a universal tendency to want to go to grand lengths to discover "the meaning of life." Even today people climb high mountains and travel wide seas to hoping to learn from a guru the essence of religion and life. This, too, is an attempt to be saved by works—the "work" of searching. Moses told the people that God came near to them on Sinai to give the Law instead of requiring such effort. Paul makes this parallel to the Word that is Christ, "the word of faith."

This is a remarkable echo of what the apostle John claimed for Jesus in John 1:1-3, 14. As the Word, Jesus was present at, and the agent of, creation. As created beings, then, when we listen to Him we are listening to a voice at the center of our being. Instead of requiring us to climb up to heaven to hear His truth, God condescended to let the Word become flesh so we could hear Him on earth.

C. The good confession, 9-10

9 That if thou shalt confess with thy mouth the Lord Jesus, and shalt believe in thine heart that God hath raised him from the dead, thou shalt be saved.

10 For with the heart man believeth unto righteousness; and with the mouth confession is made unto salvation.

The result of this Incarnation of the Word is that all people can accept it simply by accepting Christ and His saving work on the Cross and in the resurrection. No longer can religious teachers rightly say that God's will can be known only by going through Moses and the Law.

The importance of confessing "with the mouth" what one believes in the heart was born in the days of Jewish and Roman persecution of Christians. Paul insists that it is not enough to be a "closet" Christian. Even today we must be willing to pay the price for stating openly the faith that is in our hearts.

III. Hearing the Word—13-17

A. A missionary message, 13-15

13 For whosoever shall call upon the name of the Lord shall be saved.

14 How then shall they call on him in whom they have not believed? and how shall they believe in him of whom they have not heard? and how shall they hear without a preacher?

15 And how shall they preach, except they be sent? as it is written, How beautiful are the feet of them that preach the gospel of peace, and bring glad tidings of good things!

As among "new age" people in our day, some of Paul's hearers would have been quick to interpret his statement that Christ is "in thy heart" (vs. 8) as some internal force with which we are born. The apostle, however, says that saving faith in Christ requires not only accepting the Word within but the Word from without—the Good News that "God was in Christ, reconciling the world unto himself" (2 Cor. 5:19). Although this saving Word *is* the Word by which all people were created, Paul holds that it requires a "missionary" or other proclaimer to announce that this Word's name is Jesus, the Christ.

It is important to note that verse 15 is a quotation from Isaiah 52:7, a section containing "the Servant Songs," or predictions of the work of Jesus as the sin-bearer for the world. Again Paul finds in the Old Testament itself the roots of the Messiah principle that brought that era to an end. Verse 15 is also a mandate for the Church to sponsor those who are called to "Go ye therefore and teach all nations" (Matt. 28:19).

B. Hearing and obeying, 16-17

16 But they have not all obeyed the gospel. For Esaias saith, Lord, who hath believed our report?

17 So then faith cometh by hearing, and hearing by the word of God.

It was noted in the previous lesson that Jewish thought did not speak as easily as we do of the distinction between "believing" and "obeying." Here is an example, with Paul making obedience in verse 16 parallel with faith in verse 17. Once more he quotes from the Old Testament (the earliest Greek version of Isa. 53:1, which inserts the word "Lord"), showing again that it is not enough to listen to some voice from within; we must accept the message brought by Christ. As Peter would also write, this word is not merely a saving force running through creation, but "the word which by the gospel is preached unto you" (1 Pet. 1:25).

Evangelistic Emphasis

Note that it is Paul's heartfelt desire and earnest prayer that the Jews might be saved. Can you feel his genuine concern? Can you sense his wistful desire and yearning for the Jews' salvation? It seems there is no anger here, only genuine love and concern for those who do not know Jesus as Savior.

That should be a lesson for us in the 21st century. For you see, friends, it is not the worst thing for someone to die of neglect. It is not the worst thing in the world for someone to die of hunger. It is not the worst thing in the world for someone to die of a dread disease like AIDS or cancer. It really is the worst thing in the world for someone to die without Jesus.

I suspect that if we had the same concern for our friends, neighbors, and family members that do not know Christ as Savior as Paul did for the Jews, we would be out knocking on our lost friends' doors pleading with them to accept Christ. Our zeal for lost souls must be grounded in our love for the person.

Knowing Jesus as Savior is the greatest thing that could happen to anyone. It is worth sharing. If you knew the cure for cancer and you friend had cancer, you would share the cure with him, wouldn't you? We know the cure for sin and death. Surely we will share that cure with our friends.

ॐॐ

Memory Selection

How then shall they call on him in whom they have not believed? and how shall they believe in him of whom they have not heard? and how shall they hear without a preacher? And how shall they preach, except they be sent? as it is written, How beautiful are the feet of them that preach the gospel of peace, and bring glad tidings of good things!—*Romans 10:14-15*

In just these two verses we again see the tension between the sovereignty of God and our personal responsibilities in the faith. Paul begins by saying that people cannot be held responsible for their ignorance. Then he reminds us of the responsibility that we, who have already heard the gospel, have to share the good news with those who have not heard. But this responsibility is not conceived in the believer's good will. The Christian is still motivated only by the Spirit of God. The Spirit of God is both the initiator and enabler of our faith sharing. The message then motivates the messenger.

These two verses outline the human situation. God is still in control, yet the human will is free.

Weekday Problems

Jill and Kay were visiting over coffee this Wednesday morning just as they had every Wednesday morning for the past few months. They are neighbors and friends, having a great deal in common with each other. Both are wives, mothers, and homemakers. Jill has two young children. Kay's children are grown and away from home. Both families would be classified as upper middle class. Both are regular church attenders.

Jill drops her voice and speaks confidentially, "Kay, I find myself attracted to a guy who works with my husband. He has called me a few times. Yesterday, I called him just to talk."

"Jill," Kay answers, "You cannot allow yourself to do that. You simply cannot entertain thoughts like that. God will help you resist."

"I'm not sure I want to resist. Besides, everybody is doing it," Jill replies.

"I'm not doing it!" Kay said. "Jill, Christians live by a different code than the world does. You and I are called to live by a higher standard."

"Kay, you're always bringing that up. It's like you're trying to lay a guilt trip on me. That doesn't sound like the good news to me. Didn't you tell me that we live by grace and not by the law? If I'm doing anything wrong, God's love will cover my sin." Jill was exasperated.

*Are Christians still required to live by God's holy law? Explain.

*Do we have any personal responsibility for our own conduct? Explain.

Missionary Moments

First cannibal: Look! We've captured a missionary.
Second cannibal: Oh, great. I was hoping for a ham sandwich.

* * *

A resourceful missionary fell into the hands of a band of cannibals. "Going to eat me, I take it," he said. "But wait—you wouldn't like me." And with that he took his own knife, sliced a piece from the calf of his leg, and handed it to the chief. "Try it and see for yourself," he urged.

The chief took one bite, grunted, then spat it out—and the missionary enjoyed 50 years of ministry among the people.

He had a wooden leg.

* * *

Then there was the missionary the cannibal couldn't boil. He was a friar.

This Lesson in Your Life

How Are They to Hear?

We have a lot of old sayings that have woven the philosophy of self-reliance into the fabric of our society. Sayings such as, "You don't get something for nothing." Or, "If it's worth having it's worth working for." How about, "Hard work pays off." Historically, self-reliance has been considered the American way. We work for what we get.

There is something which is available to us that really is free. That something is the grace of God. The concept of grace is difficult for many of us. I remember a story about a pastor who died and found himself at the pearly gates of Heaven. St. Peter welcomed him. "Come on in," he said. "We've just switched to computers here. You need 100 points to get in. So, what have you done deserving of heaven?"

The pastor was pretty self-assured. "Well, St. Peter, every congregation I have pastored has grown. We increased the budgets every year. We brought hundreds of people into the kingdom. Total that up, please." The pastor was sure that was enough to get into heaven.

St. Peter totaled it up in the computer. "That comes to 0.7 points. You need 99.3 more points."

The pastor was flabbergasted. He began to list everything imaginable he had done that might win him some points to get into heaven. He went on and on. Finally, after he had said everything he could think of, he stopped. "Total that up, please."

St. Peter hit the total button. "That comes to 2.1 points. You still need 97.9 points to get in. Take a seat over there until you can think of something else. Next!"

As the pastor sat down a little lady came in. "St. Peter," she said, "I listened to all the great things this pastor has done. I haven't done any of those things. All I have done is ask Jesus to be my Savior and Lord."

St. Peter hit the button, "That comes to 100 points exactly!" he exclaimed. "You can come in!"

That story reminds us that there is really nothing we can do that is great enough to earn us a spot into heaven. Gaining salvation is really very simple, yet very difficult. It is as simple as the confession, "Jesus is Lord." The words are simple. The reality is difficult. You see, one cannot say, "No, Lord," with integrity. If Jesus is truly Lord, then my response to His will and His way must always be, "Yes!" When Jesus is my Lord, I will do as He desires, not as I desire. In every circumstance of my life I will walk in His footsteps, obedient to His will.

STRAIGHT

1. What was Paul's heart desire and prayer to God for the Israelites?
Paul prayed for the Israelites' salvation.

2. How were the Jews seeking to gain righteousness?
They were seeking to gain righteousness by the Law. They did not know the righteousness that comes from God and sought to establish their own.

3. According to verse 9, what two things are necessary for salvation?
Confess with your mouth, "Jesus is Lord," and believe in your heart that God raised Him from the dead, and you will be saved.

4. Verse 13 repeats a formula for salvation. What is it?
Everyone who calls on the name of the Lord will be saved.

5. Does God make distinctions between races? Explain.
No. In God's eyes there is no difference between Jew and Gentile. He is Lord of all. God richly blesses all who call on Him.

6. What Christian's responsibility is spoken of in verse 14?
We must go to those who have never heard and preach the good news.

7. Who sends the preacher to the lost (vs. 15)?
The sending is God's responsibility. We must obey His command to go.

8. Did all the Israelites accept the good news?
No. Isaiah asked God, "Lord, who has believed our message?"

9. What part of the "good news preacher's" body did Isaiah say was beautiful?
The feet. Whatever carries the good news to others is beautiful both to God and the hearers of the good news .

10. According to verse 17, where does faith come from?
Faith comes from hearing the message and the message is heard through the word of Christ.

Nowadays, "reality" television shows are extremely popular. There is a police show where the camera person is right with the police officer during an arrest. It is very dangerous.

One show featured high-speed auto chases. There were spectacular wrecks. One series is entitled something like "Amazing Rescues." One episode featured a little girl being rescued from a well.

Another was about a little boy being rescued from a collapsed cave. One featured people being rescued from dangerous flood waters. In every case, courageous people went to great risk in order to bring the victim to safety.

Picture this. The little girl is in the cave. The first person to get to her is not very handsome. Can you imagine her saying, "No thanks, I'll stay here until you send me someone more handsome." That would be ridiculous.

Can you imagine the man in the rolling, tumbling water saying to his rescuer, "I like African-Americans. Would you please send only a black person to rescue me?"

No, I suspect that the first person to get to the victim and pull the victim to safety was the most beautiful person in the world to the victim at that time.

There is a story about a young orphan boy roaming the streets of Chicago in the dead of winter some years ago. A kind police officer saw him. The officer told him, "Son, if you want a place to stay tonight, go to this address and knock on the door. When a person comes to the door simply say, 'John 3:16.'"

The boy did as he was told. He found the address and knocked on the door. When a woman answered the door he said, "John 3:16."

The woman took him in and set him in front of the warm fire. The boy thought, "John 3:16. I don't know what it means but it sure makes a cold boy warm."

When the boy had warmed up, the woman sat him down at a table loaded with food. The boy had never seen so much food in one place at one time. He ate and ate and ate. When he couldn't eat anymore he thought, "John 3:16. I don't know what it means, but it sure makes a hungry boy full."

After supper the woman drew the boy a steaming bath and scrubbed him good. She gave him pajamas and, as she put him to bed, he said to her, "John 3:16. I don't know what it means, but it sure makes a dirty boy clean."

The next morning when the boy got up, the woman was reading her Bible. The boy asked her why. She told him. Then she shared the gospel with him. Right there in front of that fire the boy gave his life to Jesus Christ.

With a big grin, he told the woman, "John 3:16. I'm not sure what it means, but it sure makes a lost boy saved."

Live the Gospel

Romans 12:1-3, 9-21

I beseech you therefore, brethren, by the mercies of God, that ye present your bodies a living sacrifice, holy, acceptable unto God, which is your reasonable service.

2 And be not conformed to this world: but be ye transformed by the renewing of your mind, that ye may prove what is that good, and acceptable, and perfect, will of God.

3 For I say, through the grace given unto me, to every man that is among you, not to think of himself more highly than he ought to think; but to think soberly, according as God hath dealt to every man the measure of faith.

9 Let love be without dissimulation. Abhor that which is evil; cleave to that which is good.

10 Be kindly affectioned one to another with brotherly love; in honour preferring one another;

11 Not slothful in business; fervent in spirit; serving the Lord;

12 Rejoicing in hope; patient in tribulation; continuing instant in prayer;

13 Distributing to the necessity of saints; given to hospitality.

14 Bless them which persecute you: bless, and curse not.

15 Rejoice with them that do rejoice, and weep with them that weep.

16 Be of the same mind one toward another. Mind not high things, but condescend to men of low estate. Be not wise in your own conceits.

17 Recompense to no man evil for evil. Provide things honest in the sight of all men.

18 If it be possible, as much as lieth in you, live peaceably with all men.

19 Dearly beloved, avenge not yourselves, but rather give place unto wrath: for it is written, Vengeance is mine; I will repay, saith the Lord.

20 Therefore if thine enemy hunger, feed him; if he thirst, give him drink: for in so doing thou shalt heap coals of fire on his head.

21 Be not overcome of evil, but overcome evil with good.

Apr. 21

Memory Selection
Romans 12:2

Devotional Reading
Romans 12:4-8

Background Scripture
Romans 12

As preceding lessons have emphasized, the apostle Paul has argued long and hard to show that salvation is by grace through faith, not by works. We know that some interpreted this teaching to mean that it doesn't matter how we live. Now Paul begins a section of his letter that shows that this was not at all the intent of the earlier chapters. The fact is, those saved by grace are expected to be eager to do good works—not to earn their salvation but in glad response to grace. They are to "live the Gospel."

The focus of this lesson is therefore to show that people saved by grace are expected to live graciously, to extend grace to others. Instead of "getting by" with sacrificing an animal under the Law of Moses, they are now to present their entire selves as a living sacrifice. Living by the law of love is seen to be as challenging as living under Law—but infinitely more fruitful and enjoyable.

৪১৫৪

Here is a true anecdote you may want to use to capture your group's attention.

A young man touring the country with a Christian drama group walked into a sanctuary to prepare for the troupe's performance later in the evening. The communion table at the front was made of stone, and in shape of an altar. Seizing the moment, the young man ran to the altar and unceremoniously flung himself atop it, on his back, and said, "Here am I. Take me, Lord!"

Some onlookers thought the young man was being quite irreligious. In his defense, he explained, "I was just doing what Romans 12:1 says: to present my body as a living sacrifice!"

What about it? Was this unorthodox behavior sacrilegious? Or does it appropriately illustrate Paul's teaching here?

Teaching Outline	Daily Bible Readings

I. Total Service to God—1-3
  A. A living sacrifice, 1
  B. A transformed mind, 2-3
 	
II. Traits of the Saved—9-21
  A. Live in love, 9-11
  B. Rejoice, with patience, 12
  C. Care for others, 13-16
  D. Overcome evil with good, 17-21
    1. Living in peace, 17-18
    2. Shunning vengeance, 19-21
	Mon. Be Doers of the Word
	James 1:19-27
	Tue. Don't Discriminate
	James 2:1-13
	Wed. Control the Tongue
	James 3:1-12
	Thu. Gentle Wisdom
	James 3:13-18
	Fri. Patience and Endurance
	James 5:7-12
	Sat. Transformed, not Conformed
	Romans 12:1-8
	Sun. Marks of Christian Living
	Romans 12:9-21

I. Total Service to God—1-3
A. A living sacrifice, 1

1 I beseech you therefore, brethren, by the mercies of God, that ye present your bodies a living sacrifice, holy, acceptable unto God, which is your reasonable service.

Paul has gone to great lengths to show that salvation is not achieved through the Jewish sacrificial system. Yet are we to offer *nothing* to God? Yes, Paul affirms. We are to offer our entire selves—in gratitude, rather than in atonement for our sins, for which Jesus Himself is the only adequate sacrifice (see 3:24-25).

Unlike the animals that were slain under the Old Covenant system of sacrifice, believers are now to offer themselves as *living* sacrifices. Here Paul urges believers to devote their bodies to God, and in verse 2 he includes their minds as components of this sacrifice. We are to glorify God as whole persons, in body, soul, and spirit.

The last two words of verse 1 are notoriously hard to translate, as a comparison of different version shows. The Greek words for "reasonable" (*logikos*) and for "worship" (*latreia*) have several different meanings. The NIV has "spiritual act of worship." The KJV's "reasonable" gives a certain rational cast to Paul's statement, as though he is cautioning against too much emotionalism in worship. More likely, we are to take the term as meaning "spiritual" in the sense of "metaphorical," or "not literal." This would mean that Paul is simply contrasting the literal slaughter of animals under the Old Law with the new "figurative" offering, the entire person, on the altar of sacrifice.

B. A transformed mind, 2-3

2 And be not conformed to this world: but be ye transformed by the renewing of your mind, that ye may prove what is that good, and acceptable, and perfect, will of God.

3 For I say, through the grace given unto me, to every man that is among you, not to think of himself more highly than he ought to think; but to think soberly, according as God hath dealt to every man the measure of faith.

Along with a body dedicated to God, we are also to give Him our minds, to be transformed and constantly renewed. Duty under the Old Covenant was often reduced to specific laws that were supposed to be applied in a variety of situations. Under Christ's Covenant, the mind is to remain constantly pliable so it can be guided by the Holy Spirit to act in a world where constantly-changing options require creativity to determine holy behavior.

Yet this creative dimension of ethics does not mean that we elevate whim over the will of God. Instead, we are to use our minds soberly and humbly, making the best choices we can according to the level of faith God gives us. This introduces more flexibility into the Christian system than was allowed under the Jewish system, where one law was supposed to fit all persons and all situations. This is why Paul will devote an entire chapter (14) to tolerance of individual viewpoints and convictions.

II. Traits of the Saved—9-21
A. Live in love, 9-11

9 Let love be without dissimulation. Abhor that which is evil; cleave to that which is good.

10 Be kindly affectioned one to another with brotherly love; in honour preferring one another;

11 Not slothful in business; fervent in spirit; serving the Lord;

In contrast to the myriad of laws (some counted 630) under the Old Covenant, Paul follows Jesus in teaching that the single law of love covers human responsibility under the New Covenant (Matt. 22:35-40). Yet the many circumstances and situations life brings us inevitably raises questions about the loving thing to do. The rest of this chapter is therefore devoted to specific instances in which

love is to guide our actions.

The first principle is to be sure that our love in sincere. To "dissimulate" is to be insincere (see the NIV); the Greek word means "without hypocrisy." This total devotion to acting in love is possible only if we totally abhor and avoid the temptation to do evil.

From verse 10 we learn that instead of competing with each other for prominence and power, living in "brotherly love" (Grk. *philadelphia*) finds us outdoing others in showing honor and consideration. How the modern workplace would be transformed by applying this principle!

Some sociologists say that applying verse 11 to the world of work radically transformed Western culture, especially through the influence of Luther and Calvin. Diligence and thrift, viewing work as service to God rather than man, helped predominantly Protestant nations prosper both materially and spiritually.

B. Rejoice, with patience, 12

12 Rejoicing in hope; patient in tribulation; continuing instant in prayer;

The constant threat of persecution for the faith made this counsel especially meaningful for Paul's original audiences. Even today, when suffering would destroy the natural joyful disposition of the Christian, we can rejoice in God's promised future, and learn patience from the experience.

C. Care for others, 13-16

13 Distributing to the necessity of saints; given to hospitality.

14 Bless them which persecute

you: bless, and curse not.

15 Rejoice with them that do rejoice, and weep with them that weep.

16 Be of the same mind one toward another. Mind not high things, but condescend to men of low estate. Be not wise in your own conceits.

Obviously, Paul has supplemented his earlier training as a rabbi by learning from the teachings of Jesus, especially the ethics of the Sermon on the Mount. The love ethic naturally finds believers tending to each other's needs. This trait was the impetus for Christians' founding the first formal hospitals and other organized ministries to those who hurt.

"Hospitality" is from a word meaning "friendship to strangers." It resulted in a network among early Christians that gave shelter to the traveler, especially to those fleeing persecution. A fruitful subject for modern Christians to discuss is how this open-home policy can be maintained in today's crowded and crime-ridden cities. A close relative of hospitality is the *koinonia,* or fellowship, described in verses 15-16. The level of fellowship Paul envisions is impossible among people who are arrogant, considering themselves too good to associate with "the lower classes."

D. Overcome evil with good, 17-21

1. Living in peace, 17-18

17 Recompense to no man evil for evil. Provide things honest in the sight of all men.

18 If it be possible, as much as lieth in you, live peaceably with all men.

Again reflecting the Sermon on the Mount, Paul rejects the "eye-for-an-eye" ethic of his Jewish background (see Matt. 5:38-44). Note that Paul's train of thought is running freely without careful organization. The counsel to be honest (vs. 17b) arises in the midst of his teaching to avoid retribution and to live in peace (17a, 18).

2. Shunning vengeance, 19-21

19 Dearly beloved, avenge not yourselves, but rather give place unto wrath: for it is written, Vengeance is mine; I will repay, saith the Lord.

20 Therefore if thine enemy hunger, feed him; if he thirst, give him drink: for in so doing thou shalt heap coals of fire on his head.

21 Be not overcome of evil, but overcome evil with good.

The principle of not rendering evil for evil seems so basic a difference between the Old Law and the New that Paul expands on it in these closing verses. Again, the influence of the Sermon on the Mount is obvious.

Refusing to take vengeance into our own hands is the only way the cycle of evil can be broken. Such passages continually raise the question of whether this policy can be expanded from personal to social ethics, and applied to the issue of nations going to war with each other.

Evangelistic Emphasis

Quite often we hear the experience of becoming a Christian described as "giving one's heart to God." So it is. The term "heart" in the Scripture refers to the emotional and spiritual center of a person. The heart is considered the essence of who one is as a human being. When one gives his heart to Christ he is turning over his will, his emotions, and the direction of his life to His direction.

We also are encouraged to "offer our bodies" to the Lordship of Jesus as well. We are to "be" different when we become Christians. We are also to "do" differently when we become Christians. We are reminded that the Christian walk is not simply some philosophy to which we adhere. Christianity is also an action that we take.

We work out our Christianity in the crucible of the world around us. People learn that we are Christians not merely by what we say, but by what we do as well. Our Christianity must be a mind, heart, and hand religion. In other words, Christianity must affect the way we think, the way we feel, and the way we act toward others.

A faith that does not affect our actions in a Christ-like fashion is not really much of a faith at all.

☜☞

And be not conformed to this world: but be ye transformed by the renewing of your mind, that ye may prove what is that good, and acceptable, and perfect, will of God.—*Romans 12:2*

There is a lizard-like animal that dwells on our earth called a chameleon. Chameleons are known for their ability to change color. A chameleon may be green, yellow, or white one minute, and the next minute it may be brown or black. The changes of color occur in response to variations in light or temperature, or as the result of fright or some other reaction to the immediate environment. It could be said, in simple terms, that chameleons change to fit into their environment.

Paul exhorts the Christian not to fit into the prevailing culture of the day. Rather, we are to be transformed into more Christ-like beings by the changing of our mind-set from a worldly point of view to a Godly point of view. We must not allow the culture to force us into its mold. We must allow the Holy Spirit to transform us into the image of Christ.

Weekday Problems

Paula did not know why, but Krystal just did not like her. Ever since Krystal came to work in that office she seemed bent on making Paula's life miserable. Krystal enjoyed making Paula the object of her sarcastic sense of humor. When Krystal invited a few of the ladies out to lunch, she always made a public show of not including Paula. When Krystal had a chance, she made Paula look bad in front of the supervisor. It began to dawn on Paula that Krystal was trying to get her fired.

Today, Paula found a rare moment when she and Krystal were the only two in the office. "Krystal," Paula said, "If I have done anything to hurt you or make you angry, I apologize. I assure you, if I have offended you in any way it was purely unintentional."

Krystal's face contorted with anger, "I hate people like you. You Christians always think you're better than everybody else. You're all just a bunch of hypocrites!"

Paula stood there in shock. She turned and walked to her desk as Krystal slammed her desk drawer and stormed out of the office.

Paula wracked her brain trying to think of what she had done to offend Krystal. She could honestly come up with nothing.

*What might Paula's next step be?

*How might Paula work to change Krystal's opinion of Christians?

Living in Love

The true measure of loving God is to love Him without measure.—*St. Benedict*

* * *

Love is the weapon which Omnipotence reserved to conquer rebel man when all the rest had failed. Reason he parries; fear he answers blow for blow; future interest he meets with present pleasure; but love is that sun against whose melting beams the winter cannot stand.—*Martin F. Tupper*

* * *

The power to love truly and devotedly is the noblest gift with which a human being can be endowed; but it is a sacred fire that must not be burned to idols.—*Maria Jane Jewsbury*

* * *

Stimulate the heart of love . . . and all other virtues will rise of their own accord, and all vices will be thrown out.—*Samuel Taylor Coleridge*

This Lesson in Your Life

How Are We to Live?

In our passage from Romans 12, Paul gives the Roman Christians a list of ways to live out their faith in relationship to God and to others. He opens the passage by telling them not to live according to the rules of their present-day society. They are to adjust their minds to God's way of thinking, being transformed into people who walk in the will of God. He knew that Christians cannot walk in the world's ways and continue to walk in the will of God. We cannot continue life as usual, living according to society's rules, and walk with God at the same time.

We see that pattern over and over in the Scripture. Noah could not continue his life as usual and build the ark at the same time. He had to adjust his life to be transformed into what God wanted.

Moses could not stay on the back side of the desert herding sheep and lead God's people out of captivity in Egypt at the same time. Moses had to allow God to transform his life.

David could not remain a shepherd boy and lead Israel as their greatest human king at the same time. He had to allow God to transform his life.

Peter, Andrew, James, and John could not continue making an honorable living, according to worldly standards, and at the same time follow Jesus as His apostles. They had to give up conformity and embrace transformation.

That is the way God works. Look at Abraham, Amos, Jonah, and Paul. Each one was doing just fine in his life according to the world's standards. Yet, enormous changes and adjustments had to be made in order for them to follow God's will. Everything had to be yielded to God and their entire lives adjusted to Him. The moment the necessary adjustments were made, God began to transform them and to accomplish His purposes through them.

You may be thinking, "But, God will not ask me to make those kinds of sacrifices." If you look at Scripture for your understanding of God, you will see that God most certainly will require adjustments and transformations of His people. Even Jesus followed this pattern. Jesus emptied Himself of His heavenly wealth and power in order to carry out God's Will for the redemption of humanity.

If I want to be a disciple of Jesus, I have no choice. I must give up my will to His. I must turn away from the world's ways and walk in the way of Christ; even if that requires a drastic change in my way of thinking and in my lifestyle.

Paul instructs us to live sacrificial lives, give up worldly ways that are contrary to God's will, and allow our lives to be transformed by God's grace. This is not simply a "good idea." It is God's way.

1. Instead of offering dead animal sacrifices, Paul encourages the Roman Christians to do what?

Paul encourages the Romans to offer their bodies as living sacrifices. We are to live for Christ.

2. Paul describes the act of sacrificial living for Christ in a holy manner as what?

Sacrificial living for God is our reasonable (or spiritual) act of worship, which is obedient service.

3. What has to take place in our lives before we can truly test and approve God's perfect will?

There has to be a Godly transformation in our lives before we can truly be active in carrying out God's perfect will.

4. How does Paul encourage Christians to view their own lives?

We are to view our own lives without pride but with sober judgment. We must remember we are what we are by the grace of God.

5. According to verses 9-10, what should be some characteristics of Christian love?

Love must be sincere. We are to be devoted to each other in brotherly love. We are to show honor to each other above ourselves.

6. How are Christians to work in their everyday jobs?

We are to work zealously, not slothfully. We must work at our jobs recognizing that through our work we are serving the Lord.

7. How are we to respond when God's people are in need?

We are to share with God's people who are in need. We are also to practice hospitality.

8. How are we to react to persecution and to those who treat us wrongly?

We are to bless those who persecute us. We must not repay evil with evil. We are to overcome evil with good.

9. What is the overarching theme of all of a Christian's relationships and actions?

Love must be our guiding light in relationships and actions.

10. How are we to treat our enemies?

With love. If an enemy is hungry, feed him. If he is thirsty, give him something to drink. This may bring about his repentance.

Paul tells us here, "If you are going to be a Christian, then act like a Christian. Acting Christian-like is different than the world acts."

For example, the world teaches us, "You owe me." The world teaches us, "I deserve all the best, even if I did not work for it. It's my right." The world teaches us, "Do unto others . . . only do it first."

Not so with Christ. Christ teaches us, "Always take the high road. Follow the Royal Way, even when it isn't convenient. Act Christ-like, even if it is at great personal cost."

Sometimes acting and reacting in a Christ-like manner pays off for us right now. When I worked as a pharmacist, there was a man who was always in a bad mood when he came into the store. He griped constantly. His prescription was too expensive. He had to wait too long. If his medicine was ready when he came in, he griped because he had to wait on his last visit. This man was the most negative person I had ever met. We all wanted to run to the stockroom when he came in because we disliked waiting on him so much.

One day God convicted me of my attitude toward this man. I realized that I had let his attitude determine my view of him. I determined to treat him as if he were the nicest fellow in the world. Not long after that, I met the man in McDonald's restaurant. I spoke to him cheerfully. I tell you the truth, he looked genuinely surprised. As I made small talk, he even smiled. I had never seen him smile before. We both got our orders and parted company. From that day on, our relationship was different. He did not become a Pollyanna, but he was pleasant. I praised God.

However, following the Royal Way does not always pay off immediately. I know a man in a neighboring city who owned a very successful restaurant and lounge. It was in a beautiful location overlooking a lake filled with cypress trees and Spanish moss. The restaurant was making big money. The bar was making even more.

During this time, the man became a Christian. God convicted him that he should not be selling alcohol at his restaurant. The conviction was so strong that he closed his bar and even quit serving low alcohol content beverages with meals. His profits plummeted. After a few years of declining business, he had to close the restaurant and sell out. His Christian convictions cost him greatly in this life.

Whatever the immediate outcome of following Christ, it will all be worth it to one day meet the Master face to face and hear Him say, "Well done, good and faithful servant!"

..WELCOME THOSE WHO ARE WEAK IN FAITH...

We Are the Lord's

Romans 14:1-13

Him that is weak in the faith receive ye, but not to doubtful disputations.

2 For one believeth that he may eat all things: another, who is weak, eateth herbs.

3 Let not him that eateth despise him that eateth not; and let not him which eateth not judge him that eateth: for God hath received him.

4 Who art thou that judgest another man's servant? to his own master he standeth or falleth. Yea, he shall be holden up: for God is able to make him stand.

5 One man esteemeth one day above another: another esteemeth every day alike. Let every man be fully persuaded in his own mind.

6 He that regardeth the day, regardeth it unto the Lord; and he that regardeth not the day, to the Lord he doth not regard it. He that eateth, eateth to the Lord, for he giveth God thanks; and he that eateth not, to the Lord he eateth not, and giveth God thanks.

7 For none of us liveth to himself, and no man dieth to himself.

8 For whether we live, we live unto the Lord; and whether we die, we die unto the Lord: whether we live therefore, or die, we are the Lord's.

9 For to this end Christ both died, and rose, and revived, that he might be Lord both of the dead and living.

10 But why dost thou judge thy brother? or why dost thou set at nought thy brother? for we shall all stand before the judgment seat of Christ.

11 For it is written, As I live, saith the Lord, every knee shall bow to me, and every tongue shall confess to God.

12 So then every one of us shall give account of himself to God.

13 Let us not therefore judge one another any more: but judge this rather, that no man put a stumblingblock or an occasion to fall in his brother's way.

Apr. 28

Memory Selection
Romans 14:13

Devotional Reading
Romans 14:14-23

Background Scripture
Romans 14:1–15:13

The grand topic of this chapter is Christian freedom. In previous chapters, Paul has labored to show that our relationship with God is determined not by works, but by grace. Here Paul applies this principle to Christian fellowship, and affirms that this relationship, too, is based on the grace we extend to those who differ from us.

Of course there are qualifications to this principle. For example, Paul is not saying that we should accept a brother or sister who insists that we are saved by works (Gal. 5:4). Neither are we to fellowship those who insist on living in blatant immorality (1 Cor. 5:9-11). Paul is dealing here with the thousands of opinions, customs, and traditions that have no bearing on the gospel of grace. He insists that since we serve a universal God, we should expect to embrace a universe of diverse people and practices.

છ૭જી

Evangelist Billy Graham once went to Australia for a campaign. Among his most ardent supporters were a group of very conservative evangelical women who believed it was a sign of worldliness to wear make-up. Putting Dr. Graham on the spot, they confronted him with the obvious question: "What do you think about women wearing make-up?

"Well," he replied, "I think any old barn needs a coat of paint now and then." His humorous reply seemed to satisfy would-be critics. Although they still didn't use make-up, most of them granted Graham the freedom of another viewpoint because he was from another culture.

What do you think? Are group members aware of more serious differences among Christians? Is humor always an appropriate way to diffuse such potential arguments? In this lesson Paul will offer guidelines for dealing with such diversity.

Teaching Outline	Daily Bible Readings
I. Dietary Disputes—1-3	**Mon.** Act to Honor the Lord Romans 14:1-6
II. Days Deemed Sacred—4-6	**Tue.** We Are the Lord's Romans 14:7-12
A. Don't judge, 4	**Wed.** Don't Cause Others to Stumble Romans 14:13-23
B. Guiding principles, 5-6	**Thu.** Build Up Your Neighbor Romans 15:1-6
III. Duties to God—7-12	**Fri.** Receive Each Other Romans 15:7-13
A. Dead or alive, we are God's, 7-8	**Sat.** Mission to Gentiles Romans 15:14-21
B. All are accountable to God, 9-12	**Sun.** Ministry to Rome Romans 15:22-33
IV. Duty to Each Other, 13	

Verse by Verse

I. Dietary Disputes—1-3

1 Him that is weak in the faith receive ye, but not to doubtful disputations.

2 For one believeth that he may eat all things: another, who is weak, eateth herbs.

3 Let not him that eateth despise him that eateth not; and let not him which eateth not judge him that eateth: for God hath received him.

It is important to identify the person Paul identifies here as "weak in the faith." Since the apostle has argued so fervently that we are saved by faith, not works, we may assume that "the faith" refers to the basic doctrine that Christ's work on the Cross, not our own works, earns salvation. A person who is "weak" on that topic is therefore one who tends to elevate a human work, practice, or custom above the faith-grace system itself.

Here Paul exhorts the Body of Christ to accept people even though they give such scruples (for example, vegetarianism, vs. 2) too much priority. The qualification, "but not to doubtful disputation" (NIV "without passing judgment on disputable matters") cuts two ways. Over-scrupulous people should not be allowed to bind their opinions on others in the Body; and those stronger in the faith should not attempt to relieve the over-scrupulous of their convictions.

Jewish scruples about diet are well-known, carried over from the clean and unclean meat restriction under the Law of Moses. It is not as widely known that Gentiles often brought their own rules into their newly discovered Christian fellowships, foods that carried the virtual label, "Taste not" (see Col. 2:16, 21; 1 Tim. 4:3, both written with non-Jews primarily in mind). Since diets have nothing to do with "the faith" that *Jesus* saves, not what we eat or don't eat, Paul clearly states his overall rule: "Live and let live."

This principle is expanded in 1 Corinthians 8 to food that has been offered to idols—although there Paul leans more to the duty of the "strong" not to partake of questionable food if it places a "stumbling-block" in the path of a weaker brother. (See more on this below, at vs. 13.)

II. Days Deemed Sacred—4-6

A. Don't judge, 4

4 Who art thou that judgest another man's servant? to his own master he standeth or falleth. Yea,

he shall be holden up: for God is able to make him stand.

Now Paul introduces the overall rule that applies both to the previous issue of what foods we may eat, and the following topic of keeping "holy" days. The principle is that we are not to "judge" or condemn practices that have nothing to do with the essence of the faith, or to impugn the motives of others. Why? Because God is their judge, and the doctrine of monotheism means we as humans are neither gods nor judges! Our brothers and sisters are not bound to please us, but their Lord.

B. Guiding principles, 5-6

5 One man esteemeth one day above another: another esteemeth every day alike. Let every man be fully persuaded in his own mind.

6 He that regardeth the day, regardeth it unto the Lord; and he that regardeth not the day, to the Lord he doth not regard it. He that eateth, eateth to the Lord, for he giveth God thanks; and he that eateth not, to the Lord he eateth not, and giveth God thanks.

Turning specifically to the issue of special days of religious significance, Paul restates in different words his "live and let live" principle. The first principle to keep in mind is that anyone who observes a "holy" day should do so with sincerity and conviction. This means we should not "fake" the observance of a holy day we may admire someone else for observing. For example, although a new Jewish Christian may want to continue to observe the Sabbath, this should not obligate a newly converted pagan, who had no Sabbath tradition, to mimic the Jewish observance merely for the sake of appearances.

The second guiding principle grows out of the first: decisions to observe or not observe a "holy" day should be made with God in mind. That is, keeping or declining to keep a holy day should not be a "secular" decision, but a choice based on our desire to keep a clear conscience before God. Of course it follows that both the observer and non-observer must also respect each other's conscientious decision.

Perhaps an illustration of this principle for our day would be Halloween. Some Christians observe the "Hallowed Evening" of Oct. 31 in connection with All Saints' Day on Nov. 1. Others associate Halloween with witches and the demonic, and cannot conscientiously observe it. According to Paul's teaching, Christians of both persuasions should refrain from condemning the other.

III. Duties to God—7-12

A. Dead or alive, we are God's, 7-8

7 For none of us liveth to himself, and no man dieth to himself.

8 For whether we live, we live unto the Lord; and whether we die, we die unto the Lord: whether we live therefore, or die, we are the Lord's.

The first point of solidarity Paul makes here in defense of a "Live and let live" policy reinforces what he said in verse 4: God, not our brothers and sisters in the fellowship, is our ultimate Master and Judge. Although we decline, for example, to make a religious observance of Halloween, we must not presume that a fellow-believer who does so is saying that "It doesn't matter what God says, I'm going to observe that day." We should rather assume that he is conscious of his living and dying under the rules of the same God we serve.

Why bring up "dying"? Perhaps Paul refers to the spiritual death an opinionated person believes will befall someone who does not keep certain holy days. If so, we would read this verse and those following as though quotation marks were around the words "live" and "die," taking them first figuratively, and then theoretically. Paul wants us to know that we actually have no control over whether God reckons our brother to be spiritually alive or dead. Since these issues are not the essence of the faith, our brother's spiritual life or death is God's business, not ours.

B. All are accountable to God, 9-12

9 For to this end Christ both died, and rose, and revived, that he might be Lord both of the dead and living.

10 But why dost thou judge thy brother? or why dost thou set at nought thy brother? for we shall all stand before the judgment seat of Christ.

11 For it is written, As I live, saith the Lord, every knee shall bow to me, and every tongue shall confess to God.

12 So then every one of us shall give account of himself to God.

Again, we may mentally place the words "dead" and "living" in quotation marks, viewing them as describing either a vital or vain status before God. If my diet or other religious custom is dedicated to God, I "live" in relation to Him, even though a critic may consider me "dead."

As a Jew, Paul has a stronger view of the unity of the "People of God" than many of us in individualistic America have inherited. Many today ignore the principle he will affirm in verse 13, that we have some responsibility regarding the scruples of others in the fellowship. Yet in the matter of personal freedom, Paul is an individualist, too. While "we shall *all* stand" before God, His judgment will be rendered on an individual basis. We have no right, therefore, to render premature judgment on others.

IV. Duty to Each Other, 13

13 Let us not therefore judge one another any more: but judge this rather, that no man put a stumblingblock or an occasion to fall in his brother's way.

Now Paul makes the point he teaches in 1 Corinthians 8. While we are not to judge each other's customs and practices when they are irrelevant to the gospel, we *are* to exercise good judgment in whether our own practice damages the faith of another member of the fellowship. This does not mean that we should refrain from doing anything someone else thinks is wrong, but from anything a weak brother is emboldened to *do* (or eat, or keep, or "observe") while thinking it is wrong (see vss. 14-23).

Evangelistic Emphasis

In this high-tech society, there seems to be a personal computer in almost every household. This is good. We call it "progress."

We hook our computers up to the Internet and we have the world at our fingertips. We can access the United States Library of Congress right from our home. We can research the merits and demerits of the latest Broadway play right from our homes. We can purchase almost anything a person could think of and have it brought directly to our doorstep without ever setting foot outside our front door.

One of the problems of the widespread use of the Internet on personal computers is that we can become alienated from other human beings. Even though a person can be entertained for hours, even days, in front of a computer, there is still a need within us all for close personal human relationships.

What better place to build a personal relationship than within the church. One of our tasks as Christians is to bring others into a personal relationship with Jesus Christ and to offer that person the warmth and safety of genuine Christian fellowship. The call of God is to all people. One responsibility of the Christian is to help those who come into the church feel like part of the family of God. We welcome and accept all who follow Christ. That's good news.

❧❧❧

Memory Selection

Let us not therefore judge one another any more: but judge this rather, that no man put a stumblingblock or an occasion to fall in his brother's way—*Romans 14:13*

Picture this scene. A baby is just learning to walk. The baby pulls up on the coffee table and walks around it. The baby walks across the floor giggling with glee while holding Dad's hands. Then, the big moment comes and the baby takes its first steps without any help. The parents laugh and clap.

Now, imagine someone placing a four-inch square beam in front of the tottering child for the baby to step over without assistance. I suspect that image brings a frown to your face. Yet, that is the same kind of thing some well-meaning Christians do to newborn Christians.

We sometimes trip up the new Christian with human rules that really have nothing to do with a genuine Christian walk. May we mature Christians be very careful only to require of the new believer what Jesus required. We must always guard against being a stumblingblock to anyone's faith.

Weekday Problems

They came in the back door of old First Church after the organ had already begun playing. There were no seats in the rear of the sanctuary, so the couple made their way down to the third row from the front. Every eye in the church was glued on the pair.

His head was shaved. He was wearing a black leather jacket with silver studs all over it and black leather pants. He had an earring in his left ear that appeared to be a two-inch cross. His tee shirt had a motorcycle symbol on the front. Her outfit caused even more commotion. Her hair was bright blue with streaks of pink. She wore a neat skirt and blouse, but had a tattoo on the back of her neck that peeked over the collar. The gold stud in her left nostril seemed to be a beacon that lit up the room.

They walked to the front and sat down, opened the hymnal and began to sing with the congregation, "Amazing grace how sweet the sound, that saved a wretch like me. . . ."

It seemed that everybody in the place was whispering.

*How important do you think it is to God how we look? Explain.

*Are your feelings about outward appearances based on Scripture or on tradition? Explain.

Unkind Judgments

Ike: Do you know a cure for insomnia?
Mike: Try talking to yourself.

* * *

Mae: I'm chilled to the bone.
Faye: Why don't you put on a hat?

* * *

Betty: I dread the thought of turning 45.
Heddy: Why? What happened to you back then, dear?

* * *

Bill: I have had to make a living by my wits.
Will: Well, half a living is better than none.

* * *

Kay: What brings you to town?
Rae: Oh, I just came to see the sights, and I thought I'd start with you.

* * *

Jack: Something just came into my mind, but it went away again.
Mack: Maybe it got lonely.

This Lesson in Your Life
Who Can Judge?

Paul begins this passage with these words: "Accept him whose faith is weak, without passing judgment on *disputable* matters" (Rom. 14:1, NIV, italics mine). Paul reminds us that we are to be tolerant with others whose ideas differ from our own concerning matters that do not strike at the heart of Christianity.

In the Christian faith there are myriads of differing ideologies. These differences might be significant, even important, yet if they do not alter the core beliefs of the faith they are to be tolerated. Please note carefully: there are certain essentials of the faith which one must embrace. There are some foundational doctrines one must both accept and implement for one to be a believer, a disciple of Jesus Christ. Yet we argue over many other issues that are only peripheral.

We must be careful not to reject a sincere believer just because she or he does things differently than we do.

Paul calls the person who is bound by religious rules a person of weak faith. Such a person has not yet discovered the meaning of Christian liberty. That person is still a legalist at heart and sees Christianity simply as a set of rules and regulations.

He has not set himself free from a belief in the efficacy of works. In his heart he believes that he can gain God's favor by doing certain things and abstaining from others, or by doing things in a certain way, or by doing right things often enough. That person is basically still trying to earn a right relationship with God, and has not yet accepted the way of grace.

Christianity is certainly not an "anything goes" faith. Still, we must be careful not to construct rules and regulations by which we exclude or judge others. Embrace one another in Christian love. For it is only by God's love, mercy, and grace that any of us has the privilege of being in the Family of God.

STRAIGHT

1. What is the proper Christian response to one whose faith is weak?
We are to accept those whose faith is weak, kindly receiving them rather than offering only condemnation.

2. To what is Paul referring when he begins the discussion on what one does or does not eat?
Paul probably refers to strict adherence to Jewish dietary laws.

3. Do a person's dietary habits determine that person's worth before God?
No. Jesus said that it is not what goes into a person's mouth but what comes out of a person's mouth and heart that defiles him.

4. Are we to judge one another according to appearances or externals?
Indeed not. The strong are not to despise the weak as superstitious or ignorant. Neither are the weak to condemn the strong for excess.

5. To whom does a servant answer?
A servant answers to her or his master, not to anyone else.

6. Who is the master to which the Christian, strong or weak, answers?
The Christian answers to the Lord, who alone aquits or condemns.

7. In verses 6-7, is Paul telling us we do not need to observe a Sabbath day?
No, Paul is saying that every day should be dedicated to God. We must not condemn one another for different ways of observance.

8. Upon whom does the Christian depend, whether in life or death?
We depend upon God, who is Lord both of the living and the dead.

9. What will happen at the final judgment seat (vs.11)?
Every knee will bow to God and every tongue confess that He is Lord. All will submit to God.

10. Who will be required to give an account before God of their lives?
All, whether believers or not, will give an account of themselves to God.

A story is told of the saintly missionary to India, Dr. E. Stanley Jones. Some years before his death Dr. Jones was asked to return to the United States to appear at a pastors' conference. When it was his turn to speak, he addressed the moral, ethical, and spiritual decline of the American clergy. Though he spoke with humility and love, he left no stone unturned. He spoke with a prophetic voice.

When he had finished, he stepped down from the platform and began shaking hands and issuing greetings to those who wished to meet him. However, one lady, a pastor's wife, met him at the bottom of the steps with eyes flashing anger.

As he greeted her she came back at him, "How dare you!"

"Madam?" he replied.

"How dare you speak to these men of God like that! You have no idea what they are going through here in this changing society. You have no right to scold them! Jesus Himself said, 'Judge not lest ye be judged.'"

"Dear madam," Dr. Jones replied, "I suppose you are referring to Jesus' words found in Luke 6:37, 'Judge not, and ye shall not be judged: condemn not, and ye shall not be condemned. . . .'?"

"That's right," she replied.

"Please, sister, read on farther in that passage," Dr. Jones said. "Jesus goes on to say, 'For a good tree bringeth not forth corrupt fruit; neither doth a corrupt tree bring forth good fruit. For every tree is known by his own fruit.' Dear madam, you are absolutely right. I am no judge, nor do I desire to be. I am simply a fruit inspector."

How about you? Is your life producing good fruit? That is the most important thing for individual Christians to focus upon. Sometimes we get so hung up on making sure the other person is doing right that we forget to make sure our own lives are pure, holy, and pleasing to God. God is your Master. God is my Master. Each of us will answer to Him individually. We must make sure, by the power of the Holy Spirit, that our houses are in order.

Now, this is not to excuse us from encouraging others on to holy living. This thought does not excuse us from discerning the difference between things that glorify God and things that do not. Yet, if our primary focus is making sure the other person is living up to our standards, then we are making a mistake.

Leave the judging to God. Encourage one another to holy living. May we live our own lives in a fashion that brings honor and glory to our Heavenly Master.

WE HAVE COME TO BELIEVE IN CHRIST JESUS...

Lesson 10

Faith and Works

Galatians 1:1-2, 6-9; 2:15-21

Paul, an apostle, (not of men, neither by man, but by Jesus Christ, and God the Father, who raised him from the dead;)

2 And all the brethren which are with me, unto the churches of Galatia:

6 I marvel that ye are so soon removed from him that called you into the grace of Christ unto another gospel:

7 Which is not another; but there be some that trouble you, and would pervert the gospel of Christ.

8 But though we, or an angel from heaven, preach any other gospel unto you than that which we have preached unto you, let him be accursed.

9 As we said before, so say I now again, If any man preach any other gospel unto you than that ye have received, let him be accursed.

2:15 We who are Jews by nature, and not sinners of the Gentiles,

16 Knowing that a man is not justified by the works of the law, but by the faith of Jesus Christ, even we have believed in Jesus Christ, that we might be justified by the faith of Christ, and not by the works of the law: for by the works of the law shall no flesh be justified.

17 But if, while we seek to be justified by Christ, we ourselves also are found sinners, is therefore Christ the minister of sin? God forbid.

18 For if I build again the things which I destroyed, I make myself a transgressor.

19 For I through the law am dead to the law, that I might live unto God.

20 I am crucified with Christ: nevertheless I live; yet not I, but Christ liveth in me: and the life which I now live in the flesh I live by the faith of the Son of God, who loved me, and gave himself for me.

21 I do not frustrate the grace of God: for if righteousness come by the law, then Christ is dead in vain.

May 5

Memory Selection
Galatians 2:16

Devotional Reading
Acts 13:26-39

Background Scripture
Galatians 1—2

It is appropriate to follow our previous studies in Romans with these lessons from Paul's letter to the Galatians, since they both focus on the principle that we are saved by faith, not works.

Yet there are differences. While Romans reads like a formal essay, Galatians seems to have been written in the heat of battle. Here Paul apparently folllows up on his and Barnabas' church-founding mission in Galatia, when they had been constantly badgered by "Judaizing teachers" (see Acts 13:50; 14:2, 19). It angered Paul for his sacrificial work in behalf of the gospel of grace to be threatened by those who wanted to require Gentiles to come to Christ through Moses, and to be circumcised. In this letter he therefore speaks out with bold emotion instead of calmly writing a doctrinal treatise. The basic message, however, is unchanged: We are justified by grace through faith, not by works.

ഔഃ

A game of "Pin the Donkey" is a lighthearted way to begin this session. Bring the usual cardboard cut-out of a donkey, along with a tail and a thumbtack. *This time, however, be sure the cut-out includes the donkey's tail.* Blindfold a few participants and challenge them to pin the extra tail over the one already on the donkey.

After a few group members have taken their turn, point out the obvious: *they have been trying to tack a tail on a donkey that already has one.* Point out that this is something like the problem Paul faced. The Good News he had preached in Galatia was complete, lacking nothing. Now, however, "Judaizing teachers" were trying to "tack on a tail." They maintained that the grace of Christ was not enough to save Gentiles; they must add the work of circumcision to the simple gospel of grace. Paul bluntly calls this attempted addition a distorted gospel.

Teaching Outline	Daily Bible Readings
I. Paul's Authority—1:1-2	**Mon.** Grace in Christ 1 John 2:1-6
II. Perverted Gospel—6-9	**Tue.** Commandment to Love 1 John 2:7-17
A. A puzzling development, 6-7	**Wed.** Living by the Spirit 1 Corinthians 8
B. A curse on false teachers, 8-9	**Thu.** All for God's Glory 1 Corinthians 10:23-32
III. Pertinent Comparisons—2:15-21	**Fri.** Commissioned by Christ Galatians 1:1-5
A. Between Jew and Gentile, 15-16	**Sat.** Not of Human Origins Galatians 1:11-24
B. Sin after salvation, 17-18	**Sun.** Saved by Faith, not Works Galatians 2:15-21
C. Between death and life, 19-21	

Verse by Verse

I. Paul's Authority—1:1-2

1 Paul, an apostle, (not of men, neither by man, but by Jesus Christ, and God the Father, who raised him from the dead;)

2 And all the brethren which are with me, unto the churches of Galatia:

Just as he did at the beginning of his letter to the Romans, Paul emphasizes his authority as an apostle, no doubt to waylay objections from those who he knew would disagree with his teaching. Although the term "apostle" at first meant only a messenger or "one sent" on a particular mission, it took on an "official" meaning in reference to the original 12 men Christ called to be His special aides. Although a disciple named Matthias was named to take the place of Judas (Acts 1:26), Paul's call on the Damascus Road constituted a 13th apostleship, "one born out of due time" (1 Cor. 15:8). In verses 15-24 he will explain that this apostolic commission was "not of man." It came directly from Christ, independent of the other apostles.

Despite his insistence on the authority of the apostolic office, Paul had no personal pride to defend. He admitted that he was "the least of the apostles, that am not meet to be called an apostle, because I persecuted the church of God" (1 Cor. 15:9).

His letter is addressed to "the churches of Galatia." This could refer to the churches he and Barnabas had established on their first missionary journey in Antioch of Pisdia, Iconium, Lystra, and Derbe (Acts 13-14), or to the older "Galatia," a much larger area of Asia Minor (now Turkey). However, it seems unlikely that Paul would have known about Judaizing teachers in the larger area, where, as far as we know, he planted no churches.

II. Perverted Gospel—6-9

A. A puzzling development, 6-7

6 I marvel that ye are so soon removed from him that called you into the grace of Christ unto another gospel:

7 Which is not another; but there be some that trouble you, and would pervert the gospel of Christ.

We will learn later that insisting on circumcision and perhaps other institutions from Moses' Law was what "removed" some Galatian Christians from Christ and His grace. Although adding circumcision to salvation by grace may seem to be "another gospel," Paul says it is actually a perversion of the true gospel.

B. A curse on false teachers, 8-9

8 But though we, or an angel from heaven, preach any other gospel unto you than that which we have preached unto you, let him be accursed.

9 As we said before, so say I now again, If any man preach any other gospel unto you than that ye have received, let him be accursed.

Paul feels so strongly about adding anything to the simple gospel of grace that he takes the unusual step of calling down a curse on those who teach otherwise, even repeating it for emphasis. The word for "accursed" in the original is *anathema.*

The Galatians may have been in awe of these Judaizing teachers, some of whom may have come directly from the "mother church" in Jerusalem, where the council on such issues had been conducted (Acts 15). Paul, however, knowing that Satan can go to great lengths to deceive, warns that even though an angel brought the doctrine of circumcision (or other works) to add to the gospel of grace, he is to be accursed.

III. Pertinent Comparisons—2:15-21

A. Between Jew and Gentile, 15-16

15 We who are Jews by nature, and not sinners of the Gentiles,

16 Knowing that a man is not justified by the works of the law, but by the faith of Jesus Christ, even we have believed in Jesus Christ, that we might be justified by the faith of Christ, and not by the works of the law: for by the works of the law shall no flesh be justified.

In context, it is clear that "We Jews" here must refer to Paul and other Jewish Christians. In verses 9-14, the apostle had argued that it is wrong to show racial favoritism. Although he refers to Gentiles as "heathens" (vs. 9) and "sinners" (vs. 15), he is only using terms in common use to distinguish Jew from Gentile.

The point is that since Jewish Christians had, by coming to Christ, admitted that the Law was inadequate, how can they now require Gentiles to submit to it? Instead of being saved by Law, both Jew and Gentile are saved by "the faith of Christ" (NIV "faith in Jesus Christ"). In the last part of verse 16, Paul quotes Psalm 143:2 to show that even the psalmist, who lived under the Law itself, knew that the works it required were inadequate to save.

B. Sin after salvation, 17-18

17 But if, while we seek to be justified by Christ, we ourselves also are found sinners, is therefore Christ the minister of sin? God forbid.

18 For if I build again the things which I destroyed, I make myself a transgressor.

Of course whether Jew or Christian, "all have sinned" (Rom. 3:23). In speaking here of being "found sinners," Paul refers to the specific sin of attempting to "tack on" legal requirements of the Law of Moses to the true gospel of salvation by grace through faith. Furthermore, the Judaizing teachers were claiming that their message was in fact a part of Christ's will, thus implicating Jesus Himself in the sin!

The reference in verse 18 to building recalls the Hebrew writer's description of salvation as part of a house built not by Moses but by God, and therefore being a worthier structure than Moses' temporary building (Heb. 3:3-4). The purpose for Moses' "house" was fulfilled, "nailed to the cross" (Col. 2:14). Paul argues that it would be a gross transgression to choose to rebuild the old structure by asserting the ongoing validity of circumcision, instead of living in the grander house built by Christ.

C. Between death and life, 19-21

19 For I through the law am dead to the law, that I might live unto God.

20 I am crucified with Christ: nevertheless I live; yet not I, but Christ liveth in me: and the life which I now live in the flesh I live by the faith of the Son of God, who loved me, and gave himself for me.

21 I do not frustrate the grace of God: for if righteousness come by the law, then Christ is dead in vain.

Paul continually faces the delicate task of showing that the Law itself, valuable though it was, pointed to its own inadequacy. One way he does this is to compare it with a husband whose wife is bound to him as long as he lives, but who is set free from the bond when her husband dies (Rom. 7:1ff.). The only thing that would make such a husband-and-wife union "wrong" would be to think it still exists after the death of one of the partners. The law of the land says the law binding a woman to her former husband is now as "dead" as the husband! This is essentially Paul's argument in verse 19. The dispensation of Law under Moses was a case of "planned obsolescence," and we do it no honor by extending it into the dispensation of grace.

Ironically, the New Covenant involves a "death" as well. Not only has the Law "died"; so has Paul, by submitting his own desires to the will of Christ. So completely has this "death of desire" occurred that it is as if Jesus lives in Paul's flesh. Yet, as countless other dedicated Christians testify, it was in dying to himself that Paul found new life in Christ. Now that he has experienced the joy of living under this New Covenant by faith, he could not imagine trying to return to living by law under the Covenant that had "died."

Verse 21 is starkly simple, but profound. By insisting on continuing the demands of the Law, the Judaizing teachers were frustrating God's plan to save the world by grace. The supreme gift of grace, the death of Christ "while we were yet sinners" (Rom. 5:8), was a complete waste of His precious blood if we could have been saved by the Law. Paul is asking a probing question: Why would anyone cling to works such as circumcision when it is Christ's "work" that makes believers righteous?

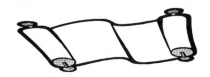

355

Evangelistic Emphasis

Notice that Paul begins his letter to the Galatians with these words: "Paul, an apostle—sent not from men nor by man, but by Jesus Christ and God the Father" (NIV). Paul was sent on a mission with full authority of representation. He was an ambassador sent by God.

Do you remember the command of Jesus in Matthew 28:18-19a? Jesus said, "All authority in heaven and on earth has been given to me. Therefore go and make disciples of all nations." Jesus has all authority. We are given the authority and the command to go and make disciples. We could begin our letters in a similar way, "David (or whatever your name is), a messenger sent by God."

We make disciples in God's name. Sometimes in our zeal to see our churches grow, we forget we are working in the name of Jesus. We say, "If we don't get some new members in here soon, our church will die." That is not a legitimate reason to do evangelism. Our motivation for winning souls to Christ should not be to perpetuate an institution. We must bring people into the Kingdom out of our love for Christ and obedience to His Great Commission. When we do that, our churches will naturally grow.

એિંટ્ટ

Memory Selection

Knowing that a man is not justified by the works of the law, but by the faith of Jesus Christ, even we have believed in Jesus Christ, that we might be justified by the faith of Christ, and not by the works of the law: for by the works of the law shall no flesh be justified.—*Galatians 2:16*

This is a key verse in Galatians. Three times in this letter, Paul tells us that no one is justified by observing the law; and three times he underscores the indispensable requirements of placing one's faith in Jesus Christ. Do you think Paul wanted the Galatians, and us in the 21st century, to catch on that a person cannot have her or his sins wiped away by observing the Old Testament law more carefully?

Friends, we are justified by faith in Jesus Christ. That is the essence of the gospel message. Paul said in Romans, "For all have sinned and come short of the glory of God" (3:23). All of us have sinned. Furthermore, we cannot perform enough good works or observe enough laws to erase that fact. We need something that renders us "not guilty." That something is a someONE. He is Jesus. By faith in him we are justified.

Weekday Problems

Eugene was complimenting himself as he trimmed the shrubs around the church. "You know, there probably isn't anyone in this congregation that does more than I do around here. Here I am, giving up my Saturday morning to make the church look nice. There's no telling what our church yard would look like if I weren't around. Hmmph! There's no telling what our church building would look like if it weren't for my family."

Eugene gazed past the shrubs at the stained glass window. "My daddy gave the money for that window. Folks tell me it's the most beautiful one. I know it cost the most. Speaking of money, Gladys and I always make a big pledge during the annual stewardship campaign. Why, our pledge is one of the top 10 pledges in the church. And I know there are more than 30 families in the church that make more money than we do. Yes, we really are big givers." Eugene was really proud.

"And we're good church members! I know they couldn't get anyone to do as good a job as I have done as Building Committee chairman. And Gladys is president of the Women's Group."

Eugene smiled to himself, "No sir, I don't imagine there's a better pair of Christians in this whole church; maybe even the whole town."

*What do you think Paul would say to Eugene if Paul could read Eugene's thoughts?

*What verse (or verses) in our passage would apply to Eugene's situation?

Q & A on Essential Bible Facts

Q: Where was Solomon's Temple?
A: On the side of his head.

* * *

Q: When was money first mentioned in the Bible?
A: When the dove brought the green back to the ark.

* * *

Q: Why didn't the last dove return to the ark?
A: Because she found sufficient grounds to stay away.

* * *

Q: Why are there so few men with whiskers in heaven?
A: Because most men get in by a close shave.

* * *

Q: How do we know they used arithmetic in early Bible times?
A: Because the Lord said to go forth and multiply.

This Lesson in Your Life

Living by the Truth

Dr. Ron Crandall, one of my seminary professors, told us this story one day in class. The incident happened to him while he was pastor of a local church.

One of his parishioners came to see him one Monday morning. The day before, Dr. Crandall had preached a message focusing on salvation by faith not by works. The man was not a regular church attender. In fact, he was somewhat of a rough fellow, skeptical and suspicious.

He knocked on the door, "Preacher, can I come in?"

"Sure, Bob (not his real name), come on in. Have a seat." So Bob, puffing on his pipe, came in and sat down.

"This will only take a minute. I wanted to ask you about yesterday's sermon. Now, you said that a person can become a Christian and he doesn't have to do anything to earn it?" Bob asked.

"Basically, that's right," Dr. Crandall answered.

"And when that person becomes a Christian, he doesn't have to deal with the eternal consequences of sin?" Bob continued.

"That's right, Bob. When a person becomes a Christian all his sins are forgiven. His spirit has the privilege of living forever with God in heaven. And it's all free. Jesus offers this gift to us without price. All it requires is that we put our faith and trust in Him."

"Well," Bob thought, still puffing on his pipe. "In that case, a man would be a fool not to be a Christian. Yep," Bob got up to leave, "a man would be a plumb fool not to be a Christian." And Bob left without ever giving his life to Christ.

To some, the gospel is too good to be true. We think we have to do something to earn it. Yet, Jesus offers us eternal life as a gift.

We simply accept the gift. However, when we accept the gift, the gift changes our lives. The Christian does not live a holy life of Christian service in order to gain salvation. No, the Christian lives a holy life of Christian service because the Christian no longer lives for her or himself, but Christ lives within that person. The Christian lives his life out of gratitude for what Christ has done for him, not out of some neurotic desire to earn something that has already been given freely.

Thus, we do good works because Christ lives within us. Christ is the source of all the life we have. We derive all our energy, all our zeal, and all our life from His grace.

1. Under whose authority was Paul sent to the Galatians?

Paul was sent by Jesus Christ and God the Father, not by any human authority.

2. According to 1:6, had the Galatians drifted slowly from the message Paul preached?

No. Apparently they turned away in a short time, for Paul says they had quickly deserted his message.

3. How did Paul describe this "new gospel" to which the Galatians turned?

He said it was really not another gospel, but no gospel at all. It was bad news, not good news.

4. What was the effect of this "new" gospel within the church at Galatia?

It was confusing and troubling, and was perverting the true gospel Paul had already preached and they had accepted.

5. What did Paul say that showed he was convinced the gospel he preached was the truth (1:8-9)?

If he, or even an angel, preached anything different, that person should be accursed, or eternally condemned.

6. According to 2:16, how is a person justified?

A person is justified not by works of the law, but by faith in Jesus Christ.

7. If a Christian sins, does that mean that Christ is the source of sin?

Of course not. Sin can always be traced back to something or someone other than Jesus. His grace does not promote sin.

8. How does Paul describe in 2:18 the act of turning back to sin?

He describes that act as rebuilding that which we have already destroyed. If we do that we become lawbreakers.

9. How does Paul describe his conversion to Christianity and subsequent life in Christ?

He says that he has been crucified with Christ. Now Christ lives within him, and Paul lives by faith in Jesus.

10. How does Paul finish this verse, "If righteousness come by the law, then . . ."?

Then Christ died in vain. That is, if righteousness could be gained by observing the law alone, Christ died for nothing.

359

Are you really convinced that God loves you? Did you know that God desires a relationship with you that is real and personal? That is one reason Jesus came. He came to re-establish the love relationship with humanity that was broken by humanity's sin in the Garden of Eden.

God loves us. He can live anywhere in the universe, yet He chooses to live in your heart. Even if there are a thousand steps between you and Him, He will take every step to close that gap.

God gives us His love freely through Jesus Christ. It is a *gift*! There is nothing we can do to earn it. Paul wrote in Ephesians 2:8-9, "For it is by grace you have been saved, through faith—and this not from yourselves, it is the gift of God—not by works, so that no one can boast." That is one lesson Paul was teaching here in Galatians. We cannot adhere closely enough to the Law of Moses to earn our way into salvation. It's a gift, remember! And a gift is always free.

Paul told us in Galatians 3, "Are you so foolish? After beginning in the Spirit, are you not trying to attain your goal by human effort?" It cannot be done.

You see, we must trust in the merits of Christ's death on the cross for our salvation, that is, our justification.

Picture this. One day you decide you are going to swim all the way from North America to England non-stop. So, you go to New York harbor and dive into the water. You are swimming strong. The miles in the water seem to slip by. After a couple of hours of swimming a boat pulls alongside and the pilot of the craft hails you, "Do you need help?"

"No," you reply. "I'm swimming to England non-stop."

"You'll never make it," the boat's pilot shouts back. "It is humanly impossible."

"I can make it," you shout back. "I know I can." You swim on.

Friends, the truth of the situation is that a human being cannot swim, unaided and non-stop, across the Atlantic Ocean. It cannot be done. If a person wants to gain England in the water, one must get in the boat.

Our spiritual lives are much the same. We cannot live for Christ with holy, righteous lives strictly by human effort. It cannot be done. We must get into the boat, the Old Ship of Zion. If we could gain righteousness (and heaven) by human effort, then Christ's death on the cross was simply a tragic, cosmic mistake. But His death was not a mistake. We need a Savior.

If you are reading this and find yourself trying hard to live a Christian life under your own energy, please stop it. Let Christ live His life through you.

God sent His Son to redeem us...

Heirs with Christ

Galatians 3:6-9, 23–4:7

E ven as Abraham believed God, and it was accounted to him for righteousness.

7 Know ye therefore that they which are of faith, the same are the children of Abraham.

8 And the scripture, foreseeing that God would justify the heathen through faith, preached before the gospel unto Abraham, saying, In thee shall all nations be blessed.

9 So then they which be of faith are blessed with faithful Abraham.

23 But before faith came, we were kept under the law, shut up unto the faith which should afterwards be revealed.

24 Wherefore the law was our schoolmaster to bring us unto Christ, that we might be justified by faith.

25 But after that faith is come, we are no longer under a schoolmaster.

26 For ye are all the children of God by faith in Christ Jesus.

27 For as many of you as have been baptized into Christ have put on Christ.

28 There is neither Jew nor Greek, there is neither bond nor free, there is neither male nor female: for ye are all one in Christ Jesus.

29 And if ye be Christ's, then are ye Abraham's seed, and heirs according to the promise.

4:1 Now I say, That the heir, as long as he is a child, differeth nothing from a servant, though he be lord of all;

2 But is under tutors and governors until the time appointed of the father.

3 Even so we, when we were children, were in bondage under the elements of the world:

4 But when the fulness of the time was come, God sent forth his Son, made of a woman, made under the law,

5 To redeem them that were under the law, that we might receive the adoption of sons.

6 And because ye are sons, God hath sent forth the Spirit of his Son into your hearts, crying, Abba, Father.

7 Wherefore thou art no more a servant, but a son; and if a son, then an heir of God through Christ.

May 12

Memory Selection
Galatians 3:26

Devotional Reading
Galatians 4:17-22

Background Scripture
Galatians 3–4

The need for Paul to defend his new-found faith against "Judaizing teachers" often required him to draw sharp distinctions between Christ and Moses. On the other hand, as we have seen, he also showed how Christ's way was an outgrowth of the Old Covenant, and therefore closely related to the faith of Abraham. This close relationship is the apostle's emphasis in today's lesson.

Specific points of harmony to emphasize include:

• Abraham was made right with God by faith, just as Christians are.

•The Law of Moses was a necessary "elementary education" leading to Christian "graduation."

•The centuries-old division between Jew and Gentile is bridged in Christ, where all can become "children of Abraham," and therefore heirs of God, members of His family, by faith.

ॐ

Ask members of your group what events young children look forward to most. Christmas, of course, will be one. Birthday will be another. Many kids also look forward to the day when they're old enough to go off to school. Then, after elementary school loses its excitement, they look forward to graduating to junior high, then high school.

In this lesson Paul compares the Old and New Covenants with this familiar process. The Jews had the privilege of entering "elementary school" under the great schoolmaster Moses, and the Law. When the Messiah came, however, they were offered the opportunity to "graduate" from the lower grades and to enjoy the privileges of "higher education."

The question Paul asks Jewish Christians who oppose salvation by grace is: *Why would you want to return to elementary school?*

Teaching Outline	*Daily Bible Readings*
I. Abraham Saved by Faith—3:6-9	**Mon.** One Body, One Bread 1 Corinthians 10:14-22
A. Abraham believed God, 6-7	**Tue.** Gentiles to Be Blessed Galatians 3:1-9
B. We can share Abraham's faith, 8-9	**Wed.** The Promise Through Faith Galatians 3:10-14
II. The School of Faith—23-25	**Thu.** Heirs Through the Promise Galatians 3:19-29
A. Shut up from faith, 23	**Fri.** No Longer Slaves Galatians 4:1-7
B. Graduating to Jesus, 24-25	**Sat.** Don't Turn Back! Galatians 4:8-16
III. The Family of Faith—3:26—4:7	**Sun.** Freedom in Christ Galatians 4:17—5:1
A. Children by faith, 3:26-28	
B. Heirs of Abraham, 3:29—4:2	
C. Redemption from the law, 3-5	
D. Sons, not servants, 6-7	

Verse by Verse

I. Abraham Saved by Faith—3:6-9
A. Abraham believed God, 6-7

6 Even as Abraham believed God, and it was accounted to him for righteousness.

7 Know ye therefore that they which are of faith, the same are the children of Abraham.

The Jewish faith is above all a family- or clan-based faith. Much of the Jewish opposition Paul faced stemmed not just from a desire to be saved by the "work" of circumcision, but from the fear that this long heritage would disappear if its external mark were neglected.

Paul's reply is that those who are saved by faith are Abraham's children, along with his more direct descendants, the Jews, because Father Abraham himself was "declared righteous" or saved by faith, not circumcision.

B. We can share Abraham's faith, 8-9

8 And the scripture, foreseeing that God would justify the heathen through faith, preached before the gospel unto Abraham, saying, In thee shall all nations be blessed.

9 So then they which be of faith are blessed with faithful Abraham.

Paul supports his argument by citing the "gospel" (good news) of Genesis 12:3, which envisions that "all families of the earth," not just Jews,

would be granted entrance into Abraham's family. This pronouncement occurred *before* the law of circumcision, which is not required of Abraham and his family until Genesis 17:9-14; see also Rom. 4).

II. The School of Faith—23-25
A. Shut up from faith, 23

23 But before faith came, we were kept under the law, shut up unto the faith which should afterwards be revealed.

Although Paul has previously shown the similarity of the Abrahamic and Christian faiths, he must point out a difference as well. Although faith was implicit under the Law, it was not emphasized because the *object* of faith, the Messiah, had not appeared to broadcast the message that God receives all people, not just the circumcised. Before Christ, Judaism was a closed system. Not only were the Jews "shut up" in it, Gentiles were largely "shut out" by it. It was only in God's good time that the message of salvation by faith was revealed through His son.

B. Graduating to Jesus, 24-25

24 Wherefore the law was our schoolmaster to bring us unto Christ, that we might be justified

by faith.

25 But after that faith is come, we are no longer under a schoolmaster.

Now Paul comes to his famous analogy of Judaism as an essential but early level of education, and Christianity as the next stage. A "schoolmaster" A "schoolmaster" (from the same Greek word that gives us the term "pedagogue") was a person, often a slave, placed in charge of a wealthy family's children to be both tutor and guardian. He was not the primary "teacher," as in the modern sense of the word "pedagogue," but served more in the role of a governess in well-to-do English families of earlier days. The pedagogue was responsible for taking the children to and from their formal studies, then for seeing that they did their "homework" and learned household duties as well.

It is clear from this analogy that Paul does not disrespect the Mosaic "dispensation." Without a schoolmaster, children not only fail to get an education; they forfeit much of their usefulness to the family and to the larger society. The only time we might think such "elementary education" is overrated is if it is still the way an 18-year-old is trained! Paul is challenging the Jews, whose Law had served its purpose by bringing them to Christ, to turn over their "education" now to Him instead of insisting on not being "promoted."

III. The Family of Faith—3:26–4:7
A. Children by faith, 3:26-28
26 For ye are all the children of God by faith in Christ Jesus.

27 For as many of you as have been baptized into Christ have put on Christ.

28 There is neither Jew nor Greek, there is neither bond nor free, there is neither male nor female: for ye are all one in Christ Jesus.

This line of thought continues the portrayal God's people as a family. "All" believers, Paul says, whether Jew or Gentile, have been brought to Christ as the head of the family of faith. They arrived there by different tutors, or pedagogues,the Law of Moses in the case of Jews and the moral law in the case of Gentiles. That "legal" stage of their education was necessary, but not sufficient; and it has been replaced now by the "law" of faith.

Why is baptism introduced at this point? Perhaps Paul wants us to think of it as the new "mark" of the believer, replacing circumcision, as he does in Colossians 2:11-12. Whatever the reason, it is clear that Paul does not think of baptism as a work of righteousness as some Jews viewed circumcision. It is the "mark" of one who trusts, not one who works.

Being baptized "into Christ" and in order to "put on Christ" are vivid ways of describing the radically changed relationship before and after salvation by faith. The phrases describe Paul's own sense of wanting so intensely to follow Christ that his own personality was "melded" with Christ's. It is as though we are to "get into Christ's skin" or put Him on as a close-fitting garment.

B. Heirs of Abraham, 3:29–4:2

29 And if ye be Christ's, then are ye Abraham's seed, and heirs according to the promise.

4:1 Now I say, That the heir, as long as he is a child, differeth nothing from a servant, though he be lord of all;

2 But is under tutors and governors until the time appointed of the father.

Although Paul's main argument continues here, the imagery shifts slightly from believers as children in a family to heirs of their father's fortune. Abraham is the head of the family, and the "promise" or fortune is that all families of the world shall be blessed through him. Earlier Paul asked why anyone who has graduated into high school would want to return to grade school. Now he asks why anyone who is the heir of a fortune would want to return to childhood, when he enjoyed no more of his father's inheritance than a servant might.

C. Redemption from the law, 3-5

3 Even so we, when we were children, were in bondage under the elements of the world:

4 But when the fulness of the time was come, God sent forth his Son, made of a woman, made under the law,

5 To redeem them that were under the law, that we might receive the adoption of sons.

Although all people are "children of God" in the sense of having Adam as their father, Paul holds that both Jew and Gentile have sinned, living under the authority of worldly "elements" instead of under God. In other words, they sold themselves to sin. Yet, in His own good time, God redeemed them or "bought them back" from this slavery, by offering up His only-begotten Son. Now, through Him, both Jew and Gentile can be adopted back into God's family.

D. Sons, not servants, 6-7

6 And because ye are sons, God hath sent forth the Spirit of his Son into your hearts, crying, Abba, Father.

7 Wherefore thou art no more a servant, but a son; and if a son, then an heir of God through Christ.

Paul draws together several of his preceding figures of speech in this statement. We were estranged from God but now, through Christ, are sons. We were slaves of sin but now heirs of righteousness. The new element introduced here is the Holy Spirit, which Paul always associates with the Gospel, not the Law. In 3:2-5 he argued explicitly that the gifts of the Spirit were experienced by these early Christians not while they were under the Law but after they came into grace, through Christ. Now the Spirit enables those delivered into God's family to express a relationship so intimate that they view God not just as Creator or Judge, but as "Abba," the Aramaic way of speaking of an intimate father, the term Jesus Himself used for God (Mark 14:36).

Evangelistic Emphasis

What would you do for your child? If you are a normal, red-blooded parent who loves her or his children your answer would probably be, "I will do almost anything for my child."

We will go to summer league baseball games and sit out in the broiling hot sun just to watch our children play. We do it because we love them. We will go to a dance recital that lasts two hours too long just to watch our child perform for seven minutes. We do it because we love him. We will do without things we want, even things we need, in order to make sure our children have what they need to be successful in whatever they undertake. We sacrifice because we love them. We endure emotional discomfort when we discipline our children. We want them to grow up to be decent human beings. We do that because we love them.

Think of all the good things we human parents do for our children just because we love them. Now, consider this. God loves His children even more than we love ours. We cannot even begin to fathom how much God's love for His children exceeds our human love for our children.

We are God's children. We have been born again into His family. We have been adopted into His home. I feel all safe and secure when I think of that. That is certainly good news.

ഇ൞ര

For ye are all the children of God by faith in Christ Jesus.—*Galatians 3:26*

When we are born into a family we bear the family name. Even when a child without a permanent home is officially adopted into a family, the adoptive parents proudly bestow the family name on the child.

Likewise, all who are born into the family of God bear the name "Christian." Whether Jew or Gentile, male or female, rich or poor, there are no first class or second class children in God's family. We are all blessed to bear the family name, and to be heirs of the father.

Yet, we are not *little* children. We are not taken care of by nannies and tutors. Formerly, as God's children, we were under the care of another, that is, the Law of Moses. We were restrained, if you will, by the rules and regulations of the Law. Now, in Christ, we have reached maturity in the faith. We have reached the level of spiritual adulthood in which we are entitled to all the rights and privileges—as well as the responsibilities—that come with being a grownup child of God. We are heirs of all the benefits He provides, and we can enjoy these family blessings here and now.

Weekday Problems

Sister Bluff huffed into Pastor Young's office, closed the door forcefully, and sat down with a thud. "Pastor, you've got a big problem here at Olde Oaks Church. Everybody is upset. You're just taking us to the bad place in a handbasket."

"Sister Bluff, it's obvious you're upset, but I don't think everybody is upset. What seems to be the problem?" replied Pastor Young calmly.

"Well, you're going and changing everything. You've started using projectors in the sanctuary. You've started using guitars and drums in the worship service. People that aren't 'our' kind of people are beginning to come to Olde Oaks. We don't like that a bit. Some of those young people don't even know how to act in church!" Sister Bluff said all that in one breath.

"Well, sister, maybe all these new people aren't 'your' kind of people, but they certainly are God's kind of people. They are people who need a Savior. Apparently there are a lot of folks out there who need a Savior, because our attendance has doubled since we made the changes you mentioned."

Sister Bluff got up and headed for the door, "But those people don't belong here!" she blurted as she walked out.

*What might have been some of the problems the early church had in mixing Jews and Gentiles?

*What are some of the purposes of the church?

School Daze

Teacher: What does "trickle" mean?
Wise guy: To run slowly.
Teacher: Good. And what does "anecdote" mean?
W.G.: It's a short, funny tale.
Teacher: Now give me a sentence with both words.
W.G.: Our dog trickled down the street wagging her anecdote.
* * *

Lad: Hey Dad! I got 100 in school today!
Dad: Great! What in?
Lad: Two subjects, 50 in spelling and 50 in math.
* * *

Mom: I think our son is going to be an astronaut.
Dad: How's that?
Mom: His teacher told me that he's taking up space.
* * *

Lad, reporting to Dad: I made like Abe Lincoln today.
Dad, taking the bait: How's that?
Lad: I went down in history.

This Lesson in Your Life
God's Blended Family

Consider the Galatians' plight. Here was a group of Gentiles who responded in a positive way to Paul's preaching of the gospel in their area. They trusted Christ alone for their salvation. Paul had convinced them that Christ was enough.

Then, some Christians who had converted from the Jewish faith show up. These Jewish Christians are convinced that a number of the ceremonial practices of the Old Testament are still binding in the New Testament Church. "Hey, guys, you aren't doing it right," they said. These "Judaizers" began to convince many of the Gentile Christians of Galatia that to be a true Christian one must also follow the Jewish Law. In fact, the Judaizers even went so far as to argue that Paul was not an authentic apostle. They accused him of "watering down" the gospel by removing certain legal requirements in his desire to make the gospel more appealing to Gentiles.

So, here was the Galatian church. On the one side were the Jewish converts who believed that real Christians did things the Old Testament way. On the other side were the Galatians who were trying to believe that one could be justified by faith in Jesus Christ—nothing less and nothing more.

I suspect it was kind of like a modern day family where a man with children marries a woman with children. The two existing families become one new family. Yet each family comes to the new one with habits, ways of doing things, and traditions that may seem odd to the other family. In the new family the family members must determine what is essential to keep and what can be let go. They must become a blended family.

It is much the same way in our spiritual lives. When new people come to the faith, quite often they are different than we are. They do things differently. They view things differently. They too must become a blended family, determining what practices are essential or foundational as opposed to those things that have merely become comfortable.

We must cling with fierce determination to such doctrines as the Cross, justification by faith, sanctification through obedient love, and grace, to name but a handful. Other doctrines that are not essential or even detrimental, such as the legalism that Paul spoke out against in Galatians, must slip by the wayside and be allowed to dissolve in the sea of God's love.

We may have been Christians most of our lives and worshiped in the same church for the last 50 years. Still, we must remember that we, too, were saved by grace alone through faith in Jesus Christ. God brought us into the family. He will continue to blend whosoever will into His family.

STRAIGHT

1. What was it that made Abraham righteous?
Abraham's faith. "He believed God and it was credited to him as righteousness" (Gal.3:6)

2. Abraham was the physical father of the Jewish race. Who are the spiritual children of Abraham?
The spiritual children of Abraham are all those who believe and place their faith in Jesus Christ.

3. What Old Testament promise foresaw the coming of the Gentiles to faith in Christ Jesus?
God said to Abraham, "All nations will be blessed through you." This came from Genesis 12:3, 18:18, and 22:18.

4. What served as a "school-master" to lead people to Christ?
The law was put in charge as a school-master to lead us to Christ.

5. What has taken us out from under the supervision of the Law (Gal. 3:25)?
Now that faith has come, we are no longer under the supervision of the Law.

6. When we put our faith in Jesus Christ, what happens to us (Gal. 3:26)?
We become sons and daughters of God through faith in Jesus Christ.

7. What outward sign shows that we have been clothed with Christ's righteousness?
Baptism into the Christian faith is a visible sign that we have put on Christ.

8. Does God make distinctions between His Christian children?
Indeed not. "There is neither Jew nor Greek, slave nor free, male nor female, for you are all one in Christ Jesus" (Gal.3:28, NIV).

9. What was the guardian of the people of God in the Old Testament?
The Law of Moses was the guardian of God's Old Covenant people.

10. What or whom has God sent to lead and guide us today?
God sent His Son and subsequently the Holy Spirit to guide us. The Spirit gives us an especially close relationship to God the Father.

I read a story several years back in the *Reader's Digest* about a man and woman who had two children. One child was their own flesh and blood. The other was adopted. One day an acquaintance was over visiting. The woman and the visitor were in the den having a cup of tea and making conversation while the two small children were in and out, caught up in their game of the moment.

The visitor remarked, "They get along so well together." Then in a hushed, more confidential tone she asked, "Which one is yours?"

The mother looked puzzled, "Why, both of them are ours."

The visitor smiled sweetly, "Yes, I know, but which one of them is adopted?"

The mother gazed at the children for a long moment. She then replied sincerely, "I forget."

Paul reminds us in this week's passage that God makes no distinctions among His children. In this age, He has no particular "chosen people." One believer receives no special, preferential treatment or benefits from God over the other believer. It does not matter to God who our parents were. It does not matter to God what our financial standing is. It does not matter to God what our social status is. It does not matter to God whether our skin is black, brown, or white. It does not matter to God whether we were born in North America, Central Africa, or Communist China. When God looks at us, He sees us through the eyes of love. Paul tells us that when we were baptized into Christ we have clothed ourselves with Christ. When God looks at us He sees us dressed in Christ's righteousness.

When we become Christians, we become children of God, born again into His family. When we become part of that family then we become sisters and brothers of each other and of Jesus, joint heirs with Christ. We inherit that which has been prepared for the children of God, that is, eternal life in heaven. Being joint heirs also means that we have the privilege of enjoying all the blessings and benefits that come from being a child of God today.

God gives us His love and enables us to love one another in unselfish ways. He gives us joy in our lives that does not depend upon fleeting circumstances. He gives us peace that enables us to sleep at night. He sends us patience that brings even more peace. He makes us kind and good. He grows within us faithfulness to Him and to the ones we love. Gentleness is evident in our lives. We become people of self-control. People are trying all sorts of quick-fixes to gain the character traits that come with being a child of God. Actually, such traits come as the fruit of the Holy Spirit. The Christlike character that grows in our lives is a blessed benefit to all who call upon the Lord.

Called to Freedom

...through LOVE become slaves to one another.

Galatians 5:1-15

S tand fast therefore in the liberty wherewith Christ hath made us free, and be not entangled again with the yoke of bondage.

2 Behold, I Paul say unto you, that if ye be circumcised, Christ shall profit you nothing.

3 For I testify again to every man that is circumcised, that he is a debtor to do the whole law.

4 Christ is become of no effect unto you, whosoever of you are justified by the law; ye are fallen from grace.

5 For we through the Spirit wait for the hope of righteousness by faith.

6 For in Jesus Christ neither circumcision availeth anything, nor uncircumcision; but faith which worketh by love.

7 Ye did run well; who did hinder you that ye should not obey the truth?

8 This persuasion cometh not of him that calleth you.

9 A little leaven leaveneth the whole lump.

10 I have confidence in you through the Lord, that ye will be none otherwise minded: but he that troubleth you shall bear his judgment, whosoever he be.

11 And I, brethren, if I yet preach circumcision, why do I yet suffer persecution? then is the offence of the cross ceased.

12 I would they were even cut off which trouble you.

13 For, brethren, ye have been called unto liberty; only use not liberty for an occasion to the flesh, but by love serve one another.

14 For all the law is fulfilled in one word, even in this; Thou shalt love thy neighbour as thyself.

15 But if ye bite and devour one another, take heed that ye be not consumed one of another.

Memory Selection
Galatians 5:13

Devotional Reading
1 John 2:7-17

Background Scripture
Galatians 5:1-15

May 19

The book of Galatians has rightly been called the apostle Paul's "Emancipation Proclamation." Nowhere is Paul's commitment to freedom in Christ expressed more strongly than in today's passage.

As many in modern times have also found, however, freedom often comes with a price. The focus of this lesson is therefore not so much on freedom itself as on one of the responsibilities that come with freedom: *Insisting strongly on staying free, while living in peace.*

Paul had once had Timothy, a half-Jew brother in Christ, circumcised to make peace with "Judaizing teachers" (Acts 16:1-3). His mood in Galatians 5 is not so peaceable. Although he counsels Galatian Christians not to "devour" each other, he sticks with a position much like that of Martin Luther. When it comes to freedom in Christ, *"Here I stand!"*

ഇരു

The dilemma Paul faced in writing to the Galatians can be introduced by asking group members to recall instances in history when people had to sacrifice *peace* as the price of *freedom*. For example, our nation's founding fathers found that they could not stay free without going to war against England. The peace of "the body politic," British rule in the Colonies, was forfeited in order to stay free. Other classic examples include World Wars I and II, when Americans gave up sons and daughters in war in order to remain free.

The point is similar to the one Paul makes in this lesson. Peace is an ideal to be sought; but when others would destroy it by limiting freedoms, peace-loving people must speak out in defense of "the liberty wherewith Christ hath made us free."

Teaching Outline	Daily Bible Readings
I. Called to Freedom—1	**Mon.** Bloom Where You're Planted 1 Corinthians 7:17-24
II. Cancelling Christ's Work—2-6 A. *A* law involves *the* Law, 2-4 B. Faith: a superior law, 5-6	**Tue.** Am I Not Free? 1 Corinthians 9:1-12 **Wed.** Free, Though a Slave 1 Corinthians 9:15-23
III. Confusion in the Church—7-12 A. Alien leaven, 7-9 B. Troubling influences, 10-12	**Thu.** New Birth, Living Hope 1 Peter 1:3-12 **Fri.** Free to Serve 1 Peter 2:11-17
IV. Called to Peace—13-15 A. The law of love, 13-14 B. The law of self-destruction, 15	**Sat.** Freedom from Fear 1 Peter 3:13-22 **Sun.** Called to Freedom Galatians 5:4-15

Verse by Verse

I. Called to Freedom—1

1 Stand fast therefore in the liberty wherewith Christ hath made us free, and be not entangled again with the yoke of bondage.

Paul has argued skillfully and earnestly for salvation by grace through faith, against salvation by keeping the Law, especially circumcision. Now it is time to note that Christ did not set us free from the Law merely in a moment of anger against "legalists," but to give us an ongoing principle of living in a state of "responsible freedom." It was unthinkable to return to a state of bondage; we are to *stand,* or be steadfast, in maintaining the principle of salvation by faith.

II. Cancelling Christ's Work—2-6
A. *A law involves the* Law, 2-4

2 Behold, I Paul say unto you, that if ye be circumcised, Christ shall profit you nothing.

3 For I testify again to every man that is circumcised, that he is a debtor to do the whole law.

4 Christ is become of no effect unto you, whosoever of you are justified by the law; ye are fallen from grace.

From what we know of the "Judaizing teachers" who hounded Paul on his missionary journeys, they were influential and respected members of the Jewish community in the cities where he preached. Apparently Gentiles who had been attracted by Paul's message, and who, along with the Jewish believers were a part of the churches of Galatia, were considering giving in to these forceful teachers' demands that they be circumcised. Surely it would be a small gesture to compromise and submit to circumcision for the sake of harmony and peace.

To such a thought Paul virtually shouts *"No!"* For him, a much larger principle than circumcision is at stake. As in the case of Timothy (Acts 16:1-3), circumcision as a gesture of peace was one thing. In the Galatian churches, however, Paul's opponents were making it a condition of salvation. In that light, to be circumcised would be brazenly to claim that Christ's work on the Cross was not enough to purchase salvation.

Furthermore, circumcision was not the only rule at stake. Since agreeing to be circumcised for salvation is in effect saying that *law* saves, what about the Sabbath, animal sacrifices, and all the other commands of the Law? They must be observed, too. It is this substitution of the Law for the grace of the Cross that wrings from Paul such strong language as to say that those who take that position have "fallen from grace."

B. Faith: a superior law, 5-6

5 For we through the Spirit wait for the hope of righteousness by faith.

6 For in Jesus Christ neither circumcision availeth anything, nor uncircumcision; but faith which worketh by love.

Admittedly, keeping a rule may carry with it a measure of reassurance since we can see that something has been "done" about salvation. This comfort, however, is short-lived because we proceed to break other rules. By saying that those saved by faith "wait for the hope of righteousness" (the Spirit's promise), Paul does not mean that we do not experience personal guiltlessness and freedom now. He is admitting that our salvation will be publicly "proved" only at the return of Christ when He claims us as His own.

Since, however, we *are* saved by Christ's work, not our own, both circumcision and uncircumcision are matters of indifference. Gentiles might miss the latter point: they cannot be saved by boasting that they are *not* circumcised any more than Jews were saved by boasting that they *were*. The entire focus or weight in the discussion of salvation has shifted from what we do or don't do to what Christ has done for us. As proved in the example of Timothy's being circumcised, Paul opposes circumcision only when others make it a condition of salvation.

III. Confusion in the Church—7-12

A. Alien leaven, 7-9

7 Ye did run well; who did hinder you that ye should not obey the truth?

8 This persuasion cometh not of him that calleth you.

9 A little leaven leaveneth the whole lump.

The phrase "run well" is taken from the Greek races, which provided a favorite metaphor for Paul. The Galatian Christians had been "fast off the blocks" in the Christian race by accepting the work of Christ on the Cross as the effective means of salvation. Paul may not have known the name or names of those who now would now "hinder" (NIV "cut in on you") them by teaching works-salvation, but he knows that their message is not from the One who called the Galatians to Himself.

Paul then changes his metaphor of salvation from a race to the Jewish practice of shunning leavening, such as at Passover (see Exod. 12:15-20). Just as a little leaven permeates the entire lump of dough (probably a common proverb; note that the NIV places the saying in quotation marks), so a "little law" carries with it the much larger and fatal implication that law, not Christ, saves.

B. Troubling influences, 10-12

10 I have confidence in you through the Lord, that ye will be none otherwise minded: but he that troubleth you shall bear his judgment, whosoever he be.

11 And I, brethren, if I yet preach circumcision, why do I yet suffer persecution? then is the offence of the cross ceased.

12 I would they were even cut off which trouble you.

Changing to a personal tone instead of doctrinal, Paul expresses confidence that the Galatians will resist legalist teachers and come down on the side of grace. He is equally confident, however, that the Judaizing teacher or teachers who trouble them will suffer judgment.

Verse 11 seems to imply that some of these teachers claimed that Paul upheld their insistence on circumcision—coming to Christ through Moses. Perhaps they seized as evidence the fact that Paul had Timothy circumcised. Paul responds with the logical argument that he would not subject himself to the attacks of the Judaizers if indeed he agreed with them.

In a rare instance of sarcasm, Paul uses more biting language than ever in verse 12. Why, he suggests, don't those who boast so much of using the knife in circumcision, go ahead and castrate themselves?! This was not so far-fetched in the world in which the Galatians lived. Priests in some pagan religions would often do just that, as a sign that the flesh was so evil that they would literally cut away its power over them. The Jewish teachers who opposed Paul could not have missed Paul's blunt way of placing circumcision and emasculation in the same class of degrading practices.

IV. Called to Peace—13-15
A. The law of love, 13-14
13 For, brethren, ye have been called unto liberty; only use not liberty for an occasion to the flesh, but by love serve one another.

14 For all the law is fulfilled in one word, even in this; Thou shalt love thy neighbour as thyself.

Now Paul turns abruptly to another charge often made by his opponents: that salvation by grace instead of Law was "antinomian," or opposed to living by high moral standards. Ironically, those he urges to live by faith instead of trusting Law he now calls to live morally, not indulging "the flesh." However, this is to be out of free choice, not out of trust in any power in rule-keeping to save. What better way to live in harmony with the "circumcision party" than to "out love" them in service? In so doing, they in fact show that love, not circumcision, fulfills the Law, just as Jesus had taught (Matt. 23:39, citing Lev. 19:18).

B. The law of self-destruction, 15
15 But if ye bite and devour one another, take heed that ye be not consumed one of another.

Paul again turns to the Roman sports arenas for another graphic word picture. The words "bite" and "devour" described the animals that fought to the death in some of the exhibitions. Although Paul allows no compromise on the issue of salvation by circumcision, he knows that if those who accept his teaching merely fight with the circumcision party, the result will be a Body torn to shreds. His admonition is a reminder to reformers in the modern Church: the Body is not nourished by a diet of harsh criticism, but by love.

Evangelistic Emphasis

I suspect that too often people of our day primarily think of Christianity as a set of rules to follow. They think of Christianity as a list of regulations that would keep them from doing what they want to do in the first place. Many see Christianity as inhibiting or, worse, bondage. They do not know that Christianity is freedom.

I have seen people who are bound up, who are held in bondage by unchristian lifestyles. I know a man that has lost his family and cannot keep a job because he is under the bondage of alcohol. I know a man who cannot get a job and has not been able to stay out of jail for very long because he is under the bondage of illegal drugs. I know a woman who does not have enough money to feed her family or pay her bills because she is under the bondage of a gambling habit.

Some people think that Christianity is simply a list of inhibiting rules. They won't accept Christ as Savior because they don't want to lose their freedom. In actuality, Christianity is a way of life that gives us freedom. There are so many types of bondage humans could avoid if they only knew the liberating power of the truth of the gospel.

Folks need to hear the gospel. They need to be freed from the burden of sin. You will share the good news of the liberating power of Jesus, won't you?

✺✺✺

For, brethren, ye have been called unto liberty; only use not liberty for an occasion to the flesh, but by love serve one another.— *Galatians 5:13*

Although citizens of the United States are free, we are not people without laws. In general, I am free to do what I want, but I am not at liberty to go into a bank and withdraw money that I have not deposited there. In the U.S. we call that bank robbery. There are laws against that.

Although Christians are called to be free, we are not people without moral laws. We Christians no longer base our salvation on our ability to keep perfectly the Law of the Old Testament. There is liberty in Christ Jesus. Still, when one considers the feelings and concerns of another, we are bound by the law of love. We still follow rules that fulfill Christ's rule: "Do unto others as you would have them do unto you." The law of love still dictates that we treat others with kindness and respect, and that we think them above ourselves. We do not use the law of liberty as license, but as a guide to keeping the law of love.

Weekday Problems

Robert prayed, "Lord, please give me the words to say and the grace to say them properly."

Robert had been leading a discipleship group in his home for some time. The group began when Robert's pastor noticed several new families coming from a very legalistic, cult-like congregation into their church. Robert was a wise, mature, and grace-filled Christian who was the perfect choice to instruct those who had been bound up in legalism.

For almost a year now, Robert had been lovingly teaching his group about the freedom of the grace-filled Christian life. There were two of the members of the group who had been shunned by the former congregation because they filed for divorce. Neither the man nor the woman was completely without fault in the breakup of the marriage.

That is where the problem arose. The two decided to start living together. "We know God approves because we love each other," they said. "We are no longer in bondage to the Law. Besides, we are already married in God's eyes."

Robert knew he had to speak to them.

*How would you approach this situation if your were in Robert's shoes?

*Share a time in your own life when your life was in conflict with God.

So Why Worry?

Worry is what gives small things a big shadow.

* * *

Don't tell me that worry doesn't do any good. I know better,the things I worry about don't happen.

* * *

The reason why worry kills more people than work is that more people worry than work.—*Robert Frost*

* * *

I am an old man and have known a great many troubles, but most of them never happened.—*Mark Twain*

* * *

We probably wouldn't worry about what people think of us if we only knew how seldom they do.

* * *

Bob: You sure look worried.

Rob: Man, I've got so many troubles that if anything bad happens to me today it'll be at least two weeks before I can worry about it.

This Lesson in Your Life
The Point of Freedom

Fred was a "good ol' boy" from Louisiana. Every afternoon after work he would stop off at the local bar and have a few beers with his buddies. Every Saturday he got with his buddies to watch a football game or go fishing or hunting or just drink a few more beers.

One week Fred's wife's church was having a revival. In a weak moment Fred agreed to go with her to the preaching service. Lo and behold, he heard the gospel clearly and invited Jesus to be the Savior and Lord of his life. All of a sudden Fred's buddies noticed that he wasn't drinking with them every afternoon. They did not see him anymore on Saturdays.

One day at the barber shop Fred ran into one of his old drinking buddies. "Fred, since you got religion you don't do any of those things you love to do," his friend said.

Fred replied, "You're partly right. Since I got saved I don't hang around with you guys anymore, but I still do everything I want to. God just changed my 'want-to's.'"

Without really knowing it, Fred caught on to one thing Paul was saying in this passage in Galatians. When we come to know Jesus as Savior and Lord, we still can indulge in our heart's desire. However, what the Christian's heart desires tends to be more Christlike than worldly. When we truly love Christ, we begin to follow in His footsteps of right living. We begin to "clean up our act" out of our desire to please Him more than out of a desire to avoid punishment. Our lives are no longer ruled by a list of do's and don'ts, but by a preference to do that which pleases God. Oh yes, we still adhere to Christ's laws of right living, but we do it as a loving response.

For example, many people employ the tired old argument, "You don't have to go to church to be a Christian." There is a lot of truth to that statement. Going to church doesn't make one a Christian anymore than watching golf on television makes a person Tiger Woods. There are not enough church services that one could attend in order to earn the title "Christian."

But to look at church attendance in that way is a legalistic point of view. Ask this question: "Why would any person who owed her or his eternal life to Jesus Christ *not* want to be in church somewhere?" You see, when you ask the question instead of making the statement, you discover the problem. Going to church is not an attempt to earn enough points to get us to heaven, but a response to the grace of God, by which we were saved. Our whole lives as Christians should be lived not as following rigid rules but as a loving response to God's grace, mercy, and love.

STRAIGHT

1. To what is Paul referring when he speaks of "the yoke of bondage?"
He is referring to the servitude of strict adherence to the Jewish laws.

2. In this passage, what does the act of circumcision represent?
Circumcision represents turning away from acceptance of justification by faith in Christ and back to adherence to the Law for justification.

3. What else is true if we feel bound to obey the Jewish law of circumcision?
Paul says in verse 3 that we are then obligated to obey the whole Law.

4. What can cause us to fall away from grace?
We fall from grace when we try to be justified by law and become alienated from Christ.

5. Which has more value to Christ—being circumcised or not being circumcised?
In Christ Jesus neither circumcision nor uncircumcision has value. The only thing that counts is faith expressing itself through love.

6. Who is "the one who called you" or "him that calleth you" in vs. 8?
That phrase refers to God Himself as the one who called the Galatians.

7. What is the "yeast" to which Paul refers in vs. 9?
The yeast is the false teaching of the Judaizing teachers.

8. Does our freedom mean that we are to throw off all restraint?
No. Our freedom should not be used to indulge our sinful nature, but rather to serve one another in love. We are still under moral law.

9. What command sums up the whole Law, regarding human relationships?
Love your neighbor as yourself.

10. What happens when a spirit of contention invades a body of believers?
When believers begin to "bite and devour one another" they will eventually be destroyed by each other.

Once upon a time an outdoorsman was hiking a mountain trail near a cliff. As he traversed the narrow ledge the ground gave way and over the side he went. He would have plunged to his death had he not managed to grab a root that was sticking out of the cliff.

He began to pray, "God, if you're up there, please do something to help me get out of this mess. Please save me."

About that time a cloud drifted over the man and a deep voice spoke from the cloud, "I am up here. I hear you. I will save you. Trust me and let go of the root."

The man looked up at the cloud. Then he looked way down to the bottom of the canyon. He looked back up at the cloud and shouted, "Is there anybody else up there I can talk to?"

In a sense, the outdoorsman was in the same fix as the Galatians. The Galatians were being convinced by the Judaizers that the old, tried-and-true method of walking with God through the Law was still the best method. But God, through Paul, was convincing them that faith in Jesus Christ was actually the best method (the only method) for walking with God. In a sense, the Galatians were still trying to hang onto the Law (the root), rather than trust God by grace through faith alone in Christ Jesus.

Paul had convinced them and was trying to re-convince them that the Law was unable to justify. They had to let go of the Law and trust Christ's merits for their justification and salvation.

However, that teaching can be confusing at times. We do know that we cannot be saved by the Law, yet we still must follow many portions of the Law even after we have put our faith completely in Jesus Christ. Paul said Christ has set us free. Paul said not to turn back to the burdens of the Law. Do we reject all the Law and become people of lawlessness? Indeed not!

We are called to liberty, but it is not liberty to do anything we want to indulge our physical nature. Our liberty is not freedom from virtuous and moral restraints. Our freedom is liberty from the servitude of sin, and from thinking that we are saved by keeping religious rites and ceremonies.

There really aren't enough laws that could be written down that would govern every single aspect of right living. We come up with too many new situations and circumstances that are not covered by past laws. Such a ponderous list of laws would smother us. Still, there is one law that we could practice that would cover all the do's and don'ts of human relationships.

The one law? Jesus stated it clearly: *Love your neighbor as yourself.*

Live by the Spirit

Galatians 5:16–6:9

This I say then, Walk in the Spirit, and ye shall not fulfil the lust of the flesh.

17 For the flesh lusteth against the Spirit, and the Spirit against the flesh: and these are contrary the one to the other: so that ye cannot do the things that ye would.

18 But if ye be led of the Spirit, ye are not under the law.

19 Now the works of the flesh are manifest, which are these; Adultery, fornication, uncleanness, lasciviousness,

20 Idolatry, witchcraft, hatred, variance, emulations, wrath, strife, seditions, heresies,

21 Envyings, murders, drunkenness, revellings, and such like: of the which I tell you before, as I have also told you in time past, that they which do such things shall not inherit the kingdom of God.

22 But the fruit of the Spirit is love, joy, peace, longsuffering, gentleness, goodness, faith,

23 Meekness, temperance: against such there is no law.

24 And they that are Christ's have crucified the flesh with the affections and lusts.

25 If we live in the Spirit, let us also walk in the Spirit.

26 Let us not be desirous of vain glory, provoking one another, envying one another.

6:1 Brethren, if a man be overtaken in a fault, ye which are spiritual, restore such

an one in the spirit of meekness; considering thyself, lest thou also be tempted.

2 Bear ye one another's burdens, and so fulfil the law of Christ.

3 For if a man think himself to be something, when he is nothing, he deceiveth himself.

4 But let every man prove his own work, and then shall he have rejoicing in himself alone, and not in another.

5 For every man shall bear his own burden.

6 Let him that is taught in the word communicate unto him that teacheth in all good things.

7 Be not deceived; God is not mocked: for whatsoever a man soweth, that shall he also reap.

8 For he that soweth to his flesh shall of the flesh reap corruption; but he that soweth to the Spirit shall of the Spirit reap life everlasting.

9 And let us not be weary in well doing: for in due season we shall reap, if we faint not.

Memory Selection
Galatians 5:16

Devotional Reading
Colossians 3:5-17

Background Scripture
Galatians 5:16+6:18

May 26

In his letters, the apostle Paul typically tends to theological concerns first, then shows how theology should express itself in practical living. This lesson focuses on that second stage, in this case, the way salvation by grace through faith should be expressed in everyday living.

The text draws a sharp distinction be-tween living by "the flesh" and "the spirit." Previously Paul has aligned "flesh" with human attempts to be saved by keeping the Law, and "spirit" with salvation by grace through faith. Now he shows that these two ways of thinking about salvation also re-sult in very different life-styles. It may be surprising to some that emphasizing the Law, which many felt would *curb* fleshly behavior, actually encourages *pride*, which, in Paul's mind, is as fleshly as blatant im-morality.

ℬℭ

This session can be aptly introduced by recalling the old anecdote of an eld-erly lady who was being encouraged by her minister. "I'm sure you gain great comfort from reading the Bible," he said, "especially those great sections like the Ten Commandments."

"Oh my no!" exclaimed the perceptive old lady. "I don't read the Commandments much because they put such bad ideas in my head."

Many Jews in Paul's day felt that dwell-ing on the Law would curb wrong-doing. Paul, however, pointed out what this woman had discovered: *over-emphasizing rules can result in focusing on the sin the rules are designed to overcome*. In this les-son, he urges us to overcome the flesh (NIV "sinful nature") not by focusing on rules that try to curb the worst in us, but the Spirit that appeals to our best.

Teaching Outline	Daily Bible Readings
I. Two Ways to Walk,16-18	**Mon.** A Mystery Revealed Ephesians 3:1-13
II. The Works of the Flesh,19-21	**Tue.** Filled with God's Fullness Ephesians 3:14-21
III. The Way of the Spirit,22-26	**Wed.** One Body, One Spirit Ephesians 4:1-7
A. Fruit of the Spirit, 22-23	
B. Crucifying the flesh, 24-26	**Thu.** The Earnest of the Spirit 2 Corinthians 5:1-10
IV. Well-doing and Well-being,6:1-9	**Fri.** Now Is the Time 2 Corinthians 6:1-12
A. Looking to self and others, 1-5	
B. Actions and consequences, 6-9	**Sat.** The Fruit of the Spirit Galatians 5:16-26
1. Teaching and earning, 6	
2. Sowing and reaping, 7-9	**Sun.** You Reap What You Sow Galatians 6:7-18

Verse by Verse

I. Two Ways to Walk, 16-18

16 This I say then, Walk in the Spirit, and ye shall not fulfil the lust of the flesh.

17 For the flesh lusteth against the Spirit, and the Spirit against the flesh: and these are contrary the one to the other: so that ye cannot do the things that ye would.

18 But if ye be led of the Spirit, ye are not under the law.

It is important to tie this section on the Christian "walk" (practical ethics) with Paul's previous emphasis on salvation by grace through faith, as opposed to law. Just as there are two opposite ways of salvation, grace vs. works, so there are two ways of "walking"—spirit vs. flesh.

To walk in the flesh means to be guided by our "sinful nature" (NIV). Although this often results in "fleshly" or bodily sin, such as adultery, it also includes "mental" sins such as lust, envy, covetousness, and idolatry. Under a law-based system, we may think to curb fleshly works by concentrating on rules against them. Unfortunately, however, that merely keeps the forbidden act in focus, and provides no inner moral power to keep the law.

On the other hand, Paul counsels us to walk "in the Spirit." It is not always clear whether he is speaking in this section of the Holy Spirit or the individual Christian's spirit. Although most translations capitalize "Spirit" in verse 1, the original Greek was written in all capitals; and the capital letter in English versions rests on the context. This, however, is not a crucial problem because Paul associates both the Holy Spirit and the human spirit with salvation by grace precisely because the in grace-based ethics the Holy Spirit stays in closer touch with the human spirit than is the case in law-based religion.

Tying all this to the present passage, Paul urges us to walk ("live") by the Spirit because the rules of mere law had been proved ineffective in the war between man's sinful and spiritual natures. For example, the law against adultery was clear, but keeping it in mind focuses the believer on the forbidden act, and lacks motivating power, so that "ye cannot do the things ye would." On the other hand, focusing on grace calls us to live above adultery out of gratitude for grace, rather than out of obligation to the Law; plus the Spirit "helps us in our infirmities" (Rom. 8:26), strengthening us "in the inner man" (Eph. 3:16).

II. The Works of the Flesh,19-21

19 Now the works of the flesh are manifest, which are these; Adultery, fornication, uncleanness, lasciviousness,

20 Idolatry, witchcraft, hatred, variance, emulations, wrath, strife, seditions, heresies,

21 Envyings, murders, drunkenness, revellings, and such like: of the which I tell you before, as I have also told you in time past, that they which do such things shall not inherit the kingdom of God.

These specific examples of "fleshly" works need little elaboration. Although some of the terms (such as "adultery") may be translated in various ways (such as the NIV's broader term "sexual immorality" here), all of them are clearly related to man's "sinful nature." Also, a detailed analysis of each term would still not yield a complete list, since other terms could be added under Paul's sweeping phrase "and such like." If the list were more than suggestive, it would have the same limitations as the more elaborate Jewish Law.

III. The Way of the Spirit,22-26
A. Fruit of the Spirit, 22-23

22 But the fruit of the Spirit is love, joy, peace, longsuffering, gentleness, goodness, faith,

23 Meekness, temperance: against such there is no law.

In contrast to the works of the flesh are these character traits that indicate a person is walking in the Spirit. Note that while the items in the first list are called "works," emphasizing sins that we do out of willfulness, their counterparts are "fruits" or results not just of our own working but of the Spirit working in us. Of course this is not automatic. If they did not require any effort on our part, Paul would not exhort us consciously to allow the Spirit to produce these traits in our lives.

Again, there is no attempt to "codify" these traits into a list of legal requirements. Yet it is clear that focusing on these attitude-related traits of the spirit (or Spirit!) has the power to prevent or counter the effect of each trait in the previous list of fleshly works. This capacity is why Paul can say that "against such there is no law." There is no need for a law against murder, for example, if the Spirit's gift of love rules the human spirit.

B. Crucifying the flesh, 24-26

24 And they that are Christ's have crucified the flesh with the affections and lusts.

25 If we live in the Spirit, let us also walk in the Spirit.

26 Let us not be desirous of vain glory, provoking one another, envying one another.

Some people have come to Christ and been disillusioned that they were not automatically rid of all desires of the flesh. Note, however, that verse 24 contains the seeds of both God's work and our cooperation. If we "are Christ's," we can expect His working in our life; but it is the believer himself who has, in coming to Jesus, "crucified" the sinful nature's cravings of the flesh.

Yet one important result of this "crucifixion" is that we do not boast of how we "cured ourselves." Verses 25-26 are a call to those who are saved by grace to live *graciously,* refraining from the anti-spiritual competitive and boastful attitudes that lie behind so many conflicts in human relationships. Failing to heed this call could result in the "oxymoron" of a Christian *boasting* that he was saved by grace!

IV. Well-doing and Well-being, 6:1-9

A. Looking to self and others, 1-5

1 Brethren, if a man be overtaken in a fault, ye which are spiritual, restore such an one in the spirit of meekness; considering thyself, lest thou also be tempted.

2 Bear ye one another's burdens, and so fulfil the law of Christ.

3 For if a man think himself to be something, when he is nothing, he deceiveth himself.

4 But let every man prove his own work, and then shall he have rejoicing in himself alone, and not in another.

5 For every man shall bear his own burden.

When a person living by law sees a brother or sister fall, she is likely to "hurl the book" and have a condemning spirit. A person living by grace recalls that she herself was saved by grace, and extends a gracious spirit to the backslider. In this way she bears the brother or sister's burdens.

On the other hand, verses 3-5 probably refer to the person who boasts of his own position in Christ and looks down on the downfallen. Instead of being able to rejoice that Christ bore her own burden, and that she was saved by grace, she must bear the burden of her own ineffective works.

B. Actions and consequences, 6-9

1. Teaching and earning, 6

6 Let him that is taught in the word communicate unto him that teacheth in all good things.

In a section of miscellaneous exhortations, Paul briefly mentions the principle that those who benefit from one who teaches and preaches the gospel should share (NIV for "communicate") financial compensation with those who so spend their time (see also 1 Cor. 9:9).

2. Sowing and reaping, 7-9

7 Be not deceived; God is not mocked: for whatsoever a man soweth, that shall he also reap.

8 For he that soweth to his flesh shall of the flesh reap corruption; but he that soweth to the Spirit shall of the Spirit reap life everlasting.

9 And let us not be weary in well doing: for in due season we shall reap, if we faint not.

In a final word against the charge that his doctrine of salvation by grace leads to "antinomianism," or living by no rules, Paul indicates that God is fully capable of looking into the heart. Those who trade on God's grace as an excuse for living in the flesh will share in the eventual corruption for which all flesh is destined. Those who untiringly manifest the fruits of the Spirit, will share in the everlasting life that is the nature of Spirit.

Evangelistic Emphasis

Let me ask you a question. Before whom are you playing your life? Really? Whom are you trying most to please? I ask you to consider your answer carefully. The best answer is, "I am playing out my life to please God." I am not so sure all of us could honestly answer in that fashion.

I know people that are living their lives primarily to please other people. The people they are trying to please may be good people. They may be trying to please parents. They may be trying to please a certain social group. They may be trying to make sure they are accepted in a certain financial strata. Their family may be their primary audience.

I know pastors whose main goal is to keep their congregations happy. I have been guilty of that now and again. We do not want to ruffle feathers, so we do what is convenient even if God desires us to move in a direction that might be uncomfortable for us.

We must remember we are not fooling God. He knows whose opinion we value most. He knows if we are seeking first His Kingdom or if we are seeking first approval from another source.

Before whom are you playing your life? Whose applause to you seek?

ဆာ

This I say then, Walk in the Spirit, and ye shall not fulfil the lust of the flesh.—*Galatians 5:16*

Paul says, "Walk in the Spirit. . . ." By this he means to challenge Christians to live under the influence of the Holy Spirit. He is calling us to allow the Holy Spirit to reside fully in our lives. He is encouraging us not to resist Him, but to yield to all the Spirit wants to do in our lives.

If a person would yield completely to the leading of the Holy Spirit, that person would have no great problems with the urgings of the carnal nature. Never has there been a better, safer, or easier rule to follow that would help us overcome any corrupt or sensual nature within us.

Now, view the second part of the verse not as a command, but as a promise. "Walk in the Spirit and I promise you will not want to fulfill any sinful desires." This is a deep truth. The only way to overcome sinful desires is to yield completely to the Holy Spirit in our lives. The Spirit gives us the power to be victorious over the sin nature.

Weekday Problems

"Walt, you are the only one I've felt comfortable talking to about this. What do you think I ought to do?" Jerry asked. It was like Jerry had handed Walt a hand grenade with the pin already pulled. Walt prayed a quick prayer, took a deep breath, and began his answer to Jerry.

Jerry and Walt were neighbors and long-time friends. They attended the same church. They played golf together. They talked regularly about their lives. But Walt wasn't ready for this.

Jerry just told Walt that he had been frequenting pornographic internet sites for some time. He started out searching soft porn sites which specialized in what some call "tasteful nudity." Then Jerry began seeking hardcore pornography. The hardcore sites required a subscription fee. Jerry found himself spending over a hundred dollars a month just to look at filthy pictures. He was staying up all hours of the night. He was addicted.

"I need help!" Jerry pleaded.

Walt answered, "Jerry, you cannot play around with this. Paul says, "Crucify the flesh." I say, get rid of your computer—NOW!"

*How would you try to help Jerry if you were in Walt's position?

*What other means might help Jerry to "crucify the sinful nature?"

The Difference Between You and Me

When you get angry, it's because you are ill-tempered. When I get angry, it's my nerves.

* * *

When you don't like someone, it's because you are prejudiced. In my case, I happen to be a good judge of character.

* * *

When you compliment someone, it's just because you use flattery. I am a natural-born encourager.

* * *

When you take a long time to do a job, you're unbearably slow. When I take a long time, it's because I believe in quality workmanship.

* * *

When you spend your paycheck in 24 hours, it's because you are a spendthrift. When I do, it's because I am by nature a generous person.

* * *

When you stay in bed until 11 a. m., you're lazy. As for me, I was exhausted by yesterday's hard work.

This Lesson in Your Life
Choices and Consequences

It has been years ago now, but I remember some things about the summer Olympic Games held in Los Angeles in 1984. One of the things I remember well was the performance of a diminutive female gymnast named Mary Lou Retton. She was a gold medal winner and she led the women's gymnastics team. She was only a teenager at the time. She did not even have her driver's license.

After one of her victories, an interviewer asked her about her life as an Olympic quality athlete. She said she gave her life to gymnastics. When her friends were sleeping late, she was turning off the alarm, hauling herself out of bed to be driven to the gym for a morning workout. When her friends were getting out of school in the afternoon and going to hang out at the local hamburger establishment, she was going back to the gym for her afternoon workout. Her friends could eat anything and everything they wanted. She carefully monitored her diet. She wanted to be the ideal weight and build for gymnastics. .

Mary Lou made up her mind to be a gymnast in the Olympics. When she said Yes to that dream, she had to say No to anything and everything that might distract her from that dream. She gave up what others might deem a normal childhood to gain the goal she sought all her life.

Life is like that. To say Yes to certain goals means an automatic No to all that might distract from that goal. That is certainly true in our spiritual lives. When we say Yes to Jesus and ask Him to be our Savior and Lord, that means an automatic No to those things that would keep us from His Lordship.

Satan tries to do everything he can to get us to say No to Christ and Yes to him. The things that would keep us from Christ may not necessarily be bad things. Notice, the writer to the Hebrews exhorts us, "Let us throw off everything that hinders and the sin that so easily entangles, and let us run with perseverance the race marked out for us. Let us fix our eyes on Jesus, the author and perfecter of our faith" (Heb. 12:1b-2a, NIV). He says, "everything that hinders *and* the sin that entangles." There are some things that are not sin that could keep us from being all that God wants us to be.

We have choices to make every day. Do I want to seek the goal of a pure and holy life, entirely pleasing to God, or do I want to live life according to my own rules? It really is a personal choice. But if you choose to live life your way, there are consequences to that choice.

STRAIGHT

1. When does Paul mean by "living" or "walking" by the Spirit?
Paul is reminding us to live a life led and guided by the Spirit of God; to yield our lives completely to the Spirit's influence.

2. What two forces are constantly at battle in the spiritual realm (5:17)?
The sinful nature and the Spirit are always contrary to each other.

3. List some of the acts of the sinful nature or "works of the flesh."
Sexual immorality, impurity, debauchery, idolatry, witchcraft, hatred, discord, jealousy, fits of rage, selfish ambition, dissensions, etc.

4. What happens to those who continue to practice these acts of the flesh?
Those who live like that will not inherit the Kingdom of God.

5. List the fruit of the Holy Spirit as they are found in Galatians 5: 22-23.
Love, joy, peace, long-suffering (patience), gentleness, goodness, faith (faithfulness), meekness (gentleness), and temperance (self-control).

6. How does Paul tell us to treat the "flesh" or "sinful nature" within each of us?
Paul tells us to crucify the sinful nature, or to put it to death.

7. What is one way we can fulfill the law of Christ?
We can bear one another's burdens and thus fulfill the law of Christ.

8. Can we fool God?
Of course not. God knows what our real character is and will judge us accordingly.

9. What does a person get who strives to please his sinful nature?
He who sows to please his sinful nature will reap destruction.

10. What does a person get who dedicates himself to pleasing the Spirit?
The one who sows to please the Spirit, from the Spirit will reap eternal life.

Once upon a time I was invited to a family pool party at a neighbor's house. The pool was filled with laughing, diving, splashing kids. One boy was an exception. He was not having a good time at all. Although he had on his swim trunks, he would not get into the water. He did not want to float on one of the inflatable toys. He would not dive. He even screamed when the other kids splashed him, whether they did it by accident or on purpose just to hear him bellow. He lived right next door, so he could have gone home. Yet, he stayed and was miserable. He never caught on that the fun was in the water. I wondered why he even came at all.

That day the Lord said to me, "David, if you watch this carefully I will teach you something." He said, "This pool party is like the Christian life. It's not much fun just watching others. If you really want to experience the joy and fun of My way of living, you have to get in the water."

You know, I don't think there is anything any more miserable than half a Christian. There is no one more forlorn than one who wants to enjoy full fellowship with God but who will not jump in and experience the fullness of God's grace and love for themselves. Too many folks hold some of themselves back from God.

It was once said of a Texas politician, "He developed saddle sores from riding the fence so long." I suspect there are people who are trying to live the Christian life that way, too. They have made half a commitment to Christ. They are trying to keep one foot on God's side and the other foot on the world's side.

Quite often folks view the Christian walk much as they do paying their bills. On payday we get our wages and deposit them in our checking account. Then we go home and begin to write out checks for our bills. We pay the doctor, the pharmacist, the utilities, the house note, the car note, and what ever other debt we may have. And as we are writing checks, we are hoping to have some money left over to spend on a few things we want to do. Some of us view the Christian walk the same way. We give God what we feel we owe Him of ourselves and we hope we have some of our time, energy, and money left over to do things that are strictly self-indulgent.

Friends, God wants it all. He wants us to crucify within us all that does not glorify Him. He wants us to dedicate to Him *all* of ourselves. The beautiful thing about that is, when we give to God, whatever the gift, God returns it to us in blessings. Go all out. Jump in the pool. Give it all to God.

Then say, "I'm giving myself to the One 'who is able to do immeasurably more than all we ask or imagine'" (Eph. 3:20).

Amen!

The Way of the Righteous

Psalms 1:1-6; 19:7-10

Blessed is the man that walketh not in the counsel of the ungodly, nor standeth in the way of sinners, nor sitteth in the seat of the scornful.

2 But his delight is in the law of the LORD; and in his law doth he meditate day and night.

3 And he shall be like a tree planted by the rivers of water, that bringeth forth his fruit in his season; his leaf also shall not wither; and whatsoever he doeth shall prosper.

4 The ungodly are not so: but are like the chaff which the wind driveth away.

5 Therefore the ungodly shall not stand in the judgment, nor sinners in the congregation of the righteous.

6 For the LORD knoweth the way of the righteous: but the way of the ungodly shall perish.

19:7 The law of the LORD is perfect, converting the soul: the testimony of the LORD is sure, making wise the simple.

8 The statutes of the LORD are right, rejoicing the heart: the commandment of the LORD is pure, enlightening the eyes.

9 The fear of the LORD is clean, enduring for ever: the judgments of the LORD are true and righteous altogether.

10 More to be desired are they than gold, yea, than much fine gold: sweeter also than honey and the honeycomb.

Memory Selection
Psalm 1:6

Devotional Reading
Psalm 19:1-6

Background Scripture
Psalms 1; 19

The fourth quarter of this series focuses on the books of Psalms and Proverbs. These Old Testament selections recall the children's song: *"Make new friends, but keep the old./One is silver and the other gold."* For the modern Christian, the timeless truths in the poetry of the Psalms and the wise sayings of Proverbs are "old friends," often as pertinent to us as they were to the ancient Hebrew.

This first lesson calls us from the "rat race" to the altar, from activities that we think "get us ahead" to true righteousness before God and others. They help us re-center our hearts on the truly lasting things of life, and to recall the fact that following God's will is more important than gaining material goods or temporal power. We learn here what true and durable happiness is all about. If we can recall that this poetry was originally written to be *sung,* we will sense that placing God at life's center is not a burden, but a joy.

ℰℛℭℛ

A simple object lesson from a children's science class can focus your group's attention on Psalm 1. "Plant" a small, leafy branch from a bush in a pan of soil, and bring it to class along with a pitcher of water and a spray bottle.

First spray a fine mist of water on the branch and note that such careful water-ing helps real trees grow strong and sink deep roots. Then, in contrast, slosh hard dashes of water on the branch from the pitcher, noting how the soil is washed away and the "tree" uprooted.

Psalm 1 shows us how to survive such forces as life's damaging "floods." It reminds us that "watering" our lives with the gentleness of God's will and Word keeps us rooted and grounded, able not only to stand ourselves but to offer shade and sustenance to others.

Teaching Outline	Daily Bible Readings

I. The Importance of Roots, Ps. 1:1-6
  A. A well-planted tree, 1-3
  B. . . . vs. wind-blown chaff, 4-5
  C. The discernment of God, 6
II. The Incomparable Law, Ps. 19:7-10
  A. The way of perfection, 7a
  B. The way of wisdom, 7b
  C. The way of rejoicing, 8a
  D. The way of purity, 8b
  E. The way of cleanness, 9a
  F. The way of truth, 9b
  G. The value of the Law, 10
	Mon. Choose Righteousness
	    Psalm 1:1-6
	Tue. God Loves Righteousness
	    Psalm 33:1-5
	Wed. God's Steadfast Love
	    Psalm 33:10-22
	Thu. God Loves Good Deeds
	    Psalm 11:1-7
	Fri. God Is a Righteous Judge
	    Psalm 7:9-17
	Sat. The Heavens Tell of God
	    Psalm 19:1-6
	Sun. God's Law Is Perfect
	    Psalm 19:7-14

Verse by Verse

I. The Importance of Roots, Ps. 1:1-6

A. A well-planted tree, 1-3

1 Blessed is the man that walketh not in the counsel of the ungodly, nor standeth in the way of sinners, nor sitteth in the seat of the scornful.

2 But his delight is in the law of the LORD; and in his law doth he meditate day and night.

3 And he shall be like a tree planted by the rivers of water, that bringeth forth his fruit in his season; his leaf also shall not wither; and whatsoever he doeth shall prosper.

Since the Psalms were probably assembled in a formal collection after the Jews returned from Babylonian captivity and rebuilt the Temple, they are often called "The Hymnbook of the Second Temple." Most modern English translations print them as poetry, reminding us that many of them were composed to be chanted or sung in worship.

The very practical thrust of Psalm 1 also reminds us that worship should be related to everyday life. This is clear from the three verbs in verse 1: they deal with *walking, standing,* and *sitting,* in other words, with living, in the world of work and family, trade and government, recreation and relationships. These verbs are paired with three types of people: the *ungodly*, the *sinner*, and the *scornful*. The psalm-ist (traditionally considered to be King David) affirms that we are most "blessed" or happiest when we decline habitually to walk, stand, and sit, to find our primary relationships, with people who ignore God's teachings. This blessedness, which means more than immediate and superficial happiness, is usually realized every day; and even when it is deferred it is a firm hope for those who trust God.

The truly blessed person finds his delight in meditating on and following God's law. It is God's will that provides the rootedness we need in life's storms, and the productivity ("fruit") and joy we need in trials. The imagery calls us back to Eden, where Adam and Eve enjoyed Paradise in the presence of the Tree of Life.

B. . . . vs. wind-blown chaff, 4-5

4 The ungodly are not so: but are like the chaff which the wind driveth away.

5 Therefore the ungodly shall not stand in the judgment, nor sinners in the congregation of the righteous.

In stark contrast to the life rooted and "fruited" in the will of God, the anti-godly will be blown away like the chaff from the winnowing floor at harvest-time. Even when those who cheat and connive and hurt others grow wealthy, faith knows that God will eventually bring them to judgment. The "congregation" from which they are banned is not the current assembly of the faithful, for, as Jesus would teach, the "tares" or weeds are allowed to grow alongside the good growth (see Matt. 13:27-30).

C. The discernment of God, 6

6 For the LORD knoweth the way of the righteous: but the way of the ungodly shall perish.

The fact that true faith deals with things unseen is both a comfort to the believer and a frustration to the unbeliever, who believes only in what he can see. The righteous believer may be persecuted in this life, but by faith he has confidence that in the life to come it will be revealed that he is "like a tree planted by the rivers of water." By the same token, he refrains from judging the hearts and motives of others, knowing "Man looketh on the outward appearance, but the LORD looketh on the heart (1 Sam 16:7).

Note the "parallelism" of this verse, with the second line stating the opposite of the first (often the second line only restates the sense of the first)—one of the features of Hebrew poetry.

II. The Incomparable Law, 19:7-10

Psalm 19 continues to discuss the importance of God's way, in two distinct categories: His *world* and His *Word.* Verses 1-6 have dwelt on

the way Creation speaks of God's glory ("general revelation"). Now the psalmist turns to the glories of God's Word ("special revelation").

A. The way of perfection, 7a

7a The law of the LORD is perfect, converting the soul:

These verses may be viewed as a commentary on why meditating on and living in God's law, as described in Psalm 1, produces such "rootedness," blessing, and fruit. Again, the poetic structure is obvious from the carefully balanced pattern of the thoughts in verses 7-9: *The law is* (thus), *producing* (this).

Six synonyms are used for God's will: *law* (vs. 7a), *testimony* (7b), *statutes* (8a), *commandment* (8b), *fear of the Lord* (9a), and *judgments* (9b). Such a collection of terms can refer to only one entity: the Law (Heb. *torah*) of Moses, which is the word used in both 1:2 and here in 19:7a.

In light of our previous studies in Romans, where Paul argues *against* the Law as a means of salvation, how can the psalmist say that the Law can be so perfect as to convert the soul? "Convert" means to change, and the psalmist insists that a person changes only by accepting God's will over the ways of the world. He is speaking more of the overall influence of the Law for holiness, rather than claiming that it saves apart from God's grace. In fact, at their best, the Jews held that the Law *was* grace; Paul was arguing against abusing the intent of the Law by corrupting it into a system of works-salvation.

B. The way of wisdom, 7b

7b the testimony of the LORD is sure, making wise the simple.

"Testimony" refers to the word of witness accompanying any assertion, as in a court of law. The psalmist assures us that the witness of God's will through the Law is dependable, and is so wise as to transform a simpleton into a sage.

C. The way of rejoicing, 8a

8a The statutes of the LORD are right, rejoicing the heart:

"Statutes" is another legal term, referring to the laws enacted by a court of law, in this case by the heavenly court over which God is Judge. Today in our own country many are reassessing the death penalty because of apparent errors. In contrast, God's rulings are not subject to error. Submitting to them is not a burden, as those that the Pharisees would require (Matt. 23:1-4), but rather a joy. For example, a substance abuser may chafe against God's statute against harming the body, until the "monkey on his back" proves to be a greater burden than abstinence; then God's law is seen to be not a burden but the path to freedom.

D. The way of purity, 8b

8b the commandment of the LORD is pure, enlightening the eyes.

The word translated "pure" also means "clear" or, as in the NIV, "radiant." This reading provides better balance and harmony with the idea that God's will "enlightens" the eyes. Throughout Scripture runs the theme that we live in darkness without a knowledge of God's will, which is often spoken of as a "dawning" that clarifies right and wrong and throws light on the pathway to God. As Paul said, "I had not known sin, but by the law: for I had not known lust, except the law had said, Thou shalt not covet" (Rom. 7:7)

E. The way of cleanness, 9a

9a The fear of the LORD is clean, enduring for ever:

Because God's Law moves us to awe and reverence (not "terror"), His will can be called "the fear of God." It endures because it is "pure" in the sense of ore that has been refined to the extent that the residue lasts indefinitely because it has no more impurities.

F. The way of truth, 9b

9b the judgments of the LORD are true and righteous altogether.

God's judgments (NIV "ordinances") are true because He is Truth personified and cannot lie (Heb. 6:18).

G. The value of the Law, 10

10 More to be desired are they than gold, yea, than much fine gold: sweeter also than honey and the honeycomb.

Finally, God's commandments are exalted above the value of gold to the wealthy and honey to the gourmet. We can only imagine how different the world would be if all placed obedience to God's rules in everyday life above the value of the most precious metal and the finest foods.

Evangelistic Emphasis

Those who have worked in prison ministries, like Kairos, know the importance of support groups and Bible study. Amazing transformations have come to hardened criminals sentenced to prison for the rest of their lives. In a weekend of witness, Bible study, praise, and fellowship, many inmates make a fresh start. Those for whom the change becomes a new way of life are bound together in weekly prayer and Bible study groups. In such prayer and share groups, "true cell groups," they are both held accountable and supported.

The writer of the very first psalm knew that the company we keep shapes and forms who we become. "Happy are those who do not follow the advice of the wicked, or take the path that sinners tread, or sit in the seat of scoffers." (Ps.1:1) The path to real happiness lies not in conforming to standards of those who mock God, and whose outlook is cynical. Rather if one would find true peace and contentment it comes from living with God's word day by day.

Our evangelistic responsibility is not finished with sharing the good news in preaching or witness. Those who seek to start anew need the nurture of a supportive group. All of us who would walk with God need the discipline of a daily study of the Scriptures and a regular meditation on God's word. Salvation is a lifelong process. We always need to be open to God's converting grace.

&)(&

For the Lord knoweth the way of the righteous; but the way of the ungodly shall perish.—*Psalm 1:6*

The psalmist has posed a choice for the reader—one with eternal consequence. We can trust in self. We can choose to live only for our own pleasure or success. That way of life has no root or sustaining power. It is like chaff that drifts with the wind.

But the Lord knows the way of the righteous. The person who puts his trust in God lives in a right relationship with God. In love, trust, and obedience the person becomes what God intends. That person is understood at the depth of her being. The Lord watches over those who trust in Him. The Lord cares for those who live as children, relying on God's love.

The choice is ours to make. In what or in Whom do we trust?

"The Lord watches over the way of the righteous, but the way of the wicked will perish.

Weekday Problems

Sue was a nice young woman, attractive, competent, pleasant. She worked with a group of secretaries. Her work was always done well. But Sue had a problem that made other workers in the office shy away from her. She was "hyper-critical." It sometimes seemed as if she thought her mission in life was to point out the mistakes and imperfections of others. She had an opinion about every current event and was always negative. She had an opinion about every person and it was always negative. If something went wrong in the office, she was quick to tell you who was at fault. And it was never ever her responsibility.

In Psalm 19 the writer points to the great value of the instruction given in the law. From the ancient instructions of Moses the servant of God can be made aware of his or her shortcomings. The law redirects the focus of attention from the other person's failures to oneself and what may be lacking in one's own life. In open honesty the psalmist prays: "Who can discern his errors? Forgive my hidden faults. Keep your servant also from willful sins; may they not rule over me" (vss. 11-13, NIV).

Jesus also speaks to this critical attitude in Sue and in us: "Do not judge, so that you may not be judged. Why do you see the speck in your neighbor's eye, but do not notice the log in your own eye. You hypocrite, first take the log out of your own eye, and then you will see clearly to take the speck out of your neighbor's eye" (Matt. 7:1, 3, 5).

'In My Estimation . . .'

I believe the Bible is the best gift God has ever given to man. All the good from the Savior of the world is communicated to us through this book.—*Abraham Lincoln*

* * *

It is impossible to rightly govern the world without God and the Bible.—*George Washington*

* * *

The Bible is no mere book, but a Living Creature, with a power that conquers all that oppose it.—*Napoleon Bonaparte.*

* * *

The Bible has been the Magna Charta of the poor and oppressed. The human race is not in a position to dispense with it.—*Thomas Huxley*

* * *

It is impossible to enslave mentally or socially a Bible-reading people. The principles of the Bible are the ground-work of human freedom.—*Horace Greeley*

This Lesson in Your Life

In Psalm 1, the psalmist warns that having fellowship with scoffers and with people who think they are self-reliant provides not lasting satisfaction. Instead, he points to the true source of happiness: "Happy are those (whose) delight is in the law of the Lord, and on his law they meditate day and night." The "law" referred to in the psalm includes not only the Old Testament rules and regulations. The Law or Torah (Instruction) includes the whole story of God's redemptive action in the life of Israel. True joy comes to those who find fresh delight each day in reading and praying the Scriptures.

An ancient method of "praying the Scriptures" is called "Lectio Divina." This method of meditation and prayer has been used by many spiritual guides since the sixth century. It involves a repeated reading, aloud if possible, of a short passage of Scripture. The second step is meditating on the meaning of the Bible passage. In reading stories about Jesus, the reader is encouraged to use his/her imagination. As you focus for a time on the story, you try to involve all the senses. What do you see? What are the colors of the sky? What can you smell by the Sea of Galilee? What do you feel in the warm sand or cool water? What do you hear in the waves along the shore. You imagine that you are there. Then you listen to God's word to you through the Scripture. As you live with the words of the biblical passage, they begin to shape your prayer, giving words and form to it. Finally, at least part of the time, one may move into a wordless prayer, a quiet listening, an awareness of the holy presence of God in contemplation. In such awareness of the very presence of God there comes renewal. Indeed we are like "trees planted by streams of water." "The fruit" is growing in the capacity to care with God's compassion, to love with God's' own indiscriminate grace.

The prayer, "Let the words of my mouth and the meditation of my heart be acceptable in they sight, O Lord, my rock and my redeemer" is appropriately offered by preacher and congregation before a sermon. It is a plea that what is said and heard, what is thought and felt, what is decided and what is acted on will be pleasing to God. Indeed this prayer is a helpful way to begin each day. It asks that every encounter provide the opportunity to make an offering to God of our words and thoughts. In every relationship of our daily lives we can make of our communication with others and of our inmost meditations a sacrifice pleasing and acceptable to God.

STRAIGHT

1. According to Psalm 1, who are the happy (blessed)?
Those whose delight is in the law of the Lord, and who meditate on His law day and night (vs. 2)?

2. Who are those who are "like a tree planted by streams of water?"
Those whose delight is in the law of the Lord and who meditate on the law day and night (vs. 2).

3. To what does the psalmist compare the wicked?
The wicked are like chaff that the wind drives away (vs 4).

4. What is the difference between the righteous and the wicked in the final consequence?
The Lord watches over the way of the righteous, but the way of the wicked will perish (Ps. 1:6).

5. According to Psalm 19, what declares the glory of God?
The heavens declare the glory of God (vs. 1).

6. What is "firmament?"
Firmament refers to the great dome above the earth, or the skies.

7. What are the synonyms used for the law in Ps. 19:7-9?
Testimony, statutes, commandment, and judgment are words used by the psalmist as synonyms for the law.

8. What is more precious than gold, even much pure gold?
The law is more to be desired than gold.

9. What is the value of the Law?
God's servant is warned by it and rewarded for keeping it (vs. 11).

10. According to the psalmist, what is an acceptable offering to the Lord?
The words of one's mouth and the meditations of one's heart are the sacrifices which are pleasing to God.

Everywhere people go, "the heavens declare the glory of God, as Psalm 19:1 reminds us. Wherever we find ourselves there is a silent, persistent witness to God's greatness. Even the passage of each day and night is a silent witness to God's order. Though not expressed in human speech that ears can hear, yet there is a witness to the ends of the world. No one is left without this silent, overwhelming witness to the majesty of creation.

It was an unusual Thanksgiving Day. My wife and I forsook the traditional feast at home for exploring a wilderness area long beckoning us, Clark Creek in the Tunica Hills of West Feliciana Parish in Louisiana. Our dinner that day was a sharp contrast to our family tradition—turkey, cornbread dressing, pecan pie, all served on the china and crystal reserved for special occasions, complete with linen napkins and polished silver. This year we perched on a rock in sight and sound of the Clark Creek falls. We feasted on brown bread, mild cheese, tart apples, and wonderful, thirst-quenching water. Our denim hiking caps served well as table cloth, plate, and napkin. We spied the tracks of a raccoon, an early visitor, who could not wait but promised to come back. A nosy armadillo crisscrossed our trail, but had some difficulty locating the exact address. A wild turkey flew overhead, grateful to be on the wing. We shared the sights and sounds the native Americans heard and enjoyed in the autumn. The rocks worn smooth by centuries of rushing water were reminders of the links uniting us with past and future generations. Pilgrims and their descendants come and go, but nature's gifts of sun and soil, leafy trees and rushing water continue to sustain and renew the life they opened for us.

We remembered friends and family with whom we shared Thanksgiving Days before, those scattered around the world and those gathered with the saints in glory. But this day we were mindful that our extended family includes the ancient ancestors who hiked the trails before Columbus sailed, and the unborn generations who will discover for themselves the white water, the autumn colors, the steep ravines and delicate wild flowers. Our extended family includes the majestic turkey, free and wild, the plodding armadillo, the feisty raccoon, the flock of birds ever singing, sometimes seen. Our family includes the stately trees, reviving the soil with a myriad of leaves, and purifying the air we breathe. Our family includes the red dirt hills, the sandy beach, the rich loam soil from which we come and to which we shall return. No audible words testified to God's greatness, but the witness to His glory was everywhere. "The heavens declare the glory of God and the firmament showeth his handiwork."

Hope in God

Psalm 42

As the hart panteth after the water brooks, so panteth my soul after thee, O God.

2 My soul thirsteth for God, for the living God: when shall I come and appear before God?

3 My tears have been my meat day and night, while they continually say unto me, Where is thy God?

4 When I remember these things, I pour out my soul in me: for I had gone with the multitude, I went with them to the house of God, with the voice of joy and praise, with a multitude that kept holyday.

5 Why art thou cast down, O my soul? and why art thou disquieted in me? hope thou in God: for I shall yet praise him for the help of his countenance.

6 O my God, my soul is cast down within me: therefore will I remember thee from the land of Jordan, and of the Hermonites, from the hill Mizar.

7 Deep calleth unto deep at the noise of thy waterspouts: all thy waves and thy billows are gone over me.

8 Yet the LORD will command his lovingkindness in the daytime, and in the night his song shall be with me, and my prayer unto the God of my life.

9 I will say unto God my rock, Why hast thou forgotten me? why go I mourning because of the oppression of the enemy?

10 As with a sword in my bones, mine enemies reproach me; while they say daily unto me, Where is thy God?

11 Why art thou cast down, O my soul? and why art thou disquieted within me? hope thou in God: for I shall yet praise him, who is the health of my countenance, and my God.

Memory Selection
Psalm 42:11

Devotional Reading
Psalm 43

Background Scripture
Psalms 42–43

Some have called our times "The Therapeutic Age." Psychological therapy and counseling have largely taken the place of religion in the lives of many people. Today's passage also focuses on the need for "therapy," describing distress and depression in terms that will be familiar to many in your group.

However, God is the "counselor" to whom the psalmist turns—the One who knows above all others about the "psyche" or heart because He created it. This is the God who Himself experiences heartbreak when people rebel against Him, and who, unlike any human counselor, is ever-present in our darkest hours. It is no accident that, in the New Testament, one word used for "worship" is *therapeuo*, from which we get our word "therapy." We do not need to discount the value of psychological counseling to focus, as the psalmist does, on the healing power of worship.

ഇൽ

This session can be started with a discussion on the leading causes of mental and emotional distress such as that experienced by the author of Psalm 42. Topics to be brought out include conflict within the home, loneliness, financial and work-related stress, the fast pace of modern times, illness, a sense of meaninglessness, and old age.

For centuries, faith served as an antidote for depression and distress, and the job description for ministers included "the cure of souls." Note, however, that for many today, psychology and counseling have taken the place of faith, with therapists serving as "ministers." Without dismissing the need for sound psychology, point out that the author of Psalm 42 turned instead to prayer and worship. Can distressed people today benefit from this response?

Teaching Outline	Daily Bible Readings

I. Longing for God—1-3
  A. Divine thirst, 1-2
  B. Tears as food, 3
II. Long-standing Memories—4-6
  A. Of worship in the assembly, 4
  B. Of the God who delivers, 5-6
III. Laments amid Hope—7-9
  A. Floods of grief, 7
  B. Prospects of hope, 8-9
IV. Living in Hope—10-11
	Mon. Hope in Distress
	    Psalm 42
	Tue. In God I Trust
	    Psalm 56:1-7
	Wed. I Am Not Afraid
	    Psalm 56:8-13
	Thu. My Hope Is from God
	    Psalm 62
	Fri. You Are My Hope
	    Psalm 71:1-8
	Sat. I Will Continue to Hope
	    Psalm 71:12-24
	Sun. God Is My Hope and Help
	    Psalm 43:1-5

Verse by Verse

I. Longing for God—1-3
A. Divine thirst, 1-2

1 As the hart panteth after the water brooks, so panteth my soul after thee, O God.

2 My soul thirsteth for God, for the living God: when shall I come and appear before God?

This psalm is a remarkable example of the Bible's forthright honesty. Its authors dare to pose the hard questions, which abound in this psalm:

When shall I come and appear before God? . . . Where is thy God? (twice) . . . Why art thou cast down, O my soul, and why art thou disquieted in me? (twice) . . . Why hast thou forgotten me? . . . Why go I mourning because of the oppression of the enemy?

This feature of the Psalms (and of other "Wisdom" books such as Job and Ecclesiastes) is a powerful lesson against pious pretensions. God had rather we confront Him with honest questions than gloss over our doubts with false faith.

At first the psalmist gives no external reason for his doubts and distress. He seems only to feel bereft of God's presence. Even the strongest believer may sometimes experience a nameless void instead of a voice from heaven. Some have called this feeling that God has abandoned them a "holy discontent." It is this that wrings from the author the moving confession that he is as thirsty for God as a deer for water. With Job, he longs for an audience with the Supreme Judge of the Universe (see Job 23:3-5). The hope is that he would put his complaint into words and receive an answer if he could only appear before God personally

B. Tears as food, 3

3 My tears have been my meat day and night, while they continually say unto me, Where is thy God?

Some kinds of depression comes and goes, while others seem to hang over us like a permanent cloud. We may feel so deprived of energy and hope that we lose our appetite. In eloquent irony the psalmist says, "No matter; my tears are a constant diet anyway."

"They" in the second line of the verse apparently refer to the psalmist's enemies or other tormentors. Unbelievers and enemies of faith often ask the suffering believer, "Where is thy God?" Of course the sufferer has already asked the same question, since God has made a Covenant to bless those who serve Him (Deut. 38:1-14). Sometimes, as in cases when Israel abandoned God for idols, the question is easily answered. Here, however, it is important to note that the psalm does not tell us why God allows the believer to suffer. The challenge is to maintain hope and faith despite God's silence.

II. Long-standing Memories—4-6
A. Of worship in the assembly, 4

4 When I remember these things, I pour out my soul in me: for I had gone with the multitude, I went with them to the house of God, with the voice of joy and praise, with a multitude that kept holyday.

The NIV makes "these things" refer to going with the multitude of other worshipers to the Temple to worship. The sufferer is recalling instances of abundant faith, specifically in the public assembly, as a defense in times when faith wilts under pressure. A similar expression is powerfully worded in Psalm 73, where the psalmist confesses that "my steps had well-nigh slipped" . . . until I went into the sanctuary of God (vss. 2, 17). Grief can be so intensely private and subjective that the last thing we want to do is to assemble with others in worship. Yet the psalmist testifies that it is precisely in overcoming this tendency to withdraw from others and from public worship that our faith can be restored.

B. Of the God who delivers, 5-6

5 Why art thou cast down, O my soul? and why art thou disquieted in me? hope thou in God: for I shall yet praise him for the help of his countenance.

6 O my God, my soul is cast down within me: therefore will I remember thee from the land of Jordan, and of the Hermonites, from the hill Mizar.

The suffering believer has questions for himself as he tries to deal with his sadness. Yet he is not so much trying to pinpoint the precise reason for his depression as confronting himself with why it is so often easier to be "cast down" than to be lifted up in faith. One answer is that the immediate anguish of the moment can blot out our memories of past times when God demonstrated His presence.

In verse 6 the sufferer has the mental courage to dwell on the time when God led Israel across the Jordan River, which springs from the hills of Mount Hermon. ("Mizar," which means "little hill" and has not been identified, was perhaps a part of the complex of Mount Hermon.) Remembering happier times is a powerful antidote for depression, and well worth the considerable emotional effort required. Israel as a people was also often encouraged to renew their contact with such sacred memories, especially the exodus from Egypt, in times of national crisis (see Isa. 43:16-17).

III. Laments amid Hope—7-9
A. Floods of grief, 7

7 Deep calleth unto deep at the noise of thy waterspouts: all thy waves and thy billows are gone over me.

For "waterspouts" the NIV has "waterfalls," tying this verse with the cataracts of the Jordan not far from the point where Israel had crossed into the Promised Land. "Deep calleth unto deep" probably describes the successive, deep waves of depression that flooded over the psalmist like pounding seas. The language recalls Jonah 2:3,"The floods compassed me about: all thy billows and thy waves passed over me." Obviously the suffering psalmist feels that he is about to "drown" in his sorrows.

B. Prospects of hope, 8-9

8 Yet the LORD will command his lovingkindness in the daytime, and in the night his song shall be with me, and my prayer unto the God of my life.

9 I will say unto God my rock, Why hast thou forgotten me? why go I mourning because of the oppression of the enemy?

Now the psalmist's mood begins to rise as he feels the healing effects of creatively remembering previous times of God's faithfulness. He is not out of the tunnel of darkness, but he can begin to trust that the light at the end isn't an oncoming train! "Lovingkindness" is a word that appears so often with the word for "covenant" that it can often be translated "covenant love." This implies that despite ongoing questions, the sufferer has an underlying trust that God will keep covenant with him and rescue him.

Note the realism in verse 9, where questions and faith are expressed in the same breath. Now the source of the suffering is the psalmist's enemies. Although he still has questions about why God allows this situation, he can address them to God as being as dependable as a "rock." This ambivalence is common in the throes of despair. Again, God does not answer the question *Why?*, but challenges the believer to keep the faith even when God is silent.

IV. Living in Hope—10-11

10 As with a sword in my bones, mine enemies reproach me; while they say daily unto me, Where is thy God?

11 Why art thou cast down, O my soul? and why art thou disquieted within me? hope thou in God: for I shall yet praise him, who is the health of my countenance, and my God.

The psalmist's enemies seem not only to be attacking him with their swords, but "twisting the knife" by restating the taunt, "Where is thy God?" The sufferer not only must deal with the emotional pain but with the added derision hurled at him by his enemies. Of course they are not interested in knowing where God is, but in rubbing the salt of doubt into the psalmist's wounds.

Yet the sufferer cannot allow his lament to close on a negative note. God has rescued him (and his people, the Jews) before, laying a solid basis for hope, to which the psalmist calls himself. This combination of past deliverance with no present proof of certainty is the essence of faith. Verse 11 is a good illustration of what Hebrews 11:1 means when it defines faith as "the substance of things hoped for, the evidence of things not seen."

Evangelistic Emphasis

The writer of Psalms 42 and 43 takes us on a Ferris wheel ride, up and down, up and down in an endless cycle. We are moved from a thirsting for the living God to a persistent hope. We move down into despair, groaning in misery, and then up to a quiet waiting in trust. Then once again we are plunged into despair and doubt only to be lifted up by the vision of praising God continually. Around and around, up and down in a recurring circle. In this ever-circling Ferris wheel there is a center, a hub. In the continual struggle between faith and unbelief, in the conflict between trust and doubt, we can know that at the center is One who holds us.

When the poet's unanswered "Why?" is the loudest and his sense of being overwhelmed is the greatest, he still addresses God. It is not *despite* his sense of the absence of God but rather *because* of it that he grows in faith. He discovers that within himself are the gifts that God has provided for his journey. There are memories of other days. There is the gift of God's steadfast love new every morning. There is the gift of imagination with which to dream of a better future. All these are provided by God, who is at the center of the wild swings from heights to depths. He is ever held by the steadfast love of God. That is good news for all of us who sometimes are "cast down and disquieted within."

༄༅༈

Memory Selection

Why art thou cast down, O my soul? And why art thou disquieted within me? Hope thou in God: for I shall yet praise him, who is the health of my countenance, and my God."—*Psalm 42:11*

In a beautiful way, the psalmist lets us in on the inner struggle of his heart. Seeing the moods of despair and depression that seem almost to overwhelm him, he yet speaks to that inmost self. There is more than homesickness, more than the debilitating weakness of a persistent illness, more than the taunting of enemies who interpret his suffering as the judgment of God. There is down in the depths of his being a sure confidence in God. He waits, he hopes, he trusts in God. The day will come when once more he shall sing the praise of God, and experience the holy presence of God. Looking on the countenance or face of God will bring healing, wholeness, and salvation. Then he shall praise God continually. It is as though glorifying God is the whole purpose and fulfillment of his existence.

Weekday Problems

When Opal was a small girl of six or seven, one of her household chores was to empty out the ashes from the big furnace in the basement. The dark, vast, cold, damp basement filled her heart with fear and dread. Her imaginative mind could see dragons and witches, robbers and ghosts. She was frightened every time she went down into the dark basement. Time and again her family would hear her little voice drifting up the stairwell singing "Be not dismayed what e're betide, through every day, o'er all the way God will take care of you." Singing a song of faith helped to quiet her fears.

So the psalmist testifies: "By day the Lord commands his steadfast love and at night his song is with me" (Ps. 42:8). Music we sing or hum picks us up and carries us with it. How blessed are those who early on have hid in their hearts the great hymns of faith or familiar refrains of gospel music. In their darkest hours they remember them and even sing them. They find their spirit is buoyed.

For many, walking in the dark valley, the words of the 23rd psalm come back, as though they had been written just for them, just for that hour.

In the musical "The King and I," Anna shares her secret: "Whenever I feel afraid, I hold my head erect, and whistle a happy tune . . . every single time the happiness in the tune convinces me that I'm not afraid."

Doubting Our Doubts

Never be afraid of doubt, if only you have the disposition to believe.—*Samuel Taylor Coleridge*

* * *

Every step toward Christ kills a doubt. Every thought, word, and deed for Him carries you away from discouragement.—*Theodore Ledyard Cuyler*

* * *

In the darkest night of the year,/When the stars have all gone out,/That courage is better than fear,/That faith is truer than doubt.—*Washington Gladden*

* * *

Why didn't someone tell me that I can become a Christian and settle the doubts afterward?—William Rainey Harper

* * *

Doubt comes in at the window when inquiry is denied at the door.—*Benjamin Jowett*

This Lesson in Your Life

Abraham Lincoln once wrote: "I am now the most miserable man living. If what I feel were equally distributed to the whole human family, there would not be one cheerful face on earth." The poet of Psalms 42 and 43 knew this same misery and depression. In these psalms we also get some clues as to how to deal with depression.

Christian faith affirms the freedom of each person to choose how the person will respond. We have no control over the events that come to us but we always have a choice of how we will respond. Especially in blue moods, when we are more sad than glad, we need to use that freedom that makes us distinctively human. To give into passing moods is to become a victim of life. We may not be able to reverse what has happened, but we can choose how we will respond.

All of us are blessed with memories. In that memory are recollections of good times. Sometimes we need simply to take out of our memory bank those recollections of times when we knew joy, companionship, peace and joy. This is what the psalmist does. "These things I remember, how I went with the throng and led them in procession to the house of God with glad shouts and songs of thanksgiving"(Ps. 42:4). As he remembered leading the pilgrims in that joyful procession, he could hear the glad shouts, feel the rhythm of the music, and taste again the joy of the celebration. It was a strategy learned by Maria in "The Sound of Music." "When the dog bites, when the bee stings, when I'm feeling sad, I simply remember my favorite things and then I don't feel so bad."

Christian faith provides through the story of Jesus an opportunity for a new relationship with God. It is a relationship not based on our goodness or our achievements. It is a relationship based only on God's love. We can trust ourselves to this steadfast love of God made known in Christ, convinced that nothing can separate us from the love of God which is in Christ Jesus (Rom. 8:29).

When Pastor Martin Niemoeller was in he United States after World War II, he was interviewed by Dr. Kenneth Hildebrand, pastor of Central Church of Chicago. Dr. Niemoeller had defied Hitler and led the Confessional Church movement in resistance to Hitler's demands. As a consequence he spent three years in solitary confinement in concentration camps. "How did you endure three years of solitary confinement?" Dr. Niemoeller smiled and replied, "A man doesn't know what he can stand until he is put to the test." It is then that we can recall that "The Lord commands his steadfast love" (Ps. 42:8).

1. What verses, very similar in form, are repeated as a refrain in Psalms 42 and 43?
Psalms 42:5, 42:11, and 43:5: "Why are you cast down, O my soul? And why art thou disquieted in me? Hope thou in God: for I shall yet praise him.

2. To what is the human thirst for the living God compared?
To a hart or deer panting or longing for flowing streams (Ps. 42:1-2).

3. What event does the psalmist remember in his despair?
The psalmist remembers how at a time of holy festival he led the multitude in procession to the Temple of God with songs of praise (42:4).

4. What comforts the heart of the psalmist in the night?
At night he finds the song of God is with him.

5. In Psalm 43, what does the psalmist ask God to send to lead him to God's holy hill?
He asks God to send out His light and truth to lead him (vs. 3).

6. When the psalmist gets to the Temple, with what musical instrument will he praise God?
"I will praise you with the harp, O my God" (vs. 4).

7. What are the questions which the psalmist asks of God?
Why have you forgotten me? (Ps. 42:9). Why have you cast me off? (43:2). Why must I walk about mournfully? (42:9, 43:2).

8. What question is asked by the psalmist's enemies?
"Where is your God?" (Ps. 42:3, 10),

9. What questions are asked by the psalmist?
"Why are you cast down?" and "Why are you disquieted within me?" (Ps. 42:5, 11; 43: 5).

10. What requests does the psalmist make of God?
He asks God to vindicate him and to defend him against ungodly people (43:1), and for light and truth to lead him to God's holy presence (43:3).

In his book "Falling into Greatness" Lloyd Ogilvie tells of Louise Mohr, a truly great woman who has helped thousands in their need. In her earthy, unpious, sometimes gutsy description of the abundant life, she has reached many who were not reached by traditional religion. But now she needed help herself. After a long illness, her beloved husband Sidney had died. While she was still recovering from that loss, her eyesight was beginning to fail. The doctor told her there was nothing that could be done to arrest further deterioration. Then came a deep concern about a major health problem for a close friend. It seemed the problems just piled up, higher and higher.

One day, when she had had all she could take, she sat down to write God a letter. With her customary frankness, no mincing of words, no pulling of punches, she told God just what she thought about the whole mess.

We learn from the psalms that prayer is not always composed of beautiful words, well-crafted phrases, and eloquent petitions. Sometimes in the prayers of the psalms we hear doubt, anger, bewilderment, and exasperation. We read a strange mixture of doubt and faith, anger and trust, the absence and presence of God all melded together. "I say to God, my rock, why have you forgotten me?" (Ps. 42:9). For you are the God in whom I take refuge; why have you cast me off?"(Ps. 43:2). In a similar manner, Louise in her letter to God expressed her impatience and frustration with the way things were going in her life.

The next day Louise saw her next-door neighbor. In response to a neighborly, "How's it going?" she began relating the problems that were piling up. Louise shared with her neighbor that she had even written a letter to God, lodging a strong complaint about His management and expressing in very clear terms just how she felt about the way things were going.

A couple of days later Louise received a letter: "Dear Louise: You think you've got problems! I've got the whole universe to run, with people who have problems as big or bigger than yours. But I know and care about you. I will give you what you need to endure. You will have faith to trust Me. Love, God."

Of course her neighbor, with a sense of humor and a caring spirit, had written the letter. It was just what Louise needed. From a friend came the reminder that God's grace was sufficient. There was no immediate change of her circumstance; but with the letter came a renewal of the gift of confidence like that which came to the psalmist: "For I shall yet praise him, who is the health of my countenance, and my God" (Ps. 43:5).

I LIFT UP MY EYES TO THE HILLS...

The Lord, Our Keeper

Psalms 23; 121

The LORD is my shepherd; I shall not want.

2 He maketh me to lie down in green pastures: he leadeth me beside the still waters.

3 He restoreth my soul: he leadeth me in the paths of righteousness for his name's sake.

4 Yea, though I walk through the valley of the shadow of death, I will fear no evil: for thou art with me; thy rod and thy staff they comfort me.

5 Thou preparest a table before me in the presence of mine enemies: thou anointest my head with oil; my cup runneth over.

6 Surely goodness and mercy shall follow me all the days of my life: and I will dwell in the house of the LORD for ever.

121:1 I will lift up mine eyes unto the hills, from whence cometh my help.

2 My help cometh from the LORD, which made heaven and earth.

3 He will not suffer thy foot to be moved: he that keepeth thee will not slumber.

4 Behold, he that keepeth Israel shall neither slumber nor sleep.

5 The LORD is thy keeper: the LORD is thy shade upon thy right hand.

6 The sun shall not smite thee by day, nor the moon by night.

7 The LORD shall preserve thee from all evil: he shall preserve thy soul.

8 The LORD shall preserve thy going out and thy coming in from this time forth, and even for evermore.

Memory Selection
Psalm 121:1-2

Devotional Reading
Psalm 80:14-19

Background Scripture
Psalms 23; 80; 121

It has long been observed with only a trace of humor that a minister's task is "to comfort the afflicted and afflict the comfortable." Much of the prophetic writings of the Old Testament minister the rod of affliction, when warranted; but the Psalms are unequaled in ministering comfort. The two psalms in this lesson are classic portrayals of God as the Great Comforter and Protector.

Although such portrayals speak with special poignancy to people in crisis, the effective teacher realizes our need to drink deeply of such spiritual nourishment in the good times as well. Focusing on God's constancy, power, protection, and love in the quiet atmosphere of a Bible study will enable group members to call on Him when they face times of strife, fear, and sorrow.

ഇൽ

The 23rd Psalm has spoken meaningfully to millions of believers who have never even seen a sheep because we sense that we ourselves have needs that are akin to a sheep's needs.

This session can be started by asking group members to share some of the characteristics people and sheep have in common. Guide the discussion to include such traits as: (1) sheep have a poor sense of direction, and need guidance; (2) they have a tendency to be better followers than leaders; (3) they are relatively defenseless against predators; (4) they are so easily frightened that they will not drink from a rushing stream as readily as from a quiet pool; (5) they require careful land management, since their tooth formation causes them to uproot grass instead of "clipping" it so it will grow back; (6) yet for all their inadequacies they are useful, providing both wool and meat.

Point out that Psalms 23 and 121 show that we can depend on God to care for our needs as a good shepherd tends his sheep.

Teaching Outline	Daily Bible Readings
I. Guiding Our Steps—Ps. 23:1-4 　A. Meeting our needs, 1-2 　B. Tending to the spirit, 3-4 II. Giving Us Victory—5-6 III. Guarding Us from Evil—Ps. 121 　A. Yahweh, not mountain gods, 1-2 　B. Alive, not inert, 3-4 　C. Master of the elements, 5-6 　D. Watchman of our ways, 7-8	**Mon.** Restore Us, O God 　　　Psalm 80:1-7 **Tue.** Tend Your Vine! 　　　Psalm 80:8-19 **Wed.** Our Refuge and Strength 　　　Psalm 46:1-11 **Thu.** God Heard My Cry 　　　Psalm 40:1-10 **Fri.** Keep Me Safe Forever 　　　Psalm 40:11-17 **Sat.** The Lord Is My Shepherd 　　　Psalm 23:1-6 **Sun.** The Lord Will Keep You 　　　Psalm 121

Verse by Verse

I. Guiding Our Steps—Ps. 23:1-4
A. Meeting our needs, 1-2
1 The LORD is my shepherd; I shall not want.
2 He maketh me to lie down in green pastures: he leadeth me beside the still waters.

Several factors come together to make the imagery of God as a Shepherd and His people as sheep a highly meaningful portrait. The ancient Middle East itself provided the pastoral setting that made the picture immediately recognizable. Flocks of sheep and the work of the shepherd were as common then as are skyscrapers in modern cities. As the "For a Lively Start" section indicates, even people who are far removed from such a rural setting identify with the picture painted in Psalm 23 because the needs of people everywhere are so similar to those of sheep.

First, Yahweh (identified by the caps-and-small caps "the LORD") is appropriately described as a Shepherd because both people and sheep tend to wander into dangerous places without a leader. Note our total dependence on the Shepherd for well-being: It is only because "The LORD *is* . . . " that "I *shall* . . . ."

As Creator, God knows where to take us for "green pastures" even better than an ordinary shepherd. This

may apply in general to material needs such as food, clothing, and shelter. Obviously, however, this is not an automatic law. Since believers are sometimes found in poverty, we are reminded that God is sovereign over this Covenant to care for us; and that even amid physical needs the Shepherd tends to our spirits.

This guidance is essential because, since the Fall, it has been clear that, left untended and uncorrected, human nature leads us not to the pastures that would best nourish us but to the wastelands of sin. Yet the Creator-Shepherd-God knows that "all we like sheep have gone astray" (Isa. 53:6), and leads us to better grazing than our nature would ordinarily provide.

The phrase "still (NIV 'quiet') waters" reminds us that sheep are often too frightened to drink when they have only rushing water. The fact that God knows our own fears as "sheep" is indicated in His strategy in leading Israel out of Egypt. He "did not lead them on the road through the Philistine country, though that was shorter. For God said, 'If they face war, they might change their minds and return to Egypt.' So God led the people

413

around by the desert road toward the Red Sea" (Exod. 13:17, NIV). Even now, confronted with fear and uncertainty, believers are assured that if they will trust God He will provide them with the quiet pools where they can drink deeply of His peace, then face the worst.

B. Tending to the spirit, 3-4

3 He restoreth my soul: he leadeth me in the paths of righteousness for his name's sake.

4 Yea, though I walk through the valley of the shadow of death, I will fear no evil: for thou art with me; thy rod and thy staff they comfort me.

Our need to have our souls "restored" is nowhere more apparent than in Isaiah 53, cited above to show that we tend to stray into sin. That chapter is also the crowning jewel of God's remedy for sin, describing not only our tendency to stray but the suffering Servant who gives His life to bring us back into the sheepfold (vs. 12). It is this gift of grace, not our own goodness, that places us on the path of righteousness.

Anyone who has lost a loved one can identify with the imagery in verse 4 of a sheep on a treacherous mountain trail with a deep and rocky valley ready to claim it with the first misstep. Yet we can have confidence in the protection of the Good Shepherd who gives His life for the sheep (Jn. 10:15). He is armed with a staff to use in fending off wild animals. It also has a

hook to catch us if necessary. Most important, the Shepherd is willing to brave the same terrain over which we must cross, even death itself, in order to reassure and protect us.

II. Giving Us Victory—5-6

5 Thou preparest a table before me in the presence of mine enemies: thou anointest my head with oil; my cup runneth over.

6 Surely goodness and mercy shall follow me all the days of my life: and I will dwell in the house of the LORD for ever.

The psalmist shifts the imagery now from sheep to a ruler such as David himself, traditionally viewed as the author of this psalm. The picture of being able to dine sumptuously in the very presence of an enemy God has helped the king defeat describes the height of victory over spiritual enemies as well. The picture of a cup that "runneth over" invites us to do more than merely *cope* with life's "enemies" or difficulties; it invites us to *flourish*, or triumph over them superlatively.

Verse 6 summarizes both the pastoral and the princely images in the preceding verses. So complete is the psalmist's confidence in God that he is assured that even when he is weak, God's strength will support him; even when he strays, God's guidance will direct him back home. Here is an echo of the apostle Paul's assurance that nothing can separate us from God's love (Rom. 8:36-39).

III. Guarding Us from Evil—Ps. 121

A. Yahweh, not mountain gods, 1-2

1 I will lift up mine eyes unto the hills, from whence cometh my help. 2 My help cometh from the LORD, which made heaven and earth.

Moving to the first of 14 "Psalms of Degrees" (NIV "Ascents") we find the psalmist expressing the same confidence in God's protection as we found in Psalm 23. The precise meaning of the title "degrees" is unknown. Some scholars believe these psalms were sung as the Israelites streamed in ascending "degrees" up the hillsides surrounding Jerusalem on their way to the Temple. Others envision official singers mounting the Temple steps as they sang these songs especially composed for feast days.

"The hills" of verse 1 are probably a reference to the places where pagans thought their mountain-gods dwelt. The NIV expresses verse 1 as a question: "Where does my help come from?" The answer of the psalmist is, "Certainly not from any 'gods of the hills,' but from Yahweh, who made both hills and heaven."

B. Alive, not inert, 3-4

3 He will not suffer thy foot to be moved: he that keepeth thee will not slumber.

4 Behold, he that keepeth Israel shall neither slumber nor sleep.

The author continues the contrast between the true God and pagan deities by noting that Yahweh is able to protect the faithful because he does not need to take time out to sleep as people, or presumably false gods, do. Prophets such as Elijah and Isaiah emphasize the difference between in-animate gods and the true God in humorous satire (see 1 Kings 18:27; Isa. 44:9-17). In short, the true God is alive, while others are inert.

C. Master of the elements, 5-6

5 The LORD is thy keeper: the LORD is thy shade upon thy right hand.

6 The sun shall not smite thee by day, nor the moon by night.

Verses 5-8 can be translated as exhortations: "May the Lord be your keeper," etc. This divine Protector of which the psalmist sings is in control of the elements. Again, although the rain does not always fall when, or in the amounts, we wish, we are assured that even the floods and droughts of a fallen world are not greater than the "Keeper" who is also Creator.

D. Watchman of our ways, 7-8

7 The LORD shall preserve thee from all evil: he shall preserve thy soul.

8 The LORD shall preserve thy going out and thy coming in from this time forth, and even for evermore.

We need this Protector on the journey of the spirit even more than on the physical roads we may travel. Of course the watch-care promised here is for those who seek it. As James would write many years later, we are always to confess that our fortunes are subject to God's will (Jas. 4:13-16). In return, His guidance and protection are unlimited by time and space.

Evangelistic Emphasis

There is good news in the shepherd's psalm, Psalm 23. For all who wander aimlessly, the Lord provides leadership. Like a shepherd the Lord leads us to places of renewal and restoration. The Lord shows us paths of righteousness. If we wait and listen, we can discern God's calling, nudging, pulling, leading. We are not alone. That's good news.

When we walk through the valley of the shadow of death, we are not alone. When we face the reality of our dying, we leave all that is familiar for a strange and unknown experience. We are not spared the experience of death, but we are assured that when we face that new and often frightening reality of dying, we are not alone. God's presence is there to comfort. That's good news.

When we pass through death to life hereafter, we are given no descriptions. We don't need blueprints or roadmaps. It is enough to know that we shall be with the God. We will dwell in the house of the Lord forever. That's good news!

At a gathering in a coffee house, a professional actor was invited to recite the 23rd psalm. With the full range of his rich, deep voice, he read with dramatic power. When he finished, he received a standing ovation. Then a simple believer was asked to read it. When he finished, all knelt in prayer. The actor knew the psalm, but the simple believer knew the shepherd. That made all the difference.

℘℧

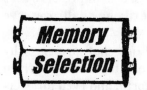

Memory Selection

I will lift up mine eyes unto the hills, from whence cometh my help. My help cometh from the Lord, which made heaven and earth.— *Psalm 121:1-2*

A pilgrim on the way to Jerusalem was mindful of the dangers of his journey. Robbers may lurk in the hills. Disease may descend, or heatstroke from the sun. This pilgrimage to the Holy Temple was not an easy journey. It was fraught with dangers. In the lonely watch of the night the traveler was anxious for himself and for his companions.

He realized that his security rests not in the armed strength of that band of pilgrims, for they were no match for armed brigands. He did not have remedies for diseases of the dessert. His safety did not rest in speed, for he plodded along by foot or donkey. His strength came from the One who made the heavens and the earth. God's power is the greatest. God's will is for our good. In the confidence in God's faithfulness and steadfast love, the poet and his company could rest secure.

Weekday Problems

Nettye loved the Bible. Her favorite passage was Psalm 121. When her son was overseas during World War II she began the practice of reading (or praying) this psalm everyday. After his safe return she continued her daily praying of the psalm each day. Day by day she held before her the image of God as her "keeper." During her last days of illness and confinement in the hospital, she asked her pastor to read this psalm and then she would recite it with him, word for word. The psalm spoke to her of the trustworthiness of God.

In some ways she took on the qualities of the Lord she praised so often in the words of this psalm. She was worthy of the trust of others and she extended a measure of protective care and loving concern. In her community she was a keeper, a keeper of memories, a preserver of values.

Nathaniel Hawthorne tells about a boy who grew up in the shadow of a mountain with a great stone face on a mountainside. Every day he looked at the face and admired its qualities of strength and character. Then one day it was noticed that his own face had taken on the features of the face on the mountain that he had gazed upon each day.

So Nettye daily gazed at the portrait of God as keeper in Psalm 121. She gradually took on the very qualities of abiding compassion, persistent care, and unceasing love which it conveyed. She became like the Keeper to whom she trusted her life anew each day.

Did You Hear the One About . . . ?

Cop: Lady, you were doing 85 miles an hour!
Lady: Oh, isn't that splendid! And I only learned to drive yesterday!

* * *

Tom: Do you know how to get down from an elephant?
Jerry: No, how?
Tom: You don't, silly. You get down from a goose.

* * *

Bill: When I'm near death, I'll ask my wife to cook my last meal.
Will: Why?
Bill: Because then I'll feel more like dying.

* * *

First Mom, at the high school football game: What position does your son play?
Second Mom: I think he's one of the drawbacks.

This Lesson in Your Life

Isaac Bashevis Singer once said, "I only pray when I am in trouble. But I am in trouble all the time, and so I pray all the time." Psalm 80 was written in a time of trouble for the psalmist and all Israel. His psalm can teach us much about prayer. Prayer is not reserved for the moments of peace, joy, ecstasy when we are overwhelmed by the beauty of God's creation, or the wonder of the divine love mediated through others' kindness. We pray in those good times to be sure, mindful of God's blessings.

This psalm leads us to pray when we feel forsaken and forgotten. "How long will you be angry? You have fed them with the bread of tears." The prayer expresses the bewilderment of the people that the nation God has called and guided, shepherded and nurtured, is now being ravaged and destroyed. Prayer begins where we are. Sometimes that involves a protest or a question, such as "Why have you broken down the walls?"

The psalm teaches us that prayer includes the whole range of our experience. God can be found in our suffering as well as in our salvation. Indeed sometimes the suffering is a part of salvation.

The prophet Isaiah uses the image of the vineyard to represent Israel. The prophet is clear that the wasting of the vineyard so carefully tended is because Israel failed to practice justice and righteousness (Isa. 5:1-7).

Yet along with the despair and bewilderment there is a deeper trust. God is addressed. The psalm focuses on the Divine. After lifting up the dark despair and the agonizing Why?, the psalmist returns again and again to God with the simple petition: restore us, cause us to return, let your face shine, is a request that God be present for us. Turn O God from wrath to grace.

The psalms lead us to "tell it like it is" to God, not in pretty language, but honestly opening our hearts and wounds that we may be healed. Yet this psalm leads us to a deeper trust, even when we cannot understand.

As we read the psalms in the light of the cross, we are reminded that Christ's suffering was not wasted. God worked in and through the crucifixion to bring about salvation. So in prayer we offer our doubts and fears, our hurts and agonies, that finally we might move through them, even made stronger by them. We ask the very God we question to cause us to return, to make us aware of God's presence, to make us whole.

STRAIGHT

1. What duties of the shepherd are described in Psalm 23?

The shepherd makes the sheep lie down in green pastures, he leads them beside still water, and he leads them in a right path.

2. In Psalm 23, what are the signs of hospitality and welcome prepared by the Lord for his guests?

He prepares a table, anoints his guest's head with oil, and fills his cup to overflowing.

3. In Psalm 23, what will follow the pilgrim all the days of his life?

Goodness and mercy will follow him all the days of his life.

4. In Ps. 23 how long will the poet dwell in the house of the Lord?

He will dwell in the house of the Lord forever.

5. What is the source of saving help for the poet of Psalm 121?

His help comes from the Lord, who made heaven and earth.

6. According to Psalm 121, when does God sleep?

Never.

7. From Psalm 121, how long will God keep our "going out and coming in"?

The Lord will keep our going out and coming in from this time on and forevermore.

8. In Psalm 80, what refrain is repeated three times?

"Turn us again, O God, and cause thy face to shine; and we shall be saved (vss. 3, 7, 19).

9. In Isaiah 5, how is "Why have you broken down the walls?" answered by Isaiah's parable?

The Lord "looked for judgment, but behold oppression; for righteousness but behold a cry!" (vs. 7).

10. What New Testament passage echoes the imagery of the shepherd in Ps. 23:1 and 80:1?

John 10:11: "I am the good shepherd."

419

I saw a rabbit on the Interstate. His brown coloring, ordinarily helping him blend in with his surroundings, made him stand out against the white expanse of pavement. His sensitive ears, able to pick up the slightest sounds of danger, were overwhelmed with the alien sounds of 18-wheelers, racing engines, and blaring horns. His sensitive nose was confused with the odors of exhaust fumes and careless litter. It was as though his whole defense network was overloaded. Unable to sort out the confusing signals, he was frozen in the middle of the highway. By any measure, he was where he did not belong.

I don't know what brought him to that conglomerate of concrete ribbons in his morning search for some tender morsel of green grass. I hope he managed to hop to safety. I know he was out of his element. He was where he had no business being. He was trespassing where he did not belong.

I've sometimes felt like that rabbit on the interstate. It is the strange feeling of being where you don't belong. It is the feeling of the prodigal when he comes to his senses and realizes his destiny is not found in slopping the hogs. It is the feeling of Joseph left in the pit by his brothers, cut off from everything and everyone near and dear to him. It is Jonah in the belly of the whale, when he was supposed to be in Nineveh. It is being "in the pits" when we are meant to soar like the eagles. It is being where we don't belong.

I hope that little rabbit made it safely off he Interstate and found a lush green field in which to run and romp, and feed and play.

I pray the Lord will lead us to the place where we belong. The psalmist found it so:

"The Lord is my Shepherd. He makes be lie down in green pastures. He leads me beside the still waters. He restores my soul."

RISE UP, O GOD, JUDGE THE EARTH...

God of Justice

June 23

Psalms 82; 113:5-9

God standeth in the congregation of the mighty; he judgeth among the gods.

2 How long will ye judge unjustly, and accept the persons of the wicked? Selah.

3 Defend the poor and fatherless: do justice to the afflicted and needy.

4 Deliver the poor and needy: rid them out of the hand of the wicked.

5 They know not, neither will they understand; they walk on in darkness: all the foundations of the earth are out of course.

6 I have said, Ye are gods; and all of you are children of the most High.

7 But ye shall die like men, and fall like one of the princes.

8 Arise, O God, judge the earth: for thou shalt inherit all nations.

113:5 Who is like unto the LORD our God, who dwelleth on high,

6 Who humbleth himself to behold the things that are in heaven, and in the earth!

7 He raiseth up the poor out of the dust, and lifteth the needy out of the dunghill;

8 That he may set him with princes, even with the princes of his people.

9 He maketh the barren woman to keep house, and to be a joyful mother of children. Praise ye the LORD.

Memory Selection
Psalm 82:8

Devotional Reading
Psalm 72:11-19

Background Scripture
Psalms 72; 82; 113

This lesson reminds us that the God praised in the preceding lesson as the Source of all comfort is also the Judge of all the earth. Some are slow to consider this aspect of God. They want Him to rush to their aid in time of trouble, but in good times they seem unconcerned about what He thinks about their behavior toward others.. The psalms considered here

affirm that God is the Great Comforter *because* He is concerned about justice.

This lesson was especially hard for ancient Israel to learn. Since they were God's "chosen people," He helped them defeat those who opposed their conquest of the Promised Land. This, in turn, sometimes caused lapses in Israel's "social conscience",they too easily assumed that since God was "on their side," they need not be too concerned about how they treated others. The present lesson is a healthy corrective for such assumptions.

જીભ

Try introducing this lesson by leading your group in an assessment of your church's involvement in righting wrongs. Are programs or ministries in place to feed the hungry, or provide housing and clothing for the poor? Are steps being taken to care for widows and orphans,two groups who were often singled out in

Scripture as needing special care?

Include in your discussion the causes of such needs. Do we have a tendency to dismiss them by assuming that the needy "bring it on themselves"? Even if this is true in some cases, do Christians still have some responsibility for their needs? Are funds or hand-outs always the best way to meet needs?

Allow such question to lead into the theme of today's lesson. God's people must be concerned about justice and meeting human needs because the God they worship is the God of justice.

Teaching Outline	Daily Bible Readings
I. The Just and the Unjust—Ps. 82:1-2	**Mon.** God of Everlasting Righteousness Psalm 119:130-144
A. God, the source of justice, 1	
B. Man and the lack of justice, 2	**Tue.** God of Love and Justice Psalm 119:149-160
II. Services to Be Rendered—3-4	**Wed.** Justice, God's Throne Psalm 97:1-12
III. Judgment on the Unjust—5-8	**Thu.** A Plea for God's Justice Psalm 82:1-8
A. The shaken foundation, 5-7	
B. The Call for Justice, 8	**Fri.** God Helps the Needy Psalm 113:1-9
IV. The God of Justice—Ps. 113:5-9	**Sat.** God's Justice for Rulers Psalm 72:1-7
A. A Ruler who serves, 5-6	
B. A God who exalts, 7-9	**Sun.** God Delivers the Needy Psalm 72:11-19

Verse by Verse

I. The Just and the Unjust—Ps. 82:1-2

A. God, the source of justice, 1

1 God standeth in the congregation of the mighty; he judgeth among the gods.

The ascription, "A Psalm of Asaph" reminds us that while King David seems to have written most of the songs in our collection, a few others also contributed. Asaph was a leader of singers in the time of David (1 Chron. 6:31, 39). His name appears at the headings of Psalms 50, and 73-83.

The main thrust of the psalm is to affirm that the true God is the source of justice, even when it is administered by the "mighty" among human judges. Although human laws differ from culture to culture, some principles of law are the same throughout all societies, because both people and the principle of law are created by the one God.

The psalm therefore affirms "ethical monotheism," the principle that there are absolute principles of right and wrong that are rooted in the one true God, not invented by "gods" or judges in various societies. Of course the particular details of right and wrong may differ, but the universal sense of "rightness" or justice comes from God.

The word "gods" is probably to be understood here and in verse 6 as "judges," although this would admittedly be a rare use of the term. Certainly it cannot be taken to imply that the psalmist believed that Yahweh is only one among many gods. The Hebrew word is *elohim*, which can refer to angels, and some scholars think it refers here to "principalities and powers," or spiritual entities who also exert their influence on humanity's concept of justice. This meaning, however, is hard to apply in verse 6 (see below). It is better to take the verse to mean that in any gathering ("congregation") of high and mighty judges, even including so-called "gods" (see the NIV), Yahweh stands out as the author of the principles by which they judge.

B. Man and the lack of justice, 2

2 How long will ye judge unjustly, and accept the persons of the wicked? Selah.

Because God is the source of justice (vs. 1), He has the right to correct mere human judges and others who commit or tolerate injustice. Here He is angry at judges who accept bribes or for other reasons become "respecters of persons" (Acts 10:34; Jas. 2:1-4) by rendering decisions that favor the wicked. The cry "How long . . . ?" implies the answer supplied elsewhere in Scripture: until evil has reached its appointed level and Judgment Day dawns (see Rev. 6:10-11).

The term "Selah," which appears often in the Psalms, was apparently a musical notation directing the way the piece was to be chanted or sung, although its meaning is now obscure. Some scholars think it signified a "rest" or pause, while others think it was a sign that the preceding word was to be emphasized or accented.

II. Services to Be Rendered—3-4

3 Defend the poor and fatherless: do justice to the afflicted and needy.

4 Deliver the poor and needy: rid them out of the hand of the wicked.

It is not enough to be against injustice in general. God's people are also to stand positively for specific acts of justice and benevolence. It is common for skeptics to ask why God would allow poverty and wrongful death. Here it is clear that such evils arise not from God but from unjust people (although admittedly God allows them free will

to act on orders from Satan). Here the psalm takes on the character of the prophetic books. Injustice and idolatry were the two sins of which the prophets most often accused the Jews, and which they maintained led to the downfall of the nation (see Micah 2:1-3; Amos 5:21-27).

III. Judgment on the Unjust—5-8
A. The shaken foundation, 5-7

5 They know not, neither will they understand; they walk on in darkness: all the foundations of the earth are out of course.

6 I have said, Ye are gods; and all of you are children of the most High.

7 But ye shall die like men, and fall like one of the princes.

The unjust judges are accused of willful ignorance. The decisions they render in favor of the wicked plunge society into moral darkness and upset the absolutes or foundations of moral order on which God created the worlds. All this is despite the trust God placed in them by elevating them to positions of authority—again, figuratively, "gods," and "children of God."

In John 10:34 Jesus quotes this passage to show the same degree of esteem with which God views humans, a rank that is defamed by wicked judges. As a result, God pronounces judgment on them; their end will be the eternal death earned by evil people instead of the eternal life with which God endows the faithful.

B. The Call for Justice, 8

8 Arise, O God, judge the earth:

for thou shalt inherit all nations.

Now the author's viewpoint changes from God to the psalmist, or to the worshipers reciting the song. They call for God to bring an end to injustice, and to show that all nations are subject to His authority. Here is one of the clear examples of the biblical claim that God is not just the God of Jews and Christians, but of all the earth, whether or not they recognized Him as such.

IV. The God of Justice—Ps. 113:5-9
A. A Ruler who serves, 5-6
5 Who is like unto the Lord our God, who dwelleth on high,

6 Who humbleth himself to behold the things that are in heaven, and in the earth!

Psalm 113 continues to praise God as a just ruler who has compassion on those whom earthly judgments have failed to recognize. Recalling the picture of God standing among a gathering of lesser judges (Ps. 82:1), we see here a remarkable difference. A human ruler or judge may have "pride of place," coveting the robes and other trappings that elevate him above the common people he judges. In contrast, our supreme heavenly Judge condescends to come down from behind the bench and identify with those who have been wronged. Such a picture will become central to the supreme example of such an act— the incarnation of Jesus, who did not view His divine position as something to cling to, but gave it up to identify with flesh and blood sufferers (Philip. 2:5-8).

B. A God who exalts, 7-9
7 He raiseth up the poor out of the dust, and lifteth the needy out of the dunghill;

8 That he may set him with princes, even with the princes of his people.

9 He maketh the barren woman to keep house, and to be a joyful mother of children. Praise ye the Lord.

To envision God raising up the poor and needy and placing them at the banquet tables of princes requires a longer perspective on life than a this-worldly view. Certainly there are instances of such surprising transformations in this life. Men first saw in David a poor and simple shepherd boy, but God elevated him to be king. Again, God saw to it that the poor widow of Zarephath was blessed with unlimited amounts of oil and meal (1 Kings 17:9ff.). A few barren women such as Sarah and Rachel were enabled to "keep house" (NIV "have a home as a happy mother of children"). Such glimpses of God's grace are only a foretaste of a future state and the banishment of Satan's rule of injustice that so often dominates this realm.

Evangelistic Emphasis

In Psalm 113 we are repeatedly enjoined to praise the name of the Lord. The name of God was of special significance. To know the name of God was to know something of the mystery of God. To call the name of God was to invoke God's holy presence. God's personal name, "Yahweh" came to be considered too holy to be spoken; so when a reader came to the holy name "Yahweh" the term "Lord" was substituted. To praise the name of God is to worship His very being. Praise is an action that has no other purpose but to glorify the Giver of life. Such praise is at the heart of our prayer life.

But praising the name of God is not limited to worship on Sunday or to personal times of prayer. God's name is glorified when we teach a child to read, when we help a person regain a sense of self worth, when we protect children from crippling diseases through vaccines, when we feed the hungry and house the poor.

The opposite of hallowing God's name is profaning it. The profaning of the Name occurs when the needy are sold for a pair of shoes, or the poor are trampled into the dust (Amos 2:6-7). We take the name of God in vain when we piously sing about the sweet name of Jesus and then are callous to the children of God who suffer around us. Praising and glorifying the name of God involves both acts of worship and deeds of love.

಺಄಄

Arise O God, judge the earth; for thou shalt inherit all nations.—*Psalm 82:8*

This ancient prayer holds in tension the "already" and the "not yet" of God's rule.

The faithful believer knows that God rules over all the powers and forces in nature and history. He is "Lord of lords and King of kings." Yet there is much around us and within us that denies the rule of God. As long as people do not let the will of God determine their way and destiny, then other gods seek to play that role.

We pray for God's saving judgment on all that denies the reality of the Kingdom of God. To pray, "Rise up O God and judge the earth for all nations belong to you" is akin to praying "Thy kingdom come." It acknowledges both that God is already sovereign and yet that His will is not fully done.

Weekday Problems

Lawi is a 12-year-old African boy who lives with his family in a small village. One day, as Lawi was baby-sitting with his little brother, their little hut caught fire. It was quickly enveloped in flames. Lawi was outside, but he ran into the blazing hut. His baby brother was trapped by a burning rafter which had fallen on him. Hurriedly he worked to free his brother. Finally, as the flames danced around his head, Lawi freed the baby, and carried him outside just as the hut caved in.

The villagers had gathered but they had been too frightened to go inside. They said "Lawi, you are very brave. Weren't you frightened? What were you thinking of as you ran into the burning hut?" Lawi answered: "I wasn't thinking of anything. I just heard my little brother crying."

This young African boy fits the psalmist's description of the character of Israel's ideal king: "He delivers the needy when they call, the poor and those who have no helper. He saves the lives of the needy" (Ps. 72: 12-14). How long has it been since you heard your brother or sister crying? How long has it been since you stopped and did something about it?

Church Bulletin Bloopers

Women's Luncheon: Bring a sandwich. Polly Phillips will give the medication.

* * *

Karen sang a beautiful solo: "It is well with my solo."

* * *

Congratulations to Tim and Rhonda on the birth of their daughter Oct. 12 thru 17.

* * *

If you choose to heave during the Postlude, please do so quietly.

* * *

Hymn: "I Love Thee My Ford."

* * *

Newsletters are not being sent to absentees because of their weight.

* * *

As soon as the weather clears up, the men will have a goof outing.

* * *

Thank you, dead friends.

* * *

Diana and Don request your presents at their wedding.

This Lesson in Your Life

The common thread of the psalms selected for study today is the theme of justice. As the psalmist prays for the king, he prays for an ideal ruler, one anointed by God "to judge the poor with justice, to defend the cause of the poor and deliverance to the needy" (Ps. 72:2,4). In his directions to the "divine council" the Lord exhorts them, "Give justice to the weak and the orphan, maintain the right of the lowly and the destitute; rescue the weak and needy, deliver them from the hand of the wicked" (Ps. 82:3-4). In his description of the character of God the psalmist proclaims, "He raises the poor from the dust and lifts the needy from the ash heap to make them sit with princes" (Ps. 113:7-8).

Marian Wright Edelman, one of the prophets of our time, helps us to translate the psalmist's concern for justice into concern for children in our day. She calls for us to to consider that in a single hour, 400 children will drop out of school, 90 children will be born into poverty, 32 will be born at low birth weigh, 10 will be arrested for violent crime, two will be wounded by gunfire. At the current rate of child gun deaths, 6,000 children born this year will not live to be 20. A gun takes the life of a child every two hours.

Marian insists that every child deserves the early education that he needs to get a strong start in life. Education is far less expensive than ignorance, long term welfare, and prisons. It is estimated that it cost $65,000 per year to keep a prisoner locked up in a state penitentiary. Why are we willing to spend so much more to lock up children and youth after they get into trouble than we are willing to invest in programs to get children ready to learn and succeed and stay out of trouble?

A middle-class father in New York City had one son, an only child. He was very proud of his boy. The father wanted to do everything to help him succeed. He took him to Little League Baseball practice. They read books together. The father enrolled him in the best private schools. But the dad was still worried about bringing him up in New York City. There was so much violence there. So he moved his family to the suburbs to make sure his only son was safe. One day the child was caught in a crossfire of gunfire. The child was killed. Friends tried to comfort the grieving father. "You did everything you could to raise this child to be successful." The father replied, "No, no, I didn't. I didn't pay enough attention to other people's children."

To paraphrase Dr. Edelman, Don't tell me that God is pleased that with all God's gifts to America, the richest nation in the world, we allow the children to be the poorest part of our population. Don't tell me that God is pleased that with all our military power we can't protect all of God's children from gunfire. Don't tell me that God is pleased that with an unparalleled budget surplus we can't educate all of God's children.

STRAIGHT

1. According to Psalm 113, when should God's name be blessed.
From this time on and forever more God's name is blessed (vs. 2).

2. According to Ps. 113, where is the Lord's name to be praised?
From the rising of the sun to its setting (vs. 3).

3. According to Psalm 113, what does God do for the poor and needy?
He raises the poor from the dust and lifts the needy from the ash heap to make them sit with princes (vss. 7-8).

4. According to Psalm 113, what does God do for a barren woman?
He gives the barren woman a home, making her the joyous mother of children (vs. 9).

5. In Psalm 82, what is God's instruction to the divine Council?
Give justice to the weak and the orphan; maintain the right of the lowly and the destitute. Rescue the needy (vss. 3-4).

6. In Psalm 87, what is God's assessment of the gods?
They have neither knowledge nor understanding, they walk around in darkness (vs. 5).

7. In addition to Psalm 82, where else in the Bible is the plea, "Arise, O God" found?
Whenever the bearers of the ark set out, Moses would say, "Arise, O Lord" (Num. 10:35).

8. In Psalm 72, what prayers are offered for the king?
May he judge your people with righteousness and your poor with justice. May he defend the cause of the poor, and give deliverance to the needy (vss. 2,4).

9. What is the prayer for the nation in Psalm 72?
May righteousness flourish and peace abound (vs. 7).

10. How is the character of the king described in Psalm 72:12-14?
He delivers the needy and the poor. He has pity on the weak and saves the lives of the needy. From oppression and violence he redeems their life.

John Wesley admonished his preachers to "visit from house to house." I'm sure he never imagined the perils of visiting in the 21st century. For example, one day I came home from an afternoon of pastoral visiting, cut, bruised, and bleeding. I had walked through—more accurately run into—a glass door. Trying to explain only makes it seem even sillier. I was inside the comfortable home of a parishioner, sipping a frosty root beer when it started to rain. It was one of those summer showers that come up without warning. I hurriedly set down my drink to dash out to my car and put the windows up. In my rush to get out, I failed to notice the glass door, which was shut. It was a "shattering" experience. As I picked myself up from the floor, amidst a few thousand slivers of glass, I was more embarrassed than hurt. Even in this, there may be some lessons to be learned.

One lesson I should have learned 50 years ago is that most houses have doors that need to be opened if you want to go in or out. Another old lesson made a fresh impression. The old adage "haste makes waste" took on a new and "pointed" meaning. But I also see it as a parable of a lot of idealism: looking ahead (in this case to the car on the street) one fails to see the immediate present (like a door to be opened to get to the street).

So it sometimes occurs that one is in love with humanity but can't stand "Mrs. So-and-So" who lives down the street. There is a reformer out to change the whole penal system, but he has not visited the first inmate in the city jail. Then there is the ecumenical Christian who prays long and earnestly for church union but won't speak to his fellow pew-sitter with whom he has had a long-standing feud. There's the activist who is loud about lobbying Washington for help with the hungry but doesn't know the name of a single hungry child in his city.

It is important to have great dreams, challenging goals, lofty aspirations; but it is needful as well to keep one's eyes open to the needs at hand. It's possible to be so obsessed with details we miss the big picture. We can miss seeing the forest for the trees, but it is also possible to miss seeing the variety and beauty of individual trees when staring at the forest as a whole. It is tempting to be so enamored of the big picture we stumble over the bodies of the homeless and the hungry at our door.

It was this strong word which the Lord gave to the divine council: "Give justice to the weak and the orphan; maintain the right of the lowly and the destitute. Rescue the weak and the needy" (Ps. 82:3-4). The principle is put even more clearly in 1 John 4:20: "He who does not love his brother whom he has seen, cannot love God whom he has not seen."

...TELL THE COMING GENERATION...

Teach the Wonders of God

Psalm 78:1-8

Give ear, O my people, to my law: incline your ears to the words of my mouth.

2 I will open my mouth in a parable: I will utter dark sayings of old:

3 Which we have heard and known, and our fathers have told us.

4 We will not hide them from their children, shewing to the generation to come the praises of the LORD, and his strength, and his wonderful works that he hath done.

5 For he established a testimony in Jacob, and appointed a law in Israel, which he commanded our fathers, that they should make them known to their children:

6 That the generation to come might know them, even the children which should be born; who should arise and declare them to their children:

7 That they might set their hope in God, and not forget the works of God, but keep his commandments:

8 And might not be as their fathers, a stubborn and rebellious generation; a generation that set not their heart aright, and whose spirit was not stedfast with God.

Memory Selection
Psalm 78:4

Devotional Reading
Psalm 135:1-7

Background Scripture
Psalms 78:1-8

An old hymn states poetically the focus of this lesson:

> How shall the young secure their hearts
> And guide their lives from sin?
> Thy word the choicest rules imparts,
> To keep the conscience clean.

Psalm 78 emphasizes the importance of believers bringing children up under-standing who they are, and *whose* they are. It summarizes the moral and spiritual history of Israel from Egypt to the Promised Land. The story line rises to heights of faith, then plunges to the depths of unbelief and disobedience.

The records of many nations in the ancient world include only victories and accomplishments. In contrast, this psalm exhorts us to "tell it like it is," contrasting God's steadfast blessings and faithfulness with the people's wavering commitment. The theme, then, is *Lest we forget. . . .*

৪০০৪

Open this session by a discussion of the best way to hand along the Christian faith to children. Psalm 78's Jewish setting assumes a tight-knit family structure, with much of the children's education provided by the parents. Discuss (1) the differences in family life today, and (2) how the modern Christian home can ensure that children learn the story of the faith.

In early America, parents could assume that the school would hand down the tradition. Recent court rulings emphasizing the separation of church and state have challenged this practice. One result has been a marked growth in private Christian schools, and in home-schooling. Somewhere in the mix, the Church and the Sunday School are involved. Are the family devotionals of earlier years still workable? What other means of "traditioning" youth can your group suggest?

Teaching Outline	Daily Bible Readings

I. Hearing from the Fathers—1-3
  A. History as parable, 1-2
  B. Treasures from the fathers, 3
 	
II. History of Salvation—4-5
 	
III. Hope for the Future—6-8
  A. Lest we forget, 6-7
  B. Learning from mistakes, 8
	Mon. Proclaim to All Generations
	  Psalm 89:1-7
	Tue. Ruler of Heaven and Earth
	  Psalm 89:8-18
	Wed. From Everlasting to Everlasting
	  Psalm 90:1-6
	Thu. God's Name Endures
	  Psalm 102:12-22
	Fri. Remember God's Wonders
	  Psalm 77:11-20
	Sat. Teach the Children
	  Psalm 78:1-8
	Sun. Praise Ye the Lord!
	  Psalm 135:1-7

Verse by Verse

I. Hearing from the Fathers—1-3
A. History as parable, 1-2

1 Give ear, O my people, to my law: incline your ears to the words of my mouth.

2 I will open my mouth in a parable: I will utter dark sayings of old:

Curiously, the psalm seems to open as though God Himself is calling His people to listen to His law (Heb. *torah*), then moves to the voice of a wise teacher, perhaps the psalmist Asaph himself. This literary device immediately calls for obedient ears to pay attention to the authority of the psalm.

The law (Heb. *torah,* or NIV "teaching") often refers to the Pentateuch, or first five books of the Old Testament. Here it is best understood as "precepts" or teaching (as in the NIV), since the following subject matter is on a particular subject whether found in the Pentateuch or not.

The teacher intends to teach in "a parable" (vs. 2). The word also means "proverb," and in fact is the Hebrew title of the book of Proverbs. This is the teaching method that Jesus would perfect. In fact, Matthew 13:35 quotes this verse in describing Jesus' favorite way of teaching. In citing this psalm, Matthew uses the Greek word *paraboles,* whose make-up helps us understand the value of parables. Literally the word refers to something that has been "thrown alongside" something else. An example is the parable that the prophet Nathan told David, of the king who stole a man's pet sheep. This story was "thrown alongside" David's theft of Uriah's wife, Bathsheba, and David perceived immediately that it referred to him. This illustrates why the psalmist says he will use parables. They have the ability to draw the hearer into the story, and invite him to bridge the gap between story and event, making the meaning more personal.

Verse 2 says that the parable will reveal "dark sayings," that is it will help us understand what was previously hidden. Since the meaning of historical events (NIV "things of old") is not always clear, one purpose of the biblical revelation is to show how those events apply to our own lives. The psalmist would have agreed with the modern saying that those who ignore history are condemned to repeat its mistakes.

B. Treasures from the fathers, 3

3 Which we have heard and known, and our fathers have told us.

The meaning of the events in Israel's history was not unknown to the psalmist because it had been handed down by the "fathers"— older, wiser sages among the people. As is true of most eastern peoples, the Jews honored the elderly for their wisdom: "Gray hair is a crown of splendor; it is attained by a righteous life" (Ps. 16:31). The psalmist's own elders had obeyed the command in Deuteronomy 6:7, "Thou shalt teach [the commandments] diligently unto thy children, and shalt talk of them when thou sittest in thine house, and when thou walkest by the way, and when thou liest down, and when thou risest up."

II. History of Salvation—4-5

4 We will not hide them from their children, shewing to the generation to come the praises of the LORD, and his strength, and his wonderful works that he hath done.

5 For he established a testimony in Jacob, and appointed a law in Israel, which he commanded our fathers, that they should make them known to their children:

"Them" refers to the "dark sayings" in verse 2, which the psalmist promises to illuminate so their meaning is no longer dark, or hidden. Specificially, he calls elders and parents to teach the younger generation God's *praise, strength, and wonderful works* (NIV "wonders"). Certainly the teaching will also include Israel's failure, but it is significant that the emphasis is on the positive: the nature of God as a loving, powerful Father.

This exhortation implies a difference between *event* and *interpretation*. For example, the escape of the Jews from slavery in Egypt could have been recorded by any historian. The fact that God was behind the plagues that led to their liberation, the parting of the waters, the Israelites' wandering in the wilderness, and the conquest of the Promised Land, all this is seen only by the eye of faith. Surely there is still an urgent need for parents and older people to help youth read history through the eyes of faith, accompanying the mere description of events with praise and prayer for God's power and guidance.

In verse 5, "testimony" is from a legal term describing an affidavit, or the description of an event by a witness. Coupling this term with, again, the "law," the verse refers to God's having made a Covenant with Jacob, father of the twelve tribes of Israel, testifying to His having chosen them to be His people. The story of this "election" is to be continuously handed down to Hebrew children. By extension, the "testimony" is to be repeated by believing parents and church leaders today, so no generation allows the story of salvation to die.

III. Hope for the Future—6-8

A. Lest we forget, 6-7

6 That the generation to come might know them, even the children which should be born; who should arise and declare them to their children:

7 That they might set their hope in God, and not forget the works of God, but keep his commandments:

The task of "traditioning" children is to move from one generation to the next, for three specific purposes: so the flame of *hope* never dies, so the next generation does not forget God's *wondrous works*, and so they will honor and keep His *commandments.*

Unfortunately, many people today ignore this responsibility toward youth. They forget that even though Christ fulfilled the Law, the events recorded in the Scriptures of the Old Covenant,the story of God's relationship to His people,"were written for our learning, that we through patience and comfort of the scriptures might have hope" (Rom. 15:4). The result is an entire generation of youth who value nothing but the moment. Having not been told the story of God's love and judgment on the Jews, they have little concept of being connected to a "history of love",and their own ability and responsibility to live by love and law are stunted.

B. Learning from mistakes, 8

8 And might not be as their fathers, a stubborn and rebellious generation; a generation that set not their heart aright, and whose spirit was not stedfast with God.

Although the accent, as noted above, in our recital of "salvation history" to youth is on the positive aspects of God's love, the psalmist does not ask us to read this story with rose-colored glasses. The history of the "fathers" includes the story of Israel's stubborn rebelliousness and recurring tendency to disobey God.

Far from pronouncing a legalistic judgment on them for this national and personal character, the psalmist asserts that the people's faithlessness indicates "heart trouble." Their spirit, not just their acts, are to be faulted, and their inconstancy is to be blamed. This indictment is yet another indication that the Old Covenant is not a merely legal list of rules, as Christians sometimes view it. God called His Old Covenant people to obey *from the heart*, not just to go through the motions. It was their need to have God's word "hidden in their hearts," not just the failure to keep external rules, that prompted the Spirit, through the psalmist, to call them to be more faithful in traditioning the younger generation.

Evangelistic Emphasis

Psalm 78 calls one and all to the task of telling of the wonders of God. It brings the awesome reminder that humanly speaking, in every era the faith of the people of God is only one generation away from extinction.

There is an ancient legend that tells of Jesus' return to glory. When He approached heaven after His crucifixion and resurrection He encountered the angel Gabriel, who asked, "What is your plan, Lord, for continuing your work?"

Jesus replied, "I have left Peter and Andrew, James and John, and the other disciples."

"But Lord, what is your plan?" Gabriel persisted.

Jesus responded: "They will tell others of God's plan of salvation, and others will tell others, and they will tell others until the whole world knows of God's saving love."

"But Lord, suppose others fail to tell others?"

Jesus replied, "I have no other plan."

ℰ❍ℭℛ

Memory Selection

We will not hide them from their children, shewing the generation to come the praises of the Lord, and his strength, and his wonderful works that he hath done."—*Psalm 78:4*

Christians have a great story to tell. God has acted in the life of Israel to reveal God's nature and God's will. The Word of God has become incarnate in Jesus that we might better know, trust, and serve God.

The story is not about abstract propositions that God is revealed. Rather it is in a story that occurs in the midst of history, in God's deliverance of Israel from slavery, in God's bringing them into the promised land that we come to know this God of justice and mercy.

In the life of Jesus, His teachings, His welcome to sinners and outcasts, His miracles, His death and resurrection, we come to know the measure of God's redemptive love. We have come to know God through these ancient stories of our faith, preserved for us in Scripture. It is our charge and privilege to teach these Bible stories to the next generation.

Weekday Problems

If we would, in the psalmist's words, "tell the next generation the praiseworthy deeds of God, the wonders He has done," we will need to read the Bible regularly. A survey reports that 80 percent of adult Americans said they believe the Bible to be the "revealed word of God." When these same Americans were asked to name the first four books of the New Testament, 53 percent could not name even one. How can we teach what we do not know?

If we would teach the Bible to our families, we need to read the Bible together as a family. Carl Sandburg pointed out that before Lincoln had learned to read as a boy, he heard his mother saying certain Bible verses day by day as she worked. Lincoln had learned these verses by heart. The tones of his mother's voice were in them; and sometimes as he read these verses as an adult, he seemed to hear the voice of Nancy Hanks speaking in them.

If we would be faithful interpreters of the Word, we must, most of all, live the Bible. Said an Indian Brahman to a missionary: "If you Christians in India, in Britain, or in America were like your book, you would conquer India in five years.

Teach the Children Well

It is essential that the student acquire an understanding of and a lively feeling for values. He must acquire a vivid sense of the beautiful and of the morally good. Otherwise he,with his specialized knowledge,more closely resembles a well-trained dog than a harmoniously developed person.—*Albert Einstein*

* * *

Not to know what has been transacted in former times is to be always a child . . . If no use is made of the labors of past ages, the world must remain always in the infancy of knowledge.—*Cicero*

* * *

Dad: How's your new teacher?
Lad: O.K., I guess, but she really gets historical.
Dad: I guess you mean "hysterical."
Lad: Nope. She's always digging up the past.

This Lesson in Your Life

The book of Acts tells us that after the outpouring of the Holy Spirit on the Day of Pentecost the believers gathered together and "they devoted themselves to the apostles' teaching" (Acts 2:42). Can you imagine the people clustered together listening while Peter or Andrew, James or John told the stories of Jesus? So many of His teachings Jesus communicated through parables: the story of the lost coin, the story of the lost sheep, the story of the lost son and waiting father, the story of the publican and Pharisee who went to the temple to pray, the story of the good Samaritan. The apostles would never tire of telling about the wonders they had seen, the healing of the blind, the deaf, the lame. They would tell again and again about His trial, arrest, and crucifixion. They would never fail to feel the wonder, the mystery, and the joy of the appearances of the risen Lord. These stories were passed on even unto us.

Your own home can be a "church," a place of learning, where the stories of the faith are shared, and the traditions of the faith are passed on. John Westerhoff, an influential writer on Christian Education today, stresses the crucial role of the family as the chief agency by which the Christian faith is transmitted. Whatever the church does is only a supplement to what parents live and share with their children.

The primary teachers of the Bible are parents. To tell and retell the stories of the Bible is to leave a rich deposit in the memory bank of your children.

Do you have Bibles in your home? Are they dusty? Are they well read? Are they well marked? Do you read the Bible by yourself? Do you read the Bible aloud with others of your family?

Much of the learning in our homes is not by intentional effort to transmit the faith. Ross Snyder says the family is "a cracker-barrel discussion at the crossroads store where the roads running to and fro meet." When family members are available to each other at meals, on vacation, working together they share stories of their own experiences. Values are transmitted. Faith is shared.

Westerhoff affirms that we should focus not on how we can make our children Christian but on how we can be Christian with our children. If we really love our children, if we really want them to grow in Christian faith, we need to spend more time working at our own growth in the faith. Faith cannot be given to children; it can only be shared with them.

Our teaching is most effective by example. It is well to be able to recite the Ten Commandments. It will be even more effective if one keeps them. All a father's preaching about telling the truth is nullified when he tells his child, "Just tell them I'm not at home." All the literature on drug abuse is not as effective as a parent who lives a drug-free life. Character is not so much taught as caught.

1. What are the things the people have heard and are instructed to tell their children?

They are to tell of the glorious deeds of the Lord and the wonders that he has done (Ps. 78:4).

2. What are their ancestors commanded to teach?

The decrees and laws of the Lord(vs. 5).

3. Who are they to teach?

They are to teach their children (vs. 5).

4. What is the expected result of their teaching?

The next generation will know the law and teach it to their children so that they will set their hope in God and keep His commandments (vss. 6-7).

5. How are their ancestors described in Psalm 78?

Their ancestors were stubborn and rebellious, whose heart was not steadfast and whose spirit was not faithful to God (vs. 8).

6. Where else in the Old Testament is Israel sternly charged to teach the children?

After issuing the great commandment, Moses charged Israel to recite it to the children, talk about it at home, and write it on door posts (Deut. 6:4).

7. In the great commission (Matt. 28:19-20), what does Jesus command the disciples to do?

"Go ye therefore, and teach all nations, baptizing them in the name of the Father, and of the son, and of the Holy Ghost."

8. Whom did Paul encourage to teach (1 Tim. 6:2; 4:13; 2 Tim. 2:24)?

Paul urged Timothy, "These things teach and exhort" (1 Tim 6:2); "Give attention to teaching" (1 Tim. 4:13, RSV); and he said that the Lord's servant must be an apt teacher (2 Tim 2:24).

9. What are the gifts spoken of in Ephesians 4:11?

The gifts were that some would be apostles, some prophets, some evangelists, some pastors and teachers.

10. What is the purpose of these gifts (Eph. 4:12)?

The gifts Christ gave were to equip the saints for the work of ministry.

In a burst of unexplainable energy, I finally got around to going through a stack of old books. To my amazement and embarrassment I found two books from the library of the church where I grew up. They were 40 years overdue. I noted that the date slip indicated there would be an overdue charge of 2 cents per day. I quickly calculated that I owed approximately $420 for each 40-year-overdue book. If there was a modest interest charge as well, I probably owed my home church $1,500.

Although they did not charge me the $1,500 overdue fine, it occurred to me that I really owed my home church much more than that. It was there that I first learned the story of the Bible, sang the hymns of the church, heard the gospel and the claim of Christ. Although I resisted the momentary urge to write out a check for the overdue fine plus interest, I did realize that to that fellowship of caring folk, teachers, pastors, counselors, and friends, I owe more than I ever can repay.

The true "repayment" is to pass on the stories that I learned from those books. While I cannot adequately say Thank you for introducing me to the biblical faith, I can pass on what I have learned to others. What a blessing to come to know Abraham and Sarah, Moses and David, Ruth and Naomi, Mary and Joseph, Peter and Paul! How can I thank faithful teachers for making these persons come alive for me? It was from that community of believers, some of whom were gifted to be teachers and pastors, that I was introduced to Jesus. Many of them have gone on to glory. I can show my gratitude by sharing the faith, expressed in the stories of Scripture with others.

That is what the ancient psalmist calls us to do: "We will tell to the coming generation the glorious deeds of the Lord and his might, and the wonders that he has done" (Ps. 78:4).

Perhaps that's why the old hymn of Catherine Hankey is still a favorite for many: "I love to tell the story of unseen things above/Of Jesus and his glory, of Jesus and his love./I love to tell the story, because I know 'tis true;/It satisfies my longing as nothing else can do./I love to tell the story, 'twill be my theme in glory, /To tell the old, old story of Jesus and his love."

HOW MANIFOLD ARE YOUR WORKS!

Lesson 6

Creator and Sustainer

Psalm 104:24-35

O LORD, how manifold are thy works! in wisdom hast thou made them all: the earth is full of thy riches.

25 So is this great and wide sea, wherein are things creeping innumerable, both small and great beasts.

26 There go the ships: there is that leviathan, whom thou hast made to play therein.

27 These wait all upon thee; that thou mayest give them their meat in due season.

28 That thou givest them they gather: thou openest thine hand, they are filled with good.

29 Thou hidest thy face, they are troubled: thou takest away their breath, they die, and return to their dust.

30 Thou sendest forth thy spirit, they are created: and thou renewest the face of the earth.

31 The glory of the LORD shall endure for ever: the LORD shall rejoice in his works.

32 He looketh on the earth, and it trembleth: he toucheth the hills, and they smoke.

33 I will sing unto the LORD as long as I live: I will sing praise to my God while I have my being.

34 My meditation of him shall be sweet: I will be glad in the LORD.

35 Let the sinners be consumed out of the earth, and let the wicked be no more. Bless thou the LORD, O my soul. Praise ye the LORD.

July 7

Memory Selection
Psalm 104:24

Devotional Reading
Psalm 65

Background Scripture
Psalms 65; 104

441

Psalm 104 is one of the Bible's "nature psalms",hymns of praise to God for the wonders of the natural world, the creation. It joins Psalm 19 in affirming that "the heavens declare the glory of God; the skies proclaim the work of his hands" (vs. 1, NIV).

From the earlier verses in today's passage the teacher can emphasize how all life is dependent on God, as illustrated by the rich variety of sea-life. In verses 31-35 the focus broadens to creation in general, and the praise that is due the all-powerful God who can send both earthquakes and pastoral serenity. The smooth connection between sea-life and humanity shows the connectedness of all life. Here is an opportunity to emphasize our responsibility to be good stewards of the environment, which actually belongs not to us but to God.

ഇരുന്ന

This session can be effectively introduced by a discussion of the wonders of nature which, as Psalm 19 affirms, "declare the glory of God." What specific wonders have caused group members to reflect on God's creative power and glory? Responses may include everyday wonders such as a brilliant sunset . . . geographical marvels such as the Grand Canyon . . . biological miracles like human birth or the marvel of how body and mind work together . . . and "environmental miracles" such as the vastness of the seas or of space, which has only recently begun to be explored.

Point out that the passage for this lesson emphasizes how all this glory depends on a gracious God, and how we owe it to Him to care for a world filled with such wonders.

Teaching Outline	Daily Bible Readings
I. 'Natural' Wonders,24-26	**Mon.** The Creator's Love Psalm 136:1-9
A. Wisdom of creation, 24	**Tue.** Sustainer of Land and People Psalm 147:1-11
B. Marvels of the sea, 25-26	**Wed.** God Sustains Mortal Life Psalm 103:15-22
II. Nature's Dependence,27-30	**Thu.** God Established the World Psalm 93: 1-5
A. God's provision, 27-28	
B. Dependent life-cycle, 29-30	**Fri.** God Set Earth's Foundations Psalm 104:1-9
III. Normal Response,31-34	**Sat.** God, Sustainer of Life Psalm 104:10-23
A. Confessing God's power, 31-32	
B. Praising and meditating, 33-34	**Sun.** Praise to the Creator Psalm 65:1-13
IV. Negative Note,35	

Verse by Verse

I. 'Natural' Wonders—24-26

A. Wisdom of creation, 24

24 O LORD, how manifold are thy works! in wisdom hast thou made them all: the earth is full of thy riches.

Along with many modern scientists, the psalmist (perhaps David) is in awe at the number and variety of species in creation, some of which are still being discovered. David had special occasion to become intimately acquainted with nature early in his life as a shepherd dwelling in the open fields. Although he could kill a lion who would feast on his flock, he could still appreciate the wisdom of the "food chain" and other instincts God built into wildlife. These biological "riches" (NIV "creatures") that belong to God as Creator are probably referred to here.

B. Marvels of the sea, 25-26

25 So is this great and wide sea, wherein are things creeping innumerable, both small and great beasts.

26 There go the ships: there is that leviathan, whom thou hast made to play therein.

Although the Hebrews were not known for the knowledge of the sea, David knows about it at least through inspiration and probably through experience. The remarkable aspect of the spirit of this psalm is that the sea typically struck fear, not joy, in ancient people. Some scholars believe that the term "the deep" (Heb. *tehom*) in Genesis 1:2 was taken from the name of a pagan god (*Tiamat*); and that the creation account deliberately describes it as part of the creation, not a god.

The number of species in aquatic life is thought to far exceed those on land. They include "creeping" life such as giant sea worms, microscopic ("small") animals beyond number, and "great beasts" as large as whales (to which the term "leviathan" may refer), and giant squid.

Although the sea is also noted for ferrying the ships of mankind, the emphasis here is on earth's oceans as a playground for sea life. Many naturalists have marveled at the capacity, for example, of otters for play, a function that seems to have little to do with the creaturely drive to propagate the species. This element of exultation is in contrast to the dark side of creation, which includes deadly species and damaging storms and earthquakes. All this is viewed in Scripture as a result of the Fall, not of creation itself. As it came from the hand of the Creator, nature was only a source of joy.

II. Nature's Dependence—27-30
A. God's provision, 27-28

27 These wait all upon thee; that thou mayest give them their meat in due season.

28 That thou givest them they gather: thou openest thine hand, they are filled with good.

The countless life forms of earth and sea "wait" for God (NIV "look to") for their food, This shows that, unlike God, creation has only "contingent" being—its existence depends on God's good grace. Only the Creator is "non-contingent," or dependent on no other being for His existence. Again, it is a matter of perplexity that through the Fall of Adam, sin resulted in an earth whose hand is sometimes not "filled with good," as when wildlife suffers from drought. For the psalmist, however, this negative note is all the more cause for awe at nature's stark dependency on its Creator.

B. Dependent life-cycle, 29-30

29 Thou hidest thy face, they are troubled: thou takest away their breath, they die, and return to their dust.

30 Thou sendest forth thy spirit, they are created: and thou renewest the face of the earth.

The note of awe at the darker aspects of nature continues as the psalmist reflects on the Creator's capacity to take life at will. Perhaps the poet was thinking of the "food chain" that requires the strong to feed on the weak to sustain the cycle of nature; for in the next breath (vs. 30), he confesses that while some animals die, others are sustained, and the marvelous cycle of nature is enabled to roll on. The life process itself is such a joyful wonder that the deaths it entails cannot overwhelm the joy. Perhaps something like this view lies behind the Jewish salutation, *l'chaim,* "to life." The whole concept reminds us that God is not only the Creator but also the Sustainer of life.

III. Normal Response—31-34
A. Confessing God's power, 31-32

31 The glory of the LORD shall endure for ever: the LORD shall rejoice in his works.

32 He looketh on the earth, and it trembleth: he toucheth the hills, and they smoke.

Having recited the awesome works of God, the author now steps back from creation and sings praises that are appropriate to what he has described. The mighty works of creation speak not only of the existence of a Creator but of His eternity as well: He "endures for ever." Furthermore, it is not only the playful otter that rejoices;

God Himself is glad to participate in the creative process. Even though the earth be destroyed, the glory of the "non-contingent" Creator will endure forever.

As proof of the eternal nature of God, verse 32 asserts His power over the finite world. This verse is no primitive attempt to say that every earthquake is the result of God's "looking" at the earth or every volcanic eruption the result of His "touch." It is sheer, worshipful poetry, meaning, again, that all creation is dependent upon, and subject to the will of, its Creator.

In passing we may note that the fact that *God* has the power to cause such catastrophes on earth does not mean that we who have been made stewards of it can also wreak havoc on creation. Instead, we are to be faithful to Father Adam's vocation of "tending the Garden."

B. Praising and meditating, 33-34

33 I will sing unto the LORD as long as I live: I will sing praise to my God while I have my being.

34 My meditation of him shall be sweet: I will be glad in the LORD.

When believers consider creation and the might of the Creator, what can they do but sing praise? God's being is eternal, and as long as the psalmist has his admittedly transient being he will spend it in praise, and in meditating on the Creator's goodness.

Meditation has received new emphasis in some circles in our day, es-pecially among religions based on eastern thought. Often the mind is fixed on a phrase or "mantra," or at times cleansed of all thought. In contrast, the Bible speaks of meditation mainly with God and His will as its object. Otherwise, the mind is open to influences other than godly forces.

The last phrase of verse 34 is a special invitation to those who are habitually unhappy. If God is glad about His creation, surely we who are a part of it can share His joy.

IV. Negative Note—35

35 Let the sinners be consumed out of the earth, and let the wicked be no more. Bless thou the LORD, O my soul. Praise ye the LORD.

Realistically, the psalmist knows that unbelievers will not share his joy and thanksgiving to God for the created order. Instead, the unbeliever is more likely to look at the creation from the viewpoint of its "fallen" condition, and send up complaints instead of praises. The psalmist's response does not pretend to follow a Christian ethic of a forgiving spirit, but pronounces a curse calling for such sinners to be removed from the creation they decline to appreciate. In contrast, the psalmist will "bless the Lord"; and the last phrase, translated "Praise ye the LORD," is literally *Hallelujah!*, "Praise to Yah!," (a shortened form of Yahweh).

Evangelistic Emphasis

Psalm 104, the lovely song in praise of the diversity and wonder of the world, affirms that God is Creator. In the beginning was God. By His Word were all things made. God saw everything that he had made, and it was very good.

That is good news for those who feel lost. For those who find no meaning in existence the psalm insists we are not here by accident. For those who lack a purpose for their lives, the psalm affirms that we are here by the plan and design of a loving God. For those who feel adrift in a vast sea without compass, rudder, or skipper, here is witness to a loving, caring, and providing God.

Science may help us explore various theories of how the world was made. The universe is vaster than that imagined by the psalmist. The awesomeness of creation is increased by the more we know about it and the awareness of how much more there is we do not know. More fundamental to the way we live is the question, Why? The psalmist is clear that the earth and the heavens beyond are no accident. They are no hoax by a cruel or indifferent deity. The world and all who dwell therein, people and animals of every kind, plants and trees, oceans and mountains are here because of a loving God.

The delightful children's hymn by C.F. Alexander puts it well: "All things bright and beautiful/All creatures great and small/All things wise and wonderful/The Lord God made them all.

ℰℭℛ

Memory Selection

O Lord, how manifold are thy works! In wisdom hast Thou made them all: the earth is full of thy riches.—*Psalm 104:24*

The psalmist exclaims with amazement at how many creatures the Lord in his wisdom has made. Wild animals, birds and storks, people, even the mysterious monster of the sea—the Lord has made them all. Streams and springs, plants and grass, trees and mountains, moon and sun—the Lord God made them all.

The world of nature in all its variety and complexity displays the wisdom of the Lord. The world of nature from this faith perspective is not to be exploited for our own selfish purposes, but every use is shaped by a reverence for the Creator. As the poet Jarfoslav Vajda puts it, "God of the sparrow/God of the whale/God of the swirling stars/How does the creature say Awe?/How does the creature say Praise?"

Weekday Problems

Jamie had grown up in a family that shared meals together. At every meal they paused to say grace. In the hectic rush of college, she ate her meals on the run. But now that she was married and had children of her own, she realized how much she missed that tradition. Saying grace at meals was not a practice to which her husband was accustomed. However, at her suggestion he was willing to give it a try. What they discovered was the simple practice at each family meal was an important reminder that all of life is a gift from God.

The psalmist reminds us of our daily dependence upon God: "They all look to you to give them their food in due season. When you open your hand, they are filled with good things. When you take away their breath, they die" (Ps. 104:27, 28, 29).

Jesus taught His disciples to pray, "Give us this day our daily bread." The words remind us that day-by-day, even moment-by-moment, we are dependent upon God for the gift of life. In daily life we are farther and farther removed from basic food production. Children think milk comes from cartons. The bounty in the supermarket belies the reality that the human family is never more than one harvest from famine. The Bible reminds us that God is our daily provider: "When you open your hands, they are filled with good things." Offering thanks to God at mealtime is an acknowledgment of our dependence and God's grace.

Ask the Animals

Two goats were wandering over a trash dump when one of them found part of a reel of movie film. It was able to loosen part of it from the reel, and to eat a few frames.

"How was it?" asked the other goat.

"Oh, not bad," said the first goat, "but I thought the book was better."

* * *

A man's car stalled on a country road, and a cow came up beside it and said, "The trouble is in the carburetor."

Astonished, the man ran down the road to a nearby farmhouse and told the man who answered the door, "That brown cow up the road told me what was wrong with my car!"

"I wouldn't pay her no attention," said the farmer. "She don't know much about cars."

* * *

Q: Which came first: the chicken or the egg?

A: The chicken, of course. God can't lay eggs.

This Lesson in Your Life

Rabbi Heschel taught that there are three ways humans can respond to creation. We may exploit it, we may enjoy it, or we may accept it with awe. The writer of Psalm 104 clearly accepts creation with awe.

Though we may know more about the universe than did the ancient poet, our increased knowledge only increases our sense of awe and wonder. Our planet earth is a small speck in the Milky Way, which is 100,000 light years in diameter. One light year is something a little less than 6 million miles. This vast Milky Way galaxy is but one of countless masses of stars and planets. This awareness of vastness and immensity of the universe only serves to increase our respect, devotion, and awe.

Rachael Carson reminds us that a child's world is fresh and new and beautiful, full of wonder and excitement. If she could bestow one gift on every child, she writes, it would be a sense of wonder so indestructible that it would last throughout life, as an unfailing antidote against the boredom and disenchantments of later years.

In Alice Walker's novel "The Color Purple," Shug shares her conception of God with Celie. The dialogue is reported by Celie in a letter to her sister Nettie. "God made it. Listen: God love everything you love—and a mess of stuff you don't. (God) just wanting to share a good thing."

Shug asserts that God is turned off, angered, "if you walk by the color purple in the field somewhere and don't notice it."

Celie concludes, "I been so busy. I never truly notice nothing God made. Not a blade of corn (how he do that?) Not the color purple (where it come from?) Not the wild flowers. Nothing."

Long before there was smog, acid rain, oil spills, toxic wastes, and global warming, the psalmist was an environmentalist. He knew about the inter-connectedness of all things. He saw the hand of a providing God in providing grass for cattle and plants for people, water for trees, which in turn provide shelter for birds. More and more we are led to realize that the family of God encompasses more than humankind. There is an intricate, complex, and marvelous chain of life, where each part of creation depends upon another, and eventually upon God.

Much of the modern concern for protecting the environment comes out of fear of making life difficult for generations to come. The psalmist's sense of stewardship begins with joining all creation in the praise of God.

STRAIGHT

1. In Psalm 104: 1-2, how is God clothed?
God is clothed with honor and majesty, and wrapped in light as with a garment.

2. According to verse 3, where is the royal residence set?
He lays the beams of His chambers on the waters.

3. According to verse 3 what serves as God's chariot?
He makes the clouds His chariot.

4. Who are God's messengers and ministers, according to verse 4?
He makes the angels His messengers and flaming fire His ministers.

5. What creatures are mentioned in Psalm 104: 10-23?
Wild fowls, and animals such as wild asses, birds, storks, cattle, mountain goats, coneys (badgers), lions, people.

6. What is "the leviathan" mentioned in verse 26?
It is an enormous sea monster.

7. In verse 31, what is the poet's wish-prayer?
He wishes that God's glory might endure forever and that the Lord might rejoice in His works.

8. What vow does the poet make in verse 33?
He promises to sing to the Lord as long as he lives.

9. What is the psalmist's wish-prayer in verse 34?
He prays that his meditation may be pleasing to the Lord.

10. In verse 35, what is the psalmist's prayer?
Let sinners be consumed from the earth and let the wicked be no more.

449

On an air flight from New Orleans to San Francisco, I was excited to hear our pilot describe the spectacular scenic wonders we would be flying over—Bryce Canyon, the Rocky Mountains, Yosemite National Park—a three-hour panoramic tour. We would be flying over mountains and plains, lakes and rivers, cultivated fields and vast wildernesses. We would be flying over some of the most diverse and beautiful terrain on the planet. Tourists would travel across the ocean to glimpse wonders we would see on that flight. Pioneers had spent months by covered wagons traversing the territory we would see in the next few hours.

I could hardly contain my excitement. You can imagine my shock and dismay when the flight attendant requested all passengers to lower the window shades so that some passengers could watch the movie, "Meat Axe Murder" or some such thriller. Imagine shutting out the great natural beauty of God's green earth to watch some gory murders on the screen. My first impulse was to dash about the cabin raising all the shades and pointing out to the bored and sleeping passengers the wonders they were missing. My wife and my seat belt restrained me from this preacher-like response. After all, I was on vacation.

I've wondered how often that pattern is repeated. We prefer to live in a world of our own created darkness, playing with our illusions and our fears. In our preoccupation with the petty or demonic, we shut out the light of the presence of God's love.

The writer of Psalm 104 helps to open our eyes to the beauty of God's creation. His words help us to see in it God's design, majesty, and providence. This sacred psalm reminds us that we live every moment in the presence of God. The light of God's presence can dispel our darkest fears if we but let that light shine in our hearts and minds. Then we can join the psalmist's prayer: "May the glory of the Lord endure forever. I will sing praise to my God while I have being."

GOD ENDUES HUMANS WITH GREAT HONOR...

The Crown of Creation

Psalm 8

O LORD our Lord, how excellent is thy name in all the earth! who hast set thy glory above the heavens.

2 Out of the mouth of babes and sucklings hast thou ordained strength because of thine enemies, that thou mightest still the enemy and the avenger.

3 When I consider thy heavens, the work of thy fingers, the moon and the stars, which thou hast ordained;

4 What is man, that thou art mindful of him? and the son of man, that thou visitest him?

5 For thou hast made him a little lower than the angels, and hast crowned him with glory and honour.

6 Thou madest him to have dominion over the works of thy hands; thou hast put all things under his feet:

7 All sheep and oxen, yea, and the beasts of the field;

8 The fowl of the air, and the fish of the sea, and whatsoever passeth through the paths of the seas.

9 O LORD our Lord, how excellent is thy name in all the earth!

July 14

Memory Selection
Psalm 8:4

Devotional Reading
Psalm 100

Background Scripture
Psalms 8; 100

The twin focus of this famous psalm is (1) the majesty of God and (2) the honor it is for persons to reflect something of this glory. Few of the songs in this ancient "Hymnbook of the Second Temple" can claim to exalt God to such heights in so few words. Ironically, however, since the psalmist also ties persons to this exalted God, insisting that they reflect at least something of His glory, the psalm requires also that we honor persons.

In contrast to "secular" humanism, here is a view of persons that respects them because they reflect God's glory, not because they are inherently good. It is humbling to note that despite the magnificent phrases that exalt God, more than half the psalm speak of this reflected glory of persons. Of course instead of inviting egotism, this royal positioning calls us to live up to the honor of being called the children of God.

ഇ)യ

Sometimes authors "add light" to the idea that Jesus is the *Son* of God by spelling it *Sun,* reminding us that Jesus is the Light. With a similar device, this lesson can be introduced with the idea that believers can be considered "moons of God"!

Remind group members of the reason we can see the moon as a silvery disk on a dark night. It can appear so bright that we even speak of the liquid that gets a hillbilly "lit," *moonshine*. Yet we know that the moon doesn't really shine at all. Unlike the sun, the moon is a dark rock. If it appears to be bright, it is only because of reflected light from the sun. In Psalm 8, King David affirms that people, lowly as we are, reflect the glory of God.

(An alternative way to begin the class is to play a tape or CD of Michael W. Smith's contemporary Christian song, "How Majestic Is Your Name," which is based on Psalm 8.)

Teaching Outline	Daily Bible Readings
I. The Majesty of God—1-2	**Mon.** God's Abundant Goodness Psalm 145:1-7
A. Name above names, 1	**Tue.** God's Works Praise Him Psalm 145:8-13
B. Strength to be weak, 2	
II. The Lowliness of Man—3-4	**Wed.** God Watches Over All Psalm 145:14-21
A. Compared with the heavens, 3	**Thu.** Let Everything Praise Him! Psalm 150
B. Insignificant creature, 4	
III. The Significance of Man—5-8	**Fri.** Praise God, All Creation! Psalm 148:1-6
A. A step below angels, 5	**Sat.** God's Wondrous Deeds Psalm 75
B. Master of beasts, 6-8	
IV. The First and Last Word—9	**Sun.** Worship God Who Made Us Psalm 100

Verse by Verse

I. The Majesty of God, 1-2
A. Name above names, 1

1 O LORD our Lord, how excellent is thy name in all the earth! who hast set thy glory above the heavens.

It is highly appropriate that several Christian hymns have been composed from this well-known Hebrew song. It begins, as all worship should, with exalting God, and ascribing glory to His name. Note that since the first "Lord" is spelled LORD, with caps and small caps standing for God's personal name, the psalm begins, "O Yahweh, our Lord, how excellent is thy name!"

For the ancient Hebrews, one's name stood for his character traits (hence "Jesus" means "Savior"). Eventually, as noted previously, the rabbis came to consider the name Yahweh to be too holy even to pronounce, so the Hebrew for "LORD" would be written in its place. Even today, many Jews and "Messianic Jews" will not write "Yahweh," and even spell "God" G-D, to avoid tempting anyone to speak the holy name that is above all names

God's glory is "*above* the heavens" because He in fact is creator of the heavens. The more common word for "glory" is not used here (as it is in verse 5, below), but one that has the connotation of "comeliness" or "beauty." The psalmist is saying that as glorious as the starlit heavens may be at night, as beautiful as billowing white clouds may be against a deep-blue sky, or as marvelous as the wonders of space may be, God's grandeur is greater.

B. Strength to be weak, 2

2 Out of the mouth of babes and sucklings hast thou ordained strength because of thine enemies, that thou mightest still the enemy and the avenger.

This verse is quoted by Jesus in Matthew 21:16, referring to little children in the Temple acknowledging His Messiahship, in contrast to "more mature" Pharisees who would not. God is so great that He doesn't have to be arrogant, but can condescend to allow children to confess His name, and even to be born as a baby, and slain on a cross.

It is more difficult, however, to determine what this line may have meant to its original hearers. We may get a clue by remembering that the warrior king, David, wrote the psalm. Perhaps we are to take "babes and sucklings" (NIV "children and infants") as referring to himself and his soldiers who were ordained with enough strength to defeat armies who oppose God, as David himself as a mere boy slew the giant Goliath.

II. The Lowliness of Man—3-4
A. Compared with the heavens, 3

3 When I consider thy heavens, the work of thy fingers, the moon and the stars, which thou hast ordained;

In the Old Testament, "heaven" (and especially "the heavens") usually refers to the atmosphere around the earth, rather than the eternal resting place of the saved. This is obvious here by the reference to the moon and the stars following the term. Even people in David's time, about 1,000 B.C., knew enough about the skies to be in awe. Today, with such knowledge expanded by telescopes and space travel, it is even more awesome to consider the infinity of space and the impressive and mysterious nature of the stars and planets that populate it. The more we know about the marvelous nature of the heavens, the greater the contrast with mere man.

B. Insignificant creature, 4

4 What is man, that thou art mindful of him? and the son of man, that thou visitest him?

It is tempting to make a philosophical question of this sentence, and to speculate on the make-up and nature of persons. Often, for example, Bible students will go from this question to Paul's description of man as "body, soul, and spirit" (1 Thess. 5:23). In context, however, the question is not asking about what man is composed of but how, creature that he is, he could possibly have been "visited" by God! No doubt the psalmist expects us to read the question as though it is, "What is *mere* man, that you exalt him so!

Although "the son of man" is used of the Messiah in several places in both the Old and New Testaments, here the phrase is probably only a repetition and expansion of the previous word "man," an example of the common "parallelism" of Hebrew poetry. Although, the letter to the Hebrews will quote the phrase in reference to Christ (Heb. 2:8), it is in the context of exalting Christ, not emphasizing the insignificance of (mere) man. The following verses will show why the psalmist can speak of insignificant man being touched with grandeur.

III. The Significance of Man—5-8
A. A step below angels, 5

5 For thou hast made him a little lower than the angels, and hast crowned him with glory and honour.

As insignificant as man is, he occupies a high place in the order of creation, one that is only a step below the angels. The word for angels, *elohim,* is also often translated "God," but the King James Version's "angels," which follows the earliest

Greek translation, agrees with Hebrews 2:8. The point is the psalmist's amazement upon reflecting that man is only *third* in the created order, only below God and the angels.

There are many ways in which this position appears exalted above the beasts, as described below. As far as we know, animals do not dream of "being saved" or existing in an afterlife, and presumably therefore lack a soul, with which persons are endowed. Beasts do not invent stories for entertainment; and despite the amazing ability of a few apes who have been taught sign language, their communication skills are far below that of persons. The psalmist is not boasting, but exclaiming about and exulting in the privilege of being human.

B. Master of beasts, 6-8

6 Thou madest him to have dominion over the works of thy hands; thou hast put all things under his feet:

7 All sheep and oxen, yea, and the beasts of the field;

8 The fowl of the air, and the fish of the sea, and whatsoever passeth through the paths of the seas.

Elsewhere, Bible writers can wax eloquent about the marvelous traits of animals. To humble Job, God points out that he cannot give the peacock its gorgeous feathers (Job 39:13) or frighten an enemy by pawing the ground like a magnificent war-horse (39:19-25). Here, however, King David returns to the created order of Genesis 1:28, when man was placed in charge of the earth and the creatures upon it. As magnificent as some animals are, persons have been made stewards over them.

The psalmist is obviously using this fact to describe the "humble exaltation" of persons. Although they are "a little lower than the angels," they are a little higher than beasts. They were given the authority to "subdue" the earth, also from Genesis 1:28. In earlier times, this has been taken as an excuse to *exploit* the earth, including its wildlife. More recently we have been made aware that man's position over the earth and animals includes the command to *replenish* it, and to be more concerned for the welfare of that over which we have been placed.

IV. The First and Last Word—9

9 O LORD our Lord, how excellent is thy name in all the earth!

Why does the psalmist close with the identical words with which he opened the psalm? Probably because, as poetry, or song lyrics, it is subject to such stylistic devices as repetition; and he is inspired to "close the circle" of his poetic utterance by both beginning and ending it with an outburst of praise to God. He began by praising God, continued by showing that one reason we praise Him is the exalted place He has given to persons, and now can close with the same applause because he has proved his case.

455

Evangelistic Emphasis

William Willimon tells of the plans made by a little boy named Leroy and his mother for his fifth birthday party. He wanted all his young guests to be treated as royalty. Everyone was to be a king or queen. So he and his mother set to work fashioning crowns (cardboard covered with aluminum foil), capes (purple crepe paper), and scepters (broom sticks painted gold.) They had a royal good time, parading up and down the street, and feasting on ice cream and cake.

That night when his mother was tucking him into bed, she asked Leroy what he had wished for when he blew the candles out. "Oh, I wished that everyone could be a king or queen, not just on my birthday but everyday."

Something like that has happened in Jesus Christ. In Him we are a royal priesthood. A similar status is spoken of in Psalm 8. "What are human beings that you are mindful of them? Yet you have crowned them with glory and honor." What good news we have to share with people who feel they are nobodies, without worth, no good and forgotten. They have been made a little lower than God, crowned with glory and honor. They are God's regents on earth, called to be a part of God's royal priesthood, God's own people.

☙❦

What is man, that thou art mindful of him? And the son of man, that thou visitest him?—*Psalm 8:4*

As our knowledge of the universe expands, the question, "What is man?" becomes more poignant. Our solar system is only a part of a cosmic island with a diameter of 100,000 light years. Within this one galaxy there are 100,000 million stars of the same kind as our sun. The Milky Way is only one galaxy amid hundreds of millions of similar islands. What is man?

An ancient legend of creation describes the day when all the little seeds of life came before God. He let each of them choose what they wanted to be. Some saw how much water there was, and they wanted fins to swim in it. So God made the fish. Others thought there was more air than water and asked for wings to fly in it. So God made the birds. One quiet little seed was left. "I don't want wings or fins he said. Just let me be made in Your image. I'll make my own wings and boats." God was well pleased, and made a man.

Weekday Problems

We live up or down to the expectations laid on us. Comedian Dick Gregory shares his painful memory of a teacher who shamed him often. He sat in the back of the classroom in a seat with a chalk circle drawn around it. It was known as the idiot's seat. The teacher thought he was stupid. She viewed him as a troublemaker.

One day the teacher asked how much each child's father could give to the community chest. Dick had money in his pocket from shining shoes and selling papers. He decided that he was going to top whatever Helen Tucker pledged for her daddy. The teacher called each name alphabetically. "Helen Tucker?"

"My daddy said he would give $2.50."

Dick knew he could top that; but the teacher never called his name. He stood up and raised his hand. "You forgot me. My daddy said he'd give $15!"

The teacher replied, "We're collecting this money for you and your kind, Richard Gregory. Furthermore, we know you don't have a daddy. Sit down Richard." Then she added, "Where are you going, Richard?"; for he walked out of school that day, and he didn't go back very often.

The psalmist helps us see with better vision, persons made a little less than God, crowned with glory and honor.

Persons, Lowly and Grand

The higher a man is in grace, the lower will he be in his own esteem.—*Charles Spurgeon*

* * *

Humility must be carefully distinguished from a groveling spirit. Though we may be servants of all, we should be servile to none.—*E. H. Chapin, adapted*

* * *

To say that a man is a person . . . is to say that he is a beggar who participates in absolute being, mortal flesh whose value is eternal and a bit of straw into which heaven enters.—*Jacques Maritain*

* * *

Surely, if all the world was made for man, then man was made for more than the world.—*Pierre Duplessis*

* * *

Bounded in his nature, infinite in his desires, man is a fallen god who has a recollection of heaven.—*Alphonse de Lamartine*

This Lesson Your Life

Many a person has felt a kinship with the writer of Psalm 8. Overwhelmed by the majesty of the starry heaven on a clear night, he wonders with the psalmist, "What is man?" It is easy to feel lost in the vastness of space. Yet it is this human being who measures the vastness of the universe. While dwarfed by the immensity and power of stars, yet it is still the human being that calibrates their weight and distances. J. Wallace Hamilton observes: "For all the wonder of the glittering worlds that swirl around him, the greatest wonder is still at the small end of the microscope. One bit of mind stuff, one touch of gray matter with power to think outweighs all the stars that burn and blaze through space."

"You have made them a little lower than God, and crowned them with glory and honor" (Ps. 8:5).

"What are human beings that you are mindful of them, mortals that you care for them? You have given them dominion over the works of your hands" (Ps. 8:4, 6). In the psalmist's song he spells out a role for mortals in God's wondrous creation. Man is given dominion over all that God has made.

"Dominion" has too often been misunderstood as a license to exploit, to waste, and to ravage. James Mays describes this misunderstanding: "Dominion has become domination; rule has become ruin. Subordination in the divine purpose has become subjection to human sinfulness." In the context of this psalm, "dominion" is the role of a steward to manage the estate on behalf of another. It is the role of Adam in Eden, placed there to tend the garden, to till the ground.

The psalm begins and ends with the affirmation of God's sovereignty: "O Lord, our Sovereign, how majestic is your name in all the earth" (vss. 1, 9). The responsibility of having "dominion over the works of God's hands" is framed with praising the majestic rule of God. Though crowned with glory and honor, as God's anointed ones, people are only standing in for God, regents ruling in God's name. While given great responsibility, there is a higher authority to which the human race is accountable. Serving a God of righteousness and justice, there are standards of fairness for all, mercy for the poor and needy, and compassion for the oppressed and dispossessed of the earth. Because, in the words of Genesis 1:31, Every part of creation is to be cherished.

1. In Psalm 8, what question is prompted by the poet's viewing of the heavens?
What is man that Thou art mindful of him?

2. What is the status of man in this psalm?
He is made a little lower than God, and crowned with glory and honor.

3. What is the responsibility of man?
He is given dominion over the works of God's hands.

4. Over what does man have dominion, according to Ps. 8:7-8?
Over all sheep and oxen, beasts of the field, birds of the air, and fish of the sea.

5. What does the "name" of God represent?
The "name" of God represents God's nature, character, and essence.

6. In Psalm 100, who is summoned to worship the Lord?
All the earth is called to worship (vs. 1).

7. What actions are appropriate in coming into the presence of the Lord, according to Psalm 100?
Shouting for joy, worshiping with gladness, and joyous singing.

8. What knowledge is necessary for worship in Psalm 100?
That the Lord is God, that it is He that hath made us, and we are his.

9. In Psalm 100:4, how is God's house to be approached?
We are to enter His gates with thanksgiving and His courts with praise.

10. What reasons are for thanksgiving called for in Psalm 100:5?
The Lord is good: his steadfast love endures forever, and his faithfulness to all generations.

What is man? The materialist has one answer. We are just of particle of matter, for a brief time a human body, and then returned to dust. Peter Marshal reminds us that in a good museum one can see laid out in saucers the constituent elements of the human body. We will find a little phosphorus, silicon, iron, carbon, lime, water, etc. There is enough iron to make a half dozen 10-penny nails. There is enough lime to whitewash a chicken coup. There is enough phosphorus to tip the heads of a thousand matches. There, they will tell you, is man. The creature called man is a physical body made up of identifiable chemicals.

The psalmist says there is more to man than the elements that compose his body. That describes the house but not the tenant. This creature, made by God from the dust of the ground, has the breath of God breathed into him. He is capable of knowing, serving, and praising God. He is a little less than God.

What is man? In a mass society many feel they have been reduced to a number. All Americans have a social security number, now issued soon after birth. From ordering prescription drugs to inquiring about mortgage payments, the automated operator has you enter your social security number. The state issues you a driver's license number, a necessary identification for cashing checks. You have a number at your bank, another number for each charge card, with an expiration date. The friendly clerk at the video store never asks for your name, only the last four digits of your telephone number. For the pollsters we're part of a percentage, for market researchers a unit, sometimes for production managers a cog in a process. Against the dehumanizing effects of computers, the efficiency of going by numbers, the intimidation of statisticians who count you every way but special, the psalmist offers a different view. "You are crowned with glory and honor."

What is man? The fatalist would say he is no more than a puppet manipulated by powers beyond his control. Like a clock he has been wound up to function in a predetermined way. His end is set from the beginning. He is the victim of circumstance. For every action there are forces outside himself that affect his behavior.

A little boy had mislearned the Lord's Prayer. Listening to him say his prayers at night his mother was surprised to hear his earnest prayer: "Our Father, who art in heaven, how do you know my name?" It is that mystery which is confessed by the psalmist.

460

Joy in Forgiveness

Psalm 32

Blessed is he whose transgression is forgiven, whose sin is covered.

2 Blessed is the man unto whom the LORD imputeth not iniquity, and in whose spirit there is no guile.

3 When I kept silence, my bones waxed old through my roaring all the day long.

4 For day and night thy hand was heavy upon me: my moisture is turned into the drought of summer. Selah.

5 I acknowledged my sin unto thee, and mine iniquity have I not hid. I said, I will confess my transgressions unto the LORD; and thou forgavest the iniquity of my sin. Selah.

6 For this shall every one that is godly pray unto thee in a time when thou mayest be found: surely in the floods of great waters they shall not come nigh unto him.

7 Thou art my hiding place; thou shalt preserve me from trouble; thou shalt compass me about with songs of deliverance. Selah.

8 I will instruct thee and teach thee in the way which thou shalt go: I will guide thee with mine eye.

9 Be ye not as the horse, or as the mule, which have no understanding: whose mouth must be held in with bit and bridle, lest they come near unto thee.

10 Many sorrows shall be to the wicked: but he that trusteth in the LORD, mercy shall compass him about.

11 Be glad in the LORD, and rejoice, ye righteous: and shout for joy, all ye that are upright in heart.

July 21

Memory Selection
Psalm 32:1

Devotional Reading
Psalm 51:1-12

Background Scripture
Psalm 32; 51

Psalm 32 is one of seven that have traditionally been called "penitential psalms" (Pss. 6, 32, 38, 51, 102, 130, and 143). Their theme is one of the most basic religious issues: what to do when we realize that we have offended the deity, and taking whatever steps are necessary to put things right.

Many believers will identify with the feelings expressed by the psalmist, some of which have a decidedly modern ring. He feels estranged from God and shut up in the prison of self-condemnation, until he faces up to and acknowledges his sin. Then he experiences the joy of release and comfort, and is ready to receive instruction from the God he has offended.

Each stage is crucial. Failing to confess sin obviously blocks an honest relationship with God. Failing to accept and rejoice in His forgiveness reflects poorly both on our faith and on the reality of His grace.

ೞೞ

Your group can more readily identify with this lesson if it is introduced by recounting the experience of King David, traditionally considered to be the author of Psalm 32, and his sin with Bathsheba.

Recall the anguish David felt when punished for his sin by the death of his and Bathsheba's son (2 Sam. 12:15-17).

Note the courage of his confession, recounted in Psalm 51:3-4. Then emphasize the dramatic reversal of his feelings, from devastation to "moving on," after accepting God's discipline and forgiveness (2 Sam. 12:19-20).

People whose relationship to God is damaged by specific sin can be restored only by going through the stages described of David, and in this psalm: confession, repentance, and, a step that can be as difficult as the first two, internalizing God's gracious forgiveness and living again in the joy of His salvation.

Teaching Outline	Daily Bible Readings
I. Blessing of Forgiveness—1-2	**Mon.** Sins,Ours and Our Fathers Psalm 106:1-12
II. Anguish of Denial—3-4	**Tue.** The Lord Heals and Forgives Psalm 103:1-14
III. Relief of Confession—5-7	**Wed.** Restore Us, O God Psalm 85
A. Forgiveness, 5	**Thu.** In God Is Forgiveness Psalm 130
B. Protection, 6-7	**Fri.** Blot Out My Transgressions Psalm 51:1-9
IV. Living in Forgiveness—8-11	**Sat.** New and Right Spirit Within Psalm 51:10-19
A. Willing obedience, 8-9	**Sun.** Happy Are the Forgiven Psalm 32
B. Rejoicing in grace, 10-11	

Verse by Verse

I. Blessing of Forgiveness—1-2
1 Blessed is he whose transgression is forgiven, whose sin is covered.

2 Blessed is the man unto whom the LORD imputeth not iniquity, and in whose spirit there is no guile.

Anyone who has known the emotional suffering of being "at outs" with God knows something of the relief implied in the word "blessing" here. It is a "beatitude" (as in the "Blessed are . . ." phrases of the Sermon on the Mount) to move from having offended the God who loves us to experiencing His grace again in the forgiveness of sin. Although many modern translations use the word "happy," the religious usage of "blessed" through the years seems to more appropriately endow the word with the profound joy of perceiving that the God who had gazed sadly at our sin has now "covered" or hidden it, banishing it from the record.

In verse 2, the word "impute" (NIV "count against") recalls the emphasis of the apostle Paul in Romans 4:6-8, where he cites this very psalm to describe God's grace. The term was used in banking and accounting circles, when a debt that was legally "on the books" was set aside, just as when a debt is "forgiven" today. The emphasis is therefore not on the debtor hav-

ing paid off what he owed, but on the one to whom the debt was owed graciously canceling the debt as though it were paid in full.

II. Anguish of Denial—3-4
3 When I kept silence, my bones waxed old through my roaring all the day long.

4 For day and night thy hand was heavy upon me: my moisture is turned into the drought of summer. Selah.

The experience of inwardly "groaning" (NIV) because of internalized guilt has a surprisingly modern ring. Every counselor and therapist, not to mention sinners themselves, knows the power of guilt not only to eat away at the soul but at the body as well. The connection between body and soul or spirit is today a medically-documented fact, both negatively and positively.

Although it is not clear that this refers specifically to David's having "kept silence" about his sin with Bathsheba, we can well imagine his being reluctant to admit his having committed adultery and murder (by leaving her husband Uriah exposed on the front line of battle). Unconfessed sin is like a cancer, sapping our strength ("moisture") like a hot summer day.

As mentioned earlier, although the precise meaning of the term "Selah," which appears in so many psalms, is unknown, many authorities believe it to have been a musical notation.

III. Relief of Confession—5-7
A. Forgiveness, 5

5 I acknowledged my sin unto thee, and mine iniquity have I not hid. I said, I will confess my transgressions unto the LORD; and thou forgavest the iniquity of my sin. Selah.

It is noteworthy that the only thing mentioned that David "did" about his sin is that he acknowledged or confessed it. Although this does not mean that he did not also offer the proper sacrifice commanded under the Old Covenant, it does emphasize that it is God who forgives, not man who earns forgiveness by some act of atonement.

It is intriguing to think of David, a forerunner and sometimes a "type" or foreshadowing of the Messiah, benefitting from the forgiveness of the Cross on which Messiah's blood would be shed. Somehow the supreme sacrifice of Jesus is involved even here, a thousand years before it occurred, since His blood flowed backward as well as forward (see Rom. 3:25).

B. Protection, 6-7

6 For this shall every one that is godly pray unto thee in a time when thou mayest be found: **surely in the floods of great waters they shall not come nigh unto him.**

7 Thou art my hiding place; thou shalt preserve me from trouble; thou shalt compass me about with songs of deliverance. Selah.

The "this" for which the godly pray apparently refers to the relief that comes from forgiveness referred to in verse 5. The "godly" in verse 6 are the sinners of verse 5, reminding us that no saint is sinless (see Rom. 3:23). The crucial difference between the godly and the ungodly is that the godly seek the God who has turned His face from them in their sin while He can be found. Of course the possibility of not finding Him is not that God is not always ready to forgive, but that the sinner is capable of denying his sin so long that He is unable to repent and thus seek the God he has offended (see Heb. 6:4-6).

For sinners who do seek forgiveness, verse 7 praises God for becoming a haven and a protector. From what? Although the psalms are filled with appeals to God to save the righteous from their enemies, the context suggests that David is here praising God for protecting him from the ravages of unconfessed and therefore unforgiven sin. Deliverance from guilt is every bit as glorious as salvation from any external enemy.

IV. Living in Forgiveness—8-11
A. Willing obedience, 8-9

8 I will instruct thee and teach thee in the way which thou shalt go: I will guide thee with mine eye.

9 Be ye not as the horse, or as

the mule, which have no understanding: whose mouth must be held in with bit and bridle, lest they come near unto thee.

The speaker shifts here from David to God Himself. Because David the sinner has acknowledged and repented of his sin, God the forgiver condescends to gently guide the forgiven sinner into the paths of righteousness. "Instruct" must therefore refer to more than merely communicating knowledge. The language implies that as God receives a sinner back into His fold, He helps him understand the insidious way sin interfered with his relationship to God, thus helping prevent further missteps.

Verse 9 reminds us that the returning sinner must be more willing than a stubborn horse or mule if this teaching and guiding process is to be effective. The KJV imagery here is that a sinner must not be like a contrary animal that must be restrained by bit and bridle to keep it from biting or butting its handler. The NIV picture is the opposite, saying that a stubborn horse or mule "will not come to you" without a tug on bit and bridle. The point is the same, of course: God's protection of a returning sinner against falling into further sin depends on the forgiven one's willingness to be guided.

B. Rejoicing in grace, 10-11

10 Many sorrows shall be to the wicked: but he that trusteth in the LORD, mercy shall compass him about.

11 Be glad in the LORD, and rejoice, ye righteous: and shout for joy, all ye that are upright in heart.

In closing the psalm, the author exults in the state of grace to which God has returned him. He has stood on the brink of living out of grace, then pulled away from the temptation by confession and repentance. Now he finds joy in having chosen to acknowledge his sin and live in God's mercy.

The direct command of verse 11 reminds us that living in the joy of spiritual health after the Great Physician has pronounced us healed and forgiven is as important as acknowledging our sin in the first place. Unfortunately, many believers think so ill of themselves for having sinned that they cannot bring themselves to rejoice in forgiveness. For them, grace is too good to be true. Joy is a command here because continuing to live in sorrow is more than a "low self-image"; it betrays mistrust in the reality of God's grace.

Gladness in being received again by a forgiving father balances the anguish expressed in verses 3-4. As denial made the sinner's "bones wax old," restoration to a state of grace should manifest in the healing of the whole person. The specific mechanism between body and soul here may be obscure, but it is no doubt connected to the fact that the God against whom we sin, and to whom we confess, is also the God who created us, body and soul.

Evangelistic Emphasis

Dr. A. J. Cronin tells the story of a young nurse placed in charge of a little boy brought to a hospital. The boy was desperately ill; his throat was choked with membrane. A tube was inserted to help him breathe. The young nursed dozed off. When she roused up she realized that the tube was blocked. She panicked. Hysterically she called the doctor; but when he arrived the child was dead.

The doctor was furious over such negligence. In anger he wrote a report to the health board demanding the immediate expulsion of the young nurse. He called her into his office read her his report. She stood there in pitiful silence, this thin, gawky Welsh girl, half fainting with pain and remorse. "Well, have you nothing to say for yourself?" The frightened girl stammered a plea, "Give me . . . give me another chance." He didn't give her plea a second thought as he sealed his report. That night he couldn't sleep. A strange echo of words kept whispering, "Forgive." The next morning he tore up his report. This slim, nervous girl became one of the honored nurses in England.

The psalmist found that through penitence and confession, there is pardon and forgiveness. That is the good news shouted by the Bible. There is forgiveness with God. There is a chance to begin again. We can be changed. God creates a new and right spirit within.

૭૦൬

Memory Selection

Blessed is he whose transgression is forgiven, whose sin is covered.—*Psalm 32:1*

Blessedness or happiness for the psalmist contrasts with what society today holds up as the ideal of happiness: wealth, security, health, success, reputation, cruises, condos, boats, and such. True blessedness comes not in what we possess, or even what others think of us, but from being right with God. Righteousness is not being blameless before the law. Righteousness comes in our repentance and God's forgiveness. Our sin is "covered over," blotted out.

This verse was a favorite of St. Augustine. He had it written on the wall opposite his bed during his last illness. It is quoted by Paul in his letter to the Romans (Rom. 4:7). The message is restated in 1 John 1:8-9: "If we say we have no sin we deceive ourselves, and the truth is not in us. If we confess our sins, he who is faithful and just will forgive our sins and cleanse us from all unrighteousness."

Weekday Problems

We gathered early that morning for study, prayer, and sharing. The morning was beautiful. The sun was reddening the eastern sky. The birds were joined in a morning chorus. We left the doors and windows open to let fresh air fill the room. We had started to share our experiences in trying some disciplines of the spiritual life, particularly the discipline of confession. Just then the garbage truck arrived. It sounded like it was in the next room. The raucous banging and clanging, grinding and crushing drowned out the voices of my friends sharing the ups and downs of their faih journey. I couldn't hear the others.

The noisy garbage truck shattered my mood of quietness and peace. Why did it have to come at precisely this hour? Then it occurred to me that confession was rather like putting out the garbage. With an honest looking at ourselves, we acknowledge the resentments, the angers, the wrong choices, the pride, the jealousy, and the fears. Through God's forgiveness we let them be carried away. The outside noise became not so much a distraction as another interpretation of the important practice of confession. It seemed a comment on David's prayer of penitence: "Wash me and I shall be whiter than snow. Create in me a clean heart, O God and put a new and right spirit within me" (Ps. 51:7, 10).

Pun Fun

Q: Why did the crow sit on the telephone line?
A: Because he was making a long-distance caw.

* * *

Mr. and Mrs. Smith were touring Russia during the Cold War. Their guide was a Communist named Rudolph, with whom Mr. Smith argued constantly. As the Americans were at the airport planning to leave, Mr. Smith said, "Look. It's snowing out."
"No sir," the guide insisted, "it's raining."
"I know snow when I see it," Smith retorted.
"Now now," his wife said. "Rudolph the Red knows rain, dear."

* * *

A housewife in Tibet smelled something burning in the kitchen. She rushed in, saw smoke pouring from the oven, and exclaimed, "Oh, my baking yak!"

* * *

Once there was an Indian named Shortcake. When he died, his squaw bury Shortcake.

This Lesson in Your Life

Psalm 32 uses three ways of speaking of wrongdoing. "Transgression" comes from a word suggesting rebellion, defiance, or disobedience. Adam's defying the Lord's prohibition against eating the fruit of the special tree was transgression. "Sin" comes from a root word meaning missing the mark. An archer aims for the bull's eye on the target, but misses. A human being is meant to trust, love, and serve God. When his or her life is wasted in pursuit of trivialities that astound the angels, he or she misses the mark of what was intended. That is sin. "Iniquity" or "guilt" suggests the destructive and enduring effects of disobedience. The whole person is sick. What is needed is not a treatment of the symptoms but a cure for the disease. The psalmist's life is characterized by transgression, sin and iniquity/guilt.

The psalmist points to the crucial role of acknowledging sin. When he did not confess his sin, his body wasted away. He tried to hold it all in while keeping up outward pretenses. He deceived others and himself. By his denial of a problem, deep disorientation festered inside.

Everything depends on acknowledging one's sin. There is no healing until he makes known who he really is. He must quit playing games with God. He can't conceal his iniquity. But when he confesses his sin, he finds forgiveness, healing, health, and wholeness. Walter Brueggemann points out that long before Freud, this psalmist understood the power of speech, the need for spoken release and admission, the liberation that comes when one speaks to the One who listens and who can respond.

Several years ago Karl Menninger pointed out that when moderns discarded the concept of sin they did away with any sense of personal responsibility. All the evil doing in which we become involved to any degree tends to evoke guilt feelings and depression. They may be reacted to and covered up by all kinds of escapism or rationalization. Menninger recognized what Psalm 32 recognizes: there are devastating consequences—physical, emotional, and spiritual—when we fail to acknowledge our sinfulness.

In the concluding verse of the psalm there is a joyful picture of those who trust in the Lord, the righteous, the upright in heart, glad in the Lord and rejoicing. It is not that they are without transgression, sin, or guilt. But in acknowledgment and confession they have found forgiveness. They are right with God. Happy are those whose transgression is forgiven and whose sin is covered.

1. According to the superscription preceding Psalm 51, what was the occasion of its writing?

The psalm was written by David when the prophet Nathan confronted him, after David had sinned with Bathsheba.

2. In verses 10-12, for what does David pray?

He prays for a clean heart, a right spirit, God's presence, the Holy Spirit, and a willing spirit.

3. Against whom had David sinned (vs. 4)?

David declares to God, "Against you and you alone have I sinned."

4. What promise does David make in verses 13-14?

He promises to teach transgressors God's ways and to sing of God's deliverance.

5. According to verse 17, what sacrifices are acceptable to God?

The sacrifice acceptable to God is a broken spirit, a broken and contrite heart God will not despise.

6. According to Psalm 31:1-2, who are the blessed or happy ones?

Those whose transgression is forgiven, whose sin is covered, those to whom the Lord imputes no iniquity, who are without deceit.

7. What happened when the psalmist did not confess his sin (Ps. 32:3)?

When he kept silence, his body wasted away.

8. What happened when the psalmist acknowledged his sin to God? (Ps. 32:5).

God forgave him.

9. How is God described in Psalm 32:7?

God is a hiding place.

10. What contrast is drawn between the wicked and those who trust in the Lord (Ps. 32:10)?

Many are the torments of the wicked, but steadfast love surrounds those who trust in the Lord.

When I was in college I went to Europe on a Norwegian steamer. We pretty much had free run of the boat, except that on certain doors there were posted warnings: No Trespassing! We were not invited on the captain's deck, lest we tell him how to set the ship's course. We were not allowed in the crew's quarters, lest we infringe upon their privacy. We were not permitted in the engine room, lest we injure ourselves. To trespass was to be where we did not belong.

Sometimes, in life, we invade the Captain's deck, or try to take over, to be "like God." We would rather be master than servant. God, however, is our true Master. When we put ourselves in that position, we are where we do not belong.

Sometimes we trespass against our neighbor. To trespass is to rob persons of their dignity, to demean them. It is to use people for our own advancement, treating persons as things. It is to support rules and traditions which deny to others a fair chance at jobs or schools because of race, gender, or sexual orientation.

Sometimes we trespass against ourselves. William Barclay tells of Charles Lamb's description of the career of Samuel LeGrice. Lamb said there were three stages—a time when people said, "He will do something," a time when people said, "He could do something, if he would," and finally a time when people said, "He might have done something, if he had liked." He missed the mark. He spent his life where he had no business being.

So Jesus teaches us to pray, "Forgive us our trespasses." The psalmist reminds us of the crucial importance of acknowledging our sin to God if we find forgiveness and cleansing. Thomas Langford insists that penance is being honest; it involves looking at ourselves straightforwardly. A lady engaged a professional photographer to take her picture. Unhappy with the result, she complained the portrait did not do her justice. The photographer replied that what she needed was not justice but mercy. So do we all.

Kierkegaard insisted that no one who is aware of God's presence can regard himself in a strong position for making demands. If we shout "I demand justice!" a voice from heaven will reply, like an echo, "I demand justice!" Who is bold enough to think he can pass that test! But if we fall to our knees and cry out, "Grace!" the answer comes back, "Grace!"

Paul proclaims, "Since all have sinned and fall short of the glory of God; they are now justified by his grace as a gift, through the redemption that is in Christ Jesus, whom God put forward as a sacrifice of atonement by his blood effective through faith" (Rom. 3:23-25).

Let All the Peoples Praise God

Psalms 67:1-5; 96:1-9

God be merciful unto us, and bless us; and cause his face to shine upon us; Selah.

2 That thy way may be known upon earth, thy saving health among all nations.

3 Let the people praise thee, O God; let all the people praise thee.

4 O let the nations be glad and sing for joy: for thou shalt judge the people righteously, and govern the nations upon earth. Selah.

5 Let the people praise thee, O God; let all the people praise thee.

Psalm 96

1 O sing unto the LORD a new song: sing unto the LORD, all the earth.

2 Sing unto the LORD, bless his name; shew forth his salvation from day to day.

3 Declare his glory among the heathen, his wonders among all people.

4 For the LORD is great, and greatly to be praised: he is to be feared above all gods.

5 For all the gods of the nations are idols: but the LORD made the heavens.

6 Honour and majesty are before him: strength and beauty are in his sanctuary.

7 Give unto the LORD, O ye kindreds of the people, give unto the LORD glory and strength.

8 Give unto the LORD the glory due unto his name: bring an offering, and come into his courts.

9 O worship the LORD in the beauty of holiness: fear before him, all the earth.

July 28

Memory Selection
Psalm 67:3

Devotional Reading
Psalm 97:6-12

Background Scripture
Psalms 67; 96

Adopting the theme of the two psalms in today's lesson would cure two common ills in Christian worship: *boredom* and *self-centeredness.*

Many people under age 40 who have dropped out of church indicate that the services have ceased to minister to their needs, answer their questions, or provide an outlet for expressing religious feelings. In short, the services, for them, are boring. When such comments are brought to some church leaders, they respond that changing the service would push many worshipers beyond their "comfort zone," and disturb long-standing traditions. In such a situation, both sides often center not on what pleases God or wins souls, but on what is self-satisfying.

Psalms 67 and 96 portray worship as lively and exuberant, anything but boring. The focus is on pleasing God, not the self, and on testifying to unbelievers so powerfully that they too are led to confess the glory of God.

ഓരു

This session can be introduced by reading or summarizing the prophet Isaiah's humorous satire on idols, in Isaiah 44:9-17. Isaiah seems exasperated by the folly of an artisan smelting metal and hammering it into the shape of an idol, or carving one out of wood, then bowing down before it. For the prophet, nothing is more ludicrous than a craftsman fashioning a mere object, then worshiping what he created as though it were alive.

Today's lesson grows out of the implications of Isaiah's satire. Both Isaiah and the psalmist know that, unlike idols, the true God is *alive.* This means that His worship should be *lively,* filled with joy and exuberance. This kind of worship not only offers appropriate praise to God; it has the power to attract the idol-worshiper described by Isaiah. Spirit-filled worship has an evangelistic edge.

Teaching Outline	Daily Bible Readings

I. Prayer for Blessing—Ps. 67:1-2
II. Praise from the Nations—3-5
III. Proclaim God's Glory—96:1-3
  A. Sing a new song!, 1-2
  B. Speak of His wonders, 3
IV. Proclaim His Power—4-6
  A. The true God vs. idols, 4-5
  B. Worship His majesty, 6
V. Publish His Beauty—7-9
	Mon. Ruler Over All the Earth
	Psalm 47
	Tue. Praise God, Earth's Judge
	Psalm 98
	Wed. Sing Praises to God
	Psalm 68:1-6
	Thu. All Peoples Praise!
	Psalm 148:7-14
	Fri. Declare God's Glory!
	Psalm 96:1-6
	Sat. Let All Rejoice!
	Psalm 96:7-13
	Sun. Let the Peoples Praise!
	Psalm 67:1-7

Verse by Verse

I. Prayer for Blessing—Ps. 67:1-2

1 God be merciful unto us, and bless us; and cause his face to shine upon us; Selah.

2 That thy way may be known upon earth, thy saving health among all nations.

The prefix to this psalm in most Bibles is "To the chief musician on Neginoth. A Psalm of David." *Neginoth* (plural of *neginah*, in the heading of Ps. 61) are either stringed instruments such as the lyre, or music composed for them. This and other psalms with the prefix are therefore compositions made in response to such irrepressible urges as Isaiah's, who said, "We will sing my songs to the stringed instruments all the days of our life" (Isa. 38:20).

Note that one expectation the psalmist has for asking God's blessing is that His "saving health" (NIV "salvation") might be made known "among all nations." Although the Israelites' worship was directed to God, not to Gentile nations, the psalmist was aware that evangelism occurs indirectly every time believers gather for worship. The very act of assembly and praise is a testimonial to the true God.

II. Praise from the Nations—3-5

3 Let the people praise thee, O God; let all the people praise thee.

4 O let the nations be glad and sing for joy: for thou shalt judge the people righteously, and govern the nations upon earth. Selah.

5 Let the people praise thee, O God; let all the people praise thee.

Next, the psalmist anticipates one outcome of true worship: that it will be an infectious influence among the nations to whom it is a witness, and that Gentiles will join the chorus of praise. Now we note that worship and praise have an *ethical* aspect as well as being evangelistic. Attracted to the worship of Yahweh, the Gentiles ask what kind of God He is. The psalmist anticipates that, discovering that He is a God who judges righteously, the worshipers will also want to be just and righteous. Many of the gods of the Gentiles were notoriously capricious and unjust; and it is a universal rule that worshipers tend to become like the God they worship.

III. Proclaim God's Glory—96:1-3
A. Sing a new song!, 1-2

473

1 O sing unto the Lord a new song: sing unto the Lord, all the earth.

2 Sing unto the Lord, bless his name; shew forth his salvation from day to day.

The two parallel phrases in verse 1 suggest that it may have been composed not only as a "call to worship" but to be sung in worship. It invites a singer or chorus to chant or sing the first line, "O sing unto the Lord a new song," and another singer or group to respond with, "Shew forth his salvation from day to day." A "new song" is not necessarily one that has never been sung before but a new and fresh outburst of song.

Singing was an important part of Jewish worship, especially under the leadership of David, who "spake to the chief of the Levites to appoint their brethren to be the singers with instruments of music, psalteries and harps and cymbals, sounding, by lifting up the voice with joy" (1 Chron. 15:16).

Verse 2, however, calls believers to sing of God's salvation in the midst of everyday life, not just in formal worship. Although we may wonder how we, the creature, can possibly "bless" the Creator, the word also means to "pay homage" to the One we serve and adore.

B. Speak of His wonders, 3

3 Declare his glory among the heathen, his wonders among all people.

The emphasis on worship as an influence on unbelievers appears again. This time, the psalmist anticipates that the service will include, in sermon or song, a recital of the "wonders" God has done in the midst of His people. Typically, this somewhat formal recollection might include the miracle of creation (Isa. 42:5), and go on to the wonder of the exodus from Egypt, praising God for the monumental and formative event that welded the Israelites into a nation, and who "maketh a way in the sea, and a path in the mighty waters" of the Reed Sea (43:16).

So effective was this kind of public testimony that the book of Judith, in the Apocrypha, tells a moving story of an army about to advance against the Jews, then hesitating to attack after being warned that God worked so mightily among them that they would be unconquerable as long as they obeyed Him.

IV. Proclaim His Power—4-6

A. The true God vs. idols, 4-5

4 For the Lord is great, and greatly to be praised: he is to be feared above all gods.

5 For all the gods of the nations are idols: but the Lord made the heavens.

The praise of Yahweh becomes more assertively evangelistic here, as the song advances the truth that Yahweh is superior to the so-called "gods" of the heathen. The psalm recalls the ridicule of the prophet Isaiah as he taunts those who craft an idol out of wood and bow down before it, then burn the other end of the wood in the fire! (See Isaiah 44:9-17, and "For a Lively Start," p. 472.) In contrast, the true God is alive, and created the heavens that declare His glory (Ps. 100:1ff.)

Any reflection on the folly of idol worship should include the "idols" in our own culture. These include anything such as materialism or wealth or power that we allow to compete with the true God for our allegiance. As the apostle Paul reminds us, even covetous is a form of idolatry (Col. 3:5).

B. Worship His majesty, 6

6 Honour and majesty are before him: strength and beauty are in his sanctuary.

Now the psalmist focuses not on the surrounding Gentiles who may witness the Israelites in worship but on God Himself. "Honour and majesty," . . . "strength and beauty" are translated "strength and glory" in the NIV. The words remind us of the awesome "throne scene" in Isaiah 6:1-4, where the prophet has a vision of God that is described in just such terms.

V. Publish His Beauty—7-9

7 Give unto the LORD, O ye kindreds of the people, give unto the LORD glory and strength.

8 Give unto the LORD the glory due unto his name: bring an offering, and come into his courts.

9 O worship the LORD in the beauty of holiness: fear before him, all the earth.

Coming full circle, the psalmist returns to the theme that it is not only the Jews who are to praise God in such lofty terms; all "kindreds of the people" (NIV "families of nations") are invited to join in the song of praise.

Such worship is "due" the Lord simply because of who He is, as revealed through His "name." The Jews often connected one's name with his character. In God's case, the name Yahweh is thought to refer to His eternal being, as contrasted with the temporary being of mortals. In explaining His name to Moses, God says His name means He is the great "I am" (Exod. 3:14). Here, verse 8 reminds us that we are to worship God for this quality of being implied in His name, not just for what we have received from Him or in order to win further favors.

Verse 9 can be translated to mean we should be clothed in beautiful holiness as we worship, or that "the beauty of holiness" refers to God. Most scholars prefer the latter meaning: "Worship the Lord in the splendor of his holiness" (NIV).

Either way, the phrase may strike a strange note in a day when "holiness" is not commonly spoken of as "beautiful." This element returns us to the ethical dimension of worship. Both the inherent righteousness of God and the righteousness that He "imputes" to man are values to be cherished above the aesthetic or physical beauty that modern societies virtually worship.

Evangelistic Emphasis

"Declare his glory among the nations, his marvelous work among all the peoples" (Ps. 96:3). The psalmist's summons is not only to praise and worship, but also to evangelism. The word "declare" or "proclaim" suggests a herald who goes before a king, victorious in battle. The herald announces the king's wondrous works, his mighty acts, his glory. So God's people in every age are to tell of God's salvation, proclaim God's wondrous works, declare God's glory. The church exists to proclaim the good news, God reigns. It is the same message of Jesus, "The kingdom of God is at hand. Repent and believe the gospel" (Mark 1:14). Jesus' message called for a decision. Submit now to God's sovereignty. Enter now into God's kingdom. The witness of Jesus' disciples today also calls for a response. The good news is the same. "Say among the nations, 'The Lord is king!'" (Ps. 96:10).

The church has no other mission than to share this good news: God reigns! We pray and struggle to know how to show forth God's salvation in our lives, that people might see what it means to be whole. We pray and struggle to live now under the sovereignty of God. So we continually pray: "Thy kingdom come, thy will be done."

ℰℴℭℛ

Let the people praise Thee, O God; let all the people praise Thee.—*Psalm 67:3*

Leander Keck insists that the center of worship is praise. To praise God is to acknowledge joyously, not grudgingly, that we did not make ourselves. God is to be praised because God is God. While many good results may flow from the worship of God, the experience of praising Him needs no pragmatic justification. It is right for creatures to praise God. Because there is no ulterior motive, no carefully calculated hoped for results, worship can be described as "pointless praise."

Psalm 67 calls us to glimpse the universal nature of praise. "Let *all* the people praise Thee." Each time we gather to praise God we are part of a greater fellowship, embracing people of many denominations, many cultures, many languages, many races. Somehow it enlarges our vision and expands our hearts to be mindful that it is with all God's people on earth and all the company of heaven that we join in "pointless" praise of the holy Lord, God of power and might.

Weekday Problems

Henry went to church every Sunday. He didn't enjoy it. He didn't want to go. He would rather sleep late on Sunday morning. But he goes regularly because even though he hates it, he knows the discipline will do him some good. Henry believed that like jogging a mile or swimming laps, the discipline of church going has a value, unpleasant as it may seem.

But one Sunday, sharing in the singing, praying, and listening, God touched Henry. His spirit was ignited by divine fire. Henry found that it is a transforming experience to know God, and even more important to be known by God. He experienced worship in the way Robert McAffee Brown described it: "When people are known by God they do not first of all write books, or start analyzing their religious experience. They sing, or they pray, or they sing and pray at the same time."

For Henry, Sunday worship has become not just a grim "work out," like the jogger trudging by his house, straining and sweating to live longer. Sunday has become like running to meet your lover, embracing your wife when back from a dangerous mission, like a child dancing wildly when he hears there's a circus in town.

"For great is the Lord and greatly to be praised" (Ps. 96:4).

Praise with a Gladsome Mind!

Let us with a gladsome mind
    Praise the Lord, for he is kind
For his mercies aye endure,
    Ever faithful, ever sure.

Let us blaze His name abroad,
    For of gods he is the God; . . .
Who by all-commanding might,
    Filled the new-made world with light.

He the golden tress-ed sun
    Caused all day his course to run;

Th' horn-ed moon to shine by night,
    'Mid her spangled sisters bright.

He his chosen race did bless,
    In the wasteful wilderness;
He hath, with a piteous eye,
    Looked upon our misery.

All things living he doth feed.
    His full hand supplies their need;
For his mercies aye endure,
    Ever faithful, ever sure.

—John Milton

This Lesson in Your Life

The psalmist points to the essence of worship when he writes: "Worship the Lord in the beauty of holiness; fear before him all the earth" (Ps. 96:9). Robert Shaw, the famed choral conductor and arranger, stated that the basic conditions for worship are a sense of awe and an acknowledgment of pain. When we gather for worship we bring with us a variety of experiences of the past week and the past years. We come with heavy hearts, tears not yet dry from grief. We come with frustration that things have not gone well. We come with disappointments, jobs lost, relationships broken, hoped for opportunities closed. We come with anxieties for others, their pains, their hurts, their stress. We come knit with others whose suffering we feel: homeless, aging, handicapped. We are one with children without safe neighborhoods, or good schools, or health care, or enough food. The hymns or the prayers, the psalms or the silence, help give expression to the pain we carry as we gather to worship.

The other minimal condition for worship suggested by Robert Shaw is a sense of awe. We have come into the presence of the Holy One. We come as we are, bearing pain, but we come not first to focus on our needs or even our concerns for others but to be aware of the Lord, who draws us into his Holy presence. It is this sense of awe and mystery that the young prophet Isaiah knew in the temple. "In the year that King Uzziah died, I saw the Lord sitting upon a throne, high and lifted up; his train filled the temple. Above him stood the seraphim; and one called to another and said: 'Holy, holy, holy is the Lord of hosts; the whole earth is full of his glory'" (Isa. 6:1-2a, 3).

Grady Hardin insists that awe is the definitive spirit of worship. All emotions or feelings in worship are valid as worship to the extent that they accord with awe. Awe is the direct personal relatedness to God who is the object of worship. Awe is the awareness by thought and feeling that God is God, and we are creatures. Awe is the awareness that nothing in life has real meaning except our being accepted by God and that on our own we cannot cause this acceptance.

It is this sense of awe and mystery at the heart of worship that is expressed in the vision of John: "Then I looked and I heard around the throne the living creatures and the elders and the voice of many angels, numbering myriads of myriads, and thousands of thousands, saying with a loud voice: 'Worthy is the Lamb who was slain, to receive power and wealth and wisdom and might and honor and glory and blessing'" (Rev. 5:11-12).

STRAIGHT

1. In Psalm 67:2, what should be the result of God's blessing?
That God's way be made known upon earth and God's saving power known among all nations.

2. In Psalm 67:3,5, who is summoned to praise God?
All the peoples are to praise God.

3. What are the people commanded to do in Psalm 96:1-3?
They are to sing to the Lord, bless his name, tell of his salvation, and declare his glory.

4. What reasons for praise are given in Psalm 96: 4-6, 10, 13?
The Lord is great, He made the heavens, He will judge the people with equity, and He is coming to judge the earth.

5. In Psalm 96, what attributes of God are found with His presence in the sanctuary?
Honor and majesty, strength and beauty.

6. What are the people instructed to give or ascribe to the Lord in Psalm 96:7-8?
They should give to the Lord glory, strength, and an offering.

7. How is appropriate worship described in Psalm 96:9?
"Worship the Lord in the beauty of holiness; Fear (tremble) before him all the earth."

8. In Psalm 96:11-12, what parts of creation join in the celebration of the Lord's coming?
The heavens, the earth, the sea, the field, and trees of the forest.

9. In Psalm 96:13, how is the judgment of God described?
He will judge with righteousness and the peoples with his truth.

10. In Psalm 67:1, for what does the psalmist pray?
That God would be gracious, bless us, and make his face to shine on us.

In the Sequoia National Park are groves of giant Sequoia trees, towering 10 and 20 stories high. Some of the trees are estimated to be 2,000 to 3,000 years old. They were growing here when Columbus came to the shores of the new world. They were here at the beginning of Abraham's migration from his father's land.

For all their age and height, these giants have shallow roots. Yet they have withstood the ravages of storm, ice, and snow. They bear the scars of forest fires. Still they survive. How can they stand so straight and tall, millenium after millenium when their root system is so shallow? The answer is that they always grow in colonies. You will never find a Sequoia by itself. It thrives and survives only in the company of other Sequoias. Their root systems intertwine and intermesh. Although no one tree has roots enough to sustain it through mighty winds and torrential rains, each one borrows strength from the others. Together they have survived through the centuries.

Christians who survive, who maintain a vitality and enthusiasm in their faith, are not loners. In communities of faith, where they share in small groups for prayer and praise, in study and service, in care and nurture of one another, they continue to grow. Their faith is made strong. Bonded in common covenant and mission, they lend strength to one other.

Not only are individual disciples strengthened when they are joined together in prayer and praise, but congregations find strength in the midst of a secular world by reaching out to other communities of faith. A congregation is stronger if it realizes it is not God's only outpost in the neighborhood or city. When congregations reach out to each other, across racial, ethnic, class, and denominational lines, pooling strength and sharing resources, each is made the stronger for its task.

A California pastor, Browne Barr, has made a study of high-flying snow geese. They have been tracked on a flight of 1,700 miles from St. James Bay in Canada to coastal Louisiana—in 60 hours! A study of birds that fly in formation shows that this pattern affects aerodynamic efficiency. A flock of 25 birds can fly about 70 percent farther than a lone bird. So geese fly in formation! The geese make a honking sound. It is not the impatient honking of the motorist behind you. Their honking is a means of keeping in touch, encouraging one another during flight.

When we gather to worship, we share our common memory of what God has done in Christ. We pray for one another. We bow in awe before the God who made us. We "fly farther" when we unite our hearts and voices in worship.

Lesson 10

Embrace Wisdom

Proverbs 3:13-18; 4:1-9

Happy is the man that findeth wisdom, and the man that getteth understanding.

14 For the merchandise of it is better than the merchandise of silver, and the gain thereof than fine gold.

15 She is more precious than rubies: and all the things thou canst desire are not to be compared unto her.

16 Length of days is in her right hand; and in her left hand riches and honour.

17 Her ways are ways of pleasantness, and all her paths are peace.

18 She is a tree of life to them that lay hold upon her: and happy is every one that retaineth her.

Prov. 4:1 Hear, ye children, the instruction of a father, and attend to know understanding.

2 For I give you good doctrine, forsake ye not my law.

3 For I was my father's son, tender and only beloved in the sight of my mother.

4 He taught me also, and said unto me, Let thine heart retain my words: keep my commandments, and live.

5 Get wisdom, get understanding: forget it not; neither decline from the words of my mouth.

6 Forsake her not, and she shall preserve thee: love her, and she shall keep thee.

7 Wisdom is the principal thing; therefore get wisdom: and with all thy getting get understanding.

8 Exalt her, and she shall promote thee: she shall bring thee to honour, when thou dost embrace her.

9 She shall give to thine head an ornament of grace: a crown of glory shall she deliver to thee.

Memory Selection
Proverbs 3:13

Devotional Reading
Proverbs 3:1-8

Background Scripture
Proverbs 3+4

The four lessons in this unit are taken from the book of Proverbs, the centerpiece of the "Wisdom Literature" of the Old Covenant Scriptures. Although the books of Job, Psalms, Ecclesiastes, and Song of Solomon are also considered Wisdom Literature, it is the Proverbs that are specifically intended to impart wise sayings for godly living.

The focus of the proverbs in today's lesson is on *the advantage in everyday life of gaining godly wisdom.* This is not always obvious. Sometimes, in the business world for example, it may seem as though cheating or lying or cutting corners and producing an inferior product give us an edge over a competitor. This lesson emphasizes the opposite: The person who is wise in the ways of God, not the ways of the world, is the one who has the advantage.

&)C&.

Discussing the practical value of following God's will is a good way to begin this session. Ask group members what advantage a godly person has *in this life,* in contrast to the person who ignores God. Responses may include (1)honesty in dealing with others is likely to result in their being honest with us; (2)building a business on a reputation for fairness usually brings more business, and financial blessings; (3)God promises to care for those who do His will; (4)treating our bodies wisely usually results in health, in contrast to sickness and addiction from abusing our bodies; (5)we can sleep peacefully at night knowing that we have done our best to do God's will.

Of course the highest and best motive for following God's ways is out of love for Him, not for personal gain. We know that we will be rewarded in heaven, whether or not we are blessed in this life. The proverbs, however, are more concerned to show that righteousness usually results in rewards in this life, not just in the life to come.

Teaching Outline	Daily Bible Readings

I. Better than Wealth—Prov. 3:13-15
  A. Definition of terms, 13
  B. More precious than riches, 14-15
II. Benefits of Wisdom—16-18
  A. Long life and honor, 16
  B. Pleasantness and peace, 17-18
III. Be True to Parental Wisdom—4:1-4
IV. Buy the Principal Thing—5-7
V. Blessings from Wisdom—8-9
	Mon. Learning About Wisdom
	      Proverbs 1:1-7
	Tue. Wisdom Brings Security
	      Proverbs 1:20-33
	Wed. Accept God's Words
	      Proverbs 2:1-15
	Thu. Trust God's Wisdom
	      Proverbs 3:1-12
	Fri. Keep Wisdom and Prudence
	      Proverbs 3:21-26
	Sat. Hold on to Instruction
	      Proverbs 4:10-17
	Sun. Choose Knowledge over Gold
	      Proverbs 8:1-12

Verse by Verse

I. Better than Wealth—Prov. 3:13-15
A. Definition of terms, 13

13 Happy is the man that findeth wisdom, and the man that getteth understanding.

As we begin a study from the book of Proverbs, it is helpful to reflect on the meaning of the term. A proverb is literally a "before-word" (*pro* = "before" and *verb* = "word"). A proverb is therefore a wise saying that equips us with wisdom to face life before we run into problems that would hinder our walk with the Lord. While those who ignore God's Word encounter life "in the raw," believers are supposed to become acquainted with it so they are pre-armed and ready to meet life's events before they come.

The biblical proverbs all stem from "wisdom," as in verse 1. To the ancient Jews, the word did not refer to being wise in philosophical thought, as in the sentence "Socrates was a wise man." Neither did "wisdom" refer to "head knowledge" gained from facts considered apart from God, or technical skills. Instead, wisdom was living in "the fear of the Lord" (Prov. 1:7). Wisdom is the capacity to discern God's will and the willingness to submit to it.

All this means, as in verse 1, that while the world may define happiness in terms of success, beauty, wealth, or power, a "happy" person is really one who is acquainted with God's Word and is willing to walk in His ways.

Although verse 2 separates "understanding" from wisdom, the two words are practically synonyms. Proverbs is written as Hebrew poetry, and the two words are probably the result of "parallelism", that feature of Hebrew poetry that "rhymes" ideas instead of words. The Hebrew word for "getteth" in reference to understanding means to "draw out," implying that godly understanding requires effort on our part in "drawing out" from the Word just how we should apply it in the world.

B. More precious than riches, 14-15

14 For the merchandise of it is better than the merchandise of silver, and the gain thereof than fine gold.

15 She is more precious than rubies: and all the things thou canst desire are not to be compared unto her.

Making "merchandise" of wisdom does not mean we can trade on it for material gain, although the commercial overtones of the term are important. The wise man is saying that we really do *gain* or *profit* from wisdom, although the enrichment may be of the spiritual life rather than the bank account. Placing wisdom in this light leads to the metaphors in verse 15. Wisdom is of greater "gain" that any precious jewels or other material re-ward, although, as we shall see, it does lead to blessings during life in the body.

II. Benefits of Wisdom—16-18
A. Long life and honor, 16

16 Length of days is in her right hand; and in her left hand riches and honour.

Long life is the first "this-worldly" blessing of living with godly wisdom promised here, and the second is, after all, material gain and the respect that goes with it, when rightly used. This theme of gaining reward in this life from submitting to the wisdom of God is stated again and again without apology in the book of Proverbs. A superficial reading of such promises easily prompts a skeptical response, causing us to ask, "Why do some good people die young, while others are short-lived, or poor?"

The answer lies in the fact that such promises are made in the framework of God's Covenant with Abraham. The material blessings promised to his faithful descendants are clear (see Deut. 28:1-5, 11). However, the fulfillment of this Covenant promise depended on Israel's faithfulness; otherwise she would not be blessed, but cursed (Deut. 27:15ff., esp. vs. 26). It was inevitable that many good people would suffer when the majority fell into idol worship and other sins. Material blessings, therefore, are not an automatic sign of being "in covenant" with God. Jesus corrected that common misunderstanding by saying that "the rain falls on the just and the unjust" (Matt. 5:45).

However, we must not discount the *general* rule that appears so often in Proverbs: *Generally,* those who sincerely try to do God's will are blessed in this life; and *always* they will be blessed in the next. When bad things happen to people of faith, they have God's permission to spiritualize His promise to bless them in this life, postponing their actualization until heaven.

B. Pleasantness and peace, 17-18

17 Her ways are ways of pleasantness, and all her paths are peace.

18 She is a tree of life to them that lay hold upon her: and happy is every one that retaineth her.

The affirmation here is subject to trial in the arena of life. Homes guided by parents who are guided by godly wisdom are simply more pleasant and peaceful than those without such guidance. Businesses operated on godly principles provide a more pleasant workplace. On the personal level, verse 18 reminds us of the "tree of life" in the Garden of Eden (Gen. 2:9), and assures us that its life-sustaining power is available to those who live by the wisdom of God.

III. Be True to Parental Wisdom—4:1-4

1 Hear, ye children, the instruction of a father, and attend to know understanding.

2 For I give you good doctrine, forsake ye not my law.

3 For I was my father's son, tender and only beloved in the sight of my mother.

4 He taught me also, and said unto me, Let thine heart retain my words: keep my commandments, and live.

The quality and closeness of Jewish family life is seen here to be the vehicle for transmitting wisdom, the law, and the commandments. Three generations are envisioned, one before the author, and one after. The oft-discussed breakdown of the family in modern American life adds to generational differences in posing obstacles to "traditioning" youth to this extent. Youth obviously have greater difficulties absorbing wisdom's commandments when parents and grand-parents do not practice them.

IV. Buy the Principal Thing—5-7

5 Get wisdom, get understanding: forget it not; neither decline from the words of my mouth.

6 Forsake her not, and she shall preserve thee: love her, and she shall keep thee.

7 Wisdom is the principal thing; therefore get wisdom: and with all thy getting get understanding.

The advice and encouragement here is still aimed at the children of verse 1. Wisdom is spoken of in the feminine gender simply because the Hebrew word (*hookah)* is feminine (as is the Greek, *Sofia*). Of all the things a wise parent wants a child to gain, wisdom "is the principle thing," along with the understanding to put it into practice.

V. Blessings from Wisdom—8-9

8 Exalt her, and she shall promote thee: she shall bring thee to honor, when thou dost embrace her.

9 She shall give to thine head an ornament of grace: a crown of glory shall she deliver to thee.

The wise parent continues to counsel youth to put wisdom in first place, with the promise that this will result in *real* blessings, whether tangible or not. The "crown of glory" may not rest in this life on everyone who chooses wisdom, but it will be seen to be real in the form of an eternal relationship with God.

Evangelistic Emphasis

The wise teacher in Proverbs instructs his child on the importance of the company he keeps. No matter how deeply moving the experience of conversion, no matter how sincere the commitment to Christ as Lord, the persons we live, work, and play with will either re-enforce that commitment or weaken it. "Do not enter the path of the wicked and do not walk in the way of evil doers. Avoid it; do not go on it: turn away from it and pass on" (Prov. 4:14-15).

When we try to win acceptance from the cynical and scornful, their unbelief rubs off on us. When we try to be part of an elite group that has different standards concerning alcohol, drugs, and sex, we are tempted to lower our moral standards. When we try to keep up with a fast set, spending money to impress others, we erode our sense of stewardship. When we try to gain popularity with a group that disparages minorities, we discover our convictions are weakened by compromise. Salvation is an on-going process requiring nurture, discipline, and support groups.

The youth ministries of a congregation are more than "keeping the kids off the street." They are an essential part of providing peer group support for young disciples of Christ. Such surrounding of youth with healthy and moral recreation options is as important a way to share the gospel as any crusade or revival.

৯০৪৪

Memory Selection

Happy is the man that findeth wisdom, and the man that getteth understanding."—*Proverbs 3:13*

The true source of blessedness and contentment does not lie in the accumulation of possessions or the admiration of others. The true source of happiness is to be found in the knowledge of God. This knowledge is not primarily information about God, but more a trusting in His steadfast love. To trust means we do not need to know all the answers. It is enough to know that God knows us and cares for us.

Dietrich Bonhoeffer, imprisoned and executed for his opposition to Hitler, wrote, "Not everything (evil) that happens is the will of God, yet through every event, however untoward, there is always a way through to God." A German sailor in World War I wrote to his family: "If you should hear that I have fallen, do not weep. Remember that even the deepest ocean in which my body sinks in death is only a pool in the hand of My Savior." That is the wisdom, the understanding, the trust that brings true happiness.

Weekday Problems

Susan was a new student at Central High. She came from a loving but strict family. Every Sunday she attended church and Sunday School. But the kids at school seemed on a fast track. She felt alone and left out. When she went to parties she was under a lot of pressure to drink. Her new friends insisted that she hadn't lived until she had gotten "high." When the handsome football captain invited her out, she thought she had it made. But he pressured her to have sex.

She was living a double life—a model Christian daughter at home and church, but a wild and sophisticated chick at school. She was thoroughly miserable. Finally she was able to discuss her inner conflict with Joyce in her church youth group, who said, "I used to worry about what other kids thought. Now I know what God thinks of me is more important."

Susan went on a church youth mission tour. It was a great trip, full of fun, and a chance to bond with new friends. She found a new joy in her life as she dropped out of the fast set at school. She found a new peace as she worked with others in repairing houses, visiting the Children's Home, and packing boxes for relief. She felt better about herself, closer to God and to her family. The wise counsel of Proverbs was proved in her life: "Do not enter the path of the wicked, do not walk in the path of the evil doers."

What is your church doing to help youth cope with the pressures to conform to a "party, party" culture?

Wisdom and Wise Cracks

Teacher: Make a sentence beginning with "I."
Student: I is . . . .
Teacher: No, you must say "I am."
Student: O.K., I am the ninth letter of the alphabet.

* * *

Prof: Now, students, we'll use my hat to represent the planet Mars. Any questions?
Rolf: Yes, sir. Is Mars inhabited?

* * *

Teacher: If I laid two eggs on the chair and three on the table, what would I get?
Pupil: Your picture in Ripley's "Believe It or Not."

* * *

Lem: What's your son going to be when he graduates from college?
Clem: An old man . . . a very old man.

This Lesson in Your Life

In Proverbs 4, children are repeatedly enjoined to heed the instructions of their parents. "Listen to a father's instruction, be attentive" (vs. 1). "I give you good precepts: do not forsake my teaching" (vs. 2). "Let your heart hold fast to my words" (vs. 4). "Hear, my child, accept my words" (vs. 10). "I have taught you the way of wisdom" (vs. 11). "Keep hold of instruction, do not let go" (vs. 13). "My child be attentive to my words; incline your heart to my sayings" (vs. 20).

It is clear the parent is charging his child with the responsibility of remembering the instruction and obeying the way of life laid out for him. In our day we often pass on Christian values through family traditions. Lillian Africano shares her memories of visiting her grandmother's house. Dutiful visits were expected of all the children. When Lillian had chosen a movie over going to grandmother's house once too often, her Aunt Rose drew her aside. "Lily, I want to talk to you. You know the man who takes off his clothes is going to feel cold some day. Your family is like a suit of clothes. Sometimes the clothes feel tight, but you would be wrong to throw them away." Family gatherings and traditions help us know who we are. Children need to listen and remember. Children who give attention to only the newest fad, and dismiss the counsel of their elders, risk walking in harm's way.

If children have an obligation to be good learners, parents have the responsibility to be faithful teachers. Parents are the primary interpreters of the Christian faith to their children. If children don't learn the stories of the Bible at home, if they don't share in prayer as a part of everyday life, if they don't catch the importance of faith in God from their parents, then they are deprived. No matter how many radios, TVs, or computers they may have, something important is missing.

Part of parental teaching is taking the time to listen. Debra Smoot remembers her Aunt Lois. Aunt Lois always listened, no matter what kind of question Debra asked. With most adults children talk to kneecaps or belt buckles. But Aunt Lois would hunker down, nose-to-nose with the kids. The smallest child could look into her eyes. Aunt Lois would always repeat the question to make sure she understood it. She made each one feel important. So the answers she gave were valued because she valued the person asking the question.

STRAIGHT

1. In Proverbs 3:13, who are those who are happy?

Those who find wisdom and get understanding.

2. In Proverbs 3:14-15, to what is wisdom compared in value?

Wisdom is better than silver and gold, and more precious than jewels.

3. In Proverbs 3:19-20, what did the Lord do by wisdom, understanding and knowledge?

The Lord by wisdom founded the earth; by understanding he established the heavens; by his knowledge the deeps broke open.

4. In Proverbs 3:21, 24, what condition is required for sweet sleep?

Keep sound wisdom and prudence; when you lie down your sleep will be sweet.

5. What six actions are prohibited by the instructions in Proverbs 3:25-32?

Do not be afraid of panic or storm, withhold goods, say to neighbor go and come again, plan harm, quarrel with anyone, envy the violent.

6. What is God's attitude toward the scornful and toward the humble (Prov. 3:34)?

Toward the scornful he is scornful, but to the humble he shows favor.

7. What did the writer's father teach him (Prov. 4:3-4)?

My father taught me, Let your heart hold fast my words; keep my commandments and live.

8. According to Proverbs 4:7, what is the beginning of wisdom?

The beginning of wisdom is this: Get wisdom, and whatever else you get, get insight.

9. What will be the result for the writer if he accepts his father's words (Prov. 4:10)?

The years of his life will be many.

10. According to Proverbs 4:23, from what do the springs of life flow?

The springs of life flow from the heart.

Much advice is shared in the book of Proverbs. Sometimes the instructions seem to be in tension with each other. Proverbs 3:5 declares: "Trust in the Lord with all your heart, do not rely on your own insight." Dag Hammarskjold, the former General Secretary of the United Nations voices this deep trust, "What I ask for is absurd: that life shall have meaning. What I strive for is impossible: that my life shall acquire a meaning. I dare not believe, I do not see how I shall ever be able to believe that I am not alone.

"I don't know who or what put the question. I don't know when it was put. I don't even remember answering. But at some moment I did answer 'Yes' to Someone or Something and from that hour I was certain that existence is meaningful and that therefore my life in self-surrender had a goal. You dare your 'Yes' and experience a meaning. You repeat your 'Yes' and all things acquire a meaning. When everything has a meaning, how can you live anything but a 'Yes'"?

But the Book of Proverbs not only calls us to "trust the Lord with all our heart." It also calls us to shoulder our responsibility. "Get Wisdom, get insight" (Prov. 4:5, 7). The wise teacher addresses us as if it were up to us. While we cannot change our circumstances, we can determine how we respond. It is up to us to do our part. Our freedom to respond is what makes us human.

Harold Russell demonstrates what human responsibility means. His autobiography was made into a movie, "The Best Years of Our Lives." Russell was a sergeant in charge of a demolition unit in World War II. In training for combat he lost both hands. Eventually he was fitted with two hooks that he learned to use skillfully. His initial reaction was one of resentment when strangers would approach to talk about his hooks. Finally he recognized that they were only trying to be friendly. He tells of the day when he chose how he would respond. In a Chinese restaurant a stranger had watched his eating with chopsticks. The man came over and started a conversation. "I was noticing how well you managed with those things.

"These?" Russell held up the chop sticks.

"No—I, er, I mean those," said the man, nodding at he hooks. "I couldn't help notice how skillful you are with them. You can do just about everything with them, can't you sergeant?"

Russell replied with a twinkle in his eye, "Everything but pick up a dinner check."

Russell reminds us that along with trust in God, we have a responsibility of choosing how we will respond. "It is not what you have lost, but what you have left that counts. Too many of us squander precious energy, time, and courage dreaming of things that were and can never be again, instead of dedicating our selves to the realities and tasks of today."

The wisdom of Proverbs maintains this healthy balance between trust ("Trust in the Lord with your whole heart") and responsibility ("Get wisdom, get insight").

Run from Evil

Proverbs 6:16-29

These six things doth the LORD hate: yea, seven are an abomi nation unto him:

17 A proud look, a lying tongue, and hands that shed innocent blood,

18 An heart that deviseth wicked imaginations, feet that be swift in running to mischief,

19 A false witness that speaketh lies, and he that soweth discord among brethren.

20 My son, keep thy father's commandment, and forsake not the law of thy mother:

21 Bind them continually upon thine heart, and tie them about thy neck.

22 When thou goest, it shall lead thee; when thou sleepest, it shall keep thee; and when thou awakest, it shall talk with thee.

23 For the commandment is a lamp; and the law is light; and reproofs of instruction are the way of life:

24 To keep thee from the evil woman, from the flattery of the tongue of a strange woman.

25 Lust not after her beauty in thine heart; neither let her take thee with her eyelids.

26 For by means of a whorish woman a man is brought to a piece of bread: and the adulteress will hunt for the precious life.

27 Can a man take fire in his bosom, and his clothes not be burned?

28 Can one go upon hot coals, and his feet not be burned?

29 So he that goeth in to his neighbour's wife; whosoever toucheth her shall not be innocent.

Aug. 11

Memory Selection
Proverbs 6:20-21

Devotional Reading
Proverbs 6:6-15

Background Scripture
Proverbs 6:16-35

Evangelistic Emphasis

The topics in this passage are not linked by a common theme. Yet the entire passage can be said to be focused on "wisdom" or "wise living," since that is the theme of the entire book. We may therefore tie the three topics together under the overall title—

Wisdom in Three W's
(1) What God Hates (vss. 16-19
(2) 'Wearing' God's Will (20-22)
(3) Warning Against Adultery (23-29).

Despite the variety, it is clear that we are sitting at the feet of a wise teacher who commends three ways to live in "the fear of the Lord." Some in our own culture may question whether the author, King Solomon, is qualified to teach against adultery in light of his harem of 300 wives and 700 concubines (1 Kings 11:3). However, in the author's ethical framework his harem was not considered adulterous, only polygamous.

෨෨

FOR A LIVELY START...

You can introduce one theme in this lesson by making "phylacteries" to give each group member. A phylactery is a tiny Scripture-scroll or group of scrolls worn on the forehead, around the neck, or on the arm to remind a person of the importance of God's Law. Prepare some paper facsimiles before class (see illustration), distribute one to each group member, and suggest that they be worn during the discussion.

For each phylactery, cut four 4"x4" strips of construction paper, tie them with string, and use a large (9") rubber band to tie the ornament on class members' foreheads or arms.

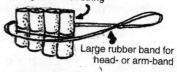

Four 4-inch-wide "scrolls," tied together with string

Large rubber band for head- or arm-band

Teaching Outline	**Daily Bible Readings**

I. What God Hates—6:16-19
  A. Pride, lies, and violence, 16-17
  B. Willful flaws, 18
  C. Sins against others, 19
 	
II. 'Wearing' God's Will—20-22
  A. Consider the source, 20
  B. Keep them with you, 21-22
 	
III. Warning Against Adultery—23-29
  A. Protection of the Law, 23-24
  B. Self-destructive behavior, 25-29
	Mon. Avoid Sinful Companions
	Proverbs 1:8-19
	Tue. Walk in Integrity
	Proverbs 10:1-12
	Wed. Righteousness Leads to Life
	Proverbs 10:13-25
	Thu. Empty Expectations
	Proverbs 10:27-32
	Fri. Wickedness Self-Destructs
	Proverbs 11:1-8
	Sat. Avoid Evil; Fear the Lord
	Proverbs 16:1-9
	Sun. Don't Envy the Wicked
	Proverbs 24:1-9

Verse by Verse

I. What God Hates—6:16-19
A. Pride, lies, and violence, 16-17
16 These six things doth the LORD hate: yea, seven are an abomination unto him:

17 A proud look, a lying tongue, and hands that shed innocent blood,

The author of Proverbs was fond of using a number-plus-one as a way to draw attention to several "wisdom" truths. Compare the six-plus-one formula in verse 1 to the three-plus-one items listed in Prov. 30: 15: "There are three things that are never satisfied, yea, four things that saith not, It is enough" (see also 30: 18, 21, 29). Here, although God hates any sin, and the list is almost endless, the formula underlines seven that are particularly detestable.

The "proud look" (NIV, "haughty eyes") of verse 2 is a clear picture of an arrogant person, nose held high and eyebrows arched. A "lying tongue" reflects the person who had rather tell a falsehood than the truth. Since, as Jesus would say later, God's Word is truth (John 17:17), a liar positions himself directly opposite God. The person who sheds "innocent blood" is a murderer, violating the Sixth Commandment.

B. Willful flaws, 18
18 An heart that deviseth wicked imaginations, feet that be swift in running to mischief,

God also hates the practice of plotting evil schemes and the habit of being quick to seek ways to commit "mischief." The original term actually means "evil," or what modern laws might call *criminal* mischief. Note the *intentional* aspect of these sins. They are not mistakes which well-meaning people might stumble into, but creatively evil practices that require deliberate scheming.

C. Sins against others, 19
19 A false witness that speaketh lies, and he that soweth discord among brethren.

We were told in verse 17 that God hates a lying tongue; now the wise man narrows the definition to focus on deliberate violations of the Ninth Commandment against bearing false witness, or telling lies that slander another person, whether in a court of law or only casual gossip.

The person who "soweth discord" is guilty of sedition. Earlier Solomon warned against being a "naughty person, a wicked man," who sows discord (vss. 12, 14). Why would anyone deliberately sow such seeds in an otherwise peaceful group? Usually in order to manipulate others and control the group, like the aged apostle John's enemy, Diotrophes, who loved to have preeminence in the church (2 John 9).

II. 'Wearing' God's Will—20-22
A. Consider the source, 20

20 My son, keep thy father's commandment, and forsake not the law of thy mother:

Here the wise man wants to assure children that his counsel, which ultimately comes from God, is also a part of a godly parent's teaching. We have previously remarked about the special respect normally given to elders in traditional eastern and mid-eastern societies. The verse also reminds us of the way God planned for His commandments to be handed along by *families*, not just by priests or other official religious leaders. Here are the roots of the strong ties among many Jewish families even today.

B. Keep them with you, 21-22

21 Bind them continually upon thine heart, and tie them about thy neck.

22 When thou goest, it shall lead thee; when thou sleepest, it shall keep thee; and when thou awakest, it shall talk with thee.

The reference here is to "phylacteries," which were originally small scrolls of parchment or vellum containing Scripture texts and worn on the forehead or as an arm band by devout Jews. This was the traditional way of interpreting Exodus 13:9, 16, where God told His people to keep the memory of His rescuing them from Egypt as "frontlets between thy eyes."

As verse 22 indicates, these tokens of faith were originally intended to be traveling personal reminders of God's guidance. Among some, this simple purpose came to be expanded to a superstitious belief that a phylactery had magical powers to protect the wearer from evil. ("Phylactery" comes from a Greek word that also gives us the term "prophylactic," which refers to a protective substance such as fluoride in toothpaste.) Still later, pride led some Jews to increase the size of their phylacteries and wear them for display or "to be seen of men" (Matt. 23:5).

III. Warning Against Adultery—23-29
A. Protection of the Law, 23-24

23 For the commandment is a lamp; and the law is light; and reproofs of instruction are the way of life:

24 To keep thee from the evil woman, from the flattery of the tongue of a strange woman.

The "prophylactic" or protective power of God's commandments mentioned above was of course inward, in the soul, rather than contained in an amulet. As Psalm 119:105 says,

"Thy word is a lamp unto my feet, and a light unto my path." Note the positive rather than negative description of God's Word as "reproof," which is intended not merely to correct believers or rob them of joy but to protect them from self-destructive disobedience.

Specifically, the wise man focuses on the protection of God's guidance against sexual sin, returning to a theme elaborated on in chapter 5. An "evil" or "strange" woman (that is a stranger to God's will; see NIV "wayward wife") of course stands also for a man with the same wayward tendencies. The wayward person is cast as a woman because the section began with counsel to a son rather than to a daughter (vs. 20).

B. Self-destructive behavior, 25-29

25 Lust not after her beauty in thine heart; neither let her take thee with her eyelids.

26 For by means of a whorish woman a man is brought to a piece of bread: and the adulteress will hunt for the precious life.

27 Can a man take fire in his bosom, and his clothes not be burned?

28 Can one go upon hot coals, and his feet not be burned?

29 So he that goeth in to his neighbour's wife; whosoever toucheth her shall not be innocent.

The flirtatious and seductive person is no modern invention of the magazines on the rack at the super market. Knowledge of a woman's ability to lure the lustful by batting her eyelids (RSV "eyelashes") is apparently as old as mankind.

Verse 26 refers to a prostitute, or a wife who acts like one, who degrades the otherwise beautiful sexual relationship by selling it to an outsider. In turn, this reduces the man who keeps the prostitute in business to an object of merchandise, such as a loaf of bread. The adulterer "hunts" illicit sex as though it is as life-sustaining as bread, the "staff of life."

Again, verses 27-29 sound as modern as lurid magazines and soap operas. Many are the adulterers who think that it can be treated as a harmless "fling" with no repercussions. Solomon has a more realistic view: it is like trying to carry the hot coals of one fire to start another by clutching them to his breast. Neither this nor walking barefoot on glowing coals is without "burning" consequences. The after-effects may appear in the form of guilt, in a poorer relationship with one's spouse, in a lawsuit, the break-up of a marriage, or possibly not until Judgment Day when an unrepentant adulterer's lack of "innocence" (vs. 29) is brought to light. Whenever the consequences appear, the warning here is like that in Numbers 32:23, "Be sure your sin will find you out."

Evangelistic Emphasis

In Proverbs 6:16-19, seven behaviors are listed that are hated by the Lord: haughty eyes, a lying tongue, hands that shed innocent blood, a heart that devises wicked plans, feet that hurry to run to evil, lying witness who testifies falsely, and one who sows discord in the family. When our message of the good news of God's love is not heard or accepted the fault may be in the messenger.

The very persons who need most to hear of God's redeeming love may be turned off by the way of living of those who profess to follow Jesus. When others observe that we misrepresent a car we're trying to sell, they are not inclined to listen to our witness of Christ's' transforming love. When they see us insisting we had the green light at the intersection when clearly we ran the red light, they are not likely to be inspired by our testimony to Jesus. When they see in us a belligerent, dominating, controlling behavior with spouse and children they are not moved when we sing about "amazing grace that saved a wretch like me." When others see the "welcome" sign outside our church but inside find a cold reception for strangers, and haughty looks for those who are different, they must wonder about the God we serve. Such a gap between what we profess and what we practice is an abomination to the Lord. No wonder God hates our hypocrisy. It is a hindrance to God's saving work.

&)CR

Memory Selection

My son, keep thy father's commandment, and forsake not the law of thy mother: Bind them continually upon thine heart, and tie them about thy neck. — *Proverbs 6:20-21*

The Scripture verses we learn as a child, we carry with us all our years. In long hours of vigil waiting for a report from surgery, these passages remind us of God's steadfast love. "God so loved the world." When we walk through the valley of grief, we remember we are not alone. "Thy rod and thy staff they comfort me." When we are moved by the wonder and beauty of creation, the words we memorized as a child help to shape our prayer: "The earth is the Lord's and the fullness thereof." The words we "hide in our hearts" become the channels for God's living word to us in special times of stress or discouragement, in moments of joy and ecstasy.

Bible verses memorized function as the Proverbs promise: "when you walk, they will lead you, when you lie down, they will watch over you; and when you awake they will talk with you."

496

Weekday Problems

Jim and Judy had been married five years. Jim was a lawyer who frequently traveled on assignments. He became involved in his civic club and served on several church committees. His days and evenings were full. Judy was a pediatrician. As the newest doctor in her practice, she was on call every otherweek end and most holidays.

Judy and Jim seemed to have less and less "good" time together. Whenever one was free, the other had commitments. What few conversations they had seemed to end in arguments, shouting, or tears. So they had fewer and fewer conversations. Both had been reared to honor the sacredness of the marriage covenant. But they wondered what had gone wrong with their marriage. They went to their pastor for counseling. They agreed to give their marriage a new priority. They would make the effort to take off their masks and share their feelings with each other. Their counselor quoted Ruel Howe: "Dialogue is to love what blood is to the body. When the flow of blood stops, the body dies. When dialogue stops, love dies and resentment and hate are born."

Jim and Judy prayed together that God would give them strength to be open, to share the being and truth of their souls with each other. Their covenant of marriage kept them together. Neither walked out. They resolved, with God's help, to talk and share, and to make "good" time to spend together.

Little-known Bible Facts (?)

Where is medicine first mentioned in the Bible?
In Exodus, where God gave Moses two tablets.

* * *

Did you know that the Bible mentions tennis?
It says that "Joseph served in Pharaoh's court."

* * *

Where does the Bible forbid some hair styles?
Where it says "Let him who is on the house, top-knot come down."

* * *

Where does the Bible mention smoking?
Where it says that Rebekah "lighted off her camel."

* * *

Who is the most wicked man in the Bible?
Moses, because Exodus 32:19 says he broke the Ten Commandments all at once.

This Lesson in Your Life

In Proverbs 6:24-36, the parent gives stern warning to his son to avoid adultery. He echoes the Ten Commandments: "You shall not commit adultery. You shall not covet your neighbor's wife" (Ex. 20:14, 17). Jesus goes beyond the outward act to the inner motives of the heart: "You have heard that it was said, 'You shall not commit adultery.' But I say to you that everyone who looks at a woman with lust has already committed adultery with her in his heart" (Matt. 5:27-28).

Marriages are in trouble today not only because we give less authority to God's commandments, and not only because we feed the lusts that exploit others as objects. Marriages are in trouble because we neglect to work at the relationship and help it grow deeper with the years. Certaintly we need to honor the covenant of marriage, and keep our promise to stay together even when there are difficulties and conflict. But a marriage relationship is more than a duty. Married love is more than a contract.

The Greeks had three words for the English word "love." *Eros* refers to that romantic dimension of marriage. It brings the glow and sparkle between a man and a wife. In the Bible sex is viewed as a good gift of God, a way of expressing love. Because the passions and desires of the body are good and holy, they are to be saved for their full expression between two persons in the marriage covenant.

The second Greek word for love is *philia*, as in **Phila**delphia, the city of brotherly love. This kind love suggests that your spouse is also your best friend. There is no real relationship without some risking. We cannot know another unless we are willing to let ourselves be known as well. The joining of two into one in holy matrimony intermingles two lives, their interests, their aims, and their dreams. The deepest sharing comes when two people move in the same direction, when their lives have a common calling, when they seek to serve a common Lord. They are walking in the same direction. They have the same goals. The two are made one.

The most distinctive word for Christian love is agape. This is a self-giving love, without expectation of return. The kind of person to whom we are married after 40 years or more is in part a product of how well that mate has been loved. If the bride becomes hard, brittle, defensive, and always fault finding, it may be because she hasn't been loved. But if she becomes a warm, caring, and giving person, radiating warmth and love, it is probably because she knows what it is to be loved.

Who of us is capable of giving such love? It is a gift. "We love because He first loved us." (1 John 4:19)

1. What seven things are an abomination to the Lord according to Proverbs 6:16-19?
Haughty eyes, a lying tongue, hands shedding blood, a heart devising wicked plans, feet hurrying to evil, a lying witness, one who sows discord.

2. What should a child do with his father's commands and his mother's teaching (6:21)?
He should bind them upon his heart and tie them around his neck.

3. What will God's teachings do for the child (6:22)?
When he walks, they will lead him; when he lies down, they will watch over him; and when he awakes, they will talk with you.

4. What things of God serve as a lamp and a light (6:23)?
The commandment is a lamp and the teaching is a light.

5. What is the purpose of reproofs or discipline (6:23-24)?
To keep one from adultery, and the smooth tongue of the adulteress.

6. What is the difference between a sexual relation with a prostitute and another's wife, according to 6:26?
A prostitute's fee is only a loaf of bread, but the wife of another stalks a man's very life.

7. What punishment can a thief expect when caught (6:30-31)?
He will pay sevenfold; he will forfeit all the goods of his house.

8. What is the consequence of adultery (6:32-33)?
He who does it destroys himself. His sing will bring wounds, dishonor, and disgrace.

9. What is the response of the husband toward the man who commits adultery with his wife?
He shows no restraint when he takes revenge (6:34).

10. What compensation should be paid to the husband whose wife has sex with another man?
He will accept no compensation, and refuses a bribe no matter how great (6:35).

Much of the Book of Proverbs is in the form of a wise father giving advice to his son. Part of the wisdom of the father here is advising his son to stay out of harm's way—and of charm's way. "Can fire be carried without burning one's clothes? Or can one walk on hot coals without scorching the feet?" (Prov. 6:27-28).

A problem about staying out of trouble is that while we often pray, "Lead us not into temptation," but never wait before God in stillness for us to be receptive to the guidance of God's Holy Spirit. If we're trying to cut down on calories, we don't need to hang around the bakery. If we struggle with a drinking problem, we do well to stay away from bars and from a gang that pressures us to go along. If we find ourselves spending a large amount of time alone with another's spouse, listening to his/her problems or pouring out our own trouble, we need to be aware of the danger. What begins in an entirely innocent meeting can develop attachments that compromise our marriage covenant.

The warnings of the wise father in Proverbs have relevance for today. There are limits in relationships for appropriate behavior. To go beyond these is to court disaster. The widespread break up of marriages today is a symptom showing that we do not work at the relationship of marriage. It is not enough to avoid temptation. A good relationship takes attention, time and work.

In a similar vein to the father in Proverbs, Charlie W. Shedd wrote letters of advice to his son Philip, in the months before Philip's marriage. In one of those letters he gives suggestions of how to treat a woman in public. At the heart of his sage and sometimes humorous advice is to find ways continually to give affirmation to his wife. Shedd encourages his young son to find ways to show his respect and caring for his soon-to-be bride. Among his gems of wisdom imparted to his son, Charlie Shedd suggests:

"When you enter a room, walk proud! Act like you are thinking, 'How could I be so fortunate?' Say something nice about her when you introduce her. It will lift her spirits. She will know you really appreciate her. When the conversation lags, ask her a question. Be sure you choose a subject on which she is something of an authority. Smart people make others feel smart. Never fuss over little points in her story. It doesn't matter if the incident occurred in Louisiana or California. On the way home take her hand and tell her how proud you were to have her along. Too often we give compliments to hosts, friends, co-workers but neglect to let the one closest to us know how really special they are. Sometimes when you are with her mother alone, tell her how much you appreciate her daughter. No woman alive could keep this to herself, and nothing does more for your wife than a compliment coming in sideways."

Watch What You Say

Proverbs 15:1-4, 7-8; 17:4-10

A soft answer turneth away wrath: but grievous words stir up anger.

2 The tongue of the wise useth knowledge aright: but the mouth of fools poureth out foolishness.

3 The eyes of the LORD are in every place, beholding the evil and the good.

4 A wholesome tongue is a tree of life: but perverseness therein is a breach in the spirit.

7 The lips of the wise disperse knowledge: but the heart of the foolish doeth not so.

8 The sacrifice of the wicked is an abomination to the LORD: but the prayer of the upright is his delight.

17:4 A wicked doer giveth heed to false lips; and a liar giveth ear to a naughty tongue.

5 Whoso mocketh the poor reproacheth his Maker: and he that is glad at calamities shall not be unpunished.

6 Children's children are the crown of old men; and the glory of children are their fathers.

7 Excellent speech becometh not a fool: much less do lying lips a prince.

8 A gift is as a precious stone in the eyes of him that hath it: whithersoever it turneth, it prospereth.

9 He that covereth a transgression seeketh love; but he that repeateth a matter separateth very friends.

10 A reproof entereth more into a wise man than an hundred stripes into a fool.

Memory Selection
Proverbs 15:1

Devotional Reading
Proverbs 16:16-30

Background Scripture
Proverbs 15+17

Aug. 18

In this unit, called "Words for the Wise," we come now to a lesson specifically on words themselves. The topic is a favorite one for Solomon, which underlines the importance of speech and its connection to "wisdom" or living in "the fear of the Lord."

The wise man's counsel on this subject invites comparison with the ambiguous signals our own society gives us about speech. On the one hand is an "anything goes" standard in the movies and television, and the advice that mental health is possible only if we "let it all hang out." On the other hand, the "politically correct" movement would place severe restrictions on many forms of speech that were previously considered harmless. In the midst of such opposite trends, this lesson invites God's own Word to instruct our words.

ഇൗരു

Ask group members what they think about the popular saying, *"Sticks and stones can break my bones, but words can never hurt me."* While there may be a kernel of truth in the saying, words in fact have the power to wound, as well as to heal.

Ask what other popular sayings deal with speech, and briefly discuss their truth and/or shortcomings. You may need to supply some, such as: *Actions speak louder than words. . . Do as I say, not as I do . . . A picture is worth a thousand words . . . . Practice what you preach . . .* and, from the Bible, *Silence is golden,* and A *word fitly spoken is like apples of gold in pictures of silver.*

Note that God has underlined the importance of speech by giving us His Word; and that this Word has important counsel about our own speech, as in the lesson to follow.

Teaching Outline	Daily Bible Readings
I. Wholesome tongue—15:1-4	**Mon.** Loose Talk Destroys Proverbs 11:9-14
A. Soft vs. grievous words, 1-2	**Tue.** Sins of the Lips Proverbs 12:13-22
B. Healing words, 3-4	**Wed.** Words Foolish and Gracious Proverbs 15:12-14, 23-30
II. Wise lips—7-8	**Thu.** Pleasant as Honeycomb Proverbs 16:21-29
III. Wicked words—17:4-5	**Fri.** Stop Before Quarreling Proverbs 17:14-20
IV. Winsome speech—6-10	**Sat.** Power of Life and Death Proverbs 18:6-8, 19-21
A. Their impact, 6-8	**Sun.** Informed by Knowledge Proverbs 20:15-22
B. Their result, 9-10	

Verse by Verse

I. Wholesome tongue—15:1-4
A. Soft vs. grievous words, 1-2

1 A soft answer turneth away wrath: but grievous words stir up anger.

2 The tongue of the wise useth knowledge aright: but the mouth of fools poureth out foolishness.

Everyone with any experience at all knows the power of words both to smooth tempers and to stir up strife. Why, then, do we not always choose "soft" words instead of "grievous"? Sometimes it is because we need to speak out against a falsehood or injustice. Failing to do so can make us guilty of crying "Peace, peace, when there is no peace" (Jer. 6:14). Long-term, the habit of avoiding conflict as a matter of principle does not contribute to healthy relationship.

Here, however, the sage Solomon is warning against inflammatory speech deliberately designed to stir up anger. The difference is often a matter of heart and attitude. A deadly example of choosing "grievous" words is occurring at this writing, in the tense situation between Muslims and Jews in Palestine. Both sides have plenty of "knowledge," as in verse 2,

knowing very well what to say that "pushes the buttons" that enrage the other side. At present this knowledge is not being used "aright," but foolishly.

B. Healing words, 3-4

3 The eyes of the LORD are in every place, beholding the evil and the good.

4 A wholesome tongue is a tree of life: but perverseness therein is a breach in the spirit.

Verse 3 may have nothing to do with the power of words, since the Proverbs typically switches from one topic to another without transitions. Yet it is also possible that the fact that an omnipresent God sees both the evil and the good is inserted here to remind us that He is fully aware of both the words we choose and in the intent behind them. This relates our speech to God's judgment, as though He is recording our every conversation. As Jesus would say later, "By thy words thou shalt be justified, and by thy words thou shalt be condemnded" (Mark 12:37).

Verse 4 reminds us that words

have the power to be "wholesome" in the sense of nourishing (NIV "healing"). The comparison of such speech with a "tree of life" reminds us of the life-sustaining qualities of that tree in the Garden of Eden. The person who habitually seeks to build up and encourage others often never knows how far-reaching such speech can be. In Hebrew parallelism, the opposite is also stated: Perverse speech breaks the spirit (cp. NIV, "A deceitful tongue crushes the spirit").

II. Wise lips—7-8

7 The lips of the wise disperse knowledge: but the heart of the foolish doeth not so.

8 The sacrifice of the wicked is an abomination to the LORD: but the prayer of the upright is his delight.

Although knowledge is often sharply distinguished from wisdom in Proverbs, it is not belittled unless it is used apart from wisdom. Verse 7a links the two in a positive relationship. Then in 7b, the proverb teaches that it is not only foolish merely to distribute cold facts or "head knowledge"; it is also foolish not to provide facts that can be helpful in a given situation.

Again, as in verse 3, the insertion of verse 8 may depart for a moment from the subject of the power of words. However, a case can be made for understanding it to refer to the words of prayer that accompany a sacrifice, teaching us again that the God who knows the heart accepts genuine prayers with

our offerings but detests and rejects those that are hypocritical. (Speech, "the fruit of our lips," can itself be considered a sacrifice or offering, as when we praise God; see Heb. 13:15.)

Imagine in passing the contrast between the biblical God who "delights" in sincere offerings or praise, and the unfeeling and artificial gods of pagans, or the remote and uninvolved "divine principle" of the philosopher. The Bible freely attributes a wide range of emotions to the true God.

III. Wicked words—17:4-5

4 A wicked doer giveth heed to false lips; and a liar giveth ear to a naughty tongue.

5 Whoso mocketh the poor reproacheth his Maker: and he that is glad at calamities shall not be unpunished.

A new element is injected here as Solomon includes the responsibility of *hearing* aright with the responsibility of speaking constructively. Like speaker, like listener: those who habitually lie are attuned to lies, and those who do wickedness flock like birds of a feather to those with naughty tongues. The affinity between wicked doers and hearers reminds us of the non-biblical proverb, "There is no honor among thieves." Why would one who uses his tongue for evil seek out those whose speech is informed by godly standards?

In verse 5 the author establishes a "vertical" link between evil speech and heaven, tying ethics to theology. Mocking or "putting down" the poor mocks God because the poor are made in His image (Gen. 1:27). It also belittles those for whom God has special concern, thus both belittling God's values and showing how little we have in common with Him in this area. The second line of verse 5 establishes similar negative connections, shining a glaring spotlight on the gulf between the God of compassion and those who are glad when others suffer calamity.

IV. Winsome speech—6-10

A. Their impact, 6-8

6 Children's children are the crown of old men; and the glory of children are their fathers.

7 Excellent speech becometh not a fool: much less do lying lips a prince.

8 A gift is as a precious stone in the eyes of him that hath it: whithersoever it turneth, it prospereth.

In a refreshing shift in tone, Solomon shows the positive power of words over against the preceding negatives. Once more, verse 6 may break the train of thought; or it may invite us to think of how children who use words wisely are a joy to their elders, and the "glory" it is for children when their parents are verbally supportive of them.

Verse 7 is based on simple appropriateness. It is out of character both for a fool to say "excellent" things and for a prince to lie; when either occurs it seems as unfitting as a gold ring in a hog's snout (a proverbial saying itself from 11:22).

B. Their result, 9-10

9 He that covereth a transgression seeketh love; but he that repeateth a matter separateth very friends.

10 A reproof entereth more into a wise man than an hundred stripes into a fool.

Verse 9 brings us to a very practical situation related to everyday life. "Covering a transgression" in this context does not refer to attempting deceitfully to cover up a wrong, but to refraining from mentioning a damaging deed for the sake of harmony between friends. Such situations frequently arise in a trio of friends, or among three chidren in the same house. When one of them becomes jealous of the bond between the other two, it is tempting to relate something that was done or said that would turn them against each other. ("You think she can be trusted, but did you know she peeked into your diary?")

The result of the *convicting* or *reproving* word is the topic of verse 10. The responsibility here focuses on the hearer rather than the speaker. A wise person profits from criticism, while a fool resents it. Wisdom here appears in the form of a certain security of identity that enables us to accept reproof without its crushing us, as opposed to being so insecure that any criticism is taken as a personal attack against which we must retaliate to save face. This truth is stated in other forms in 9:8 and 13:1.

Evangelistic Emphasis

Because of our negative reaction to over-zealous witnesses, we are sometimes reluctant to speak of our faith at all. Convinced that what we are speaks so loudly, we conclude that we don't need to say anything at all. But the good news is always expressed imperfectly in our lives; and in some instances we may be the one God chooses to speak the word of help or healing. It may be a simple sharing of what God means to us. Evangelism is one beggar telling another beggar where there is bread.

Robert Luccock tells of a nurse who was asked to sit beside the bedside of a young woman, stabbed in a drunken brawl. She had but a few hours to live. The nurse thought what a pity it was that such a face should have been marred by such hard lines. The patient opened her eyes and said, "I want you to tell me something and tell me straight. Do you think God cares about people like me? Do you think God can forgive anyone as bad as me?" The nurse reached out to God for help and reached out to the poor girl until she felt one with her. She said, knowing it is true, "I'm telling you straight. God cares about you and He forgives you." The young woman gave a sigh and slipped back into unconsciousness. The hard lines of her face changed as death approached. Such is the power of words to communicate the Word.

෨෦ӕ

Memory Selection

A soft answer turneth away wrath: but grievous words stir up anger."—*Proverbs 15:1*

The way we respond to the words or actions of another makes a great difference. We can meet anger with anger, and tempers flare. We can meet insult with insult and the conflict escalates. We can meet shouting with shouting, and we generate more heat than light.

We cannot control what others say or do to us, but we can choose how we will respond. We can choose to respond, not in kind but in kindness. The "soft" answer shows sensitivity to the hurt or pain that brought on the other's outburst. The gentle answer shows respect for the other person although his words or actions may not be pleasing. The mild reply allows the speaker to hear the truth in another's rebuke, without becoming defensive. The gentle reply allows one to move beyond the facts stated to the feeling behind the statement. A way is opened for a deeper sharing, a fuller understanding, and a new relationship. All these possibilities are destroyed with a sharp word that ignites tempers.

Weekday Problems

The Jones family have a habit of telling each other that they like each other. They affirm each other. On every occasion they take the opportunity to speak and act affectionately. The result is they enjoy being together. Theirs is a strong and healthy family.

Just the opposite is true of the Smith family. There are almost never any words of affirmation from parents to children. Family conversations are a continual stream of criticism and correction. They don't really enjoy being together. The children never recognize their own gifts and goodness because their parents never say a kind or encouraging word. No wonder the children do poorly at school. They don't feel good about themselves. The children need more praise and less scolding.

Sunday school teachers help children from both of these families. One third grader said of her teacher, "One thing I like about my teacher is she is glad to give me a second chance." The more children receive praise from their teachers and their parents the better they are able to achieve.

But praise also is needed from children to parents. One mother's day was made when she received from her son a card with this message: "You taught me to appreciate the finer things in life. I really do appreciate you."

*When was the last time you told your spouse you appreciate her?

*When was the last time you praised your child?

Words About Words

Will: That sergeant! I never heard a man talk so fast in my life.
Bill: Why shouldn't he? His father was a tobacco auctioneer and his mother was a woman.

* * *

Wife: Well, did they like your banquet speech?
Husband: I'll say! When I sat down they said it was the best thing I'd ever done.

* * *

Gracie: Doesn't it bother when your kids tell lies?
Maizie: Not as much as when we have people over and they tell the truth at the wrong time.

* * *

Gossip? I never heard anyone like her. She tells everything she knows, and a lot of it even before it happens.

This Lesson in Your Life

The wise teacher of Proverbs teaches the power of words. Words can hurt and words can heal. The wise teacher of the young encourages restraint in speech: "The mouths of fools pour out folly" (Prov. 15:2)." A torrent of words may spew forth without really saying anything. An editor asked a reporter what a prominent public official had said in his speech. "Nothing" was the answer.

"Well, keep it down to a column," the editor replied.

If you don't have something to say, it may be better to keep quiet. "Even fools who keep silent are considered wise; when they close their lips, they are deemed intelligent" (Prov. 17:28)." To Lincoln is attributed the remark, "Better to remain silent and be thought a fool than to speak out and remove all doubt."

The wise teacher warns against idle gossip. "For lack of wood the fire goes out, and where there is no whisperer, quarreling ceases" (Prov. 26:20). "A perverse person spreads strife, and a whisperer separates close friends." In the letter of James we are reminded, "So also the tongue is a small member, but it boasts of great exploits. How great a forest is set ablaze by a small fire! And the tongue is a fire" (James 3:5).

Henry van Dyke has proposed three rules that would greatly curtail the output of unkind gossip if followed. "Never believe anything bad about anyone unless you positively know that it is true. Never tell even that unless you feel that it is absolutely necessary. Remember that God is listening while you tell it." The wise teacher underscores the importance of words when used rightly, "To make an apt answer is a joy to anyone, and a word in season, how good it is."

A young girl, only four years old, was killed by a reckless teenage driver. She was playing on the sidewalk in front of her house. Careening around a corner, traveling too fast, the driver lost control. A precious young life was snuffed out. At the funeral service, the pastor did not say anything the grieving parents did not already know and believe. But he put into words the faith which sustained them in that hour. The hearing of that expression of their faith brought healing and renewing. There is a power in words. "A word in season, how good it is."

Thomas More understood the sacredness of a word spoken, an oath taken. He was to be executed because he refused to give his sworn approval to the king's annulment and remarriage. If he would only swear to what he believed was wrong, he could be free. In Robert Bolt's play, "A Man for All Seasons" More explains his refusal to his daughter, Meg. "When a man takes an oath, Meg, he's holding his own self in his hands. Like water. And if he opens his fingers then, he needn't hope to find himself again."

STRAIGHT

1. What will turn away wrath (Prov. 15:1)?
A soft answer turns away wrath.

2. What comes from the mouth of a fool (Prov. 15:2)**?**
The mouths of fools pour out folly.

3. Who watches everyone in every place (Prov. 15:3)**?**
The eyes of the Lord are in every place, keeping watch on the evil and the good.

4. To what is a gentle tongue likened (Prov. 15:4)?
A gentle tongue is a tree of life.

5. What is spread by the lips of the wise (Prov. 15: 7)**?**
The lips of the wise spread knowledge.

6. What is an abomination to the Lord, and what delights Him (Prov. 15:8)?
The sacrifice of the wicked is an abomination to the Lord, but the prayer of the upright is his delight.

7. Who are those who insult their Maker (Prov. 17:5)?
Those who mock the poor insult their Maker.

8. Who are the crown of the aged (Prov. 17:6)?
Grandchildren are the crown of the aged.

9. What fosters friendship and what alienates friends (Prov. 17: 9)?
One who forgives an affront fosters friendship, but one who dwells on disputes will alienate a friend.

10. What strikes deeper into a discerning person than a hundred blows into a fool (17:10)?
A rebuke strikes deeper into a discerning person than a hundred blows into a fool.

Recurring throughout the Book of Proverbs, in almost every chapter, are sayings about words and their power to do good or evil. No one has tapped the power of the spoken word as much as Annie Sullivan, the teacher of Helen Keller. As Helen's one link to the outside world, Annie's passion for words is portrayed in William Gibson's play, "The Miracle Worker."

Deaf, blind, and mute 12- year-old Helen was like a wild animal. Annie, half blind herself, struggled to release the young girl from the terrifying prison of eternal darkness and silence. Annie insisted that Helen had to learn that everything had a name. Words could be her eyes, her connection with everything in the world outside her and inside too. With words she can think, have ideas, be reached. Day after day Annie, with fanatical dedication, spelled words into Helen's hand. But at first Helen couldn't make the connection between the teacher's touch in her hand and the objects she touched.

One day Helen had a temper tantrum at the dinner table. She swung a pitcher of water at Annie. Annie carried Helen bodily out of the room. She forced Helen's hand to work the pump and then guided her hand under the spout as the water tumbled into the pitcher and doused Helen's hand. Annie took over the handle to keep the water coming and did automatically what she had done so many times before. She spelled into Helen's free palm, "WATER." "It has a name," Annie said. *"Water."*

Suddenly Helen dropped the pitcher and stood transfixed. There was a change in her face. A light came into it which had never been there before. Her lips trembled, trying to remember something the muscles around them once knew, until at last it found a way out. Painfully, a baby sound emerged, buried under the debris of years of dumbness. "Wah. Wah," she said. And again, "Wah. Wah." Helen plunged her hand into the dwindling water and spelled into her own palm. Then she groped frantically. Annie reached for her hand and Helen spelled into Annie's hand. Helen dropped to the ground and patted it swiftly and held up her palm. Annie spelled into it "GROUND." Helen spelled it back. Helen whirled to the pump, patted it, held up her palm. Annie spelled into it 'PUMP.' Helen spelled it back. Now Helen was in such an excitement that she seemed possessed. She ran and fell on the porch steps, clasped them, and reached out her hand. Annie spelled "STEPS." Annie called Mrs. Keller, and when Helen encountered her mother's skirt and held out her hand, Annie spelled into it "MOTHER."

As the play ends, Annie and Helen are alone in the yard. Annie has found Helen's hand, and almost without knowing it she spells slowly into it, her voice whispering, "I LOVE HELEN." The wise teacher of Proverbs puts it well: "Pleasant words are like a honeycomb, sweetness to the soul and health to the body" (Prov. 16:24).

Care for the Poor

> ## Proverbs 19:17; 22:1-4, 8-9, 16, 22-23; 23:10-11

H e that hath pity upon the poor lendeth unto the LORD; and that which he hath given will he pay him again.

22:1-4

1 A good name is rather to be chosen than great riches, and loving favour rather than silver and gold.

2 The rich and poor meet together: the LORD is the maker of them all.

3 A prudent man foreseeth the evil, and hideth himself: but the simple pass on, and are punished.

4 By humility and the fear of the LORD are riches, and honour, and life.

22:8-9

8 He that soweth iniquity shall reap vanity: and the rod of his anger shall fail.

9 He that hath a bountiful eye shall be blessed; for he giveth of his bread to the poor.

22:16, 22-23

16 He that oppresseth the poor to increase his riches, and he that giveth to the rich, shall surely come to want.

22 Rob not the poor, because he is poor: neither oppress the afflicted in the gate:

23 For the LORD will plead their cause, and spoil the soul of those that spoiled them.

23:10-11

10 Remove not the old landmark; and enter not into the fields of the fatherless:

11 For their redeemer is mighty; he shall plead their cause with thee.

Memory Selection
Proverbs 19:17

Devotional Reading
Proverbs 19:1-8

Background Scripture
Proverbs 19:17;22:1-4, 8-9,
16, 22-23; 23:10-11

Aug. 25

511

King Solomon became known far and wide as one of the wealthiest of Israel's kings. When the Queen of Sheba saw his possessions and his wisdom at work she said, "Behold, the half was not told me: thy wisdom and prosperity exceedeth the fame which I heard" (1 Kings 10:7). It may therefore come as a surprise to some that the Proverbs of this wealthy king are filled with expressions of concern for the poor, and exhortations to tend to their needs.

Although the scattered texts gathered for this lesson focus mainly on caring for the poor, they also show that Solomon was aware of some facts about the poor that we may think of as modern ideas. For example, the rich and the poor may have more in common than they suspected; and at times the poor need something more than material goods. They need self-respect and initiative as well.

&)03

One difficulty in a lesson like this is that the definition of the term "poor" is obviously relative. You can try to defuse this issue by facing it head-on, challenging your group to define the term. Of course the poorest person in an industrial nation may be rich compared to a starving child in a war-torn rural society in Africa. On the other hand, some people feel that they are poor if they have less material goods than most others in their social circle. Others may rightly observe that people can have plenty of material wealth and be "poor" in graciousness and generosity. We even speak of people having "poor" social or communication skills.

Relative though the term "poor" may be, point out that lacking enough food, clothing, and shelter to keep body and soul together is an objective fact of life for some people. This lesson challenges believers to knife through the relativism of terms and help meet such needs.

Teaching Outline	Daily Bible Readings
I. Poverty's Investment—19:17	**Mon.** Plight of the Poor Proverbs 19:1-8
II. Perspectives Involved—22:1-2	**Tue.** God Pleads for the Poor Proverbs 22:7-9, 16, 22-23
III. Prudence Is Essential—3-4	**Wed.** Give to the Poor Proverbs 28:20-27

IV. Poor Management—22:8-9, 22:16
  A. Sowing sin, 22:8
  B. Blessings of generosity, 22:9, 16
	Thu. Defend the Rights of the Poor
	Proverbs 31:4-9

V. Prohibitions to Obey—22:22-23; 23:10-11
  A. Against robbing the poor, 22:22-23
  B. Against stealing property, 23:10
  C. Advocate for the poor, 23:11
	Fri. Don't Withhold Good
	Proverbs 3:27-35
	Sat. Generosity Rewarded
	Proverbs 11:17-18, 24-28
	Sun. Happiness in Giving
	Proverbs 14:20-22, 31-34

Verse by Verse

I. Poverty's Investment—19:17

17 He that hath pity upon the poor lendeth unto the LORD**; and that which he hath given will he pay him again.**

Solomon views helping the poor as an investment on which we can expect "interest" or a return in the form of blessings from God. This is hardly the same as the "gospel of wealth" that is sometimes preached, which holds that contributing to certain radio or TV ministries is bound to make us rich in material wealth. The "pay" to be expected from God when we have "pity upon the poor" (NIV "are kind to the poor") is more likely to be in the form of spiritual blessings than material.

This emphasis on caring for the needy runs not only through the book of Proverbs but the entire Bible. Unfortunately, some quote Jesus' statement, "The poor you will always have with you" (Matt. 26:11, NIV) as an excuse not to minister to the poor. The fact is, those in poverty were of special concern to Jesus, who announced that a central feature of His Messianic mission was to them (see Matt. 11:5). When leaders in the early Church discussed what part of the Old Covenant should be carried over into the New, they called on converts "to remember the poor" (Gal. 2:10), which is consistent with the exhortations in this lesson.

II. Perspectives Involved—22:1-2

1 A good name is rather to be chosen than great riches, and loving favour rather than silver and gold.

2 The rich and poor meet together: the LORD **is the maker of them all.**

In discussing poverty and wealth, Scripture consistently warns both the poor and the rich against placing material gain at the top of our list of priorities. In these verses, the "riches" of a good reputation earned by an exemplary life are held to be above the value of silver and gold.

It is not often noted that the poor can be "materialistic" as well as the rich. Here, however, we are told that both rich and poor find fellowship in the arena of values that elevate a good name over material wealth. In this arena the poor and the rich "meet together," because both are created by the same God. The wealthy are therefore never to consider themselves better than the poor, and both are to value spiritual wealth over the material. Of course this gives no license for the wealthy to dismiss the needs of the poor by telling them that a good reputation is more important than food. The wisdom of the passage is to be applied to ourselves, not pasted on others.

III. Prudence Is Essential—3-4

3 A prudent man foreseeth the evil, and hideth himself: but the simple pass on, and are punished.

4 By humility and the fear of the LORD are riches, and honour, and life.

Another qualification of giving to the poor is that the poor themselves are to be expected to take responsibility for their condition when possible. Some fall into poverty because they have exercised poor judgment, such as not foreseeing hard times ahead and saving up for them. They are then "punished" neither by God nor Satan, but by their own lack of foresight.

Furthermore, verse 4 reminds the poor of the value standard stated above: true riches come by fearing the Lord, not by accumulating material wealth.

Neither of these two qualifications is to be used by the rich as an excuse not to help the poor. They do, however, imply that sometimes offering them budget-planning services that teach how to live within their means and save for hard times may be a more valuable ministry than giving them cash or food. The wise man foresaw the modern saying: "Give a man a fish and you feed him for a day. Teach him how to fish and you feed him for a lifetime."

IV. Poor Management—22:8-9, 22:16
A. Sowing sin, 22:8

8 He that soweth iniquity shall reap vanity: and the rod of his anger shall fail.

Although these verses have a more general primary application, it is appropriate to consider them in the context of giving to the poor, and keeping ourselves from becoming poor. Verse 8 applies first as a general principle that we "reap what we sow" (see also Gal. 6:7-8). For "vanity," the NIV has "trouble." Although the wrath of angry, wicked persons can cause immediate suffering, the wise man sees that eventually God will bring them into judgment. It is poor life-management to waste one's energy in wickedness.

B. Blessings of generosity, 22:9, 16

9 He that hath a bountiful eye shall be blessed; for he giveth of his bread to the poor.

16 He that oppresseth the poor to increase his riches, and he that giveth to the rich, shall surely come to want.

On the other hand, it is good management to be generous to the poor, instead of oppressing them or taking advantage of them in order to line our own coffers. Note that placing these widely separated verses together describes opposite lifestyles and their consequences side-by-side.

Verse 9 repeats the promise made in 19:17, that God will reward those who care for the poor. This is balanced by the warning in verse 16 that "giving to the rich" (compare the saying, "gilding the lily") will bring poverty. This last phrase may refer to the practice of trying to bribe the wealthy and powerful in return for special favors, which often results only in further oppression.

V. Prohibitions to Obey—22:22-23; 23:10-11
A. Against robbing the poor, 22:22-23

22 Rob not the poor, because he is

poor: neither oppress the afflicted in the gate:

23 For the LORD will plead their cause, and spoil the soul of those that spoiled them.

The poor are often easy targets because of their lack of political clout. Many governments have been organized in ways that seem designed to perpetuate this situation, with power vested in the "ruling class," which consists of the wealthy. Solomon's immediate predecessor, King David, gave us a tragic example of this truth when he used his kingly power to "rob" Uriah the Hittite of his wife, Bathsheba.

In theory, democracy is designed to prevent precisely the situation envisioned by Solomon, who, although a wealthy king, was given the wisdom to see the danger of such a system. However, no form of government is immune from the temptation of those in power to oppress the powerless.

Verse 23 assures that the poor are not in fact powerless, for God will actually come to their aid and be their advocate. In the case of David's theft of Bathsheba, this came in the form of Nathan the prophet saying to the king, "Thou art the man." Sometimes God's advocacy occurs in the form of political change that topples the oppressive ruling party. At other times the results of God's advocacy are harder to see, and may become evident only in the next life.

B. Against stealing property, 23:10

10 Remove not the old landmark; and enter not into the fields of the fatherless:

In many ancient lands, widows and orphans were especially subject to oppression by the greedy and powerful. Some-times this took the form of moving a stone or other natural landmark or boundary marker on property inherited by the widow or children of a deceased male landowner, to make it appear that the land belonged to someone else. Through the prophet Isaiah, God's passion for justice brought Him to pronounce judgment against such practices: "Woe unto them that join house to house, that lay field to field, till there be no place, that they may be placed alone in the midst of the earth!" (Isa. 5:8).

The special vulnerability of widows, orphans, and other relatively powerless people was the basis for the prophet Nathan's parable against David's "theft" of Bathsheba (see 2 Sam. 12:1-4). David was enraged at the rich man who stole the poor man's lamb, until he realized that the parable really referred to him. As the modern saying goes, "power corrupts, and absolute power corrupts absolutely."

Applying all this to our day, we can note that the relative powerlessness of the poor and of other minorities in our own society has been the object of a great deal of civil rights legislation; but that, as David's case shows, continued vigilance is required.

C. Advocate for the poor, 23:11

11 For their redeemer is mighty; he shall plead their cause with thee.

As in 22:23, the "fatherless" of verse 10 have an advocate or "redeemer" in God himself. It is in society's best interest to protect the interest of the poor instead of finding itself arguing against God.

Evangelistic Emphasis

The wise teacher of Proverbs reminds us: "Those who are generous are blessed, for they share their bread with the poor." (Prov. 22:9) In the time of the prophet Isaiah the people felt their prayers were not getting through. All their liturgies and fasts seemed to no avail. Isaiah suggests their public and pious fasting did no good and only made them more contentious. The word of the Lord was: "Is not this the fast I have chosen? . . . Is it not to share your bread with the hungry?" (Isa. 58:6, 7).

The most effective witness to our faith may not be elaborate ritual, public prayer, or televised sermons. The witness that points to a God of love and compassion may be as simple an act as sharing bread with the poor. We may not preach like Paul, but we can help to house the homeless. We may not have the gifts of Billy Graham to move the hearts of thousands, but we can help a lonely wanderer experience God's love through a warm meal. We may not have the influence of a Mother Teresa, but a simple act of generosity may help others be found of God. We may not have millions of dollars to invest in colleges and hospitals, but we can take an elderly widow to the doctor. In the final judgement we are judged not because we are not Mother Teresa or Billy Graham. We are accountable for using the gifts we have. "Those who are generous are blessed."

ಀಧ

Memory Selection

He that hath pity upon the poor lendeth unto the Lord; and that which he hath given will he pay him again.—*Proverbs 19:17*

The wise teacher of Proverbs reminds us that when you are kind to the poor, you actually show kindness to God. In helping a poor person you are helping God in His work of caring for the poor. In Matthew 25:31-46 Jesus tells of the great surprise at the judgment of all the nations. The righteous are invited to the kingdom prepared for them, for when he was in special need, they had ministered to him. The righteous ask, "When did we see you hungry and give your food or thirsty and give you something to drink?" The king answers, "Just as you did it to one of the least of these you did it to me."

Kathleen Norris tells of the evening she was invited to join in the procession of nuns when they entered the chapel for evening prayers. They walked slowly, two-by-two. The Prioress, who was her partner, whispered: "We bow first to Christ who is at the altar and then we turn and face our partner and bow to the Christ in each other."

Weekday Problems

Louise is chairperson of a group called "FISH" in Anaheim, California, an organization that seeks to respond to the emergency needs of other people. One day she received a call from a mother of seven children who was to have surgery the next day. She needed someone who would care for her children for a week. Louise called her list of 40 volunteers, but no one was available to help.

When Danny, her husband, came home from work Louise told him it looked like they themselves would be taking care of seven children for a week. Dan's reply was "Okay, but if this is the work of the Lord, someone will respond." At 11 o'clock that night, the telephone rang. A young woman, Stephanie, was calling from a nearby city. She had heard about the woman's need through her church. She was taking a week's vacation and would be glad to spend it with the children.

Two weeks later, when Louise called together the FISH steering committee, she invited Stephanie to their meeting. "Sure, I'd be glad to come," said Stephanie. "Could you arrange transportation?"

"Won't you be able to drive?" asked Louise.

"Oh," Stephanie replied, "I thought you knew. I'm blind."

What's your excuse when Jesus calls on you?

Who's That Knocking at My Door?

Knock, knock.
Who's there?
Wendy.
Wendy who?
Wendy red, red robin
    comes bob-bob-bobbin' along. . . .

* * *

Knock, knock.
Who's there?
Tarzan.
Tarzan who?
Tarzan stripes forever.

* * *

Knock, knock.
Who's there?
Atch.
Atch who?
God bless you!

This Lesson in Your Life

Running through the selection of proverbs to be studied this week is the theme of care for the poor. Some of the proverbs bring a stern warning of judgment when the poor are oppressed. "Do not rob the poor because they are poor, or crush the afflicted at the gate, for the Lord pleads their cause and despoils of life those who despoil them (Prov. 22:22). The poor and afflicted may seem helpless and vulnerable. But in the larger scheme of things, the Lord is on their side. When one tries to take advantage of them, exploit them with high prices, rigged scales, low wages, shoddy goods, that one will in the end find himself plundered, punished, even robbed of life itself. It is the Lord who pleads their cause. In taking advantage of the poor, one is in truth insulting God.

Again the wise teacher warns: "Oppressing the poor in order to enrich oneself will lead only to loss." When the wealthy use influence, bribery or authority to cheat the poor by changing the ancient stones that mark the boundary (Prov. 23:10-11), they will discover sooner or later that in fact they have been messing with the Lord. The orphans who seem so defenseless, with no one to defend them or take care of them, have in fact Another on their side. Who might that be? The Lord Himself. He will plead their cause. He will make the case against the callous and cheating ways of the powerful and indifferent.

The ancient words of the wise teacher have a contemporary bite. In our rich and prosperous America, we have allowed too many children to fall through the cracks. Too many children do not share in the prosperity of our land. Marian Wright Edelman reminds us that many of the poor of our day are children. Too many children wake up in dens of dope rather than in homes of hope. Too many children wake up with hunger in their bellies and in their spirits, and without parents or friends who care, affirm, and lovingly discipline them. Too many children are abused or neglected by parents who themselves were often abused or neglected. Too many children are sick from disease we could have prevented. Too many children die from guns we could have controlled. Too many girl children have babies without a husband, and without parenting skills. Too many children grow up in poverty without a seat at America's table of plenty. There are too many youth whose only hope for employment is drug dealing, whose only belonging is gangs, whose only haven is the streets, and whose only tomorrow is prison or death.

When we live in comfort, indifference and callused complacency we need to hear and heed the warning of the ancient wise teacher. It is the Lord who pleads their case. Their redeemer is strong. "Those who are generous are blessed, for they share their bread with the poor" (Prov. 22:10).

STRAIGHT

1. Who lends to the Lord (Prov. 19:17)?
Whoever is kind to the poor lends to the Lord.

2. What is more important than riches (Prov. 22:1)?
A good name is to be chosen rather than riches.

3. What do rich and poor share in common (Prov. 22:2)?
The Lord is the maker of all both the rich and the poor.

4. What is the reward of humility and fear of the Lord (Prov. 22:4)?
The reward is riches and honor and life.

5. What is reaped from sowing injustice (Prov. 22:8)?
Whoever sows injustice will reap calamity.

6. Why are the generous blessed (Prov. 22:9)?
Because they share their bread with the poor.

7. What is the end result of oppressing the poor (Prov. 22:16)?
Oppressing the poor will lead only to loss.

8. Why should one not rob the poor or crush the afflicted (Prov. 22:22)?
Because the Lord pleads their cause, and the Lord will despoil life those who despoil them.

9. To what does "removing ancient landmarks" refer (Prov. 23:10)?
"Ancient landmarks" were boundary markers. Moving the markers was a way of robbing others of land the Lord had given families of Israel.

10. Who will defend and plead the cause of the orphan (Prov. 23:10-11)?
The Lord is the redeemer who will plead their cause.

William Wilimon relates this story. Millard and Linda Fuller walked out of a successful law practice in Alabama a few years ago, sold their possessions, and gave the money to the poor. Searching for a new focus for their lives, the Fullers founded "Habitat for Humanity." It is now an international movement of volunteer Christian house-building for the poor.

Fuller was invited to speak at the Chapel of Duke University. Tall, lanky, well tanned, not from golf but from building houses, Fuller spoke with a graceful southern drawl. "You know, we Christians are good at differing with one another on just about everything. Habitat for Humanity is bringing together a broad array of Christians and people of good will around a simple principle: all God's people ought to have simple, decent, affordable housing."

In a project in Charlotte, N.C., workers came from 28 states. After devotions, they grabbed their hammers and went to work. An Episcopal priest and the most conservative Baptist preacher in town began hammering together. Fuller observed, "When you're on the roof of a house, working for God, it don't matter if you're liberal or conservative. All that matters is that you can hit the nail on the head. Those two preachers didn't know each other before they started work on that house. Now they're good friends. That's the theology of the hammer."

In New London, Conn., the Habitat workers presented a woman a house for her family, complete with shrubbery and appliances. As they gave her the keys to her house and a Bible, they asked her to say something to the workers if she wanted to. She was so overcome that she was only able to say a few words. Fuller relates, "But on the way back to her seat she began to shout. Sometimes when people get so full of the Spirit and joy, they just start shouting, 'Glory Hallelujah!' Well, she just started shouting because she was so happy to have at last a decent house for her family. There were a lot of reserved New Englanders there. They were unnerved. They didn't know what was gonna happen next, whether the Lord himself might appear any minute. It was wonderful!"

The workers of Habitat come from many churches, classes, and races. Those who receive the house work along beside them. It is called "sweat equity." On any given Saturday one might see a bank president and a high school drop-out, a university professor and a mother on welfare, a freshmen in college and a retired engineer. Rich and poor, young and old, liberals and conservatives work side by side. As Proverbs puts it, "The rich and the poor have this in common: the Lord is the maker of them all."